DATE DUE

DEMCO 38-296

REVOLUTION
and
CHANGE
in
CENTRAL
and
EASTERN
EUROPE

Also available from M.E. Sharpe, Inc.

**EAST-CENTRAL EUROPEAN ECONOMIES
IN TRANSITION**
John P. Hardt and Richard F. Kaufman, eds.

ENVIRONMENTAL ACTION IN EASTERN EUROPE
RESPONSES TO CRISIS
Barbara Jancar-Webster, ed.

ETHNIC CONFLICT IN THE POST-SOVIET WORLD
CASE STUDIES AND ANALYSIS
Leokadia Drobizheva et al., eds.

ETHNIC POLITICS IN EASTERN EUROPE
A GUIDE TO NATIONALITY POLICIES,
ORGANIZATIONS, AND PARTIES
Janusz Bugajski

THE GYPSIES OF EASTERN EUROPE
David Crowe and John Kolsti, eds.

THE POWER OF THE POWERLESS
CITIZENS AGAINST THE STATE IN
CENTRAL EASTERN EUROPE
Vaclav Havel, et al.
John Keane, ed.

**RESTRUCTURING AND PRIVATIZATION
IN CENTRAL EASTERN EUROPE**
CASE STUDIES OF FIRMS IN TRANSITION
Saul Estrin, Josef C. Brada, Alan Gelb, Inderjit Singh, eds.

THE ROAD TO DISILLUSION
FROM CRITICAL MARXISM TO
POSTCOMMUNISM IN EASTERN EUROPE
Raymond Taras, ed.

**WOMEN IN THE POLITICS OF
POSTCOMMUNIST EASTERN EUROPE**
Marilyn Rueschemeyer, ed.

REVOLUTION
and
CHANGE
in
CENTRAL
and
EASTERN
EUROPE

Political, Economic, and Social Challenges

Minton F. Goldman

*With a Foreword
by Karl W. Ryavec*

M.E. Sharpe
Armonk, New York
London, England

Library of Congress Cataloging-in-Publication Data

Goldman, Minton F.
Revolution and change in Central and Eastern Europe:
political, economic, and social challenges / by Minton F. Goldman.
p. cm.
Includes bibliographical references and index.
ISBN 1-56324-757-7 (c: alk. paper).
ISBN 1-56324-758-5 (p: alk. paper)
1. Europe, Eastern—History—1989– .
2. Post-communism—Europe, Eastern.
3. Europe, Eastern—Politics and government—1989– .
4. Europe, Eastern—Economic conditions—1989– .
5. Europe, Eastern—Social conditions—1989– .
6. Yugoslav War, 1991– . I. Title.
DJK51.G654 1996
940'.09717—dc20
95-52512
CIP

To Maureen
for her invaluable help, encouragement, and patience

Contents

Foreword

With this book Professor Minton Goldman has performed a timely and useful service for teachers, scholars, and students of Central and Eastern Europe. The wide-ranging changes recently set in motion in this historically rich region of over 100 million people between Western Europe and Russia constitute the latest significant example of decolonization, albeit of a special variety, of a large area of the world. Long under either foreign rule or forced outside influence, the twelve countries of *Mitteleuropa* (Middle Europe) are now embarked on the difficult course of potential five-sided or quintuple transformation on the new historical tide flowing from the failure of communism and the breakup of the Soviet Union. The transition now facing the area has five main aspects: attitudinal and cultural, societal, political, economic, and diplomatic. This is a high number of "transition challenges" to face at one time. The so-called developing countries or "Third World," on whose experience most of our scholarship on political and economic development is based, did not have to cope with the powerful and limiting after-effects of communism as they underwent development, nor did they have to re-establish private enterprise. Even the most traditional countries possess private enterprise, however basic in nature. Not so some ex-communist countries. As Goldman correctly says, "Communism had distorted everything it touched." (p. 51.) Accordingly, post-communist change is a very special and highly difficult, and problematic, challenge. Yet the challenge and its outcome are crucially important, not only for Central Europe itself, but also for Western Europe, Russia, and the United States as well as for international relations. Twice in this century world wars engulfed the region and brought the world's major powers into either deadly conflict or close and even desperate alliance. And today the attempt to stop the internecine war in Bosnia and prevent its escalation is but another indication of the continuing importance of Central Europe for world politics and the major powers.

The main focus of Goldman's welcome book is the progress and problems of post-communist development. It covers the several aspects of the transition in the region as a whole as well as in all the countries specifically. In the first two chapters the reasons for the collapse of communism and the commonalities of development are explained, and in the following nine chapters the extraordinary and interesting diversity of the various countries' rejection of communism and their progress to date in the post-communist transitions are examined country by country. All chapters are subdivided into sections and subsections, thereby allowing easy accessibility to particular topics. The book clearly sets forth the difficulties encountered in moving from communist monolithic authoritarianism to pluralistic democracy, in transforming command economies into free-market economies, in coping with threats to progress and stability such as continuing communist influence and predilections and outbreaks of divisive nationalism and ethnic discrimination and conflict. Problems such as dealing with polluted environments, anti-Semitism, and the difficult situations of women in the post-communist period are covered. In addition, the book is notable in dealing with the international aspects of the transitions. There is attention to the foreign policy of the individual states, especially in relation to one another but also toward Russia and the other newly independent states, Western Europe, and the United States.

This book benefits from the author's many years of experience in teaching and writing about the region's domestic and foreign policies and his extensive experience in the field, especially his numerous interviews with government officials and academics in most of the countries covered. The author has used a wide variety of recent good primary and secondary source materials in producing this up-to-date, clearly written, well organized, wide-ranging, and valuable examination of the first years of the post-communist changes in Central and Eastern Europe. As Goldman makes clear, transformation will not take place overnight, but he has given us an excellent guide to the issues, processes, and the initial steps of this great voyage of transition that is so necessary for the area and so important for Europe, the United States, Russia, and world politics itself.

Karl W. Ryavec
Professor of Political Science
University of Massachusetts at Amherst

Introduction

The Region of Central/Eastern Europe

Central and Eastern Europe today consists of twelve countries: Poland, Hungary, the Czech Republic, Slovakia, Romania, Bulgaria, Albania, a rump Yugoslav state consisting of the Serb Republic and Montenegro, and the former Yugoslav republics of Slovenia, Croatia, Bosnia-Herzegovina, and Macedonia. Before 1993, the Czech Republic and Slovakia made up Czechoslovakia. Before October 1990, going back to the end of World War II, when the German state was partitioned by the four victorious Allies (Britain, France, the United States, and the Soviet Union), there was the German Democratic Republic, sometimes called East Germany, which is now part of the Federal Republic of Germany.

The region has a distinctive but somewhat sad political past. With the exception of the East German state, created out of the Soviet zone of occupation, all the countries of the region were occupied and administered for many centuries by powerful outside empires (German, Austrian, Russian, and Ottoman Turkish), which left their own legacies with the peoples they ruled. In all cases, but especially for the countries in the southern part of Eastern Europe, known as the Balkans (Romania, Bulgaria, central and southern Yugoslavia, and Albania), foreign rule was repressive, abusive, and beyond the ability of the people living under it to influence or reform short of revolution. Russian rule of central and eastern Poland and Turkish rule in the Balkans was harsh, with German rule in western Poland a bit less brutal and Austro-Hungarian rule of Czechoslovakia, southern Poland, Slovenia, and Croatia somewhat more enlightened and progressive though by no means liberal. For some countries of Central and Eastern Europe, this foreign control ended in the late nineteenth century, while others became independent only at the end of World War I.

The nation-states of Central and Eastern Europe, when compared with those in the West, are young. They have had far less experience with self-rule and very little experience with parliamentary democracy, although some countries did have democratic government in the early years of the interwar period (1919–39). This effort at Western-style parliamentary democracy was brief and severely flawed. By the eve of World War II, when the countries of Central and Eastern Europe were either invaded by or became allies of Nazi Germany, their liberal-looking governments had degenerated into fascist tyrannies, with the exception of Czechoslovakia, where a moderately successful parliamentary democracy was cut short by the Nazi invasion that began on October 1, 1938.

In the failure of democracy in Central and Eastern Europe during the interwar period, one can find a cautionary lesson for today. Many of the problems that burdened and undermined the democratic governments of that era seem to have reappeared in the 1990s to compromise democratic development today. The earlier democratic experience was undone by excessive political factionalism and party conflict that paralyzed parliaments; by pervasive economic poverty resulting from a maldistribution of wealth; by strong conservative tendencies that included a distrust of democracy and a predilection for strong authoritarian leaders who could unify and stabilize society; and by divisive ethnic conflict throughout the region. The final blow came from the Germans and Russians, who brutally imposed their will on the region—the Germans from the late 1930s until their defeat at the end of World War II, and the Russians from the early post–World War II era until the late 1980s.

The peoples of Central and Eastern Europe have always been vulnerable to the expansionism of their powerful neighbors, the Germans in the west and the Russians in the east. Germany and Russia have always been deeply interested in the Central and East European peoples for reasons of security, global strategy, economic opportunity, and ideology. For example, Germany has always had an *Ostpolitik,* or eastern policy, calling for German influence over and, if possible, control of Central and Eastern Europe because of its importance to German security against the real or imagined threat of Russia. At the same time, Russia before, during, and after the Soviet/communist era saw influence over, if not control of, the middle region, as it has sometimes been called, as essential to Russian security vis-à-vis the West, from at least the time of the Napoleonic invasion of Russia in the early nineteenth century through the German invasions of Russian territory in the two world wars. Moreover, both Germans and Russians viewed the middle region as a potential source of raw materials and a potential market for domestic exports important to their economic well-being. Finally, in the World War II era both Nazi Germany and the Soviet Union viewed the middle region as ripe for the adoption of their national ideologies, national socialism and communism, and Russia before and after the communist era considered the peoples of Central and Eastern Europe a logical object of their attention and concern because of their shared Slavic and Orthodox Christian background. The impact of this region's vulnerability to the historical, compulsive, and frequently violent intrusiveness of its powerful neighbors on its development cannot be underestimated.

Perhaps a significant reason for this vulnerability is the region's extraordinary conflict-producing ethnic diversity, which exists on both macro and micro levels of society. On a macro level, the region comprises large ethnic groups that have their own state systems, such as the Polish, Hungarian, Czech, Slovak, Romanian, Bulgarian, Albanian, Serb, Slovene, and Croatian peoples. Historically, these large majorities have had difficulty living together in peace and harmony as a result of deep-seated prejudices toward each other that seem indestructible and have exerted a mischievous influence on overall political development. On a micro level are the multiplicity of culturally diverse ethnic minorities living in the societies dominated by the large majorities. Special cases are Hungarian minorities living in southeastern Slovakia, in northwestern Romania in an area called Transylvania, and in the Vojvodina province of northwest Serbia; a large Turkish minority living in southeastern Bulgaria; Serb minorities scattered in Croatia, Bosnia-Herzegovina, Montenegro, and Macedonia; and a large Albanian population living in the Kosovo province of southeastern Serbia and in northern Macedonia. In many instances, relations between minorities and majorities have been traditionally difficult and in some instances have given rise to confrontation, conflict, and civil war that have divided and weakened the region and encouraged outside interference.

After World War II, the adoption of communism and the subordination of the region to the Soviet Union in a process called satellization, which rendered the countries of Central and Eastern Europe, with the exceptions of Yugoslavia and Albania, dependent on the Kremlin, paradoxically brought a measure of stability and security to most of the middle region. But the communist systems and their subservience, most of them to the Soviet Union, turned out to be a developmental straitjacket. As satellites they could pursue no policy at home or abroad without the acquiescence of the Soviet leadership, which used a variety of political, economic, and military devices to assure the conformity and obedience of its satellites. Soviet communism was imposed on them, so the Kremlin argued "for their own good," but in reality this control carried enormous strategic, political, economic, and even psychological benefits for the Soviet political system. For forty years after World War II, the countries of Central and Eastern Europe were prevented from fulfilling their destiny of maximizing the benefits of their resources to assure the best quality of life that those resources could have provided had their governments been free of external control.

The rejection of communist rule at the end of the 1980s was a watershed event for the region. Very few people, including foreign-policy experts and scholars of the region, expected to see the collapse of communist rule before the end of the century. Until the political upheavals of 1989, no area that had come under communist rule had yet rejected and replaced it. Moreover, initially there was little evidence that the perestroika-inspired reforms of Soviet domestic and international behavior under Soviet president Mikhail Gorbachev would lead the Kremlin to ease up on its control of the region and allow it to adopt reforms that eventually would result in the collapse of communist dictatorship and Soviet power. But perestroika seemed to have a momentum of its own in both the Soviet Union and Central and Eastern Europe that the Kremlin could not interrupt. Indeed, Gorbachev's decision to let nature take its course and allow the satellites to liberalize their political and economic systems in 1989 and 1990, in response to mounting public pressures for change of the kind that was going on in the Soviet Union itself, was responsible, more than any other event, for the erosion and collapse of communist rule and the transition to noncommunist political systems in the early 1990s.

Certainly, what is happening in the countries of Central and Eastern Europe is important to the United States. These countries are now potential friends and allies of Washington in its relations with Russia, which remains a challenge to American interests abroad. They are also potential markets for American investment and American exports. They also are trying in various ways to make a success of liberal government, which the United States wants to encourage as part of a large and historical American strategy of furthering democracy. As the countries of Central and Eastern Europe move into uncharted territory, struggling to establish democracy and preserve newly achieved national sovereignty, they are seeking substantial Western, and in particular American, political, economic, and strategic support, which, as yet, has not been forthcoming.

REVOLUTION
and
CHANGE
in
CENTRAL
and
EASTERN
EUROPE

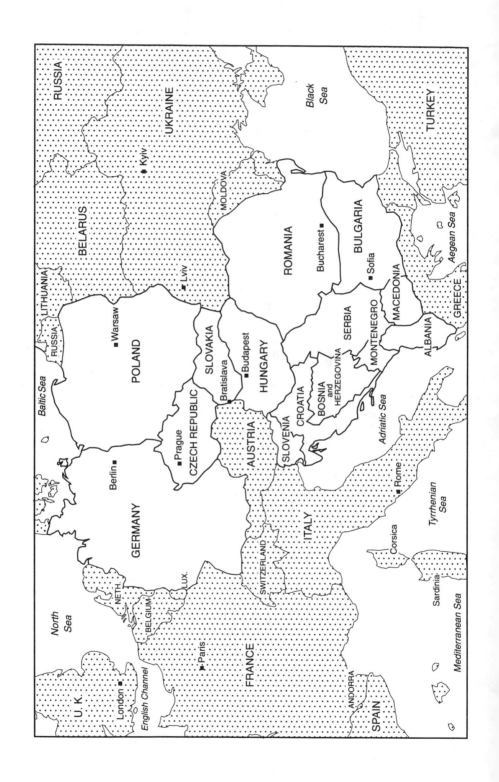

1

Roots and Causes of Communist Collapse

Communist political systems in Central and Eastern Europe collapsed at the end of the 1980s primarily because of long-standing internal weaknesses that denied them the popular legitimacy needed for long-term survival. They collapsed also as a result, paradoxically, of Soviet policy toward them in the late 1980s that encouraged their adoption of perestroika-style reformism but called for restraint when reform got out of hand and endangered their survival. The West also had a hand, though an oblique one, in the collapse by doing what it could when it could to undermine their credibility at home as well as abroad.

Internal Weaknesses

The major internal weaknesses of the communist systems in Central and Eastern Europe were political, economic, and environmental. Subservience to the Soviet Union, which had helped to get most of them started after World War II and subsequently had heavily influenced their domestic and foreign policies, also greatly weakened them by making them appear as little more than colonial-style dependencies of the Kremlin. By the late 1980s, despite efforts in some countries to reform communist rule, all the communist systems had lost whatever legitimacy they may have had, which at best was very little. They were ripe for overthrow.[1]

1. Political Weaknesses

The Central and East European communist systems, which largely resembled the Soviet dictatorship, remained throughout most of their history repressive, rigid, and corrupt. They denied opportunities for public criticism and opposition. Their representation of the popular will was artificial, inadequate, and perverse, reflecting not what people thought but what Communist Party leaders wanted them to think. The communist systems inevitably became less instruments of the change and improvement promised in their ideology and more like a straitjacket that stunted growth by their coercive, intrusive, and frequently inept management of national life.

Repression

Like the Soviet Communist Party, the communist parties of Central and Eastern Europe monopolized politics and were undemocratic in their organization and behavior. Communist parties tolerated no critics, rivals, or opponents, refusing to share leadership with any other group except in a superficial and ineffectual way. They controlled the personnel and functioning of the government, the working of the economy, and the organization and behavior of society. They closely monitored the personnel and policy implementation of governmental agencies, using a complex and ubiquitous network of intrusive controls that pervaded all aspects of administrative life. Their authority extended to cultural areas of national life, including the church, the media, and artistic expression. While there were some exceptions to this broad scope of communist party power, by and large there was very little in the public or private life of all the Central and East European societies that escaped party influence.

Communist parties were always an elite whose membership was limited to a small percentage of the total population of a country, usually 6 percent or a little more. Communist party leaders usually were co-opted into power by a process of self-selection that excluded influence of the rank-and-file membership or of the voting public, which had little if anything to say about what the party did and how it was organized. Indeed, communist parties had a high degree of internal discipline preventing discussion or debate, not to mention criticism, of leadership policy. By the end of their rule, the communist parties had become highly bureaucratized and professionalized, with many members, including the leadership, more interested in protecting their power and perquisites than in developing socialism and achieving the communist ideal.

The communist governments, at all times subservient to the communist party, which micromanaged much of their administrative behavior, on the surface resembled Western-style parliamentary systems. The working of the legislatures on many levels of administration and the holding of frequent elections for the membership of these seemingly popular government bodies were supposed to provide the political system with an aura of democracy, in which people were supposed to think they had some role to play in policy making. But these communist governments operated very differently than the Western democracies. For example, most national and local legislatures had little or no influence over policy making because their membership had neither the power nor the inclination to force prime ministers and cabinets to be responsive to them. Indeed, most members of the legislature belonged to the Communist Party and were obedient to its leadership; they lacked the time and information needed to learn enough about a policy to question it, much less reject it. Nor did the communist legislatures have the constitutional authority to terminate the life of a cabinet with a Western-style no-confidence vote. Moreover, the Communist Party's close control of every aspect of elections, in particular the nomination and election of legislative candidates, excluding persons who might be independent and critical of or opposed to national policy, guaranteed the discipline and docility of the members of legislative bodies. Thus, representation was more apparent than real, and the communist legislatures generally became ratifiers of, rather than challengers to, government policies, even those disliked by voters.

While the communist legislatures did provide Central and East European peoples with a vague understanding of the rudiments of self-government and a certain degree of political stability that increased the efficiency of party and government policy making, their authoritarian and largely unresponsive character encouraged popular ridicule of them. Communist societies learned that their legislatures could do little to influence party leaders, who made and implemented policy quite independently of them.

There were, of course, exceptions to these conditions, especially toward the end of communist rule. For example, from the 1970s onward, the Polish Parliament, called the Sejm, frequently criticized policies by Communist Party leaders and on a few occasions actually got a reversal of them. Moreover, the membership of the Sejm was diverse, with deputies representing Catholics and the intelligentsia, who were critical of the party's repressive and grossly inept behavior in managing the economy. There was also an occasional streak of independence in a few other communist legislatures, notably Czechoslovakia, Hungary, and Slovenia.

Rigidity

Without peaceful means of achieving change in their structure and functioning, the Soviet-style dictatorships of Central and Eastern Europe overall gradually became brittle and either unwilling or unable to introduce systemic change when circumstances warranted it, namely, in the late 1960s and throughout the 1970s and 1980s, when societies began to chafe at the flaws and failings of communist rule. This was especially true in the political sphere where Communist Party leaders, with few exceptions, were fearful of liberalization, even a little of it, believing, and rightly so as matters turned out, that liberalization, if allowed, would be difficult to control and might eventually jeopardize their own power and that of the Communist Party. Moreover, if a communist leadership did contemplate political reform, no matter how modest in scope, the Soviet Union in most instances opposed and blocked it to discourage modification of the authoritarian status quo, which could weaken its influence in the region. The Kremlin remained adamantly opposed to political reforms that might allow the surfacing of popular criticism of communist rule and popular dislike of Russia, which was seen as the region's historic enemy. Thus, in Hungary and Poland in 1956, in Czechoslovakia in 1968, and in Poland in 1980 and 1981, the Soviets moved aggressively to suppress movements that seemed to threaten the communist dictatorship and its intimacy with the Kremlin. Even Gorbachev, who endorsed political reform in Central and Eastern Europe in the late 1980s, initially did so with caution and caveats, warning that "liberalization" should not be at the expense of the Communist Party's monopoly of power and should under no circumstances lead to a Western-style pluralistic political order that would jeopardize the national commitment to communism and close political, economic, and military ties with the Soviet Union.

For all their claims to be "democratic," these rigid and essentially static regimes in fact had lost touch with the people and remained either ignorant of or indifferent to the real depth of popular discontent. In many instances, they concealed or lied to themselves and to their citizens about severe and dangerous problems facing the society. Moreover, by the end of the communist era, these regimes were led by people who not only seemed more interested in their own careers than in promoting the well-being of society promised in the communist ideology to which they all swore allegiance, but also had little, if any, accountability to the public. Selfishness, arrogance, secrecy, deception, and "professionalism" had become the chief features of communist parties and governments. The characteristics of Communist rule helped to destroy whatever faith and credibility the peoples of Central and Eastern Europe may have ever had in it.

Corruption

The communist political systems in Central and Eastern Europe were also corrupt. East European bureaucrats frequently took bribes, lied, and concealed mistakes, with no obligation to be responsive to people's needs. Especially aggravating to ordinary citizens was the privilege that allowed administrators to live in near-luxurious circumstances while the rest of society suffered from economic deprivation and misery. When the full extent of corrupt behavior by officials, including party leaders, who may have been the most corrupt because they had the largest opportunities to be so, became known in the fall of 1989, most peoples of Central and Eastern Europe were furious and sought retribution.

2. Economic Scarcity and Deprivation

All Central and East European economies developed some version of the highly centralized and autarchic economic model developed by Stalin in the Soviet

Union in the 1930s. Communist economies in many, though not all, Central and East European countries must be given credit for impressive achievements, such as redistribution of wealth, modernization of the infrastructure, and expansion of industrial capabilities, the so-called socialist prerequisites for the eventual achievement of communism.

But Soviet-style communist economies, even when modified substantially—as, for example, in the case of Hungary's New Economic Mechanism, Yugoslavia's Workers' Councils, and Poland's tolerance of private entrepreneurialism in agriculture—never achieved a level of individual well-being that was commensurate with each country's resources and capabilities, that compared favorably with living standards in the West, and that at least implicitly, if not explicitly, was promised in communist ideology and pledged by Communist Party leaders. By the 1980s, despite their compulsive micromanagement of economic life, communist leaders had failed conspicuously to provide people with a level of material well-being nearly comparable to Western living standards. Everything that people needed in daily life, such as food, clothing, housing, and household and other amenities taken for granted in the West but considered luxuries in Central and Eastern Europe, was perennially in short supply or simply not available. And worse, for many people living conditions had not only not improved or even stayed the same under communist rule but had deteriorated from what they had been in the precommunist and pre–World War II era, when for many there was an abundance, or at least an adequacy, of everything that became scarce under communism.

The more people in Central and Eastern Europe learned about life in the West, the angrier they became about the inadequacies in their own countries, which had promised so much and delivered so little. Despite the strict censorship of news and the limits on travel to the West, as well as relentless propaganda about the superiority of the communist system, people in Central and Eastern Europe knew that they were poorer than people in Western Europe, including the less-affluent countries of Spain, Portugal, and Greece, and worse off than some Third World countries, such as Taiwan, South Korea, and Singapore.[2]

The economic scarcity and deprivation that characterized communist economies can be attributed to misguided investment priorities, to managerial mediocrity and ineptitude, to limits on the kind of reform that could have expanded output, and to perverse behavior patterns of the vast majority of people, who, in seeking to cope with the harshness and austerity of daily life, made things worse for themselves.

Misguided Investment Priorities

Central and East European Communist Party leaders set the same misguided priorities as their Soviet counterparts. Full employment, the hallmark of the communist economic systems, required keeping unprofitable enterprises working. Also, East European governments spent heavily on defense and far too little on consumer-goods production. Communist leaders favored heavy industry at the expense of other sectors, such as agriculture, health and welfare, and housing. Communist governments also emphasized quantity over quality. Their economies produced shoddy goods, which in many instances no one wanted to buy, leaving enterprises with huge unsold inventories that eventually had to be disposed of below cost. The waste of resources in such situations was enormous. Furthermore, real costs and values of property and production were never precisely known, while enormous amounts of capital were absorbed to maintain the system's operation. With no real incentives, individual productivity was extremely low by Western standards. And, in one of their worst miscalculations, Central and East European leaders virtually ignored technological development, perhaps because research and development did not yield immediate payoffs. Moreover, technology was scarce also because East European countries were isolated from the West and conducted their business primarily with one another and the Soviet Union, missing the latest advances in such important areas as computer information systems.

Managerial Mediocrity and Ineptitude

Communist Party emphasis on conformity, loyalty, and obedience to ideology in the recruitment of managerial leadership too often resulted in the elevation to positions of responsibility throughout the party and state structures of unimaginative and administratively inept people who put deference to superiors ahead of competence in administration. Eventually, bureaucracies were riddled with mediocrities, an especially disastrous situation given the extraordinary control over national economic life wielded by bureaucrats. When mistakes and misjudgments occurred, as they frequently did in various policy areas, such as industry, agriculture, banking, and trade, the negative impact on society's well-being was catastrophic.

Limits on Reform

No amount of tinkering with the Soviet-style economy measurably improved its efficiency, although some economies, notably in Hungary, Czechoslovakia, Yugoslavia, and East Germany, did better by their citizens than others, for example, in Poland, Bulgaria, Romania, and Albania. Radical systemic change in the form of a major curtailment of state control over national economic life, which might have been able to increase output and raise living standards eventually, perhaps, to near-Western levels, was ruled out by communist leaders, since state control over the national economy was a source of their power and prestige. They also could do nothing without the approval of the Kremlin, which adamantly opposed systemic change, first, because it could undermine central control over economic life and weaken the foundation of the command economy rooted in communist ideology and, second, because it could serve as a subversive precedent for systemic change in Soviet society, which the Soviet Communist Party was unwilling to introduce, even under Gorbachev's perestroika.

Making matters worse was the fact that workers in the Central and East European communist countries could do little on their own to improve living conditions. Unions, which in the West could lobby aggressively for change, were little more than agents of the Communist Party and the state. Union leadership frequently belonged to the party and was loathe to criticize policies and complain about conditions causing hardships for workers. Communist unions never represented workers before management, as in the West, but controlled them, discouraging their assertiveness by bribes in the form of handouts of scarce goods, school scholarships, and preferred vacation facilities. Not surprisingly, workers lost faith in their unions. By 1989, workers were angry over the sacrifices and suffering they had endured for the sake of achieving the better life their communist leaders had promised but never delivered. Central and East European unions could not and did not help to assuage the deficiencies of communist economies, for example, by pushing for different priorities congenial to the individual. To that extent unions did little to facilitate the kind of economic reform that might have enabled communist regimes to perform more efficiently and enhance their legitimacy.

Distortions and Perversities

People tried to cope with the harshness and austerity of daily life as best they could. A black market flourished in almost all the East European economies. But this illegal activity benefited only a small percentage of people, because black-market prices, which were much higher than prices of goods sold in state-run stores, kept many goods beyond the reach of most ordinary consumers. Hoarding was not unusual. Furthermore, shoppers spent an enormous amount of time in long lines, which frustrated and exhausted them. Quite possibly the authorities complicated the process of shopping in order to reduce consumer demand for goods the regime simply did not want to produce in large quantities. People also were angry over special stores created for customers with hard currency, especially tourists from the West, that were well stocked with scarce goods, in particular imports, beyond the reach of ordinary consumers.

3. Environmental Degradation

Citizens of the Central and East European countries were aware of the environmental degradation that contributed to the harshness of daily life. By the late 1980s, they were desperate for an improvement in physical living conditions.

Causes of Pollution

Environmental pollution occurred as a by-product of the official obsession with industrial development. In the name of industrial progress, the communist governments allowed rivers and lakes to become polluted. The air of large East European cities had pollution fifty times the safe limits; much of the region's arable farmland was polluted with overdoses of fertilizer; and forests were destroyed from polluted industrial waste of all kinds.

Central planning, with its high subsidies and monopolistic practices, encouraged the careless use of energy. The more energy was used, the greater was the fallout of pollution. For example, the East European economies consumed enormous amounts of lignite, a soft brown coal plentiful in the region. Lignite is a poor fuel because more of it has to be burned to heat a room or drive a steam turbine than hard coal. It also has a high sulfur content. But the communists burned it anyway and did so very wastefully. Eastern Europe used 50 percent to 100 percent more energy than the United States to produce a unit of gross national product.

Contributing to pollution was the fact that the major polluter was the government, which was solely responsible for controlling pollution. State-owned factories that polluted had no real interest in following antipollution rules. Furthermore, there was no agency capable of policing industry to diminish pollution. The East European countries also lacked cleanup technology: there were no power-plant scrubbers, and sewage systems were primitive and inefficient. Advanced Western antipollution technology was too expensive to import.[3]

Impact

The consequences of environmental degradation were serious. Pollution contributed to many illnesses, a comparatively high infant mortality rate, and a shorter life span for both men and women than in the West. The dirty and unpleasant physical environment caused by pollution contributed significantly to the depressed standard of living and low morale that provoked opposition to communist regimes.

4. Subservience to the Soviet Union

Bulgaria, Czechoslovakia, East Germany, Hungary, Poland, and Romania became "satellites" of the Soviet Union soon after the communists took power. Satellization, which was intended to assure Soviet control over and security in Central and Eastern Europe, had constitutional, political, economic, military, and diplomatic dimensions.[4] Satellization was a major cause of popular hostility to the Central and East European communist political systems, which were always seen by the peoples whom they governed as alien, imposed by a powerful and disliked neighbor, and, therefore, illegal and immoral.

Dimensions of Satellization

The satellite nations were obliged by Moscow to adopt authoritarian dictatorships patterned after the Soviet model. These dictatorships denied citizens influence over their own government and thus the opportunity to criticize subservience to the Soviet Union. They were the most important means of assuring Soviet influence. Regular and frequent bilateral summit meetings between the Central and East European leaders and the Kremlin assured their obedience to and conformity with Soviet will in areas such as leadership succession, internal party discipline, and the formation of domestic and foreign policies. Local law-enforcement agencies had to work closely with Soviet KGB personnel deployed throughout different Central and East European countries to identify and suppress groups and individuals who might form a political opposition or harbor anti-Soviet views. When the dictatorships collapsed and were replaced by parliamentary democracies, the Kremlin lost the means of controlling the region and satellization came to an end.

The economies of the satellites were subject to a similar degree of Soviet influence and control. The Council for Mutual Economic Assistance, or CMEA, set up by Stalin in 1948 to develop close trade links among member countries, enabled the Kremlin to influence the economic priorities and policies of its satellites. The economic dimension of satellization also involved Soviet exploitation. The Kremlin oriented the trade of the satellite countries toward the Soviet Union and severely restricted the region's economic contacts with the West. The CMEA also fostered an intraregional economic integration that was so complex as to make it almost impossible for individual countries to chart their own course of internal economic development independently of the Kremlin and other socialist neighbors. The CMEA certainly discouraged its East European members from reforming their centrally controlled economic organization.[5]

The Kremlin also had a strong influence over the military establishments of its East European satellites through the Warsaw Treaty Organization, or Warsaw Pact. The pact was supposed to be a collective security organization of socialist countries to protect them against an attack by NATO. In reality, however, the pact made it possible for the Soviet Union to control the East European defense system. The commander in chief of the pact was a Soviet officer; the Soviets were the chief suppliers of weapons to pact members; the command and control agencies of the national military establishments of member states were integrated and dominated by the USSR; and the pact's annual military maneuvers in different countries, involving hundreds of thousands of troops, were a not-so-subtle reminder to those countries of their vulnerability. Furthermore, many high-ranking officers of the national armies in positions of responsibility completed their advanced military studies in Moscow, where they came under the influence of Soviet colleagues and established strong and continuing working relationships with them. The pact could and did intervene in the internal affairs of a member state in the event of a challenge to Soviet will, as in the case of Czechoslovakia in August 1968, when the Kremlin led a collective invasion to suppress the liberalization movement of Czechoslovak party leader Alexander Dubček. The so-called Brezhnev Doctrine, which justified Warsaw Pact interference in Czechoslovakia's internal politics, was a constant reminder that the USSR could and would move forcefully against any threats to its influence in the region.[6]

Finally, the Central and East European countries that belonged to the CMEA and the Warsaw Pact were forced to pursue an artificial and unpopular diplomatic intimacy with the Soviet Union. This intimacy meant a readiness to accept Soviet leadership in world affairs and at the very least to embrace Soviet anti-Western policies that precluded the cultivation of friendship and cooperation with Western countries, with which they had strong historical links. While satellites, they could never join Western organizations such as the Organization for European Economic Cooperation, which was responsible for implementation of the Marshall Plan; the European Community, now called the European Union, which fostered economic integration; and the North Atlantic Treaty Organization (NATO), which provided a system of collective defense and security for its members.

Satellization depressed and demoralized Central and East European societies by reminding them of their historic vulnerability to the Soviet Union. Contributing to this psychological malaise was a pervasive belief that subservience to the Russians, the region's historic enemy, would be permanent. Finally, satellization fueled a strong anti-Russian nationalism and helped provoke the massive popular demonstrations against communist rule in 1989.

Yugoslav and Albanian Exceptions to Satellization

The Kremlin would have liked to have controlled Yugoslavia because of its wealth and influence over the rest of the region and always considered the Yugoslav communist system, despite its commitment to Marxism-Leninism, a threat to Soviet international interests. The Kremlin, however, could never satellize Tito's regime because it was too strong. The Yugoslav Communist Party was loyal to Tito and could not be seduced into betraying him. Moreover, Tito was very popular with the Yugoslav public as well as with the party, largely because of his heroic leadership of the antifascist resistance during World War II and because he was willing to resist Soviet pressures on him to accept Kremlin leadership and follow Kremlin advice on setting up his communist government. He was in every sense a genuine national figure around whom most of the country's diverse ethnic groups could rally.

Furthermore, the costs to the USSR of forcing its will on Tito's Yugoslavia were prohibitive. The Kremlin lacked the military power to replace Tito with a more compliant communist leader. Nor could it rely on the cooperation of Yugoslavia's East European neighbors to cooperate with a Soviet invasion of Yugoslavia. The Kremlin also risked a worsening of its already strained relationship with the West, especially the United States, which had warned against a Soviet takeover of Yugoslavia. Although the West had no great affection for Tito because of his commitment to communism, despite his campaign against the fascists in World War II, it preferred him in power to a Soviet puppet who would place Yugoslav resources at the disposal of the USSR and strengthen its already extensive influence in Central and Eastern Europe. Yugoslavia thus escaped satellization, remained independent of the USSR, and charted its own national path to communism, which was more significant for its self-proclaimed independence of Soviet communism than for divergence from it. Indeed, Tito's communism bore a striking resemblance to the Soviet model.

Albania also escaped satellization because the costs of bringing it under Soviet influence were even more prohibitive than the costs of subduing Tito's Yugoslavia. Albania was small, mountainous, and very poor. Controlling Albania was simply not worth an expensive Soviet effort. And although Albania became a nuisance to the Kremlin because of its support of Mao Zedong when the Kremlin was feuding with him, it was never a serious strategic threat to Soviet security or other Soviet international ambitions. Moreover, like Yugoslavia, Albania imitated much of the Soviet model, and there was very little chance it would abandon communism.

Gorbachev's Policies

Gorbachev's policies of reform and restraint toward Central and Eastern Europe in the late 1980s, were intended to rejuvenate and legitimize communist rule in Central and Eastern Europe. But paradoxically, those policies ended by disrupting and eventually destroying Communist rule, along with Soviet influence in the region.

1. Reform

In the late 1980s, Gorbachev wanted Central and East European leaders to adopt some aspects of Soviet perestroika to resolve problems with and assure the durability of their socialist systems since Soviet influence in the region depended on them. In particular, Gorbachev advocated a loosening of party and state control.[7] But in urging liberalization, Gorbachev apparently understood neither the fragility of communist rule nor the possibility that reform might further weaken it.[8] He did not seem to take seriously the fear of many Central and East European communist leaders that a little reform would inevitably generate pressures for a lot of reform as popular expectations rose and would weaken rather than strengthen them and the system.[9]

As matters turned out, Communist Party rule was weakened when reform was adopted and weakened when reform was not adopted. For example, when Polish and Hungarian communist leaders of their own volition, and, of course, with the Kremlin's blessing, allowed a substantial liberalization of their political systems in 1989, they whetted the appetites of their citizens for more liberalization and, ultimately, for the replacement of single-party rule, which they were hoping to preserve, with political pluralism, which they really did not want. And when the conservative communist leadership of East Germany, Czechoslovakia, Romania, and Bulgaria resisted liberalization, unprecedented numbers of people demonstrated in Dresden, Leipzig, Prague, Bucharest, and Sofia against the authorities, demanding not only liberalization but also democratization and, to Gorbachev's dismay, an end to Communist Party dominance.

2. Restraint

In responding to the explosion of popular pressure for the end of communist rule throughout most of Central and Eastern Europe, Gorbachev kept the Soviet Union on the sidelines, helping to facilitate the collapse of Communist Party rule and with it the end of Soviet power in Eastern Europe. His restraint contrasted sharply with the aggressiveness of his predecessors, who had always been ready to protect and preserve communist rule in Central and Eastern Europe. Indeed, he rejected the Stalinist notion, reaffirmed by Khrushchev and Brezhnev, of a universal socialist model developed and defended by the Soviet Union. In July 1989, in a speech to the Council of Europe in Strasbourg, he renounced Soviet interventionism in Central and Eastern Europe, in effect affirming the death of the Brezhnev Doctrine, which had been used to justify Soviet intervention in Czechoslovakia in August 1968.[10]

Restraint logically grew out of an acknowledgment that, in trying to coerce its East European allies to adhere strictly to Soviet policies, Khrushchev and Brezhnev had sacrificed long-term success for short-term achievement. The Kremlin had successfully suppressed challenges to communist control and Soviet influence from the mid-1950s to the early 1980s only to alienate local populations, intensify their latent hostility to communism and the Soviet Union, and undercut their reliability as allies in the protection of East bloc security vis-à-vis the West. Moreover, intrusive Soviet policies always carried the cost of antagonizing the West and discouraging Western trade and strategic concessions to the USSR.

Furthermore, Soviet efforts to keep conservative leaderships, such as those of East Germany, Czechoslovakia, Romania, and Bulgaria in power could have precipitated civil war in their countries, which would have embarrassed the USSR and alienated the West. Soviet interference, especially if it provoked a civil war, also would have been extremely costly in terms of further debilitating an already dilapidated Soviet economy, increasing hardship for ordinary people and, consequently, the likelihood of social turmoil and revolution.

There also was little strategic logic in trying to keep the Soviet Union's allies as satellites. The United States and West Germany, the two most powerful members of NATO, no longer seemed, at least to Gorbachev, to be threats to Soviet security. Eastern Europe, therefore, had much less military value to the Soviet Union than it had in the era of the cold war of the late 1940s.[11] At the same time,

Gorbachev hoped to develop new relationships with his East European socialist allies similar to those with Finland and Austria. Soviet relations with these two countries were based on an understanding that they would live in harmony and friendship with the Soviet Union and eschew policies injurious to each other's interests. During a visit to Helsinki in October 1989, Gorbachev implied that the Soviet–Finnish relationship could be a model for Soviet ties with Eastern Europe.[12]

But as communist rule eroded and eventually collapsed in Central and Eastern Europe beginning in the summer of 1989, Soviet power also eroded and with it the means of satellization. What Gorbachev's predecessors had always feared and tried to prevent now occurred. The Kremlin lost direct control of a region important to its security. The historical buffer zone Stalin had created in the region after World War II was gone. The end of satellization also made possible the reunification of Germany in October 1990, another potential liability for Soviet security that past Soviet leaders had been determined to avoid. Gorbachev had no choice but to accept reunification, and on Western terms, that is, an all-German government linked closely to the West, a situation feared and opposed by Stalin, Khrushchev, and Brezhnev. Reunification meant increased German influence throughout Eastern Europe.[13]

Policies of the West

Policies of the West also contributed to the collapse of communist rule in Central and Eastern Europe, but only indirectly. It is an exaggeration to attribute the collapse of communist rule to Western hostility and willingness to undermine it, as some conservatives in the United States, who would like to give all the credit for the collapse to the foreign policy of presidents Ronald Reagan and George Bush, have argued.

Nevertheless, the West was undoubtedly a catalyst of communist collapse in Central and Eastern Europe. Though Western countries recognized communist governments, dealt directly with them, and were prepared to coexist with them indefinitely, they never made a secret of their hope that someday those governments would move away from internal dictatorship and intimacy with the Soviet Union. Sometimes acting in concert, other times acting unilaterally, the major Western powers (Germany, France, Britain, and the United States) tried to make their hope for the collapse of communist rule a reality. The Western powers tried to influence communist rule in Central and Eastern Europe in three ways: by calling attention to violations of human rights, by restricting trade in strategic and related goods, and by expanding détente with the Soviet Union to improve the international environment, reduce Soviet anxieties about the West, and encourage it to loosen its grip on Central and Eastern Europe and to pursue the very policies of reform and restraint adopted by Gorbachev that helped erode communist power.

1. Focus on Human Rights

Western nations consistently objected to alleged human-rights violations by communist governments in Eastern Europe. At a meeting in Helsinki, Finland, in 1975 of the Conference on Security and Cooperation in Europe (CSCE), an organization of thirty-five European countries including the Soviet Union and its Warsaw Pact allies, to discuss economic, strategic, and cultural issues, Western countries focused attention on human rights. The meeting, which occurred during a short period of improved relations, or détente, between East and West, resulted in the Helsinki agreement on human rights, which called upon signatory governments to respect the fundamental liberties of its citizens, notably freedoms of thought, conscience, expression, press, and religion. The governmental leadership of the USSR and other communist-led countries reluctantly signed this agreement, seeing trouble in it for their policies but wanting to conciliate the West in exchange for concessions, especially in trade and arms-control agreements.

The human-rights provisions of the Helsinki agreement in fact were troublesome for the communist governments in the USSR and Central and Eastern Europe. They encouraged dissident groups to agitate for political relaxation. Some even went so far as to monitor their governments' compliance and complain about violations. For example, the Charter 77 group in Czechoslovakia established in early 1977 signed a document criticizing the Prague government's violation of the Helsinki agreement through its harassment of political dissidents. In Poland the Helsinki agreement helped to sensitize people to the importance the West attached to their political oppression. The Helsinki agreement thereby gave a lift to the nascent antigovernment opposition, at least psychologically, if not materially.

Helsinki also provided Western governments, especially the United States, with the legal as well as moral justification for exerting pressure on the East European communist governments to liberalize their political environment, to be more tolerant of protest and dissent, and to ease up on harassment of religious institutions. This pressure helped weaken defensive East European dictatorships trying to cultivate popular and international legitimacy.

2. Restrictions on Trade

The West used trade as a lever to influence and undermine the Communist Party regimes in Eastern Europe. They limited trade and investment in communist countries to express opposition to the antidemocratic policies of the Communist party leadership. They also withheld economic support to prevent communist governments from raising the standard of living and thus making communism more tolerable or even acceptable to its citizens. In the pursuit of this policy, however, the United States was more aggressive than the West Europeans, who seemed to need trade for their economic well-being much more than the Americans. Moreover, they did not seem to be as ideologically hostile to the Soviet communist system as the United States was, especially under presidents Carter and Reagan.[14]

3. Détente with the Soviet Union

The West, especially the West Europeans, tried to encourage the USSR to loosen its grip on Central and Eastern Europe by strengthening détente and weakening the historical Soviet argument that its close ties to the region resulted from their shared vulnerability to a Western attack motivated by Western hostility toward communism. The Kremlin was receptive to a strengthening of East–West détente. In the 1970s under Brezhnev, the Kremlin wanted relief from the expensive weapons buildup and an expansion of trade. A limited improvement in East–West relations lasted from the 1972 Nixon–Brezhnev summit to the conclusion of the SALT II agreements in 1979. The Soviet invasion of Afghanistan in December 1979 severely strained détente, especially Soviet relations with the United States. But in the late 1980s, with the advent of Gorbachev, East–West relations improved. The West supported Gorbachev because of his extensive reform program, called perestroika, which promised liberal change at home and less aggressive behavior abroad. Western support of Gorbachev made the Kremlin feel less threatened and encouraged the Kremlin to move forward with its reforms, in particular, a new leniency in Eastern Europe.

4. Differentiated Policies

The Federal Republic of Germany under both Social Democratic and Christian Democratic leadership from the 1970s onward, while eager to weaken communist regimes, which were viewed as a threat to its security and an obstacle to the reuniting of the divided German nation, was inclined to proceed in a conciliatory way, gradually developing political and economic links to individual Central and East European countries to encourage their autonomy of the Kremlin without alarming it. Germany was at all times the most vulnerable to an attack by Soviet-led Warsaw Pact forces located on the borders of Poland and Czechoslovakia. In 1968, the Bonn government formally recognized the Romanian communist government. And in 1971, Bonn concluded treaties with Poland and East Germany acknowledging the post–World War II boundaries of these countries. These gestures, indirectly at least, diminished their isolation and their sense of dependence on the Kremlin.[15]

But the West Germans were careful to avoid allowing their policy toward Central and Eastern Europe, sometimes called *Ostpolitik*, to alarm the Kremlin by going out of their way to strengthen détente with the Soviet Union, reassuring the defensive Brezhnev that Western Europe and especially Germany wanted good relations with the Soviet bloc. Moreover, the Germans gave enthusiastic and unstinting support to Gorbachev and his perestroika, which they hoped would transform Soviet domestic and foreign policies. Indeed, by 1989, when change was imminent, German foreign minister Hans Dietrich Genscher helped convince Gorbachev that the Soviet Union had nothing to lose by allowing the East European countries to reform themselves, to have greater autonomy, and to increase their contacts with the West. Always an enthusiastic supporter of Gorbachev and his perestroika, Genscher was behind a large German program of financial and economic assistance to the Soviet Union to bolster Gorbachev's leadership.

The French also cultivated ties with the Central and East European countries, partly to offset the rapid expansion of German influence. France also saw friendship with the Central and East European countries not only as beneficial to France's strategic and economic interests in the region and as a counterweight to a strong German state but also as an opportunity to encourage reform, especially in the area of human rights. French governments in the 1970s and 1980s, therefore, under both conservative and socialist leadership, always kept lines of trade and communication open with Central and East European communist leaders. Both presidents Giscard d'Estaing in the 1970s and François Mitterrand in the 1980s met with Central and East European leaders. Although these meetings did give some recognition and support to communist leaders, they also gave the French an opportunity to criticize the repressive behavior of those leaders. President Mitterrand, in particular, was very active in the human-rights area. Eager to demonstrate to the French electorate that the Marxian socialist origins of his Socialist Party did not preclude its vigorous opposition to communist dictatorship, Mitterrand made human rights a big issue in French relations with communist governments and offered Soviet and East European dissidents a safe haven in France.

Like Germany, the French tried hard to keep their political fences mended with the Kremlin as they strengthened ties with the leaders of Central and Eastern Europe. While they did not shy away from criticizing Soviet violations of human rights, the French deemphasized ideological differences with the Soviet Union and expressed support for East–West détente. Thus, when the Soviet Union invaded Afghanistan, the French muted their criticism, despite pressure from the United States to confront and condemn the Kremlin. And when the Americans imposed sanctions against the Soviets in early 1980, the French gave only lip service to enforcement. Indeed, France, like Germany, did much to reassure the Soviets of the West European commitment to détente, thereby doing its part to help diminish Soviet insecurity and the strategic logic of maintaining a repressive grip on Eastern Europe.[16]

The United States was more ideological and punitive than the West Europeans in dealing with the Central and East European communist governments and with the Kremlin. Historically hostile toward all forms of communism, Washington refused to distinguish among communisms in different countries based on the degree to which a particular country was or was not a threat to American strategic interests. Moreover, a rigid anticommunism struck many American leaders as the right way to deal with the Soviet Union and its European satellites. Indeed, to many American commentators and political leaders, the more subtle and nuanced approach of the West Europeans appeared as passivity and appeasement. Many American politicians also thought that nothing could be done to make the Soviets loosen their grip on the Central and East European countries, so it was pointless to try. Why make any concessions to the Soviets if they would make none back, at least none that were meaningful in American eyes?[17]

Thus, Washington used power openly and forcefully to weaken communist rule in Central and Eastern Europe. For example, the Carter administration (1977–81), by focusing heavily on human-rights violations, tried to discredit communist governments and encourage an expansion of dissident activity and the emergence of a political opposition that conceivably some day might challenge Communist Party rule. In 1977, Carter visited Warsaw expressly to underline U.S. concern about human-rights violations by the Polish government under Communist Party chief Edward Gierek, a hard-liner who insisted on a neo-Stalinistic political conformity in Polish society. The Reagan administration (1981–89) severely criticized President Wojciech Jaruzelski's declaration of martial law in December 1981 to suppress Solidarity and other political opponents of the regime. The Reagan administration consulted with the Vatican on ways to encourage political dissent and imposed sanctions on Polish trade with the United States, depriving it of a valuable source of hard currency earnings. American economic sanctions ultimately helped bankrupt the Polish economy, contributing to the economic crisis in the late 1980s that would lead to the collapse of Communist Party rule in 1989. Reagan also condemned the Ceauşescu regime in Romania for its violations of human rights. In the mid-1980s, when the U.S. ambassador to Bucharest David Funderburk began sending reports back to Washington about the Ceauşescu regime's brutal treatment of its citizens, the administration canceled most-favored-nation treatment of Romanian trade, and this accelerated the decline of an already weak economy. These policies helped to delegitimize communist rule in Central and Eastern Europe and to that extent must be given some credit for contributing to the eventual collapse of communist and Soviet power in the region in 1989.

The Processes of Collapse

The emergence of opposition to communist rule that led to its collapse in 1989 and 1990 had antecedents in the late 1970s and early 1980s in small minorities of intellectuals critical of the repressive behavior of communist governments. This antiregime opposition was ruthlessly persecuted in Czechoslovakia, Poland, Romania, and other countries. But it survived by dint of its sheer determination to force change.[18] A communications revolution in the 1980s helped fuel the growth of political opposition. People learned about the flaws of their political system from outside sources such as broadcasts by the British Broadcasting Company (BBC), the Voice of America, and Radio Free Europe. Videocassette recorders carried uncensored films, political discussions, and dissident platforms.[19] At the same time, different social groups, which had been separate and independent of one another in articulating grievances against the regime, began to cooperate in opposing communist rule. Workers had tended to concentrate primarily on economic issues, such as low pay, poor living conditions, and lack of influence over the workplace, as well as over the political system, while intellectuals had been concerned with political liberalization, in particular the lifting of censorship, the toleration of pluralism, and the democratization of the government. Driven by a shared hostility toward communist rule, these groups eventually found common ground and by the end of the 1980s joined together to pressure communist leaders to reform and ultimately to resign.[20]

Although there were many commonalities, the collapse of communist rule did vary in scope and pace in different countries beginning in the summer of 1989. At least four large patterns are discernible: an evolutionary and gradual pattern in Poland and Hungary, where the Communist Party agreed to liberalize and ultimately give up its rule in response to popular demands for radical political change; a pattern in East Germany, Czechoslovakia, Bulgaria, and Albania, where conservative Communist Party leaders tried to resist popular pressures for change but eventually stepped aside in favor of reformers outside the party or inside it ready to move forward with meaningful political liberalization; a pattern in Romania, where Ceauşescu was so opposed to liberalization that he tried to use force to prevent it, with disastrous consequences for his rule and even his personal safety—he was executed; and, finally, the pattern in Yugoslavia, where political liberalization gave rise to a vehement nationalism among the different ethnic groups that made up the country and eventually provoked a violent civil war that destroyed the Titoist state.

1. Poland and Hungary

The popular political upheavals of 1989 began in Poland and Hungary, which were always less tightly controlled by party leaders and the Kremlin than other Central and East European countries. As early as 1988, reform-oriented communists, anticipating an explosion of popular hostility, tried to avoid it by agreeing to reforms liberalizing the political system. In Poland the pressure for change came largely from workers, intellectuals, farmers, and the Catholic Church. By contrast, in Hungary party reformers took the initiative in liberalizing the Hungarian communist system, displaying a pragmatism and flexibility that were intended to help ensure the survival of the party's leadership in a new era of radical change that could no longer be avoided. But Polish and Hungarian communist reformers were simply too late to stave off the collapse of party rule.

2. East Germany, Czechoslovakia, Bulgaria, and Albania

Political change was more traumatic in these countries, which experienced massive public demonstrations against the government. In the fall of 1989, fed up with the incompetence and hypocrisy of the communist system and with its subservience to Moscow, thousands of people took to the streets of Leipzig, Prague, Budapest, Bucharest, Sofia, and Tirana to demand a lifting of censorship, multiparty politics, freedom of religion, and the resignation of conservative communist leaders in favor of reformers. These popular demonstrations were unprecedented in the tightly controlled systems of East Germany, Czechoslovakia, Bulgaria, and Albania. They frightened hard-line leaders, put them on the defensive, and eventually forced them out of power in favor of people either inside the party, as in Bulgaria, or outside it, as in Czechoslovakia and Albania, committed to dismantling the traditional communist system. Communist leaders who survived were those ready to make a complete break with the old order, or at least to make a believable appearance of doing so, but their willingness to compromise came too late to salvage their credibility with voters, who, given the opportunity, eventually voted them out of power.

A dramatic event emblematic of the ubiquitous erosion and collapse of communist power occurred on November 9, 1989, in East Berlin, where citizens attacked the Berlin Wall, pushed a hole through it, and opened it for passage into West Berlin, with no response from the East German authorities. East Germany was special in still another way. The collapse of communist rule there led to its eventual reunification with West Germany in October 1990.

3. Romania

The most violent response occurred in Romania, which experienced a mini–civil war in which the Ceauşescu regime refused to the last to undertake radical change. It had to be dislodged by the army, which had joined the opposition to rid the country of an abusive and incompetent government.

On the one hand, Romania had a very conservative rural population skeptical of the radical political and economic change advocated by liberal reformist elements in the countryside. These people did not support the overthrow of communist rule, but neither did they oppose it. People in the cities, however, hated the inept and reactionary dictatorship by Ceauşescu and finally openly challenged it in December 1989 when it resisted pressures for reform and used force against the opposition. Romania now literally split apart, with the countryside remaining passive, while city people, supported by the Romanian army, which shared their hatred of the regime, cooperated to bring it down. Yet the aftermath was anticlimactic. Although Ceauşescu was killed, his successor seemed a reincarnation of him in many ways, setting the stage for a long period of conflict between reformers and reactionaries that continued well into the mid-1990s.

4. Yugoslavia

A unique kind of challenge to communist rule occurred in Yugoslavia, starting with political reforms in the late 1980s in the republics of Slovenia and Croatia, where Communist Party leaders had always been somewhat more liberal than those in other Yugoslav republics. Before long, newly elected nationalist-inspired governments in Slovenia and Croatia separated from the Yugoslav state. The independence of Slovenia and Croatia, which helped trigger the independence of Bosnia-Herzegovina and Macedonia, precipitated the disintegration of the Titoist state. It also contributed to the outbreak of war in the newly independent republic of Croatia and Bosnia-Herzegovina as the different ethnic groups, now freed of communist control, indulged their historic prejudices and began a campaign of landgrabbing. The most aggressive of these groups turned out to be the Serb minorities who were encouraged by the Serb Republic government of President Slobodan Milošević.

Conclusions

Communist systems had been ripe for revolt for many years, with flaws that rendered them inept and hypocritical and deprived them of the popular legitimacy needed to assure their long-term survival. They collapsed in 1989, rather than earlier or later, largely because of the Soviet Union, which under Gorbachev encouraged reform to correct these flaws but then refused to defend them against popular demands for more change and eventually for the complete abandonment of communism and satellization. And, although the West was a catalyst, not a cause, of the collapse of communist systems in Eastern Europe, its role should not be underestimated. Western countries, in particular the United States, had been trying to weaken the East European communist political systems internally and externally for several decades. The West also had succeeded in lulling the Kremlin into a sense of security that helped to encourage a more flexible Soviet approach to the region and eventually to allow change to run its natural course. Moreover, the longer the Kremlin remained passive, the more difficult it became to reverse that behavior—and the West helped to make sure of that.

While the causes of collapse were rather similar throughout the region, the actual process of communist collapse varied from country to country depending on the differences, however subtle from an outsider's point of view, in how the communist system actually worked in each country. In the more highly developed north, namely, in Poland, Hungary, and Czechoslovakia, there were people even within the Communist Party with strong liberal instincts ready to lead a radical and profound shift away from orthodox communist rule. In the Balkans, however, which were less developed politically and economically and lacked the kind of liberal elite found in the northern countries, the collapse was more traumatic and more violent.

2

Problems of Postcommunist Development

After the collapse of Communist Party rule, the Central and East European governments tried to develop Western-style democracy, some version of the free-market economy, societal peace and unity, and a diversified foreign policy with new links to the West. But six years into the postcommunist era, although they have made great strides, they face horrendous problems in their search for political stability, material well-being, stability and tranquility at home, and security abroad.

Establishing Democratic Government

Postcommunist governments in Central and Eastern Europe tried to democratize the parliamentary institutions inherited from the communist past. Single-party dictatorships gave way to political pluralism with free, open, and competitive elections for national parliaments. Freedom of the press, of assembly, of thought, and of religion was guaranteed in law. And communist-style parliamentary government was modified to operate more like the Western model, with the acceptance of parliamentary approval of and control over ministerial leadership through the "no-confidence" vote, which requires that a cabinet resign if it loses majority support in parliament.

But the postcommunist parliamentary systems do not yet work as they do in London, Paris, and Bonn. They are burdened by a proliferation of political parties, strong authoritarian tendencies of leaders and governments, a nostalgia for the communist past accompanied by a pervasive voter cynicism and apathy, and, in some but not all countries, a disquieted military with lukewarm sympathy for the new democratic order.

1. Proliferation of Political Parties

Once pluralism was legalized by the outgoing communist leadership, there was quite literally an explosion of new party groups eager to obtain power, or at least influence, over government. More than a dozen parties frequently competed for voter support in parliamentary elections, and many more party groups struggled to reach the threshold of support needed to enter the electoral process. At one point in the early 1990s Romania was reputed to have almost a hundred different political organizations styling themselves as a party.

Impact

Although party proliferation might be considered an asset to democratic development because it provides voters a maximum amount of choice in parliamentary and other elections, the impact has been negative. As a result of the multiplicity of parties competing for voter support in the parliamentary elections of the early 1990s, no single party was usually able to win a majority. To construct a majority of support in the legislature, prime ministers and their cabinets had to rely on coalitions made up of several small parties that had agreed to back a prime minister in return for representation in his cabinet in proportion to their strength in Parliament. Many Central and East European ministerial leaderships in the early 1990s had to engage in extensive deal making to form a coalition, making them beholden to their coalition supporters. This meant that prime ministers had to proceed cautiously in the formation of controversial policies that could provoke conflict within the coalition, disrupt it, and possibly destroy it. With weak ministerial leadership, the new parliamentary democracies of Eastern Europe seemed ill suited to the task of addressing complex social and economic problems that required difficult and unpopular policies.[1]

Causes

Most of the earliest noncommunist parties established at the end of communist rule and eager to lead in the postcommunist era, such as Poland's Solidarity, the former Czechoslovakia's Civic Forum, and Romania's National Salvation Front, were really not political parties at all. Begun as mass protests against communist rule and led by a core of long-time dissident activists, they provided a focus for the mobilization of broad-based, spontaneous popular pressure against communist power. They were never more than broad alliances with vague, non- or anti-ideological, and strongly moralistic programs and with informal, somewhat loose internal structures designed to avoid alienating any of their constituencies.

Although some received the bulk of voter support in the early postcommunist years, they lacked stability and cohesion. When they confronted the new task of exercising power, they began to experience severe internal conflict within their leaderships and among parliamentary deputies and activists on the local levels, which eventually led to splits and the emergence of new political groups.[2]

Another source of party proliferation was the deep traditional cleavage between city and country in most Central and East European societies, which has its origins in the pre–World War II era, when industrialization was beginning. Communist rule intensified it by neglecting agriculture and marginilizing rural society. While rural-based parties reflected popular resentment and distrust of city life as godless, alien, corrupt, and privileged, urban-based parties talked about developing better living facilities, acquiring consumer goods and services, education for one's children, and an easier, more comfortable material existence, as well as access to political power. This cleavage had a special impact on the less-developed Balkan countries, where the professional middle class and intelligentsia of the urban centers waged endless battles with the countryside in parliamentary elections.[3]

The use of proportional representation (PR) in the election of parliaments also contributed to party proliferation. PR was supposed to make postcommunist parliaments sensitive to the nuances of different constituencies. But by assigning seats in parliament following an election on the basis of the percentage of votes won by each party, PR multiplied the number of parties that were able to win seats. PR made it virtually impossible for a party to win a majority or even a large plurality of popular votes. Indeed, it encouraged voters to support very narrowly focused special-interest parties that could attract only a small percentage of the electorate.[4]

Explosions of nationalism among the region's many ethnic minorities also contributed to party proliferation by giving rise to several different kinds of political parties focused primarily on national identity, such as Romania's Hungarian Democratic Union, a party pledged to the protection of the interests of the Hungarian minority in Transylvania, and Bulgaria's Movement for Rights and Freedom, which is concerned with the well-being of the Turkish minority. At the same time, many large parties committed to the interests of the ethnic majority were highly nationalistic. Some, notably Romania's National Salvation Front and Slovakia's Public Against Violence, eventually split between moderates and radicals over how far and how fast to advance the cause of their constituents against minorities seeking to gain political influence.[5]

Finally, the proliferation of political parties was encouraged by popular but constitutionally weak presidential figures who were unwilling or unable to build broadly based umbrella-like party organizations.[6] Leaders like President Lech Wałęsa of Poland and President Václav Havel of Czechoslovakia initially refrained from developing large party organizations because of a determination to stay above politics and to act as leaders of all the people in their countries and not as leaders of only those who supported a presidential party. They left the nitty-gritty of party formation and voter mobilization to others. When they finally realized the need for a party organization to enhance their leadership, they had difficulty developing a devoted political constituency either because, as in the case of Wałęsa, they had lost much of their original popularity or, as in the case of Havel, others, such as Prime Minister Václav Klaus in the Czech Republic, had formed their own strong organizations. Of course, in the case of Romania's Ion Iliescu, who did form his own party, his alienation of many social groups prevented his National Salvation Front from becoming a truly broadly based, catch-all party.

2. Authoritarian Tendencies

Another problem for democratic development, not unconnected to party proliferation, has been popular sympathy in some Central and East European countries for authoritarian styles of leadership, despite memories of communist repression. Increasingly, voters seem to miss the guidance and discipline provided by strong leaders in the communist and precommunist eras. Even in Poland, where most people seem dedicated to individual freedoms and democratic government, there was some acceptance of an argument by President Lech Wałęsa that the crises of the moment in Poland require the kind of directive, forceful executive leadership prime ministers and cabinets seemed unable to provide. Indeed, many Poles, including Wałęsa, hold a very positive image of Marshal Piłsudski, the authoritarian "man on the white horse" to whom Polish society looked for unity and security in the late 1920s and early 1930s. President Iliescu of Romania and President Slobodan Milošević of the Serb Republic are other East European leaders in the postcommunist era who display a strong authoritarian style. They have a lot of popular support despite their readiness to suppress opposition, censor news, and monopolize the media.

Indeed, press censorship is more prevalent than one might suspect. It is practiced in a variety of ways in Slovakia, Romania, Serbia, and Albania and to a lesser extent in Hungary and Poland, which are reputed to be, along with the Czech Republic, the strongest democracies in the region. For example, the authorities in Serbia and Slovakia frequently threaten critical journalists with physical violence. They allow independent newspapers but control them closely by imposing taxes and regulating their production and distribution facilities, especially the acquisition of supplies. Given the high cost of putting out a newspaper or journal in the cash-strapped societies of Eastern Europe, it is impossible, or at least very difficult, for newspapers to survive without some kind of government support or cooperation.[7]

Also, governments insist that newspapers adhere to certain "values" in the presentation of information to the public. For example, the Polish government has reportedly told the press to respect "Christian values," which presumably means newspapers cannot lobby aggressively in favor of abortion rights, which are opposed by the Catholic Church. The Polish government also calls upon the press "to tell the truth" in its reporting another implicit limit on what they can print.[8]

Popular tolerance of authoritarian styles of political behavior in several Central and East European societies is attributable to several factors, not the least of which is a lack of familiarity with and understanding of the complexities and inefficiencies of democratic government. Although the countries of Central and Eastern Europe did have Western-style parliamentary democracy in the period between World War I and World War II (1919–39), in most Central and East European countries it was shallow and short-lived. Democratic governments in the interwar years were burdened by extreme factionalism caused by the proliferation of narrowly focused combative political parties that undermined national unity, the capacity for consensus making, and the ability of government to address pressing socioeconomic problems. This factionalism, which required ministerial leaders of most Central and East European countries to rely on unstable multiparty coalitions that would break up at the first hint of a controversial policy, severely undermined the faith of people, especially the middle class, in the efficacy of democratic rule.

By the 1930s, incessant conflict paralyzing national politics, occurring as it did at moments of socioeconomic crisis, such as the world depression and the appearance of widespread unemployment, encouraged growth of popular support of strong leaders such as Marshal Piłsudski in Poland, Admiral Horthy in Hungary, and the authoritarian monarchies in Romania and Bulgaria. Strong leaders inclined toward authoritarian rule, moreover, strengthened their appeal to various constituencies such as the landed aristocracy, the urban middle class, and the rural peasantry by insisting on the need to limit political freedom to discourage the spread of communist ideas from the Soviet Union. By the eve of World War II most Central and East European governments had become fascist dictatorships.[9]

After World War II, forty years of communist rule strengthened popular tolerance of authoritarian political behavior by teaching people that politics in the sense of choosing leaders and influencing public policy was the Communist Party's business, not theirs, and by punishing those who by criticizing or opposing the regime rejected this notion. By giving the peoples of Central and Eastern Europe the appearance but not the reality of self-government, communist rule, for all its democratic rhetoric, deprived them of a real understanding of how democracy works and ill prepared them for the liberal transformation to occur in the early 1990s. Finally, communist rule suggested the logic, and perhaps the necessity, of popular acceptance of a political trade-off inimical to democracy. This trade-off, on which communist rule in fact was based, required people to accept a substantial diminution, and in some cases a complete loss, of personal political freedom in return for the assurance of material security, stability, and predictability that democratic government by its nature cannot guarantee and frequently cannot achieve despite its best effort.[10]

The apparent tolerance of authoritarian leadership, especially of Slovakia's Prime Minister Mečiar, Romania's President Iliescu, Croatia's President Tudjman, and Serbia's President Milošević, also may be related to the weakness or lack of the kind of developed civil society found in Western democracies. Civil society means the existence of a web of autonomous political and social organizations able to act more or less responsibly within an established institutional framework. But most of the former communist-ruled countries had only embryonic forms of civil society in their precommunist history, and those structures that did exist were not repressed by the communists. Moreover, the closest thing to an autonomous political or social organization, the opposition, wherever it existed under communist rule, provided inadequate schooling for the practice of democracy as the "art of the possible." The opposition had a lot of experience with confrontation but hardly any with compromise and consensus building. Without a framework for compromise and consensus building, politics becomes, as it has become in postcommunist Central and Eastern Europe, a lot of noise, confrontation, and conflict leading to political paralysis that makes people impatient, angry, and susceptible to demagogy. Indeed, communist authoritarian rule left most of the societies of Central and Eastern Europe with only a very primitive understanding of how real democratic government works.[11]

It might be expected that the spirit of the dissenters under communism, who spoke the language of democracy and called for political liberalization, would translate into an ability to make democratic government work once it was established following the collapse of communist rule. But dissent was not synonymous with democracy, and the dissident movements in some former communist countries, such as Poland and Czechoslovakia, did not produce a liberal tradition. With little if any experience with democratic political parties, interest groups, and distinct social organizations, dissent was more an expression of shared opposition to a common enemy. The dissenters in Eastern Europe during the last years of communist rule therefore could not be expected to provide, and did not provide, the cohesive political leadership needed in the new democratic era.[12]

3. Cynicism and Skepticism of Democracy

In part, the present tolerance of authoritarian behavior in some Central and East European countries is a by-product of voter apathy, as seen in the low level of popular interest in political life, particularly in declining turnouts in parliamentary and local elections. The number of people actively involved in the day-to-day building of new parties and movements is still quite limited and well below the level of popular involvement in the political life of most of the societies of Western Europe. Political apathy comes from a popular mistrust of the political-party form inspired by the simplicity of the monolithic communist experience, as well as by a traditional mistrust and rejection not just of formal organization but of power itself and by a long-held perception of politics derived from the long authoritarian past as a morally corrupt, dirty business to be shunned by respectable, decent people.[13]

The communist system played on and strengthened these historic sentiments by its unresponsiveness to popular feelings while encouraging popular political participation. Workers were especially cynical not only because the so-called "workers' state" of the communists had failed to deliver on its promises to them but also because the postcommunist parliamentary systems did not seem to be doing much better by them, seemingly unable to cope with unemployment, inflation, and a conspicuous decline in living standards that, they expected, would improve once the communists were ousted from power. Workers became impatient with the slow-moving parliamentary system and either cannot or will not come to terms with its complexities and inadequacies, which burden all democratic government, even the most well developed ones in the West, of which, arguably, many people in Central and Eastern Europe know and understand little. Workers have allowed themselves to be manipulated by politicians who seek their electoral support by promising them security and stability.[14]

In fact, many East European workers suspect that most politicians, whatever they say to the contrary, are communists, or corrupt, or both, because many of the people who are running Eastern Europe in the early postcommunist era had been in positions of political or economic control under communism. People find it hard to reconcile the continuing influence of former communists in governmental bureaucracies with the shift to democracy. The explanation that many former communists are the only people with administrative experience is not understood and credible with a lot of voters, even though many of those same voters turn around and, out of desperation over the harshness of daily life, support former communists in the hope they will do a better job of running the country and of solving its problems than the noncommunist incumbents.[15]

4. Nostalgia for the Communist Past

Not so paradoxically, another problem for postcommunist democratic development is a new popular nostalgia for some aspects of the communist past evident in the increasing numbers of voters who support former Communist Party members in parliamentary elections. While most former communists certainly remain under a cloud, blamed for almost everything that was wrong with the past, they retain a certain appeal for voters disappointed by the failure of the democratic leadership to improve living conditions, and they have been trying to cultivate this appeal in the hope of a return to power. For example, they are quick to point out that in the past people could count on order, stability, and predictability, with everyone guaranteed at least enough food and in most cases a job, a home, and affordable health care. Most former Communist parties also insist they *have* broken with the dictatorial and centralizing tactics of the past and speak of a commitment to pluralistic democracy and of support for free-market reform. They call themselves "socialists" and insist on their role as a loyal opposition. They speak also of patriotism and express no interest in links with the Russian Communist Party. They express widely felt fears and suspicions of hastily implemented radical reforms that have caused hardship and empathize with voters who would like to preserve the paternalistic aspects of communist rule, especially policies guaranteeing citizens a job, health care, housing, education, and other entitlements.

By the beginning of 1995, former communists were in control of either executive or legislative branches of government in Poland, Hungary, Slovakia, Romania, and Bulgaria. They do not appear to be a threat to democracy. For example, most of the former Hungarian communists, including Prime Minister Gyula Horn, are promarket, procompetition, and proreform socialists. Former communists in Poland, who won a plurality in the October 1993 parliamentary elections as well as President Aleksandr Kwasniewski, have indicated similar commitments. They seem willing to accept and work within the democratic system and give up power voluntarily if they are voted out of office. But former communists in power in Slovakia, Romania, and Serbia seem skeptical of, if not hostile to, democracy and willing to act in authoritarian ways to suppress criticism of their policies.

5. The Military

A wild card in the future development of Central and East European politics is the military, which is not altogether comfortable with the new postcommunist order. Defense expenditures have been cut in all states except Romania, where Ceauşescu's notorious neglect of the army led to an increase of appropriations by the post-Ceauşescu leadership, which wanted to repay the army for its support in the revolution that toppled Ceauşescu. Many military personnel have complained that not enough has been done to weed out the so-called "red colonels" or political officers whose job it was in the communist era to assure the ideological reliability and political subservience of the military. Many military leaders resent extensive investment in the nonmilitary infrastructure, such as health, education, and welfare. They resent curtailment of defense expenditures that deprive them of the expensive weapons and status of primary importance they had in the communist era. In response the new governments have been continuously shifting personnel to get aggressive and neocommunist officers into the reserves or retirement. The armies of Poland, Hungary, and the Czech Republic, however, seem to be more accepting of democratization than those in Bulgaria and Romania, where military leaders are uneasy over the severe economic problems that have reduced the standard of living of military personnel. The potential of the military to back conservative leaderships in some countries for the sake of national well-being, as well as for its own sake, is a potential liability for democratic development.[16]

6. Prospects of Democratic Development

There is no guarantee that Western-style parliamentary democracy will work in postcommunist Central and Eastern Europe the way it does in Western Europe. At the moment, the Central and East European countries are in a transitional phase of political development, experimenting with Western processes and seeking ways of tailoring them to the peculiarities of their local environment. They are not likely to return to the authoritarianism of the communist era, but they also are unlikely to replicate exactly the Western democratic models, which may not be suited to their specific needs and capabilities.[17]

Introducing a Free-Market Economy

The new leaders of postcommunist Central and Eastern Europe, eager to improve living conditions, saw the communist command economy as the biggest obstacle to economic growth and development. Many political leaders and their economic advisers throughout Central and Eastern Europe today believe that only the introduction of a free-enterprise economy based upon the capitalist principles of supply and demand can restore economic health, raise living standards, and ultimately assure political stability.

1. Basic Principles

On the advice of Western economists as well as their own experts, most Central and East European governments are pursuing at different speeds and in special ways some or all of the following policies to free up the economic life of their country. They are (1) privatizing large and small enterprises in industry, agriculture, and service areas such as banking, insurance, and retail sales, while retaining local determination of wages in enterprises still under state control; (2) ending monopolies—either state or private; (3) accepting bankruptcies and unemployment as the free market expands; (4) terminating centralized control of both planning and pricing and allowing prices to be influenced by supply and demand; (5) dismantling the bureaucratic planning pyramid, including the retirement of the former communist *nomenklatura*; (6) abandoning subsidies to producers and consumers; (7) using fiscal policy to restrict demand; and (8) making currency convertible.[18]

In addition, East European governments are trying to establish a legal infrastructure that will define the rules of the marketplace, particularly regarding property, contract, and tort. Other infrastructures—accounting, managerial, statistical—also are being installed. Habits of accuracy and full disclosure are slowly taking the place of socialism's habits of false and deceptive statistics, cover-ups, and other kinds of deceptive economic and financial practices.[19]

Governments have also aggressively recruited foreign investment. Foreign direct investment in the region rose from $2.3 billion in 1990 to $11 billion in 1992, especially in Hungary, which had half of all foreign investment in the region in 1993.[20] Some Central and East European governments have encouraged foreign investment by easing restrictions on foreign ownership of property, providing tax incentives in the form of "tax holidays" and allowing repatriation of profits.

2. Problems, Obstacles, and Constraints

But a variety of problems is slowing up and in other ways compromising the shift to a free-market economy. The most important of these concern (1) the rate of change and the political costs of moving too far too fast to the free market by what has been called "shock therapy," (2) privatization of state-owned and state-operated enterprises, (3) a decline in trade, (4) paucity of foreign investment, and (5) cost-cutting policies that have increased the hardships most people are enduring as the old economic paternalism of the communists is dismantled.

Pros and Cons of Shock Therapy

Initially, reformers in some countries, such as Poland and the former Czechoslovakia, wanted to proceed rapidly in dismantling the state-controlled economy and in developing free-market policies in a strategy called "shock therapy." They assumed that the longer it took to reform the economy, the longer people would have to suffer hardships caused by the withdrawal of the state from most aspects of economic life. Furthermore, postcommunist leaders were told by Western governments and banking institutions such as the International Monetary Fund that financial assistance for the transition to a free-market economy would not be forthcoming unless curtailment of state control over the economy proceeded quickly and efficiently. But fearing an explosion of social tensions, politicians and political parties, especially the former communists, urged steady but slower, incremental change to minimize hardship. Many Central and East European leaders were aware that voters were less enthusiastic about the free-market economy than they. While many people disliked the low living standards that communist governments brought, they did like the relative economic security communist rule had provided and still expect the state to assure a minimum level of material well-being. Postcommunist governments in most Central and East European countries have also tried in different ways to cushion the effects of the transition to a free-market economy. They have continued to subsidize some enterprises simply to keep people employed. They have kept control of prices for some food staples, for rent, and for public transportation to assure their availability to everybody, especially the poorest groups, such as retirees and the elderly on fixed pensions. They have continued to sustain unemployment benefits for long periods of time.[21]

Privatization

Privatization is essential to the revitalization of economic life in Central and Eastern Europe, if only because it provides high rewards for successful performance. In particular, the quality of management will improve when managers' personal interests are directly related to the performance of their enterprises. Privatization also will stimulate competition among different economic sectors, and competition will revitalize the stagnant economy inherited from the communist past. Finally, privatization should generate foreign investment while also bringing in direct revenue for the government.[22] But privatization has been slow and is far from complete. It has gone further in Poland, the Czech Republic, and Hungary, but has barely started in most Balkan countries. The problems of diminishing the enormous role played by the state in the running of the economy under communist rule are many, complicated, and a long way from being resolved.

There are too few local buyers, who have the funds to purchase state properties that are for sale. The only people who do have the wealth to buy state industries are a small elite, in many instances former Communist Party officials who had managed the industries now being sold. Indeed, managers of enterprises under communist rule who still had their jobs in the early 1990s have an advantage in claims to state industries. They are usually the only people who know exactly how the enterprises functioned, and they frequently are the only people with sufficient cash to buy the enterprises.[23]

It is still too early to determine the success or failure of government efforts in Poland and the former Czechoslovakia to sell large numbers of state enterprises to citizens by giving them vouchers that they can eventually exchange for shares in those enterprises, making these people in effect investors and part owners. This procedure looks simple, but in practice it has been extremely complicated and difficult to administer, and its economic impact is barely evident.[24] While the commercial banks and stock exchanges that ultimately will make privatization work have started up, they are not yet well developed. Many banks lack adequate credit for the financing of private ownership, in part because they are obliged to buy government securities to finance social spending. They also are still granting credit to sustain unprofitable enterprises that the government does not want to see closed down because they employ so many workers. The banks have many such loans out, which they probably will never recover. In addition, price distortions caused by continuing price controls on raw materials and on finished products have made it virtually impossible for a would-be entrepreneur to figure out exactly what he is getting in a business.[25]

The primitive financial infrastructure has also tended to discourage much-needed foreign investment in privatization and the overall development of private enterprise. Because of the difficulties of doing business on a day-to-day basis in some countries, foreign investors have been unwilling to invest more than a marginal amount. At the same time, because they also have tended to "skim the cream" by investing in the most promising state enterprises being sold while leaving the restructuring of more problematic enterprises to others, there have been calls, especially in Hungary, for keeping firms in local hands. Foreign investment, therefore, has been an uncertain and unreliable source of much-needed capital and technology.

Questions of ownership have also complicated privatization efforts. In many instances, the state is not the uncontested owner of an enterprise and therefore cannot sell it. Many enterprises were confiscated after World War II, and claims against them are now being raised. The claims of these various owners need resolution before the state can sell the property. This struggle for "ownership" is complicated by the lack of understanding of property titles, which were virtually nonexistent in many East European nations under communist rule. The "owner" often turns out to be the individual or group that managed the enterprise's operations and revenue.[26]

Negative Consequences of Privatization

Privatization increased unemployment as new owners streamlined overmanned companies. Moreover, the new, rapidly expanding private sector cannot absorb most of the unemployed. This means that many people may never be able to find a job and will have to rely on casual work with long periods of unemployment and dependence on welfare. Also, working conditions in many instances have not improved from what they were under state control. The old Workers' Councils have remained but have lost their clout because managers will not put up with anything that interferes with their efforts to develop profitability. Under these circumstances, workers are understandably skeptical about what capitalism can do for them.[27]

3. Other Difficulties of Introducing a Free Market

The expanding private sector has produced a new, small entrepreneural elite that consists of people who have managed to do well in the transition, notably, government bureaucrats and managers of profitable companies and agricultural cooperatives. Many of these new entrepreneurs are conspicuous consumers who show off their wealth, much to the disgust of most people who have all they can do to stay afloat. With the gap among the economic classes widening in Eastern Europe, sharp class divisions are developing and social tensions are increasing, with conflict over the distribution of goods and services.[28]

A decline in the region's trade with the Soviet Union and its successors, in particular Russia, increased the difficulty of introducing a free-market economy.

The decline in trade, which meant shortages of energy needed for local industry as well as a decline in revenue from export enterprises, occurred when Moscow started insisting on payment for its exports in scarce hard currency. At the same time, the USSR and after it Russia simply lacked the means to pay for most of what was wanted when the Central and East Europeans themselves demanded payment for their exports in hard currency. Meanwhile, Russian oil, on which the East Europeans had become dependent in recent years, became almost prohibitively expensive, forcing some oil-dependent industries in the region to curtail output.[29]

Making matters worse was the disintegration of the Council for Mutual Economic Assistance (CMEA). Whatever its flaws, the CMEA had provided the region guaranteed markets for manufactured exports, however poor their quality. Although the postcommunist East European leaders wanted an end to the CMEA, viewing it as an economic straightjacket and another instrument of Soviet control, the absence of an alternative mechanism to facilitate interstate trade also compromised both economic recovery from the stagnation of the 1980s and the successful development of market-based national economies.[30]

The West has not been as much help in the transition to a free-market economy as Central and Eastern European leaders had originally hoped. Despite Western enthusiasm for free-market reforms and frequent advice forcefully given to Central and East European leaders to push on with them, it has failed to provide substantial amounts of economic and financial assistance needed to ease hardship and suffering caused by the dismantling of the communist command economy. For example, Western aid has not been enough to help the financially hard-pressed Central and East European governments pay for the kind of broad social safety net required to assure social stability in a period of rapid and traumatic change. The West has been especially niggardly in the Balkan countries, which need financial help the most, because of dissatisfaction over the slow pace of their free-market reformism.[31]

With a decline in trade and the absence of adequate financial help from the West, with a need to service enormous debts to the West incurred in the last decade of communist rule when some communist leaders went on a buying spree to try to overhaul their stagnant local economies, and with rising costs of essential social services, postcommunist governments have had to pursue harsh cost-cutting policies that increased the hardship of daily life for most people.[32] Although many areas were affected, such as housing, education, and especially employment—as governments stopped subsidizing inefficient enterprises, closed them down, and increased unemployment to double-digit numbers—two areas that most affected the quality of life for many citizens have been the health-care system, touted so long by the communists as the most praiseworthy achievement of their rule, and the environment, which the communists had virtually ignored and which was so polluted in many instance as to require immediate remedial action.[33]

Deterioration of the Health-Care System

Postcommunist governments in Central and Eastern Europe have had to curtail subsidies to an already-debilitated health-care system, leaving personnel poorly paid and hospitals short of supplies, from simple items like syringes and surgical gloves to complex diagnostic equipment like CAT-scan machines. Health care facilities, such as village clinics, have difficulty providing patients with free medical care—more and more people who need health care must pay for it, at least partially, out of their own pockets. The poorest groups in society and those who need health care the most have been hit the hardest. The majority of people have to settle for whatever is available at minimal cost, which means that they are obliged to accept in many instances inadequate or second-best care.

Tardiness in Cleaning up the Environment

At the same time, while they certainly acknowledged the severity of pollution, spoke about the need for national clean-up policies, and in fact began cleaning up dirty public buildings, the postcommunist governments of Central and Eastern Europe have not accomplished very much in diminishing pollution of the land, air, and water in their countries. The major reason is cost, which is staggering and beyond the resources of the financially strapped governments of the region. Despite support for national clean-up policies, people do not want to make the sacrifices needed to pay for them. They do not—and in many instances cannot—pay higher taxes, and they do not want to see enterprises where they are employed shut down by the government because they cannot afford to install expensive high-technology pollution-control devices.[34]

Also, environmental political groups, the so-called Green parties, which actively opposed communist rule and arguably helped to end it, have failed to exert pressure on the postcommunist governments of the early 1990s. They have had little influence with the electorate, despite popular concern about pollution, for several reasons. Like most other political groups in the early 1990s, they were deeply divided over organizational and policy issues, and these divisions were worse for them than for other parties because the Greens were among the smallest of the groups to emerge on the eve of communist collapse. They lost members to other emergent parties that co-opted their concern with the environment. They had little influence with the electorate also because they paid little attention to other issues, such as economic hardship resulting from free-market reforms, which were more important for voters than the polluted environment. In turn, voters became less interested in the environment as some of the worst offenders among state-controlled enterprises were shut down by the government.[35]

Finally, although money is coming from the World Bank to help reduce the

pollution of air and water, and although some Central and East European governments have started to recruit money at home by asking people to buy bonds to
finance the kind of clean-up they say they want in order to improve living
conditions and to raise environmental standards to conform to those in the West,
available capital for investment in the environment remains scarce. The West has
not been forthcoming in help for the environment for the same reasons it has
been niggardly in its assistance in other areas of national life in Central and
Eastern Europe. Moreover, a degree of short-sightedness in the West that pre-
vents appreciation of the political dangers of not helping to make the environment inherited from the communists more livable.[36]

4. A Balance Sheet of Economic Change

Poland, Hungary, and the Czech Republic have made great strides away from the
communist command economy toward the free market. By early 1996, over 50
percent of Poland's gross national product came from the free section of the
economy. While living conditions remain difficult in all three countries, inflation
and unemployment have been reduced to single-digit numbers, and most people,
according to recent public-opinion polls, are optimistic about a further improvement of living conditions. The rate of foreign investment has quickened in a few
countries, notably the Czech Republic, Hungary, and Poland, providing capital
for more economic expansion. But the economic picture in other countries is less
bright. In places such as Slovakia, Romania, Bulgaria, Albania, and Serbia,
economic reform has been slow and slight. The state still controls much of the
country's economic life as inefficiently as in the past. Privatization has barely
begun, and there is still little, if anything, in the nature of a capitalist infrastructure, such as banks, stock markets, and a reformed legal system that protects and
encourages free enterprise. Finally, all the societies of the former communist
countries are continuing to experience the hardships caused by free-market reforms, notably, skyrocketing living costs, which have been especially hard on
retirees on fixed pensions, the elderly, and low-paid workers who could not
boost their wages quickly enough to compensate for the new inflation; an unprecedented and unanticipated explosion of unemployment, in a few countries
reached double-digit numbers in the early 1990s and has eased up only in the
Czech Republic; and continuing government retrenchment in services such as
health care that most people do not yet have the wherewithal to take care of by
themselves. While many people in Central and Eastern Europe in the mid-1990s
would acknowledge satisfaction with the demise of the communist system and
express a cautious optimism about the future, they would insist that life remains
difficult, that the new abundance of food and other goods lacking in the communist era is still beyond their reach, and that there is still a need for some government regulation of the economy to assure a minimum standard of living and
guaranteed jobs.[37]

Promoting Social Stability

The pace of political and economic democratization has contributed to social tensions throughout the region, which have taken different forms, such as explosions of ethnic conflict, a revival of anti-Semitism, discrimination against other minorities, such as the Roma people (Gypsies), and the marginalization of women.

1. Ethnic Conflict

Historic conflict-producing prejudices and animosities among the myriad of large and small ethnic groups in Central and Eastern Europe had been held in check by the communist dictatorships. But once they were replaced by pluralistic systems, these prejudices and animosities surfaced and led to social tensions and in some instances to hostile intergroup confrontations and civil war. Moreover, though they refused to tolerate social conflict, the communists laid the groundwork for it.

Communist parties kept ethnic identities alive as a temporary means of maintaining administrative unity and societal cohesion. They refrained from homogenizing multiethnic societies like those in Yugoslavia and Czechoslovakia.[38] In the postcommunist era, national majorities, notably Romanians, Bulgarians, and Slovaks, led by politicians eager to use ethnocultural nationalism to win popular support, showed an extreme sensitivity to their newly achieved sovereignty and independence by discriminating against minority groups, despite the fact that democracy, which these majorities said they were practicing in one form or another, is supposed to protect minorities against such discrimination. Majorities have only grudgingly granted minorities the right of political expression.[39]

In Czechoslovakia, the strength of feelings of Slovaks and Czechs led to the split of the country into two separate states at the end of 1992. In Yugoslavia, a vicious civil war accompanied the transition from Communist rule. The grievances of the Hungarian minorities in Romania and Slovakia have aroused the concern of the government in Budapest. The large Albanian minority in Serbia is restless. Bulgaria's Turkish minority is agitating for rights, and in the Czech Republic, former German residents of the Sudetenland now want restitution of property confiscated by Prague at the end of World War II. Poland has a sizable minority of German-speaking people in Silesia who are also concerned about their future cultural well-being and have expressed interest in strengthening links with Germany.

The development of ethnocultural nationalism undermines democratic development. Nationalist-inspired conflicts are narrowly focused and sometimes all-consuming, crowding out other issues. They also deny the reality of commonalities, shared interests, or even mutual dependence. Ethnically based claims to autonomy also strike at the heart of the process of democratization because they compete with the individual-rights–based legitimation of a liberal democratic order. The political organization of nationalist movements and the state institutions and processes they spawn are rather based on group dominance and do not easily tolerate competing demands. They are exclusive rather than inclusive and tend to extremism rather than moderation. In this way the politics of ethnic nationalism is contrary to the essence of the liberal democratic process.[40]

2. Revival of Anti-Semitism

The communists never tried to eliminate anti-Semitism from its entrenched place in the national society and, indeed, in some instances used it to strengthen their legitimacy among the ethnic majority. Today, many people accept the myth that Jews are responsible for the miseries suffered under communism. Certainly some Jews in most East European countries embraced communism after World War II, in part as a reaction to nazism. But the overwhelming majority of Communist Party members were non-Jews, something anti-Semites in Eastern Europe seem to ignore. In addition, because a tradition of anti-Semitism taught the population to see Jews as a unified entity, many East Europeans fail to differentiate between the actions of individuals and the Jewish community as a whole. They think that because a few Jews were communists, all were responsible for communism.[41]

Some postcommunist politicians are using anti-Semitism to cultivate popular support. They circulate anti-Semitic graffiti, articles, and homilies, such as the *Protocols of the Elders of Zion*. In opposing the move to capitalism, they blame the economic hardships caused by the transition away from socialism to the free-market economy on Jews. Shortages, high prices, and unemployment are all Jewish responsibilities, they say, as Jews achieve economic success. Successful Jews are singled out for contempt and condemnation, which comes naturally to people who have long accused Jews of usury and other economic evils. Finally, anti-Semitic demagogues resonate even with those who have had no contact with Jews but who are nonetheless convinced that their personal troubles as well as those of their country are the fault of Jews.[42]

A number of positive steps have been taken to counter the revival of anti-Semitism. Political leaders in Central and East European countries have spoken out forcefully against it. President Wałęsa of Poland established a presidential commission on anti-Semitism. The Hungarian government has encouraged a revival of interest in Judaic studies in Budapest. Some church leaders, including Pope John Paul II, have condemned anti-Semitism as antithetical to Christian principles. Despite these gestures and despite the smallness of the Jewish population left in the region after the Nazi Holocaust, anti-Semitism persists on the official as well as the personal levels of the societies of some Central and East

European countries. No broad-based programs to educate about anti-Semitism and about the Holocaust have yet been established in any East European country, and there are oblique—and sometimes not so oblique—attacks on Jews by conservative nationalistic politicians and church officials.[43]

3. Discrimination Against the Roma (Gypsies)

The Roma population in Eastern Europe has also suffered from the effects of nationalism. The Roma have emerged as great losers from the overthrow of communism and the end of the rigid controls it imposed on daily life. Under communism, the Roma had at least some economic and social protection, but when communism collapsed, there was a revival of open prejudice and persecution of the Roma people. With the closing of the unprofitable factories, mines, and construction projects that provided work for most Roma, even if at the most menial jobs, Roma people have been at the mercy of communities where citizens and government officials are actively hostile to them. They have become scapegoats for the hardship most people are experiencing as the region dismantles the socialist state and moves toward the free-market economy.[44]

Governments have done little to diminish prejudice against the Roma. There is simply not enough money available to help the Roma improve their living conditions, and many officials argue that helping the Roma is hopeless. Roma, they believe, waste the money they receive on welfare and soon return to stealing, their "ancient" way of surviving, according to officials who have dealt directly with them. And, these officials say, when an apartment is given to a Roma family, it is soon occupied by three or four times the number of people it was intended to house. Some officials also say that Roma parents are to be blamed for the difficulty of breaking the cycle of poverty and prejudice by not encouraging their children to go to school and work hard. Roma parents, officials argue, seem to think that education is not needed for survival and that their children can live by their wits.[45]

Furthermore, political leaders in many instances do not like to deal with popular prejudice toward the Roma, fearing a backlash if they are seen to be giving the Roma "too much" of the communities' scarce resources. Therefore, however well intentioned some Central and East European leaders might be, they are doing little, if anything, to protect the Roma.

Roma leaders are alarmed by the prejudice against their people, but they, too, have had little success in improving the situation. While they have set up many social and political organizations to lobby on behalf of Roma interests and gain recognition of the distinctiveness of Roma culture, language, and history, they have been unable to influence policy makers. Roma organizations have little impact on policy because they are divided, conflict ridden, and personality oriented. The Roma themselves have not yet developed effective political institutions to help protect their interests in a hostile environment.[46]

4. The Marginalization of Women

Very few women, when compared with men, are active in postcommunist party politics, and even fewer have been elected to parliament or appointed to high positions in government,[47] though there have been some notable exceptions, as in the case of Prime Minister Hanna Suchocka of Poland in 1992 and 1993. Political marginalization of women is worse in the conservative societies of the Balkan countries, where there are large clusters of Muslim peoples, than in those of the north-central part of the region. In Romania, Bulgaria, and Albania, women are virtually without any political influence whatsoever. The systematic exclusion of women from high positions in politics has made women less visible and denied them role models to encourage them to become more interested in politics and to fight for increased influence in the political system.

Women themselves must bear some responsibility for political marginalization. Most women lack interest in issues that do not directly affect daily life in the home and family, though, again, there are exceptions. Women's organizations do exist, but they are not the aggressive instruments of change that they are in the West, especially in the United States, and that they need to be in Eastern Europe to make a difference for women politically. Moreover, the small minority of women who do gain influence in politics or in other areas of national life do not encourage other women to become more active outside the home and family. Under these circumstances, a majority of women in postcommunist Central and Eastern Europe have expressed a preference for pursuing the traditional gender roles of wife and mother.

Other conditions make it difficult for women to become politically active. Women have suffered more than men from the economic hardships of privatization. Lacking the education and technical skills that men tend to have acquired, they find it far more difficult to get rehired when their places of employment are shut down or privatized and they lose their jobs. At the same time, the new multiparty systems are not interested in recruiting women. Many political parties in post-communist Central and Eastern Europe are narrowly focused, single-interest organizations that do not care about gender equality or consider it very low on their list of priorities. National political leaders also do not consider women's interests or an enhanced political role for women to be of major importance. They therefore do little to help women get ahead, with forceful affirmative-action programs, for example. Indeed, financially hard-pressed governments are unwilling to spend precious resources on facilities that could help women broaden their interests outside the home and family, such as day-care centers. Finally, in Poland the Catholic Church has been a big obstacle to gender equality, having literally gone on an offensive against the social and political advancement of women since 1989. And in Albania the poverty of the country and the revival of Islamic traditions that call for the passivity of women make it nearly impossible for women to assert themselves outside the home. It is difficult for women to gain equality in Albania also because of the near-total absence of any familiarity with democratic concepts. These conditions work to preserve stereo-typical roles for women in that country.[48]

Diversifying Foreign Policy

After years of isolation, the Central and East European countries have been looking to Western Europe and the United States for close political, economic, and military ties. But the Central and East European countries also understood the strategic and economic logic of keeping fences mended with the former Soviet Union and with its successors, in particular, the Russian Federation, Belarus, and Ukraine, which are powerful and potentially troublesome neighbors but also neighbors who can help Central and Eastern Europe economically and strategically. Finally, the postcommunist governments in the region are looking to one another for help in the solution of strategic and economic problems, trying to forgive and forget old animosities and to focus on ways to cooperate with one another and increase their independence of powerful outsiders.

1. Western Europe

The postcommunist Central and East European governments have sought an expansion of trade with the West, economic and financial assistance in "Marshall Plan" proportions, and membership in the European Union (EU). They say they deserve and should receive Western cooperation and help because they have done what the West had always wanted them to do—they abandoned communist rule and established their independence of the Soviet Union. But the reactions of particular West European countries have been mixed.

Germany

In keeping with its long-standing vision as a bridge builder between East and West and as a country that views the stability, prosperity, and friendship of the Central and East European peoples as important to its own material well-being, Germany has been the most supportive of the integration of the East European economies with the West. Moreover, with the Berlin Wall down, the Bonn government felt morally obligated not to abandon the peoples of former commu-nist countries and not to allow a new economic gulf to develop between them and the democratic and well-off societies in the West. It pressed the European Union to strengthen links with the most advanced postcommunist govern-ments—notably, Poland, Hungary, and the Czech Republic—while being less sympathetic to the leadership of Romania and Bulgaria.[49]

France

The French have been reluctant to integrate the Central and East European economies with those of Western Europe. The late French President François

Mitterrand warned that Eastern Europe may be decades away from full membership in the EU. Mitterrand's position, no doubt, derived in part from a concern that the admission of the East European countries would strengthen Germany's already-substantial influence in the organization, given existing German political and economic links to the former communist region. France also has had economic reasons for proceeding cautiously. Paris does not want West European markets flooded with cheap agricultural products from Eastern Europe. In September 1991, France blocked a European Community plan to open doors to East European exports. The French also opposed a package of trade concessions to Poland, Czechoslovakia, and Hungary, expressing fears about the negative impact on French farmers. The French told other members of the EU that its politically powerful farmers would not tolerate more relaxed restrictions on Polish beef exports in the early 1990s. The French thus put a monkey wrench in the EU plan, proposed by its executive commission, to abolish all trade curbs on textiles and allow a 60 percent reduction in tariffs over three years on imports of meat, vegetables, and fruit from Eastern Europe.[50]

The European Union

The European Union initially resisted the immediate membership of the postcommunist governments. Some EU countries feared mass migrations of Central and East European people westward to escape economic hardship at home, especially as the single regional market for the EU, now in the process of development, would make movement within and between member nations difficult to control. Other EU members argued that integration with Central and Eastern Europe must be put off because the region's economies are not yet able to take their places alongside the more productive and affluent economies of the West. This argument cites the way in which much of the East German economy precipitously collapsed following reunification of the two Germanies in October 1990. But, in addition, EU governments worried that their own textile, footwear, coal, and steel industries would suffer in competition with low-cost producers in Central Europe. Another EU argument against immediate full membership for the East European states was the probable impact on its delicately balanced administrative institutions, in which every interest has been represented, every ruffled feather smoothed, so to speak. Designed for the original six founding members (Germany, France, Denmark, and the Benelux), these institutions are already under stress in catering to the needs today of twelve members. If membership were expanded further by the admission of the East European states, the function of every EU institution, so the argument went, would have to be renegotiated. Finally, cost was a reason for the reluctance of the EU to admit the Central and East European countries. Money from the EU's regional fund spent on investment in less-developed member economies, which accounts for about a quarter of the Community's budget, plus the cost of supporting EU farmers under a common agricultural policy—this accounts for half of EU spending—would amount to $6 billion to $10 billion a year. No EU member seemed ready to pay these sums.[51]

Nevertheless, in an effort to reward the Central and East European countries for their progress toward political pluralism and the market economy in the early 1990s, the EU has made some substantial concessions. Some East European agricultural and other exports now come into West European markets. Pablo Benavides, the EU's chief negotiator with the East European countries, said in late 1991 that these agreements with Poland, Czechoslovakia, and Hungary are the first step toward their full membership in the Union.[52] In June 1993, EU leaders took another step toward integrating the Central and East European countries with Western Europe. They extended a formal invitation to membership in the European Union to Poland, Hungary, the Czech Republic, Slovakia, Romania, and Bulgaria. As soon as they meet required economic and political conditions (including explicit recognition and protection of minority rights), they can become EU members. The EU also agreed on a package of trade concessions involving an accelerated reduction of tariffs and quotas that had been blocking many of Eastern Europe's most competitive exports: duties on industrial products will be eliminated two years earlier than planned, tariffs on textiles, previously scheduled to end in 1998, will be dropped in 1997. Behind these gestures was a recognition by EU leaders that they had erred in not getting more involved in ending the Yugoslav civil war and a determination to show more initiative toward the rest of the region.[53]

Furthermore, in April 1991, thirty-nine industrialized countries set up the European Bank for Reconstruction and Development to channel funds into Eastern Europe to help facilitate the transition to a market economy. The World Bank also has helped with loans. The Organization for European Economic Cooperation and Development, a research and statistical organization that grew out of the Marshall Plan, created the Center for Cooperation with European Economies in Transition to provide a wide range of international expertise on specific problems faced by the East European countries.[54] In recent years EU members have expanded trade with Eastern Europe, and by 1994 they replaced the former Soviet Union and Russia as the chief trade partners of the region. But the downside of this situation is that the trade remains one-sided. EU members sell more than they buy, provoking complaints from East European leaders about EU protectionism, namely, the refusal of EU members to allow the sale of East European agricultural and industrial exports. The EU's imposition of high tariffs and quotas against East European goods has slowed the region's economic recovery.[55]

NATO

If Central and East European economic integration with Western Europe has been slow, military integration has been even slower.[56] Beginning in 1990,

Poland, Hungary, and Czechoslovakia signaled interest in joining NATO. Historically caught between the competing ambitions of Russia and Germany, they certainly did not want to rely on themselves alone for the region's security. They saw membership as symbolically affirming that they are now part of Europe and the West.

NATO responded with an offer of modest links with Central and East European countries to provide some limited security against a resurgence of Soviet and post-Soviet Russian influence. In June 1991, NATO foreign ministers agreed to tell the former Eastern bloc countries that NATO would not accept any coercion against emerging democracies, to offer wider cooperation between East and West in military matters, and to acknowledge a close linkage between the security of Western countries and that of the East European countries.[57]

But this was not enough for some Central European leaders. In October 1993, President Vaclav Havel of the Czech Republic, long an advocate of NATO membership for the new East European democracies, renewed his appeal, arguing that NATO has new responsibilities in the post-Soviet era to guarantee the internal stability of a democratic Europe and to serve as an instrument of collective defense against an outside aggressor. He insisted that the Czech Republic, Poland, Hungary, and Slovakia have Western values and traditions and should immediately become partners with Western Europe and the United States in a new, enlarged NATO. Because these countries lie adjacent to the traditionally unstable Balkans and the great Eurasian area of the former Soviet Union, which is also unstable, these East European countries urgently need links to a militarily strong West European Alliance.[58]

NATO members are sympathetic to these arguments, as well as to the strategic vulnerability of the area to Russian influence. They have tried to accommodate the former communist countries without offending Moscow. At a meeting of NATO defense ministers in Travemünde, Germany, in late October 1993, the Clinton administration proposed a kind of partial membership of the former Warsaw Pact countries, including Russia, into the Western Alliance. The U.S. proposal, a compromise between the extremes of no ties and complete ties between Central and Eastern Europe and NATO, was called the "Partnership for Peace." It envisaged the negotiation of joint military training, joint military exercises, and the gradual standardization of military equipment between NATO and the East European governments. But U.S. Defense Secretary Les Aspin made clear at Travemünde that NATO was not ready to offer the security guarantees the East European countries were seeking but merely, as he put it, "a certain amount of security comfort."[59]

NATO's eastward expansion remains a controversial issue in the West. NATO members do not want to antagonize the Kremlin, which remains very sensitive to the prospect of military links between its former allies and NATO. Although in August 1993 President Boris Yeltsin of Russia indicated no objection to Poland's and the Czech's Republic joining NATO, within six weeks he reversed himself.

No doubt he was responding to pressures from the Russian army, on whose political support he depended. His government, in particular, Russian intelligence chief Evgenii Primakov, who became Foreign Minister in January 1996, asserted that Russia could not accept East European membership in NATO and would have to take countermeasures. Yeltsin periodically has reiterated, often with an unpleasant shrillness, Russian opposition to an expansion of NATO and anger over the prospect of it. The Western governments cannot ignore Russian concerns and are reluctant to do anything that would strengthen the anti-NATO and anti-Western positions of Russian ultranationalists like Vladimir Zhirinovskii and frustrated army leaders, who have never really accepted the loss of Russian influence in Eastern Europe, especially since it is so important to the security of their country. NATO members also worry that extending the pledge of collective self-defense to the new governments of the Central and East European countries could get the West involved in unwanted conflicts over ethnic issues like those tearing apart the former Yugoslavia.[60] They continue to resist the demands of the Central and East European governments for the full membership that would bring them the security guarantee in Article XVI of the 1949 NATO treaty.

2. The United States

The United States has major strategic, economic, and ideological interests in postcommunist Central and Eastern Europe and, therefore, has been responsive to approaches of the postcommunist governments for closer, stronger, and more long-lasting relations with Washington than had been possible in the communist era. The United States wants the region to move forward with democratic reforms. It also is concerned about the security of the region and does not want a resurgence of Moscow's influence. Finally, the United States has a vested interest in the economic well-being of Eastern Europe and the restoration of the free-market economy that will permit an expansion of trade.[61]

But there are constraints on what Washington can do. Both the Bush and the Clinton administrations in fact have proceeded cautiously and with restraint in developing political, economic, and military ties with Central and East European countries. Washington has always been a bit skeptical about the will and the capacity of the new noncommunist leadership to adopt capitalism and democracy. The Bush administration was sensitive to the fact that in some countries, such as Romania and, more recently, Hungary, Poland, and Bulgaria, former communists were still in charge. And both the Bush and the Clinton administrations were concerned about the slow pace of free-market economic reforms in many East European countries, especially the Balkans.

Reflecting the deep conservative instincts of the Republican party, the Bush administration was convinced that it was better for Eastern Europe to help itself rather than to rely on large infusions of foreign capital. And the Clinton administration was eager to give priority to the solution of domestic problems. Finally, the United States at all times has other major aid priorities in the Middle East and Latin America, as well as in Russia and in other former Soviet republics that are strapped for cash, are having difficulty implementing free-market reforms, and are sensitive to Western initiatives in an area the Kremlin once controlled.

Nevertheless, the United States has given some economic and financial support to Central and Eastern Europe, partly because of the extensive political, economic, strategic, and ideological interests it has in the region and partly because of support in Congress for helping the region make the difficult transition to political and economic democracy. Senator Bob Dole, the former Republican majority leader, was an advocate of American aid to Central and Eastern Europe and has called for a rethinking of U.S. aid priorities. Large numbers of Americans, especially those with roots in Eastern Europe, supported Dole's position. They constitute a voting bloc that has been crucial to the Republicans in recent presidential elections. Finally, the West Europeans, especially Germany, have lobbied aggressively with both the Bush and the Clinton administrations for generous Western aid to the new East European countries.

Although the Bush administration was unwilling to undertake a major aid program, it was sensitive to the negative impact of the Persian Gulf crisis (summer of 1991 to March 1992) on several Central and East European countries. The interdiction of Iraqi oil exports provoked a shortage of energy, and the price of oil skyrocketed. In response, Bush reportedly urged the International Monetary Fund to change its lending regulations so that it could provide extra money to pay for high-priced oil imports.

The Bush and the Clinton administrations also continued to diminish restrictions on trade with Eastern Europe. They offered modest amounts of economic and financial assistance to Poland and Hungary, encouraged private American investment in Czechoslovakia, and tried to find ways of accommodating their demands for closer military relations with the West. But by the end of 1995, Washington was still not prepared to undertake a major economic and financial aid program to Eastern Europe. The Clinton administration was discouraged by perceived violations of human rights, especially conditions that interfered with the holding of truly free and open parliamentary elections, and continued to warn some East European countries, especially Yugoslavia, of American sensitivity to human-rights violations. And new as well as continuing crises in the Middle East, Somalia, Haiti, and Cuba in 1993 and 1994 monopolized Washington's attention. The Clinton administration increasingly had to balance the needs of Central and Eastern Europe against the increasing need for aid to Russia as political and economic conditions there deteriorated sharply in 1993 and 1994. Under these circumstances, Washington has not been able to develop a clear and effective policy toward Central and Eastern Europe.

In recent years, a new problem has developed in U.S. relations with some

Central and East European countries. They are selling weapons and military technology to countries with which the United States has difficult, if not dangerous, relations in the Middle East, southern Asia, and sub-Saharan Africa. The United States has protested these sales but to no avail. They continue because, as East European leaders have told Washington, they are necessary for economic survival. All the Central and East European countries need the hard currency earned from these sales to finance economic recovery and reform, especially as aid from the West has been so skimpy. The Central and East European leaders have asked specifically for Western aid in reconverting weapons industries to the production of consumer goods. This aid has not been forthcoming, and the problem remains unresolved.

3. The Soviet Union and Russia

At least four major issues troubled East European relations with the Kremlin before and after the demise of the Soviet state in December 1991. These are (1) the termination of the Warsaw Pact and the CMEA; (2) the withdrawal of Soviet troops; (3) the restoration of traditional trade links; and (4) the prospect of Central and East European membership in NATO.[62]

The Warsaw Pact and the CMEA

With the fall of communism, the new East European leaders briefly toyed with the idea of preserving, but radically altering, the Warsaw Pact and the CMEA to be in accord with the new political realities and avoid antagonizing Moscow. But people felt strongly about breaking old ties with Moscow and wanted Soviet-dominated organizations dismantled.[63] When in 1990 the Kremlin made a clumsy attempt to preserve some of its old influence in the region with new treaties that called upon them to refrain from joining organizations considered inimical to the interests of the signatories, the East European countries became more resolute than before in severing the old ties.

Faced with the disintegration of its own economy and political upheaval among the union republics, Gorbachev eventually agreed to the termination of the Warsaw Pact and the CMEA, even though doing so in effect punctuated the collapse of Soviet power in the region. The Soviet political and military establishments, to their credit, accepted the new situation.

Trade

Regardless of their feelings about the CMEA, the new East European governments did not want to sever trade links with the Soviet Union. Soviet trade with Eastern Europe declined sharply in the early 1990s and has not yet resumed. Moscow simply does not have the money to buy much from Eastern Europe.

Moreover, the political and economic turmoil throughout Russia has so far para-lyzed its capacity to produce and sell abroad, even the oil that is so desperately needed by the East European countries. This situation has left the East European countries in a bind. Their industries were dependent on Soviet purchases, and they have not been able to make up for the loss of this market, especially in light of the fact that their exports to Western Europe are not yet competitive.[64]

Withdrawal of Soviet Troops

Central and East European governments also had to work out how to get the military forces of the former Soviet Union off their soil. Starting in early 1990, the East European countries that still had large numbers of Soviet troops de-ployed on their territory were East Germany, Poland, Hungary, and Czechoslo-vakia. During bilateral discussions with Soviet officials on the troop-withdrawal issue in 1991, Poland and Czechoslovakia, which were concerned about the fate of the Baltic states, were very careful not to chastise Moscow for its attempted crackdown in Vilnius, Lithuania, in early 1991. And in the political crisis of August 1991, when an inner circle of conservative Russian leaders tried to over-throw Gorbachev, the East European governments were very careful not to take sides, even though they were fearful that the anti-Gorbachev coup might succeed and bring to power conservative military leaders who might try to reassert Rus-sian political and military influence abroad. Needless to say, they were relieved when the putsch against Gorbachev failed.[65]

The troop-withdrawal discussions led eventually to agreement on the condi-tions for withdrawal. There were some temporary difficulties reflecting a mea-sure of bitterness on both sides, but these difficulties did not interrupt the withdrawal process, which continued throughout 1991. All Soviet forces were withdrawn from the region by the end of 1992.

East European Membership in NATO

Russia opposes the inclusion of East European countries in NATO for three reasons. First, East European membership in NATO would greatly strengthen Western political, economic, cultural, and military influence in a region that is historically important to the territorial security of the Russian state. Second, it could and probably would encourage some of the former Soviet republics in the near abroad, in particular the Baltic states and possibly Ukraine, to seek membership in NATO, further weakening Russian influence in regions of strategic importance to Russia's security and material well-being. Finally, East European membership in NATO would inevitably strengthen the most radically nationalistic elements on the Russian political spectrum, increasing pressures on the political center, which presently governs Russia, to pursue aggressive policies toward the outside world, in particular the West, in ways that could provoke a new cold war.

The East European countries must expect trouble from Moscow should they succeed in persuading NATO to admit them. The mere willingness of the West to discuss East European demands for NATO membership has strained Western, and especially American, relations with Russia. The East Europeans could well end up provoking Russia to the very behavior they want to prevent by their membership in NATO: a Russian effort to expand political and military influence westward, starting, perhaps, in the Baltic states, and possibly menacing Poland, which has been more aggressive than other East European countries in lobbying for membership in NATO.[66]

Are the East Europeans justified in their fears of a resurgent Russia? Sergei A. Karaganov, an adviser to President Yeltsin and deputy director of the Russian Institute for Europe, did not think so. He was reported to have said that the East Europeans were exaggerating what they perceive to be a Russian threat to their sovereignty and independence. He is quoted as saying that

> about 95% of the rhetoric of Russian imperialism is just "hot air." It is a kind of medicine for injured pride and a divided nation. Even Zhirinovsky's most fervent supporters, polls indicate, are more interested in domestic issues like crime and unemployment than imperialist expansion.[67]

Still, the East Europeans worry about Russia and maintain their pressure on NATO to admit them. The course of events seems to vindicate their feelings of insecurity. The explosion of war in Chechnya in December 1994 seemed to convince East Europeans that the Russians had changed very little in their readiness to use military force to get their way and to ignore every other consideration that inspired restraint when their strategic and economic interests were perceived to be endangered. Poland, in particular, reacted strongly to the Russian military invasion of Chechnya and demanded, along with other countries, including the United States, an end to the fighting.

4. Intraregional Diplomacy

In the postcommunist era, the Central and East European countries have many incentives to forgive and forget old prejudices. They have many common foreign-policy interests: they want to become part of Western Europe, in particular, they want membership in the European Union and NATO; they fear a resurgence of Russian influence in the region; they also worry about the impact of the continuing wars in the former Yugoslavia, which could eventually involve them, especially the Balkan countries that are located near areas of conflict.[68]

Diplomatic leaders of the northern countries of Poland, Hungary, the Czech Republic, and Slovakia have met regularly to discuss economic, environmental, and strategic issues of common concern. They are trying to reduce pollution, foster intraregional trade, and consider ways of furthering their ambitions to draw closer militarily and economically to the West and strengthen their security vis-à-vis postcommunist Russia. These countries are sometimes referred to as the Visegrád Group after the city where, in 1990, they held their first multilateral summit after the collapse of communist rule. Diplomats of the Balkan countries have also met periodically to discuss problems in areas of mutual concern and to strengthen ties with peripheral countries such as Ukraine, Georgia, Turkey, and Greece.[69] While the Central and East European counties have not created any regional organizations to replace the Warsaw Pact and the CMEA, and while integration of the kind going on in Western Europe is still far away, they have collectively laid the basis for bilateral and multilateral cooperation among themselves and strengthened ties with neighbors outside the region.

Conclusions

In the postcommunist era, the countries of Eastern Europe are moving into uncharted waters. They are developing new political systems, economic structures, and social orders quite different from those they had in the era of communist rule. They seem to be developing versions of Western-style pluralistic parliamentary democracies, free-market capitalist-style economies, and open, unfettered social environments in which people are experiencing a new freedom in personal behavior they never had under communist rule.

But change has not been easy. Communism had distorted everything it touched. When Communist Party rule collapsed, the whole structure of society, institutions, processes, and values collapsed along with it. People lost one way of doing things, but they have had difficulty finding an alternative. Popular behavior and thought could not be transformed overnight. The societies of Central and Eastern Europe are in a sort of political and economic limbo. This condition is fertile ground for a hunt for scapegoats and a search for a common identifiable enemy, as well as for radicalism of both the neofascist and neocommunist sort. It is a time in which the new postcommunist states are vulnerable to hatred of the world, are seeking self-affirmation at any cost, and are displaying a personal selfishness and an excessive, primitive consumerism based on the principle that everything is now permitted. The success of political and economic democratization is by no means assured.

An important aspect of communism had been its monotonous conformity, a similarity of greyness that had spread throughout the wide region of its rule from Berlin to Vladivostok. Red stars had been everywhere; administrative institutions, at least in their physical appearance and to some extent in the way they functioned, had been similar all over Eastern Europe. Even allowing for rather sharp environmental and cultural distinctions in different national settings, social and economic life showed the same characteristics and the same problems and weaknesses wherever one went. Consequently, the different peoples of Central and Eastern Europe are paying more attention to their special characteristics and the unique features of their national identities. They are beginning to remember ancient achievements, ancient sufferings, ancient enemies and ancient allies, ancient statehood and their ancient borders, and last, but certainly not least, ancient animosities toward one another.

All this has led to an explosion of nationalism with hatred toward "outsiders," such as immigrants, and ethnic minorities. Postcommunist governments are under intense pressure to right historical wrongs and avenge historical injustices. Also, many peoples are in a hurry to enjoy the individuality that had been denied them for so long by the communist dictatorships and have been quick to organize and express their displeasure if they think things are not working out. In this way diversity has taken another form: an explosion of political pluralism that is complicating development of democratic government, which requires some consensus to succeed. Indeed, there is not enough unity, cohesion, and direction in governmental organization and behavior, and some East European peoples are looking back nostalgically to a simpler, more disciplined political era, when there was little political choice but when governments made policies and solved problems, if not always in a congenial manner.

The Central and East European countries are looking to the West to end the isolation imposed on them by the Soviet Union in the communist era. This isolation had denied them the cultural, socioeconomic, and political contacts with the West they needed for their own growth and development. As the Central and East European countries broaden their foreign relations in the postcommunist era, however, they risk antagonizing the Kremlin, which has some regret over its loss of influence in a region of historic importance to Russia and contemplates, perhaps, a restoration of that influence at some future time. Not surprisingly, the new governments of Eastern Europe want to strengthen political, economic, and especially military links to Western Europe and the United States. They want membership in the European Union and NATO, and they want good relations with the United States. But the West, for its own reasons, has reacted with ambivalence to East European initiatives, welcoming them but not accommodating East European demands for intimacy and largess, and at the same time, although the East Europeans have tried to avoid provoking a hypersensitive Russia by their turn toward the West, they may have made the Kremlin uncomfortable. Russian leaders of all persuasions are uneasy over the strong military and political links of Eastern Europe to the West.

Certainly, the entire region of Central and Eastern Europe has made a dramatic shift away from communism, and its struggle to develop Western-style democratic political systems and economies is one of the great events of the late twentieth century. But as the shift takes place, the internal development of each of the former communist states in the region takes on new meaning. As the following chapters show, each country found its own way to break with communism, and each is finding its own way to develop democracy with varying degrees of speed and success.

3

Albania

For several centuries, Albania was a dependency of the Ottoman Turkish Empire. It gained independence in the early twentieth century. During the interwar period, Albania was ruled by an authoritarian monarch known as King Zog I. Albanian independence in the interwar period, however, was short lived. In the late 1920s, Albania came under the influence of Mussolini's Italy. Mussolini viewed Albania as important to Italian security and control of the southern Adriatic. By the eve of World War II, Italy controlled most of Albanian territory. Albanians, consequently, knew little of Western parliamentary democracy when the communists took power at the end of World War II.

Communist Dictatorship

With this past, as well as a threat after World War II to its newly won political independence from Tito's Yugoslavia, the Albanian Communist Party, which came to power in the late 1940s, quickly adopted a harsh and brutal dictatorship. While it never became a Soviet satellite because it was too far away geographically from the USSR for Moscow to control, Albanian communism resembled the Stalinist version of Soviet communism in many important respects.

1. Political Repression

The Albanian communist leadership insisted on society's total obedience to its rule and established state control over almost every aspect of Albania's political, economic, and social life. Although it had the appearance of a parliamentary democracy, Albania's communist government ignored popular will and severely

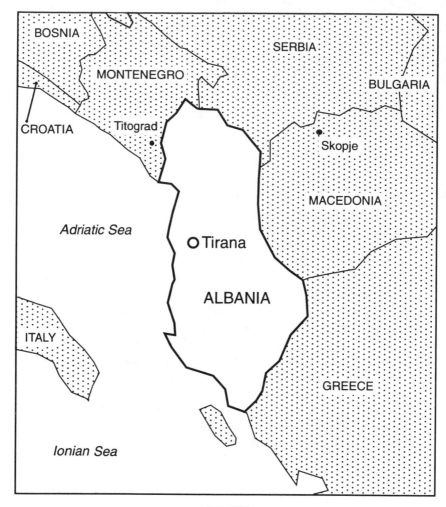

ALBANIA

Geography
1. Location: southeastern Europe, bordering the Adriatic Sea and the Ionian
   Sea, between Greece, Serbia, and
   Montenegro
2. Area: total — 28,750 square kilometers; land area — 27,400 square kilometers; comparative area — slightly
   larger than Maryland
3. Boundaries: with Greece — 282 kilometers; with Macedonia — 151 kilometers; with Serbia and Montenegro

— 287 kilometers (114 with Serbia
and 173 with Montenegro); with the
Adriatic Sea and the Ioniain Sea —
362 kilometers
4. Climate: mild temperature; cool,
   cloudy, wet winters; hot, clear, dry
   summers; interior cooler and wetter
5. Terrain: mostly mountains and hills;
   small plains along coast
6. Natural resources: petroleum, natural
   gas, coal, chromium, copper, timber,
   nickel

7. Land use: arable land — 21%; permanent crops — 4%; meadows and pastures — 15%; forest and woodland — 38%

People

1. Population: 3,413,904 (July 1995 estimate)
2. Age structure: 0–14 — 32% of population (female — 520,186; male — 563,953); 15–64 — 62% of population (female — 1,026,321; male — 1,104,371); 65 and over — 6% of population (female — 112,252; male — 86,821) (July 1995 estimate)
3. Growth rate: 1.16% (July 1995 estimate)
4. Life expectancy at birth: total population — 73.81 years; female — 77.02 years; male — 70.83 years (1995 estimate)
5. Ethnic divisions: Albanian — 95%; Greek — 3%; Vlachs, Gypsies, Serbs, Bulgarians — 2% (1989 estimate)
6. Religions: Muslim — 70%; Albanian Orthodox — 20%; Roman Catholic — 10%
7. Languages: Albanian, Greek
8. Literacy: total population 72%; female — 63%; male — 80%
9. Labor force: total — 1.5 million; agriculture — 60%; industry and commerce — 40% (1986 estimate)
10. Environment: deforestation, soil erosion, water pollution from industrial and domestic effluent

Government

1. Type: emerging parliamentary democracy
2. Capital: Tirana
3. Independence: November 28, 1912, from Ottoman Empire
4. National administration:
   a. Chief of state: President of the Republic (1996 — Sali Berisha)
   b. Ministerial leadership: Prime Minister and Council of Ministers (1996 — Aleksander Gabriel Meksi, prime minister)
   c. Legislature: unicameral — People's Assembly (*Kuvendi Popullor*)
   d. Judicial branch: Supreme Court (has not accepted ICJ jurisdiction)
   e. Political parties: Albanian Socialist Party, Democratic Party, Albanian Republic Party, Social Democratic Party, Democratic Alliance, Omonia (Greek minority party)
5. Local administration: unitary system with 26 districts

Economy

1. Gross domestic product: $3.8 billion; agriculture — 55% (1994 estimate)
2. National product real growth rate: 11% (1994 estimate)
3. Per-capita national product: $1,110 (1994 estimate)
4. Inflation rate: 16% (1994 estimate)
5. Unemployment rate: 18% (1994 estimate)
6. Budget: revenue — $1.1 billion; expenditures — $1.4 billion
7. Industrial output: food processing, chemicals, lumber, oil, cement, chemicals, mining, basic metals, hydropower
8. Agricultural output: livestock raising, temperate-zone crops
9. Exports: $112 million (1993 estimate) — asphalt, metals, metallic ores, electricity, crude oil, vegetables, fruits, tobacco
10. Imports: $621 million (1993 estimate) — machinery, consumer goods, grains
11. Trade partners: Italy, Macedonia, Germany, Czech Republic, Slovakia, Romania, Poland, Hungary, Greece
12. External debt: $920 million (1994 estimate)
13. Economic aid received in 1993: $303 million
14. Transportation: railroads — 543 kilometers; highways — 18,450 kilometers; ports — Durrës, Sarandë, Shëngjin, Vlorë; airports — 11 (5 with paved runways)

punished dissidents of any kind. The Albanian communists got the reputation of being the most reactionary Marxists in Eastern Europe. Their political system, more than any other in the region, resembled the Stalinist dictatorship in the Soviet Union during the 1930s.

2. Economic Underdevelopment

Throughout communist rule, despite pledges by the Communist Party to improve the living conditions of farmers and workers, Albania remained the least economically developed country in Europe, with the lowest standard of living on the continent. The small towns and villages where most of the Albanian population lived were poverty stricken. Albanian agriculture lacked the technology and machinery needed for modern cultivation. The rural population was very conservative and suspicious of the large urban centers, such as Tirana, with their factories and tenements.

3. International Isolation

In this period, the Albanian communist leaders allied themselves with the Kremlin. But when the Soviet Union reconciled with Yugoslavia after a bitter ideological and political dispute that occurred in 1947 and 1948 and nearly led to war between the two, Albanians no longer saw the Soviet Union as a friend. Indeed, relations between Tirana and Moscow deteriorated sharply during the 1950s as a result of the Kremlin's condemnation of many aspects of Stalinist rule practiced by the Albanian communists. Soviet Communist Party leader Nikita Khrushchev's "de-Stalinization" policies threatened the legitimacy of the Albanian dictatorship. By the end of the decade, the Albanian communist leadership had added the Soviet Union to a long list of countries it distrusted.

The only major exception was Mao Zedong's China, which the Albanian communist leadership admired for its loyalty to Stalinist totalitarianism. The Albanian Communist Party also admired Mao's willingness to stand up to the Soviet Union and its allies and practice its own brand of communism in the 1960s and 1970s. But after Mao's death in 1975, China rejected much of his neo-Stalinism, especially in the economic sphere, and the Albanians eventually broke with Beijing in the late 1970s. For the next ten years, Albania was completely isolated, with few foreign friends.

4. Resistance to Change

Indeed, insecurity and poverty explain why Albania remained a Stalinist dictatorship until the early 1990s. In the post-Stalinist era, as leaders of other socialist countries in Eastern Europe diverged from Stalinism, the Albanians remained loyal to it, denouncing Soviet party leader Nikita Khrushchev's "de-Stalinization" and refusing to adopt any aspect of it. Rather, in the 1960s, Albania consolidated its Stalinist system, much as China was doing, and pursued a miniversion of Mao Zedong's cultural revolution to reinforce Stalinist norms. As happened in China in this period, there were ruthless purges of political moderates in and outside of the Communist Party; people were moved from the cities to the countryside; and there was a campaign to obliterate foreign influence of any kind anywhere in Albanian society.

Even after the death of long-ruling Albanian party leader Enver Hoxha in April 1985, a stern disciple of Stalin, the prospects for change in Albania's totalitarian system still seemed slight. Hoxha's successor, Ramiz Alia, reiterated the Albanian Communist Party's commitment to Stalinist domestic and foreign policies. When Soviet Communist Party leader Mikhail Gorbachev moved to loosen up the Soviet system with his policy of perestroika in 1986, Alia's initial reactions were critical. He believed that the introduction of Gorbachev's reformism into Albania would destabilize the Tirana regime, and he called Gorbachev's perestroika a revisionist policy that would lead to the total restoration of capitalism in the Soviet Union.

As some Central and East European countries and the Soviet Union undertook perestroika-style reforms, the Albanian communists resisted change of any kind and continued to maintain their strong grip over their country. They continued to punish dissidence with a neo-Stalinistic repression that was, arguably, the most draconian of all the socialist regimes, with the possible exception of Romania under Nicolae Ceauşescu. The absence of a democratic tradition and a pervasive popular sympathy for strong-leadership–oriented government explain why, at least initially, there was no popular outcry against Alia's rejection of perestroika and his continuation of Hoxha's neo-Stalinistic rule.

Another reason for resistance to change in the late 1980s was the situation in the province of Kosovo in the neighboring Yugoslav Republic of Serbia inhabited by a large Albanian minority. The Albanians in Kosovo held demonstrations in 1989 and 1990 against the repressive policies of the Serbian president Slobodan Milošević, who had deprived them of administrative autonomy in violation of the Yugoslav constitution. Albanians in Kosovo organized opposition political parties, which, in addition to advocating full autonomy and republic status for Kosovo, demanded political pluralism and the introduction of a free-market economy. The communist leadership in Tirana was terrified of a replication of this anticommunist ferment inside Albania.[1]

Beginnings of Reform

President Ramiz Alia turned out to be less closed-minded about change than his predecessor. Something of a pragmatist, he did see some flaws in Albania's socialism. Reform-minded colleagues in the late 1980s began to suggest cautiously that some aspects of Soviet perestroika could be introduced into Albania to make its socialist system function more efficiently, and some party members began to speak openly of the need for reform, though they all insisted on the continuing dominance of the Communist Party, Alia listened.[2]

1. Incentives

Alia's willingness to consider the possibility of change was partly a result of growing social tensions. Young people, who made up most of the Albanian population (at least one-third of the Albanian population in 1989 was under 15 years of age, with the median age of the country at 25), were frustrated by the pervasive economic stagnation that seemed to doom them to a life of misery. They wanted a relaxation of political control and increased economic opportunity. Western radio and television broadcasts, increasingly accessible even in this closed society, presented attractive alternatives. Albanian youth began to act in aberrant ways, at least from the regime's perspective. They showed a disinterest in the study of Marxism-Leninism. They were attracted to religious activity; and some young people openly displayed anger toward communist authority by violence. Albanian officials complained of willful destruction of socialist property and violent behavior on the streets by Albanian youth.

In 1986, Premier Adil Çarçani acknowledged the country's serious economic problems. He spoke of shortages of energy and imported raw materials. In 1987, President Alia criticized poor planning and control by enterprise managers and complained about a serious decline in output in the chrome industry, a major source of hard-currency earnings. Indeed, by the late 1980s, the Albanian economy was bankrupt, unable to absorb new workers, and plagued by chronic shortages of such basic foods as milk, meat, and bread. Burdened by Europe's highest annual population growth (2.9 percent), the Albanian government did not have the resources to improve living conditions.[3]

Alia's new interest in reform was also a response to political developments elsewhere in Eastern Europe in the late 1980s. The Albanian intelligentsia learned of reform movements in other central and East European countries in 1989 by tuning into foreign radio and television. In addition, the Albanian state media provided wide and surprisingly objective coverage.

No event in Eastern Europe had a greater impact on Albanian communist leaders than the revolution in Romania. At the end of 1989 the execution of Ceauşescu, whose brutal methods of rule were, to be sure, worse than those of Hoxha and Alia, had a sobering impact on Alia and his colleagues. They were determined not to suffer the same fate. They wanted to avoid the kind of political ferment that was challenging and toppling Communist Party regimes elsewhere in Eastern Europe in late 1989 and early 1990.[4]

2. Scope of Reform

At the Ninth Plenum of the Albanian Communist Party's Central Committee in January 1990, President Alia discussed a "democratization" of the country's economic life. He meant the preservation of socialism through reform of an obsolete administrative system, on which he blamed the country's economic stagnation and social unrest. Alia proposed the decontrol of prices for some consumer goods; the acceptance of private enterprise, mostly in the service area; and the toleration of variations in personal income for farmers to encourage them to sell produce in the open market.[5]

Most of the Albanian political establishment accepted the need for some economic reform. In early February 1990, a Central Committee plenum approved a decentralization of economic decision making, giving local authorities and enterprises greater autonomy, an acknowledgment of the importance that market forces played in regulating production. And in order to stimulate agricultural production and deal with food shortages in the cities, cooperatives were permitted to sell their surplus products freely.[6]

Alia, however, hesitated to introduce a large-scale political liberalization. He and the conservative party bureaucracy did not want to compromise the Communist Party's monopoly of power. The Albanian party bureaucracy was hostile to any change that would diminish its power and perquisites. Conservative bureaucratic officials opposed his request for a more liberal emigration policy to give the country's young people, who mostly wanted to find work, a chance to leave. Typical of the bureaucracy's conservatism in the summer of 1990 was the position of Xheli Gjoni, a candidate member of the party politburo. Gjoni condemned Albanian youth seeking to emigrate, calling them enemies of their country.[7]

Nevertheless, the party leadership did agree to make the party more responsive to popular concerns. By this time Alia and his colleagues recognized the need to conciliate an alienated and frustrated public in order to strengthen the party's public image at home and in the West in the hope of securing some of the Western economic and financial assistance going to other Central and East European countries, such as Poland and Hungary.

The party leadership announced in early February 1990 that primary party organizations (cell and local branches) would hold open meetings and allow workers to play a greater role in the selection of party officials. Competition would be introduced in the election of officials, and their terms of office would be limited.[8]

There was an equivalent softening of restrictive government policies. In April 1990, Alia announced the Parliament's formal endorsement of the right to travel abroad, the lifting of restrictions on religious activities, and the abolition of the death penalty for illegal emigration.[9]

3. Consequences of Reform

Having opened the door to change, Alia was confronted with conditions he had hoped to avoid. Albania's small literary and scientific intelligentsia began to speak out critically about the communist government's repression, lamenting its frequent violations of human rights. In late 1989, Neshat Tozaj, a writer well known among the Albanian intelligentsia, published a novel criticizing human-rights violations by the Ministry of Internal Affairs. Other intellectuals, including the future leader of Albania's first legal opposition party Dr. Sali Berisha, also called attention to violations of human rights by communist officials and advocated the adoption of an Albanian version of glasnost. The intellectuals did not, however, unite in a political organization that could lend force to their ideas.[10]

Soon, however, a large number of Albanian youth echoed these sentiments. Over 4,000 young people tried to leave the country in the summer of 1990. The picture reported in the Western press of young Albanians climbing the sides of overcrowded vessels bound for Italy where they hoped to find work and better living conditions was the first clear evidence that the closed society of Albania was about to disintegrate.

Alia, trying to head off more unrest, responded with promises of new reforms. He announced enactment of a law that would allow free parliamentary elections.[11] In a major speech to the People's Assembly on November 13, 1990, Alia also proposed measures to separate the party from the state. He said the Albanian Communist Party would give up its constitutionally guaranteed monopoly of power. He also promised a new constitution to guarantee human rights and pledged to open the country to foreign investment.[12]

By the end of 1990, popular pressure for more political change increased. Many Albanians, especially in the large urban centers like Tirana, aware of the democratization occurring elsewhere in Central and Eastern Europe, renewed demands for the equivalent in Albania. Some even discussed the possibility of imitating the bloody Romanian revolution and violently removing the communist leadership. In mid-November, people took to the streets for the first time in forty-five years of communist rule. They attacked the symbols of dictatorship: the monuments and buildings from the Stalinist era and symbols of the late Enver Hoxha. In December, dissident students led antigovernment demonstrations in Tirana, Shkodër, Elbasan, and Durrës.[13]

These events reached a climax with the formation of Albania's first formal opposition party, the Democratic Party. One of its founders, economics professor Gramoz Pashko, a self-styled "dissident," underscored the new party's commitment to a multiparty system, protection of human rights, a free-market economy, good relations between Albania and its neighbors, and integration with Europe. In December the national trade union declared its independence of the Communist Party, asserting that it would no longer act as a party lever, and promised to fight for higher pay and better conditions for workers.[14]

The Albanian leadership seemed willing to conciliate the protesters with further political liberalization. In early December 1990, the party's Central Committee decided to allow the formation of a multiparty system in Albania. In addition, several reformers were selected as full or candidate members of the party's Central Committee, including the economists Fatos Nano and Ylli Bufi.

The government acted equivalently. On December 28, Albania's Council of Ministers set up a state commission to draft a new law liberalizing rules governing the press, radio, television, and publishing and formally defined the jurisdiction of the directors of the various media. The council also legalized the first opposition newspaper, *Relindja Demokratie,* the organ of the new Democratic Party. For the first time during communist rule, Christmas was celebrated with well-attended Catholic and Orthodox services.[15]

Perhaps the clearest sign that liberalization was under way was the publication on December 31, 1990, of the complete text of Albania's new draft constitution, to replace the 1976 document. The draft was free of communist dogma and avoided reference to past totalitarian practices. There was no reference to the Albanian Communist Party. The new document lifted the ban on religion and sanctioned foreign investment. It introduced a governmental system that appeared to be very similar in structure to the parliamentary democracies in Western Europe while providing for a strong presidential office. The constitution seemed to suggest a final break with the Stalinist past.[16]

Resistance to Further Liberalization

As Alia pressed forward with his reforms in 1990 and 1991, he continued to meet resistance. Conservative forces in the party were still trying to slow the pace of change. In the summer of 1990, party leaders promoted Gjoni, chief of the Tirana city party organization, to the Politburo. Gjoni strongly opposed the more-liberal faction of the party elite headed by Foto Cami, blaming him for the breakdown of law and order in the country. Gjoni launched a fierce campaign against the families and relatives of the young emigrants.[17]

Party conservatives also attacked Alia, blaming political liberalization for the outbreaks of social turmoil and accusing him of leading the country to anarchy. They warned of an impending civil war. A hard-line lobby, the "Enver Hoxha Voluntary Activists Union," worked for the preservation of the old authoritarian order. This organization had the sympathy of the military and security agencies of the Albanian government and organized rallies all over the country in support of the late Hoxha.[18]

1. Alia's Response

Alia refused to engage the conservatives. With his eye on parliamentary elections scheduled for March 1991, hoping they would produce an assembly willing · to reelect him as president of the republic, Alia proceeded with caution in responding to the conservative offensive, with which he had some sympathy and which had a lot of popular support in the countryside. He would not denounce the late Hoxha, as reformers wanted. But he was determined to continue the process of liberalization, arguing that, while there had been much good in the past, the party under Hoxha in its Stalinist policies had made many mistakes that now had to be corrected.[19]

In the months preceding the elections, Alia tried to steer a middle course, assuaging the hard-liners without losing the support of the reformers. To strengthen his hand with the conservatives, in February 1991 Alia announced assumption of personal control over the country. He appointed a nine-member presidential council, whose members, with the exception of Fatos Nano, were conservatives. The council included Çarçani and Gjoni.[20]

At the same time, Alia tried to keep his fences mended with party liberals, appointing Nano to succeed Çarçani as prime minister. He also accommodated a demand by the political opposition to postpone parliamentary elections, originally scheduled for February 10, for a month to give it time to organize and convey its message to the electorate. The Alia government also provided the opposition parties—there were now several, although they were still quite small —with space for campaign headquarters, some telephones, and some automobiles. On the eve of the day of the elections, Alia said that the Communist Party would accept defeat if that were the will of the people.[21]

2. The Parliamentary Elections of March 1991

The parliamentary elections held on March 31, 1991, were the first contested elections in Albania since 1923. The two major contenders were the Communist Party and the newly established Democratic Party. To the dismay of voters in the large urban centers who had supported candidates of the Democratic Party, the communists won a comfortable majority of 169 out of 250 seats.[22]

Albanians living in the countryside had voted overwhelmingly for communists. These voters were afraid of an outbreak of lawlessness and anarchy if reformers were elected to lead the country—indeed, Alia lost his seat in parliament to Gjoni. In addition, communists benefited from the enormous resources at their disposal. They still controlled the media. Also, government control over the distribution of newsprint supplies made it very difficult for the opposition to publish its organs, *Rilindja Demokratie* and *Republika*. Communist control over radio, television, and the printed media, made it nearly impossible for the opposition to send its message to the electorate. They also used the old electoral trick of bribing some rural voters who wanted reform to win their support: on the eve of the elections. The regime announced decisions to allow enlarged private farms and unlimited ownership of livestock.[23]

Communists also benefited from the failure of the Democrats not only to develop an effective electoral organization, but to communicate with rural voters, who made up a majority of the electorate. Most rural voters knew little if anything about the noncommunist organizations challenging the Communist Party in the election. Finally, according to Dr. Sali Berisha, who had succeeded

Pashko as leader of the Democrats, the communists won because they had cheated. In late May 1991, during a visit to Washington to brief American officials on recent Albanian political developments, he told members of the U.S. Congress that there had been killings and beatings of opposition candidates. He said the regime had imposed severe restrictions on opposition access to news outlets.[24]

Nevertheless, the elections did confirm what was already evident—a steady Albanian movement away from communism. Although the conservative Gjoni intoned that the election results showed that Albanians still had faith in Marxism-Leninism, the opposite was more true, given the fact that the Democratic Party, only four months old and hamstrung in so many ways by the communists, had been able to win 38 percent of the popular vote.[25]

3. Reaction of the Hard-liners

Following the elections, hard-liners inside the party made a last desperate effort to block further departures from the old order. Gjoni was elevated to full membership in the party politburo in April 1991. In the party's official newspaper *Zeri i Populitt*, the hard-liners published an editorial hailing the late Enver Hoxha as a great leader and saying that there was no need for the party to apologize to the Albanian people for the costs of building socialism.[26]

Ascendancy of Reformers

Party reformers, however, pressed on, and even Gjoni prepared for compromise. In the hope of being elected leader of the party at its Tenth Congress in June 1991, Gjoni criticized Hoxha's leadership in the keynote address and promised further reform. This political *volta face* did not fool the reformers, who rejected Gjoni. They supported Nano, the former prime minister, as party chairman.

1. More Liberalization Within the Communist Party

Reformers now took steps to strengthen their influence on party decision making. They got the congress to dilute conservative influence at the top of the party hierarchy by replacing the hard-line politburo with a fifteen-member party presidency. The congress also changed the name of the party to the Socialist Party, with no reference to communism. *Zeri i Popullit* dropped the hammer-and-sickle insignia from its masthead and published startling criticisms of Hoxha and his family. A new party program formally abandoned the goal of creating a communist society. It called for a market economy with a safety net that would minimize hardships of the new system. While advocating privatization, the Socialists favored preservation of agricultural cooperatives and retention of state control over vital industries such as those involving national defense.[27]

2. Further Liberalization of the Government

With no stomach for the violence and civil war that would surely have occurred had he used force to resist popular pressures for change, Alia, who was chosen president of the republic by the newly elected Parliament, was now eager to lead the effort at reform. He was convinced it was the only way to salvage the party's leadership of the country. He called for an Albanian version of democracy in national political, economic, and social life, in particular, freely contested elections for managers of industrial enterprises and farms and for representatives in Parliament. Alia hoped that multicandidate elections and the secret ballot for elections to municipal councils, the national parliament, and internal party positions would allow people to vote conservatives out of power. He also sought limits of ten years on terms of office for government positions, with a fifth-year peer review of performance and the possibility of dismissal, and limits of five years for holding party office.[28]

The new Parliament enacted much of this reform program into law throughout the remainder of 1991. It approved a Law on Constitutional Powers, including many provisions of the new draft constitution intended to replace the 1976 constitution. The Law on Constitutional Powers endorsed political pluralism and the establishment of a multiparty system. It also guaranteed human rights and the equality of all forms of private ownership—state, collective, and private. Finally, the Law on Constitutional Powers explicitly banned party activity in the government ministries of defense, internal affairs, justice, and foreign affairs.[29]

Alia's reforms and the Socialist Party's attempt to change its image and break with its past, however, did not slow down the momentum of popular opposition to communist rule. Strikes and street demonstrations continued and eventually led to the resignation of Prime Minister Nano in June 1991. Alia replaced him with Ylli Bufi, a nonpartisan, nonideological economist. Bufi formed a coalition cabinet of experts, in which half of the twenty-four ministers were drawn from newly formed opposition groups and half from the former communists. The former communists, however, were still influential. They retained control of the ministries of foreign affairs and public order, formerly the Ministry of Internal Affairs.[30]

Showing confidence and flexibility, political opposition groups accepted this power sharing, despite reservations about the continuing influence of former communists over key bodies of the national government. Berisha and other opposition leaders were willing to work with reform communists to forestall anarchy, a real possibility given growing popular dissatisfaction with conditions throughout the country. The more likely the prospect of increased violence, the opposition reasoned, the more difficult it would be to make the transition to democracy. The opposition also did not want to provide Alia and the military with any pretext for declaring the country to be in a state of crisis and instituting a dictatorship.[31]

3. Continuing Economic Deterioration

While political change was taking place in 1990 and 1991, economic conditions were deteriorating. On July 28, 1991, the Council of Ministers reported that as of midyear exports had reached only 22 percent and imports only 33 percent of their planned targets and that industrial production had fallen 50 percent.[32]

During 1991, factories closed for several months for lack of spare parts, raw materials, and power. Increased unemployment, in turn, drained the state treasury because the government paid idle workers 80 percent of their normal wages. By early 1992, Albania was importing 70 percent of its energy supplies, at high prices. Inflation in 1991 ran at 30 percent. Agricultural production was in a slump, and food reserves were dangerously low. There was a chronic shortage of eggs and meat, even on the expensive free market. Throughout 1991, there was never enough flour or cooking oil. There was also a drastic decline in revenue from hard-currency exports such as oil, electricity, and chromium, and the foreign debt, which previously was nonexistent, climbed to the equivalent of $400 million.[33]

This economic misery provoked peasant seizures of land and livestock owned by the state in a real revolution against the old collectivist order. But more telling was the continuation during 1991 of the exodus of young Albanians looking for work and better living conditions in Italy and Greece. While the emigrants said they were fleeing because of chronic unemployment and food shortages, some Albanian political figures, including Prime Minister Bufi, believed that conservative elements opposed to reform had incited the migration in order to embarrass the reformist leadership and bring back a communist-style dictatorship.[34]

4. More Economic Reform

In the summer of 1991, the government was ready for a further reduction of state control over the economy to increase productivity. Prime Minister Bufi proposed an extensive reduction of government expenditures for administration and the military while calling for an acceleration of privatization of small and medium-sized enterprises. He also granted substantial autonomy to managers of large state enterprises. In the beginning of September 1991, the government announced preparations for a reform of the banking and currency systems. He wanted to give the Albanian central bank greater independence over the money supply, investment, and interest rates. Banks were to help initiate privatization and encourage individuals to set up their own private businesses.[35]

But by the end of 1991, Albania was still the poorest country in Europe. Most Albanians were still living with oxen- and donkey-drawn carts. They worked in grimy steam-powered factories and had farm equipment dating back to the 1950s. Towns and villages had few shops, and workers walked to their jobs or traveled on rickety buses. Moreover, Albania had to import 70 percent of its energy supplies, at high prices, because the Persian Gulf crisis had put oil on the open market at a premium. Inflation in 1991 ran at 30 percent.[36]

By early 1992, the economy was still in the doldrums. Many industrial plants were working at only 5 percent of capacity, and unemployment was widespread. Although agricultural output had increased as a result of the successful privatization of almost 90 percent of collective farms, food reserves were dangerously low, and there were shortages of basic items, such as bread.[37] Endless lines formed outside empty shops in the hope that food relief would become available. Mob looting of government warehouses became commonplace. Making matters worse was the apparent impotence of law-enforcement authorities, who in the more-relaxed political order introduced by the communists were openly derided and attacked by citizens.[38]

The End of Communist Rule

Unlike Deputy Premier Pashko, who favored continued cooperation with the communists to deal with the deteriorating economic and political environment, Berisha wanted their removal from political power and parliamentary elections to bring this about. He hoped a new Parliament with a noncommunist majority would produce a government that could address pressing economic and social problems. He had in mind ambitious schemes for privatization of state property, increased attention to the expansion of consumer-goods production, and a drastic reduction of state expenditures.[39]

1. Berisha Challenges the Socialists

In December 1991, when Socialist members of Parliament seemed to be stalling on the issue of early elections and stonewalling reforms to open up the economy to free enterprise, Berisha decided to take them on. He was encouraged to call them on their delaying tactics by demonstrations in the streets of Tirana and other Albanian urban centers by young people furious over continuing economic hardships, especially unemployment and food shortages. Berisha and other Democratic Party members in the cabinet decided to bring the Bufi government down and force the issue of parliamentary elections by resigning their cabinet posts.[40] Bufi retreated and gave up the prime ministership. A caretaker government of technocrats took over until parliamentary elections, scheduled for March 22, 1992.[41]

2. The March 1992 Parliamentary Elections

Parliamentary elections held in March 1992 finally brought an end to Albanian communist rule. Berisha's Democratic Party won an overwhelming majority of the popular vote.[42] While support for the Democrats in the city areas was expected because they were strongholds of reform, support for them in the country-side, which had voted for the communists in the last parliamentary election, came as a pleasant surprise. People in the small towns and villages of rural Albania were disappointed by the failure of the Socialists to improve conditions as they enacted major reforms, such as decollectivization. Albanian farmers, who now had their own land, said they were disgusted by their inability to cultivate it. They complained about the lack of tools, fertilizer, and seed.[43] Most Albanians also hoped that the Socialists would move faster than they did to end Albania's international isolation and open up the country to European ideas and values—Berisha's recent visits to Western countries, in particular the United States, had been publicized on national radio and television. Albanians hoped that, with new ties to the West, their country might receive much-needed economic and financial help. The end of communist rule occurred on April 3, 1992, when the newly elected Albanian Parliament chose Democratic Party leader Berisha as president of the republic, Albania's first noncommunist chief executive since the end of World War II.[44]

Postcommunist Albania

Albania's new democratic leadership confronted serious political, economic, social, and international problems dangerous to the country's stability and security. While some of these problems were inherited from the communist past, others were the direct result of the collapse of communist rule, not only in Albania but elsewhere in Central and Eastern Europe. The Albanian economy continued to deteriorate well into 1993 and 1994, prolonging the hardships of the communist era that many people hoped would go away once communist rule came to an end. Social problems rooted in the past and made worse by the collapse of communist rule, along with the weak economy, threatened the stability and success of democratic development. While relations with the West improved in postcommunist Albania, relations with Balkan neighbors, which had substantial Albanian minorities, became problematic as Yugoslavia disintegrated and civil war exploded or threatened to explode.

1. Political Problems

Political problems threaten the success of Albania's effort to develop a Western-style parliamentary system. New political party groups are not yet viable vehicles of mass popular participation. The majority of Albanians living in the countryside do not have meaningful party affiliations, and parties themselves have yet to mobilize the voting public. A variety of different party groups have tried to model themselves on political parties in other newly emancipated Central and East European countries, but they have not yet developed coherent political programs. One possible exception has been the ruling Democratic Party of President Berisha, which has a wide base of support that cut across all segments of society. But the Democrats have experienced a divisive factionalism that has severely weakened Berisha's leadership of the country; has offered Socialists an opportunity to regain influence even though it is not at all clear that they have broken completely with their discredited past; and has encouraged the state to continue a strong influence over the political environment, reminiscent of the authoritarian past.

Factionalism in the Democratic Party

After the March 1992 parliamentary elections, polarization occurred among President Berisha's followers, who split over the issue of his increasingly auto-cratic style of leadership. He was in their view using presidential decrees as an alternative to getting parliamentary support for his policies. One prominent par-liamentary faction, led by Gramoz Pashko, who together with Berisha had founded the Democratic Party in late 1990, formed a new party organization called the Democratic Alliance. Pashko had been shut out of the new cabinet, and, when Berisha resigned the leadership of the Democratic Party, Pashko disliked the fact that he arbitrarily chose Eduard Selami, the party secretary and an intellectual in his early thirties, to be his replacement. Other high-ranking members of the party thought they were better qualified to succeed Berisha and accused him and his supporters of a rightist coup. For this behavior, Pashko's supporters were expelled from the Democratic Party. They then joined the Dem-ocratic Alliance.[45]

The Socialists Seek a Political Comeback

Meanwhile, the former communists were working hard to make a political come-back. They had an advantage as the second-largest party in the new Albanian Parliament. They emphasized their changed identity, insisting that they were not a throwback to the past, and said they had a new program of paced and moderate socioeconomic change.[46]

Although they tried to convince voters of their new persona by criticizing the late Enver Hoxha, their criticism was only halfhearted. They expressed no re-morse over their past mismanagement of the country. Furthermore, the party's credibility—whatever was left of it—suffered when a former communist prime minister, Fatos Nano, was accused of having misappropriated $8 million during his short leadership of the country in 1991.[47] Nano's arrest compromised the Socialists by encouraging a group of moderates in the party to separate, form their own group called the Social Democrats, and align themselves with the Democratic Party.[48]

Still, the potential of the Socialists for a political rejuvenation and a chance, however remote, of returning to power is real. The Socialists are cultivating the support of a poverty-stricken electorate by promising to minimize the hardships caused by free-market reforms. The Socialists have scored points with the public by accusing Berisha and his party of dictatorial tendencies, pointing to political trials that contradict the Democratic Party's commitment to a liberal political environment.[49]

It remains to be seen whether the Socialists will help or hurt Albanian democratic development. They could strengthen the credibility of democratic government in their pursuit of moderation. They also could undermine democracy if they seek a return to political authoritarianism.

Politicization of the Judiciary

One prerequisite for a successful democracy is a vigorous and independent judiciary, which Albania still did not have three years after the end of communist rule. For example, office space for judicial officials remained in short supply, requiring judges and prosecutors to share the same space, which kept alive the old communist idea that both are on the same team, so to speak.

Albanian courts lack modern electronic equipment and must rely during trials, even high-profile ones, on stenographers' taking notes that are sometimes inadequate or in error. The system is so short of money that it cannot afford to guarantee legal defense to people unable to pay for their own lawyer—and most Albanians are in that boat. Investment of scarce capital in the judiciary is considered a luxury, and the improvement of its machinery is low on the list of investment priorities, which favor economic development.[50]

A more-serious defect in the postcommunist Albanian judicial system, however, is political pressure on its decision making. Berisha is partly responsible in that, in the name of "anticommunism," he replaced officials appointed by the Hoxha and Alia regimes with his personal cronies to assure the judiciary's cooperation with his policies. Berisha tried to use the judiciary to strengthen his personal leadership and undermine the opposition Socialists. If judges did not cooperate, they risked being fired. A good example of how the postcommunist government used the judiciary involved former President Alia, who was accused of violating a law forbidding dual office holding common in the communist era, when the head of the party was usually the head of state. It made no difference to Berisha's judiciary that this law was not in effect when Alia was in power and was passed only after his retirement. Alia was convicted.[51]

Harassment of the Media

Albania still has a large degree of government control over its media. The Berisha government has continued the same kind of pressure on the media as its communist predecessor. It harasses journalists who criticize its personnel or policies. In

January 1994, the government amended the criminal code to provide for prosecution of "anyone who 'injures the dignity' of the president or insults ministers and parliamentary deputies." It does not make any difference if the accusations are proven to be true. And the government can close a newspaper if it publishes so-called "official secrets," a term that has not been publicly defined. While the number of journalists accused of violating these sweeping rules remains small, the fact that they are on the books discourages the kind of open, free, and aggressive press that is needed by a real democratic government—as opposed to a government that looks democratic but acts differently—and means that Albania still has a long way to go before its political system can be considered truly liberal and a decisive break with the country's authoritarian past has taken place.[52]

Berisha's Decline

Berisha steadily lost popular support in 1994, especially in Parliament, where the politicians, even those in his own party, were becoming increasingly annoyed by the gap between what he said and what he did. He called himself a liberal and pledged to further Albanian democracy. He acted otherwise, however, at least in the view of Parliament. Toward the end of the year, he was in open conflict with Parliament over a new draft constitution designed to transform Albania into a Western-style parliamentary democracy. Fearful that he could not muster the two-thirds majority of Parliament needed to have the constitution approved, he decided to obtain direct popular acceptance of it in a referendum, which was held at the end of November.

It was not so much that politicians and people disliked this constitution—they actually favored it, though some were concerned that it gave too much power to the president and thus invited a restoration of dictatorial rule. Many voters resented the high-handed way Berisha went about campaigning for public support of it. He called the document "his constitution." He lobbied aggressively for it over the state-controlled media, and he was overbearing and offensive in his refusal to allow discussion and criticism of the charter.[53]

Many inside and outside government thought he was acting like Hoxha or Alia. While he wanted democracy for Albania, it looked like he did not understand the meaning of it or how it worked. After all, Berisha had no first-hand experience with democracy, except to the extent that he had visited democratic countries, in particular, the United States. Instead of trying to "sell" his constitution to Parliament, he chose to circumvent it. He seemed to lack the interest in and capacity for the kind of conciliation and compromise essential to the success of democratic government. Although Berisha lost the referendum—a majority of Albanian voters rejected the constitution as a criticism of his handling of power—a majority of Albanians seemed to have faith in the new postcommunist government and in Berisha himself.

But this faith began to wear thin during 1995, as Berisha's authoritarian style became more pronounced. Socialist Party leaders accused the Berisha government of trying to undermine and subvert their party to prevent a resurgence of its influence. They pointed to the arrest and conviction in 1994 of Socialist leader Nanos who received a sentence of twelve years in prison that was intended, as the Socialist leadership argued, to weaken and discredit the party. The Socialist position was not without merit and several human rights groups, including Amnesty International, called for Nanos's release. Although Democratic politicians denied the Socialists' accusation, they apparently were put on the defensive and reduced Nanos's sentence several times to allow his release in 1998.[54]

The Democratic campaign against the Socialists and other opposition groups on the eve of parliamentary elections scheduled for May 1996 continued throughout 1995. The enactment of two laws in the fall of 1995 effectively disqualified many Socialist politicians from participation in the elections. One of these laws prohibited people who had held high office under the communists from running for office until 2002. Another law required prospective parliamentary candidates to be screened to determine if in fact they had been high functionaries in the governments of presidents Alia and Hoxha. The screening process put promptly into effect resulted in the disqualification of more than one hundred prospective Socialist candidates for parliamentary seats. Once again, the Democrats insisted they were not trying to destroy their political opposition, but their protestations were not credible in light of the events surrounding the parliamentary elections held at the end of May 1996.[55]

Finally, the Berisha government put through a new electoral law designed to work in favor of the Democratic Party and against the Socialists. The new law increased the number of parliamentary seats to be filled by the single-member-district voting system, and diminished the number of seats filled by proportional representation. This helped the Democrats and hurt the Socialists by making it more difficult for smaller parties to win seats and then ally with the Socialists to form a majority in Parliament. The new electoral arrangement was denounced by the Socialists and other parties as a blatant effort to manipulate the electorate and limit its choice.[56]

The May 1996 Parliamentary Elections

Although the opposition Socialists nevertheless expected victory in the parliamentary elections held at the end of May 1996, pointing to popular dissatisfaction with the Berisha government's slow pace of economic reform, bureaucratic corruption, and the president's heavy-handed style, the opposite occurred. Berisha's Democratic Party won over 50 percent of the popular vote, the Socialists slightly less than 25 percent, and small left-leaning parties not enough to give them an opportunity to make a coalition with the Socialists. Partly, the Socialists had themselves to blame for their poor showing. A few hours before the polls closed on May 26, they pulled out of the election, accusing the Democratic Party of large-scale shenanigans (such as ballot-box stuffing, voters casting more than one ballot, and violence against opposition supporters)—they said Berisha had not fulfilled his promise when the electoral campaign started at the end of April that the elections would be free and democratic.[57]

It remains an open question whether voter fraud in fact was responsible for tipping the balance in favor of the Democrats. By mid-1996, however, one thing was clear: Berisha had undermined the credibility of his country's fragile parliamentary democracy and strengthened critics who insisted that he was no longer the Democrat he proclaimed himself to be and was well on the way to restoring dictatorial rule in Albania. And what disturbed the opposition groups, in particular the Socialists, was the West's official silence on the complaints of fraud by international monitors and human-rights groups such as the New York–based Human Rights Watch as well as by Albanians themselves. Presumably the West, especially the Clinton administration, wanted to avoid weakening or antagonizing Berisha, who was viewed as a friend and whose government had contributed in the Western view to stability in the region, especially in the restraint it showed toward the volatile Albanian community in the Serb Republic province of Kosovo.

2. Economic Problems

Perhaps the biggest liability for postcommunist Albania is continuing economic hardship for most Albanians, who eventually might lose patience with the democratic order. In 1993, it was possible to argue that Albania had no economy at all or certainly had the least-developed economy in continental Europe.

Industrial and Agricultural Stagnation

Forty percent of the Albanian workforce was unemployed in 1993, and this figure did not count the 10 percent of the population that had fled abroad to find work. The country's only railroad line was not functioning. Electric power, heat, and water in Tirana were interrupted for long periods of time. Desperate for firewood, people in Tirana cut down trees that for centuries had lined roads, leaving thousands of stumps. Hospitals had virtually no resources, and schools had no textbooks, since 27 million of the heavily ideological books of the past were scrapped. In most of the country, hardly a factory chimney was seen smoking. Many plants were dismantled by their workers, partly in an explosion of anger against past oppression and partly to steal tools or such basic goods as window frames to put in their own homes. Where people were working, the average wage by mid-1993 was less than $30.00 a month.[58]

In the agricultural sector, things were not any better. Instead of promoting large collectives, which could produce enough to maintain a low but adequate nutritional level, the land was split up into small inefficient units of 3.5 acres on average. Farm productivity declined to one-tenth of that in the European Union. Albania was forced to import expensive foreign grain. It was necessary to raise the price of bread, although, to head off the explosion of social tension bound to be provoked by this action, the Berisha government compensated 1.8 million of the hardest-hit citizens. There was also staggering unemployment in the countryside, the result of an inadequate amount of land to farm. In the past, the government had provided seed and other necessities and mechanical equipment. As state control over the economy diminished, people increasingly had to fend for themselves and get their own supplies. To make matters worse, the government still had not regularized the rules governing private ownership of land, in particular, owners' deeds, and there was much quarreling about ownership issues.[59]

Government Responses

The Berisha government tried radical reforms to improve the health of the Albanian economy. In 1992 and 1993, it slashed government spending, made Albanian currency convertible, and eliminated barriers to foreign trade. It also tried to free up prices, except for staples such as bread and milk, and expand the private sector in agriculture, although 90 percent of the land already had been distributed by the Socialists in 1991.[60]

While privatization proceeded quite rapidly in retailing services, transportation, and housing, with about 100,000 out of a total population of 3.2 million employed in private enterprise, there are problems. For example, Albania lacks the legal framework for a market economy, and the government is trying to develop it through legislation on taxes, legal accounting, bankruptcy, and banking and credit creation. But the government is still left with the obsolescence of the industrial sector and the high cost of modernization of plant and equipment.[61]

The Albanian government also tried to lure foreign investment into the country, although a major infusion of private capital has not materialized because of the poor economic infrastructure and because of political instability.[62] The government has also sought foreign economic and financial aid, and received more foreign aid per person than any other country. This foreign aid financed 50–60 percent of the national budget. But foreign aid has yet to make a difference in living conditions for most Albanians. The Albanian government is partly to blame. The administrative ineptitude of government officials, who are incapable of spending what they receive, has slowed down aid delivery. The country still lacks an adequate pool of competent officials. There is also a tendency, inherited from the communist past, for managers of state owned enterprises to avoid initiative and responsibility and pass decisions they themselves should make to a higher level.[63]

Nevertheless, in 1993, polls showed that President Berisha was still popular with many Albanians. These polls also showed a popular optimism about the future of the country, with 77 percent of Albanian respondents saying they think the country is moving in the right direction and 71 percent saying that the country's economic situation will improve.[64]

3. Social Problems

Perhaps the most pressing of postcommunist Albania's social problems involves the rejuvenation of the heavily politicized education system inherited from the communist past. Another problem has to do with gender inequities. As in most other Central and East European countries, women have not fared well in the postcommunist era. At the same time, however, though Albania is predominantly Islamic, there is no threat of a fundamentalist incursion.

Education

The communist regime bequeathed a system of higher education that was inadequate, inept, overcentralized, and elitist. The country had only two universities, with only 8,000 students enrolled out of a total population of 3.5 million people with a median age of 25. Textbooks were in short supply, and academic salaries were so low—ranging from $20.00 a month for faculty to $130.00 for top administrators—that many educators had to take second jobs to survive. Finally, up-to-date learning in the physical and social sciences was minimal as a result of the tough government political control and propagandization of universities and the country's isolation, which deprived Albanian educators of contacts with colleagues in the West.[65]

The Berisha government made some progress toward improving the quantity and quality of Albanian higher education. It expanded the number of enrolled students by early 1995 to about 25,000. It encouraged an updating of curricula with the help of visiting professors from the West. It sent Albanian faculty abroad with financial help from such organizations as the European Union's "Tempus" program.[66]

But Albania still has a long way to go in upgrading its university system and meeting the demands of its youth for quality higher education. Some government officials, such as economic adviser Fatos Cocoli, suggest that the private sector must help because the Albanian government will never have enough resources to develop a system of higher education that satisfies on both qualitative and quantitative levels the demands of the postcommunist era. Another suggestion has been to charge tuition to provide revenue for funding higher salaries for faculty to allow them to devote all their time to teaching and research. But there are problems. Without the existence of quality-control agencies, the government would have difficulty assuring that private institutions are maintaining academic standards. The government is also reluctant to impose tuition charges given the impoverishment of the society and the inability of many young people to pay for the education they need and the government wants them to have in order to help the country through the transition to a new liberal order.[67]

The Predicament of Albanian Women

Severe economic problems, in particular, runaway inflation and unemployment, that impoverished much of Albanian society in the mid 1990s have hurt women the most. Unemployment is higher among women than among men because women have no ability to protect their socioeconomic interests. They also have been affected psychologically by the continuing economic crisis. Their preoccupation has been with survival, leaving little if any time and energy to think about themselves. Indeed, the hardships they are enduring have all but destroyed any interest they might have had in getting involved in politics and promoting gender equality. They are especially unhappy in the cities, where they are confined to their apartments except when shopping for scarce and expensive food that requires them to wait on endless lines as they used to do under the communists. Albanian women see little that is good for them either in the Islamic religion, which emphasizes the subservience of women to men, or in the collapse of communist rule.[68]

Women in Albania seem to have been better off under Communist rule. At least under communism there was a pretense of fostering equality, with communist governments providing women opportunities to work outside the home and earn income that could help improve living conditions for them and their families. Postcommunist leaders have shown little interest in women's issues and have not done much to help women improve their social and economic condition. At the same time, women's groups affiliated with the Communist Party have disappeared, and nothing has taken their place. The new political parties do not seem interested in recruiting women, to say nothing of nominating them in elections for seats in national and local legislative bodies.[69]

While the political situation of women in other former communist countries in Eastern Europe is not strong, the worst case for women exists in Albania. The country's impoverishment and the conservative, antifeminist teachings of Islam are the biggest roadblocks to the entry of women into politics and to an improvement of their living conditions in Albania. And, there is nothing to suggest a change in this situation in the near future.

A "Nonproblem": Religion

According to one sympathetic observer of postcommunist Albanian political development, the country deserves to be lauded for its apparent religious toleration. The religion of the overwhelming majority of Albanians is Islam. Yet despite the long period of antireligious propaganda by the communists, there has been no explosion of religious fervor in the postcommunist era when discrimination against religion and religious practices ended. Albanians seem to be indifferent, at least for the moment, toward Islamic fundamentalism, pursuing their Islamic faith in the dignified and restrained manner of Islamic neighbors in Bosnia and Turkey. Albanian women do not generally wear the veil.[70]

There are several reasons for the mildness and almost secular and tolerant quality of Islam in Albania. Albanians adopted the religion largely out of expediency when the Ottoman Turks conquered the country in the early fifteenth century. Albanians did not become Muslims because "they saw the light," so to speak, or were inspired by some great religious hero. They adopted Islam as a matter of self-preservation. Also, the influence of countries that were fervently Islamic—notably those in the "fertile crescent" of the eastern Mediterranean, such as Syria and Iraq, and others to the south and east, such as Saudi Arabia, Iran, and Pakistan—have never had much influence on Albania. Albanian Islam has been affected more by the Christianity of the societies surrounding it in the former Yugoslavia.[71]

But while there is no imminent threat of Islamic fundamentalism, Albania is still vulnerable. It could become the site of fundamentalism should countries like Iran, which are fundamentalist, take an interest in Albania at its own request as a measure of defense against expansionist policies of its Balkan neighbors, notably Serbia and Greece.

4. International Problems

Postcommunist Albania is building on the efforts taken by the Alia government toward the end of its rule to end the country's historic isolation. While the Berisha government focused on strengthening ties with the West, it was very active in looking out for Albania's interest in the southern Balkans, which has become in the early 1990s an area of political turbulence that threatens Albanian stability and security.

Western Europe

The postcommunist Albanian government continues to build on the ties already established in the late 1980s with some West European countries. The new democratic leaders asked in June 1990 to join the European Conference on Security and Cooperation (ECSC), saying that Albania would adopt the principles of the 1975 Helsinki Accords on which the ECSC is based.[72]

United States

Postcommunist Albania has focused a lot of attention on the United States, which took a special interest in the country's gradual transition away from communist rule given its historic reputation of being the most Stalinistic of the communist systems set up in Central and Eastern Europe after World War II. In March 1991, Washington announced a restoration of ties between the two countries.[73] There had been a lot of popular support for friendly ties with the United States, even before the complete collapse of communism. When Secretary of State James A. Baker visited Tirana in early June 1991, 300,000 Albanians gathered in central Tirana to welcome him. This public display was not only anticommunist but also a strong expression of faith that somehow the United States could and would help Albania.[74]

Baker offered a modest program of economic aid worth about $6 million. But he cautioned the Alia leadership that the future of Albanian–American relations would depend on Albania's continued pursuit of political and economic liberalization. As in the case of other East European countries, while the United States was gratified by the departure of communist politicians from positions of leadership, it awaits more concrete development of liberal political and economic institutions before considering an extension of large amounts of economic aid.[75]

In the meantime, however, foreign investment from the United States has trickled into the country, mainly in the form of joint ventures involving Western multinational corporations such as the Coca-Cola Company, the European Bank for Reconstruction and Development, and the Albanian government. This foreign investment, however, is more significant as a symbol of future expansion than as a meaningful contribution to the present growth of the country's still poverty-stricken economy.

The Balkans

In the early 1990s, events in the south Balkan region threatened to destabilize Albania. The most dangerous problems involve the Kosovo province of Serbia, Montenegro, Greece, and Macedonia. All four areas have Albanian minorities. The Albanian government worries about the well-being and safety of kinsmen living in these countries.

Kosovo. Tirana is especially concerned with the plight of the large Albanian majority living in the Kosovo province of Serbia. The Albanian majority in Kosovo for a long time had been subject to repression by the Serbian government. Then, in 1990, President Slobodan Milošević of Serbia reduced Albanians in Kosovo to second-class citizens by abolishing the autonomy they had enjoyed under the Yugoslav Federation constitution. He dissolved their local parliament and closed down Albanian-language radio, television, and newspaper publications.

Alarmed by the increasingly repressive policies of the Milošević government in Kosovo, newly elected Albanian President Berisha sought outside diplomatic help. In June 1992, during a meeting with President Bush in

Washington to discuss the civil war in Bosnia and the prospect of its spreading to other parts of Yugoslavia, he spoke about new threats of Belgrade to the ethnic Albanian population in Kosovo. While Albania certainly wanted to avoid a confrontation with Serbia over its policy toward Kosovo, Berisha told the administration it could not dismiss a fear that Milošević was planning to apply the ethnic-cleansing policies he had approved in Bosnia, against Muslim civilians, to the Albanian population in Kosovo.[76]

Throughout 1993, the situation of Albanians in Kosovo further deteriorated as Belgrade began arming the Serb minority, creating groups of paramilitary fighters, presumably to fight against the ethnic Albanian majority. Albanians in Albania worried that the Milošević leadership someday will use Bosnia-style ethnic-cleansing policies against their kinsmen in Kosovo to dampen any interest in independence or union with Albania, which Milošević vehemently opposes. In an interview in Tirana in June 1993, Albanian army chief of staff Lieutenant General Ilia Vasho said that Serbia had concentrated 100,000 troops in Kosovo.[77]

Albania is no match for the militarily superior Republic of Serbia. Largely made up of unpaid conscripts serving fifteen-month stints, the Albanian army is reducing its force from 300,000 to a maximum of 200,000, with 80 percent of the smaller force to be reservists. Because of Albania's poverty and its hostility toward all other countries in the decade before the fall of communism, the military received no foreign arms or equipment since the break with China in 1978. Albania produces only small infantry weapons, and its air force flies nothing later than Korean War–vintage Soviet MIGSs.[78] And even if there is no war but simply a mass exodus of Albanians from Kosovo to escape Serb repression, Albania will have difficulty coping and will have to turn to the West for help. The area of Albania most likely to be affected is the border town of Kukës, which is in the poorest part of the country and is accessible only by a deeply rutted road through the mountains. Unemployment in Kukës is already 70 percent, with its copper and chromium mines operating at severely reduced levels, and food is in short supply. Consequently, should there be a radical Serbian crackdown in Kosovo, this region, and Albania as a whole, would soon be in the midst of a major crisis.[79]

Certainly Albania wants to avoid an Albanian–Serb conflict. President Berisha has suggested, along with Ibrahim Rugova, the leader of the Albanians in Kosovo, that Kosovo be placed under United Nations control until the final status of the region determined through negotiations, an action that Milošević strongly opposes. Berisha also demanded, to no avail, however, that the lifting of international sanctions against Serbia be linked to the peaceful solution of the Kosovo question.[80]

Montenegro. To strengthen its hand in the event of trouble with Belgrade over the Kosovo problem, the Berisha government has been pursuing a discreet policy toward Montenegro. It is cautiously trying to exploit a perceived weakening of relations between Belgrade and Skopje. Berisha apparently was looking for an opportunity to drive a wedge into the rump Yugoslavia by encouraging the Montenegrins to remain aloof or even to oppose a Serbian effort to pursue ethnic cleansing against Albanians in Kosovo. Montenegro was not happy with Milošević's harsh approach to the Albanian minority in Kosovo. Berisha, trying to play on this difference, called for the lifting of sanctions imposed on Yugoslavia for Montenegro alone, which suffered from them as much as Serbia. The West did not respond to this call. Berisha also received President Momir Bulatović of Montenegro in Tirana in September 1993. Although no important agreements were concluded, the meeting was symbolically important and not appreciated by the sensitive Milošević.[81]

Greece. Albania continues to have problems with Greece. When the communists ruled Tirana, Greece frequently complained about discrimination against the Greek minority (about 70,000 to 80,000 people, although the Greek government says 400,000) living in southern Albania, a region the Greek government has frequently called "northern Epirus" and has claimed belongs to Greece. While the complaints by Athens of Albanian assimilation of the Greek minority were probably exaggerated, the interest of Greek conservatives in bringing "northern Epirus" under Greek control was real, and their concern about assimilation was not totally unwarranted given the refusal of the Tirana government to allow schooling for Greeks to be in the Greek language. Still, Greece could not with justice claim Albanian unfairness. In Albania's first multiparty elections in March 1991, the Alia regime allowed the Greek minority to have its own political party, Omonia, which fielded candidates and won five seats in the new Albanian Parliament.[82]

In the next few years, Albanian fears about a separatist agenda of Greek Albanians increased. Although the Greek community in Albania was by no means unanimous about joining Greece, some local politicians quietly advocated separatism and lobbied with the Berisha government for increased local autonomy. Then, in early 1992, on the eve of the March parliamentary elections, the Albanian Parliament outlawed Omonia, calling it an ethnic party with no place in Albania's so-called homogeneous, unitary polity.[83]

This Albanian action infuriated Athens and strengthened its belief that Tirana, which it accused of violating the human rights of its citizens of Greek extraction, was determined to obliterate Greek culture. It also angered the Council of Europe, which put intense pressure on the Albanian government to retreat. Eventually, to avoid compromising Albania's new campaign to strengthen ties with the West, the Berisha government retreated. Omonia reappeared, but with a new name, the Union of Human Rights, and managed to obtain two parliamentary seats in the March 1992 elections.[84]

Muddying the waters of the Albanian–Greek relationship was the influx of Albanians into Greece when communist control eroded in the early 1990s. Thousands of impoverished Albanians had emigrated to find work and a higher standard of living in Greece, Italy, and other parts of Western Europe. It is reckoned that 500,000 Albanians have settled in Greece, many of them living and working there illegally.[85] The Greek government came under tremendous domestic pressure to halt this emigration of Albanian poor into northern Greece, which could ill afford to take care of them. When Prime Minister Constantine Mitsotakis went to Tirana to discuss this problem, as well as that of the Greek minority in Albania, he achieved little. While there was an agreement with Albania to halt the migration, the authorities in Tirana did not implement it. Albania was benefiting too much from the money earned by the emigrants. According to one source, Albanian workers in Greece sent home $1 billion during 1994. As a result, the Greek government continued to expel the refugees, a policy that infuriated the Albanian government. Tirana accused Athens of using torture to send the Albanian immigrants home.[86]

Albanian–Greek relations took a turn for the worse in July 1993, when the Berisha government expelled a Greek Orthodox priest who it said had fanned separatist feeling among Albania's Greek community. Athens retaliated by deporting some 30,000 illegal Albanian refugees and canceling several scheduled ministerial meetings. Moreover, Greece raised the specter of territorial claims on southern Albania, insisting that Albania should be willing to grant ethnic Greeks the same rights it was demanding for the two million ethnic Albanians living in Serbia. But this somewhat aggressive Greek reaction seemed to backfire. Instead of weakening Berisha and pushing him to grant the Greek minority in Albania a special status, it strengthened the president and provoked a public outcry against a Greek effort to influence Albanian policy making.[87]

Moreover, the Albanians were taken aback by the Greek reference to Albanian policy toward Kosovo, suspecting that it was part of Greece's ill-concealed sympathy for Serbia in the ongoing civil war in the former Yugoslavia. Albania feared that Athens had cut a deal with Belgrade on the future of southern Albania and of Kosovo.[88]

Nevertheless, the Berisha government felt obliged in July 1993 to try to improve relations with Athens, which also had incentives to resolve differences and normalize ties with Tirana. Berisha started with some conciliatory gestures toward the Greek minority in southern Albania, promising to foster Greek culture. The Greek government seemed to reciprocate this gesture by easing up on its expulsions of Albanians. But the chances of a real reconciliation are slight. Neither the Albanian nor the Greek government can afford, because of domestic pressures, to appear too conciliatory to the other side. For example, the Greek government is under continuous pressure by people who dislike the Albanian émigrés in Greece and want them forcibly returned to their homeland. Others believe that Tirana is determined to assimilate the Greek minority and to discourage even a hint of separatism, not to mention a full-blown movement of the Greek minority for annexation to Greece. Berisha told the Greeks that "Albanian territory does not have an inch of foreign soil."[89]

Berisha continued to exert pressure on the Greek minority in 1994, apparently to force their return to Greece and thereby eliminate the possibility, however remote, of an effort by Albanian Greeks to join their territory to Greece. The irony of this fear, which Albanian political leaders have had for much of the post–World War II era, is that many Greeks living in southern Albania are citizens of Albania, loyal to the Albanian state, and not interested in joining Greece. Their only concern is to get the government in Tirana to stop making trouble for them and allow them to live their lives in peace. It would seem that those who favor annexation to Greece are a minority of activists.

It is not clear that the Albanian government accepts this view. In September 1994, Albanian authorities convicted several Greek activists of espionage in the service of Athens. During the trial, the defendants were allegedly mistreated. They allegedly were deprived of their right to question witnesses, and the Albanian prosecutor never made clear how the accused could have obtained the secret information they were supposed to have turned over to the Greek government. The Greek government was angered by the trial and demanded the release of the accused. By early 1995, Albanian relations with Greece had reached their lowest point in many years.[90]

Macedonia. Complicating Albania's relations with Greece is the former Yugoslav republic of Macedonia. When Macedonia declared its independence of Yugoslavia at the end of 1991, Albania supported it. Albania has also taken Macedonia's side in its conflict with Greece over the formal name of the state. The Greeks have opposed Macedonia, which separated from the Yugoslav state at the end of 1991 and received western recognition of its independence in early 1992, calling itself "Maccdonia," which is also the name of the Greek province where a Macedonian minority resides. Albania, in addition, has strengthened economic ties with independent Macedonia. But there is a cloud over the relationship between the two countries involving Macedonia's large Albanian minority of about 30 to 40 percent of the country's total population. The Albanians have demanded that ethnic Albanians in Macedonia be granted equality with ethnic Macedonians.

While expressing sympathy for the Albanian position, however, the Macedonian government has not made any real progress toward accommodating Tirana on this issue. It fears that the ethnic Macedonian culture will be threatened by the local Albanians. Complicating this issue is the wish of many Albanians inside Macedonia for greater autonomy and, ultimately, annexation to Albania or complete independence. The Albanian government in Tirana gives no support to this incipient separatism, arguing that the preservation of Macedonia's territorial integrity is in the strategic interests of Albania. But, should events develop where Macedonia somehow is partitioned between Greece and Serbia, the Albanian government would certainly try to obtain the territory inhabited by the Albanian minority.[91]

Other Balkan Countries. Albania's relations with other Balkan countries are somewhat better. President Berisha has said that Albania has good relations with other former Yugoslav republics, notably Slovenia and Croatia, which do not want a Serb-Albanian conflict over Kosovo. Berisha also spoke of very good Albanian relations with Turkey, where a large Albanian minority is trying to act as a bridge builder between the two countries and heal the wounds of centuries of occupation by the Ottoman Empire. Helping the cause of reconciliation is the fact that Turkey has refrained from discrimination against its small Albanian community.

Conclusions

President Ramiz Alia deserves credit for Albania's peaceful transition from communist authoritarianism to pluralistic parliamentary government. He was a very skillful leader who showed a degree of flexibility that set him apart from other communist leaders in Central and Eastern Europe, such as Romania's Ceauşescu, East Germany's Honecker, Czechoslovakia's Jakeš, and Bulgaria's Zhivkov.

But Albanian political liberalization was very slow and gradual, making it appear at times that the country would never completely discard communist rule, largely because most of Albanian society, which was rural and conservative, was not easily won over to the liberalization policies advocated by the political opposition based in the cities. The process of change, however, continued because the Alia leadership saw reform as the only chance the Albanian Communist Party had of preserving its leadership of the country into the 1990s. Alia and other Albanian communist leaders were alive to the implications for them of communist collapse everywhere else in the region, as well as in the Soviet Union.

In the postcommunist era, however, severe economic hardship is taxing the country's new democratic order to the breaking point. Despite accusations by his critics that he is becoming increasingly authoritarian—as, indeed, he is, partly in response to the pluralistic and conflict-ridden political environment that makes it difficult for him to lead and reform his country—President Berisha is not a dictator. He is committed to the democratic process and does not seem ready to sacrifice the newly won liberal political institutions for the sake of moving quickly through the reforms needed to improve economic performance and raise standards of living.

So far he has managed to chart an intelligent course through the complex, unpredictable, and potentially dangerous diplomatic waters of Balkan international politics. Under his leadership, Albania seems to be moving away from the old isolationist order and developing new links with foreign countries, especially in the West, that can help Albania economically and enhance its security.

4

Bulgaria

Like other Central and East European countries, Bulgaria came under communist rule in the late 1940s. Shortly thereafter, Bulgarian communists transformed their country into an orthodox socialist dictatorship and a loyal Soviet satellite. By the early 1950s, the pattern of Communist Party rule for the next thirty-five years had been set.

Bulgarian Authoritarianism

Bulgarian communist leader Todor Zhivkov, in power from 1954 until the end of 1989, was an ideological hard-liner. During his rule, Bulgaria became one of the most repressive regimes in Eastern Europe, characterized by a harsh censorship, an ubiquitous secret police, a ruthless suppression of dissent with no workers' strikes and no *samizdat* publications, and a Soviet-style highly centralized autocratic command economy involving a thorough destruction of free enterprise and the extension of state control over almost all aspects of Bulgarian economic life.

Bulgaria's repressive authoritarianism under the communists had deep roots in the country's history, in particular, the many centuries of authoritarian government under the Ottoman Turkish Empire and in the brief period of independence from 1909 until the end of World War II. Most Bulgarian people had little experience with and understanding of Western parliamentary democracy and less sympathy for political liberalism. For most of the communist era, the Bulgarian people tolerated without serious challenge the communist dictatorship forced on them by the Soviet Union after World War II.[1]

BULGARIA

Geography

1. Location: southeastern Europe, bordering the Black Sea, between Romania and Turkey
2. Area: total — 110,910 square kilometers; land area — 110,550 square kilometers; comparative area — slightly largely than Tennessee
3. Boundaries: with Greece — 494 kilometers; with Macedonia — 148 kilometers; with Romania — 608 kilometers; with Serbia and Montenegro — 318 kilometers (all with Serbia); with Turkey — 240 kilometers; with the Black Sea — 354 kilometers
4. Climate: temperate; cold, damp winters; hot, dry summers
5. Terrain: mostly mountains, with lowlands in north and southeast
6. Natural resources: bauxite, copper, lead, zinc, coal, timber, arable land
7. Land use: arable land — 34%; permanent crops — 3%; meadows and pastures — 18%; forest and woodland — 35%
8. Environment: air pollution from industrial emissions; rivers polluted from raw sewage, heavy metals, detergents; deforestation; forest damage from air pollution and resulting acid rain; soil contamination from heavy metals and metallurgical plants and industrial wastes

People

1. Population: 8,775,198 (1995 estimate)
2. Age structure: 0–14 — 19% of population (female — 800,413; male —

841,697); 15–64 — 66% of population (female — 2,927,880; male — 1,910,133); 65 and over — 15% of population (female — 735,706; male — 559,639) (July 1995 estimate)
3. Growth rate: –0.25% (1995 estimate)
4. Life expectancy at birth: total population — 73.68 years; female — 77.1 years; male — 70.43 years (1995 estimate)
5. Ethnic divisions: Bulgarian — 85.3%; Turk — 8.5%; Gypsy — 2.6%; Macedonian — 2.5%; Armenian — 0.3%; Russian — 0.2%
6. Religions: Bulgarian Orthodox — 85%; Muslim — 13%; Jewish — 0.8%; Roman Catholic — 0.5%; Uniate Catholic — 0.2%
7. Languages: Bulgarian, with secondary languages corresponding to ethnic breakdown
8. Literacy: total population — 98%; female — 97%; male — 99%
9. Labor force: total — 4.3 million; agriculture — 20%; industry — 33% (1987 estimate)

Government

1. Type: emerging parliamentary democracy
2. Capital: Sofia
3. Independence: September 22, 1908, from Ottoman Empire
4. Constitution: adopted July 12, 1991
5. National administration:
   a. Chief of state: President of the Republic (1996 — Zheliu Zhelev)
   b. Ministerial leadership: Prime Minister and Council of Ministers appointed (1996 — Zhan Videnov, prime minister)
   c. Legislature: unicameral — National Assembly (*Narodno Sobranie*)
   d. Judicial branch: Supreme Court, Constitutional Court
   e. Political parties: Bulgarian Socialist Party, Union of Democratic Forces, People's Union, Movement for Rights and Freedoms, Bulgarian Business Bloc, Fatherland Union, Bulgarian Agrarian National Union
5. Local administration: unitary ystem with 26 districts

Economy

1. Gross domestic product: $33.7 billion (1994 estimate)
2. National product real growth rate: 0.2% (1994 estimate)
3. Per-capita national product: $3,830 (1994 estimate)
4. Inflation rate: 122% (1994 estimate)
5. Unemployment rate: 16% (1994 estimate)
6. Budget: revenue — $14 billion; expenditures — $17.4 billion (1993 estimate)
7. Industrial output: machine building and metal working, food processing, chemicals, textiles, building materials, ferrous and nonferrous metals
8. Agricultural output: livestock raising, grain, oil seeds, vegetables, fruits, tobacco
9. Exports: $3.6 billion (1993 estimate) — machinery and equipment, agricultural products, manufactured consumer goods, fuels, minerals, raw materials, metals
10. Imports: $621 million (1993 estimate) — fuels, minerals and raw materials, machinery and equipment, consumer goods, agricultural products
11. External debt: $12 billion (1994 estimate)
12. Trade partners: former CMEA countries — 51% (Russia, Poland — 3.7%); developed countries (Germany, Austria); less-developed countries (Iran, Libya)
13. Economic aid received in 1994: $700 million in balance-of-payments support
14. Transportation: railroads — 4,294 kilometers; highways — 36,932 kilometers; ports — Burgas, Lom, Nesebŭr, Ruse, Varna, Vidin; airports — 355 (116 with paved runways)

1. Persecution of the Turkish Minority

A striking aspect of Bulgaria's authoritarianism beginning in the mid-1950s was Zhivkov's long-term policy of assimilation of the country's Turkish minority of two million people, or 15 percent of the total population. His policy threatened Turkish cultural identity and aimed to deprive the Turkish people of everything Turkish—their names, language, customs, traditional clothing, and Muslim faith. At the same time, because it considered people of Turkish extraction an integral part of Bulgarian society, the Bulgarian government denied them permission to emigrate to Turkey.[2]

Zhivkov's policy was inspired by Bulgarian nationalism fed by a hypersensitivity to national identity born of an inferiority complex caused by the brutal Turkish occupation of Bulgaria for several centuries and Bulgaria's defeat in the Second Balkan War and in the first and second world wars.

Communist ideology dismissed ethnic differences and justified Zhivkov's belief that all citizens of Bulgaria are Bulgarians. But the most compelling justification for Zhivkov's discrimination against Bulgarians of Turkish extraction had to do with a determination to limit or even obliterate a potential of the Turks for political influence. The Communist Party leadership, which was ethnically Bulgarian, was afraid that the country eventually might be overwhelmed by the Turkish minority, despite the fact that it was only about 15 percent of the total population. Throughout the 1980s, the Turkish birthrate in Bulgaria had been increasing as that of the Bulgarian majority remained static.[3]

2. The Economic Dimension

In the beginning of communist rule after World War II, the centrally controlled Soviet-style command economy seemed well matched to Bulgarian needs and resources. The Bulgarian economy was underdeveloped and primarily agricultural. The communists developed an industrial base, first in the area of heavy industry and subsequently in electronics. Zhivkov dreamed of making Bulgaria a leading producer of advanced-technology goods in the Eastern bloc. This technology could be exported and could be used to improve Bulgarian economic productivity. In the 1970s, the communists tried to improve output and raise living standards by some modest adjustments of their sluggish and inevitably stagnant economy, called the "New Economic Mechanism" (NEM), which provided for some decentralization of managerial decision making. The NEM also encouraged foreign investment.[4]

The NEM had a positive impact on agriculture. The government integrated various phases of food production involving cultivation, processing, and distribution, allowing farmers to sell what they produced on plots set aside for private use in public markets at prices determined by supply and demand. The result of this incentive-generating reform was a surge of agricultural output. But by the early 1980s, it was clear that the NEM had done little to improve the antiquated, dilapidated, and grossly inefficient industrial sector. The annual growth rate declined from 11 percent to 3.7 percent.[5] After thirty years of communist rule, Bulgaria still had an economy of scarcities in the consumer sector. Many consumer goods were perennially in short supply and of shoddy quality. The Bulgarian environment was as drab as it had always been. While Bulgarian living standards were higher than those in neighboring Romania under Ceauşescu, they were below the levels prevalent in Hungary, Czechoslovakia, and Poland and far below levels in Western Europe, as any Western visitor could see for himself in Sofia.

The Impact of Soviet Perestroika

In the mid-1980s, the Bulgarian communist leadership showed some interest in the economic aspects of Gorbachev's perestroika as a means of improving economic performance, raising living standards, and strengthening the country's socialist system. On the other hand, there was little, if any, official interest in the political aspects of perestroika, in particular, glasnost or a toleration of pluralism.

1. Interest in Economic Reform

In May 1987, Zhivkov introduced changes advocated by Soviet president Mikhail Gorbachev. The government allowed a commercial bank to be established and called for increased worker participation in the management of enterprises in all fields. Echoing Gorbachev's call for financial accountability in Soviet industrial enterprises, Zhivkov warned that unprofitable Bulgarian factories would not receive state money and would have to declare bankruptcy and close down.[6] And at the end of July 1987, Zhivkov called attention to the needs of consumers. He criticized Bulgarian enterprises for misleading the consumer by reclassifying products from "ordinary" to "deluxe" to disguise price increases and for not paying enough attention to what the consumer really needed and wanted.[7] Indeed, by the end of 1987, it looked as if Bulgarian socialism was getting a new lease on life in the economic sphere. Most state companies formed self-management teams and allowed workers to participate in the selection of managerial officials. Many enterprises were now able to negotiate their own business deals and conducted foreign trade independently of the central bureaucracy.

But there were limits on how much the Zhivkov regime could actually improve Bulgaria's economic performance. For example, many factory managers would not take initiative or accept responsibility for critical production decisions heretofore made by, or with instructions from, central ministries. Furthermore, Moscow played its part in retarding Bulgarian economic growth and development. While he urged his East European allies to embrace at least some aspects of perestroika to make their economies operate more productively, Gorbachev, evidently worried about a weakening of the Bulgarian Communist Party's leading role in setting policy, advised Sofia to slow down economic reforms. In deference to the Kremlin, a special party conference, convened in January 1988 in Sofia, did not endorse implementation of the July 1987 reform program and sounded a note of caution with regard to future change.[8]

2. Resistance to Political Reform

In the late 1980s, there was virtually no effort at reform in the political sphere. The Zhivkov regime was not interested in liberalizing the political environment. It had no intention of introducing political freedoms, at least as far as the Turkish minority was concerned.

Renewal of Hostility to the Turkish Minority[9]

To emphasize the regime's commitment to political discipline and conformity, Zhivkov appeared on national television in the spring of 1989 to tell Bulgaria's Turkish community that there would be no glasnost or democratization for them. He repeated the fiction that most of the ethnic Turks were historically Bulgarians who had been forcibly converted to Islam and a Turkish identity during the pre–World War I Ottoman period of Bulgarian history. He blamed disturbances among Bulgaria's Turkish minority on an anti-Bulgarian campaign carried on by Turkey. The Bulgarian authorities also launched a broad reign of terror against ethnic Turks in the second half of 1989, including forced emigration, a counterproductive policy full of contradictions. For example, it was motivated by pervasive popular prejudice of ethnic Bulgarians against the Turkish people, but it was also based on an assumption that most Bulgarian Turks would not emigrate to a country where living conditions for émigrés would be much harsher than in Bulgaria. Zhivkov also believed that the Turkish government would not open its doors to thousands of émigrés from Bulgaria.

The Bulgarian leadership turned out to be wrong. About 300,000 Bulgarian Turkish people, terrified by the intensification of official harassment, abruptly left Bulgaria in 1989 for the safety of Turkey. Moreover, the mass exodus of Turks turned out to be a fiasco for the Bulgarian economy and an embarrassment for the Zhivkov regime. Most of the Turkish emigrants were engaged in agriculture, livestock breeding, transport, and construction. Coinciding with the harvest season, one that promised exceptionally good yields after several years of setbacks, the departure of the Turks meant that crops were not harvested. Officials claimed that losses were minimal, but the domestic market was upset, and in the last months of 1989 many food items and other consumer goods were unavailable.[10] Meanwhile, the Turkish government declared that it would accept all refugees from Bulgaria. Although the exodus was so great and so unexpected in Ankara that the Turkish government temporarily had to close its frontier with Bulgaria, it eventually did absorb most of the emigrants.

Aversion to Pluralism

In addition to persecuting the Turkish minority, the Zhivkov regime affirmed rejection of Soviet glasnost. The Zhivkov leadership rejected out of hand any form of political pluralism. It refused to tolerate any criticism of the Communist Party. While Zhivkov did try to emulate Gorbachev's effort to limit the Communist Party's excessive influence over the day-to-day working of the government apparatus, complaining that the Bulgarian Communist Party had exercised "unlimited power" and had seized the government's functions leading to "uncontrollable omnipotence of party bodies and functionaries," he was careful to avoid restricting the party's leadership role. The Bulgarian Communist Party continued to dominate most aspects of Bulgarian life.[11]

The Collapse of the Zhivkov Regime

By 1989 there were several large social groups dissatisfied with Zhivkov's leadership and eager for perestroika-style reformism in Bulgaria. These groups became a new and unprecedented political opposition.

1. The New Political "Opposition"

The new opposition came from an evolving middle class made up of people from poor backgrounds who owed their education and subsequent professional success to the communists. At first, the new intelligentsia had little reason to challenge or oppose the communists, who had made a point of favoring these people while discriminating against the old middle class of the interwar period. Zhivkov artfully cultivated their loyalty by acknowledging their achievements, flattering them, and reminding them obliquely of the regime's munificence toward them.[12] But in terms of psychology and outlook, skepticism toward inherited dogmas, and desire for material success and personal autonomy, this Bulgarian middle class began to adopt the outlook of its Western contemporaries.[13] Frustrated by the regime's failure to adopt the political reforms of Soviet perestroika, many educated Bulgarians, particularly in the Sofia region, joined clubs for the support of a Bulgarian version of Soviet perestroika.[14]

The new opposition consisted of other groups, politically passive in the past, which in the late 1980s also became critical of the regime. Some were concerned with human-rights abuses, in particular official discrimination against the

Turkish minority. Workers organized *Podkrepa* (Support), an independent trade union, in February 1989 that quickly enrolled thousands of members. In addition, in different parts of the country ordinary people joined new organizations that were committed to the protection of human rights and religious freedom. For example, in 1988 the Independent Association for the Defense of Human Rights was set up to address the issue of Muslim rights and to oppose Sofia's assimilation policies.[15]

In November 1989, encouraged by the popular attacks on Communist Party rule in East Germany and Czechoslovakia, which they used as a model, large numbers of middle-class Bulgarian citizens in Sophia staged antigovernment demonstrations calling for democratization.[16]

2. Zhivkov's Response

At first, Zhivkov was adamant. True to his Stalinist instincts, he warned the intelligentsia against agitating for political reform, which he disparagingly referred to as "national nihilism." But the opposition persisted and became more vocal. Watching developments elsewhere in Central and Eastern Europe, especially the explosion of popular hostility toward conservative party leaders like East Germany's Honecker and Czechoslovakia's Jakeš, Zhivkov became worried about his own fate. He adopted a conciliatory stance, acknowledging "the positive role" of nongovernment groups, and pledged extensive change in all areas of Bulgarian life, including politics.

Unwilling to use force to suppress this new opposition and in the absence of any Soviet support, Zhivkov resigned as party leader on November 9, the day East Germany opened the Berlin Wall. He really had no alternative. Disgusted by his nepotistic behavior, in particular, the elevation of his son, Vladimir, to high academic and political office not long after he had done the same for his daughter, a majority of his politburo colleagues had lost confidence in him and were not only eager to see him go but willing to give him a push. Moreover, Foreign Minister Petar T. Mladenov and party politburo member Andrei Lukanov hoped that timely change, including the departure of Zhivkov, who had come to symbolize everything that was wrong with Bulgaria at the end of the 1980s, might enable the Communist Party to preserve its leadership of the country. Mladenov and Lukanov envisaged a perestroika-style path of political development that had been opposed by Zhivkov and his neo-Stalinist supporters. When Zhivkov resigned, Mladenov took Zhivkov's place as head of the Bulgarian Communist Party, which changed its name to the Bulgarian Socialist Party (BSP). Lukanov became prime minister.[17] The changes apparently had the Kremlin's blessing. Speculation had it that Gorbachev had no special affection for Zhivkov, despite his past loyalty, and encouraged Mladenov to finesse his removal.[18]

Post-Zhivkov Political Liberalization

Now under reformist leadership, the Bulgarian Communist Party endorsed a major liberalization of the political environment. In the short term, it saw accommodation as the only means of quieting down the opposition, restoring order, and strengthening its rapport with society in the new, post-Zhivkov era.

1. Pluralism

In December 1989 and during the early months of 1990, the new Bulgarian Socialist Party (BSP), made up of former Communist party members eliminated all references to communism and Marxian socialism in its program and policies. It endorsed political pluralism, gave up its political monopoly, and accepted a greatly reduced role in Bulgarian life. It also consented to the legalization of political opposition groups and promised to eliminate the domestic role of the state security forces and to ease censorship in order to enable the media to focus attention on the flaws and abuses of the old regime. It pledged toleration of popular demonstrations, halted the persecution of Bulgarian Turks, and invited those who had fled to return to Bulgaria. Finally, the BSP agreed to elections for a new parliament to replace the existing communist-dominated one, stipulating that the newly elected parliament, to be called the Grand National Assembly, would enact constitutional reform that would make Bulgaria a democratic and pluralistic state with a market economy and a social safety net for the poor.[19]

As proof of his commitment to political pluralism, Mladenov made concessions to the new, hastily formed opposition groups that were trying to build voter constituencies. For example, ignoring the opposition of Lukanov and other party leaders, Mladenov chose June 10 as election day to give the opposition time to get organized. Lukanov wanted parliamentary elections much earlier to take full advantage of the BSP's control of the state and of the weaknesses of new political groups challenging the party's leadership. In another concession to the political opposition, Mladenov agreed to proportional representation in upcoming parliamentary elections to establish his credibility with the new political groups with small and scattered voter constituencies.[20]

The impact of these reforms was immediate. Opposition groups multiplied. Discussion clubs quickly transformed themselves into political parties. By early 1990, there were almost fifty new political party groups. The most important remained the BSP. A new coalition of opposition groups, the Union of Democratic Forces (UDF), established in early December 1989, had supporters mainly in the city areas and among the intelligentsia and professional people. The UDF called for a multiparty system and a market economy. Zheliu Zhelev, an advocate of "shock therapy," was the party leader. He denounced Bulgaria's socialist system as degenerate, calling it a corrupt form of state socialism with a totalitarian superstructure.[21]

2. Changes in BSP Leadership and Internal Organization

At an extraordinary congress that began at the end of January 1990, Mladenov resigned the party leadership in favor of Aleksandr Lilov, who had been purged from the leadership in 1983 by Zhivkov for being too liberal and for supporting the elevation of younger and better-educated party officials to positions of leadership. Lilov was elected chairman of a newly created executive body of the BSP, called the Supreme Council, which took the place of the former Communist Party's Central Committee. Lilov denounced the totalitarian practices of the past and asked the BSP to be more open to a diversity of views. He spoke of its development in a "Euro-socialist" direction, taking as a model the democratic socialist parties of Western Europe.[22]

The BSP January 1990 congress also liberalized the party's internal organization and procedures. The membership of the new BSP Supreme Council was to be elected individually, rather than by slate, as had been the case with the old Central Committee membership. Only 10 percent of the old Central Committee membership appeared in the new Council. In turn the politburo was replaced by an eleven-member presidency eventually to be elected.[23] The BSP emerged from the congress still the leading force of the country, despite the abolition of the constitutional guarantee of its leading role. Indeed, the BSP, unlike most other former Communist parties in Eastern Europe, experienced a new influx of members.[24]

3. A Softening of Policy toward the Turkish Minority

Another aspect of liberalization affected the Turkish minority. The postcommunist leadership encouraged Turkish émigrés to return to their homes and agreed to restitution of their property, which had been sold or confiscated by the state when they left. In October 1990, the Bulgarian government established a kind of junior college in Sofia to teach Muslim culture, and a Muslim high school was opened in Shumen, a center of ethnic Turks in northeastern Bulgaria. And in February 1991, the authorities allowed the reopening of a Turkish-language newspaper.[25]

4. The June 1990 Parliamentary Elections

To prepare for the elections scheduled for June 10, the BSP quickly rid itself of the most conservative elements in its top leadership, formally expelling Zhivkov in December 1989. Although he was eventually arrested on charges of abuse of power in January 1990, demonstrations against him continued in Sofia and other Bulgarian cities. People blamed him for gross mismanagement of the Bulgarian economy during his long 35-year rule. The BSP tried to appear as a party of moderate change, committed to decommunization of Bulgarian society but with due regard to minimizing hardship. It warned that the "shock-therapy" approach of the UDF would endanger pensions and cause suffering.[26]

Parliamentary elections were held on June 10, 1990. The BSP won 47.15 percent of the seats in the new Grand National Assembly, enabling it to control important government posts, such as the premiership, the army, and the police. The 90 percent turnout of voters was striking when compared with the low voter turnout in the parliamentary elections in other East European countries following the collapse of communist rule. Bulgarians in all walks of life were elated by the new freedom to speak out after a long period of repression.[27]

It was a solid victory for the BSP. However, while the BSP benefited from its democratic rhetoric and the sweeping political reforms it promised, its victory could be explained by the weakness of the opposition.

The political opposition had lacked funds to mount a proper campaign. There were shortages of typewriters, xerox machines, and even paper, making the distribution of party programs almost impossible. Although newspapers and magazines were available and the government-controlled electronic media did present "perspectives" other than the official line on television and radio programs, access to the mass media was still controlled by the state and biased toward the BSP.[28]

The BSP success was also at the expense of the country's Turkish minority. Throughout the campaign the BSP had blatantly discriminated against the party of the Turkish community known as the Movement for Rights and Freedom (MRF).[29] The MRF had been left out of the parliamentary discussions between government and opposition groups held in January and February 1990 leading up to the campaign and had not received much access to the media during the campaign. Moreover, Turkish-Bulgarians abroad could not vote, and the government had placed limits on many of the MRF's campaign activities. In response, the Turkish minority overwhelmingly supported the MRF, encouraging it to become exactly what the ruling elite opposed: an alienated particularistic organization that could exert a divisive influence over national politics. In any event, by playing the so-called "Turkish card" to curry favor with voters hostile to the Turkish minority, the BSP cultivated the image of a nationalist, patriotic party that had a lot of popular appeal.[30]

The BSP also benefited from the strong conservatism in the countryside. Farmers believed that Bulgaria had not done badly under communist rule. In addition, as several influential BSP members explained, party policies still corresponded to the interests of a majority of Bulgarian voters who craved "security of work, security of income, and social security in the broad sense." The BSP emphasized calm, well-being, and stability and eschewed the rhetoric of radical reform that tended to frighten many Bulgarian voters who worried about unemployment. An important part of this conservatism was the pervasive popular hostility to the Turkish minority, which the BSP shrewdly coopted, thereby weakening challenges to it coming from such nationalist organizations as the Fatherland Party of Labor, the National Democratic Party, and the Bulgarian National Radical Party, which were never able to mobilize much voter support despite popular sympathy for their views.[31]

But it was also true that the BSP had been successful because local authorities, who were for the most part BSP members, took advantage of their control over jobs, housing, and other necessities in the small towns and villages of rural Bulgaria to persuade voters to support Socialist candidates. This intimidation, indirect and oblique, was impossible for outside observers supervising the elections to prove, though they sensed what was happening.[32]

Furthermore, the BSP had a very appealing and reassuring image of unity of purpose, organization, and behavior. In contrast, the UDF struck many voters as a collection of odd believers in odd causes. Consistent with its liberal and democratic orientation, the UDF lacked cohesion and discipline of the kind people saw in the BSP. Indeed, working to the advantage of Bulgaria's former communists seeking to hold on to power was the opposition's lack of the kind of charismatic leaders, such as Poland's Wałęsa and Czechoslovakia's Havel, who could inspire support of a broad popular constituency.[33]

Finally, the BSP benefited from the fact that voters did not hold against the BSP the close ties its predecessor had maintained with Moscow. There was nowhere near the dislike of Russians in Bulgaria that other Central and East European peoples had. Indeed, Bulgarians had some positive feelings toward the Russians, partly as a result of the Russian effort to liberate Bulgaria from Turkish rule in the late nineteenth century and partly because the Soviet government did not impose on Bulgaria at the end of World War II the kind of punitive policies, such as reparations, imposed on other East European allies of the Nazis.

Decline of the BSP in 1990

The euphoria of the BSP over its electoral success was short lived. Despite an enormous popularity, the BSP's grip on political power was tenuous after the June 1990 parliamentary election. In addition, the BSP was held responsible for a deterioration of economic condition. By the end of 1991, the BSP could no longer govern and had to yield leadership of the country.

1. Political Difficulties

The BSP had to preside over a society split between generations; between people living in the cities and the countryside; and between Bulgarians who felt strongly about the need to promote ethnic purity in society and the minorities, in particular the Turks, who stood to suffer from such prejudice.[34] Indeed, the country's youth were especially dissatisfied. Newly appointed Prime Minister Lukanov and his cabinet confronted a wave of student strikes and spontaneous street demonstrations by UDF activists. They were angered by alleged BSP electoral manipulations. This opposition eventually forced President Mladenov's resignation in early July 1990. The Grand National Assembly now elected Zhelev, the head of the UDF, president of Bulgaria. He was the first noncommunist head of Bulgaria in over forty years.[35]

Another problem for the Lukanov government in the aftermath of the June 1990 elections, was an intensification of anti-Turk chauvinism among such ultra-nationalist groups as the Fatherland Labor Party, which resented the government's conciliatory gestures toward the Turkish minority in 1990 and early 1991. The Turkophobes were angered by the election in June 1990 of 23 MRF candidates (out of 400 deputies to Parliament) by Turkish voters. They feared the Turks might encourage a secessionist movement that could compromise the country's territorial integrity. They also feared subversion of Bulgarian culture by Bulgarian Turks. And they were incensed by a decision in January 1991 by the Ministry of Education to allow the teaching of the Turkish language in public schools.[36]

As the economy worsened and unemployment increased, the BSP was under pressure from the nationalists to enact job quotas for Bulgarians where Turks were in a majority. The nationalists also demanded that the Lukanov government follow the Zhivkov regime's policy of excluding ethnic Turks from managerial positions in state-owned industrial enterprises. In late July 1990, in places like the southeastern town of Kurdzhali, which had large concentrations of people of Turkish cultural origin, the nationalists staged protests against the Turks by preventing their access to municipal buildings, closing down factories, blocking roads, and preventing people from shopping.[37]

The BSP also had a problem in mobilizing parliamentary support for the tough economic reforms needed to improve living conditions. Since links with the Turkish-controlled MRF were out of the question, the BSP looked to the UDF, which refused to cooperate with the former communists. The UDF correctly suspected that influential conservatives in the BSP wanted to delay democratization of Bulgarian society. Moreover, the liberal wing of the BSP, committed to rapid movement toward the free-market economy and reconciliation with the West, found the BSP leadership too conservative for the good of the country, formed its own organization called the Alternative Socialist Party, and eventually joined the opposition.[38]

Making matters worse for the BSP leadership were its own internal differences over policy. Liberal reformers sought rapid, radical reform, after the fashion of Poland, while moderate conservatives, led by Lilov, advocated a very slow pace of change. The liberal reformers were youthful, energetic, and outspoken in their advocacy of change, but they lacked the influence of the conservatives, who still controlled the levers of power.[39]

The BSP politicians also were distracted by their pursuit of Zhivkov. After his arrest, he was brought to trial on charges of corruption and the commission of illegal actions. At his trial, beginning in February 1991, Zhivkov fought back, saying he made mistakes but never committed any crimes. He never made any decisions alone, he said, and, he insisted, others had always been involved. The government's preoccupation with the trial and punishment of Zhivkov turned out to be a time-consuming, energy-wasting exercise that distracted attention from economic problems.[40]

2. Economic Problems

The BSP also confronted severe economic problems that threatened further social turmoil. People were angry as the economy deteriorated and things just seemed to fall apart: facades of buildings were sooty, and many had peeling plaster; there were giant potholes in the streets and highways; road tunnels were closed indefinitely for repairs; people endured hours-long waits at gas stations to fill their cars; there were frequent power cuts and production shortages; and such essentials as butter, cheese, sugar, eggs, and detergents were rationed.[41]

While the problem-ridden Bulgarian economy, of course, was a victim of the kind of communist mismanagement found elsewhere in Eastern Europe, in particular, the excessive emphasis on capital- and industrial-goods production at the expense of consumer-goods output, it suffered from other conditions of the moment. For example, Bulgarian farmers withheld livestock from government slaughterhouses in anticipation of vastly higher prices that would follow when price controls were lifted. Making matters worse was a decline in exports.

There were other complications undermining the Bulgarian economy in the early 1990s. In compliance with Western requests, Bulgaria stopped arms shipments to the Middle East during the Persian Gulf War, forfeiting a valuable source of hard currency. Furthermore, oil supplies from the Soviet Union, formerly its principal supplier of petroleum products, declined, partly because Sofia could not meet Soviet demands for payment in hard currency. Trade with the former Soviet Union was disrupted also as a result of the political turmoil there. Bulgarian hopes for replacement deliveries of oil from Iraq, where it had a $2.6 billion credit, were dashed by the international trade embargo imposed after the August 1990 invasion of Kuwait. Finally, the government contributed to the Bulgarian economy's problems when it limited the export of scarce agricultural commodities and suspended payments on its $10.6 billion foreign debt, thereby cutting itself off from trade credits and other forms of overseas help. This made it almost impossible to finance imports, and soon after the election basic commodities began to disappear from the shelves, forcing the government to introduce rationing.[42]

The prospects for economic improvement, however, were not altogether bleak. Sales of computers at cut-rate prices to developing countries begun in the early 1980s continued. Bulgaria also joined the International Monetary Fund and the World Bank. But swift help from the West was not forthcoming, and the inefficient production and distribution systems, along with the lack of foreign investment, left Bulgaria in a serious economic depression in 1990.[43]

In October 1990, Prime Minister Lukanov proposed a comprehensive program of economic reform based on recommendations by a team of U.S. experts headed by Richard Rahn, then vice-president of the U.S. Chamber of Commerce. The program called for rapid denationalization of major state-owned holdings, the privatization of agriculture, and reliance on the market to set prices and wages. Lukanov warned that there was no alternative to this program and that inevitably it would be accompanied by increased unemployment and a short-term decline in living standards for the majority of the population. Because of the hardships involved, Lukanov refused to ask the National Assembly to approve the plan unless the political opposition agreed in advance to support it. Despite the fact that Lukanov's proposals coincided with their own recommendations for reform, the opposition refused to back the prime minister, hoping to topple his regime. They also maintained that the BSP wanted privatization because many of its supporters, in particular former communist officials, were the only people with enough money and resources to buy the state enterprises they themselves had managed. The opposition argued that these people were only serving their own interests and should not be the group to implement reform.[44] By the end of 1990, young people aged 30 and under had begun a mass exodus to Canada, Sweden, Austria, and Greece to escape Bulgaria's poverty and the prospect of chronic unemployment. The departure of these young people, many with skills and a university education, though something of a safety valve that temporarily relieved unemployment and discouraged a social explosion, was an embarrassment to the Lukanov government and further weakened the prime minister's leadership.[45]

3. The End of BSP Leadership

Seeing an opportunity to attack Lukanov, whom the workers blamed for the worsening economic situation, *Podkrepa* engineered a general strike. The strikes went on for two weeks and were accompanied by large anti-BSP demonstrations in Sofia and other cities. People took to the streets to protest the government's failure to live up to its promises of social security. Frustrated, Lukanov resigned on that same day, taking his five-month-old Socialist government with him.[46]

Lukanov was succeeded by Dimitur Popov, a nonparty technocrat and

Bulgaria's first noncommunist prime minister in over forty years. Petar Beron, who had succeeded Zhelev as head of the UDF and was Popov's chief rival, lost any chance of becoming prime minister when he was publicly accused of having served the communists. Although the BSP supported Popov's coalition, which was made up of eight socialists, three UDF members, and two members of the Bulgarian Agricultural National Union (BANU), BSP influence in fact had diminished. Indeed, the BSP agreed with the other parties to hold another round of parliamentary elections in 1991, even though it feared substantial losses in such elections because of growing hostility toward it in the liberal urban centers.[47]

The Final Collapse of Communist Power

Without waiting for new elections, Prime Minister Popov's government began a major long-term shake-up of the Bulgarian economy. He called for an abandonment of subsidies for many basic goods and utilities as part of an overall effort to create a market economy. Anticipating increases in the price of heating, public services, and many food items, the government struck a deal in advance with trade unions to allow a modest increase in wages and a hike in the minimum wage to soften the blow of change.[48]

1. Popov's Problems

Popov's government had inherited an enormous foreign debt of $11 billion from the Zhivkov era. Unpaid interest on the national debt by mid-1991 was about $400 million. Popov started to free up the economy by decontrolling prices and curtailing subsidies to state-owned enterprises, creating hardship for many Bulgarians. Unprofitable enterprises collapsed, and production dropped by 10 percent, putting 70,000 workers out of a job. Price decontrol fueled inflation, and to dampen it, Popov required that the employer had to give the state one lev for every lev paid out in wage increases. But this put such a lid on wages that Bulgarians were forced to limit themselves to the barest necessities.[49]

As Popov diminished state control over the economy, the Bulgarian people suffered severe economic hardships. Energy was in short supply, with frequent interruptions of heat and light to consumers. Most streets in Sofia and other cities were unlit at night. Endless lines formed at gas stations, with waits for service of up to twelve hours. Basic foods also were in short supply, with sugar, cheese, flour, eggs, and cooking oil rationed. In mid-August 1991, about 21,000 Bulgarian miners in 81 of the country's 90 mines again struck. The strike threatened to interrupt the supply of coal to plants producing over a third of the country's electricity. The miners, however, like those in other sectors of Bulgarian society, were unable to achieve any improvement in their living conditions.[50]

Circumstances in 1991 increased economic hardship, complicating Popov's reform program. The country's still-enormous foreign debt, made more burdensome by its inability to trade its poorly manufactured goods on the open market, contributed to its impoverishment. Bulgarian trade declined sharply in 1991 for three reasons: the collapse of the CMEA trading bloc, with which Bulgaria had done 80 percent of its export business; the insistence of the former Soviet government on payment for its oil in hard currency, which Bulgaria lacked; and the eventual collapse of the Soviet state in December 1991. This trade decline caused severe shortages of energy needed by Bulgarian industry.

By the end of 1991, the economic record was not good. Although the Popov government had undertaken many initiatives to transform the economic system, and especially to open up opportunities for its most enterprising citizens, the economy remained weak. Output had fallen 8 percent and real domestic product 23 percent in 1991. Unemployment was at 10 percent, not bad by Western standards but rather high for a society that had been used to virtually full employment for several decades. In early June 1991, inflation was running at 330 percent a year.[51]

On the other hand, Popov's free-market initiatives encouraged the West to take a chance on Bulgaria, and in March 1991 the IMF said it would disburse more than $550 million in loans for Bulgaria, $109 million of which were to offset the oil crisis provoked by the Iraqi invasion of Kuwait and the subsequent international trade sanctions imposed on Baghdad. The Paris Club, an informal grouping of the world's largest creditor nations, had agreed to reschedule its $2 billion share of Bulgaria's foreign debt over the next ten years. But as the October 1991 parliamentary elections approached, little had changed in the economic life of the country, and Bulgarians were angry.[52]

2. New Parliamentary and Presidential Elections

In July 1991, the Bulgarian Parliament adopted a democratic constitution, which opened the way for open, free, and competitive parliamentary elections, held in October. In these elections, the embattled Popov government and its BSP supporters in the Parliament lost to the UDF, with a plurality of 34.4 percent. The BSP lost the election and consequently had to give up leadership of the country. But it by no means had been decisively defeated. It was a very close second to the UDF and still had the loyalty of at least 33 percent of the Bulgarian electorate. Thus, while the elections ended forty years of communist rule, the BSP remained an influential political force the UDF could not afford to ignore. Other important results of the election concerned the level of voter participation and the strength of the MRF. Over 90 percent of the Bulgarian electorate voted in this election, suggesting that an overwhelming majority of voters, whatever their political preferences, appreciated and took advantage of an opportunity they had not had in a very long time to express their will. While there was still strong support throughout the country for the conservative policies of the BSP, the election left little doubt about popular Bulgarian support for the new democratic political order. Furthermore, in winning 7.5 percent of the popular vote, the MRF displayed a resilience that would enable it to exercise some influence over national politics and aspire to become a "swing party," whose support might be needed by the other large parties, such as the BSP and UDF, to govern the country.[53]

The process of communist collapse was completed in the presidential elections held in January 1992. Incumbent President Zhelev ran against Velko Vulganov, a Socialist. Zhelev won with 53 percent of the vote. He was elected for five years and was the first Bulgarian president to be elected by direct popular vote. He benefited from several popular foreign policies, notably his support of Gorbachev and Yeltsin in the August 1991 attempted coup in Moscow, his backing of the Western allies in the Persian Gulf War, and his accurate assessment of the dangers of civil war in Yugoslavia for the Balkans in general and Bulgaria, a neighbor of Serbia, in particular.

With Blaga Dmitrova, a former dissident and poet, as vice-president, Zhelev quickly reaffirmed his support for economic reform. He declared that, if Bulgaria could attract sufficient foreign investment, it would catch up in a few years with Poland, Hungary, and Czechoslovakia.[54] And, despite its slender victory in October 1991, the new UDF government led by Prime Minister Filip Dimitrov, which took office in November, announced an ambitious reform program, including an expansion of democratic freedoms and further movement toward the market economy. Bulgaria was finally on the threshold of a new postcommunist era of political development.

Problems of Postcommunist Political Development

Throughout 1992 and 1993, the new UDF government faced some of the same difficulties that had undermined the BSP leadership before it. They led eventually to a decline in UDF popularity and a BSP return to power.

1. Growing Turkish Political Influence

Without an absolute majority of seats in parliament, Dimitrov had to form a coalition with the MRF, which had won 7 percent of the popular vote, and the BSP, which had a third of the seats in the parliament. The UDF coalition gave the Bulgarian Turks an opportunity to play a pivotal role in national politics, something the former communists had feared and had tried to prevent through a ruthless policy of forced assimilation. The MRF wasted no time in advising the UDF leadership that its cooperation in producing the majority needed to govern the country would come at a substantial price. The MRF wanted several ministerial posts and a meaningful MRF participation in the formation of Bulgarian foreign policy. For its part, the UDF responded very cautiously, recognizing its cabinet would need popular acceptance to function effectively that might be hard to achieve given the national prejudice toward Bulgarians of Turkish back-ground.[55]

2. The Role of the BSP

The BSP remained an important force in Bulgarian politics despite its electoral setbacks. It had many able and enlightened members, who rapidly learned demo-cratic politics and could easily pass for left-wing social democrats. They rightly claimed to represent political constituencies not only among members of the former ruling apparatus but also among pensioners and unskilled workers in heavy industry. The BSP remained strong in the countryside. Farmers who ex-pected to lose from the privatization of agriculture either because they were too old to farm on their own or because they would not gain from the restitution of land to former owners looked to the BSP for help.[56]

In the early 1990s, the UDF was not sure how to deal with the BSP. Should the BSP be treated as a normal democratic opposition with full rights and free-doms? Or should it be considered a subversive organization with agents through-out the administration and political power out of proportion to its electoral strength? The UDF leadership in 1992 was split between conservatives and liberals on this issue, with Prime Minister Dimitrov inclined to take a hard line against the former communists, convinced that they could not be trusted to continue the country's transition away from socialism to capitalism and democ-racy. In 1992, the Dimitrov government tried publicly to discredit the BSP and punish it. It prosecuted a number of former high-ranking BSP officials and forbade former prime minister Lukanov from leaving the country until cleared of the criminal charges for which he was being investigated. And the UDF–MRF majority in the Grand National Assembly put through legislation denying pen-sions to a number of retired BSP members who had served in the government under Zhivkov.[57]

The question of how much political and economic influence former commu-nists should be allowed in postcommunist Bulgaria was raised in the preparation of a decommunization law. While satisfying the needs of the UDF to punish and weaken the former communists still in positions of influence in 1992 by trying to keep them out of high administrative positions, the legislation was criticized for denying a political role to talented people whose skills could help Bulgaria in the postcommunist era. Some argued that a ruthless enforcement of the law could provoke the BSP to take revenge should it win the next parliamentary elections. The UDF would then be the victim of its own policy.[58]

3. The Problem of "Restitution"

Closely related to this issue was the question of restoring land and property seized by the communists after World War II. Pushed through Parliament by the

Dimitrov government, legislation entitled most precommunist owners to full recovery of land and property. But implementing this law was slow and difficult. Scattered lands had been incorporated into large agro-industrial complexes, which were difficult to break up. Acrimonious disputes broke out in villages and within families that inherited holdings of variable value or where some members wanted to farm and others wanted to build, join a cooperative, or sell. Some people believed that the UDF sponsors of this law were influenced by those members of Parliament who expected to acquire property. But another incentive for restitution was ideological: it was another way the UDF–MRF government could send a signal to the BSP of its hostility to the communist past, since a law providing for political rehabilitation that would allow the filing of claims to confiscated property was extended to the Bulgarian monarch dethroned by the communists in 1946.[59]

4. The Decline of the UDF

By the end of 1991, factionalism had begun to disrupt the UDF. A group of pragmatic political figures in the UDF, including Blaga Dmitrova, was critical of Zhelev and other UDF founders who had been instrumental in challenging communist rule at the end of the 1980s. This new generation of UDF political leaders was impatient with the "old-timers," especially their willingness to cooperate with the former communists, who were deeply distrusted and disliked. For these "young Turks," nothing the BSP could say or do could change the party's discredited image, and they wanted nothing to do with it. They favored a complete and absolute break with the past and considered anyone who disagreed with this radicalism as a traitor to democracy and, worse, a "pinko," or communist sympathizer. This conflict of generations within the UDF was certainly not peculiar to Bulgaria. The same thing was happening in other noncommunist political parties elsewhere in Central and Eastern Europe and reflected a kind of retarded revulsion against the communist past and an impatience with the slowness of the postcommunist political system in rejecting it.[60]

By late 1992, the UDF government had become unpopular and lost support in the parliament. Its aggressive, confrontational leadership eventually alienated important support groups whose interests it had not taken sufficiently into account in its policy making. For example, it lost the support of *Podkrepa* and alarmed high-ranking military officers with the prospect of a purge. It also lost the support of the MRF, which complained about the government's neglect of Turkish interests and, indeed, a perceived discrimination against them.[61] For example, the Turkish minority was especially affected by hardships accompanying the curtailment of state control over the economy and resented the absence of any meaningful remedial action to ease those hardships, such as distribution of land to Turkish peasants from the state land bank. The MRF also resented Dimitrov's failure to act on Turkish claims for land confiscated by the Zhivkov regime. The MRF withdrew from the coalition and supported a parliamentary vote of no-confidence in Dimitrov. And in December dissension within the UDF reached a climax when UDF ministers and other influential UDF politicians accused Zhelev of "disloyalty."[62]

Zhelev replaced what was left of the Dimitrov government in December 1992 with a caretaker government of nonparty professionals led by Prime Minister Liuben Berov to keep the country going until new elections. The new "care-taker" government soon solidified its position when Berov struck a deal with the BSP and the MRF to give him a majority that enabled him to run the country throughout 1993.[63] But the strength of Berov's government was more apparent than real. Members of Berov's coalition were soon fighting over when parliamentary elections should be held. The BSP preferred elections at the end of 1995, when it thought its chances of winning an absolute majority conceivably would be better than in 1993 and 1994. The UDF, on the other hand, wanted elections much earlier, before the BSP would have time to strengthen its appeal among the voters. The UDF asked President Zhelev to get Parliament, which had the authority to dissolve itself (the president did not have the dissolution power), to set elections by the end of 1994. Zhelev initially resisted this pressure. He backed up Berov's leadership, provoking the anger of his own party and weakening its image among the electorate, which had little sympathy for the partisan conflict in Sofia that distracted the government's attention from the economy and the need to improve living conditions.[64]

5. The Return of the BSP to Power

By comparison with the UDF, the BSP in 1994 looked like a calm, professional political force deserving of popular support and national leadership. Its standing with the public improved as the UDF's image deteriorated. By the end of the year, it was looking forward to a return to power with the hope of being able to govern without having to rely on a coalition with either the UDF or the MRF. Zhelev, tired of protecting Berov, decided to accommodate UDF demands for early parliamentary elections, a move the UDF would subsequently regret.

Elections were held in December 1994. Key issues were economic. By the end of the year, 70 percent of the population was on the verge of poverty, with 740,000 people out of a total population of 8.5 million unemployed. The BSP leader Zhan Videnov promised a slow transition to the free market to ease hardship on people with low incomes.[65]

Not surprisingly, the elections went badly for the UDF. The BSP won the absolute majority in Parliament that it wanted. It obtained 125 out of 240 seats in the Grand National Assembly. The UDF won only 68 seats, a stunning setback for the first major noncommunist party to rule the country since the fall of the communist regime. According to BSP leader Videnov, who had succeeded

Aleksandr Lilov in 1992, the voters were punishing the UDF for policies that kept living standards low, as well as for its excessive partisanship. The fighting between the leadership and many in the parliamentary group of the UDF was too much for Bulgarian voters weary of hard times and eager for leadership that could introduce change without making things worse. The BSP victory could be seen as a message to the government to proceed toward the market economy more slowly and sensitively. BSP leader Videnov succeeded Dimitrov as prime minister in December 1994. Living standards continued to fall, however, and in due course, Videnov himself would be blamed for moving too slowly on economic reform.[66]

Postcommunist Economic Problems

Following the October 1991 parliamentary elections, the UDF government quickly indicated the broad direction in which it intended to lead the country in the economic sphere. Prime Minister Dimitrov pledged to move forward with privatization, encourage private entrepreneurship in agriculture, and stimulate foreign investment. He freed up the currency to make it convertible and allowed the lev to reach its true market level, which was 24 lev to the U.S. dollar, not the old official rate of 2 lev to the dollar.[67]

1. Difficulties with Privatization

Privatization of state-owned industrial enterprises was slow. The UDF enacted legislation providing for the sale of large industrial enterprises by public auction, the price to be based on estimates by the Privatization Agency. About 20 percent of the shares of each enterprise were to go into a social security fund, and another block of shares was to be offered to workers at discounted prices. The rest were to be sold on the open market. The UDF government wanted to avoid the voucher system adopted by Czechoslovakia out of fear of promoting a "casino economy." The Bulgarian government, however, had difficulty unloading the huge, overmanned, antiquated, and polluting heavy industries. Fortunately, it had fewer of these than most other socialist countries because the communists had concentrated on agriculture and light industry.[68]

The UDF was not able to improve Bulgaria's economic performance. In 1992 and again in 1993, there was another 20 percent drop in overall production, and unemployment climbed to 23 percent, an unacceptable figure that threatened social turmoil and political instability and strengthened the chances of a return to power of the socialists. Indeed, an overwhelming majority of Bulgarians indicated a strong desire to preserve a substantial part of the old welfare system put in place by the late communist regime, including full-employment policies and controlled and subsidized prices for food. Moreover, the World Bank warned that, if large-scale privatization did not get under way, its second disbursement of a previously granted $250 million would not be forthcoming. Although the Grand National Assembly passed a privatization law, hardly any progress toward privatization of the large state-owned industrial enterprises had been made by the end of 1993. At the same time, relations between Bulgaria and the IMF deteriorated as the government of Prime Minister Berov tried to address popular discontent over the hardships caused by the transition to a free-market economy. Berov asked the IMF to ease its rulings on budgetary restraint to allow Bulgaria to maintain a budget deficit equal to 8 to 10 percent of gross domestic product to allow the government more flexibility in spending on the social net. Reluctant to ease the terms under which it extended credit, it took Beron's request under advisement.[69]

2. Prospects of Economic Improvement

Chances for economic improvement in the mid- and late 1990s are nevertheless hopeful. Bulgaria has a highly educated workforce that is now extremely cheap by international standards. There are plans to produce Rover cars, half for sale in markets abroad. Bulgaria also has a well-developed agriculture and plans to enlarge its tourist industry. Moreover, it is strategically located between Europe and the Middle East and can hope for a revival of the Russian and Ukrainian markets.

On the other hand, the standard of living for most Bulgarians had not improved by the end of 1994, five years after the demise of the Zhivkov regime. Inflation had doubled to 120 percent a year, and output in key industries remained stagnant. Retirees were hardly able to survive on pensions of $24 a month most received from the state. The BSP victory in the December 1994 elections confirmed a pervasive public pessimism about the country's economic prospects in the mid-1990s. Furthermore, the IMF and the World Bank have withheld large disbursements of credit to Bulgaria until the government makes large cuts in social spending and speeds up the country's move toward a free-market economy. Prospects for such policies are dim because the BSP was elected to power by the poorest elements in Bulgarian society. Indeed, in the late 1990s, the BSP will have to walk a fine line between its impoverished supporters intent on holding the party to its promises of looking after them and the international bankers from whom it wants to borrow a lot of money and who insist on the pursuit of an austerity that the society is reluctant to accept.

3. Nuclear Energy and the Environment

Adding to Bulgaria's economic woes in the mid-1990s is an environmental problem involving Bulgaria's nuclear power plants, which were the country's chief source of cheap energy but were judged to be dangerous by Western engineers. For example, the plant at Kozlodui in northwestern Bulgaria, near the Romanian frontier, was unsafe. In 1990, inspectors from the International Atomic Energy Agency found radioactive contamination of groundwater around the plant and concluded that the contamination had resulted from several serious accidents. The agency also found that 217 workers had suffered excessive exposure to radiation in five hot spots in the plant. And in 1991, another agency mission found that four of the six reactors, which were old, Soviet-built models, should be shut down immediately. The other two were modern and relatively safe but were not enough to meet the country's energy needs. While these reactors supply about 40 percent of Bulgaria's electricity when they are operating, in 1992 only three of the six were working, with the others shut down for repair or maintenance, to the despair of 5,000 engineers, technicians, and other workers at these plants. But the Bulgarian government cannot afford to upgrade them. It must patch them up from time to time with some small technical and financial help from the West. Nevertheless, it continues to rely heavily on them for cheap electricity, even as production continues to be inadequate and dangerous to the environment.[70]

Women and Postcommunist Development

As in other Central and East European countries in the postcommunist era, despite communist efforts to promote equality among men and women, Bulgarian women in the professional sphere were not treated equally. Discrimination continued in regard to employment opportunities, wages, and promotions. Women had lower-paying jobs than men, they had nowhere near the influence over government that men enjoyed, and they suffered the indignity of not being taken seriously by male colleagues and administrative superiors. They were even ridiculed in the media for taking the communist regime's commitment to equality and emancipation too seriously. The message of Bulgarian society to women on the eve of the postcommunist era was to return to what was termed their "authentic culture" of homemaking and child rearing.[71]

In the early 1990s, Bulgarian women were worse off than men. An already-gender-segregated labor market was disrupted by free-market reforms, and women suffered far more loss of jobs and decline in standard of living than did men. The situation for women was made worse by a conservative social environment in which husbands preferred wives at home instead of at the workplace. Recently, other disturbing tendencies include a growing "invisibility" of women in the male-dominated media and an increase of pornography that degrades and humiliates the female sex. Finally, women in postcommunist Bulgaria are suffering physically from environmental pollution that the government in Sofia seems to be in no rush to reduce, never mind remove. Bulgaria has experienced a sharp decline in birth rates and the highest number of gynecological patients in Europe.[72]

The outlook for improvement in the social and physical status of women in Bulgaria is not especially bright. Women won less than fifteen percent of the seats in the Bulgarian Parliament in the early 1990s and those who were successful turned out to be deeply divided among themselves over party issues. They have had great difficulty developing a "feminist agenda" to promote equality for women. Women's issues are still barely mentioned in the mass media or in political forums like party meetings.

Working against women is the parlous state of the economy, where unemployment remains one of the most serious problems facing the country.[73] But there are grounds for a cautious optimism. With an expansion of economic output, the need for female labor will increase. The July 1991 constitution affirming the country's dedication to parliamentary democracy reaffirms human and minority rights. Finally, there is no Catholic Church in Bulgaria to advocate policies that encourage female submissiveness or in other ways adversely affect the well-being of women, such as the kind of near-absolute ban on abortion the Catholic Church successfully badgered the Polish government into adopting. [74]

Postcommunist Foreign Relations

In the 1990s, Bulgaria has had to keep an eye on its borders, where regional unrest threatens to slow internal reform. Of most importance are Bulgaria's relationships with its neighbors Greece and Turkey, with the former Soviet republics, in particular Russia, and with the West.

1. Greece

Probably the most delicate of foreign relationships is the one with Greece, because with its substantial Turkish minority, Bulgaria is caught in the long-running Greek–Turkish antagonism. Post-communist Bulgarian governments want to preserve good relations with Greece, while at the same time continuing a reconciliation with Turkey. For reasons of national security and regional stability, Bulgaria cannot afford to have difficulties with either Greece or Turkey. But in the 1991 parliamentary elections, the predominantly Turkish MRF had become Bulgaria's third largest political force, leading some Greek politicians and journalists to worry out loud that Bulgarian Turks—and, indirectly, the Turkish Republic—might gain an excessive influence in Bulgaria's internal affairs.

Another source of tension in Bulgaria's relations with Greece is the former Yugoslav republic of Macedonia. Bulgaria supported Macedonia's independence of Belgrade, but this position was criticized in Athens, where there is fear of a resurgence of Macedonian irredentism. The Greek government did not want Macedonians in Greece and Bulgaria forming a greater Macedonian state. There is good reason for the Greek concern. When Macedonia declared its independence, Sofia and Ankara quickly recognized the new Macedonian state. Athens now worries that the new Macedonian state will raise claims of territory in northern Greece inhabited by kinsmen.

Greece worries also that Bulgaria itself may raise claims to territory in the former Yugoslav Republic of Macedonia that have their origins in the Treaty of San Stefano of January 1878 ending the Russo-Turkish War of 1877–78. In that treaty, Russia agreed to the transfer of a large portion of Macedonia from Turkey to Bulgaria to create a "greater Bulgaria," now autonomous of the Turkish Empire, which had conquered it centuries earlier. San Stefano was reversed at the Congress of Berlin in June 1878 by Great Britain, France, and Germany, to the dismay of the Bulgarian state. From that time onward, Bulgarians cherished the hope of someday recovering Macedonian territory. Indeed, the Bulgarians tried to regain Macedonian territory in the two Balkan wars of 1911 and 1913 and during World War I and World War II, when the Sofia government aligned Bulgaria with the Germans in the hope they would help.[75]

But postcommunist Bulgarian governments have shown little interest in raising claims to Macedonian territory, which is underdeveloped and problem ridden. President Zhelev assured Athens that, while Bulgaria accepted Macedonia's independence of Yugoslavia, it would not endorse the idea of a Macedonian nation that included territory belonging to Greece. He also assured the Greeks that Bulgaria would make no claims on Macedonian territory. But a complication of the Macedonian issue in Bulgarian–Greek relations is the possibility that Macedonia might be the next object of Serbian territorial aggrandizement on the pretext of protecting the interests of small Serb minority in Macedonia. A Serbian invasion of Macedonia might be acceptable to Greece, as a means of discouraging development of the idea of a "Macedonian nation," but such a move would threaten Bulgaria and provoke a confrontation between Bulgaria and Serbia.[76]

2. Turkey

Bulgaria had difficulties with Ankara in the early 1990s. There was a legacy of bad feelings as a result of the communist policy of the late 1980s to "Bulgarianize" the country's Turkish minority. Moreover, Bulgaria watched with some discomfort the expansion of Turkish military power, which conceivably could threaten Bulgarian security.[77] But relations improved for several reasons. First, the Dimitrov government was committed to democratization and, in particular, to altering the past policy toward the Turkish minority and allowing a measure of equality. Also, to maintain its leadership in Parliament, the UDF worked with the MRF following the October 1991 parliamentary elections. Furthermore, Sofia fully appreciated the importance of good relations with Turkey, which, like Greece, was a member of NATO, for strengthening Bulgarian ties with the West. Finally, many educated Bulgarians favor a positive policy toward Turkey because they believe that Turkey is the country most likely to invest in Bulgaria and to provide regional economic leadership. For its part, Turkey has developed an idea for a Black Sea economic cooperation zone involving Bulgaria and other littoral powers.[78] In October 1991, Dimitur Ludzhev, an adviser to President Zhelev, visited Ankara and assured the Turkish government that Bulgaria was committed to full equality for its Turkish minority.[79] Unfortunately, Bulgarians still want to impose restrictions on and limit the political and economic influence of the Turkish minority.[80] Good Bulgarian–Turkish relations in the future will depend on how the Bulgarian government proceeds on this issue.

In Istanbul at the end of June 1992, Turkey hosted a summit of eleven nations with economic and strategic interests in the Black Sea. The five Balkan states of Bulgaria, Romania, Turkey, Greece, and Albania, plus Armenia, Azerbaijan, Moldova, Georgia, and Russia, signed a declaration of economic cooperation, with a pledge to contain regional conflicts. Turkey was especially gratified because the summit represented a first step in the development of its idea of creating a European Community–style grouping of the Balkan Black Sea countries. But more importantly, the emergence of an organization of countries that traditionally had been rivals could provide the means of lessening confrontation and conflict in the region. The willingness of Bulgaria to go along with this plan was appreciated by the Turkish leadership.[81]

3. Russia

While Bulgaria built new links to Greece and Turkey, it also worked to improve ties with Russia. Like the other former Soviet satellites, Bulgaria has had to cope with the sudden, devastating effects of a 30 percent decline in the delivery of cheap Soviet oil. Energy prices in Bulgaria soared in the early 1990s, slowing down Bulgarian economic growth and fueling inflation.[82] Bulgaria has a positive base on which to develop friendly and cooperative relations with post-Soviet Russia, not least the shared cultural traditions. President Zhelev's support for the Gorbachev–Yeltsin faction in the August 1991 attempted coup in Moscow opened the way for the new relationship between Bulgaria and Russia. In the 1990s, Sofia has focused on regenerating Bulgarian–Russian trade, which is essential to Bulgaria's future economic well-being.[83]

4. The West

Bulgarian reformers want good relations with the West. To this end, Bulgarian leaders since Zhivkov have tried to clear up questions about Bulgaria's complicity in the plot to assassinate Pope John Paul II in 1981 and have inaugurated a sweeping investigation despite the reticence of senior Bulgarian police and intelligence officials, who are reluctant to compromise colleagues and apparently have tried to destroy incriminating documents. By May 1991, the Bulgarian government had released more than 127 volumes of secret police documents. With the offer of President Zhelev to provide whatever additional relevant documents come to light, Bulgaria has increased the credibility of its stated commitment to break completely with the communist past.[84]

Nevertheless, Washington and other Western governments distrust Sofia. They have evidence that Bulgaria fostered drug smuggling and sold arms to terrorists. Moreover, Western governments remember Bulgaria's violations of the human rights of its citizens in its documented harassment of its Turkish minority—international human-rights organizations, such as Amnesty International and Helsinki Watch, have focused attention on Bulgaria's repressive policies toward its Turkish minority. Indeed, on June 15, 1989, the U.S. Senate unanimously voted to condemn Bulgaria for its treatment of its Turkish minority and voted $10 million for aid for Turkish refugees from Bulgaria.[85]

While welcoming the fall of Zhivkov, the relaxation of the political environment, and tentative moves toward economic liberalization, Secretary of State James Baker, during a visit to Sofia in February 1990, indicated that the United States still viewed the Bulgarian government as communist and that Bulgaria was on probation with the United States. While Washington offered some aid to other East European countries throwing off the Soviet yoke in the fall of 1989, it withheld aid and trade concessions to Sofia until it saw further evidence of the commitment to introduce political democracy, in particular, the holding of free and fair elections. Baker did not take on faith Prime Minister Lukanov's assurances that the communists would give up power and become an opposition party if they lost an election. He insisted on actions to back up promises, notably, government guarantees of access to the media for opposition parties.[86]

The October 1991 parliamentary elections, in which the BSP lost to the UDF, and the January 1992 direct election of President Zhelev marked a turning point in Western, and especially American, relations with Bulgaria. The United States subsequently acknowledged an improvement in the Bulgarian political environment, and relations between the two countries began to warm. The Bulgarian government had helped its cause with Washington by endorsing economic sanctions against Iraq and by its expressed willingness to send a token military force to the region, despite the severity of the impact of the embargo of Iraqi oil on the Bulgarian economy.[87]

In January 1991, President Bush cleared the way for the lifting of trade restrictions on Bulgaria. He affirmed that the Sofia government now allowed unrestricted emigration and was eligible for a waiver of the Jackson–Vanik amendment prohibiting most-favored-nation treatment of trade with countries that obstructed emigration. With the new trade status, Bulgaria could apply for loan guarantees from the Export–Import Bank and for participation in Overseas Private Investment Corporation programs.[88] Newly appointed Prime Minister Dimitrov was well received in Washington in early March 1992, when he met with Bush and asked for economic aid as well as investments in Bulgaria. He noted with satisfaction American appreciation of the changes taking place in Bulgaria.[89]

While these gestures were not the same as getting large-scale aid from the United States, they certainly were a good start. They were a signal of American satisfaction over the gradual departure from power of communists like Lukanov and the appointment of the country's first noncommunist leadership in over forty years. But Bulgaria still has a way to go in its political development before it can expect to receive the same kind of attention from the United States that has been shown to Poland, Hungary, and Czechoslovakia. Washington is concerned with the resilience of the BSP and with the slowness of Bulgarian governments in moving the country toward a free-market economy.[90] In fairness to Bulgaria, the pace of change is slow because of political instability. Neither the BSP nor the UDF, which are committed to a dismantling of the state-controlled economy and the development of capitalism, seems able to keep a grip on power long enough to implement significant change.

The civil war in Yugoslavia has recently complicated Bulgaria's relations with the United States. Bulgaria has lost a lot of money upholding U.N. sanctions against the rump state of Yugoslavia. But if it had refused to support sanctions, Bulgaria would have antagonized Washington and compromised its chances of receiving financial support from the World Bank and the IMF. Many Bulgarians believe some sort of compensation for their trouble is due them, and the United Nations has agreed in principle to this idea.[91]

Conclusions

The transition away from communism to noncommunist leadership occurred without the kind of violence seen in Romania largely because of the pragmatism of the last cadre of party leaders, Mladenov and Lilov. After the stubbornness of Zhivkov, reformers in Bulgaria showed a flexibility that set them apart from their predecessors and from communist leaders in other Central and East European countries, notably, Romania's Ceauşescu and East Germany's Honecker. But reformer communists moved too slowly to assure their survival. Although they tried very hard to hold on to power by going to great lengths to liberalize their party organization and the governments they led, and although they had a surprising resilience in the early 1990s, raising the possibility of survival as Communist parties in other Central and East European countries were deprived of power by voter majorities in parliamentary elections, Bulgarian reformist leaders had to accept the reality of their failure to improve living conditions in the short term. Their reformism was too little too late. Yet the socialists still have a broad appeal, because Bulgarian society is very conservative, fearful of radical change, and reluctant to abandon the security and stability they had under communism.

The BSP return to power, however, should not arouse fears of a return to the dictatorship and isolation of the communist era. The BSP is committed to reform, albeit at a slower pace than preferred by the UDF. It wants a free-market economy and has people in its ranks who have benefited from the dismantling of state control over the country's economic life. Moreover, Bulgaria has rejected the single-party dictatorship, embraced political pluralism, and begun reforms that will eventually bring them to some kind of free-market economy with only a minimum of state interference to protect society against the inequities and abuses that economic freedom inevitably brings in its wake. And although President Zhelev has been accused of authoritarian political behavior in leading Bulgaria through the transition to political and economic democracy, he can hardly be accused of seeking to undermine the democratic system. Zhelev is loyal to the liberal order, trying to grapple with difficult problems in a difficult political context, and is ready to step down in the event he is voted out of power.

And, despite a far-from-perfect relationship between ethnic Bulgarians and the country's Turkish minority, Bulgaria has not experienced the kind of ethnic turmoil seen in other multinational countries in Central and Eastern Europe since the collapse of communist rule. The MRF has been accepted in law and in fact as a legitimate political party and has had a modicum of success in advocating and achieving recognition of Turkish economic and cultural rights, in particular, restitution of land confiscated by the communists and permission to use the Turkish language as a medium of instruction in schools attended by a majority of Turkish-speaking people. Moreover, Turkish-speaking Bulgarians who are Muslim show little, if any, interest in Islamic fundamentalism. Finally, Bulgarians want at all costs to avoid the kind of nationalist-inspired interethnic conflict that has torn neighboring Yugoslavia apart.

On the other hand, Bulgaria has a way to go before it achieves a durable and stable democratic system. It has little experience with Western-style parliamentary democracy; it continues to confront serious economic problems that are delaying an improvement in living conditions to Western levels; and the ethnocultural nationalism still quite strong among a majority of ethnic-Bulgarians, especially as it affects the country's Turkish minority, is not conducive to democratic development.[92]

5

From Czechoslovakia to the Czech and Slovak Republics

Like the rest of Central and Eastern Europe, Czechoslovakia came under communist rule following World War II. And like its neighbors, it soon became a satellite of Moscow. From the outset, the Czechoslovak communist system was Stalinist, namely, committed to a rigid ideological orthodoxy in the political and economic spheres of national life. The Czechoslovak communists slavishly imitated Soviet policies, especially after the ascendancy in 1953 of Antonín Novotný as head of the Czechoslovak Communist Party. Under Novotný, Czechoslovakia adopted a carbon copy of the Soviet political system.[1]

The Prague Spring

In the 1960s, politicians, journalists, and ordinary citizens questioned the Stalinist dictatorship. Convinced that they could live better if they reformed the system, many Czechs and Slovaks supported liberalization of the country's political environment and economic structures. Pressures for change reached a climax in January 1968, when party chief Novotný was replaced by Alexander Dubček, a Slovak and a reformer. Dubček tried to liberalize the political system by lifting censorship and allowing open debate of national problems and policies, moves that were called the "Prague Spring."[2]

CZECH REPUBLIC

Geography

1. Location: central Europe, southeast of Germany
2. Area: total — 78,703 square kilometers; land area — 78,645 square kilometers; comparative area — slightly larger than South Carolina
3. Boundaries: with Austria — 362 kilometers; with Germany — 646 kilometers; with Poland — 658 kilometers; with Slovakia — 214 kilometers
4. Climate: temperate; cool summers; cold, cloudy, humid winters
5. Terrain: two main regions — Bohemia in the west, consisting of rolling plains, hills, and plateaus surrounded by low mountains; Moravia in the east, consisting of very hilly country
6. Natural resources: hard coal, soft coal, kaolin, clay, bauxite
7. Environment: air and water pollution in areas of northwestern Bohemia centered around Teplice and in northern

Moravia around Ostrava causing health risks; acid rain damaging forests

People

1. Population: 10,432,774 (1995 estimate)
2. Age structure: 0–14 — 19% of population (female — 981,918; male — 1,030,003); 15–64 — 68% of population (female — 3,529,411; male — 3,530,112); 65 and over — 13% of population (female — 848,599; male — 512,731) (1995 estimate)
3. Growth rate: 0.26% (1995 estimate)
4. Life expectancy at birth: total population — 73.54 years; female — 77.41 years; male — 69.87 years (1995 estimate)
5. Ethnic divisions: Czech — 94.4%; Slovak — 3%; Polish — 0.6%; German — 0.5%; Gypsy — 0.3%; Hungarian — 0.2%
6. Religions: atheist — 39.8%; Roman Catholic — 39.2%; Protestant — 4.6%; Orthodox — 6%
7. Languages: Czech and Slovak
8. Literacy: total population — 99%
9. Labor force: total — 5.389 million; agriculture — 8.1%; industry 37.9%; construction — 8.8%; communications and other occupations — 45.2% (1990 estimate)

Government

1. Type: emerging parliamentary democracy
2. Capital: Prague
3. Independence: January 1, 1993, from Czechoslovakia
4. Constitution: ratified December 16, 1992; promulgated January 1, 1993
5. National administration:
   a. Chief of state: President of the Republic (1996 — Václav Havel)
   b. Ministerial leadership: Prime Minister and Council of Ministers (1996 — Václav Klaus, prime minister)
   c. Legislature: bicameral — National Union (*Narodni Rada*), consisting of Chamber of Deputies (lower house) and Senate (upper house)
   d. Judicial branch: Supreme Court, Constitutional Court
   e. Political parties: Civic Democratic Party, Christian Democratic Party, Civic Democratic Alliance, Christian Democratic Union/Czech People's Party, Czech Social Democrats, Left Bloc, Communist Party, Liberal Social Union, Liberal Social National Party, Bohemian-Moravian Center Party
6. Local Administration: unitary system with 8 regions

Economy

1. Gross domestic product: $76.5 billion (1994 estimate)
2. National product real growth rate: 2.2% (1994 estimate)
3. Per-capita national product: $7,350 (1994 estimate)
4. Inflation rate: 12.2% (1994 estimate)
5. Unemployment rate: 10.2% (1994 estimate)
6. Budget: revenue — $14 billion; expenditures — $13.6 billion
7. Industrial output: fuel, ferrous metals, machinery and equipment, coal, motor vehicles, glass, armaments
8. Agricultural output: livestock, grain, vegetables, cattle, poultry, sugar (the Czech Republic is largely self-sufficient in food production)
9. Exports: $13.4 billion (1994 estimate) — machinery and transport equipment, agricultural products, fuels, minerals, metals
10. Imports: $13.3 billion (1994 estimate) — machinery and transport equipment, chemicals, fuels and lubricants, agricultural products
11. External debt: $8.7 billion (1994)
12. Trade partners: Germany, Slovakia, Austria, Italy, France, United States, United Kingdom, Poland
13. Transportation: railroads — 9,434 kilometers; highways — 55,890 kilometers; ports — Děčín, Prague, Ústí nad Labem; airports — 116 (31 with paved runways)

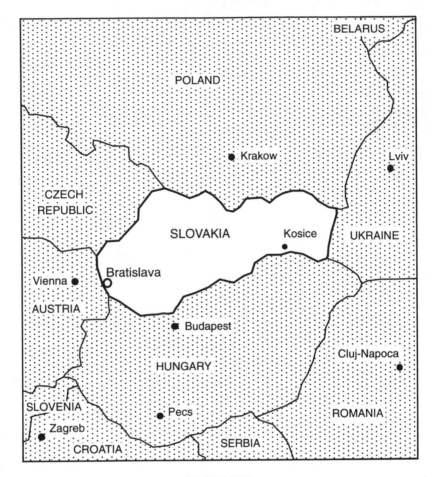

SLOVAKIA

Geography

1. Location: central Europe, south of Poland
2. Area: total — 48,845 square kilometers; land area — 48,800 square kilometers; comparative area — about twice the size of New Hampshire
3. Boundaries: with Austria — 91 kilometers; with Czech Republic — 215 kilometers; with Hungary — 515 kilometers; with Poland — 444 kilometers; with Ukraine — 90 kilometers; no coastline
4. Climate: mild temperature; cold, cloudy winters; cool summers
5. Terrain: rugged mountains in the central and northern part and lowlands in the south
6. Natural resources: brown coal and lignite; small amounts of iron ore, copper, manganese ore, salt
7. Environment: air pollution from metallurgical plants presents human health risks; acid rain damaging forests

People

1. Population: 5,432,383 (1995 estimate)
2. Age structure: 0–14 — 23% of population (female — 364,610; male — 638,346); 15–64 — 66% of popula-

tion (female — 1,817,312; male — 1,778,712); 65 and over — 11% of population (female — 364,610; male — 233,608) (1995 estimate)
3. Growth rate: 0.54% (1995 estimate)
4. Life expectancy at birth: total population — 73.24 years; female — 77.57 years; male — 69.15 years (1995 estimate)
5. Ethnic divisions: Slovak — 85.7%; Hungarian — 10.7%; Gypsy — 1.5%; Czech — 1%; Ruthenian — 0.3%; Ukrainian — 0.3%; German — 0.1%; Polish — 0.1%
6. Religions: Roman Catholic — 60.3%; atheist — 9.7%; Protestant — 8.4%; Orthodox — 4.1%; other — 17.5%
7. Languages: Slovak (official); Hungarian
8. Literacy: not available
9. Labor force: total — 2.84 million; industry — 33.2%; agriculture — 12.2%; construction — 10.3%; communications, commerce, and other — 44.3% (1993 estimate)

Government

1. Type: emerging parliamentary democracy
2. Capital: Bratislava
3. Independence: January 1, 1993, from Czechoslovakia
4. Constitution: ratified September 1, 1992; promulgated January 1, 1993
5. National administration:
   a. Chief of state: President of the Republic (1996 — Michal Kovac)
   b. Ministerial leadership: Prime Minister and Council of Ministers (1996 — Vladimír Mečiar, prime minister)
   c. Legislature: unicameral — National Council (*Narodni Rada*)
   d. Judicial branch: Supreme Court
   e. Political parties: Movement for a Democratic Slovakia, Common Choice/Party of the Democratic Left, Hungarian Christian Democrats, Hungarian Civic Party, Christian Democratic Movement, Democratic Union, Association of

Slovak Workers, Slovak National Party
5. Local administration: unitary system with 4 departments

Economy

1. Gross domestic product: $32.8 billion; agriculture — 55% (1994 estimate)
2. National product real growth rate: 4.3% (1994 estimate)
3. Per-capita national product: $6,070 (1994 estimate)
4. Inflation rate: 12% (1994 estimate)
5. Unemployment rate: 14.6% (1994 estimate)
6. Budget: revenue — $4.4 billion; expenditures — $4.8 billion (1994 estimate)
7. Industrial output: metal and metal products, food and beverages, electricity from gas and water, coking, oil production, nuclear-fuel production, chemicals and man-made fibers, machinery, paper, printing, earthenware and ceramics, transport vehicles, textiles, electrical and optical apparatus, rubber products
8. Agricultural output: livestock raising (hogs, cattle, poultry), grains, potatoes, sugar beets, hops, fruit
9. Exports: $6.3 billion (1994) — machinery and transport equipment, chemicals, fuels, minerals and metals, agricultural products
10. Imports: $6.1 billion (1994) — machinery and transport equipment, fuels and lubricants, manufactured goods and raw materials, consumer goods, grains
11. External debt: $4.2 billion (1994 estimate)
12. Trade partners: Czech Republic, Russia, Germany, Austria, Italy, United States, Poland, Ukraine, Hungary
13. External debt: $4.2 million (1994 estimate)
14. Transportation: railroads — 3,660 kilometers; highways — 17,650 kilometers; airports — 37 (12 with paved runways)

1. Soviet Opposition to the "Prague Spring"

Brezhnev and other top Soviet leaders were afraid that Dubček's plans to liberalize Czechoslovakia's socialist system would set a bad example for other East European countries, where reformist elements might urge similar change, to the detriment of Soviet-style socialism. The Soviets were also afraid that, if reform in Czechoslovakia were successful, there might be demands for change in the Soviet Union itself. Dubček's political liberalization could open the way to the election of nationalists in Prague who would seek to loosen Czechoslovak ties to the Kremlin. Brezhnev insisted, in what became known as the Brezhnev Doctrine, that the USSR had the right to protect socialism in Eastern Europe against internal as well as external threats to its survival. The Kremlin called upon other members of the Warsaw Pact to contribute forces to an invasion of Prague, which took place in mid-August 1968. The invasion was successful in replacing Dubček as head of the Czechoslovak Communist Party with Gustáv Husák, another Slovak, who turned out to be extremely conservative and subservient to the Kremlin. Under instructions from the Kremlin, Husák quickly canceled most of Dubček's liberalization and restored a repressive regime. The West accepted the *fait accompli* of Soviet power in Czechoslovakia and did nothing to support Dubček's liberalism, obliging Czech reformers to wait twenty years for another chance to reform the hard-line and submissive regime the Soviets in 1969 had put in place and called "normalization."[3]

2. The Conservative Aftermath

The values and methods of Czechoslovak communist rule after 1968 were summed up well by party ideologist Antonín Dolejsi. In an article titled "The Revolutionary Epoch Can Last Centuries," published in the party monthly *Nova Mysl* in 1983. Dolejsi flatly stated that "the present and the future belong to communism." It was an orthodox, thoroughly dogmatic article, strongly against private farming, small-scale industry, whether public or private, and any concession to the growing East European fad for small privatization. According to Dolejsi, the Communist Party was an exclusive leader of society and must constantly be on its guard against infiltrations and subversion. Despite current difficulties that the world socialist movement and his own country were encountering and the opportunities all this was giving to so-called counterrevolutionaries, he argued that "socialism would survive ... because socialism was right, and it would all work out in the end."[4]

Post-1968 Czechoslovak leaders, inspired by the thinking of people like Dolejsi, showed little sympathy for perestroika-inspired reforms in Czechoslovakia. They feared any change would bring instability and, perhaps, foreign interference in the country's internal life. Even Husák did not want the Russians back.[5] In the 1970s and 1980s, most Czechs and Slovaks tolerated, if somewhat sullenly, this reimposed conservatism. Czechoslovak workers, in particular, seemed to be satisfied with the security and stability that went with the Husák regime, which did succeed in giving Czechoslovak society a level of material well-being that, while far below that in the West, was higher than levels in other Central and East European countries. Workers and other social groups seemed satisfied with what some in Czechoslovakia called a "happy stagnation."[6]

Incentives for Economic Liberalization

By the 1980s, however, the conservative Prague regime sensed the need for some economic change in Czechoslovakia. There was much that was wrong with the country's Stalinist economic structure.

1. Economic Stagnation

By the late 1980s, the economy had become stagnant: the manufacturing base of the Czechoslovak economy was too broad and was producing too many items at the expense of quality and marketability abroad. Although there was almost full employment, with many women in the workforce, there was still a labor shortage, along with poor labor productivity. The economy wasted energy, while the cost of it was soaring in the 1970s as a result of the 1973 oil crisis. By 1980, Czechoslovakia was paying five times as much for a ton of Soviet oil as it had in 1971. There was an overemphasis on mining and forestry at the expense of more sophisticated forms of manufacturing. In 1989, an opinion poll carried out by the government found that the Czechoslovak public had lost faith in the ability of socialism to deliver a better life and favored capitalism over socialism in terms of the ability of the two systems to provide food, industrial goods, and progress in science and technology.[7]

2. The Komarek Report

A highly detailed report submitted by the State Planning Commission to the party's Presidium and called "Detailed Forecasts about the Czechoslovak Socialist Republic Until 2010" affirmed the need for radical economic reform. Written by Valtr Komarek, director of the Forecasting Institute of the Academy of Sciences, it called for a market-driven economy, arguing that unless market forces were allowed to play a role in the Czechoslovak economy, substantially altering the traditional, highly centralized, neo-Stalinist economic structure, Czechoslovakia would sink to the level of a Third World Country. It also called for the depoliticization of the economic management of the country and a radical departure from economic Stalinism.[8]

3. Regime Responses

The response of the conservative Czechoslovak leadership to the Komarek report initially was mixed. Miloš Jakeš, a political hard-liner in the Czechoslovak Party Presidium who was nevertheless believed by colleagues to have an interest in reform of Czechoslovakia's overcentralized neo-Stalinist economy and who succeeded Husák as party first secretary at the end of 1987, along with Husák, now state president, rejected out of hand the Komarek report's radical findings. Apart from ideological opposition to a significant departure from orthodox economic organization and behavior, official economists suggested that people could not easily tolerate the hardships that would result from an extensive curtailment of state control over the economy. But because of pressure from Gorbachev, Jakeš took some steps in early 1989 to improve economic efficiency and expand output: making state companies more independent of central planning and accountable for their profits and losses; setting up workers' self-management councils in factories; dividing the state bank into several autonomous commercial banks; and inaugurating Soviet-style "joint ventures" with western companies to encourage foreign investment and the introduction of Western technology. These changes, however, did not alter the autarchic character of Czechoslovak economic life and did little to improve living conditions.[9]

Pressures for Political Liberalization

Pressure was building for radical political reform. It came from a variety of sources. By 1989, most Czechs and Slovaks were fed up with the Husák regime's neo-Stalinistic repression.

1. Sources of Opposition

In January 1977, inspired by Czechoslovakia's acceptance of the human-rights provisions of the 1975 Helsinki agreements, 300 Czechoslovak intellectuals signed a document called "Charter 77" accusing the government of a systematic discrimination in education, employment, and other areas of society against citizens critical of its policies. During the 1980's despite unrelenting harassment by the Husák regime, the Charter 77 signatories, led by the playwright Václav Havel, sought perestroika-like political reforms, glasnost, and democratization for Czechoslovakia. The Catholic Church was another source of popular resentment of the regime. After a long period of political quiescence, the church hierarchy, led by František Cardinal Tomašek and encouraged by Pope John Paul II, who was elected in 1978 and was an outspoken anticommunist in the late 1970s, began to show sympathy for opponents of the Husák regime's repressive policies. Many people, especially the youth supported the church as the only truly independent institution in Czechoslovakia. They saw in the Church a way to thumb their noses at the regime, so to speak, without inviting retaliation.[10] Convinced that socialism was beyond repair, dissident groups and individuals called for a noncommunist liberal political order. By the late 1980s, small independent political organizations, close to being rudimentary political parties, such as the Renewal Party, the Stream of Rebirth, and the Democratic Initiative, took up the cause of democratic reform.[11]

2. Regime Responses

The progress of Gorbachev's political reforms in the Soviet Union, along with challenges to communist authoritarianism in neighboring Poland and Hungary in 1988 and 1989, put the Jakeš–Husák regime on the defensive. For example, while the authorities arrested and tried Havel for his role in public demonstrations against the government in December 1988, they could not ignore the thousands of public petitions demanding his release. Fearing an explosion of popular wrath in the streets of Prague, the Czechoslovak authorities treated Havel very gently, giving him a sentence of only eight months, which they subsequently shortened to four months and released him in May 1989. The authorities also ceased jamming Radio Free Europe broadcasts and authorized the publication of the works of Franz Kafka after a twenty-year ban.[12]

3. Challenges to Communist Rule

In the summer and fall of 1989, the Czechoslovak political opposition gained confidence from the weakening of communist rule in neighboring countries, noting the appointment of a noncommunist government and the beginning of an ambitious program of reform in Poland and the success of opposition groups in pressuring the Hungarian Communist Party leadership to accept political pluralism and give up its monopoly of power. In June 1989, Havel and other prominent cultural figures signed a document called "Just a Few Sentences," which called upon the government to democratize Czechoslovakia. In August there were demonstrations in Prague commemorating both the twenty-first anniversary of the invasion of Czechoslovakia and the seventy-first anniversary of the founding of the independent republic.[13] Czechoslovak liberals also received a significant lift when communist rule in East Germany collapsed in November 1989 with the resignation of conservative East German party leader Erich Honecker, the ascendancy of political reformers, and the opening of the Berlin Wall on November 9. On November 19, Havel founded a new democratic party called Civic Forum, which drew support from an emerging coalition of opposition groups. On November 24, the Forum led a massive demonstration by 300,000 people in the center of Prague. Accepting Havel's summons to oust communism rather than reform it, the demonstrators insisted on immediate democratization of the Czechoslovak political system. The demonstration, which was an unprecedented gesture of national hostility to the communist leadership, now included industrial workers, who made up 60 percent of the Czechoslovak population. Their willingness to join with the anticommunist intelligentsia in demanding democratic government was further evidence of the weakness and vulnerability of the Jakeš regime.[14]

Collapse of Communist Power

Jakeš was inclined to use force to suppress the public outcry, but, isolated, demoralized, and lacking any support from the Kremlin, he backed off and resigned at the end of November as party chief in favor of Karel Urbanek, a moderate. But Urbanek and Prime Minister Ladislaw Adamec were not sufficiently reformist to satisfy the political opposition and were soon replaced. On December 10, President Husák named Marián Čalfa, a Slovak reformist, as prime minister. Čalfa, who quickly resigned from the Communist Party, appointed a cabinet made up of prominent dissidents including Jan Čarnogurský as deputy prime minister and Jiří Dienstbier as minister of foreign affairs. For the first time in forty years communists did not hold a majority of seats in the Czechoslovak cabinet.[15] Popular pressure for an end, once and for all, of communist dominance continued to mount leading to Husák's resignation as state president and the Prague Parliament's election on December 29 of Václav Havel to replace him. Also, Alexander Dubček, ousted from the party leadership by the Soviets in 1968, was elected chairman of Parliament on December 29.[16]

The Czechoslovak Communist Party took other steps to liberalize the political system to assuage the growing popular opposition to its rule in November and December. It agreed to the abolition of its leading role; it amnestied all political prisoners; and it agreed to new laws guaranteeing freedoms of the press, of assembly, and of association that made possible a rapid pluralization of Czechoslovakia's monolithic political environment.[17]

Meanwhile, the party leadership also contemplated radical economic reform, acknowledging serious problems such as obsolete and bloated smokestack industries, Czechoslovakia's lack of competitiveness on world markets, and huge budget-draining subsidies for foodstuffs and public services. Party reformers were ready to open the Czechoslovak economy to Western investment, though with limits, and to restructure most industries, though it was not clear that he wanted them privatized. But some in the party leadership still wanted to guarantee full employment by maintaining state control over a substantial portion of the economy. Party ideologist Jan Fojtik wanted to preserve as much as possible of the paternalistic socialist order.[18]

Nevertheless, in the beginning of 1990 the Čalfa government took additional steps to punctuate Czechoslovakia's movement away from Communist Party rule. It demanded and obtained a Soviet agreement to remove as soon as possible all Soviet forces from Czechoslovak territory. It terminated all course work and academic programs in Marxist-Leninist studies at the country's universities. And it expanded private entrepreneurship, in particular, the privatization of state-controlled enterprises.[19] Finally, it agreed to hold elections for a new Parliament in June 1990, which would determine if the reforms thus far were sufficient to allow it to continue to lead Czechoslovakia.

1. The June 1990 Parliamentary Elections

The June 1990 parliamentary elections were the country's first free national elections since the end of World War II. Of twenty-two parties fielding candidates for seats in the federal Parliament, only two groups had substantial popular backing: the Civic Forum and its comovement in Slovakia, the Public Against Violence (PAV). These parties drew power from their help toppling the communists and the popularity of their leader, President Havel. They had the largest voter constituency and represented a broad spectrum of ideological views. They called for civil rights, multiparty democracy, the free-market economy, and environmental protection. Some, such as Finance Minister Václav Klaus, who spearheaded parliamentary laws in the early months of 1990 establishing the right of free enterprise with no limit on the scale of a business or the number of its employees and recommended decontrolling prices in two stages beginning in July 1990, argued for fast economic change to a market economy. Havel and others supported the introduction of free enterprise but urged caution and restraint in the movement away from socialism to minimize hardship and discourage social unrest.[20] Smaller parties focused on narrow, highly specific interests. The Slovak National Party, the Democratic Party, the Freedom Party, and the Movement for Autonomous Democracy in Moravia and Silesia all promoted forms of ethnic-based separatism. The Green Party stressed the environment, and the Romany Party defended the interests of Slovakia's Roma (Gypsy) population. The communists, rejecting their previous adherence to strict Marxist dogma, campaigned on a platform of moderate social-democratic–type reform.[21]

The Forum and the PAV received a majority of votes on both the federal and republic levels. The Christian Democratic Bloc, a bloc of parties somewhat to the right of the Civic Forum and less eager than the Forum to proceed with a rapid purge of communists from the central administrative apparatus, received the next largest number of votes. Discredited by their past leadership of the country and by recent public revelations of the degree of secrecy with which they had ruled, the communists received only 15 percent of the votes in the Czech part of the country and 13 percent of the votes in Slovakia. That the communists won as much as they did disheartened some democrats, who felt they did not deserve even that much support. The party's supporters included beneficiaries of the former regime, those fearing retribution, and individuals nostalgic for the past. The communists, however, did not get the support of the youth: they won only 3 percent of voters in the 18 to 24 age group. None of the other parties, many of which were committed primarily to local interests, obtained more than 4 percent of the electorate. Finally, political groups committed to the interests of the Hungarian minority living in southeastern Slovakia, which constituted 4 percent of the total Czechoslovak population, did quite well in winning support of the Hungarian minority, with the Hungarian Christian Democratic Party, electing twelve members to the Federal Assembly.[22]

2. The Soviet Role

The Kremlin had a role in the final collapse of communist rule in Czechoslovakia. The Kremlin decided to stay out of the political ferment in Prague in the summer and fall of 1989 partly because Gorbachev had little affection for the Jakeš–Husák leadership, despite its conspicuous loyalty to the Soviet Union in the aftermath of 1968. Gorbachev considered Husák a reactionary, too narrowly focused, and inept in both the socioeconomic and the political spheres. He regretted the Czech leadership's rejection of glasnost and democratization, believing these reforms could have rejuvenated Czechoslovak socialism.[23]

The Kremlin made no secret of its attitude toward the Czechoslovak conservatives. In an interview broadcast September 4, 1989, on Hungarian television, Kirill Mazurov, a former candidate member of the Soviet politburo, stated "in my view the old guard in Prague should without any special fuss step down from the stage of politics," and in early December the Soviets all but apologized for their 1968 intervention and formally and explicitly endorsed the new Czechoslovak communist leadership's criticism of the 1968 intervention.[24] When the Jakeš regime had to confront the massive popular demonstrations demanding radical political change in November, Gorbachev refused to endorse the use of force to counter antigovernment demonstrations in Prague in November. He also rejected a Soviet military intervention to protect the Jakeš regime. Gorbachev had decided to leave Jakeš to his fate, hoping he would be replaced by reformists who would make the readjustments in policy needed to reinvigorate communist rule. Soviet restraint in 1989 was probably decisive in opening the way for the political opposition to take power.

Establishing a Democratic Political System

Postcommunist Czechoslovakia faced many difficulties in developing a democracy. It had a proliferation of large and small competitive political parties; its executive and legislative institutions were based on unpredictable and unreliable coalitions that complicated and delayed policy making; and its top leadership (President Havel and federal Finance Minister Klaus) was deeply divided.

1. Pluralistic and Competitive Political Parties

The end of communist authoritarianism led to an explosion of political parties. As in other Central and East European countries, there was a sense of newfound freedom and of sheer enjoyment of the novelty of forming political groups free of central control. Beyond those considerations, of course, was Czechoslovakia's societal heterogeneity as a cause of the multiparty system. In addition to the large Czech and Slovak ethnic divisions, there were smaller groups that sought political influence by having their own parties, such as the Moravian Silesian Party in the Czech Republic and the Hungarian Christian Democratic Party in Slovakia. The use of proportional representation, with the two republics divided into multimember districts and a very modest 5 percent of the vote in each republic as a threshold for parties to claim seats, also contributed to the proliferation of political parties. By 1992, almost 100 political organizations, clubs, and groups competed for public support needed to enter government. Only 22 such organizations in Slovakia and 20 in the Czech Republic were large enough to field candidates in parliamentary elections. Even the largest party organizations, the Civic Forum and its successors, the Civic Democratic Party and the Civic Movement, and the Public Against Violence, could not muster more than a third of the electorate in the Czech and Slovak republics. Moreover, Czechoslovak parties tended to be preeminently republic parties, with the Civic Democrats, Civic Movement, and other parties, such as the Christian Democratic Union, primarily based in the Czech lands and the PAV, along with the Slovak National Party and the Movement for a Democratic Slovakia, primarily based in Slovakia. Czechoslovakia lacked truly national, cross-republic political organizations.[25]

2. Weak Executive and Legislative Institutions

As a result of party proliferation, the lack of parties with national constituencies, and the ethnic basis upon which the major parties rested, strong executive leadership and substantial parliamentary cohesion were elusive in the early 1990s. Czechoslovak cabinets tended to be based on coalitions that were fragile rather than stable, that is, difficult to make but easy to break and lacking the kind of unity needed to originate and implement controversial policies in the economic and social spheres. At the same time, the Parliament in Prague was so fragmented that it, too, could not adequately and expeditiously address highly controversial aspects of the transformation, especially revising the federal constitution inherited from the communists, which was ill suited to the needs of the postcommunist era and moving the country rapidly toward a free-market economy. In 1991, the Parliament was so fractious that discussions about amending or replacing the federal constitution had to be held outside its framework. Disagreement over the scope and pace of free-market reforms deeply divided Czechs and Slovaks against each other. And in 1992, the Parliament could not even elect a new president, despite the availability of a very popular candidate in the person of Havel whose support was genuinely national and cut across ethnic lines.

3. Disagreement Between Havel and Klaus

Following the June 1990 parliamentary elections, Havel and Klaus differed over the organization of the Civic Forum. Havel wanted the Forum to be a very loosely structured "catch-all" party that appealed to a truly broad national constituency and served to unify the country's ethnically diverse society behind Havel. Klaus wanted to transform the Forum into a highly disciplined cohesive political organization with a clearly defined agenda and a registered membership that could help the national leadership push controversial free-market economic reforms through the government. Klaus also wanted a strong unified party organization to help him get the presidency, and he used his disciplined political following within the Forum to become its chairman. Klaus's ill-concealed ambition antagonized Havel's followers. Havel also differed with Klaus on the role of the presidency, favoring a chief executive "above politics" that would symbolize the whole nation, not simply a party organization that had been successful in parliamentary elections. Havel somewhat naively assumed he could translate his popularity into political power and could lead the country by acting as a consensus maker. By contrast, Klaus thought Czechoslovakia's president should be like the U.S. president, able to lead a political party that was loyal to his ideas, supported his policies, and got deeply involved in mobilizing political constituencies.[26]

Finally, Havel and Klaus also were at odds over the scope and pace of movement toward a free-market economy. Klaus, a disciple of the conservative American economist Milton Friedman, preferred to privatize state controlled enterprises quickly, even at the risk of provoking hardship. He preferred a minimum of restrictions on the development of capitalism and free enterprise. Klaus spoke for the farmers and other entrepreneurs located in the countryside, where individualism was strong. Havel, on the other hand, tended to sympathize with the wage-earning groups in the densely populated urban centers, who were worried about job security and adequacy of wages. Havel emphasized the importance of a broad social safety net, including state subsidies for food and public utilities, to protect people from hardship.[27]

In February 1991, the Forum split into two separate quasi-independent groups, each with its own name: the Civic Democratic Party led by Klaus, and the Civic Movement led by Havel. Despite the pledge of the Civic Democratic Party and the Civic Movement to remain together in a coalition, they became rivals, disagreeing over key issues, helping to destabilize the national government, and weakening Havel's leadership.[28]

The split in the Forum weakened Havel's positions such as gradualism in moving toward the market economy, tolerance in dealing with former communists—including more than a few of the signatories of Charter 77, whom many radical Czech democrats wanted to purge from the political scene—and compromise in negotiations with the Slovaks, who were demanding increased autonomy from Prague. The split of the Forum also seemed to hurt the PAV, which had difficulty working with Klaus, who was seen in Slovakia as narrowly Czech. The PAV soon was overshadowed by the more radically nationalist Movement for a Democratic Slovakia (MDS). The MDS was led by Vladimír Mečiar, a former communist and now a radical nationalist calling for a reform of the Czechoslovak federation to allow Slovakia autonomy that in effect would have made it virtually an independent state or, failing that, separation of Slovakia from the federation.[29] Finally, by dividing the democrats, the split in the Forum encouraged the former communists to be more aggressive in seeking a political comeback by telling voters: "So you wish to avoid further revolutionary upheavals? Vote for those who have learned their lesson: vote for the Communists."[30]

Movement Toward a Free-Market Economy

Despite their differences, both Havel and Klaus favored dismantling the socialist economy. With Klaus pushing hard for rapid change, the Prague government initiated the closure of inefficient state-owned enterprises, removed price controls on 85 percent of goods sold, restricted the money supply to stabilize the Czechoslovak currency, and privatized thousands of shops. But this reformism initially provoked hardship and aroused controversy over the scope and pace of change.[31]

1. Inflation and Unemployment

Movement toward a free market economy provoked inflation and unemployment. Overall, the whole country experienced a 23 percent decline in industrial production in 1991. The end of subsidies caused a sharp rise in prices of about 25 percent in early 1991 and 45 percent by June. Workers' wages, despite increases, were unable to keep up with inflation, and the standard of living of many Czechs deteriorated sharply.[32] Trying to put these problems in the best light, Finance Minister Klaus said that the reforms had at least not brought the hyperinflation predicted by some economists. But unemployment, a new phenomenon for Czechoslovakia, appeared, reaching 6.3 percent by mid-1991.[33] The disappearance of the East German state in 1990 and the political and economic collapse of the Soviet Union in 1991 aggravated Czechoslovakia's inflation and unemployment. In 1991, the Soviet Union delivered only 50 percent of the energy it had agreed to sell Czechoslovakia. The lack of energy crippled many industrial enterprises. The insolvency of the entire East European market, to which Czechoslovakia traditionally sold most of its exports and from which it purchased most of its imports, also was a significant blow to the Czechoslovak economy. Overall sales to this market declined radically beginning in 1990, throwing many firms into a depression.[34]

2. Problems with Privatization

The Czechoslovak government had difficulty privatizing state-owned enterprises. People had little, if any, spare capital to purchase shares in newly privatized industries. They also lacked entrepreneurial experience, since the communist government had strictly forbidden private shops or businesses. When in the early 1990s the state auctioned off state-run stores to the highest bidders, they sold at bargain prices but to the wrong people. Those who had the money to take advantage of the auctions were former communist officials, money changers, swindlers, and black marketeers—at least that was what angry Czech citizens believed. Some managers deliberately bankrupted their enterprises so that they could buy the ruined businesses at a lower value in the privatization program with their own illicitly acquired funds and/or with the participation of foreign investors who promised to keep them in management positions.[35]

To facilitate privatization of the largest industrial enterprises, the Prague government introduced the voucher system. The government provided citizens with vouchers to be used to buy shares in these firms or in something similar to mutual funds in Western countries. The government was immediately criticized by some who called the voucher system unfair because it seemed to favor those who knew something about the enterprises and appreciated how the vouchers allowed easy acquisition of huge amounts of valuable property—namely, former Communist Party big shots and well-heeled foreign speculators who saw an opportunity to make a quick profit. Indeed, many considered the voucher system as little more than a giveaway program. But the voucher system did stimulate a lot of popular interest in privatization. Eventually people took their vouchers quite seriously. Newly established investment firms helped people use their vouchers to make investments and to learn about risk taking. By January 1992, 8.7 million Czechs and Slovaks had registered their vouchers with over 400 investment firms.[36]

In April 1993, a new stock market opened in Prague. Private investors could now buy and sell shares directly in the newly privatized companies. In addition to internal investors, they attracted increased foreign investment in the Czech economy. A big problem in the functioning of the stock market, however, has been determining the value of shares. Because people bid in vouchers rather than in cash, the monetary value of shares could not be firmly established. Until people put up hard cash for the purchase of shares, determining share prices will be difficult. Eventually, however, the market should pick up, as investment funds to which voucher owners have subscribed purchase shares in the over 800 newly privatized enterprises listed on the market.[37]

Prague's commitment to rapid and complete privatization was criticized. In 1992 Valtr Komarek, the respected director of the Forecasting Institute of the Czech Academy of Sciences, had criticized the obsession with privatization and the abrupt move to a market economy, saying that "shock therapy is out of touch with reality." He pointed to a decline of 22 percent in Czech industrial output and the explosion of unemployment, as well as the development of inflation, which had reached 58 percent by the end of 1991. He argued for caution and restraint to minimize hardship.[38] But Klaus opposed the gradualism advocated by Komarek, arguing that the longer it took to transform the Czechoslovak economy, the more suffering there would be. He called what was left of the state-controlled economy lame-duck enterprises that were draining the country of its resources and perpetuating a mediocre standard of living. He insisted that moribund Czech enterprises must be rejuvenated through free enterprise to make their output competitive in the world market and capable of earning hard currency. The kind of delay Komarek proposed was dangerous to the economic health of the country.[39]

Nevertheless, worried about the precipitous decline in living conditions, Klaus did adjust the rate of change, approving wage increases and continuing state control of some large enterprises to keep a lid on unemployment. The government also kept tight controls over rents and utility bills, thereby helping to insulate most people from the full impact of price decontrol. To ease unemployment, Klaus allowed some inefficient and unprofitable state enterprises, such as Škoda–Pilsen, to limp along with government help.[40]

3. Difficulties in Agriculture

There also were difficulties in freeing up Czechoslovak agriculture from state control. As a result of collectivization in the late 1940s and early 1950s, there was little knowledge about how to develop private farms. There was also a lack of will to do the endless work of private farming. It seemed that the collectivization experience had almost destroyed individual incentive for private farming as practiced in the West. Furthermore, large cooperatives, which to this day control 80 percent of Czech farmland, have proven to be efficient. This efficiency was the result of the autonomy farm managers enjoyed under communist rule, which allowed them to become imaginative and innovative. Also, the cooperative's profits had been shared with its workers, who consequently had more incentive to be productive than industrial workers did. Nevertheless, the Prague government wanted to put agriculture back into private hands.[41]

4. Cleaning up the Environment

A final aspect of economic life in postcommunist Czechoslovakia is environmental pollution. When the communists left office, Czechoslovakia had one of the most polluted environments in Eastern Europe. According to a study by Civic Forum, twenty-five metric tons of pollutants fall every year on every square kilometer of Czech territory, as compared with less than one metric ton in Sweden. More than 30 percent of Czech territory, including Prague, is ecologically devastated. Prague is severely polluted and frequently darkened during the day by a foul smog that endangers both health and spirit and causes many people to flee the city when the smog sets in. Havel summed up the dreadful environmental situation when he observed in June 1992 that "one would shrink from dipping a finger in rivers and there are areas where people almost cannot breathe—in those areas people die younger than elsewhere and children are born ill. Some parts of my country have turned into a lunar landscape."[42]

Czechs and Slovaks are very sensitive to the polluted environment and have staged public demonstrations demanding clean-up policies. Many voters have supported the Green Party, which focuses on environmental problems. But the Czech Greens lack the experienced and talented leadership and organizational unity needed to influence policy. Havel has faced almost insurmountable problems trying to clean up pollution. Remedial policies are costly and Czechoslovakia did not have the resources for such a massive clean-up job. Prague has had to look outside Czechoslovakia for help, turning to Germany and the United States. Moreover, because some of the pollution in Czechoslovakia came from eastern Germany, Poland, and Hungary, Czechs and Slovaks needed the support of their neighbors. For example, industrial plants in the Katowice–Kraków region of southern Poland polluted southern Czechoslovakia. Cooperation between the two countries in solving environmental problems was only beginning.[43]

5. An Economic Balance Sheet

By the end of 1992, the peoples of Czechoslovakia were by no means unanimously supportive of the move away from socialist paternalism toward a market economy. Many were afraid that radical change would diminish the extensive communist cradle-to-grave social-welfare system that had guaranteed all citizens an education, a job, a roof over their heads, and enough food to assure survival.[44] They were particularly critical of inequalities of wealth resulting from an expansion of private enterprise. While successful entrepreneurs able to earn millions of dollars in income emerged, almost 50 percent of people polled in December 1991 said their standard of living had declined, with only 6 percent of people claiming an improvement. Furthermore, Slovaks were more hard hit than Czechs as the country dismantled the communist economy. Slovakia had 11.1 percent unemployment, compared with 4.1 percent for the Czech Republic. Also, as the center of a declining arms industry, Slovakia suffered a decline in industrial output of about 23.6 percent, compared with 18.2 percent in the western part of the country.[45]

By the end of 1992, however, economic conditions, at least in the Czech parts of Czechoslovakia, had improved. By holding down wages, Klaus had helped to make Czech industry competitive. There was a steady flow of investment from abroad into the Czech Republic, which investors saw as a good base for an exploitation of the vast potential market in the territories of the former Soviet Union.[46]

Social Problems

The postcommunist Czechoslovak leadership confronted an array of sociocultural problems inherited from the communist past. Some were of crisis proportions and could not be "swept under the rug."

1. Treatment of Former Communists

From the beginning of the new era Prague had to deal with the question of how to treat former communists. Many people wanted the communists removed from positions of influence in the government and the economy and punished for the brutality and harshness of their rule before 1989. During the campaign preceding the June 1990 parliamentary elections, a large public demonstration in Prague's center demanded the return of millions of dollars worth of assets accumulated by the Communist Party during its forty-two years of rule. Several parties sought to capitalize on the public's anger, demanding that the Communist Party be outlawed.[47] Also, many reformers argued that the communists were reactionary and for that reason should be purged from political life. With a large state-controlled sector of the economy still managed by former communists, anti-communists argued that these people could use their positions to enrich themselves and obstruct reform. They would interfere with the transition to a free-market economy because the new order did not serve their personal interests. With the development of free enterprise, they would lose political influence and economic privilege. Indeed, opponents argued that the former communists still constituted a "closet party," an organization that had no procedures, no leaders, and no headquarters but that nevertheless had a presence and was therefore a potential danger for future democratic development. Even some members of Charter 77 were suspect because they, too, had been party members.[48]

Havel did not share the retributive zeal of many of his colleagues and was reluctant to undertake the sweeping purge of them advocated by hardline reformers. Havel and other Czech liberals believed that a fierce anticommunism undermined the credibility of Czechoslovakia's new democracy by showing its meaner, more hypocritical, and more radical side and that its vengeful intolerance of opposition was subversive of stable political development. Moreover, many former communists were the only people with the managerial skills and experience needed to run the country. But moderation on the communist issue was a political liability for Havel, and, to avoid alienating many of his supporters, who embraced the hard line against former communists, as well as the public at large, which was critical of his moderation, Havel did little to oppose their retributive behavior. In October 1991, the hard-liners put a new law through the federal Parliament in Prague requiring the dismissal from positions of responsibility of those who had worked as secret-police informers or who had worked in any of several key capacities for the former communist establishment. The law applied solely to people with administrative positions, excluding elected officials such as mayors and members of Parliament.[49] While these rulings went farther than those of other formerly communist-ruled states, they did not go as far as some Czechs would have liked—one proposal considered but turned down by Parliament would have applied to 100,000 former communists. In December 1991, however, Parliament passed still another law restricting the activities of former communists. It imposed a one- to five-year jail term for anyone supporting or promoting fascism or communism.[50]

The year 1992 brought little in the way of modification of the zeal of the radicals, who still sought to rid the government of former communists. When it came out that some communists, still in government, had requested Soviet intervention against the Dubček regime in the summer of 1968, the anticommunists were outraged. In early February 1992, they even accused Zdeněk Mlynář, a signatory of Charter 77, of having schemed with the Soviets in connection with their 1968 invasion. Even Dubček did not escape, though he died in October 1992. Honored at the end of 1989 for his early advocacy of liberalization and elected chairman of the federal Parliament in December 1989, Dubček was nevertheless accused by the anticommunist extremists of incompetence and lack of imagination during the Prague Spring. In November 1992, the Charter 77 group, unable to withstand this "witch-hunting" by resentful liberals, decided to disband, noting that its aims had been achieved with the emergence of the postcommunist democratic political system in Prague.[51]

2. Decommunization of Education

Closely related to the treatment of former communists in postcommunist Czechoslovakia was the question of lingering communist influence over the national education system, where administrators and faculty appointed in the communist era were suspected of doubtful loyalty to the new democratic order. As in the political sphere, there were demands that the schools and universities, which were viewed as an essential instrument of democratization, be thoroughly purged of communists. At the college level, many top administrators appointed by the communists were replaced with deans elected by new committees of students, professors, and staff members. And to deal with situations in which many instructors paid only lip service to the new politics by simply changing the names of subjects taught but retaining the same content, other reforms were enacted involving course content. The government got rid of courses in Marxist ideology and the Russian language, which Czechoslovak students had always disliked anyway, and allowed the development of new courses dealing with subjects the communists had ignored, such as modern Czechoslovak history. The decommunization of Czechoslovak education proceeded smoothly, with little opposition or violence. Administrators and faculty who were asked to leave did so without coercion.[52]

3. Street Violence

Still another social problem facing postcommunist Czechoslovakia that was not so easily and effectively addressed was the appearance of street violence. Some people, especially the youth, saw in the country's new high level of personal freedom an opportunity to indulge long-sublimated ethnocultural prejudices. A particular target was migrating Roma (Gypsy) and Vietnamese workers brought to Czechoslovakia by the former communist leadership. Economic hardship, especially unemployment attending the country's development of the free-market economy, has fueled popular prejudice against Roma and Vietnamese peoples. A striking example of this prejudice occurred in the industrial city of Teplice, northwest of Prague, on October 5, 1991, when gangs of several hundred youth called "skinheads," yelling "Czechoslovakia for Czechs," overturned a car carrying two Roma people and beat the driver so badly that he required hospitalization. The general public looked on with indifference as the beatings took place.[53] Because of little experience in dealing with the security problems of an open society, the police have had difficulty coping with the new lawlessness, which is mostly caused by right-wing gangs of young people in their late teens and early twenties, frustrated and demoralized by the high unemployment and social dislocation that has accompanied the introduction of free enterprise.[54]

4. Impact of Democratization on Women

In some respects the impact of postcommunist democratization in the political, economic, and social spheres of Czechoslovak national life was similiar to that of other Central and East European countries. In the early 1990s, Czech and Slovak women faced declining living standards. Both unemployment and competition for jobs increased as Prague steadily tried to move the country toward a free-market economy causing frequent shortages of goods and services essential to run a household. Indeed, as was true elsewhere in the region, Czech and Slovak women were more vulnerable to unemployment than men as the state-controlled economy gave way to privatization with profit rather than full employment as the driving force. Women were especially hard hit by the deregulation of prices. The new policy made shopping more difficult and time consuming than it had been under communist rule when people simply bought goods when they were available and comparison shopping was an unknown phenomenon.

Czech and Slovak women were also victims of political discrimination. New political parties in Czechoslovakia that considered themselves "democratic" paid little attention to women and the grievances they had as a result of the changes wrought by the collapse of communist rule and the development of democracy. Political leaders, and the overwhelming majority of politicians, especially influential ones, were men. They distrusted women and had few incentives to address their concerns, much less share power with them.[55]

At the same time there are some differences between the situation of Czech and Slovak women. For example, religion has a less important influence on women in the Czech lands of Bohemia and Moravia than on Slovak women. In Slovakia, the Catholic Church successfully influenced the conservative leaders in Bratislava to enact a very restrictive law on abortion that had much in common with similiar Polish legislation. Slovak women did not protest this loss of choice as Polish women did; but like Polish women, they had a distaste for abortion, were unhappy over the loss of choice and may have voted for Mečiar's party (in the June 1992 elections) for this reason. Moreover, Slovak women suffered more than Czech women from free-market reforms because Slovakia was economically less developed and less well off than the Western party of the country. The interest of Slovak women in preserving as much as possible of the old communist social net was still another reason for their support of the conservative, neo-communist policies of Mečiar.[56]

By the mid-1990s, it was still not possible to speak of a feminist movement capable of successfully influencing the political systems in Prague and Bratislava. While a few women intellectuals in Prague tried to call attention to gender issues and local women's groups proliferated, most women in both the Czech Republic and Slovakia remained relatively indifferent and willing to silently endure the economic and political inequities of their situation in the national life of their country. Women's groups have not been able to sustain, let alone increase, their membership, which actually declined in the early 1990s, and there is little evidence to suggest a reversal of this trend in the mid-1990s.[57]

Having said all this, there is some ground for cautious optimism about the ability of women to improve their situation in the Czech Republic. The Czech Union of Women, the largest women's organization in the Czech Republic, enjoys government financial backing. The Czech Social Democrats have shown a modest interest in women's issues and a willingness to help women gain some equality in the workplace. They have also shown an interest in recruiting women as party members and sponsoring their candidacy in national and local elections. Still, Czech and Slovak societies have a long way to go in achieving gender equality and in that respect bear a strong resemblance to the societies of other emergent democracies in Central and Eastern Europe.[58]

Postcommunist Czechoslovakia's Foreign Policy

In the early 1990s, postcommunist Czechoslovakia sought a reorientation of foreign policy, which for so long was governed primarily by the interests of the Soviet Union. Prague wanted closer relations with the West while remaining on good terms with the Soviet Union and, after its collapse, with its successors, in particular Russia. At the same time, Czechoslovakia had to overcome historical prejudices and develop good relations with its neighbors, notably Poland and Hungary.

1. The West

According to Havel, the Czech and Slovak peoples live in the very center of Europe, historically the crossroads of different spiritual trends and geopolitical interests. All European conflicts in the present millennium, he argued, have in one way or another touched them. Havel argued that Czechs and Slovaks must take an interest in what goes on in the rest of Europe because events elsewhere in Europe have always affected Czechs more than they have other peoples. Havel also argued that Czechoslovakia should be in NATO because, as a vibrant part of Western development, with its own distinctive contributions, it should participate in the defense of democratic Europe. Havel recalled the Munich crisis of 1938, when the great Western powers bargained away parts of Czechoslovakia to Hitler, refusing to help Czechoslovakia defend its democratic order. Survival depends, Havel said, on his country's participation in a collective defense system.[59]

2. The United States

Postcommunist Czechoslovakia has been especially eager to improve ties with the United States. America was instrumental in the founding of the modern state of Czechoslovakia in 1918 and since then has never had any but friendly relations with Czechoslovakia, even during the communist era. But there are other practical reasons for good Czechoslovak relations with the United States. In its development of a free-market economy, Czechoslovakia has sought an expansion of American investment, especially when the large aid program it expected after the collapse of communist rule did not materialize. Good relations between Czechoslovakia and the United States provided the postcommunist leadership psychological strength in dealing with its two powerful neighbors, Russia and Germany.

Czechoslovak–U.S. relations got off to a good start when Secretary of State James Baker visited Prague in early February 1990. Baker brought with him substantial American material assistance to Czechoslovakia, and his visit symbolized an end to its isolation from the West.[60] When President Havel visited Washington at the end of February 1990, he received a warm welcome from the White House, a standing ovation from Congress, and promises of investment from members of the business and banking communities.[61] In late October 1991, during another visit to Washington, Havel assured Americans willing to invest in Czechoslovakia that they could repatriate their profits in hard currency. Havel did not ask for more direct U.S. aid but for support in getting more U.S. investment. He and other Czechoslovak officials told the administration that moving toward a market economy was more difficult than expected, partly because of a failure to attract Western capital, the collapse of the communist trading system, and the problems of developing a free-enterprise system from scratch.[62]

Although the Bush administration was not forthcoming with a large program of economic and financial assistance, it did provide Czechoslovakia with a package of trade and cultural benefits, not least of which was most-favored-nation treatment for Czech exports to the American market. The administration helped Prague in other ways. The Overseas Private Investment Corporation, which provides insurance for American business firms interested in foreign investment, now operates in Czechoslovakia. The U.S. government supported Czechoslovakia's request to join the International Monetary Fund, making Prague eligible for Export–Import Bank lending programs. The U.S. government also supported a location in Prague for the European Development Bank to aid East European countries in reconstruction. Washington also reopened the American consulate in Bratislava, which had been closed in 1948.[63]

In addition to economic issues, Havel had other broad concerns. In an address to Congress during his February 1990 visit, he asked the United States to help the Soviet Union navigate the "immensely complicated" road to political and economic democracy, this despite the fact that his country had for so long been a victim of Soviet aggrandizement. The sooner and the more peacefully the Soviet Union moved toward political pluralism and a market economy, the better not only for Czechoslovakia but also for other new East European democratic governments.[64] During his second visit to Washington at the end of October 1991, Havel returned to the Soviet theme and emphasized how negatively the growing Soviet economic and political crises in the past year were affecting Czechoslovakia. Economic paralysis in the Soviet Union had put a virtual end to trade between the two countries, severely hurting the Czechoslovak economy, which was another reason why Czechoslovakia needed American investment and access to American markets.[65]

Havel also wanted U.S. support of Czechoslovakia's bid for membership in NATO. But NATO was a long way from accepting Czechoslovakia and other former communist countries as full members. The Western allies were sensitive to Russian anxieties. President Boris Yeltsin opposed Czechoslovakia's membership in NATO, which was still viewed by Russian conservatives as a threat to Russian security. In addition, the NATO allies did not want to assume the burden of defending the new governments of Central and Eastern Europe in conflicts in which Western interests would be minimal and the liabilities costly, especially if the enemy turned out to be Russia. The Bush administration told Havel that NATO could not at the moment give Czechoslovakia the security guarantee it wanted.[66]

3. Germany

Havel fostered friendship with Germany to facilitate Czechoslovakia's integration into Western Europe and to encourage German financial assistance and investment in joint ventures. He chose West Germany rather than the United

States or the Soviet Union for his first official visit abroad as Czechoslovakia's chief executive. During this visit in January 1990, he discussed practical matters such as border crossings and the protection of the environment. But the real importance of the visit was symbolic and showed the Czechoslovak state's determination not to allow the past to poison the present and the future. In other conciliatory gestures, he offered an apology on behalf of his countrymen to the 3.2 million Germans who had been expelled from their homes in the Sudetenland at the end of World War II when Czechoslovakia recovered that region from Germany. Havel also gracefully accepted German reunification in 1990 and established good relations with the new unified Germany.[67]

Chancellor Helmut Kohl of Germany was responsive to Czechoslovak initiatives. Healing the wounds between Germany and the region of Eastern Europe was important to German economic, political, and psychological well-being. But the question of the Sudetenland remained troublesome. Kohl wanted Havel's government to do more than apologize for the expulsion: he wanted Prague to acknowledge the harsh treatment of Sudeten Germans at the end of the war with a view toward indemnifying some, in particular, those still living in Czechoslovakia, who had lost property. The League of Expelled Sudeten Germans lobbied Kohl to get the Prague government to restore the property rights of the expelled. Germans. This issue was sensitive for Kohl because many descendants of the Sudeten Germans lived in southern German states such as Baden-Württemberg, where the chancellor's Christian Democratic Party faced an uphill struggle in the spring 1992 elections. But Havel was under strong pressure not to concede too much to Germany. For their part, the Czechs wanted to raise claims against Germany for the human and material damage done to Czechoslovakia during World War II. Nevertheless, at the end of February 1992, Havel and Kohl met in Prague and concluded a treaty with great symbolic importance, even if it was short of specific commitments. The Czechs acknowledged their forceful expulsion of Germans after the war, and the German side gave unqualified support for Czechoslovakia's entry into the European Community. The treaty, however, did not address the issue of restored property rights, leaving open an unresolved issue that would complicate German–Czech relations. Right-wing pressure groups have been urging the Bonn government to hold back on economic and political concessions to Czechoslovakia.[68]

In other respects, however, Czechoslovakia's relations with Germany thrived in the early 1990s, and by mid-1992 Germany had become Czechoslovakia's most important foreign investor. German entrepreneurs, taking advantage of next-door-neighbor status and long historical and cultural ties, now account for 75 percent of all foreign investment in Czechoslovakia. The overwhelming German economic presence in Czechoslovakia by far exceeded the American presence, which, incidentally, lagged behind that of Austria, France, and Switzerland.[69] But, although appreciated for its enormous contribution to the country's economic growth and development, German investment was seen by some as a mixed blessing. Czechs have become uncomfortable as hoards of German executives have filled Prague's best restaurants and hotels in ways that call to mind the German presence in the country during World War II. Czechoslovak politicians spoke of a German economic *Anschluss* and have discussed the possibility of erecting barriers to slow German investment.

4. The Soviet Union and Russia

While seeking to develop strong links to the West, Czechoslovakia reassured the Soviet Union and the Russian Republic of its friendship, readiness for cooperation, and desire to improve trade. But there were problems between postcommunist Czechoslovakia and the Kremlin. Havel wanted the 80,000 Soviet troops stationed in Czechoslovakia in 1990 to be promptly withdrawn. Although Moscow agreed to a joint Czechoslovak–Soviet commission of military and civilian officials to facilitate withdrawal, it moved very slowly. As was the case with Soviet troop withdrawals from Poland and Hungary, the Kremlin could not immediately house, feed, and employ so many returning military personnel.

But pressure inside Czechoslovakia for a prompt withdrawal of Soviet troops steadily mounted in early 1990. There were popular demonstrations against the continued Soviet military presence in Prague and other Czechoslovak cities. Strong Czechoslovak language to the Soviets may have encouraged them to act. At the end of February 1990, they signed a formal agreement to begin an immediate withdrawal of 18,500 soldiers and their weapons, with the remainder of Soviet forces to be withdrawn by July 1991. Despite logistical and political problems, in particular the dissatisfaction of high-ranking Soviet officials with the precipitous disengagement of the USSR from Eastern Europe, the Soviets lived up to this agreement, and by the end of 1991 all Soviet occupation forces had been withdrawn from Czechoslovakia.[70]

5. Poland and Hungary

Finally, postcommunist Czechoslovakia set about repairing political fences with its Central European neighbors with whom it shared problems moving away from socialism to a market economy, the need for security in connection with the disintegration of the Soviet state, and a strong interest in joining the European Community and NATO. President Havel agreed to meet periodically with his Polish and Hungarian counterparts to address these problems. The first of these trilateral summits took place in February 1991 in Visegrád, Hungary, at which the leaders of the three countries expressed sympathy for the Baltic peoples' efforts to emancipate themselves from Soviet control and reiterated a shared interest in disbanding the Warsaw Pact and the CMEA. Although no formal agreements were concluded, the Visegrád meeting was of great symbolic significance in showing Czechoslovakia's willingness to cooperate with its neighbors on the basis of mutual self-interest. Other summits followed, one in the southern Polish city of Kraków in October 1991, at which the "Visegrád" leaders reiterated their determination to achieve membership in the EU and NATO and their interest in expanding trade with one another to ease the difficulties of introducing free-market reforms. Havel hosted a third meeting in May 1992 in Prague, with a similar agenda. The three countries reemphasized their long-term goal of becoming full members of NATO and moved a bit closer toward the development of a free trade zone of their own by including a reference to it in a joint communiqué. After the summit, officials of the three governments signed a limited customs agreement as a first step toward lifting all customs barriers in a future free trade agreement.[71]

Czechoslovakia had a special problem with Hungary over the newly constructed Gabčíkovo-Nagymaros hydroelectric dam on the Danube. The postcommunist Hungarian leadership criticized the hydroelectric project for the way in which it adversely affected the flow and the fish of the Danube River and defaced the surrounding landscape, which had become pockmarked with concrete facilities. Some Hungarian politicians spoke of scrapping the project before its completion. The Slovaks, however, defended the dam, saying they needed the dam's cheap electricity to bring about the region's economic regeneration, to enable closure of two antiquated and polluting coal-powered plants, and to provide an alternative to dependence on unreliable Soviet energy supplies. Prague angered Budapest by refusing to block the completion of the dam. Ultimately, the Hungarians backed away from their opposition to the dam to avoid a clash with the Slovak government, which increasingly was coming under the influence of hypernationalistic politicians, and because the dam benefited the Hungarian minority in southern Slovakia. The dam was completed and is now in operation.[72]

The Split of Czechoslovakia

A major consequence of the move away from communism was a rejuvenation of the historical antagonism between Slovaks and Czechs. In the early 1990s, relations between the two peoples steadily soured. By the end of 1992, their political leaders had agreed to separate their countries into two independent nation-states known as the Czech Republic and Slovakia. The historical Czechoslovak state ceased to exist after December 31, 1992.

1. Roots and Causes

The split had its roots in a long history of somewhat contentious relations between Slovaks and Czechs since their joining together in 1918 to form the modern Czechoslovak state. During the interwar period (1919–39), Slovaks resented a perceived domination of the new state by the Czechs, who constituted about 60 percent of its population. Czechs were more numerous in the federal cabinet, bureaucracy, and army. Slovaks also resented a perceived Czech effort to use their influence in the Prague government to homogenize and unify the country's multiethnic population at the expense of the Slovak cultural identity. Some Slovaks yearned for independence of Prague.[73] When the Nazis occupied and annexed most of the Czech lands during World War II, the Slovaks became independent under a Nazi puppet government led by the conservative cleric Monsignor Jozef Tiso, who has been accused of cooperating with Nazi Holocaust policies, though his defenders deny his complicity.[74]

After the war the Slovaks abruptly lost their independence, were reunited with the Czechs, and were ruled by the communists, who transformed Czechoslovakia into a highly centralized dictatorship that, again in the view of Slovaks, tended to be dominated by Czechs, although Slovakia did gain some political and economic advantages. For example, from the outset of communist rule, there were two separate branches of the Communist Party, one for Czechs and the other for Slovaks; in 1968, Alexandr Dubček, a Slovak, came to power, and, although his rule lasted only several months because his liberal reform program angered the Kremlin and provoked its removal of him from power, he was succeeded by another Slovak communist, Gustáv Husák. Moreover, at the end of 1968, the Communist Party approved a division of the country into two self- governing republics, one made up of Czech lands (Bohemia and Moravia) and the other comprising Slovakia. But the Slovaks recognized that whatever autonomy they enjoyed was compromised by the strong central government still heavily influenced by Czechs.[75]

Although communist Czechoslovakia remained too highly centralized to suit the Slovaks, they fared rather well economically during the 1970s and 1980s. The Slovaks appreciated the communist "cradle-to-grave" welfare system, whatever its imperfections, and they benefited materially from the communist policy of expanding Slovak industry, especially weapons production, which increased employment and brought a modest improvement in living standards. By 1989, despite their dislike of its repressive behavior in the political and cultural spheres, many Slovaks had found communist rule tolerable, in comparison with most Czechs, who despised its violations of human rights and its managerial ineptitude that prevented them from reaching Western levels of material well-being. The collapse of communist rule at the end of 1989, therefore, was a mixed blessing for the Slovaks, who also resented the way in which it had been directed and implemented primarily by Czechs.[76]

In the early 1990s, the Slovaks had much to complain about in the new democratic order. Slovak voters and their leaders did not like the speed with which the Prague government wanted to introduce the market economy, which in the short term caused more suffering in Slovakia than in the Czech part of the country. In 1991, 42 percent of Slovaks, with good reason, had reservations about the rapid privatization Czechoslovakia Finance Minister Klaus planned.[77] By April 1992, Slovakia had 12 percent unemployment, as compared with 4 to 5 percent for the Czech economy. Bohemia and Moravia had increased exports to the West, while Slovakia experienced economic stagnation from a sharp reduction in demand for its weapons. Slovakia, the home of giant energy-consuming and polluting smelting, chemical, and weapons-producing industries built by the Husák regime after 1968, saw unemployment rise as these industries, inefficient, unprofitable, and a drain on the national wealth, gradually closed. Slovak industrial exports, almost completely dependent on two buyers, the Soviet Union and East Germany, suffered when these markets almost completely disappeared with the collapse of communist rule elsewhere in Eastern Europe and the Soviet Union.[78]

Slovaks also saw themselves left out of the programs of Western economic and technological assistance. Of 3,000 joint ventures with Western companies, only 600 had located in Slovakia by the fall of 1991. To ease the transition away from communist paternalism to a free-enterprise economic system, many Slovaks thought the number of state-owned enterprises should exceed privately owned ones to provide jobs for all its citizens. They also wanted an adequate social safety net that would minimize hardships resulting from the curtailment of state subsidies and state control over economic life, which in the past had assured full employment and "cradle-to-grave" social security.[79]

In the spring of 1990, Slovak politicians proposed a new name for Czechoslovakia that would emphasize their equality with the Czechs. While Slovak members of the Parliament in Prague were willing to remove the word "socialist" from the title of the state, they demanded that the word "Czechoslovak" be dropped in favor of "Czech" and "Slovak." For Slovaks the word "Czechoslovak" carried a pejorative thrust. They saw it as an artificial concept implying centralism and Czech domination. On April 20, the federal Parliament struck a compromise, voting to name the country the Czech and Slovak Federative Republic, with permission for Slovakia to use a hyphen in place of the "and" so that the initials would be C-SFR.[80]

But more important to the Slovaks than the name of the Czechoslovak state was its constitutional makeup. To protect their interests vis-à-vis the Czechs, the Slovaks wanted to reform the federation to enlarge their autonomy of the central government in Prague—they wanted sovereignty in the federal system. This meant enough Slovak control over economic life to allow, for example, a slower pace toward the free market than in the Czech Republic. They also wanted to have their own separate foreign relations and to be recognized as a separate administrative entity in the United Nations and other international organizations.[81]

While some radical elements from the outset of the new democratic era wanted Slovak independence of Prague, other more moderate Slovak nationalist politicians proposed a reform of the postcommunist Czechoslovak state based on power sharing between the national and republic governments in economic, financial, and other policy-making areas, including protection of minority rights. The Slovaks wanted the changes put in a treaty between the separate Czech and Slovak republics to emphasize that ultimate sovereignty rested in each of them rather than in a central government in Prague. In effect, the Slovaks were asking the Czechs to accept a radical transformation of the historical structure of the Czechoslovak state into a loose confederation of equal partners.[82]

Slovak grievances found expression in the sudden appearance of ultraradical nationalist groups in Slovakia, such as the *Stur* Association, the Slovak National Party (SNP), and the Slovak National Renewal Party.[83] The SNP won nine seats in the House of Nations of the national Parliament in the May 1990 parliamentary elections. Indeed, public-opinion polls in the summer of 1990 confirmed a rising trend of popular support for Slovak nationalism that worked in favor of the SNP and against the moderate Public Against Violence. Furthermore, with the eventual split of the Forum into separate party organizations, Slovak nationalists worried about the growing influence of federal Finance Minister Klaus and his free-market views at the expense of the more moderate policies of President Havel, who was inclined to conciliate the Slovaks. Indeed, as differences between Klaus and Havel threatened a rift in the Civic Forum, Slovaks could see only more unwelcome Czech domination.

2. Czech and Slovak Efforts to Compromise

Although Havel and Klaus were sympathetic to Slovak concerns and to a point were willing to try to accommodate Slovakia for the sake of keeping the country unified, they were unwilling to decentralize the government, weaken it, and threaten the country's unity. Indeed, Klaus believed a strong central government was necessary to see the country successfully through the transition from communism to a market economy and suspected that Slovak politicians in Bratislava and Prague wanted autonomy to slow down the rate of change toward the free market in Slovakia. He opposed Slovak proposals for decentralization in the areas of banking and budgets that would have allowed the Slovak Republic government to avoid rapid privatization and an explosion of unemployment and helped to kill a power-sharing bill in the national Parliament at the end of 1990. He also opposed a Slovak demand for local responsibility in the protection of minority rights that would allow Bratislava independence in the treatment of its Hungarian minority.

During discussions with Slovak nationalists in 1991 and 1992, Klaus began to wonder if the Czechs might not be better off without Slovakia because of its poverty, its apparent opposition to the rapid introduction of a free market, the increasingly anti-Semitic character of Slovak nationalism seen in a revival of popular interest in the World War II leadership of Monsignor Tiso, and the increasingly authoritarian behavior of Slovak Prime Minister Mečiar.[84] Indeed, much of what was happening during the early 1990s in Slovak local politics disturbed Czech liberals. For example, with his supporters enjoying a 60 percent majority, Mečiar used the Slovak Parliament in Bratislava to expand his personal influence replacing personnel in the universities, the health service, and the bureaucracy with party loyalists.[85] Mečiar was especially heavy-handed in his dealings with the Slovak media, which he believed the state had a right and an obligation to regulate. And while the Slovak constitution adopted in 1992 did not permit censorship, a new press law bristled with restrictions, including a clause that required quotations of public officials to be submitted to a watchdog commission for authorization before publication.[86]

Havel was somewhat less critical of Slovak nationalism than Klaus, who saw its ascendancy, and especially Slovak demands for complete administrative autonomy of Prague, as a dangerous threat to his free-market policies. By contrast, Havel gave priority to the unity of the Czechoslovak state and the preservation of its territorial integrity and was inclined to go out of his way to conciliate the Slovak nationalists to avoid a split of the country. Thus, he had reappointed Marián Čalfa, as his first prime minister in early 1990 and had agreed to rename Czechoslovakia the Federation of Czechs and Slovaks. He also explored ways of granting the Slovaks at least some of the autonomy they wanted, proposing at the end of 1990 the establishment of a constitutional court to resolve constitutional crises of the kind arising out of the controversy between Czechs and Slovaks. Knowing that most Czechs and Slovaks did not want to see their country torn apart, he called for a referendum to determine popular sentiment about the future of the Czechoslovak federation that would goad both Czech and Slovak politicians to work harder for a compromise constitution that would keep the country together.[87]

But in 1991, time began to run out for Havel's efforts to preserve the unity of his country. Slovak nationalist agitation gained momentum in Bratislava as radical Slovak nationalists began urging Slovakia's withdrawal from the Czechoslovak federation. In late November 1990 the Slovak Parliament in Bratislava threatened to declare republic laws paramount over those of the federal government, while the Slovak mass media called for Slovak secession from the federation if Slovak demands for autonomy were not met.[88] And, since discussions between Czech and Slovak leaders on the constitutional reform of the federation produced no agreement in 1991, Havel, in a nationally televised speech, spoke of a crisis that threatened national survival and asked the federal Parliament in Prague to grant him special presidential powers to dissolve it and rule by decree until a new Parliament more sympathetic to his conciliatory approach was elected.[89]

3. The Path Toward Separation

In parliamentary elections held in June 1992, Klaus's Civic Democratic Party, which opposed weakening the federation, won 33 percent of the ballots cast in the Czech Republic for the federal Parliament. Mečiar's Movement for a Democratic Slovakia, which was committed to autonomy or, failing that, Slovak independence, won about 33 percent of the ballots cast for the national Parliament as well as 37 percent of the popular vote for the Slovak republic Parliament.[90]

After the elections, Klaus and Mečiar renewed discussions on amending the federal constitution, trying for a compromise that would accommodate Czech and Slovak positions on the future structure of the Czechoslovak state, even though those positions were essentially the same as they had been for the past two years. Mečiar was still calling for a loose economic and defense union between Czechs and Slovaks, with each republic having its own banking and credit system and separate membership in international organizations like the United Nations and the European Union. Mečiar believed that this plan would not mean a breakup of Czechoslovakia. He also said that he wanted to slow down the pace of Czechoslovakia's transformation to a market economy. Klaus's policies, he said, hurt the Slovaks unfairly, with unemployment four times greater in Slovakia than in the Czech part of the country.[91] Klaus was equally committed to his previous positions. He insisted that only a strong central government was capable of implementing reforms for the entire country. He believed that the loose federation that Mečiar proposed would interfere with Czechoslovakia's development of a free-market economy and delay its membership in the European Union.[92]

Both Klaus and Mečiar also ruled out a referendum on separation. Already convinced that separation was inevitable and perhaps preferable to a weakened federation that would be prejudicial to Czech interests, Klaus did not want to consult public opinion, which, according to recent polls, favored the preservation of Czechoslovakia's unity.[93] Mečiar also had no sympathy for a referendum, viewing the establishment of an independent Slovakia as an opportunity to strengthen his political power, inasmuch as he would be the logical choice for leadership of the new state. Klaus and Mečiar finally agreed in late June 1992 that the issue of separation and independence should be decided definitively by the two republic-level Parliaments, that is to say, by the politicians and not the people, by September 30.[94]

In mid-July 1992, however, there was a momentary glimmer of hope that a split might be avoided. Mečiar seemed to have had second thoughts about separation. He was aware that many Slovak voters did not support a total break with the Czechs and a dissolution of the federation. A poll conducted the preceding April by Bratislava's Center for Social Analysis showed that only 19 percent of the people in Slovakia favored an independent Slovak state.[95] Mečiar also seemed to have been surprised by a new willingness of Czech politicians, after so many decades of commitment to a unified Czechoslovak state, to accept separation. The change reflected the growing influence of Klaus at the expense of Havel and the fact that many Czech deputies in the federal Parliament believed, as Klaus apparently did, that the Czech lands would be better off without the Slovaks because of the way the Slovaks had tried to delay moves to a market economy. Finally, Mečiar may have had some doubts about Slovakia's economic viability after separation from the Czech lands, which had shared their wealth with other parts of the country since unification in 1918.

These considerations may well have led Mečiar to modify the conditions for Slovak participation in a federation with them. He withdrew his demand for a separate Slovak banking and currency system, almost acknowledging that Slovakia might not be ready to go it alone economically, and backed off on previous demands that Slovakia be given its own seat at the United Nations.[96] But these concessions did not move Klaus. He insisted that the Slovaks accept the federation in its existing form, with a strong central government in Prague and with the present federal commitment to a rapid introduction of free enterprise.

Havel's effort to keep the country together was decisively compromised in early July 1992 when he failed to win the federal presidency in the first of two ballots. Given the rules governing presidential elections, whereby either Slovaks or Czechs had the power to block any candidate (a 60 percent majority was needed for election), Slovak nationalists denied Havel the presidency.[97] But Czech deputies loyal to Klaus in the federal Parliament were also to blame for the failure of Havel's bid for reelection in scheduling a second ballot too quickly after the first one to allow Havel time to lobby for support among moderate deputies.[98] When in mid-July the Slovak Parliament declared the sovereignty of Slovakia, Havel realized there was no point in carrying on a fight to keep the country together and resigned the presidency, saying he did not want to preside over the liquidation of the Czechoslovak state. He also did not want to antagonize Czech deputies in the federal Parliament whose support he would need were he to run for the presidency of a new independent Czech republic.[99]

4. The End of Czechoslovakia

On November 25, the Czechoslovak federal Parliament passed a law that divided the country into two separate republics, effective December 31, 1992. The division was approved despite reservations in the Parliament about the breakup—in September a national poll showed that only one-third of the population of the country favored a breakup. The Parliament provided Czech and Slovak politicians with a legal framework for the division so as to reassure foreign investors. The law provided for a temporary joint currency until both republics had established their own monetary systems; for the setting up of a customs union; and for the division of the federal armed forces into two separate organizations, one for the Czech Republic and one for Slovakia.[100]

Aftermath of the Split

The aftermath of the split has been different for Slovaks and Czechs. In succeeding years, the cost of the split seemed higher for the Slovaks than for the Czechs.

1. Slovakia

Cut off from the Czechs, the Slovak government became increasingly conservative as Prime Minister Mečiar wielded an enormous personal influence over the country's economic life. During 1993, he was in effect minister in charge of privatization and chief of the National Property Fund, which managed the privatization process. Mečiar used his influence to slow down privatization. By the beginning of 1994, only 5 percent of Slovakia's state-owned enterprises had been privatized, leaving nearly the entire economy under state control. This was a critical disincentive to foreign investment, which in any event had been modest when compared with the nearly $2 billion entering the Czech Republic when 40 percent of state enterprises were privatized by mid-1994.[101] Furthermore, throughout 1993, afraid of provoking additional unemployment that could destabilize the new state, Mečiar's government continued to subsidize Slovakia's inefficient and unprofitable arms industry, draining precious resources from growth and development. Still, unemployment increased in some industrial centers from 13 percent to 20 percent, and the overall rate increased from 10.4 percent at the end of 1992 to 14.4 percent by the end of 1993. And these statistics do not include hidden unemployment, especially throughout both the public and private sectors of industry. With a decline in the number of industrial workers by 11 percent and construction workers by 14 percent in 1993, the Slovak economy for most of 1994 was stagnant, with gross domestic product down by about 3.7 percent and inflation running annually at about 22 percent.[102]

During 1993, Slovakia also experienced serious administrative problems. For example, when the split occurred, Slovakia lacked many of the governmental bodies necessary to run an independent state. Although both Czechs and Slovaks had republic-level assemblies and governments before the split, the federal government in Prague controlled everything from the military to the central bank. Unlike Prague, which inherited most of the federal structure and simply removed "Slovak" from the names of ministries and agencies, Bratislava had to build much of its own civil service, foreign service, and supporting organizations.

Furthermore, despite the need for political stability, independent Slovakia has not had much of it. Mečiar's MDS suffered defections as leaders quarreled about privatization and the treatment of the Hungarian minority, with some radical nationalists calling for the assimilation of the Hungarians by restricting use of the Hungarian language in schools and local administration. Four government ministers quit or were fired in the first six months of 1993, and one minister,

Lubomir Dolgos, upset over criticism of his efforts to move forward with privatization, formed a new opposition political group in the Slovak Parliament. By mid-1993, Mečiar's party had to look for support from the ultranationalistic SNP, which favored a crackdown on the Hungarian minority despite the risks for Slovakia's relations with the Hungarian Republic.[103]

By the end of 1993, people were very dissatisfied with the economy, which had not brought them the well-being they had expected and had been promised by their separatist political leaders. Indeed, by mid-1994 it was clear that many Slovaks—about 56 percent of the population according to a Bratislava polling agency—were beginning to regret the split from the Czechs. Had the federation survived, they believed, money from the well-off western part of the country would have flowed eastward to the economically depressed parts of Slovakia, as it had in the past, and life there would have been better. Popular willingness to go along with independence in 1992 gave way in 1993 and 1994 to a pervasive sullenness and disappointment with the country's new political situation.[104]

Slovak voters increasingly blamed Mečiar for the country's problems after independence. His popularity slipped precipitously, from 80 percent in 1992 to 20 percent in 1993.[105] Popular disenchantment with him reached a climax in March 1994, when the Slovak Parliament, disgusted by Mečiar's failure to improve living conditions and angered by the discovery that he had been selling off state companies at bargain-basement prices to his political cronies, forced his resignation by a vote of no-confidence. President Michal Kováč appointed Jozef Moravčik, a former Czechoslovak foreign minister and a leader of the no-confidence vote against Mečiar, as Mečiar's successor. Moravčik's government was a "grand coalition" of groups on the right and the left, including former communists, and several small parties. As one Slovak source reportedly put it, the new government was more political than professional, lacking not only an economic program but the consensus needed to transact policy.[106]

Moravčik did not last long in office. Mečiar was still a powerful rival, and his opposition to rapid privatization still resonated with many voters.[107] In parliamentary elections in Slovakia in mid-October 1994, Mečiar's MDS won 35 percent of the vote, a plurality, but one lacking a clear mandate that would give him a strong power base in Parliament. To return to power he needed to form a coalition, which took several months of deal making with other parties. By December he had a coalition, though it was extremely fragile because it consisted of two small parties on opposite ends of the political spectrum. One party was the SNP, and the other, on the extreme left, was the Association of Slovak Workers. Neither the former communists nor the followers of Moravčik would have anything to do with Mečiar's new political grouping.

Mečiar's return to power was tentative. While his antiprivatization policies were popular, the fact that he could do no better than 35 percent of the popular vote suggested that most Slovaks remained suspicious of him as the architect of the split of Czechoslovakia, which many now regretted. Moreover, the Hungarian minority in southeastern Slovakia was worried about a new campaign of discrimination because of the influence in the Mečiar regime of the SNP and because Mečiar had condemned the demands of the Hungarian citizens of Slovakia for administrative autonomy. Their anxiety was shared by the government in Budapest, which continued to lobby in Bratislava for equitable treatment of Slovakia's Hungarian population.

Finally, Slovakia has experienced difficulties in the foreign-policy area since gaining independence. Relations with Hungary deteriorated not only because of Mečiar's tough talk to Budapest about some Hungarian military exercises that were seen in Bratislava as a threat to Slovak security but also because of Budapest's complaints about the treatment of Slovakia's Hungarian minority. Although Hungarians in Slovakia are not as badly off as either the Gypsy population or the small group of Slovak people living in Hungary, they are the object of some discrimination, in particular, the Slovak government's efforts to discourage the use of Hungarian in the transaction of official business, thereby placing Slovak Hungarians at a disadvantage economically as well as politically. But Hungarian diplomacy is not without blame for the strain in relations between the two countries in the mid-1990s. Hungarian officials are reputed to have hinted at the possibility of raising claims to territory inhabited by Hungarian people in Slovakia by saying something to the effect that Hungary originally gave up control of this land in 1919 to the Republic of Czechoslovakia, and now that Czechoslovakia no longer exists, the territory should come back to Hungary.[108]

On the positive side, Slovakia has persuaded the West to show a new interest in its economic development, in particular, its difficulties in moving away from the state-controlled economy to some version of capitalist free enterprise. For example, in June 1993, the International Monetary Fund agreed to grant Slovakia $90 million in loans. The cash inflow would buttress Slovakia's small hard- currency reserves and help the national bank ease up on its money supply, enabling it to release more credits to privatizing companies. To secure the loan, Slovak leaders had to agree to control their budget deficit by cutbacks in spending for social services and subsidies to state-controlled enterprises. The Slovak leadership also agreed to curtail imports from hard-currency countries to bolster its own currency, with a view eventually to making it convertible. As a first step, the government imposed a 20 percent surcharge on imports from the European Union, the European Free Trade Area, and the Visegrád Group, which includes Slovakia, the Czech Republic, Hungary, and Poland.[109]

Sensitive to the limits of what can be obtained economically and militarily from the West, Slovak leaders seek a strengthening of relations with the former Soviet republics, with which they have much in common, starting with the communist background of many of their top leaders. But the likelihood of Slovakia's profiting from links to the former Soviet republics is at the moment dim because of intense internal turmoil and poverty in those republics. Moreover, President Boris Yeltsin has not shown the same interest in Slovakia that he has shown in the Czech Republic. Slovak–Russian relations are correct but far from what the Bratislava government would like in terms of expanded trade.

2. The Czech Republic

Klaus's conventional free-market strategy has brought a measure of prosperity to the Czech Republic, with a budget surplus and, reportedly, a 16 percent expansion of Czech exports to Western Europe despite recession there during 1993.[110] Unemployment in Bohemia and Moravia remained low throughout 1993, hovering around 4 percent of the workforce, in comparison with the near 15 percent rate in Slovakia in early 1994. By late 1993, unemployment in the Czech Republic stood at less than 3 percent.[111] Inflation leveled off, was manageable, and did not seem to be a drag on Czech economic growth. At the same time, progress toward a free-market economy in the Czech Republic in 1993 and early 1994 occurred without provoking social tensions, because Klaus diminished state control only gradually in exchange for employment stability and societal peace. The Czech Republic seems to be thriving in the aftermath of the split. Living standards are slowly but steadily improving as foreign investment remains stable with good prospects of an expansion as a result of the Czech Republic's evident political stability and commitment to the establishment of a free-market economy. The hustle and bustle of Prague bespeaks an incipient prosperity that contrasts sharply with the drab environment of Bratislava, which is reminiscent of conditions everywhere in Eastern Europe when the communists were in control.

There is, however, a cloud on the domestic horizon that, paradoxically, concerns an ethnic minority, this time the Moravians, who want greater control over their local affairs, including a separate army.[112] Jan Krycer, leader of the Movement for a Self-Governing Democracy–Association for Moravia and Silesia (MSD-SMS), in February 1993, only a month after the split, called on the Czech Republic Parliament to name the country "Czech Lands" to emphasize the republic's different regions. He proposed a referendum to allow people living in Moravia the opportunity to vote on whether or not they identified with historic Moravia.

Klaus and Havel have reacted negatively to this Moravian challenge, fearful that concessions to Moravian ethnonationalists will threaten the unity of the new Czech Republic. They do not want to grant the administrative regions that make up the Czech Republic a budgetary and legislative authority independent of Prague. Moreover, a constitution eventually adopted by the Czech Republic government on the eve of the split proclaimed respect for the rights of minorities. Both Havel and Klaus insist that this constitution sufficiently safeguards the interests of different groups in the Czech Republic. By the end of 1994, the Czech government was still wrestling with the problem of how much authority to assign the seventeen regions into which the republic had been divided. In the interest of fairness to the Moravians, it had agreed in principle to allow the regions a role in regulating policy in the social areas, notably education, health care, and social services. Moravian particularism, however, remains a problem, though not a severe one for the new Czech Republic.[113]

Finally, parliamentary elections, held in the beginning of June 1996, the first since the split of the country, weakened Klaus's leadership. Although his Civic Democratic Party won a plurality of about 29.5 percent of voters, the opposition Social Democrats were not far behind with 26.5 percent.[114] The outcome was a surprise, at least for outsiders in the West, where Klaus was held in high repute for his successful economic reform policies, which by mid-1996 had led to a sharp reduction in inflation and rock-bottom unemployment. But Czech voters were not surprised. By 1996, they were critical of Klaus's seemingly long tenure and his perceived neglect of health, education, the environment, and burgeoning crime in the urban areas as he moved the country toward a free-market economy. Many were put off by Klaus's occasionally strong rhetoric in defense of capitalism and the free market in which he emphasized individualism, self-reliance, and diminished expectations of state services that made some people compare him with former British Prime Minister Margaret Thatcher.[115]

At the same time there was a lot of sympathy in the Czech electorate for the Social Democrats, who favored a slowdown of market reforms and more government attention to the quality of life. Initially a fringe party made up of former communists and other left-wing politicians skeptical of or opposed to the speed of Klaus's introduction of Western-style capitalism, there was nothing to suggest the party favored a return to communist authoritarianism. Indeed, quite the contrary. Many of the former communists had left the party years earlier. By the mid-1990s the Social Democrats were very close in their policies to the political center. Klaus himself tended to see the party for what it really had become, an umbrella-type organization committed to political and economic democracy that would offer voters, as he put it, "better defined choices." In the end the party came off looking softer and more concerned about the welfare of people than Klaus, who struck many voters as aloof, came off as somewhat arrogant and not very interested in the affairs of ordinary people.

In early June 1996, President Havel served as a mediator in helping Klaus and Social Democratic Chairman Miloš Zeman to seek the common ground needed to form a new government. Initially, each party was reluctant to cooperate with the other. But Havel eventually prevailed upon Klaus and Zeman to make a coalition under Klaus's leadership. In the beginning of the summer of 1996, it was anybody's guess how long this fragile power-sharing agreement would survive. What was clear, however, was the message voters had sent to the country's political leadership that it must show more sensitivity to the real concerns of most Czech people as the country continued to adopt a market economy. It was also clear that the voters did not want a halt to reform; they rather wanted a more equitable version of it that would assure that the whole population, not simply a well-off elite, benefited from the changing economic order. Finally, the Social Democrats emerged from the June election as a possible swing party whose cooperation would be essential to the functioning of any Czech government in Prague.[116]

While the Czech Republic remains close to the West, it has had some problems with the United States. In 1993, the Czech cabinet, facing severe financial difficulties, resumed weapons exports, reversing President Havel's pledge when he became president of the former Czechoslovak state to end weapons exports and dismantle weapons-producing factories. The Czech government defended its policy of arms exports by arguing its desperate need for earnings abroad. There was unused factory capacity that could and should be put to productive use. Czech officials also have said that Havel's pledge was hasty and expensive for Czechoslovakia, because the reconversion of weapons factories has been very costly, and Czechs, as well as Slovaks, who specialized in weapons production received no outside aid for reconversion. Moreover, the Czech Republic, for all its relative economic well-being in the transition, was, like other Central and East European countries, short of hard currency, which could be easily earned by arms exports to wealthy developing countries. Nevertheless, Washington does not like Czech arms sales to politically turbulent countries and has made clear to Prague that, should it export to countries on the American "black-list," it would not be eligible for certain kinds of U.S. technological assistance.[117] Another issue in Czech Republic relations with the United States is full membership for the Czech Republic in NATO. Havel was not satisfied with, but settled for, Czech entry into the American-initiated "Partnership for Peace," which provides for links to NATO but not full membership and not the security guarantee contained in Article XVI of the NATO agreement of 1949. Havel has scored points with Washington for his understanding of NATO's dilemma of reaching out to the former Soviet Union's Central and East European allies without antagonizing the Yeltsin government, which was under tremendous pressure in the mid-1990s to prevent the expansion of NATO eastward.

Since the split there has also been a slight strain on Czech relations with Germany. The Sudeten Germans continue to exert a strong pressure on Bonn to press the Czech government to make restitution. In 1993, Germany's finance minister Theo Waigel called attention to the apparent hypocrisy of the Czech Republic's condemnation of "ethnic cleansing" in the former Yugoslavia given its refusal to address the demands of the Sudeten Germans for restitution of their property. To soothe Germany in order to ensure its support for the Czech Republic's bid to become a full member of the European Union, Havel—at great political risk, because many Czechs have little sympathy for the Sudeten German case—agreed to the holding of unofficial talks with groups representing the Sudeten Germans. Although there is little likelihood that the Czech Republic would willingly pay out large sums to the Germans or restore their property, which could be extremely difficult so long after it was confiscated, Czechs remain upset and have observed that Germany's proficiency in "ethnic-cleansing" policies of its own in World War II hardly put the country in a position to talk to the Czechs about their criticism of "ethnic cleansing" in Bosnia.[118]

Relations between the Czech Republic and the Russian Federation have been good, largely in response to the efforts of President Yeltsin to cultivate former Eastern bloc countries as a counterweight to Germany. Convinced that trying to pressure the new postcommunist leaders to draw closer to Russia would be counterproductive, Yeltsin was conciliatory. He apologized for past Soviet abusiveness, which, he insisted, was not Russia's fault. For example, in August 1993, on the occasion of the twenty-fifth anniversary of the Soviet-led Warsaw Pact invasion of Czechoslovakia, Yeltsin visited Prague, met with President Havel, and condemned the 1968 invasion as an assault on the sovereignty of an independent state. He signed a treaty calling for Russo–Czech friendship that was intended to publicize the end of a difficult era in relations between the two countries.[119]

But there are some clouds on the horizon. Like other former allies of the defunct Soviet state, the Czechs worry about the possibility of a conservative leadership in Moscow with the support of the Russian military and with an interest in expanding Russian influence in Central and Eastern Europe. For the time being, however, the dominance of Yeltsin, his apparent commitment to good relations with Prague, and the development of close Czech political and economic ties with the West, including Germany, provide the Czech Republic with a measure of security and confidence in the region.

Conclusions

The peaceful transition from communist dictatorship to democratic pluralism in the former Czechoslovakia is attributable to at least three major circumstances: the readiness of an already well established democratic opposition to challenge and replace the communists; the nonviolent instincts of the Czech and Slovak people; and the neutrality of the Kremlin. But the so-called "Velvet Revolution" against communist rule was not without problems, especially in the economic and social spheres. By the end of 1996, movement toward a market economy is far from complete, especially in Slovakia, where the state continues to control more than 90 percent of the national economy. Politicians in Prague, as well as in Bratislava, fear that the "shock therapy" adopted by the Polish government and pressed on Prague and Bratislava by Western banking institutions to hasten the achievement of a free market will provoke social tensions and, eventually, political extremism dangerous to the new democratic order.

But the most serious of postcommunist Czechoslovakia's problems was the revival of interethnic prejudices, which contributed to the split of the country within three years of the revolution of 1989. The split was the result of (1) the depth of economic, sociocultural, and historic diversity between Czechs and Slovaks; (2) the failure of postindependence Czechoslovak governmental systems in the period between the two world wars and during the communist era to homogenize the multicultural society of the new Czechoslovak state successfully; (3) the readiness of the postcommunist leaders of the early 1990s to nurture and exploit for narrow political purposes a rejuvenation of ethnocultural nationalism among the Czech and Slovak peoples; (4) the opportunities for conflict offered by the democratic environment, in particular, a new freedom of discussion, debate, and advocacy enabling Czechs and Slovaks to express their long-suppressed ethnic dreams, ambitions, and prejudices; and (6) the apparent deficiencies in the leadership of the very popular Czechoslovak president Václav Havel, who seemed to lack the kind of managerial expertise needed to resolve divisive problems of government, even though, in the view of his countrymen, as well as of outsiders, he remains without doubt determined in his commitment to a democratic and united Czechoslovakia.

To the credit of Czechs and Slovaks, their controversies and eventual separation occurred without violence. The Czech and Slovak peoples had little, if any, of the deep hostility toward one another found among other ethnic groups at war with one another, in particular, Muslim Slavs and Serbs in Bosnia-Herzegovina and Armenians and Azeri in Nagorno-Karabakh. Czechs and Slovaks had more in common with each other than their differences suggested. They shared a long period of peaceful coexistence in the modern Czechoslovak state. They also had a much stronger commitment to democratic processes and the rule of law and much less of a will to physical combat than many other ethnic groups now fighting each other. Czechs and Slovaks did not have the inclination and capacity for *incivisme* found in the peoples of the multinational societies in Yugoslavia, and they lacked a tradition of violent insurgency against established political order.

While the new Czech Republic will do well despite political, economic, and social problems because its leadership is strongly democratic, because it is now economically better off than it was when linked to the less well-off Slovakia, and because its chances of drawing close to Europe economically and politically are good, Slovakia's future is considerably less bright. Slovak politicians thus far have displayed strong authoritarian instincts that have produced tensions inside Slovak society and complicated Slovakia's relations with Western democracies. Slovakia also faces serious economic problems because it remains less developed than the Czech Republic and in need of large financial and other kinds of assistance from abroad. This support will be slow to come because of Slovakia's slow pace toward the free-market economy.

Ultimately, the only realistic alternative for Slovakia is the pursuit of increased links with the Czech Republic, though this may be difficult. The Czechs are skeptical of intimacy with the Slovaks as Slovakia's economy deteriorates. At the same time, Slovak politicians remain committed to the preservation of their country's political independence, which for them is "irrevocable," no matter what the economic costs may be. Closer relations between Czechs and Slovaks may be inevitable, but reunification, at least at the moment, seems highly unlikely.

6

East Germany

The German Democratic Republic (GDR), also called East Germany, was established in 1949 by East German communists who established the Socialist Unity Party (SED). Like most other communist-controlled countries in the region, the GDR quickly became a satellite of the Soviet Union. This new state consisted of territory of the defeated Germany occupied by the Soviet Union toward the end of World War II. It included Berlin, the historic capital of Germany, and had a population of about 16.5 million people, or roughly 20 percent of the total pre–World War II German population.

East German Stalinism

The Kremlin kept a close eye on political developments in East Germany because of this country's strategic importance to Soviet territorial security and the security of neighboring socialist countries, notably Poland and Czechoslovakia. The East German communist system was especially vulnerable to Western influence because of its geographical proximity to the democracy and free enterprise of the Federal Republic of Germany (FRG). In particular, the conspicuous affluence of West Berlin contrasted sharply with the poverty and dowdiness of neighboring East Berlin, so much so that in 1961 the East German communist leadership saw fit to construct a concrete wall to halt a vast hemorrhage of East Germans to the West. By 1989, the wall had a ferocious appearance, consisting of a double row of eight-foot-high concrete walls with watchtowers, electronic sensors, and a no-man's land in between.

To deter criticism and dissent in East German society, successive Soviet leaders from Stalin to Gorbachev insisted on the GDR's strict conformity with

EAST GERMANY

Geography

1. Location: north central Europe; the former German Democratic Republic (East Germany) was bordered on the north by the Baltic Sea, west by the Federal Republic of Germany (West Germany), east by Poland, southeast by Czechoslovakia; eastern Germany now comprises the Länder of Brandenburg, Mecklenburg-West Pomerania, Saxony, Saxony-Anhalt, and Thuringia in the northeastern quadrant of unified Germany

2. Area: 108,333 square kilometers (unified Germany — 356,733 square kilometers)

3. Climate: temperate coastal, continental interior

4. Terrain: northern lowlands, central uplands

5. Natural resources: coal, potash (West — petroleum, natural gas, coal, iron ore)

People

1. Population: 16,674,632 (1988) (unified Germany — 80,274,600, 1992);
2. Structure: 52.3% male (unified Germany — 51% female)
3. Birth Rate: 12.9 per thousand, 1988 (unified Germany — 10.4 per thousand, 1991)
4. Life expectancy: female — 76.2 years, male — 70 years (1989); (West Germany 1990: female — 78.9 years, male 72.6 years)
5. Ethnic Divisions: unified Germany — 95% ethnic Germans
6. Religions: unified Germany — 45% Protestant, 37% Roman Catholic, 18% unaffiliated or other (in the 1950 census the East was 80.5% Protestant, 11% Roman Catholic)
7. Language: German
8. Literacy: 99%
9. Land use: 4.7 million hectares arable, 1.26 million hectares grassland (1989); 2.98 million hectares forest (1988) (West: 7.26 million hectares arable, 4.42 million hectares pasture [1987])
10. Environment — air and water pollution; acid rain; deforestation

Government

In 1990 the Volkskammer of the German Democratic Republic voted to accede to the jurisdiction of the Federal Republic of Germany.

Economy

1. Gross Domestic Product: unified Germany $1.398 trillion (1992) (eastern — $104 billion; western — $1.294 trillion)
2. National Product Real Growth Rate: unified Germany 1.5% (1992) (eastern — 8%; western — 0.9%)
3. Per capita national product: unified Germany $17,400 (1992) (eastern — $6,500; western — $20,000)
4. Inflation rate: western — 4% (1992); eastern NA
5. Unemployment rate: eastern — 13.5%; western — 7.1% (1992)
6. Industries: western — iron, steel, coal, cement, chemicals, machinery, vehicles, machine tools, electronics, food and beverages; eastern — metal fabrication, chemicals, brown coal, shipbuilding

---

the Soviet-style single-party dictatorship, in particular, a severe political discipline involving censorship and a ubiquitous surveillance of the public by the secret police, or *Stasi*. East German political repression at times rivaled that of other tightly controlled communist systems such as Czechoslovakia after the Warsaw Pact invasion of 1968 and the Balkan states of Romania, Bulgaria, and Albania.

The GDR system was equally harsh in the economic sphere. Eastern Germany was traditionally agricultural, the homeland of the old Prussian Junker class. The communist leadership industrialized the country and imposed a severe austerity to offset the enormous cost of this transformation. Wages were kept low to allow a maximum of national wealth to be invested in the expansion of industry, and, as was true in other communist-ruled countries, East German communists neglected the production of consumer goods, causing acute shortages of food, clothing, and housing that kept living standards far below those in West Germany and the rest of Western Europe. The government wanted to make East Germany the chief supplier of industrial exports to the rest of the Eastern bloc to assure its independence of West Germany and undercut any prospect of reunification.

After Stalin's death, East Germans hoped for a relaxation of the brutal austerity imposed on them in the early 1950s. Industrial workers struck for higher wages and a liberalization of the repressive political dictatorship. These strikes of June 1953, however, achieved little of the change workers sought. They were quickly and ruthlessly suppressed by a frightened communist leadership under pressure from the Khrushchevian Kremlin, which opposed radical departures from orthodox Soviet-style socialism. After this episode, the GDR maintained a tight control over society, discouraging opposition by continuing to punish it severely whenever it surfaced.

In succeeding years, the GDR achieved a remarkable degree of political stability. To some extent, East Germans were easier to govern than, say, Poles because of a high degree of social discipline and respect for authority. Incidents of criticism and protest were very few, and for the most part East Germans showed little of the *incivisme* seen in Polish society. This stability allowed the GDR to focus on economic growth and development, which eventually provided a measure of prosperity when compared with other East European countries. The GDR thus gained a minimum of popular acceptance until the 1980s, when discontent began to surface as a result of economic and political problems.[1]

Economic Problems

Immediately below the surface of what appeared to be a smoothly run socialist system, serious economic problems were developing. By the 1980s, they had become glaringly evident and were arousing popular dissatisfaction and complaint. The most obvious sign of trouble was the fact that East Germany had failed to achieve living standards comparable to those in West Germany. German industry was producing shoddy consumer goods, and shortages of everything worsened.[2]

1. Systemic Weaknesses

The persistence of these shortages pointed to the failure of the government policy of centralized control of pricing, which complicated efforts to gear production to profit. Price subsidies drained precious capital from investment, factories could not experiment with workers' incentives to expand productivity, heavy industry was emphasized at the expense of consumer-goods production, and inadequate and obsolete technology prevented improvement in industrial efficiency.[3] An obsession with self-sufficiency resulted in the waste of resources in the production of goods that should have been imported from those countries that had an advantage in the manufacture of them. An explosion of oil prices after the 1973 crisis sent production costs spiraling. The East German economy was never able to produce enough goods for both export and domestic consumption.[4]

The GDR economy was weakened also by its dependence on West German financial assistance and commercial concessions. By the late 1980s, 60 percent of East Germany's trade was with West Germany. East Germany relied on imports of West German technology and received West German interest- free loans. The country also received over $1 billion a year in private remittances from relatives in the West, as well as payments in hard currency that were a kind of ransom for the release of a small number of East German citizens to the West each year.[5]

Commercial and financial concessions from West Germany helped mask the weaknesses of the East German economy. Communist Party leader Erich Honecker, in power since 1971, could plausibly say to President Mikhail Gorbachev in the late 1980s that the East German economy was doing quite well on an absolute and comparative sense.

2. Resistance to Change

In the late 1990s, Honecker reacted cautiously to Gorbachev's perestroika. He dismissed suggestions from the Kremlin to consider some perestroika-style economic reformism in East Germany to improve its economic performance. Although in deference to Gorbachev Honecker paid lip service to perestroika, he insisted on continuing his conservative, neo-Stalinistic economic policies.[6]

In rejecting perestroika for the GDR, the Honecker leadership said it already had taken steps within the neo-Stalinistic structure to improve efficiency. The GDR had expanded output by decentralizing economic decision making, increasing workers' incentives, admitting technocrats to top-level administrative positions, and rationalized the use of expensive imported energy. It had created industrial combines, or *Kombinaten,* in which factories in related branches of the economy were grouped together and, with limited supervision from central authorities, were responsible for everything from research and design to foreign trade. Regional agricultural cooperatives, made up of a grain farm and two to three animal farms, coordinated local food production and feed supply.[7]

The Honecker leadership also said it would not experiment with perestroika because that would undermine its orthodox socialist ideology, which distinguished it from and made it superior to West Germany. East German socialism, the SED government believed, would lose whatever legitimacy it had if it veered significantly away from the Stalinist model of political and economic organization.[8]

Political Problems

East Germany also experienced political problems in the 1970s and 1980s. As in the economic sphere, the Honecker leadership refused to consider reform and would not relax its harsh discipline. Censorship, an ubiquitous and intrusive secret police, and the harassment of political critics continued.

1. Resumption of Popular Protest

In their pursuit of political conformity and obedience to authority, however, the East German communists tried to discourage comparisons with the country's Nazi past, using restraint in dealing with minor dissent. There were no Stalin-like purges when East German intellectuals and the Evangelical Church expressed dissent. To promote the appearance of political pluralism, the East German communists also allowed other political parties to exist as long as they pledged loyalty to the system, although the communist leadership refused to share power with them.

The GDR regime always stopped short of brutality, refusing to imitate the Brezhnev regime's draconian suppression of human-rights dissent in the Soviet Union in the late 1970s. It could not and did not deny East German citizens access to West German television, which showed them the freedom as well as the economic well-being of the West. The Honecker leadership initially did not take this cultural penetration very seriously, believing that the seamier sides of capitalism portrayed in West German television would make East Germans all the more appreciative of their own system, which gave their lives security and stability.

But the opposite turned out to be the case. Constant exposure to the West German consumer culture had an insidious impact on East German society, encouraging East Germans increasingly to compare it to their own relatively run-down, deprived society. It became increasingly more difficult for East Germans to endure the sacrifices asked of them by the Honecker leadership for the sake of the future.[9]

2. Sources of Dissent

Several diverse and influential dissident groups emerged in the 1970s and 1980s. The most important were the peace and ecology movements; the East German Evangelical Church; an active intelligentsia bent on testing the limits of regime toleration; East Germany's equivalent of "refuseniks," people who had applied for exit permits; and eventually a new youth counterculture infatuated with Western ways and enamored of Gorbachev and his perestroika, which young people insisted Honecker adopt in East Germany.[10]

The Evangelical Church, which may have been seeking the same activist role in East German society that the Catholic Church had in Poland, did what it could to encourage dissident activities. In the period after the 1975 Helsinki accord on human rights, the church criticized the militancy of East German society and the proliferation in Europe of nuclear weapons. Although the church rarely challenged the regime, it annoyed the communist leadership, which saw the potential of the church for serving as the nucleus of a possible political opposition.[11]

The advent of Gorbachev's perestroika in the Soviet Union beginning in 1986 also stimulated the growth of an East German dissidence movement. East Germans admired Gorbachev for the changes he wanted to introduce in the Soviet Union, especially glasnost. Intrigued by Moscow's freer cinema and arts scene and other changes in Soviet society wrought by glasnost, they eagerly snatched up the latest editions of *Pravda* at local kiosks to read about Gorbachev's reform policies.[12]

3. Official Reactions

Determined to avoid the kind of political liberalization going on in the Soviet Union and elsewhere in Eastern Europe and to preserve the country's conservative status quo in politics, the East German regime tried in the 1980s to impose a kind of intellectual quarantine of the country. Its target was the press. In 1988 the regime denied East German citizens access to information about Soviet reformism, especially news about the Kremlin's new tolerance of criticism and dissent in the Soviet media. East German ideological spokesmen also went on the offensive. They criticized Soviet journals that condemned Stalinism and called for more grass-roots democracy in the Soviet Union. In addition, the Honecker regime imposed a total ban in East Germany on the magazine *Sputnik,* which in German translation had enjoyed a widespread readership in East German schools, because one of its issues compared Stalin with Hitler.[13]

4. Roots of East German Conservatism

Behind the East German leadership's hostility to change was fear. Given its geographic proximity to West Germany, Honecker and other neo-Stalinists in the East German communist leadership worried that the slightest liberalization could get out of hand and threaten party dominance. Indeed, Honecker correctly suspected that East Germans were very susceptible to the notion of radical change given their ill-concealed envy of neighboring West Germany's open and prosperous society and their obvious admiration of perestroika. He believed that even a limited relaxation in the political sphere would lead to demands for substantial change, which the regime might not be able to control.[14]

Competitive with West Germany for the attention and sympathy of East German citizens, the GDR leadership saw liberal change as a capitulation to the kind of Western values epitomized by the ostentatious glitz of life in West Berlin. Moreover, Honecker and other conservative GDR leaders, sensitive to dictation by the Kremlin, wanted to demonstrate to East German citizens the independence of their socialist system despite its closeness to Moscow. In late June 1988, in an overtly nationalistic gesture of assertiveness vis-à-vis the USSR, the East German official daily *Neues Deutschland* published an article praising former East German leader Walter Ulbricht, who at the end of his career had become increasingly unpopular with Moscow. As Honecker remarked, each socialist state had the right to chart its own course of development.[15]

Honecker's conservatism actually had some support from Gorbachev's Kremlin. Gorbachev acknowledged that East Germany had not done badly in the economic sphere. In an address to the East German Communist Party Congress in 1986, the Soviet leader noted approvingly that the GDR's success had been achieved without recourse to "controversial Hungarian-style market experiments," which still had not gained full acceptance in the Kremlin.[16]

Honecker and his colleagues doubtless were encouraged in their conservatism by the knowledge that many in the Kremlin shared their aversion to perestroika-style reforms. *Neues Deutschland,* reprinted Nina Andreeva's attack on Gorbachev and her defense of the bolshevist principles that had been inspired by conservative Soviet party secretary Yegor Ligachev. And while the paper eventually published *Pravda*'s Gorbachev-inspired rebuttal to Andreeva's attack, it also published an article comparing Gorbachev's reforms with those of deposed Czechoslovak party leader Alexander Dubček's 1968 Prague Spring revisionist program.[17]

Many East Germans, who had little direct contact with dissident groups, deplored civil unrest, and could not forget how workers' strikes in 1953 had been ruthlessly suppressed, accepted Honecker's conservatism with equanimity. Indeed, contributing to a pervasive docility in East German society was the widely feared *Stasi,* which was, perhaps, the most efficient internal security organization anywhere in Eastern Europe. And they also understood how the Berlin Wall, symbolized the limits beyond which the regime would not indulge personal freedoms. Finally, East Germans did live better than their neighbors in Eastern Europe, if not as well as West Germans, and for this reason were reluctant to challenge and defy the GDR system.[18]

The End of Communist Rule

But passivity and docility did not mean loyalty to and support for the regime. Opposition, when it did come, was all the more explosive because it had been unexpressed for so long. This opposition started with the GDR's disgruntled young people and led finally to the dramatic opening of the Berlin Wall, an event that sounded the death knell of communist rule.

1. The "Exodus" of East German Youth

East Germany's rejection of communist rule began in the summer of 1989, when 11,707 East German youth emigrated to West Germany by way of Hungary and Austria. This "exodus," as it came to be known, resulted in the emigration of 55,970 East Germans in the first six months of 1989 compared with a total of

39,832 emigrants to West Germany for all of 1988. Clearly, popular dissatisfaction with the Honecker regime and pessimism about the prospect of improved living conditions, as well as of political liberalization, were widespread.[19]

The exodus had serious economic and political consequences. So many workers with valuable skills emigrated that the economy slowed. Moreover, the exodus embarrassed the regime since it had been well underway by the October 1989 celebrations of its fortieth anniversary. East German leaders were surprised by the extent of the exodus, observing that among the people fleeing the country were not only refuseniks but "some good kids from good families, even from colleagues." They grudgingly acknowledged the broad national social scope of the protest.[20]

2. Opening the Berlin Wall

Meanwhile, the celebrations commemorating the fortieth anniversary of the East German republic went forward. Thousands of people who did not want to emigrate, who wanted to stay home and change the system, took to the streets in Berlin, Leipzig, and Dresden in what became at times violent protest. At the anniversary festivities in East Berlin, tension was evident between Honecker and the visiting Gorbachev, who, while praising East German achievements in the economic sphere, warned his hosts of the risks in failing to join the tide of political liberalization.[21]

3. Weakening of Party Conservatives

Honecker's stubborn resistance to change provoked a conspiracy within the SED politburo to oust him from power. The anti-Honecker cabal included Egon Krenz, head of the secret-police apparatus, union boss Harry Tisch, Günter Schabowski, and Peter Lorenz. These people wanted some relaxation in the political sphere to strengthen the party's standing among the public. They were surprised, and perhaps intimidated, by the explosion of popular hostility, notably the exodus of youth throughout 1989 and the outbreak in September and October of antigovernment and anti-Honecker demonstrations by thousands of citizens in Leipzig, Dresden, and other East German urban centers. They informed Gorbachev of their intention to force Honecker's resignation. There was no opposition to such a move from Moscow, which seemed open to the ascendancy of reform-minded leaders in East Berlin.[22]

In mid-October, isolated in the politburo, which favored a conciliatory approach to the political opposition, Honecker resigned along with Premier Willy Stoph, who wanted to use force to suppress the demonstrations. Honecker deeply resented Gorbachev's refusal to stand by him. After all, if there had been one Communist Party chief whom the Soviets might have been expected to prop up, it was Honecker because of his longstanding loyalty to the Kremlin.

4. Krenz Replaces Honecker

Following Honecker's resignation, Krenz became party leader and Hans Modrow, a reformer who had been critical of Honecker's opposition to perestroika and had the backing of Gorbachev, was elected prime minister by the East German Parliament.[23]

Krenz immediately announced a limited political relaxation. He allowed antiregime demonstrations to continue without official interference, and he lifted restrictions on travel to the West, especially West Berlin and West Germany. On November 9, he officially opened the Berlin Wall. The opening of the wall was, perhaps, one of the most dramatic incidents in the collapse of communist rule in Eastern Europe. Within hours, thousands of East Germans swarmed across the wall and clambered on it in a mass celebration of their new freedom.[24]

The Krenz leadership evidently recognized the impossibility of regulating the flood of East Germans seeking to leave and decided to let those wanting to leave emigrate freely. He hoped that others who remained would see in this gesture a new determination of his leadership to pursue the kind of political change opposed by the Honecker regime.

5. Erosion of Communist Power

But the days of the communist leadership were numbered. The East German communists could not salvage their rule. They had to accept a comprehensive political liberalization, which inevitably eroded their power. But more importantly, time and circumstances were gradually but steadily working against the survival of their leadership of the country.

Acceptance of Political Liberalization

For example, in December 1989, Prime Minister Modrow presided over a roundtable discussion with representatives of church groups and various new civic organizations, such as the New Forum citizens movement, a large coalition of opposition groups seeking to share power with the communists and to expand East German economic, social, and cultural ties with West Germany. The roundtable discussed ways to liberalize the communist government. Free parliamentary elections were promised for the spring of 1990.[25]

Modrow soon came under intense pressure from political opposition groups to make additional concessions. They demanded he limit the power of the Communist Party and share power with them. Modrow tried to conciliate the opposition, agreeing in January 1990 to move the date for parliamentary elections back from May to March. In February, he reshuffled his cabinet, admitting eight new ministers without portfolio who were not communists. But he was still a communist and was reluctant to weaken the party's leading role in East German society. His conservative bent eventually cost him and his party any chance of staying in power.[26]

Collapse of Krenz

Party chief Krenz struck many East Germans as no different than Honecker, despite his pledges of profound change. In June 1989, he had made the mistake of sending a message on behalf of the politburo congratulating the Chinese leadership on its suppression of the prodemocracy demonstrations in Tiananmen Square. East Germans reasoned that Krenz eventually would treat them as harshly if he had the chance. In a poll taken in mid-November, only 19 percent of East Germans said they had any trust in the Krenz regime. His opening of the wall had brought little popular support. Recognizing his weakness, Krenz ultimately resigned on December 3 in favor of Gregor Gysi, a less well known but pragmatic and reform-oriented party official.[27]

Revelation of "Wandlitz"

At the end of 1989, East Germans learned about Wandlitz, a hideaway not far from the capital where the top party leadership lived in scandalously luxurious surroundings. At Wandlitz party "big shots" enjoyed a variety of imported foods, electronic goods, and other amenities from the West and Japan not available to most German citizens. Reported widely in the West, the revelation of Wandlitz was deeply embarrassing to the East German leaders, who had asked great sacrifices of the East German people while making none of their own. Wandlitz, as well as other examples of party abuses and excesses in light of its frequent calls for a puritanical austerity on the part of the East German people, helped compromised the credibility of the SED and of its new leader.[28]

On the Wrong Side of the Reunification Issue

The SED also was out of step with East German society on the issue of reunification with West Germany. Following the collapse of the Honecker regime in October 1989, popular sentiment for reunification had steadily increased, fueled by national pride, by a deep resentment of the communist past, and by a belief that reunification with the affluent West would bring an immediate improvement in living conditions.

Though willing to strengthen economic links between the two Germanies, Prime Minister Modrow was cautious about political links. He accepted the idea of reunification, as did Communist Party leader Gysi, but only through a very gradual administrative amalgamation. He believed, as did many older East Germans, that in a reunified German state East Germans stood to lose much of what they had enjoyed under SED rule. A dictatorship of big business would set policy for East Germans, he feared, and deprive them of the extensive social umbrella the Marxist regime had developed in its forty years of rule.[29]

6. The March 1990 Parliamentary Elections

As the country prepared for the March 1990 parliamentary elections, Modrow was no more successful than Krenz had been in trying to salvage the party's leadership. Concessions he had made turned out to be too little too late. The party did try to break with the past by changing its name to the Party of Democratic Socialism, but it could not overcome its discredited past.

The East German Parliament, or Volkskammer, passed an extremely simple election law for these elections. In response to pressures from the political opposition, the Volkskammer used proportional representation in fifteen multimember electoral districts to ensure that the new political organizations, which were fragmented and lacking internal unity and cohesion, would not be excluded from the new Parliament.[30]

Western Influence on the Campaign

The communists were overshadowed in the campaign by the East German branches of West Germany's Christian Democratic Union (CDU) and the Social Democratic Party (SDP). Leading West German politicians, such as Chancellor Helmut Kohl, the head of the CDU, and former Chancellor Willy Brandt, the titular head of the SDP, campaigned aggressively in East Germany, almost as if it had already been joined with West Germany into a single German state.[31]

Electoral Results

When the elections were held on March 18, 1990, East German voters overwhelmingly supported parliamentary candidates of the East German CDU. It was a popular signal to West German Chancellor Kohl to move ahead with reunification, which East Germans hoped would quickly bring an improvement in their living conditions.[32] The East German electorate did not give much support to the German Social Democrats. They had been less forthcoming about reunification than Chancellor Kohl's CDU, which promised to move ahead quickly. West German Social Democratic leaders like Willy Brandt were concerned about the costs and difficulties of a rapid reunification. This position was to some extent conditioned by the party's strategy in the Bundestag elections scheduled for December 1990 and influenced by public-opinion polls in West Germany that showed a majority of West German voters worried about the financial and social costs of a rush to unity.[33] The former communists, calling themselves the Party of Democratic Socialism won only about 16 percent of the popular vote. This meant political survival but nothing more. Under Gysi they adopted the role of a constructive opposition critical of the new capitalist order. The New Forum, which had mobilized popular support for the overthrow of the Honecker regime, however, disappeared, lacking leadership of the stature and appeal of Kohl and Brandt.

7. East Germany's First Noncommunist Government

East German Christian Democratic leader Lothar de Maizière formed a coalition with the East German Social Democratic Party to become the first noncommunist chancellor of East Germany on April 9, 1990. Under de Maizière the new East German government began the long and complex processes of dismantling the socialist system and of moving the country toward reunification with West Germany.[34]

Reunification with West Germany

Popular sentiment in East Germany at the time of the March 1990 parliamentary elections strongly favored reunification. Reunification, most East Germans believed, was the means of rapidly improving the depressed economy and achieving a standard of living on a par with that in the West. Therefore, the new East German government that took power following the March 1990 election concentrated on working with the government in Bonn to achieve reunification of the two German states as soon as possible.

The route to unification was to be Article 23 of the West German Basic Law, which allowed the East German Parliament to incorporate the states of East Germany into the Federal Republic by passing legislation to that effect by a two-thirds majority. Negotiations on reunification between the East German and West German governments began almost immediately following the March 1990 elections and the appointment of de Maizière. But, there were several problems to be resolved having to do with currency exchange, abortion rights, social-welfare policies, and the relationship of a united Germany to its eastern neighbors.

1. Internal Problems

Currency Exchange

The issue of currency was probably the most pressing. To improve their living standards as quickly as possible, East Germans wanted immediate conversion on a one-to-one basis of their currency with the West German mark. Bankers and politicians in West Germany strenuously objected to such a move because the East German currency was worth much less, and they feared inflation of the West German mark.

But at the end of April 1990, the West German government, hoping to ease social and economic dislocations as the result of reunification, agreed to the exchange of West German marks for East German currency at a rate of 1 : 1 on wages, pensions, and some savings. East Germans could exchange up to 4,000 of their marks per person at this rate. The remainder would be exchanged at the rate of 2 : 1. At the same time, West Germany agreed to bring East German pensions up to West German levels, a boon to the 2.7 million East German retirees receiving approximate 420 East German inflated marks, compared with 1,100 West German marks collected by West German retirees.[35]

Abortion Rights

Another problem complicating the reunification of the two Germanies concerned abortion policy. East Germany had few restrictions on having an abortion, while in West Germany an abortion required permission from a panel of doctors and was available only on the grounds of medical risk or social hardship, such as poverty or emotional instability.[36]

Behind these different legal situations were conflicting philosophical positions and sociological conditions. According to the East German Independent Women's Association, "every woman has a right to decide what will happen with her body." In contrast, the West German Catholic Council of Bishops argued that abortion should be outlawed because life had to be saved from the moment of conception. Abortion, in their view, was the same as murder.[37]

The conflict over abortion also was a reflection of the differing status of women in each Germany: about 90 percent of East German women were wage earners doing work outside the family, versus less than 50 percent of West German women. In East Germany, day-care facilities had been extensive and state supported, while day care in West Germany was hard to find. Furthermore, while 80 percent of East German men did at least some housework, this was true for only about 20 percent of men in West Germany.[38]

Political leaders of the two Germanies eventually reached a compromise on abortion rights. Women living in what was formerly East Germany would be able to receive an abortion on demand up to the twelfth week of pregnancy for a two-year period after reunification. But to have an abortion in West Germany, they would have to obtain permission from a panel of doctors or risk criminal prosecution.[39]

Social-Welfare Policies

Other social policies had to be readjusted. At the time of its collapse in 1990, the East German communist government had one of the most extensive social-security and social-services programs in continental Europe. Although extensively damaged by the emigration of doctors, dentists, and other skilled professionals, East

Germany's medical system still offered comprehensive, free, and reasonably high-quality health care. Infant mortality was substantially lower in East Germany than in West Germany, and social services in some sectors offered more to the East German citizen than did the highly developed welfare system in the Scandinavian countries. Rent and food subsidies and guaranteed employment were part of what East Germans were used to enjoying.[40]

During the negotiations for reunification in the spring and summer of 1990, preservation of this social support system in the new, reunified German state became a matter of great public concern and a source of controversy among politicians from east and west. The East German government tried to have aspects of the East German social-security policies guaranteed in the treaty of reunification. But its efforts were unsuccessful: subsidies for rents, transportation, and some foodstuffs were to be phased out gradually; and guarantees for security of employment and other provisions of the East German social-welfare system were dropped. The political opposition in the Volkskammer in the spring and summer of 1990, including former communists, complained that East German social policy, the one popular aspect of the old communist system, was being sacrificed for the sake of a speedy reunification.[41]

2. External Problems

The move to reunify East and West Germany was causing anxiety outside Germany. Germany's eastern neighbors, notably the former Soviet Union, Poland, and Czechoslovakia, viewed reunification with some alarm. They could not forget German aggression against them in World War II and worried that a united German state of more than 80 million people was bound to be dominant, perhaps uncontrollable, and, therefore, possibly dangerous to Europe in the next century.

Poland was most concerned and demanded a say in how the two Germanies went about reunification. In particular, the Polish government wanted a guarantee of its border with Germany and a formal disavowal of claims to Polish territory obtained from Germany after World War II. The two Germanies, pressed by the four great powers (the United States, Britain, France, and the Soviet Union), in what was termed the "two plus four" negotiations eventually though somewhat reluctantly accommodated the Poles on these points.[42]

Meanwhile, the Soviets wanted a reunified Germany to be neutral, that is, out of NATO. Soviet concerns were understandable: they centered around security at a time when Soviet defenses were weakest, namely, as the Soviet Union was breaking up into separate republics. But the political leadership of the two Germanies, as well as the Western allies, rejected this position. In an attempt to put pressure on the West, the Kremlin refused to go forward with the troop withdrawals from Eastern Europe that Gorbachev had announced in December 1988.[43]

In June 1990, the Western allies and the USSR reached a compromise favorable to the West. Eager to preserve good Soviet relations with the West, Gorbachev agreed to a reunited Germany's membership in NATO provided that NATO refrain from deploying military force in eastern Germany while Soviet forces were still stationed there. The West agreed to meet this request until 1994, by which time a Soviet withdrawal from East Germany was to be completed.[44]

3. Final Agreement

In spite of problems inside and outside Germany, negotiations over reunification went forward, and on August 31, 1990, the two Germanies signed a treaty creating one German state. The document of almost 1,000 pages scheduled formal reunification for October 3. All aspects of reunification were codified in this reunification document.

In addition to incorporating the compromises on currency exchange, abortion, and social security, the treaty resolved questions of property in East Germany (it recognized the permanence of land reforms in 1945 and 1949, which had broken up the large estates of the now-defunct Junker aristocracy), established incentives for foreign investment in the east, called for temporary assumption of East German state debts by the West German government, and declared Berlin to be the official German capital. On October 4, the former East German Volkskammer and the West German Bundestag met together for the first time as a united Parliament in the old Reichstag building located in what was the former communist eastern sector of Berlin.[45]

Problems of Postcommunist Development

Like other East European societies making the transition from the communist order to political and economic democracy, the people of eastern Germany have experienced difficulties and disappointments. Regaining economic health and cleaning up a degraded environment, decommunizing the society and strengthening its acceptance of democracy, and getting accustomed to and accepting reunification with West Germany have not been easy. Eastern Germans have shown impatience and dissatisfaction with the transition away from communism. In the mid-1990s, ill at ease, they showed their dissatisfaction in supporting the Party of Social Democracy.

1. Regaining Economic Health

The task of restoring economic health to East Germany by introducing the free market has turned out to be more complex, more costly, and more time-consuming than most East Germans had anticipated. The infusion of an enormous amount of West German capital (about $80 to $100 billion) is beginning to have an impact in rejuvenating the economy of eastern Germany. The physical appearance of eastern Germany is changing. It is becoming modernized and westernized. But living conditions have not improved sufficiently to satisfy most people living in the area once ruled by communists. Indeed, for many East Germans life has become uncertain and unpredictable and in some cases worse than it was under communist rule. In the 1990s, they were and remain impatient, frustrated, and disappointed by the failure of the postcommunist order to make a real difference in their daily lives.

Movement Toward a Market Economy

The energetic measures of Bonn to move eastern Germany steadily toward a free-market economy started with the creation in 1990 of a public agency known as the *Treuhand,* which had a three-fold mandate: to sell off companies owned by the former East German communist state; to restructure enterprises that were not attractive enough to be sold because their equipment was obsolete or grossly inefficient; and to shut down the many enterprises that were not salvageable at all. The scale on which the *Treuhand* operated dwarfs that of any other privatization agency in the world. It was given ownership of 22,000 small businesses, 8,000 industrial companies, and vast amounts of real estate, including 28 percent of the former East Germany's farmland and two-thirds of its forest land. In 1992, nearly all the small businesses—among them shops, cafés, restaurants, cinemas, and pharmacies—as well as about 3,400 of the larger companies had been sold. Many of the remaining companies, which employed about 2 million workers, were broken into smaller units to make them more attractive for sale.[46]

Coping with Unemployment

Probably the most serious consequence of the movement away from socialism to a free-market economy was an unprecedented explosion of unemployment, much greater than anyone had expected. Enterprises employing hundreds and sometimes thousands of workers went bankrupt and had to close down as soon as state subsidies ended and they were offered for sale to private investors, who preferred to purchase only factories that could turn a profit. As the economy slowed down with the transition to a free market, unemployment rose steadily, reaching 350,000 by the end of August 1990. By early March 1991, about 40 percent of the former East Germany's 8.5 million workers were either unemployed or on short work, reporting to work just to collect part of their wages. This massive unemployment, inconceivable in the communist era, shocked, depressed, and demoralized the East German workforce. Young people were hardest hit and continued to emigrate to West Germany to improve their standard of living.[47]

The economic slump was difficult to reverse. Would-be West German and other foreign investors in the East German economy remained skeptical and tight fisted with their capital. They were discouraged by the poor performance of East

German managers, who had little understanding of free-market pricing. Outside investment in eastern Germany has been slowed also by the region's dilapidated plants, outmoded products, vanishing markets, heavy debts, redundant workers, and too many workers who performed poorly because poor performance had been tolerated for so long under the communist leadership, which refused to discipline, never mind discharge, inefficient workers.

In addition, the market for local manufactures was weak, partly because East German consumers now preferred to buy Western goods despite their higher costs. Privatization of state-owned enterprises unquestionably aggravated the problem of unemployment with new owners discharging hundreds of workers in an effort to cut costs and raise efficiency.[48]

The agricultural sector in the former East Germany also contributed to unemployment. There was so much surplus production in the European Union that the shrinkage of eastern German agriculture was inevitable. By mid-1991, eastern Germany's agriculture had already lost 50 percent of its 860,000-member workforce, and 13 percent of its land was taken out of production.[49]

Although the federal government in Bonn provided huge subsidies for unemployment compensation to ease the shock of job loss, and although privatization of state-controlled enterprises favored buyers who promised to keep workers employed, people still suffered, with unemployment still rising throughout the early 1990s—it was running at about 17 percent by the end of 1994. Many East Germans were angry over how reunification had upset their lives far more than they had anticipated.

To ease the hardships of the changeover from a controlled to a free economy, in particular the rising unemployment, the government in Bonn poured about $20 billion into eastern Germany in 1991 alone and at least as much in 1992. Most of this money was invested in the rebuilding of the former East Germany's dilapidated transportation and communications infrastructure, which will have a long-term benefit for the country by strengthening its growth potential and its attractiveness to foreign investors. More than 200,000 new telephones have been installed, and the East German road system is approaching the quality level of the West German autobahn system. With this public and private investment have come additional jobs. Furthermore, the effects of unemployment on those who left the workforce permanently have been somewhat mitigated by generous pension awards and guarantees of free medical care. Other West German capital has gone into developing export industries that will sell to other East European countries.[50]

Cleaning up a Polluted Environment

Closely related to, and perhaps an important part of, the problem of regaining economic health is the task of cleaning up a polluted environment. An extreme example of the environmental decay inherited from the communists is the extensive pollution in Bitterfeld, on the west bank of the Elbe River southwest of Berlin. Bitterfeld was the home of a huge chemical complex of eighty separate factories that produced basic chemicals, aluminum, pesticides, dyes, and plastics. When the factories were in operation, they spewed out coal dust that caked the buildings with black grime, poisoned the air until it stung the eyes, and transformed brook water into muddy syrup. The worst part of the situation came out in a 1990 investigation, which revealed that Bitterfeld and its environs were poisoned deliberately by the East German government in a scheme to raise money. The communist government had taxed industries for pollution control but then had refused to build pollution-control devices, using the money collected from the fines to spend elsewhere.[51]

This revelation suggests that East German communist leaders had been far more callous and cynical about the health of East German workers than was ever suspected. In fact, they had declared environmental statistics to be a state secret. Now, even though some of the factories are being closed and a massive clean-up operation is planned, trouble continues: German environmentalists say it will take years to restore environmental health to Bitterfeld.

2. Decommunization of Society

In the postcommunist era, eastern Germany has faced problems of decommunization and democratization of society. The most potentially destabilizing of the problems involves the influential role of former communists in the new economic order, lingering communist influence in the school system, the emergence of a group of youthful troublemakers known as "skinheads," whose prejudices and aberrant antidemocratic public behavior are logical consequences of the repressive rule of the communists before 1989, and revelations about the suspected but never really understood extensiveness of the former East German secret-police apparatus known as the *Stasi* in the private lives of East German citizens.

Former Communists and the New Economy

Many eastern Germans are very upset by the expanding role of former communists in the new capitalist economy. They are faring much better than they deserve to in a system they had for so long condemned and had replaced with one that deprived society of the level of well-being enjoyed in West Germany. Many of the owners of newly privatized enterprises are former communists, and anticommunist East Germans resent this fact. But these former communist managers had accumulated the capital to buy out former state-controlled property. They also understood better than ordinary people the complex procedures involved in running the former state-owned enterprises.[52]

Democratizing Education

Unfortunately, reunified Germany has done a poor job with East German schools. Disregarding the wishes of the people, the German government abruptly removed old and publicly revered symbols of forty-five years of socialism. Communist youth organizations, such as the Young Pioneers and Free German Youth, once the sole centers of extracurricular activity, disappeared, and red flags and portraits of communist heroes vanished. Schools have a difficult time, therefore, making an objective inquiry into the communist era. This is the second time since World War II that eastern Germans have been subjected to an official policy of national forgetfulness—first with the Nazis, then with the communists. Some people, including teachers, wonder whether a society can bear such forgetfulness twice within such a short period and worry about the moral confusion likely to result among impressionable eastern German youth.[53]

Responding to "Skinheads"

A dangerous signal of the difficulty of democratizing the youth, and perhaps sections of the adult population as well, of the former East German state has been the appearance since 1990 of a virulent nationalistic and anti-Semitic racism. At least 30,000 people, most of them under 25, have become involved in militant chauvinistic politics in eastern Germany. They have purchased weapons from the 300,000 Soviet soldiers deployed in eastern Germany, who sold guns for German marks as they prepared for redeployment in Russia and elsewhere in the former Soviet Union in the early 1990s. In public rallies, they shout Nazi slogans and make Nazi salutes. They have attacked foreigners and displayed intense hostility to Jews, writing anti-Jewish epithets on walls and tombstones. They are aggressive in cities like Dresden and Leipzig, where they have attacked the gathering places of homosexuals. They have also launched attacks against new centers of pornography started up in Dresden by West German criminals, and in that activity they have gained a measure of sympathy from people who oppose the spread of the West German criminal underworld to eastern Germany.[54]

Many of the youth involved in this activity are known as "skinheads." Mostly factory workers, they speak against anybody they consider "unGerman." Their behavior seems to be a reaction to the years of strict punishments meted out to right-wing radicals by the communist government. A conflict between generations may also explain the skinhead phenomenon, since many of the young people involved in the violence against minorities and in the revival of Nazi sentiments are children of former communist secret-police personnel.

Their behavior is dangerous because eastern German society under communist rule had no prolonged experience with democracy. It is vulnerable to the appeal of antidemocratic ideas, especially given the poverty of the region and the interest in simple solutions to complicated problems facing eastern Germany in the post-communist era.

The Stasi "Legacy"

A final problem in the decommunization of eastern Germany concerns the discovery by many eastern Germans that in the communist era friends and relatives had spied on them for the former East German secret police, or *Stasi*. In 1990, researchers from anti-*Stasi* groups began analyzing files in Berlin and other cities. They were shocked by the sheer volume of paper facing them: *Stasi* files filled 125 miles of shelf space, with each mile containing about 17 million sheets of paper and weighing nearly fifty tons. These represented reports filed by ordinary East Germans on their neighbors and friends as they went about their daily business.

The all-German Parliament disagreed over what to do with all this information. Some politicians warned that the files were too explosive to become public and proposed burning them. Others wanted the files sealed for a number of years or opened only selectively. But members of the Bundestag from the new constituencies in eastern Germany insisted that the files be opened to those on whom they were kept. Fleeing *Stasi* agents did manage to destroy some of their most incriminating files, such as those documenting their support for West Germany's murderous Red Army Faction and other terrorist groups.

Nevertheless, the files are remarkably complete and reveal the *Stasi*'s voracious appetite for even the most trivial information about suspected individuals, including their bathroom and sex habits. They show that the former communist system sought total penetration and control of East German society. With about 100,000 full-time employees and over 500,000 people serving as spies and informants, it is clear that the former East German communist regime considered almost all its citizens potentially subversive.[55]

Under a law approved by the German Parliament at the end of 1991, any German citizen now has the right to examine his or her *Stasi* file. Special librarians at the *Stasi* archives can usually identify the informer despite the use of code names. Many *Stasi* victims who have seen their files have discovered that some of their friends, coworkers, and even relatives were informers for the secret police.

Moreover, the law opening the *Stasi* files also empowered government agencies to request background checks on their employees, which have resulted in the dismissal of thousands of judges, police officers, school teachers, and others in the public service who lived and worked in the former East German state. *Stasi* files have also shaken the German sports world, revealing how certain prominent Olympic champions had been informers. These people, along with many others, stand discredited, with their professional ambitions severely compromised. All Germany has become transfixed by what the German weekly *Der Spiegel* called "the horror files."[56]

Today people in eastern Germany on whom files had been kept are in shock and cannot understand the behavior of these informers, many of whom were people they had trusted. Nevertheless, they all seem to agree that knowing what happened, confronting informers, and seeking some retribution, even if they know none will be forthcoming since the new Germany has no way to compensate them for what they have suffered, are all necessary actions that must be taken for the sake of personal consolation and also in the hope that a recurrence of such outrages will never happen again. At the very least, the *Stasi* revelations have had a profoundly disturbing affect on the sense of community and shared purpose in eastern Germany.[57]

3. Psychocultural Difficulties

While many problems of reunifying Germany can be resolved with money and expertise, the cultural adjustments will be difficult. The country is not unified in spirit. Indeed, a strong hostility has developed recently between eastern Germans and western Germans. Many eastern Germans resent their better-off neighbors in the West. From an eastern point of view, the western Germans are pompous and condescending in matters involving the former East German society.

Eastern Germans are also extremely sensitive about the political situation in their part of Germany, convinced that they are being "colonized" by western political organizations and that they will not be able to develop their own indigenous politics. They resent the fact that local and state governing agencies in eastern Germany are mostly staffed by western Germans, even if this is done to facilitate the melding of the two previously independent bureaucratic systems. They also resent the way in which eastern German government employees are carefully scrutinized to determine the extent of their intimacy with the former communist government. Many eastern Germans see this scrutiny as discriminatory and counterproductive, exacerbating resentment against the west.[58]

4. New Hardships for Women

Women in eastern Germany have had an especially difficult time adjusting to reunification and democratization.[59] Under communist rule, 40 percent of the East German workforce had been made up of women, and women enjoyed a greater equality with men than did women in West Germany. Unemployment has hurt them more than it has men because men, considered to be the primary breadwinners, frequently were given priority in hiring.

Furthermore, women have been discouraged from getting involved in politics in the postcommunist era, not only because they have been distracted by the new economic hardships they must endure as a result of the rapid transition to a free-market economy, but also because the feminist movement that does exist in eastern Germany today has little sympathy for the traditional role of women as homemakers and does little to attract their attention. And as long as they remain, as they are today, underrepresented in the eastern German trade unions and political and governmental organizations, they will have difficulty getting policies that favor them.[60]

The disadvantages that have befallen women in eastern Germany have demoralized and depressed them and have accounted for some ominous social changes. Women in eastern Germany are less interested in having children than was true earlier, causing a drop in the birth rate, which in 1994 was less than half of what it had been before reunification. In addition, the number of marriages has declined 62 percent, while sterilization of males has increased significantly in the state of Brandenburg. At this rate, eastern Germany stands to lose about 25 percent of its present population by the year 2010.[61]

5. Political Revival of Former Communists

The difficulties of getting used to reunification, along with the hardships caused by the rapid transformation of eastern Germany from socialist paternalism to free enterprise and the market economy, have contributed to a political revival of former communists, whose organization, the Party of Democratic Socialism, had seemed to be at death's door following its disastrous defeat in the March 1990 parliamentary election. And in October 1990, the former communists, still under the leadership of Gregor Gysi, suffered another loss of what small credibility they still had with some eastern German voters when party officials were caught illegally transferring huge sums of money for safekeeping to the Soviet Union. Although the Democratic Socialists retained some voter support, as demonstrated in state elections in October 1990 when their candidates obtained 10 percent of the vote, the chances of a revival of the former communists, by whatever name, remain problematical.[62]

Opportunities

In the early 1990s, people could not forget or forgive the Communist Party's oppressive and inept rule and gave it little support, while approving punishment of as many former communist leaders as possible, including former SED leader Honecker. But before long, the eastern German public lost interest in retribution and became focused on the difficulties of daily life in the new democratic order. In particular, the public lost interest in the prosecution of Erich Honecker and was willing to see the government dismiss criminal charges against him on the pretext that he was too old and too sick to stand trial.

In 1993 and 1994, former communists seemed to be heading for an electoral comeback, with an intensive campaign to prove they had a new platform and had broken completely with the past. For example, the Party of Democratic Socialism insisted it had completely discarded orthodox communist ideology and was a loyal opposition committed to furthering the economic and social well-being of eastern Germans. In addition, almost all of the old leadership of the Honecker era was gone, either retired or dead. The party's new persona won it some popular support, but a major source of the new voter interest in the party was less an affection for the party itself than disappointment with the results of reunification, especially the persistence of unemployment and the prolongation of hard times for most workers and their families.

Achievements

In parliamentary elections in October 1994, the Party of Democratic Socialism won about 14 percent of the popular vote in the eastern part of the country. The party benefited from the vigorous attacks on it by Chancellor Helmut Kohl. But the real reason for its success was the growing popular disenchantment throughout the territory of the former German Democratic Republic with Bonn's management of reunification, as well as unfulfilled pledges not only to be more solicitous of the well-being of eastern German workers and their families in the movement toward a market economy. To what extent eastern German voters have bought the party's message is uncertain. The party leadership is not taking any chances, however, and pledged honorable, constructive behavior in the new Bundestag, as well as another campaign to remove from its ranks any remaining militants who still believe that the orthodox communism of people like the late Honecker still has a political future.

Conclusions

As of the mid-1990s, eastern Germans have not recovered from the swiftness of the change from communism to capitalism, and they are ill prepared for the transition from dictatorship to democracy and for the problems they face as they embrace new values and new institutions. The sudden and total collapse of the socialist order to which they had become accustomed, despite its irritants, has baffled, stunned, and demoralized many eastern Germans and has recalled similar feelings most Germans experienced in the Weimar Republic of the 1920s, when the country was trying to make democracy work despite a long history of authoritarian government dating to the origins of the German nation.

The democratization of eastern Germany is likely to take a long time. In the interim, former East German citizens are in a sort of developmental limbo. It is difficult for them to reject the paternalistic order under which they lived during the communist era, and it is almost as difficult for them to adjust to the unpredictability and to what seems to many to be the cold and uncaring character of the new economic and political systems they are told are democratic. While the Bonn government is trying very hard and sparing no cost to ease the transition, it cannot avoid the physical and psychological trauma that accompanies profound socioeconomic and political change.

Many eastern Germans now think that they are the poor cousins of western Germany and in need of charity for an indefinite period. They may well be right: of Germany's 80.5 million people, 19 percent live in the eastern part of the country but produce only 6.5 percent of German gross domestic product, with industrial output at no more than about 4 percent of Germany's total. Moreover, eastern German taxes are insufficient to pay for the local government and its services, requiring the continuation of large infusions of capital from western Germany. Although Chancellor Kohl has tried to assure eastern Germans that they are not condemned to perpetual poverty and inferiority in the new reunified Germany, he does not have the wherewithal to redeem his promises to them of prosperity around the corner. And as long as economic life in eastern Germany remains harsh, political life, especially the development of democratic values, will remain uncertain.

7

Hungary

Communists came to power in Hungary immediately following the end of World War II with the help of the Soviet Union. Once in power, they quickly established a Soviet-style dictatorship and came under direct Soviet influence. On instructions from the Kremlin, Hungarian communist leaders purged society of political opponents, introduced a highly centralized economic system, and adopted Moscow's anti-Western foreign policy.

Challenges to Soviet Policy

After Stalin's death in March 1953, Hungarians of all social groups—workers, farmers, the intelligentsia—sought a relaxation of the dictatorship. A Communist Party reformer, Imre Nagy, became prime minister in 1953. He tried to liberalize the Hungarian political system and separate it from Moscow.

1. The 1956 Revolution

Stalin's successor, Nikita Khrushchev, who had no intention of loosening Soviet ties with the East European communist governments, was convinced that Nagy's reform would erode communist and Soviet power in Hungary. In the fall of 1956, Hungary appeared to be on the threshold of open revolt, with newspapers and popular demonstrations calling for a major liberalization of the Stalinist political and economic system.

2. The Soviet Crackdown

Khrushchev responded with force. In October 1956, he sent tanks into Budapest in one of the most dramatic moments of the cold war. People met the tanks with

HUNGARY

Geography
1. Location: central Europe, northwest of Romania
2. Area: total — 93,030 square kilometers; land area — 92,340 square kilometers; comparative area — slightly smaller than Indiana
3. Boundaries: with Austria — 366 kilometers; with Croatia — 329 kilometers; with Romania — 443 kilometers; with Serbia and Montenegro — 151 kilometers (all with Serbia); with Slovakia — 515 kilometers; with Slovenia — 82 kilometers; with Ukraine — 103 kilometers
4. Climate: temperate; cold, cloudy, humid winters; warm summers
5. Terrain: mostly flat to rolling plains; hills and low mountains on the border with Slovakia
6. Land use: arable — 46%; permanent crops — 1%; meadows and pastures — 13%; forest and woodland — 28%

7. Natural resources: coal, sulphur, copper, natural gas
8. Environment: air pollution; industrial and municipal pollution of Lake Balaton

People
1. Population: 10,318,838 (1995 estimate)
2. Age structure: 0–14 — 18% of population (female — 918,281; male — 958,027); 15–64 — 68% of population (female — 3,534,218; male — 3,440,036); 65 and over — 14% of population (female — 914,221; male — 554,055) (1995 estimate)
3. Growth rate: 0.02% (1995 estimate)
4. Life expectancy at birth: total population — 71.9 years; female — 76.06 years; male — 67.94 years (1995 estimate)
5. Ethnic divisions: Hungarian — 89.9%; Gypsy — 4%; German — 2.6%; Slovak — 0.8%
6. Religions: Roman Catholic — 67.5%; Calvinist — 20%; Lutheran — 5%
7. Languages: Hungarian — 98.2%
8. Literacy: total population — 99%
9. Labor force: total — 5.4 million; services, trade, and government — 44.8%; industry — 29.7%; agriculture — 16.1%; construction — 7.1% (1991 estimate)

Government
1. Type: emerging parliamentary democracy
2. Capital: Budapest
3. Independence: 1001 (unification by King Stephen I)
4. Constitution: revised October 18, 1989
5. National administration:
   a. Chief of state: President of the Republic (1996 — Árpád Göncz)
   b. Ministerial leadership: Prime Minister and Council of Ministers (1996 — Gyula Horn, prime minister)
   c. Legislature: unicameral — National Assembly (*Orszaggyules*)
   d. Judicial branch: Constitutional Court
   e. Political parties: Hungarian Democratic Forum, Independent Small-holders, Hungarian Socialist Party, Christian Democratic People's Party, Federation of Young Democrats, Alliance of Free Democrats
6. Local administration: unitary system with 38 counties

Economy
1. Gross domestic product: $58.8 billion (1994 estimate)
2. National product real growth rate: 3% (1994 estimate)
3. Per-capita national product: $5,700 (1994 estimate)
4. Inflation rate: 21% (1994 estimate)
5. Unemployment rate: 10.4% (1994 estimate)
6. Budget: revenue — $11.3 billion; expenditures — $14.2 billion
7. Industrial output: mining, metallurgy, construction materials, processed foods, textiles, chemicals (especially pharmaceuticals), buses, automobiles
8. Agricultural output: livestock (hogs, cattle), poultry, dairy products, wheat, corn, sunflowers, potatoes, sugar beets
9. Exports: $10.3 billion (1994 estimate) raw materials and semifinished goods, machinery and transport equipment, consumer goods, food and agricultural products
10. Imports: $13.3 billion (1994 estimate) — fuels and energy, raw materials and semifinished goods, machinery and transport equipment, consumer goods, food and agriculture
11. External debt: $27 billion (1994 estimate)
12. Trade partners: Germany, Austria, United States
13. Economic aid recipient: $59 billion, OECD
14. Transportation: railroads — 7,785 kilometers; highways — 158,711 kilometers; ports — Budapest, Dunaújváros; airports — 78 (14 with paved runways)

rocks and hand-made weapons. They had no chance of resistance against overwhelming Soviet military power. With the popular revolt brutally suppressed, the Kremlin removed Nagy from power and installed János Kádár as Hungarian Communist Party Chief with orders to restore a Stalinist-style government. Kádár eventually executed Nagy and had his remains buried in an unmarked grave in a cemetery on the outskirts of Budapest.

3. Kádár's Pragmatic Socialism

Kádár remained in power for thirty-two years. During this long period of rule, he avoided political and economic extremes as much as he could. He wanted Moscow to support his leadership, but he also wanted the Hungarian people to accept his government. Although he was intolerant of popular protest and dissent, he had no stomach for the kind of repression practiced in neighboring Romania and elsewhere in the Soviet bloc. Aware of problems with the working of the Soviet-style command economy that had originally provoked popular discontent on the eve of the 1956 revolution, he tried to liberalize the country's rigid economic organization to expand output and raise living standards. He shrewdly reassured Moscow of his loyalty as he began to move Hungary away from the Soviet model. In 1968, Kádár introduced the "New Economic Mechanism" (NEM). This plan decentralized economic decision making somewhat, transferring much of it from the large ministries in Budapest to the managers of enterprises throughout the country; it called for a pricing system that would be more responsive to supply and demand; and it opened the door to a limited amount of private entrepreneurship. In the 1970s and early 1980s, Hungary's economic reforms paid solid dividends. The NEM brought greater efficiency with lower costs and improved the standard of living of average Hungarians. The socialist system consequently enjoyed a higher level of popular acceptability in Hungary than anywhere else in Eastern Europe. In effect, Kádár had bought a measure of political stability by achieving a marked improvement in national economic performance.

Economic and Social Problems

By the 1980s, Hungarian communism, despite Kádár's ingenious reforms, began to experience the same problems communist systems in other Central and East European countries were having and with the same effects, namely, the development of popular discontent with communist rule and ultimately a determination to reform it out of existence. The major problems were economic stagnation and social impoverishment. Their solution required a new and more extensive reformism after the fashion of Gorbachev's perestroika.

1. Economic Stagnation

Despite the beneficial effects of the NEM, there were shortages of consumer necessities and a decline in living standards in the 1980s. The Stalinist command economic system was partly to blame. But a variety of policies were also responsible. The state had invested heavily in smokestack industries like steel and coal mining, whose huge losses were bleeding the economy. Inefficient and wasteful of precious resources, these enterprises had to be subsidized by the government, which heavily taxed the country's small number of private enterprises, undermining this sector as well. There were similar mistakes in agriculture. Although in the 1970s the Hungarian government received huge loans from the West to modernize farms to expand productivity to increase the food supply for home consumption and for export, in the 1980s there was a slump in production partly because, to bolster the inefficient industrial sector, the government curtailed credit to agricultural enterprises, forcing many to close. In other instances, the government merged failing cooperative and state farms with efficient ones, further undermining productivity.

Hungarian membership in the Council for Mutual Economic Assistance (CMEA) was another source of trouble for the economy. Hungary had to sell its exports to Eastern bloc customers at unreasonably low prices. To satisfy this market for cheap goods, Hungary ran inefficient, out-of-date, and unprofitable industries rather than producing competitive quality goods at world prices for the Western market where they could earn high profits. Moreover, during the 1980s, Hungary financed its export industries through Western loans, borrowing money for energy imports to keep unprofitable industries going. The country's net foreign debt rose, and the bulk of convertible export earnings had to be spent on debt service.

By 1989, Hungary's economic stagnation was also attributable to the government's unwillingness to implement reforms already on the books. For example, the government refused to enforce the bankruptcy law because a close down of enterprises unable to earn a profit would cause massive unemployment. Self-interested bureaucrats also did not want to preside over any dismantling of the Stalinist economic infrastructure since it was the source of their power and privilege in Hungarian society.[1]

2. Social Impoverishment

A pervasive impoverishment beset Hungarian society in the 1980s. While a fortunate few managed to prosper, the vast majority of Hungarians by 1989 had difficulty making ends meet. The average monthly wage of $160.00 did not go very far. Hungarians worked two, even three jobs. Although economic stagnation contributed to poverty, certain policies of the communist leadership made things worse for most Hungarians.

A chronic housing shortage aggravated the situation as the state failed to continue the redistribution of existing housing and did not invest in new construction. When the government approved loans to help people build their own residences, only the well-to-do could afford to take advantage of them. The vast majority of people lived in substandard, overcrowded housing.[2]

Furthermore, to make up for a shortfall of income resulting from the decline in economic output in the 1980s, the Hungarian government began to cut corners on its welfare program. It decreased expenditures for public health, causing a deterioration in the quality of medical services. Hungary's life expectancy at birth was among the lowest in Europe. As a result, Hungary's population was no longer reproducing itself, and the country's net population started to decrease. Hungarians were disappointed, depressed, and demoralized by the evident failure of their government to live up to the promises of socialism to deliver a better life for ordinary people.

Making matters worse for most Hungarian wage earners was the government's policy of income leveling, which penalized the educated employee by keeping monthly incomes of managers and other professionals nearly identical with those of skilled workers. The salary of a medical-school graduate took seven years to catch up with the wages of a semiskilled worker of his age group.[3] The educated classes were especially hurt as the government printed money to finance its debts and inflation escalated. University professors on fixed salaries found their buying power eroded and frequently took second jobs. The strain on them was evident in the classroom. Students declared publicly their support for teachers and a willingness to strike on their behalf.[4]

Social stratification increased popular pessimism about the future. Hungarian youth for several decades had been virtually frozen in the class of their parents, unable to move upward, and were frustrated in their dreams of a better life. With poor living conditions and a bleak outlook for the future, the suicide rate, alcoholism, and drug abuse soared. Disillusionment eventually turned into hard-line opposition to communism.[5]

3. Impact of Soviet Perestroika

Sensitive to these problems and the way they undermined the vitality of their socialist system and its chances of long-term survival and encouraged by Gorbachev's perestroika, reformers at the top of the Hungarian Communist hierarchy lobbied the conservative party leadership for perestroika-style reform to rejuvenate Hungarian socialism and give the party a new legitimacy.

Károly Grosz, a reformer appointed prime minister in June 1987, proposed privatization or closure of state-owned smokestack industries that could not earn a profit. He also sought to limit the country's obligations in the CMEA. In particular, he wanted Hungary to stay away from CMEA-sponsored projects, such as the proposed natural-gas pipeline from Siberia to Eastern Europe and a large hydroelectric project on the Danube, which were likely to be of more benefit to Czechoslovakia and Austria than to Hungary.[6]

Grosz introduced a Hungarian version of perestroika. But his government went much further in Hungary than Gorbachev did in the Soviet Union in altering the still very Stalinistic character of Hungarian economic organization and behavior, despite the NEM reforms enacted two decades earlier. Grosz focused on expanding economic output and making Hungarian exports competitive in the world market by encouraging private entrepreneurship in agriculture, the service industries, and retail trade. To make state enterprises more efficient and more profitable, he increased managerial independence of central authorities in acquiring raw materials abroad and in determining wages to increase incentives.[7]

In the fall of 1987, he began the groundwork for a Western-style economic infrastructure, setting up a two-tiered banking system that consisted of a central bank and a series of commercial and specialized banks to facilitate the distribution of credit to worthy borrowers, in particular, efficiently run state enterprises and newly established private ones. The new banks made short-term loans to enterprises and issued bonds to raise capital that would make possible larger loans for longer periods to more extensive and ambitious enterprises. These banks gradually developed a substantial autonomy, though not complete independence, of the state-controlled Hungarian national bank, which continued to be the chief source of investment capital for very large industrial enterprises.[8]

In the fiscal area, the government introduced Western-style personal-income and value-added taxes while reducing taxes on business, thus departing from the traditional socialist emphasis on collective responsibility for funding public policy. By shifting the tax burden to the individual, there would be increased popular pressure on the bureaucracy to use public money judiciously. With additional discretionary funds, enterprises could improve production and maximize output.[9]

Grosz also wanted to attract foreign capital and technology into Hungary and, in the fall of 1988, allowed full foreign ownership of Hungarian companies. Joint ventures with less than 50 percent foreign participation no longer needed official registration. Hungarians could trade shares in private companies (previously Hungarians could own shares, but their holdings were restricted to the companies where they worked) and employ up to 500 citizens for private profit. Indeed, the law created a framework for a Western-style capital market and revived types of companies not seen in Hungary since before the communist takeover.[10]

Political Pluralism and Democratization

There was pressure for equivalent changes in the political sphere from alienated sectors of Hungarian society as well as from within the top leadership of the Communist Party, where reformers like Rezső Nyers and Imre Pozsgay were trying to convince their conservative colleagues to introduce a Hungarian version of Soviet glasnost and democratization.

1. Emergence of New Party Groups

In the late 1980s, economists, sociologists, technocrats, and members of other professions, aware of political reforms initiated in the Soviet Union, spoke out in underground *samizdat* form in support of similar political reform in Hungary. Sensitive to their exclusion from political power, they called for Communist Party accountability to the public and, more importantly, the establishment of other political parties to criticize and challenge party rule. Their initiatives in 1988 and 1989 led to the emergence of new parties and the reemergence of old ones. By the end of 1989, Hungary had a multiparty system in place.[11]

The Democratic Forum

In September 1987, Hungarian intellectuals established a new umbrella-type organization of political advocacy, the Democratic Forum, and invited all Hungarians interested in solving the nation's economic, social, and political problems to join. The Forum called for open and uncensored debates on national issues. At first its stated aim was to act as a loosely organized club for the discussion of the state of the nation and the ways of improving living conditions. A little later, the Forum styled itself a "bridge between the state and society," emphasizing that its aim was not to challenge the Hungarian Communist Party's "leading role." This accommodating stance did not spare the Forum attacks by Kádár and other conservative party leaders, but party politburo member Pozsgay offered his support to the movement, saying it could be a potential partner for the party. In these years, the Forum worked with the communist regime to promote political reform and dialogue, wanting peaceful change based on compromise and conciliation.[12]

Alliance of Free Democrats

On March 17, 1988, a number of urban political figures created the Network of Free Initiatives. Its declaration of principles said that the internal economic crisis and a perceived loosening of the Soviet grip created an opportunity for a broad dialogue about the direction the country should take. Originally formed to link a number of freely formed clubs and organizations with what its leaders called "social liberal" principles, the Network soon became a radical alternative to the legal and more cautious Democratic Forum. The Network sponsored debates and demonstrations and issued press statements as part of a concerted effort to force the government to the negotiating table. On October 23, 1988, the Network sponsored a popular demonstration in Budapest to commemorate the 1956 revolution, despite the government's attempt to prohibit it. On November 13, the Network became a political organization, the Alliance of Free Democrats.[13]

Unlike the Forum, the Alliance was skeptical about working with the communist regime to liberalize it and believed that real economic improvement was impossible as long as the Hungarian Communist Party remained in power. It advocated the adoption of a Western identity and Western free enterprise. It rejected a so-called "Hungarian way," that is, a program of change that would leave Hungarian society between Western capitalism and Soviet-style social-ism.[14]

Old Parties into New Ones

In 1988 and 1989, other small political groups drawn from former parties of the pre–World War II years became new political parties. The Smallholders, the Peasant Party, the Social Democrats, and the Independents reappeared. By the end of 1988, there was a proliferation of organizations of political protest and dissent, some calling themselves debating clubs and others looking like embryonic political parties offering tentative programs of political reform. Still others were alternative "unions" representing particular professions, with the intelligentsia running the largest and the most aggressive ones. This new pluralism was a clear sign that Kádár's reformism had failed to keep pace with changing needs and aspirations.

Trade-Union Activism

Even the official trade union, the National Council of Trade Unions (SZOT), had declared that the leadership was out of touch with the workers and insensitive to their concerns and complaints. In fact, SZOT, along with other newly emergent labor groups, such as the Democratic Union of Scientific Workers (TDDSZ), campaigned to increase the government's responsiveness to the people. It wanted the government to reverse its policy to allow workers to strike. In June 1988, TDDSZ joined with other smaller unions of teachers, filmmakers, and housing maintenance employees to form the League of Free Trade Unions, subsequently known as the Confederation of Free Trade Unions (LIGA), which eventually expanded its membership to include blue-collar workers.[15]

2. Party Reformers Battle Conservatives

Throughout 1989, the Hungarian Communist Party wrestled with the problem of responding to the emergence of the new political pluralism. It was divided at least into two major groups: reformers who wanted to liberalize the political system, and conservatives who wanted to maintain the traditional monolithic environment.

The Reformers

Reformist party leaders believed that a conciliatory approach to the new political ferment would in the long term benefit the party, encouraging its transformation into a flexible, more publicly responsible organization. Some reformers, notably politburo member Pozsgay, were ready to allow other parties to compete with the Communist Party in free, open, competitive elections for the Parliament, which itself should be transformed into a real, Western-style legislature. Pozsgay called for the elimination of a provision of the 1983 electoral law that allowed the Communist party veto power over candidates for public office. He also proposed a greater role for nonparty people in policy making and official acceptance of a loyal opposition in the Parliament. He recommended an easing up of censorship that would allow "underground" publications to become open.[16]

Conservative Resistance to Political Change

But party leader Kádár and his supporters in the politburo, Central Committee, and Secretariat resisted these changes. Kádár was sensitive to Gorbachev's concern that Hungary proceed cautiously with reform and avoid change that would take it out of the Soviet orbit. Kádár believed that the Kremlin would not tolerate another Imre Nagy. Kádár also feared that perestroika would fail and doubted that Gorbachev could survive infighting in the USSR. When Gorbachev removed Yeltsin in October 1987 from the top Soviet leadership even though he was a vigorous champion of Gorbachev's reform initiatives, Kádár believed the issue of future Soviet reforms was far from settled.

A Middle Ground on Political Liberalization

In May 1988, after months of occasionally bitter infighting between reformers and Kádárists, and as Gorbachev showed his determination to move forward with sweeping economic as well as political reform in the Soviet Union, reformist influence in the party increased. A special party conference voted to replace Kádár as the party's first secretary with Prime Minister Grosz and to promote Kádár to the newly created but largely ceremonial position of party president.[17]

While Grosz favored economic liberalization, he was skeptical of political pluralism, even as he acknowledged that a multiparty system and free parliamentary elections would facilitate economic change. Grosz did not want to jeopardize the Communist Party's traditional monopoly of power. Any transition to multiparty pluralism, he argued, had to be gradual to avoid a "proliferation of parties" and political destabilization. Nevertheless, Grosz was willing to accept a middle road in calling for a "qualified pluralism." He said parties in parliamentary elections would have to swear allegiance to socialism and accept the Communist Party's continued preeminence in the government, allow party control of a newly created state presidency, and agree to guarantee a certain proportion of seats in the Parliament to the Communist Party as well as the party's permanent control of the ministries of foreign affairs, interior, and defense. Most members of the Party, which was overall skeptical of pluralism and suspicious of the reformers, supported Grosz's qualifications.[18] Nevertheless, the party was ready to move forward with democratic reforms, concluding that it was inevitable, that the party's acceptance of it was the only way of assuring its leadership of the country, and that popular demands for pluralism had become too strong to ignore or resist. It was also afraid that a continuation of repressive policies would have discredited Hungary in the eyes of the West and brought a shutoff of Western funds.

Weakening of Conservative Influence

In 1989, Hungarian party conservatives could expect no sympathy for their opposition to political reform from Gorbachev, who already had introduced an unprecedented liberalization of the Soviet political system.[19] There were further setbacks for the conservative faction. In May 1989, the party's Central Committee voted to oust Kádár and send him into retirement once and for all. And in June it replaced Grosz as first secretary with a prominent reformer sympathetic to pluralistic democracy, Rezső Nyers. Along with Pozsgay and the newly appointed prime minister Miklos Nemeth, Nyers was able to move forward quickly with Hungarian democratization in the second half of 1989.[20]

3. Beginnings of Democratization in 1989

Throughout 1989, the Hungarian Communist Party took important steps to democratize the Hungarian political system, hoping that by acting in a timely fashion they could strengthen public support of the party and hold on to leadership. But by early 1990, democratization had backfired on the reformers, weakening the party and eventually precipitating the end of its rule.

Rehabilitation of Imre Nagy

An important symbolic event in the movement toward democracy in 1989 was the rehabilitation in June 1989 of Imre Nagy, a hero to Hungarians because of his efforts to reform Hungary in 1956 and because of the brutal suppression of those efforts by the Kremlin.[21] Party reformers were sympathetic to the idea of rehabilitating Nagy, viewing it as an important means of gaining popular credibility and moving out of the shadow of 1956. Over the opposition of conservatives, the government agreed in January 1989 to allow the exhumation, identification, and reburial of Nagy's remains, a beginning of the rehabilitation process. Shortly afterward, Pozsgay went further by reversing the past official view of the events of October 1956 as a "counterrevolution" and agreed to have them referred to officially as "a popular uprising against an oligarchical rule that had debased the nation." After approving his formal reburial, government leaders attended what became a sort of state funeral for Nagy.[22]

The Party Abandons Its Political Monopoly

In October 1989, the party held a special congress ending its monopoly of power in Hungary. A majority of this congress also voted to transform the party into a new West European social-democratic organization, to be called the Hungarian Socialist Party. The new Socialists quickly drafted a program that discarded Marxist-Leninist principles and identified itself as a moderate, reformist party committed to political pluralism and parliamentary democracy.[23]

The November 1989 Referendum

Another landmark in democratization was the November 1989 referendum to determine when the president of Hungary should be elected. The party wanted presidential elections to come before the parliamentary elections scheduled for March 1990 in the expectation that its candidate, Pozsgay, known for his reformist achievements, would win and thereby strengthen the party's chances of a victory in March. Moreover, presidential elections held while the communists still controlled the government, in particular the media, also would help his candidacy. The Free Democrats and other opposition groups, however, wanted presidential elections held after parliamentary elections to give them time to field a presidential candidate strong enough to challenge Pozsgay. In a dialogue with opposition groups in August 1989, the party agreed to allow Hungarian voters to decide on the timing of the two elections in a referendum scheduled in November.[24]

The referendum, which was the first free electoral experience Hungarians had in forty-two years of Communist Party rule, turned out badly for the communists. Hungarians voted to hold the presidential elections after parliamentary elections. Since the Communist Party could lose its majority in the parliamentary elections in which it would have to compete with other parties and in which its record of leadership of the country would be the key issue for voters, it risked also losing control of the government as well as other advantages it had in the fall of 1989 that could help it in presidential elections. The party's reformist leadership nevertheless accepted the unhappy results of the referendum and canceled a presidential vote scheduled for January 1990.[25]

The party's failure in the November referendum indicated its diminished role in Hungarian politics and its inability to dissociate itself from its past. A public-opinion poll held shortly after the party's October congress indicated that, if elections to the Parliament had been held then, the party would have received only 16 percent of the popular vote. The referendum was also a personal setback for Pozsgay, virtually eliminating any chance of his leading Hungary in the new democratic era. The results of the referendum, indeed, did not bode well for the party in the March parliamentary elections.[26]

The End of Communist Rule

With the November referendum, the days of communist leadership of Hungary were numbered. Again, however, in a conciliatory spirit designed to ingratiate itself with the voting public, the Communist Party made significant concessions to other political groups that would challenge it in the March 1990 elections. Of 386 seats, 210 were to be elected by the list system in multimember constituencies and 176 were to be elected on the "winner-take-all" principle in single-member districts. Confident that the public would reward it for its acceptance of radical departures from the single-party dictatorship, party reformers agreed to proportional representation that would allow small parties whose support was scattered throughout the country to win seats in the Parliament, thereby jeopardizing the chances of obtaining the plurality needed to retain leadership. But communist deputies quickly had second thoughts about this concession and pushed through the Parliament a modification of the electoral law increasing the number of single-member districts to enhance their reelection chances. Still, there was much opportunity for noncommunist groups to challenge and unseat the communists if the voters wanted that.[27]

1. The March 1990 Parliamentary Elections

The voter turnout was not as large as one might have expected given the long period in which Hungarians had been denied freedom of electoral choice. Only 66 percent of the electorate participated. Many lower-middle-class voters did not vote at all because they could not find a party other than the communists that clearly and persuasively advocated the continuation of a social safety net. The Democratic Forum, which advocated gradual change, won a plurality of seats, while the Alliance of Free Democrats, which supported a rapid transition to a free-market economy, came in second. The Socialists fared badly and were swept out of power, ending over forty years of rule. A number of other parties, including the Smallholders' Party, which had called for the immediate return of property to prenationalization owners, came in third.[28]

By ousting the communists from power, Hungarian voters were by no means endorsing the radical departures from socialism advocated by the Free Democrats. Rather, the electorate preferred the gradual pace of change from socialism to the free market advocated by the Forum. The Forum did best for other reasons. Apart from its concern with Hungarian minorities living abroad, the Forum had an appealing leader in József Antall, who easily won the prime ministership shortly after the election because he had no burdensome political baggage—he had no links with the communist regime. With Antall's election as prime minister on May 10, 1990, Hungary came under noncommunist leadership for the first time in forty-three years.[29]

2. Weaknesses of the Former Communists

Working against the former communists during the campaign, despite their reformist orientation, which most Hungarians favored, was their past record in
power. Hungarians could not forget or forgive the communists for the harshness
and ineptitude of their rule. In addition, a charge that the communist-run secret
police was continuing on the eve of the elections to spy on members of the
opposition and to keep records of various meetings and events dominated the
media.

The opposition put the communists on the defensive, calling for the immediate dismantling of the entire secret-police apparatus. The government agreed to
stop monitoring opposition political activities, dismissing the chief of the secret
police and a deputy minister of the interior and transferring control of the clandestine agencies from the Interior Ministry to the prime minister's office. But the
damage to whatever credibility the communists may still have had was already
done, hurting them further in the vote.[30]

The communists lost popular support because of their lackluster record of
championing the rights of the Hungarian minority in the Transylvanian region of
northwest Romania. When the Romanian revolution broke out in December
1989, with an ethnic Hungarian cleric provoking the wrath of Bucharest by
challenging its oppressive policies, the leading parties in Hungary turned the
Hungarian minority in Transylvania into a campaign issue. The Forum benefited
because it had most consistently enunciated Hungarian cultural nationalism by
denouncing the Romanian regime for the mistreatment of its Hungarian minority.[31]

Reform and Foreign Policy

Hungary's movement toward democracy in 1988 and 1989 antagonized conservative socialist countries like Czechoslovakia, East Germany, and Romania. The Soviet Union was benevolently neutral toward Hungarian reformism, even though it
was proceeding faster and further in 1989 than the Kremlin would have liked.
Western Europe and the United States were pleased by the political changes taking
place and encouraged Hungarian leaders to continue and expand them.

1. Hostility of Conservative Neighbors

Czechoslovakia's president Gustáv Husák and Communist Party leader Miloš
Jakeš were alarmed by Hungary's rapid movement toward political pluralism,
convinced that it would exert a subversive influence on Czechoslovak socialism.
When the Hungarian leadership attended the memorial to Nagy in June 1989, the
Czech communist leadership, worried about an equivalent evaluation of former party
leader Alexandr Dubček, distanced itself from Hungary. A Hungarian television
interview with Dubček further strained relations between the two countries.[32]

The conservative regime of Erich Honecker in East Germany worried that Hungarian reformism would stimulate internal opposition. The situation was at its worst in the summer of 1989, when thousands of alienated East German citizens, professing themselves tourists, emigrated through Hungary to West Germany in search of improved living conditions. Hungarian reformism was setting a bad example for East German society.

Romanian president and party leader Nicolae Ceauşescu heartily disliked the political liberalization program going on in Hungary, fearing that the Romanian people might demand similar reforms in their own country. He was especially disturbed by the decision of the Hungarian reformers to rehabilitate Imre Nagy. In a statement handed to the Hungarian ambassador in Bucharest by the Romanian Foreign Ministry, the Romanian government said the funeral service betrayed "anti-socialist, anti-Romanian, nationalist-chauvinistic, and revisionist manifestations."[33]

Romania's alleged mistreatment of its Hungarian minority in Transylvania was another source of tension in the relations between the two countries. Especially offensive to Hungary was the application of Ceauşescu's policy of replacing old villages with modern apartment towns, which would have destroyed much of the region's Hungarian character.

In August 1988, Prime Minister Grosz met with Ceauşescu in the Romanian city of Arad near Romania's frontier with Hungary to discuss the minority issue. Grosz asked for Romanian acknowledgment of Hungary's legitimate interest in the fate of the Hungarian minority in Transylvania, an end to the program of eliminating thousands of villages historically inhabited by Hungarian-speaking peasants, the reopening of the Hungarian consulate in Cluj, the capital of Transylvania, which was closed in June, and the establishment of a Hungarian cultural center in Bucharest. Grosz got little from Ceauşescu. The Romanian leader refused to reopen the consulate and to alter his plan of modernizing Hungarian rural districts, bringing Hungarian–Romanian relations to an all-time low by the end of 1989.[34]

2. Soviet Neutrality

Although Gorbachev was uneasy about the new wave of Hungarian economic and political reformism, which threatened to undermine communist rule, he became more sympathetic to the changes taking place, hoping for a reinvigoration of socialism and Communist Party rule. Moreover, as far as the Kremlin could determine, the Hungarian Communist Party was in charge and was expected to keep control over the country. Skeptical of Kádár's conservatism, Gorbachev did not interfere with his ouster from the party's top leadership. Nor did he interfere with the rehabilitation of Nagy in the summer of 1989, especially in light of his public abrogation of the Brezhnev Doctrine. The Kremlin accepted with equanimity the demise of communist party dominance in the March 1990 parliamentary elections, recognizing the high cost for the Soviet Union, which was having its own problems, of antagonizing the West if it tried to block liberalization in Hungary. Indeed, Gorbachev and Foreign Minister Shevardnadze responded with grace to the political situation in Budapest and took steps to befriend the country's new democratic leadership. They agreed to withdraw Soviet troops from Hungary and to dissolve both the CMEA and the Warsaw Pact, as Budapest demanded.

3. Encouragement of the West

Germany and the United States, more than other Western countries, were willing to reach out to the Hungarian reformers to encourage them. They saw Hungarian reform as a model for other communist states in the region.

German Policy

In the late 1980s, Germany was ready to conciliate the new reformist leadership in Budapest. When Grosz visited Bonn in early October 1987, he came away with five different agreements on economic, scientific and technological, and cultural matters, the most important involving a guaranteed credit from the West German government of one billion marks. Relations continued to improve, and in 1989 Chancellor Helmut Kohl commended Hungary for the liberalization of travel restrictions, for Hungary's persistent diplomacy of dialogue with the West, and for its equitable treatment of the small German minority living within its borders.

Hungary and the United States

In the late 1980s, the Grosz government wanted good relations with the United States for economic and strategic reasons. Grosz wanted Americans to invest technology and capital in the Hungarian economy, especially the consumer sector. Good Hungarian–American relations would also strengthen East–West détente and protect Hungary's links with the West against possible difficulties between the superpowers.

At the end of July 1988, Grosz met with President Ronald Reagan in Washington and visited several U.S. cities to promote investment in Hungarian industry. Reagan extended to him the same courtesies he had given to Gorbachev, signifying American recognition of Hungarian reformism as well as an expectation that it would continue to go forward. Grosz obtained a joint-venture agreement worth $115 million between Guardian Industries of Northville, Michigan, and a glass-works enterprise in southeastern Hungary. Hungary would now become a modern manufacturer of glass products to be sold in Western Europe. Grosz also discussed the expansion of an educational exchange program between Hungarian and American secondary and higher educational institutions.[35]

Bush continued Reagan's supportive policies and visited Hungary in July 1989, emphasizing American support for the Hungarian reform movement. Bush approved unlimited Hungarian access to U.S. markets and a small, $25 million aid package.[36] Bush also granted Hungary most-favored-nation treatment in trade with the United States, helping Budapest to make headway in repaying its enormous foreign debt and cope with a bloated budget deficit.[37]

Part of Hungarian strategy toward the United States involved a restoration of official ties with Israel, broken off in the Arab–Israeli War of 1967 on signal from the Kremlin. A first step came in September 1987, when the two countries agreed to exchange envoys. In mid-September 1988, Grosz met with Israeli's premier Yitzak Shamir in Budapest and agreed to urge Gorbachev to improve the living conditions of Soviet Jews and lift restrictions on their emigration. On September 18, 1989, Hungary and Israel formally restored diplomatic ties with each other.[38]

Problems of Postcommunist Political Development

The new democratic leadership in Budapest wanted political stability as it moved forward with systemic economic reform and coped with worsening social problems inherited from the communist era. The stakes were high for Hungarian democracy because most people expected that the demise of communist rule would bring an immediate improvement in living conditions. In the early 1990s, Hungarian political leaders, especially those on the right, who were impatient with democratic processes that slowed policy-making, were willing to take undemocratic shortcuts to get smooth and businesslike passage of urgently needed legislation, viewing conflict and competition as counterproductive.[39] Popular disappointment that the democratic system was not changing things fast enough led people to become apathetic toward politics and encouraged them to think nostalgically about the communist and even pre-communist past.

1. Oligarchical Decision Making

Following the March 1990 parliamentary elections, the leaders of the two large winning parties, the Democratic Forum and the Alliance of Free Democrats, secretly agreed among themselves on a wide range of issues concerning the style and content of policy making in the new government. They did not consult their own party colleagues or the other political groups supporting them in the Parliament, even though their decisions affected important aspects of Hungarian governmental structure and policy making. For example, they agreed that the president of Hungary would be Free Democrat Árpád Göncz. They agreed on the staffing of the ten permanent and five special committees of the Parliament. They also agreed to establish an independent body to supervise radio and television. They agreed to require a two-thirds majority in Parliament for the adoption of amendments to the constitution. They chose Forum leader József Antall as prime minister.[40] By passing up debate and consensus building, this "smoke-filled-room" deal making was a liability for representative and responsible government, but it did bring a measure of political stability that helped the country cope with pressing economic social problems.

Another dimension of this tendency toward oligarchy concerned Hungarian unions, which were never as subservient to the Communist Party as unions had been in other socialist countries. They had been popular with workers and had enjoyed some influence with management at the plant level since the introduction of the NEM in 1968. In the early 1990s, the new democratic government, however, did not want to contend with a powerful union movement that could complicate the introduction of a free-market economy. Indeed, Antall and his colleagues wanted to minimize opposition to controversial free-market reforms likely to cause hardship, such as unemployment and inflation, and tried to restrict their role in newly privatized enterprises. A labor code that went into effect in July 1992 tended to weaken unions by allowing an open shop, by allowing so-called "pocket unions," which are unions controlled by employers, and by allowing workers' councils to perform some of the functions of unions, such as deciding how welfare funds specificied in a labor contract are distributed. Furthermore, the labor code weakened unions by not explicitly assigning them the functions they performed under socialism, such as determining basic wages in places of employment. The government antagonized many Hungarians, who viewed strong unions as an alternative to the government bureaucracy thereby helping to encourage a degree of political apathy and cynicism.[41]

2. Voter Apathy

Hungarian voters have shown some political apathy, as in the low turnout for referenda in November 1989. And in the July 1990 referendum, on the issue of how to elect the president, directly or by the Parliament, only 13 percent of the eligible electorate went to the polls. This referendum, incidentally, which favored the direct election of the president, had to be declared invalid because of the small turnout. And in local elections on September 30 and October 14, 1990, only 40 percent of eligible voters participated in a first ballot and only 29 percent participated in the runoff.[42]

Certainly one explanation of this low showing was fatigue from having had to vote in six elections in 1990. Local government also was viewed with far less seriousness than the government in Budapest. But it is also true that most people did not think that voting mattered or that voting could improve their living conditions. Moreover, voters were overwhelmed by the rapid proliferation of political parties in 1989 and 1990—sixty-five parties registered to take part in the first national elections of the postcommunist era. While party proliferation reflected the eagerness of minority political activists, long denied the opportunity for political expression, to indulge themselves, there was a negative side. The multiplicity of parties presented voters with a confusing choice and encouraged many to lose interest in politics. Moreover, many Hungarian voters did not believe the parties adequately represented their interests and anxieties.[43]

The consequences of voter apathy were significant. As a result of the low turnout of only 46 percent in the second ballot of the March 1990 parliamentary elections, Antall's government was based on "a majority of the minority." In effect the new government did not have a clear mandate for the kind of reformism to which it was committed. Worse, at the end of June 1990, less than half of those polled by the Hungarian Institute for Public Opinion Research believed that the government knew how to lead the country out of the economic chaos left by the communists.[44]

3. Nostalgia for the Conservative Past

One alternative to the mainstream parties in postcommunist Hungary is the political right. There is evidence of a growing public sympathy for Hungary's precommunist conservative past. In September 1993, there was a large public turnout for the ceremony that accompanied the reburial of the remains of Admiral Miklós Horthy, the Hungarian leader who collaborated with Hitler and who promoted the idea of Hungarian expansion to recover lands taken away from Hungary after World War I. Horthy eventually transformed Hungary's Western-style parliamentary democracy into a fascist dictatorship modeled after the Nazi system in Germany, down to imitating Hitler's anti-Semitic policies. In 1944, he presided over the deportation of 437,000 Hungarian Jews to the Auschwitz death camp.[45]

But there is another side to Horthy that explains the popular admiration for him. He took power at a time when Hungary was deeply wounded psychologically by the loss of imperial status following World War I. The country wanted a father figure to help it adjust to the new order, in which authoritarian monarchy was replaced by democracy and Hungary was reduced to one of the smallest states in Central Europe. Many also considered Horthy's rule of Hungary as a period of material well-being, in which the Hungarian middle class prospered as a result of the extraordinary political stability his strong rule provided. Others also argued that, were it not for his pro-German policy, the Germans would have conquered Hungary and subjected it to the same abuses they visited on Poland. In this view, Horthy actually helped to save Jewish lives by his pragmatic approach to the Nazis.

Prime Minister Antall gave his blessing to Horthy's reburial, calling him a patriot to be remembered by the Hungarian people. Other Hungarians disliked the enormous public and official attention given to Horthy. To them the widespread interest in Horthy suggested the existence of a deeply ingrained prejudice against Jews and a nostalgia for the precommunist authoritarian political order—not a healthy sentiment in a new democratic system.

4. Emergence of a Radical Right

This nostalgia for the authoritarianism of the pre–World War II era resonated among the political elite in Budapest, where there was a strong current of conservatism. István Csurka, the spokesman for a hard-line conservative group in the Forum that was critical of the moderate policies of the Antall leadership, became very influential. As head of *Magyar Út* ("The Hungarian Way"), an organization founded in 1992 to promote "Hungarianness," he stood for a rabid nationalism with fascist and anti-Semitic undertones. He accused Hungarian Jews, the IMF, and others of a "Zionist conspiracy" against the Hungarian nation. Many in the Democratic Forum saw him as a bulwark against the restoration of communism in Hungary.[46]

Prime Minister Antall eventually had enough of Csurka's criticism, especially as the Forum did not want to appear sympathetic to a Hungarian version of "know-nothingism" on the eve of the May 1994 parliamentary elections. He forced Csurka's ouster from the party's parliamentary group in June 1993. Csurka, however, quickly formed his own group inside the Hungarian Parliament, saying he would continue to support the Forum, to which he was still loyal, but would also continue to criticize it.[47] Csurka and his followers, however, were able to attract only very small crowds to their nationalist and anti-Semitic tirades during the campaign for the May 1994 parliamentary elections. [48] Moreover, the extreme right can be considered to be of limited political significance. At the moment it does not seem to enjoy widespread popular support, and it has had very little direct influence on Hungarian policy making.

5. Revival of the Socialists (Former Communists)

A powerful competitor of right-wing groups is the reformist left, represented by the Socialist Party, which has traveled a long way ideologically since its loss of power in 1990. Following its formation in October 1989 at a Communist Party congress, the Socialist Party in 1990 was a shadow of the old Communist Party, with only 10,000 members—the old party had over 700,000. But the new organization soon had 50,000 members. In the March 1990 elections it won 11 percent of the popular vote, making it the fourth largest party on the Hungarian political spectrum, with a modest chance for a political comeback. But in November 1990, with the resignation of Imre Pozsgay, the party lost an influential member, which diminished its standing with the voting public.[49]

Subsequently, the party's fortunes improved as it developed a program of moderate reformism. The Socialist call for a market economy with a "human face" appealed to an increasing number of voters disenchanted by the hardships free market reforms were causing for much of Hungarian society. The Socialists also tapped into worker discontent by strengthening links with the trade unions, speaking about a "social compact" that they said meant a new concern with the well-being of the workers. They said they would try to reduce, not eliminate, unemployment. Indeed they also said they would not return to the budget-draining full employment policies of their Communist predecessors. By supporting reform while advocating moderation and a gradual pace of change, the Socialists appeared as a viable alternative to the Free Democrats and the Forum.[50]

6. The May 1994 Parliamentary Elections

Hungarian voters seemed willing to give the Socialists a chance to show what they could do for the country in the postcommunist era and to test the sincerity of their commitment to the new democratic order. In the May 1994 parliamentary elections, voters overwhelmingly favored the Socialists as an alternative to the Forum and the Free Democrats. The Socialists won a clear majority, while the Free Democrats won only 70 seats and the Forum only 37 seats in the new Parliament. The party named its chairman, Gyula Horn, the foreign minister in Prime Minister Nemeth's communist government that ended with the March 1990 parliamentary elections, as its candidate for prime minister.[51]

Why the Socialist Success?

Hungarian voters everywhere in the country, especially the unemployed, workers in danger of losing their jobs, and the elderly, returned the former communists to power out of frustration over the failure of reforms in the early 1990s to bring a significant improvement in living conditions. By the spring of 1994, inflation was running at about 20 percent and half the families in Hungary were worried about unemployment. Inflation and unemployment had caused a 12 percent decline since 1989 of per-capita income.[52] Also, the Socialists apparently had been very successful in cultivating a professional image that increased their credibility with better-educated urban blue-collar workers. The Socialists worked hard to convince voters of the party's moderation and respectability and to assure them that the party had no intention of turning back the clock on reforms that would make Hungary democratic and capitalist. Indeed, by 1994, the Hungarian Socialists closely resembled a West European–style social democratic party.[53] A final reason for the Socialist success may have been a new nostalgia of many voters for the communist era, at least the last decades of it, when living conditions had improved and the Communist Party had managed to achieve substantial autonomy of the Kremlin in domestic policy making. Many voters preferred to forget about the harsher era of communist rule in the pre-Kádár era of the late 1940s and early 1950s and think only of post-Stalinist socialism, which was not as bad as they had believed in the 1990 elections when they had decisively thrown the communists out of power despite their commitment to reform.[54]

Coalition with the Free Democrats

When the new Parliament convened in early July 1994, Gyula Horn was duly sworn in as head of a government coalition consisting of Socialists and Free Democrats by President Árpád Göncz. The Socialists formed a coalition with the Free Democrats, even though they did not need to since they had an absolute majority in the newly elected Parliament. The Free Democrats, who initially opposed an alignment with their old ideological enemies, eventually relented and joined with the Socialists to make sure they kept their word to move forward with free-market reforms, in particular, privatization and tax incentives for foreign investors.

Both Socialist and Free Democratic leaders said after the election that the major challenge was the economy, and they acknowledged that meeting voter expectations without compromising reform would be very difficult. Indeed, László Bekesi, a Socialist deputy in the Parliament with an expertise in free-market economics, observed that in the next two years Hungarians could not count on an increase in consumption or in the national standard of living.[55]

Future Problems

As they looked to the future, the Socialists could not ignore much popular resentment toward former communists, who continue to enjoy many of the privileges they had under communist rule. The communist-era elite remains largely in place as factory managers, bank executives, and business owners. Many people see this lingering communist influence as an obstacle to the country's well-being and to the success of its transition to political and economic democracy and would like the government to push communists out of positions of power even though their talents are needed to keep the economy going. Furthermore, the Socialists cannot underestimate the resilience of the Forum, which is capable of a strong, perhaps even vicious opposition. Indeed, they acknowledge that if an improvement in living conditions under a left-of-center government remains unfulfilled, the political pendulum might then swing to the Forum or, worse, toward the extreme right.[56]

The Decline of FIDESZ

A major loser in the May 1994 parliamentary elections turned out to be FIDESZ, the moderate liberal party with great expectations in the early 1990s. FIDESZ initially looked to Hungary's disaffected youth for voter support but appealed also to groups hardest hit by mounting unemployment, notably pensioners on fixed incomes. Opposed to radical nationalism and critical of the Forum's political dominance, FIDESZ had gotten off to a good start, coming in fifth in the March 1990 parliamentary elections; in local elections six months later, it captured mayoral seats in nine large cities. In the fall of 1991, the party was number one in public-opinion polls.[57]

FIDESZ attracted a lot of voter attention because it was not embarrassed about taking unpopular positions on controversial issues. For example, in the summer of 1991, FIDESZ unanimously opposed any plan to compensate former owners of nationalized property because of the burden to an already financially strapped government that could not afford to continue the expansive social-welfare system developed under communist rule. By 1993, looking to electoral victory and a chance of national leadership in the next Parliament, FIDESZ embraced a forward-looking program of modernization. Viktor Orban, the FIDESZ leader, said the party was committed to rapid economic growth through continued privatization and expanded foreign investment.[58]

But on the eve of the May 1994 parliamentary elections, FIDESZ's fortunes took a turn for the worse. In April 1994, a public-opinion poll carried out by Gallup-Hungary showed FIDESZ tied with the Forum at only 12 percent of those polled. FIDESZ, as well as the Forum, lost the confidence of many voters who were upset by the continuing unemployment—about 12.5 percent in 1994—and who were willing as a measure of last resort to support the Socialists, despite their past.[59]

The weakening of FIDESZ could signal a weakening of the liberal center in postcommunist Hungarian politics. Now that they have won democratic freedoms advocated and implemented by the liberal center in the early 1990s, Hungarian voters have given priority to an immediate improvement of living conditions, even if that means a slowdown of economic reform. Thus the key to an understanding of Hungarian political development in the late 1990s must be the economy.

Toward a Market Economy

Though determined to introduce a free-market economy as the best means of raising living standards, Prime Minister Antall was skeptical of the "shock-therapy" approach advocated by Harvard economist Jeffrey Sachs, who had been advising the Polish government, and supported by the Free Democrats and FIDESZ. Antall believed that Hungarian society would not respond well to shock therapy because of what he believed to be a pervasive streak of pessimism in the national character. Antall planned, therefore, to proceed gradually, cautiously, and with restraint.[60]

1. The Communist Legacy

In 1990, Antall faced the third straight year of recession. The annual rate of inflation was 23 percent. Seventy-five percent of the money in cash or bank accounts belonged to only 25 percent of the population, while two million people, 20 percent of the total population, lived below the poverty level. Hungary also had, and still has, the highest per-capita foreign debt in Eastern Europe. Additionally, trade with the Soviet Union declined precipitously. Moscow had not yet paid almost a billion rubles for the buses, machinery, and other Hungarian products it had imported in 1989.[61]

Having said all of the above, some positive conditions were inherited from the communists. The country had made a major head start on systemic economic reform and was further along the route to a free market than any other country in Central and Eastern Europe. Under communist rule, Hungary had allowed private businesses of up to 500 employees, had permitted foreign owners to repatriate their profits in convertible currency, and had levied an income tax. It had been a member of the International Monetary Fund and the World Bank since 1982 and had achieved most-favored-nation trade status with the United States. Its gross per-capita foreign debt was the highest in Eastern Europe, but Antall intended to pay it off rather than reschedule, enhancing Hungary's credibility with investors.[62]

2. Slow Progress of Reform

Key aspects of Antall's free-market reform program were furthering privatization, increasing foreign investment, expanding foreign trade, and building a modern economic infrastructure. But he and his successors have encountered problems that have slowed the rate of change. There have been times when they may have wondered whether the benefits of free-market reform justified the costs in hardship and suffering of many Hungarian wage earners and their families.

Privatization

Privatization of state-controlled enterprises got off to a very slow start. The State Property Agency, which was supposed to sell the state's companies, was overwhelmed by the number of transactions it had to handle.[63] Privatization was slow also because it was controversial. Many in the Antall government of the early 1990s did not want privatization of agriculture, while supporters in the Smallholders' Party wanted a completely free agricultural sector and demanded a radical alteration of existing laws restricting private ownership of land. A battle ensued in the Parliament, where debate soon gave way to endless argumentation worsened by a penchant for hairsplitting. The Parliament made little progress on privatization in 1990.[64]

Foreign Investment

To rejuvenate unprofitable and inefficient enterprises formerly under state control, the Hungarian government sought foreign investment to make up for the reluctance of Hungarian investors to buy up enterprises that would not give a quick return. The government offered attractive joint ventures with tax breaks, liberalized rules for foreign investors who created jobs in Hungary, and advertised the country's comparatively low labor costs. Antall's government was determined to proceed immediately on taking office to sell more than 150 money-losing state-run industries.[65]

But Western bankers and firms with ample capital were slow to invest in Hungarian economic development. They feared the country's high indebtedness. They were put off by obsolete manufacturing facilities. They also had difficulty understanding Hungarian accounting practices, coping with a still far from adequate infrastructure, and interacting with bureaucrats caught up in red tape and unable to expedite the documents needed to execute business transactions. For some would-be foreign investors, another major obstacle to doing business in Hungary was the primitive commercial infrastructure. The role of a new stock market was weak and too narrow—stock shares turned over very slowly, and relatively few Hungarian firms are listed on the stock exchange. Finally, by mid-1993, there was popular skepticism about growing foreign influence over the Hungarian economy. Foreign retail companies were criticized for discouraging sales of domestically produced goods and contributing to the closure of local industries already hard hit by the collapse of trade with former Eastern bloc countries, especially the former Soviet Union. Hungarian nationalists called for close parliamentary scrutiny of purchase by foreigners of newly privatized Hungarian enterprises.[66]

The Socialist government elected to power in May 1994 was also skeptical of foreign investment and reportedly canceled a joint-venture deal between a state-owned hotel chain and an American hotel-management corporation on the ground that the Hungarian property being sold, which included the Forum Hotel in Budapest, was undervalued and the price for it was too low. The American partner refused to renegotiate, and the deal collapsed. Furthermore, under pressure from the right wing of his party, which wanted to preserve a substantial safety net to ease the hardships of free-market reforms, Prime Minister Gyula Horn tried to avoid spending cuts in the 1995 budget demanded by the IMF in return for a new loan. But the problem for the Horn government in discouraging foreign investment is the country's need of it for economic modernization. If the Socialists fail to secure adequate foreign capital, they risk increasing budget deficits and slowing down economic growth essential to the improvement in living standards that Hungarians expect them to achieve as the price of continuing support in parliamentary elections.[67]

Along with foreign investment, there has been a decline in foreign trade caused by the collapse of the Soviet Union and a recession in Western Europe.

Exports were down 27 percent in the first five months of 1993, compared with the period a year earlier.[68] Postcommunist Russia has not been able to pick up the slack in trade with Hungary because its economy is in a shambles and it lacks the wherewithal to pay for what it wants to buy. The only hope in the near future is an expansion of trade with the West.

Economic Infrastructure

Hungary has been reforming its legal system to support private enterprise. The government wants clear laws similar to those in the West regarding the incorporation of businesses, personal and corporate taxation, and bankruptcy proceedings. The government has also laid the groundwork for an efficient, independent banking system.[69] But some of its initiatives have not worked out well. A newly created stock exchange took a long time to get started because most enterprises were state controlled and no one had spare cash for stock purchases anyway. Furthermore, many Hungarians were suspicious of the stock exchange, which they viewed as little more than, as the communists had put it, a "capitalist gambling table." They hardly knew what securities were, never mind how they were valued.

Unemployment

With privatization, unemployment increased substantially, to 8 percent in 1991 and higher in 1992. This was a radical change from the condition of near full employment under the communists, and it threatened political destabilization as more and more Hungarians found it difficult to make ends meet. Like citizens of other former communist countries, Hungarians were unaccustomed to being out of work, and they were depressed by this situation. In October 1990, people indicated in a poll that their daily economic hardship was the most serious problem facing the country. And in 1992, people were still saying that unemployment, poverty, and the rising cost of housing were the most pressing national problems.[70]

The government has had difficulty controlling unemployment. Many industries have been closed down because of their inefficiency, unprofitability, and lack of appeal to private investors. In many that have survived and in new ones, the pay is so poor that many workers are struggling just to maintain their present status. They are tightening their belts, adjusting family budgets to absorb inflation, and, provided they have bargainable skills and work experience, taking second jobs.[71]

Personal Psychology

Many Hungarians do not approve of the pursuit of profit. Hungarians, like other East European peoples brought up in the communist ideology, learned that private enterprise exploits workers. At the same time, they are jealous of other people's success in private economic ventures. Some have responded by encouraging bureaucratic intervention to prevent profiteering, which is given a very narrow definition and refers to anybody who earns profit from private enterprise, no matter how moderate and reasonable it may be by Western standards. Finally, it has been argued that Hungarians lack entrepreneurial skills. They remain overly cautious and extremely reluctant to invest money if there is the slightest chance of losing it.[72]

The Economic Balance Sheet

Hungary has made great progress toward a free-market economy. By the end of 1994, at least half of Hungary's gross domestic product came from private companies. Hungarian exports are increasingly being sold in Western markets, suggesting improvement in their quality and reliability when compared with exports in the communist era to communist neighbors. The superhuge behemoth industries developed by the communists are giving way to small and medium-sized enterprises that are more efficient and profitable.[73]

Threats to Social Peace

The transition to a free-market economy has brought severe social problems, such as poverty, urban crime almost unheard of in the communist era, a resurgence of anti-Semitism, strident public demands for restitution for losses suffered under the communists, the spread of AIDS, and new hardships for women. These problems threaten the stability of Hungary's new democratic order.

1. Impoverishment

Societal impoverishment is now much more obvious than it was under communism, and much more severe than Hungarians anticipated in the postcommunist era. The poorest groups in Hungarian society today, partly because they have been the hardest hit by the transition to a free-market economy, are women, youth, and the elderly. With little savings, many simply do not have enough to live on. Despite relatively high levels of female education in Hungary, women's employment has been concentrated in the lowest-level industrial jobs and in low-wage service and administrative work. These semiskilled and unskilled jobs have been the ones lost in the restructured economy. Youth are also vulnerable because more and more of them are leaving school before they finish their education and are entering a saturated labor market.[74]

The middle class has also suffered a sharp decline in living standards as a result of the free-market reforms. By November 1992, many in the government were afraid that if pushed too far the middle classes could set off a social explosion, forcing strikes and other protests. With a 20 percent fall in gross domestic production between 1989 and 1993 and a steadily increasing rate of inflation, from 17 percent in 1989 to 22.5 percent in 1993, two million people were living below the poverty level and another half million were on the poverty line in 1993. Worse, as the living standard of the majority (about 53 percent of the population) deteriorated, that of a minority (about 32 percent) that benefited from the new economic freedom increased substantially, producing a pronounced income inequality.[75]

The Hungarian Roma (Gypsies) are especially impoverished, with 66 percent living in what the government considers poor households. The poverty of the Hungarian Roma, as is true of the Roma elsewhere in Central and Eastern Europe, is largely a result of their lack of education and skills. But they also remain impoverished because of popular discrimination against them. They are usually the first to lose work in the restructuring of an enterprise to make it attractive for privatization.[76]

Despite government efforts to help alleviate poverty, such as the reduction of the list of goods and services subject to a new value-added tax of 6 percent at the end of 1992, particularly bread and milk, medicines, and household electricity, middle-class disillusionment with the steady decline in living standards toward poverty levels remained strong. A discontented middle class helped to return the Socialists to power in the May 1994 parliamentary elections.[77]

But by the mid-1990s, impoverishment may have started to decline. Forty-one percent of those considered poor were able to increase their incomes in 1993 as unemployment started to edge slowly downward in 1994. These data suggest the possibility that Hungary may have passed through the worst of the transition, with the standard of living on the threshold of rising in the mid- and late 1990s as the country's overall economic health improves thanks to the steady departures from economic organization and behavior inherited from the communist past.[78]

Homelessness, which is no longer a crime, as it was under communist rule, remains a special aspect of poverty, if only because it has become a public spectacle. Homeless people live in the railway stations of Budapest or camp out on the streets. The situation is made worse by Budapest's chronic housing shortage and by the migration of people to Hungary from countries like Romania, where living conditions are even more intolerable. Almost half of the homeless people sleeping in the railway station are Romanians.[79] In coping with the homeless, the Hungarian government has come up against the "not-in-my-backyard" phenomenon. When the Budapest City Council considered turning an empty military barracks into a shelter for the homeless in late 1990, residents of the district protested, causing the city to back down temporarily. And private charity cannot be of much help. Both the Red Cross and the Catholic Church sponsor shelters, but they are dependent on state aid, which has been modest. In the early 1990s, homelessness remained a serious problem and a potentially dangerous source of political instability for the Hungarian government.[80]

2. Anti-Semitism

Difficult living conditions have helped to encourage a revival of anti-Semitism. Hungary is unique in that it has a much larger Jewish population—approximately 80,000—than any of the other East European countries. Traditionally, most Jewish Hungarians have been attracted to the culture and cosmopolitan atmosphere of Budapest. Consequently, even the bitter memories of the Nazi era did not prevent large numbers of Jewish-Hungarians from forgoing emigration and continuing to live in Hungary. Moreover, there has been a resurgence of Jewish life since the fall of communism. A wide range of Jewish religious activities takes place on a regular basis. In addition to Jewish religious schools, a secular school that emphasizes tradition, history, and culture has opened.

Roots

The dismantling of the communist order, along with the hardships for most people caused by the movement toward a market economy in the early 1990s, helped to revive anti-Semitism, a prejudice with deep roots in Hungarian society going back centuries and closely associated with the development in the nineteenth and early twentieth centuries of Hungarian nationalism. Hungarian anti-Semitism reached a climax in World War II, when the Hungarian government joined the Axis alliance and cooperated with German policy to exterminate the Jews.[81]

Some Hungarian Jews blame the Catholic Church for obliquely encouraging anti-Semitism, saying that the church sat in silence as hundreds of thousands of Hungarian Jews were deported by the pro-Nazi Hungarian government during World War II. Hungarian Jews who survived the war have been quick to point out that Hungary's Cardinal Mindszenthy, revered for his sufferings at the hands of the communists, had conspicuously declined to speak out against Nazi crimes against Jews during World War II. They believe that he was an anti-Semite and were offended by Pope John Paul II's prayer for him during his visit in August 1991, despite his condemnation of anti-Semitism as a sin, despite his praise of Jews for their "essential contribution to the spiritual and cultural life of the world," and despite his role in the Vatican's establishment of full diplomatic relations with the state of Israel.[82]

Postcommunist Revival

Anti-Semitism reappeared in public in the March 1990 parliamentary elections, when some leaders of the Democratic Forum played upon the continuing prejudice of many Hungarians against Jews despite the destruction of most of Hungary's pre–World War II Jewish population of over 800,000 in the Holocaust. In a radio broadcast, Csurka spoke about a "dwarfish minority" robbing

Hungarians of their national culture and symbols. He called Jews "rootless cosmopolitans."[83]

Other well-known Forum members engaged in similar tactics. Furthermore, a small weekly in the provincial city of Debrecen openly blamed Jews for the calamities of the communist era. It (the imposition of Communist rule) was, the newspaper reportedly said, the revenge of the Jews for the Nazi horrors. The paper also accused the Jews of responsibility for a range of problems, from Hungary's rising crime rate to liberal abortion policies.[84]

Responses to Anti-Semitism

The Hungarian government seems sensitive to the reappearance of anti-Semitism and willing to counter it.[85] Hungary's president, Árpád Göncz, condemned anti-Semitism and promised to do everything possible to make Hungarian Jews feel at home in their own country. Moreover, a poll conducted in May 1991 found that while 12 percent of the population had negative views of Jews, 67 percent had favorable ones. Many of the country's leading writers and intellectuals have spoken out against anti-Semitism in a timely and forthright fashion. Hungarian Jews agree with this positive view, saying that expressions of anti-Semitism are isolated and that the vast majority of Hungarians are not anti-Semitic.[86]

3. Restitution

People have demanded the restitution of property confiscated by the communist regime when it came to power after World War II and the bringing to justice of communists who perpetrated crimes. The Smallholders' Party has demanded the return of all farmland nationalized by the party in 1947 to the original owners. The Hungarian government has agreed in many instances to a restoration of property or some kind of cash indemnification for those hurt under communism. But postcommunist Hungarian leaders have opposed searching for past records to identify guilty parties or to determine the fate of victims, some of whom disappeared without a trace. Today's officials simply do not want to open old wounds. Indeed, some members of the Hungarian Parliament have suggested destroying the old files of the communist secret police. That is not likely to happen, but neither is it likely that the Hungarian government will be able to satisfy Hungarians seeking retribution. With priority given to stability, justice will be served only when it does not cause more problems that it solves.

4. AIDS

As if poverty and other societal problems of the postcommunist era were not enough, Hungary faces in the 1990s an increase in AIDS. As unemployment has soared in Hungary and elsewhere in Eastern Europe and as borders have opened, the threat of AIDS in previously isolated countries has increased. The incidence of AIDS has mostly accompanied an increase in prostitution in Hungary as women try to survive in the new economy. The number of women standing along the main routes into Hungary rose visibly in the first half of 1993 as the economic conditions deteriorated for Hungarian workers. A prostitute can make a month's salary in half a night's work. Making matters worse is the way in which the increase in prostitution has been accompanied by an increase in drug use, which is another way in which the risk of AIDS is heightened.

5. Gender Discrimination

Women have been especially hard hit by the movement toward a free-market economy. Changes in welfare policies designed to reduce government spending and to cut costs of production for private entrepreneurs have hurt women more than men. For example, the retirement age for women has been advanced from 55, which is what it was under communist rule, to 60. The government has limited child-care leave to thirty days. And women who have just given birth are no longer guaranteed the same job they had prior to maternity leave. The Hungarian Parliament seems reluctant to address gender issues as a whole, in particular the problem of sexual harassment on the job. Hungary, like most other East European countries grappling with the complexity and cost of developing a political and economic democracy, has no aggressive feminist movement of the kind that has appeared in the United States. This means that Hungarian women are not likely to be able to get the Budapest government to pay much attention to women's issues in the near future.[87]

Reorienting Foreign Policy

Foreign policy has been intimately connected to domestic reform in post-communist Hungary. The success of Hungary's transformation depends to a large degree on the external environment, and that fact, plus considerations of national security, has guided recent Hungarian foreign policy. The most important focal points of Hungarian foreign policy in the postcommunist era have been relations with the former Soviet Union and Russia and with the West, in particular, the United States, Germany, and the European Union. In recent years, Hungary has strengthened ties with other countries for reasons of self-interest, notably Israel, Austria, and ex-Communist neighbors in Eastern Europe.

1. The Soviet Union

Hungary's first instinct upon emancipation from communism was to break away from the Soviet Union. In 1990, the Antall government moved quickly to establish an independent foreign policy, and in June the Hungarian Parliament voted unanimously to withdraw Hungary from the Warsaw Pact. The government also asked for the evacuation of the 50,000 Soviet troops on Hungarian territory. In March 1990, the Soviets agreed, albeit grudgingly, to the short timetable sought by the Hungarians, and the last Soviet troops departed Hungary on June 16, 1991.[88]

In 1991, Hungary also sought to protect itself against a possible reassertion of Soviet influence and to give itself maximum diplomatic flexibility. For example, in negotiations in April 1991 over a new bilateral treaty with the Soviet Union, Hungary resisted language that would ban either country from joining any alliance that could be considered hostile to the other. Concerned that Hungary might prejudice its chances of eventually joining the European Union or NATO, Prime Minister Antall said that Hungary wanted a treaty with Moscow guaranteeing its right to join groups and alliances of its own choosing.[89]

Soon, however, Hungary was dealing discreetly with individual Soviet republics, notably Russia and Ukraine, which together accounted for 90 percent of Hungarian-Soviet trade.[90] The Hungarians also found the individual republics, in particular Ukraine and the Baltic states, interested in improved relations. They wanted bilateral trade relationships as did Hungary. And, when the Soviet central government in 1991 told Hungary that it would sell only 20 percent of the oil it wanted, the Hungarian government purchased it directly from individual oil-producing regions, such as Russia's Bashkir and Tatar autonomous republics.[91]

2. The West

Hungary also realigned itself vis-à-vis the West and has tried to strengthen relations especially with Germany, the United States, and the European Union. In early 1990, Hungary turned to the West to make up trade losses from the former communist bloc and to furnish new trade opportunities. Hungarian leaders believe that Hungary's closeness to Europe has been historical, dating back to the birth of the Hungarian nation in the ninth century, and that Hungary has been able to survive and develop only by remaining open to European scientific development and cultural values. Also, as part of its desire for stability and security, the democratic leadership in Budapest wants to link Hungary with NATO, perhaps through NATO's political consultative committees, such as the North Atlantic Assembly.

The European Union

One of Hungary's primary foreign-policy objectives in the postcommunist era has been membership in the European Union (EU), first as an associate and then as a full member. Participation in the EU, the Hungarian leadership believes, would stimulate Hungarian exports and pull in foreign investment, training, and technology. Before it can be a member, however, the EU has said that Hungary needs first to build a market-based economy with convertible currency. In sum, Hungary must raise the quality of its economic productivity to Western levels.

Austria may turn out to be a valuable lever for Hungary's eventual integration into Western Europe. Bound by centuries of cultural and political tradition, Hungarian relations with Austria improved after Hungarian officials cut the barbed wire at the border at Sopron on January 27, 1989. Since then there has been a flood of citizens from each country to the other and complete freedom of travel.[92] Anticipating a move by Austria to join the European Union, Hungarian authorities are studying the possibility of applying for membership in the European Free Trade Association, which groups Austria with Sweden, Switzerland, and other neutral West European countries.

NATO

Hungary has also been eager to join NATO because of real and potential threats to its security coming from Slovakia, Romania, and Serbia, where differences with those countries over their treatment of Hungarian-speaking minorities have the potential for provoking conflict. But NATO has been cautious and restrained on the issue of membership. Hungary did accept a compromise on full membership in NATO when it agreed to participate in the American-sponsored Partnership for Peace in early 1994. The Hungarian government, like other Central European governments, hopes that the Partnership for Peace, which provides for consultation of partnership members with NATO, will soon lead to full membership in the Western alliance.[93]

3. Central and Eastern Europe

A special problem concerns large minorities of ethnic Hungarians living in these countries, and the ethnic factor looms as an important source of problems in Hungary's relations with these neighbors. Prime Minister Antall has been especially concerned about the well-being of Hungarians living in neighboring countries and declared upon assuming office in early 1990 that he wanted to be the "Prime Minister of 15 million Hungarians" (there are only 10 million in Hungary itself). And in February 1992, Minister of Defense Lajos Für insisted publicly that "the Hungarian nation in the Carpathian Basin is not limited to the citizens of the Hungarian Republic."[94]

Minorities in Slovakia, Serbia, Romania, and Ukraine

A large Hungarian minority of about 600,000 people lives in eastern Slovakia. Since the split of Czechoslovakia in early 1993, the Budapest government has feared that an independent Slovakia could harm the Hungarian minority if it pursues cultural homogenization policies. Slovakia's prime minister Vladimir

Mečiar rejected the notion of a "Hungarian community" or any other ethnic minority's claim to "community status" that is entitled to administrative autonomy on the basis of ethnic identity.[95]

Hungary has also been concerned about kinsmen in the Vojvodina since civil war broke out in Yugoslavia in 1991. Prime Minister Antall said Vojvodina was given to the Yugoslav state, not to Serbia. The Hungarian government was in effect telling the Milošević regime that, if Yugoslavia collapsed, it would consider the 1919 arrangement for Vojvodina no longer valid.[96] But Hungarians living in the Vojvodina do not suffer from the kind of discrimination endured by kinsmen in Slovakia. That situation could change but until it does Hungary does not yet have a problem with the Republic of Serbia only the well being of its Hungarian minority.

Hungary continues to have difficult relations with Romania because of its alleged discrimination against the Hungarian minority living in Transylvania. To some extent, the Budapest government's anxieties about the well-being of the Hungarian minority in Romania are justified. The Iliescu government has done little to reassure the Hungarian-speaking people in his country that their cultural identity will not be threatened. Indeed, Romanian authorities have allowed Romanian to replace Hungarian on streets, in schools, and in other public places.[97]

On the other hand, chauvinistic comments by Hungarian leaders, such as the late Prime Minister Antall and István Csurka, could be considered to have goaded the already highly chauvinistic Romanian authorities in Transylvania to become more aggressive in dealing with the Hungarian minority by obliquely raising the possibility, however remote, that Hungary might finesse a return of Transylvanian land inhabited by Hungarians. True, Hungarian leaders have insisted publicly that the loss of Transylvania to Romania in 1919 is permanent and irreversible. But they also have refused to sign a treaty with Romania defining the Transylvanian frontier between the two countries.

The 160,000 Hungarians who live in the Transcarpathian districts of western Ukraine pose no problem for Budapest. Ukraine's leadership in recent years has accepted the principle of "community status" for the Hungarian minority. It has allowed the Hungarian people in the Transcarpathian *oblast* (district) administrative autonomy and has allowed the Hungarian minority to use its own language. Moreover, there is free trade between the Transcarpathian *oblast* and metropolitan Hungary. Not surprisingly, Hungarian relations with Ukraine are very good.[98]

A recent complication of the minorities issue in Hungarian relations with its neighbors is the outspoken József Torgyán, head of the conservative Smallholders' Party, which is seeking to increase its voter appeal and become a plurality party. In July 1995, Torgyán spoke of the injustices of the 1920 Treaty of Trianon, in which Hungary was obliged by the West to cede more than half the territory it had controlled before World War I to its neighbors. He did not ask for the return of this territory, but he did level a charge that the Hungarian minorities now under the authority of Slovakia, Romania, and Ukraine were victims of discrimination and said that Hungary should not sign treaties with its neighbors guaranteeing borders with them, as the European Union demands, prior to Hungary's admission because such treaties would isolate the Hungarian minorities abroad and be tantamount to a national betrayal of them. Torgyán has attracted a lot of public attention by his speeches, which resonate with many Hungarians at a time of economic difficulty and the need of a distraction from their economic hardships.[99]

The Gabčíkovo Dam and Slovakia

Hungary has a special problem with Slovakia over the large hydroelectric dams and power plants on the Danube at Nagymaros, north of Budapest, and at Gabčíkovo, 120 miles upriver.[100] The Slovaks wanted the dams and have argued that they will enhance flood control and generate sufficient power to reduce by millions of tons a year the burning of the polluting, sulfur-laden brown coal that is Slovakia's main energy source. But the Hungarian government vehemently opposed construction of the dams by the Czechoslovak communist government, warning that they would alter the flow of the Danube and pollute one of central Europe's largest aquifers supplying drinking water for several million people in Hungary and Slovakia. In addition, the Hungarians have said that the Danube's inland delta, a unique wetlands habitat, might die out as water from the Danube is diverted to turn the eight large turbines at the dam. The Hungarians threatened to block all river and truck traffic bound for Czechoslovakia if Prague went ahead and put the dam into operation.

To avoid a potentially dangerous confrontation between the two countries, the Hungarians withdrew their threats, and both sides are now looking at ways of minimizing environmental damage. One plan under consideration is to build a system of dikes and reservoirs to lessen the impact once the dam starts to operate and sends strong surges downriver.

Civil War in Yugoslavia

Hungary has also been vulnerable to the explosion of ethnic conflict and civil war in Yugoslavia. Hungarians feel some solicitude for the Croats, who were governed by Budapest before World War I and with whom they have familial links. And they also worry that the fighting in Croatia has cut off Hungary's access to the Adriatic oil pipeline. While this event is undoubtedly temporary, it is annoying and a problem for the strained Hungarian economy. Moreover, in 1991 Yugoslav federal airplanes violated Hungarian air space on several occasions and caused some minor damage to Hungarian border villages. In addition, fighting occasionally spilled over from northern Yugoslavia into southern Hungary. With 35,000 refugees from the fighting in Yugoslavia, Hungary has to provide food and shelter from its own limited resources. Finally, Hungarian officials were upset about the economic effects of upholding the sanctions against Serbia, which cost Hungary about $1 billion in 1993.[101]

Cooperation with Poland and Czechoslovakia

Under these circumstances, Hungary has been a willing participant in efforts with Poland and Czechoslovakia (and later its successors, the Czech Republic and Slovakia) to promote a new basis of consultation and cooperation among the three, now four countries. In Bratislava in April 1990, President Havel of Czechoslovakia and Hungary's outgoing president Mátyas Szűrős agreed to set up a joint commission to deal with ethnic Hungarians in Slovakia and the Slovak minority in Hungary. Although this was a modest achievement, it was certainly a first step of the new Hungarian democratic leadership to facilitate a reconciliation among the three countries and to set the stage for subsequent discussion and resolution of problems among them, such as ethnic minorities.[102]

The Hungarians hosted a next meeting of the three Central European neighbors at the Hungarian town of Visegrád in February 1991. At this summit, the participants reiterated their desire to join Western Europe. The Czechs and the Hungarians also discussed their differences over the Gabčíkovo Dam and the Hungarian minority in Slovakia. The conference had a sense of urgency because of Soviet foreign minister Eduard Shevardnadze's sudden and unexpected resignation in December 1990. Shevardnadze had been an advocate of Soviet reconciliation with the new East European governments. The three Central European countries also were concerned about Moscow's intervention in January 1991 to suppress sentiment in Lithuania in favor of separation from the Soviet Union. The Central European countries shared a sense of regional solidarity in the face of a possible resurgence of Soviet influence in the region given the Kremlin's tough policy toward the Baltic republics.[103]

Although no binding ties were negotiated, the meeting in Visegrád was significant in carrying the three Central European neighbors a bit closer to the kind of interstate cooperation that had eluded them in the interwar period. It also punctuated the readiness of postcommunist Poland and Czechoslovakia to put aside old anger toward Hungary caused by Budapest's cooperation with the Nazis. Finally, the Visegrád meeting opened the way for subsequent summit meetings of the three in Kraków in October 1991 and in Prague in May 1992, which continued the development of the new cooperation among them.

Conclusions

Apart from the fact that it had been nonviolent, the transition from communist authoritarianism to pluralistic democracy in Hungary was, perhaps, the smoothest transition from one system of politics to another, proceeding, as it did, without the massive popular demonstrations that occurred in East Germany, Czechoslovakia, Romania, and Bulgaria. Moreover, alone of the Communist parties in Eastern Europe, the Hungarian Communist Party was very much the womb of the revolution. A liberal reformist wing of the party leadership had adroitly sold the idea of change to a skeptical and somewhat conservative, blue-collar-oriented rank and file and had undermined the capacity of conservatives at the top of the party to block change. Rational and pragmatic, these communist reformers appealed to the party's fine instinct for survival and its willingness to bend rather than break.

Hungary's nonviolent transition away from communism must also be attributed to the Gorbachevian Kremlin, which had shown a measure of sympathy for, as well as anxiety over, Hungarian reformism, viewing it in the late 1980s primarily as an experiment in socialist change important to the development of Soviet perestroika. Thus, the Soviets accepted with equanimity the removal of Kádár, the ascendancy of radical reformers like Pozsgay and Nyers, the rehabilitation of Nagy, and the prospect that Hungary would adopt political pluralism and substantially reduce the role and power of the Communist Party.

The Hungarian party, like other Communist parties in Eastern Europe, had underestimated, and therefore was unable to cope with, the pervasive, deep hostility of most people toward communism and their determination to be rid of it as quickly as possible. Nevertheless, they at least were not as discredited as Communist parties elsewhere in Eastern Europe, even if they were disliked. For this reason the way for a revival of political influence was left open.

Despite the comparatively smooth transition from monolithic dictatorship to multiparty democracy in 1988 and 1989, the continuing liberalization of Hungarian life in the 1990s has remained problematical. Political parties have not yet struck deep roots in Hungarian society and therefore cannot yet effectively mobilize the Hungarian electorate in support of national policies. Under the very cautious and restrained leadership of the late Prime Minister Antall, the Hungarian government was determined to avoid provoking social tensions by too swift a rate of change. Movement toward a market economy is still proceeding very slowly, diminishing the prospects of an immediate and substantial improvement in the standard of living. Instability in Hungary's neighbors, notably Slovakia, Romania, and Yugoslavia, which are important if only because they are home to Hungarian minorities, distract the leadership in Budapest, which is burdened further by its failure to develop the kind of economic and political intimacy with Western Europe essential to Hungary's internal well-being. Finally, the pervasive popular discomfort with the socioeconomic status quo helps to explain the success of Hungary's former communists in the spring of 1994. While Prime Minister Gyula Horn and his Socialist supporters in Parliament have neither the will nor the means to return Hungary to the kind of authoritarian rule it had under the communists before 1989, voter nostalgia for the former communists is not a good omen for Hungarian political and economic democracy, and reflects widespread pessimism about the future.

8

Poland

In the late 1940s, the Polish communists took power, entered a close alliance with Moscow, and introduced a Soviet-style socialist system. But Poland never totally conformed to the Soviet model. Large sectors of Polish society remained anticommunist. The Catholic Church successfully resisted attempts to suppress it and retained its integrity and autonomy. Also, Polish farmers never fully entered into the communist system of agricultural collectivization. Finally, an active dissident intelligentsia kept democratic ideas alive.[1]

The Fragility of Communist Rule

From the outset of communist rule in Poland, there were public protests against the Communist Party's political repression and inept economic management. The reluctance of Polish communist leaders to make systemic changes undermined their legitimacy—if they ever had any—and contributed to a progressive popular alienation that helped provoke the 1980 Solidarity crisis, the most serious display of popular hostility to communist rule since its beginning in the late 1940s.

1. The 1980 Solidarity Crisis

In August 1980, Lech Wałęsa, an electrical worker in the shipyards of the northern Polish port of Gdańsk, founded a new workers' union called Solidarity, which, unlike the official trade-union organization of shipworkers, was independent of the Communist Party. Solidarity struck against the shipyard management for higher pay, better living conditions, and increased popular influence over the working of the government.

POLAND

Geography

1. Location: central Europe, east of Germany
2. Area: total — 312,678 square kilometers; land area — 304,510 square kilometers; comparative area — slightly smaller than New Mexico
3. Boundaries: with Belarus — 605 kilometers; with Czech Republic — 658 kilometers; with Germany — 456 kilometers; with Lithuania — 91 kilometers; with Russia (Kaliningrad Oblast) — 432 kilometers; with Slovakia — 444 kilometers; with Ukraine — 428 kilometers; coastline along the Baltic Sea — 491 kilometers
4. Climate: temperate; cold, cloudy, moderately severe winters with frequent precipitation; mild summers with frequent showers and thunder showers
5. Terrain: mostly flat plain; mountains along southern border
6. Land use: arable — 50.7%; permanent crops — 6.1%; meadows and pastures — 12%; forest and woodland — 18.3%
7. Natural resources: bauxite, coal, natural gas, fertile soils
8. Environment: forest damage due to air pollution and resulting acid rain; improper means for disposal of large amounts of hazardous and industrial waste; severe water pollution from industrial and municipal sources; severe air pollution from emissions of sulfur dioxide from coal-fired power plants

People

1. Population: 38,792,442 (1995 estimate)
2. Age structure: 0–14 years — 23% of population (female — 4,349,467; male —

4,559,536); 15–64 years — 66% of population (female — 12,849,300; male —12,698,179); 65 and over — 11% (female — 2,693,407; male — 1,642,553) (1995 estimate)
3. Growth rate: 0.36% (1995 estimate)
4. Life expectancy at birth: total population — 73.13 years; female — 77.33 years; male — 69.54 years (1995 estimate)
5. Ethnic divisions: Polish — 97.6%; German — 1.3%; Ukrainian — 0.6%; Belarusian — 0.5% (1990 estimate)
6. Religions: Roman Catholic — 95% (about 75% practicing); Eastern Orthodox, Protestant, Jewish — 5%
7. Languages: Polish
8. Literacy: total population — 99%
9. Labor force: total — 17,321 million; services, trade, and government — 44.8%; industry — 29.7%, agriculture — 16.1%; construction — 7.1% (1991 estimate)

Government
1. Type: emerging parliamentary democracy
2. Capital: Warsaw
3. Independence: November 11, 1918
4. Constitution: revised December 1992
5. National administration:
a. Chief of state: President of the Republic (1996 — Aleksander Kwaśniewski)
b. Ministerial leadership: Prime Minister and Council of Ministers (1996 — Włodzimierz Cimoszewicz, prime minister)
c. Legislature: bicameral — National Assembly (*Zgromadzenie Narodowe*), consisting of Diet (*Sejm*) and Senate (*Senat*)
d. Judicial branch: Supreme Court (as of 1995 had not accepted compulsory ICJ jurisdiction)
e. Political parties: Freedom Union (Democratic Union and Liberal Democratic Congress), Christian National Union, Centrum, Peasant Alliance, Solidarity, Union of Labor, Christian Democratic Party, Conservative Party, Nonparty Bloc, Confederation for an Independent Poland, Christian Democrats, German Minority, Union of Real Politics, Democratic Party, Polish Peasant Party, Democratic Left Alliance
6. Local administration: unitary system with 49 provinces

Economy
1. Gross domestic product: $191 billion (1994 estimate)
2. National product real growth rate: 5.5% (1994 estimate)
3. Per-capita national product: $5,700 (1994 estimate)
4. Inflation rate: 30% (1994 estimate)
5. Unemployment rate: 16.1% (1994 estimate)
6. Budget: revenue — $27.1 billion; expenditures — $14.2 billion
7. Industrial output: machine building, iron and steel, extractive industries, chemicals, shipbuilding, food processing, glass, beverages, textiles
8. Agricultural output: 75% from private farms, 25% from state farms — rye, rapeseed, potatoes, livestock (especially hogs)
9. Exports: $10.3 billion (1994 estimate) — raw materials and semifinished goods, machinery and transport equipment, consumer goods, food and agricultural products
10. Imports: $13.3 billion (1994 estimate) — fuels and energy, raw materials and semifinished goods, machinery and transport equipment, consumer goods, food and agriculture
11. External debt: $47 billion (1993 estimate)
12. Trade partners: Germany, Austria, Italy, CIS, United States
13. Economic aid recipient: $8 billion pledged by West but little disbursed
14. Transportation: railroads — 26,250 kilometers; highways — 360,629 kilometers; ports —Gdańsk, Gdynia, Gliwice, Świnoujście, Wrocław, Warsaw; airports — 163 (100 with paved runways)

Throughout August, the strike spread quickly from the Gdańsk shipyards to the steel mills of Kraków. By the end of the month, Solidarity had the support of Polish citizens from all sectors of society: workers, farmers, youth, intellectuals, and the Catholic Church. It demanded political and economic change that, had it been implemented at that time, would have liberalized the communist system and, perhaps, given it a new lease on life. It also was critical of Poland's close relationship with the Soviet Union and made no secret of its dislike of the extensive Soviet influence over Polish politics.

Although initially successful in forcing the authorities to make significant concessions in 1980–81, in particular, the legalization of Solidarity as the first trade-union organization totally independent of Communist Party control. But, Wałęsa and his followers wanted too much change and were naive about how to obtain it. They were overly confidant, somewhat arrogant, and far too aggressive in their relations with the Polish authorities in 1980–81. General Wojciech Jaruzelski, the leader of the Polish Communist Party and the president of Poland in 1981, refused to accommodate Solidarity and rejected its right to exist, viewing it as a threat to the Communist Party's leadership and a provocation of the Kremlin. Moscow saw Solidarity as a threat to both communist rule and Soviet influence in Poland and as a dangerous kind of dissent that could spread to other communist-ruled countries in Central and Eastern Europe. It therefore pressured Jaruzelski to suppress it, which he promptly tried to do. He declared martial law in December 1981, driving Solidarity underground and harassing its leaders and supporters wherever he could find them.

Nevertheless, throughout the period of martial law, an active though clandestine political opposition still survived, as dissent always managed to do under Polish communist rule. Solidarity's middle-class constituencies organized a massive underground publishing and distribution network that challenged the communist regime's monopoly of the mass media. Indeed, until 1989, through complex and multifaceted political agitation, Solidarity's supporters, starting with Wałęsa, continued to mobilize workers and other social groups against communist rule. But, Solidarity endured also because Jaruzelski, though severe, would not use a ruthless, neo-Stalinistic repression. Though he surely hounded the opposition, he refused to destroy it.[2]

2. Economic Stagnation

A centrally controlled, inefficient heavy industry, which devoured most of the country's scarce raw materials and energy resources, dominated the Polish economy. Management consisted primarily of Communist Party hacks, more distinguished for their ideological and political reliability than their managerial skills. Polish managers of large industrial enterprises opposed economic liberalization, particularly private entrepreneurship, that would diminish their privileges and perquisites.[3] The agricultural sector, though largely private, was in no better shape. It languished as a result of neglect of its infrastructure. Although the private sector supplied most of Polish food, the government had little sympathy for it. And Jaruzelski made things worse for the Polish economy when he expanded Polish trade with the Soviet Union in the 1980s, largely in response to tough sanctions that the West imposed when he declared martial law in Poland at the end of 1981. By 1985, some 300 of the largest production facilities in Poland were essentially appendices of their Soviet counterparts, and 37 percent of Polish industrial production was going to the Soviet Union.[4] This relationship linked the Polish economy too closely to the run-down Soviet market, which could afford only goods of mediocre quality. Polish industry had little incentive to excel and become competitive in the world market.[5]

3. Solidarity Forces Political Reform

In the spring of 1988, workers struck in the steel mills and coal mines of the highly industrialized, densely populated, and extensively polluted region of Silesia in southwestern Poland. Again, as in 1980, workers wanted improved living conditions and political liberalization. They demanded the legalization of Solidarity, the right of other groups to form organizations independent of the Communist Party, and an opportunity for the Catholic Church in Poland to participate with the Communist Party in policy making. By the summer of 1988, the strikes began to paralyze the already debilitated economy. Polish enterprises had difficulty filling orders for exports. At home, existing shortages of food, clothing, and household appliances became worse.[6]

Desperate to end the strikes, the Jaruzelski leadership decided to negotiate with Wałęsa and representatives of other opposition groups, including the Catholic Church.[7] The opposition demanded the legalization of Solidarity, the relaxation of the political environment to allow pluralism, and respect for the Catholic Church's role in Polish society.[8] The government at first rejected these demands, but by the early weeks of 1989, it was clear that without substantive concessions to the opposition the strikes would continue indefinitely. Jaruzelski concluded that the government had to cut a deal with Solidarity to end the strikes.[9]

On April 6, 1989, the Polish government concluded an agreement with Solidarity that granted much of what it had asked for in the way of political liberalization. It provided for a major reform of the communist authoritarian system, including the legalization of Solidarity, in return for a pledge to refrain from strikes for two years, for a declaration accepting Communist Party rule, and for a promise to give no support to anticommunist organizations, such as the

Confederation for an Independent Poland.[10] The heart of the reform involved major changes in the Polish Constitution that would make the government more representative, notably, the establishment of a second chamber of the national Parliament to be called the Senate, to be elected on a completely competitive basis without assignment of a minimum of seats to the Communist Party or any other party organization. The government agreed also to allow elections to the first chamber, the *Sejm*, traditionally dominated by the Communist Party and other small parties loyal to it, to be open and competitive. The opposition did agree, however, as a concession to the authorities, that the Communist Party and its allies would have a 65 percent majority. The agreement also provided that the new bicameral Parliament would elect a president, who would have a substantial leadership role, including control over the Polish military. The president would nominate the prime minister, thus allowing the president a substantial say in the choice of and behavior of the ministerial leadership. The agreement also provided for the establishment of a truly independent judiciary, with judges nominated by the Parliament and formally appointed by the president, ending use of the court system to enforce political conformity. Judges were to have tenure and could not be arbitrarily transferred to different jurisdictions as punishment for not heeding the will of the party leadership in the handling of court cases.[11]

Erosion of Communist Power

The April 6 agreement opened the way to a democratization of Polish politics, weakening Communist Party control over Polish society. Although the Communist Party preserved its technical monopoly of power, Western-style political party organizations could develop along with an expansion of pluralism that would make possible a transition from socialist dictatorship to parliamentary democracy to an extent that neither the public nor the party anticipated. Indeed, when the government scheduled parliamentary elections in early June and presidential elections in mid-July, allowing Solidarity barely two months to campaign, many saw in this a scheme to prevent the Union, handicapped by a lack of preparation and resources, from making any gains.[12]

1. The June 1990 Parliamentary Elections

In the election campaign, Solidarity surprised everyone, mobilizing Polish voters in a sophisticated campaign worthy of the well-developed democratic systems in the West.[13] The union capitalized on the pervasive alienation of Polish voters, carefully and conscientiously instructing them on how to handle the complicated electoral system the authorities devised in order to prejudice the vote against the political opposition. Its electoral strategy paid handsome dividends. Solidarity-sponsored candidates won an overwhelming majority—more than 90 percent—

in the Senate. This was the first time a legislative body in a communist-ruled country was controlled by noncommunists. Noncommunist candidates also won every seat not apportioned to the Communist Party and its allies in the Sejm.[14]

Having underestimated the vitality and shrewdness of the opposition, the Communist Party was unable to compete effectively in the new political environment in which the June 1989 parliamentary elections were held. After forty-five years of rule with little serious challenges in Poland's highly manipulated parliamentary elections, the party had become complacent, even arrogant. Some analysts went further and argued that many party members also lacked faith in the future of their own socialist beliefs and that internal party discipline had eroded.[15]

2. The July 1990 Presidential Elections

The presidential elections of July 1989 further weakened the communist leadership. Although Jaruzelski was an obvious candidate, his reelection was problematical partly because the traditional allies of the Communist Party, the United Peasant Party and the Democratic Party, which together had always given the communists a majority in the legislature, wavered in their support, seeing their future possibly linked to the opposition. Although momentarily contemplating a withdrawal, Jaruzelski ran and won, but only by a hairsbreadth, unmistakable evidence of the party's eroding position. Indeed, his victory was anything but a mandate for firm leadership of the country.[16] Jaruzelski was helped partly and paradoxically by Wałęsa, who had urged his supporters in the Parliament to proceed cautiously in challenging communist power lest they provoke the Kremlin and to refrain from opposing the Jaruzelski candidacy.[17]

3. The Appointment of a Noncommunist Prime Minister

Following the presidential election, there was a further weakening of communist rule as Jaruzelski undertook to nominate a prime minister and a cabinet. His first choice for prime minister was the interior minister, General Czesław Kiszczak, a gesture intended to accommodate hard-line party colleagues still reeling from the party's losses in the June parliamentary elections and to reassure Poland's socialist neighbors, East Germany and Czechoslovakia, then run by conservative regimes opposed to a noncommunist head of government in Warsaw. But the appointment of Kiszczak, who had led government negotiations with Solidarity months earlier and had always been a tough opponent of Solidarity, provoked an explosion of wrath from the political opposition in Parliament. Jaruzelski then asked Solidarity to nominate a candidate. After a brief flurry of discussion and debate among Solidarity leaders in which it seemed for a moment that Wałęsa might be their choice, the union's leadership recommended Tadeusz Mazowiecki, a high-ranking Solidarity official with close links to the Catholic Church. Wałęsa preferred to influence politics from behind the scenes. Overriding the vigorous opposition of conservatives, who wanted to keep the prime ministership in the party's hands, and with the approval of Gorbachev, Jaruzelski appointed Mazowiecki as Poland's first non-Communist prime minister in over forty years.[18]

4. Formation of a Coalition Government

Mazowiecki had problems forming a cabinet. Hard-line Communist Party leaders, still smarting from their failure to get the prime ministership, now insisted that most cabinet posts, including the Foreign Ministry, be given to communists, arguing that without substantial communist participation in the cabinet, Poland would provoke its socialist neighbors and lack the capacity to solve pressing economic problems.[19] But Mazowiecki gave the communists only four ministerial posts, though they were the most influential ones: national defense, internal affairs, foreign economic relations, and transportation, though these were critical ministries that enabled the communists, at least for the time being, to retain control over key sectors of the country's economic life and the police. By the beginning of September 1989, Poland was the first socialist country in the Soviet bloc to have not only a non-Communist prime minister but also a coalition cabinet in which Communists were in the minority.[20]

The End of Communist Rule

In December 1989, the Polish Parliament abolished Article 3 of the constitution, which provided for the Communist Party's leading role. Amendments to the constitution changed the country's name from "Polish People's Republic," adopted in 1952, to "Polish Republic," the country's name before World War II; called Poland a "democratic law-based state implementing the principles of 'socialist justice'"; provided for the liberal and pluralist character of the Polish political system; and guaranteed the freedom of party formation, with all parties enjoying an equality of rights under the law.[21] Meanwhile, Prime Minister Mazowiecki pushed through a battery of reforms dismantling the socialist economy and completing political democratization.

1. Dismantling the Socialist Economy

Mazowiecki sought to curtail hyperinflation caused by scarcities and shortages resulting from communist mismanagement and to return the economy to private ownership as quickly as possible. Much of his program was inspired by advice from Harvard University economist Jeffrey Sachs, who urged the end of the state's monopoly of production and distribution, the implementation of policies to make the Polish currency stable and convertible in the West, the elimination of all subsidies, and the end of price regulation. This strategy of rapid change has been called "shock therapy."[22] By the end of 1989, both the Sejm and the Senate had approved a program of radical economic reform based on the advice of

Professor Sachs and called the Balcerowicz Plan, after Finance Minister Balcerowicz. The Balcerowicz Plan ended price subsidies and price controls; it transferred many state-owned companies to private ownership; and it allowed
employers to dismiss redundant employees. It also provided for bankruptcy proceedings, made Polish currency convertible at international exchange rates, and
inaugurated financial accountability in state-run industries involving the use of
profit-and-loss criteria.[23]

This movement away from the socialist economy caused severe hardship
throughout Polish society. Prices rose dramatically at the end of 1989: 400
percent for electricity and gas and 600 percent for coal. Freezing wages to
control inflation, the government provoked workers and added insult to injury by
asking them for a moratorium on strikes and demands for indexing wages to
prices. The end of subsidies to inefficient industries led to unemployment, which
reached 25 percent by January 1990. This enraged workers, and it was no consolation to the angry unemployed that they were being asked to sacrifice by Solidarity.[24] The most serious disruption appeared in May 1990, when rail workers
demanded a 20 percent pay increase and threatened a wildcat hunger strike.
Wałęsa's personal mediation between striking workers and the government
helped restore tranquility, but several potential foreign investors, including a
Japanese car company, abandoned possible joint ventures because of "economic
chaos" in the country. Two additional waves of strikes, involving farmers in July
and municipal transportation workers in November, rocked the Polish economy
before the end of the year, and both were harmful to Poland's reputation in
international markets.[25] Another problem in moving ahead with free-market reform was the need for Western financial assistance to ease the hardships of
change. Unfortunately, although the West gave plenty of rhetorical support for
Poland's dismantling of the communist system, it was not very forthcoming with
financial help. While the International Monetary Fund (IMF) was willing to
make loans, it would do so only if the Warsaw government adopted harsh austerity programs to control inflation that carried enormous political risks the Polish
government was reluctant to take.[26]

2. Democratizing the Political System

Along with economic reform, the new Polish leadership strengthened democracy. It scheduled local elections in the spring of 1990, rather than later in the
year, to give voters an opportunity to vote communists out of power at the
municipal level, where they had been able to resist new laws lessening state
control and expanding private enterprise. In addition, the Mazowiecki government increased the autonomy of local governing bodies, which had been subservient to the central administration in Warsaw under the communists. They were
given the authority to raise their own taxes to supplement grants from the central
government.[27] Mazowiecki also sought the removal of communists from top

leadership positions. The communist ministers for security and defense voluntarily resigned, virtually ending any influence the party still had at the top of the government. President Jaruzelski now was completely isolated and could not have led the country even if he had wanted to.[28]

Meanwhile, the Polish Communist Party tried to salvage what it could of its role in politics. At the end of January 1990, at a congress in Warsaw, the party transformed itself into a new organization called the Socialist Democracy Party. Looking toward a possible future role in Polish politics, a party congress in early 1990 approved a moderate program calling for reform and the development of a market economy but allowing the continuation of some state intervention in the national economy for equity and efficiency.[29] Although the new organization, which seemed to be modeling itself after the socialist parties of France, Spain, and Italy, was trying to offer an alternative to Solidarity, it had little popular support. Nevertheless, by adopting a moderate alternative to the harsh government economic policies, the former communists shrewdly positioned themselves for a possible resurgence of popular support.

3. President Jaruzelski Resigns

In early September 1990, President Jaruzelski decided to step down, despite four more years remaining in his term of office. With the decline of communist power, he had lost the ability to lead. At the same time, he, as well as the rest of the country, realized that Solidarity, with its majority electoral support, did have the power base needed to fill the presidential post. Jaruzelski resigned also because he had no interest in using the presidency to impede further movement toward economic and political democracy in Poland.[30] People probably will be arguing for a long time about what kind of leader Jaruzelski had been: a Soviet puppet or a national patriot. In pursuing a policy of brutal repression in the early 1980s, he had followed the Brezhnevian Kremlin. But he also helped in the restoration of democracy in Poland by not resisting it. President Jaruzelski's decision to resign could be considered the beginning of the postcommunist era.

4. The Soviet Role

Without Soviet acquiescence, Poland could not have moved away from Communist Party dominance. Gorbachev assumed that Jaruzelski could rejuvenate Polish socialism and assure its closeness to the Soviet Union and was encouraged in this assumption in the summer of 1989 by Jaruzelski's reelection to the presidency and communist control of four key ministerial posts in the Mazowiecki government, and especially by communist control of the Polish armed forces. Gorbachev had underestimated the unpopularity of the communist regime and the ability of the opposition to replace it. And even if he had second thoughts about allowing the reform process to take its natural course, there was little he could have done to interrupt it short of applying the Brezhnev Doctrine, which he had disavowed in July.

The risk of blocking the Polish reform movement by military force was high. The Kremlin might have provoked a civil war in Poland and certainly would have compromised détente with the West. And the cost of a Soviet military campaign against the Polish opposition would have been prohibitive both economically and politically given the shabby condition of the Soviet economy and the more open political environment in which people were beginning to question and criticize almost every aspect of the Kremlin's behavior by late 1989.

Problems of Postcommunist Political Development

Poland has had difficulties developing a Western-style democratic system. Factionalism in Solidarity and the divisive presidential and parliamentary elections in the early 1990s contributed to frequent cabinet changes that undermined efforts to address pressing economic and social problems. This political instability undermined the credibility of the new liberal order and helped encourage a popular yearning for the strength and security of the communist past.

1. Factionalism in Solidarity

Deep differences within Solidarity date back its beginning in 1980, when major social groups, such as intellectuals, workers, and the Catholic Church, cooperated to oppose communist rule. After the defeat of communism, this unity evaporated. Solidarity changed from a vast umbrella organization opposing communist rule to an organization of competing political factions at odds over the future direction of the country. By mid-1990, the top leadership of Solidarity was split between the supporters of Mazowiecki, who wanted to transform Solidarity into a political party, and those of Wałęsa, who wanted the union to remain the amorphous organization it had always been and a home for a wide variety of political constituencies.[31] An important aspect of this factionalism was conflict between Wałęsa and Mazowiecki, once loyal friends but now bitter political antagonists. In 1990, Wałęsa openly criticized the Mazowiecki government as elitist because it was heavily influenced by the intellectual wing of the union. He also called for a purge of all Communist bureaucrats and managers. Mazowiecki resisted, arguing that he needed the expertise of Communist bureaucrats, at least in the short term. He and his followers believed that a witch-hunt for communists would be divisive and counterproductive, if only because few, if any, Polish citizens were totally free of complicity with the communist system.[32]

The split between Mazowiecki and Wałęsa was formalized at the end of June 1990, when sixty-three top Solidarity figures resigned from the Citizens' Committee dominated by Wałęsa and began the Citizens' Movement for Democratic Action, or ROAD. Wałęsa and his supporters in response organized under a group calling itself the Center Alliance.[33] While the two factions shared common views about democracy for Poland, they differed sharply over economic reform. The Alliance said it favored a rapid transition to a market economy and the swift removal of communist bureaucrats from managerial positions. It also called for immediate privatization but with a strong safety net for unemployed workers during the transition. Wałęsa wanted early presidential elections once President Jaruzelski indicated his willingness to resign before the end of his term. ROAD favored a gradual approach to the free-market economy and only a gradual dismantling of the economic structure inherited from the communist era. ROAD, moreover, was suspicious of Wałęsa's commitment to democracy, of his aggressive advocacy of rapid economic change, and of his eagerness to get rid of former communists, with some viewing him as a dangerous kind of populist who might provoke social turmoil. ROAD also was fearful of Wałęsa's closeness to the Catholic Church because of its past support of him, especially on the issues of abortion and the church's advocacy of religious instruction in public schools.[34]

2. The November–December 1990 Presidential Elections

The conflict within Solidarity and the uncertainty everywhere in the country about who should lead the new Poland were evident in the November–December 1990 presidential elections. Following Jaruzelski's decision in September 1990 to resign before the expiration of his term, the Sejm had passed another amendment to the constitution providing for the direct election of the president of the republic. He was to be elected for a five-year term. He could serve no more than two consecutive terms. The winning candidate had to get 50 percent of the votes cast. If this did not occur on the first ballot, a second one would be held two weeks later, and only the two highest candidates could go to the second ballot. If one of the candidates withdrew or died before the second ballot, the other would be automatically elected, a potentially mischievous provision whereby a president who did not have a mandate from the people could succeed to office. In changing to direct popular election of the president, the Polish Parliament, reflecting popular will, sought to reinforce the principle of separation of powers.[35]

Poland voted for its president on November 25 and December 9, 1990. Of six candidates, three dominated the race: Prime Minister Mazowiecki, Solidarity leader Wałęsa, and Józef Tymiński, a Canadian citizen of Polish extraction and a self-made millionaire. Mazowiecki entered the race reluctantly, wanting the presidency but feeling uncomfortable running against Wałęsa, a man with whom he had been closely associated for more than a decade. He reiterated his advocacy of gradualism in the movement away from socialism and his opposition to an anti-communist witch-hunt.[36] Wałęsa called for rapid acceleration of economic reform accompanied by policies to ease the hardships of the transition, the immediate removal of communists from whatever authority they still had, and restrictions on former communists' acquisition of newly privatized enterprises.[37] Tymiński promised to apply to the Polish economy the same free-market economic principles that had led to his own business success. He was a somewhat bizarre candidate, given that he was a foreigner with no political experience in Poland. He was especially popular with young workers, who were willing to overlook his political inexperience, his abusive criticism of opponents, and the inconsistencies of his arguments because they believed he would improve their lives. Tymiński argued for letting inefficient enterprises die a natural death, something that could have caused massive unemployment. Tymiński's popular support can be attributed also to widespread disillusionment over revelations of bribery, fraud, and corruption in the Mazowiecki administration though the prime minister himself has been above reproach.[38]

In the first ballot on November 25, none of the candidates obtained the 50 percent plus of popular votes needed to win: Wałęsa won a 40 percent plurality, Tymiński came in second, and Mazowiecki was a weak third. Flustered by the lack of popular support for his leadership and by the substantial vote for Tymiński, Mazowiecki withdrew from the race and resigned the prime ministership.[39] In the runoff on December 9, Wałęsa ran against Tymiński and won the election by a 3-to-1 margin. Wałęsa's victory may be attributed to the widespread fear of growing unemployment and to the view many people had of him as a kind of savior in a time of uncertainty and danger as the country was shifting abruptly from an old discredited political order to a new unpredictable one.[40]

At the same time, however, several key social groups were dissatisfied with Wałęsa, affirming the diverse and conflict-ridden character of the electorate. For example, the intelligentsia, including former dissident Adam Michnik, editor of *Gazeta Wyborcza,* the Solidarity daily, questioned Wałęsa's fitness for national leadership, viewing him as a radical populist and would-be strong leader who might sacrifice democratic principles for the sake of policy-making expediency. Michnik and other intellectuals thought Wałęsa lacked the education and intellectual sophistication needed to manage power effectively and humanely and observed that in neighboring countries, such as Czechoslovakia and Lithuania, cosmopolitan political leaders had come to power.[41]

Farmers were another group unhappy with Wałęsa's election. Constituting 35 percent of the population, they were a relatively homogeneous economic and social constituency and had a shared sense of historical oppression under the communists. But they feared Wałęsa's plans to foster a market economy which they believed would benefit consumers more than producers. With increasingly free markets and a streamlined distribution system, the food supply had increased and long lines and hoarding had ended. But farmers were producing more than they could sell and had to destroy some of their surpluses. Moreover, Polish farmers had lost the Russian market since Russian buyers could no longer pay for Polish food. Instead, the farmers had to compete with the European Community, which was dumping some of its heavily subsidized agricultural products on the Polish market. To protect their interests, many Polish farmers wanted more government intervention. Some farmers asked for a guaranteed minimum price for their produce and warned that if they were not rewarded for their work they would stop producing.[42]

Wałęsa appointed Jan Krzysztof Bielecki as prime minister. An economist with a background in private business, Bielecki was expected to move toward a free-market economy with the fastest possible privatization of business. Wałęsa also asked the Parliament to empower the cabinet to rewrite the nation's economic laws to allow the president to issue decrees with the force of law. While accepting Bielecki, the Parliament on September 14, 1991, rejected Wałęsa's request for decree power, viewing it as a thinly veiled effort to strengthen his personal power and turn himself into a dictator so that he could effectively force through some economic "shock therapy" that could disorient and destabilize Polish society. Communists and others, including members of Solidarity, opposed rapid socioeconomic change, which was increasing hardship for the overwhelming majority of Polish workers.[43] To resolve the conflict between the president and Parliament over the scope and speed of reform, Wałęsa asked for parliamentary elections before mid-1993, when they were scheduled. He hoped the elections would rid the government of at least one source of opposition to reform, the communist hangers-on, who had been guaranteed a majority in the Sejm by the terms of the agreement between Solidarity and communist leaders in April 1989. The Parliament agreed to schedule elections for October 1991.[44]

3. The October 1991 Parliamentary Elections

The parliamentary elections of October 1991, in which a myriad of small parties participated, confused rather than clarified the political situation and did little to break the governmental stalemate. While the procedure for electing senators was straightforward and resembled the American system of senatorial elections (two senators from each of Poland's forty-seven provinces plus three each from Warsaw and Katowice), the method of electing members of the Sejm employed proportional representation. Sixty percent of Polish voters abstained in order to show their dissatisfaction with politics. Because of proportional representation, and because Poland had not developed large umbrella-type "catch-all" parties with broad policy programs capable of attracting diverse constituencies, no single party was capable of winning a majority of popular votes. More than twenty-five parties were elected to the Sejm. Mazowiecki's party, now called the Democratic Union, and the former Polish communists, who now called themselves the Democratic Left, each won about 12 percent and each received 24 out of 460 seats. The remainder of seats was divided among some twenty different party groups. [45]

Wałęsa had to form a cabinet coalition from these divergent groups, recognizing that such a coalition would be extremely fragile and would compromise reform. His response was immediate and striking. Casting himself as a kind of savior, he offered to serve as his own prime minister, a move that would have greatly strengthened him in a way reminiscent of Józef Piłsudski, the Polish president of the late 1920s, who introduced an authoritarian order to promote national discipline and stability. It was not clear whether Wałęsa was moving toward autocracy or simply trying to goad the different factions to find some common ground and produce a working alliance.[46] Parliament refused Wałęsa's offer, and in early November approved as prime minister Jan Olszewski, a former Solidarity lawyer who had the support of a center-right coalition of parties in the Sejm. Though Olszewski disagreed with Wałęsa on the pace of economic change, preferring gradualism to anything in the nature of "shock therapy," he was at the moment the only political figure of stature who could muster at least a plurality of support in the Sejm.[47]

4. The Olszewski Government

Without a majority, Olszewski was always in danger of a parliamentary vote of no-confidence. His leadership was precarious also because his supporters in Parliament were divided over such key issues as a currency stabilization program requiring spending cuts the IMF said was a prerequisite for loans. Olszewski further weakened his position in the Parliament by allowing the release of names of members of the Parliament considered collaborators with the former communist regime. These officials were furious with Olszewski, viewing his disclosure as a crude attempt to discourage their support of a no-confidence vote. He was also handicapped by difficult personal relationship with Wałęsa, who resented his ill-concealed effort to gain influence over the military at the president's expense when he appointed Radosław Sikorski as deputy defense minister without consulting Wałęsa. Wałęsa eventually asked the Sejm to dismiss Olszewski, and it promptly obliged with a vote of no-confidence in early June 1992. Olszewski thereupon resigned.[48]

Wałęsa started searching for a new prime minister, eventually nominating Waldemar Pawlak, head of the United Peasant Party. Pawlak was a relatively noncontroversial politician who was expected to loyally support presidential policy. On June 5, the Sejm elected Pawlak. But the new prime minister could not form a government precisely because he was thought to be no more than a spokesman for Wałęsa.[49] The Democratic Union proposed Hanna Suchocka, a lawyer and a supporter of rapid movement toward a market economy. Wałęsa accepted and nominated her, but he worried about working with her because she was even more aggressive than he in advocating a free market. Seven parties made a coalition to support her, and she was formally approved by the Parliament in mid-June 1992.[50]

5. The "Little Constitution"

By 1992, many Polish politicians of all persuasions, including President Wałęsa, agreed on the need to revise the Polish Constitution originally promulgated by the communists in 1952. Although it had worked for the communists because they ran a dictatorship, it had become outmoded in the new democratic era because of its provision for a strong Parliament and a weak president. Such an arrangement made policy making, especially expeditious implementation of rapid and profound socioeconomic change away from socialism, difficult, if not at times impossible. On November 17, 1992, the Parliament approved and the president signed the so-called "Little Constitution" and abolished the 1952 constitution.[51]

The "Little Constitution" seemed to strengthen the presidency by affirming the principle of direct election; by making him both head of foreign policy making and commander in chief of the military with responsibility for the defense and security of the country; by giving him power to declare martial law for up to three months and longer if approved by the Sejm, with the proviso that Parliament cannot be dissolved during a period of martial law; and by granting him prerogatives to nominate the prime minister and upon the latter's recommendation to nominate members of the cabinet, to dissolve Parliament if it fails over a three-month period to pass the budget or approve the government, to call for new parliamentary elections, to submit new legislation, to veto parliamentary bills, to convene a meeting of the cabinet, and to initiate a referendum.[52]

At the same time, the "Little Constitution" guarded against the possibility of an executive dictatorship by linking the prime minister and cabinet closely to the Sejm through provisions that the president's choice of prime minister and cabinet must receive an absolute majority of support of the lower house within fourteen days of nomination. If the Sejm rejects the new government, it must come forward with an alternative slate or else defer to the president, who may nominate another slate of cabinet leaders needing only a simple majority of support from the Sejm. If the Sejm still rejects the president's choice, it must again produce an alternative by a simple majority, and if that attempt fails, the president must either dissolve the Parliament or appoint a provisional government, which would have six months to obtain the confidence of Parliament.[53] Other limitations on presidential power included the provision that the prime minister, in putting together his cabinet, needs presidential approval only for his appointments for the ministries of internal affairs, defense, and foreign affairs. Furthermore, the Sejm may dismiss a government and create a new one independently of the president, who is not empowered to ask for the government's dismissal, although he can reshuffle the government's membership with the prime minister's approval. Finally, the president cannot prevent the Sejm from passing a law limiting his authority.[54]

The "Little Constitution," arguably, thus did not really strengthen the Polish presidency after the fashion of the French presidency. The president's authority still did not allow him to influence decisively day-to-day policy making. The prime minister and the cabinet, who *are* responsible for daily governance, have stronger ties to the Parliament than to the president. Indeed, under the "Little Constitution" the legislature has more control over the choice and behavior of the prime minister and cabinet than does the president.

6. The September 1993 Parliamentary Elections

Prime Minister Suchocka lasted in power only a little over a year. Her commitment to "shock therapy," which had increased economic hardship for most Polish wage earners, was too much for the voters, as well as for her own party colleagues and supporters in the Parliament. In the October 1993 elections, the Democratic Union lost to the Left Democratic Alliance led by former communist Aleksander Kwaśniewski, who called for a slower pace of economic reform with greater government sensitivity to the hardships caused by the introduction of a free-market economy. In November, backed by his own United Peasant Party and the Left Democratic Alliance, Waldemar Pawlak again was nominated for prime minister, and this time he was approved by the Parliament with a mandate to slow down the pace of change to a market economy. To the dismay of reformers at home and in the West, Pawlak did just that, and Poland made little progress toward a free market throughout 1994. His listless leadership, especially in the area of economic reform, eventually antagonized Wałęsa, who never had much respect for him anyway.[55] By early 1995, relations between Pawlak and the president were at an all-time low, and Wałęsa's patience with his prime minister's slowness in reforming the economy, especially in the area of privatization, was virtually exhausted. Moreover, Wałęsa was annoyed by Pawlak's less-than-enthusiastic support for Polish membership in NATO, evidenced by his appointment of Longin Pastusiak, a former communist who had been critical of NATO in the communist era, as minister of defense. Indeed, the Pawlak government's perceived pro-Moscow stance infuriated Foreign Minister Andrzej Olechowski and led to his resignation. The last straw for Wałęsa was Pawlak's 1995 budget, with its excessive spending on social services that risked a re-igniting of the inflation Suchocka and Mazowiecki had worked so hard to control and that diminished the possibility of making the Polish currency convertible.[56] In early 1995, Wałęsa tried to pull the political rug out from under the Pawlak government by threatening a dissolution of the Sejm, a gesture of dubious constitutionality. Parliamentary leaders said there were no legitimate reasons for a dissolution other than the strengthening of the presidency. But the Sejm had no great affection for Pawlak, seeing him as a political weakling, and made no secret of its wish that he step aside. Lacking the support of Alliance deputies, especially the former communists, in the Sejm, Pawlak resigned.[57]

7. A Former Communist Becomes Prime Minister

The Alliance quickly proposed Józef Oleksy, a high-ranking member of the Communist Party on the eve of its ouster, though a reformer who had wanted the party to embrace major economic change. Wałęsa at first opposed Oleksy, unwilling to see a communist in power. Eventually, he relented and agreed to name Oleksy his prime minister to avoid provoking a crisis in the Sejm. In March 1995, Oleksy gave public assurances that he would continue the country's free-market reformism.[58] The Left now more than ever before became a wild card in Poland's political future. The former communists skillfully exploited popular fears of Wałęsa's aggressive behavior and of rapid economic change that would increase inflation, expand unemployment, and in other ways lower the already depressed standard of living of most Polish wage earners. They let people believe they favored less shock and more therapy in the transition to a market economy, though they have given no indication of an intention to halt or reverse movement toward the free market.

8. Wałęsa's Controversial Presidency, 1991–95

Wałęsa viewed the presidency as the dominant institution within the national government, affecting not only the operations of the state's administrative and legislative bodies but also the style and character of the country's politics. The general public as well has come to regard the presidency as the center of government decision making. Wałęsa's views are consistent with Polish history. Polish society has long admired strong leaders, no doubt a result of the memory of the weak national government that led to Poland's extinction at the end of the eighteenth century, as well as the somewhat anarchic character of Polish society, which has always cherished the freedom of which it had been so often deprived in the recent past.[59]

Ironically, in trying to strengthen the Polish presidency, Wałęsa may have weakened it, as well as his own efforts to lead. To enhance the presidency, Wałęsa placed it above politics. He believed the Polish president should be the leader of all the people, not simply of those who voted for him. He also thought the president should be independent of any single party organization. He therefore kept his distance from several groups of political and electoral supporters, such as the Center Alliance, refusing to appoint their leaders to top government positions. He also was reluctant to establish his own strong political organization to avoid creating a political "mafia" he could not control and that would be more interested in power than in the well-being of society.[60]

Wałęsa soon recognized the liabilities of stripping the presidency of its political character. Doing so undercut his leadership by depriving him of the kind of disciplined political support in the Parliament needed to assure enactment into law of his policies. In addition to lobbying in 1992 for a strengthened presidency during discussion of the "Little Constitution," in the first half of 1993, he tried to create his own political party, the so-called Nonparty Bloc, made up of people inside as well as outside Solidarity who supported him and were willing to help him get his way in Parliament against the opposition, which, though fragmented, consisted of organizations, such as the Left Democratic Alliance, that had a degree of cohesiveness that attracted public attention. Opponents criticized this new party grouping, saying it was just another power-grabbing ploy of an aggressive president. The Nonparty Bloc was not successful in providing Wałęsa with the leverage he needed to have his way with the Parliament.[61]

Wałęsa also tried to strengthen the president's influence over the day-to-day operation of the government by authorizing his personal staff of advisers to monitor operations in the areas of national defense, foreign affairs, local government, and the economy. He also insisted, after the fashion of the president of the Fifth French Republic, that the president have a say in the selection of cabinet ministers before their candidacy for office became known to the public. He also sent a ranking member of his staff to attend all meetings of the Council of Ministers and listen to its deliberations, a move that was constitutionally permissible but politically controversial. It provoked Adam Michnik to accuse him of "incipient authoritarianism."[62]

In 1994, public-opinion polls showed that Polish voters, despite a predilection for strong leadership, were not sympathetic to many of Wałęsa's ideas about the presidency. For example, the polls reportedly showed that Polish voters did not want a "hands-on" president. The polls showed also that many voters were suspicious of Wałęsa's eagerness to become deeply involved in the day-to-day running of the country, by opposing the appointment of a cabinet minister, for example, or by efforts to force the dismissal of a minister who disagreed with him. Polish voters liked even less his occasional suggestions that Poland might someday become a dictatorship and that he would be ready to lead such a government.[63] Many educated Polish people disliked Wałęsa personally. They did not think he was up to the job. They thought he was not intellectually qualified to lead Poland in this difficult period of change. They considered him uneducated and a poor speaker, who frequently did not pronounce his words correctly. They believed he lacked the diplomatic savvy to protect and further Polish interests abroad. They frequently compared him with the Czech Republic's President Václav Havel, an intellectual and worldly figure quite unlike Wałęsa.[64]

The November 1995 Presidential Elections

In mid-November, Poland held its second set of presidential elections since the collapse of communist rule in 1989. They were controversial and hard fought, with Wałęsa and the Left Democratic Alliance leader Aleksander Kwaśniewski the leading contenders. Wałęsa was defeated by Kwaśniewski, but only by a small margin of the popular vote. Nevertheless, Wałęsa's defeat and Kwaśniewski's victory marked the end of one era and the beginning of a new and uncertain one, with former communists in control of both the legislative and the executive branches of government in Warsaw.[65]

1. Wałęsa's Defeat

Many factors explain Wałęsa's defeat, not least his abrasive style of leadership. In his efforts to strengthen the presidency, he frequently looked to many Poles very much like the communist dictators he had fought in the 1980s. Indeed, voters also resented the way in which he sought the glitz of office during hard times for most of them, as, for example, when he moved out of the simple, down-to-earth official presidential home, the Belvedere Mansion, into an ornate seventeenth-century palace. Wałęsa also suffered from the negative impact of his economic reform program, in particular, his commitment to a rapid pace of change involving a much disliked austerity accompanied by rising prices and an unprecedented loss of jobs. Many of Wałęsa's traditional supporters believed he had betrayed them in his apparent indifference to the interests of wage earners. Of course, the beneficiaries of the free economy who wanted more reform, and the sooner the better, voted for Wałęsa, but they were only a minority of the Polish electorate.

Wałęsa's gruff and demagogic behavior during the campaign, especially his crude treatment of his opponent, alienated many voters who otherwise would have supported him. He spent as much time attacking Kwaśniewski as explaining his own program. He called Kwaśniewski a liar and a thug. His campaign was hurt also by the overtly partisan behavior of the Catholic Church, which used as many resources as it dared to get voters to support Wałęsa over Kwaśniewski, whom the clerical leadership despised. Cardinal Józef Glemp reportedly called Kwaśniewski an advocate of "neo-pagan values." Marcin Król, a Catholic intellectual and editor of *Res Publica Nowa,* was convinced that the overbearing behavior of the church antagonized many Polish voters, pushing them, despite their sympathy for Wałęsa, to vote for Kwaśniewski. Indeed, many Polish voters, including Wałęsa supporters, believed he had been too indulgent of the church through his personal loyalty to many of its positions, especially regarding abortion. Wałęsa consistently had ignored a popular view that, while abortion was wrong, it was more wrong to outlaw it and deprive Polish citizens of a fundamental right of choice.[66]

2. Kwaśniewski's Victory

While Kwaśniewski was a beneficiary of Wałęsa's growing unpopularity, especially on the part of the youth, who considered Wałęsa a symbol of the past rather than an instrument for Poland's future, it is also true that many voters were willing to dismiss his communist past because he was an attractive candidate in comparison with Wałęsa. He was younger than Wałęsa and better educated, although he never received the university degree he claimed to have. He was articulate in a way that Wałęsa never was. But, most importantly, he was moderate and restrained in his political behavior. For example, he called himself a "social democrat," comparing himself with other former communist "social democrats" like those in power in Hungary and Bulgaria. He advocated caution and restraint in Poland's movement away from communist paternalism to a free-market economy. He promised more attention to the needs of the country's hard-pressed wage earners still suffering from inflation, unemployment, and depressed wages. At the same time, however, he shrewdly assured the country that he had no intention of restoring the old communist order torn down in 1989 and 1990. He was also very careful to resist the temptation to respond in kind to Wałęsa's harsh denunciations of him. He refrained from attacking Wałęsa personally, recognizing that, while most Poles were critical of Wałęsa's behavior, they still deeply admired him for his combat with the communist leadership and his role in restoring Polish democracy. In sum, despite the controversy surrounding him and the pervasive distrust of him, Kwaśniewski was successful in persuading many voters that it would be not only safe but smart to give him a chance to lead the country.[67]

3. The Future

By early 1996, events seemed to vindicate those voters who had decided to take a chance on Kwaśniewski. In a conciliatory move intended to heal the deep emotional wounds caused by the presidential contest, Kwaśniewski resigned from his party, the Socialist Democracy Party, to emphasize his commitment to represent all Polish citizens, not simply those of a particular ideological persuasion. He also tried to make amends with the Catholic Church by a visit to the holy shrine at Jelenia Góra, famous for its resistance to Swedish invaders in the seventeenth century. But here he was not successful. The church was wounded and humiliated by its failure to get Wałęsa elected and was in no mood to be large-minded about a victor whom it despised. The prior at Jelenia Góra locked the gates and announced the closure of the shrine to "enemies of the Catholic faith, regardless of high rank." Kwaśniewski's response was commendably conciliatory. Determined to avoid conflict with the church hierarchy, he simply said that he would try to work as hard as he could to "earn God's blessing," though by no far stretch of the imagination could one say that he intended to allow the church to influence his policies. For example, he pledged support of a liberalization of the draconian restrictions on abortion, a position that hardly endeared him to those with whom he has wanted to make peace.

Other evidence of his commitment to reform was his readiness in November

1995 to begin implementation of the long-awaited privatization program, whereby Polish citizens were offered ownership in hundreds of former state companies the government had been promising to sell off for almost four years. Polish citizens could buy certificates of ownership for $8 apiece. Kwaśniewski also renewed Poland's strong interest in becoming a full member of NATO and in joining the European Union. He indicated his commitment to a continued strengthening of Polish links to the West. But Washington and other NATO allies are watching Kwaśniewski to determine the sincerity of his protestations about breaking with his Marxist past. For example, the Clinton administration wanted Kwaśniewski to appoint conservatives to high positions in his government.[68]

Movement to a Market Economy

Serious obstacles, especially in the areas of privatization and the development of large-scale private entrepreneurship, accounted for an erratic and halting movement toward a free-market economy.[69] But it is also true that Polish ministerial leaders since Mazowiecki and Balcerowicz were under enormous popular pressure to ease the hardships accompanying the transformation from socialism to capitalism. While Olszewski and Pawlak bowed to this pressure, moving slowly or not at all with privatization, and were inclined to maintain a costly social security net, Suchocka resisted it, favoring "shock therapy" and a harsh austerity to quicken the dismantling of what was left of the socialist economy.

1. Obstacles to a Free Market

Privatization, which is at the center of Polish free-market reformism, has been slow despite pressure from the West, especially the United States and the IMF, to end state control of Polish economic life as quickly as possible. In addition, bloated budget deficits, inflation, and unemployment have complicated the dismantling of the socialist economy.

Problems with Privatization[70]

As the government prepared to sell off industries in the early 1990s, it found that the Polish people simply did not have the resources to buy them. The average per-capita income in 1990 was $1,920.00, barely enough money to buy food, never mind stock. The government also could not reliably assess the real value of the enterprises to be sold. Sometimes it overvalued them, but more often it undervalued them. The people who did have spare capital, mostly former communists, could buy them at "bargain-basement" prices. Poland also lacked, and still lacks, an effective banking system and the computer information systems to facilitate banking operations. In 1991, it often took banks weeks, not hours or days, to cash checks and transfer funds from one location to another. Furthermore, banks had antiquated record-keeping systems and were not experienced at managing deposits. As a result, banks lacked the funds to lend to customers. In addition, the state-controlled banks had a burden of bad loans made to obsolescent state industries like arms and steel making. These loans became uncollectible because the industries that borrowed the money collapsed when the Russian market for their output started to disappear in 1990 and 1991.

Privatization was hamstrung also because the communications infrastructure was inadequate. Poland had an old telephone system inherited from the communist era in which, for reasons of security, all lines had to go through Warsaw. Poland also lacked people with free-market managerial skills who could profitably run large complex industrial enterprises. Nor did Poland have business schools and other educational institutions to train people in business administration. Furthermore, many of the large enterprises the government wanted to unload were so inefficient, with obsolete plants and equipment, that no one wanted them. Paternalistic to a fault, many unprofitable companies provided expensive recreational and housing facilities for workers that no private owners would maintain because of their drain on profit. In one instance, workers had a large swimming pool and a soft-drink bottling plant.

Social conditions were not conducive to an expansion of private entrepreneurship. The Polish public feared, with good reason, that the shift to a market economy would unfairly favor people with spare cash. In all likelihood, this select group would consist of the country's former communist administrators, who could now enjoy new advantages accruing from their accumulation of skills and wealth under communist rule. Moreover, successive prime ministers were reluctant to tell the workers, who had been instrumental in bringing about the fall of communism, that many of their factories were virtually worthless and eventually would have to be closed. Finally, the economic culture of Poland still had strong traits of socialism, with many people expecting full economic security and hesitating to seek out economic opportunities or to take risks.

To facilitate privatization, the Polish government, in June 1991, introduced an imaginative program to increase the reservoir of potential buyers of state concerns. The government set a price for the enterprise to be privatized and converted it into shares, 40 percent of which went to the employees of the enterprise or to the government and 60 percent into national wealth management funds. From these, 27 million adults received vouchers, the equivalent of American-style mutual funds. Shares were distributed so that one investment group took primary responsibility for overhauling a particular enterprise. Fund managers were not allowed to own shares, except to the extent that fees paid to them were shares as opposed to cash. The Polish government hoped that this program, beginning in 1992, would allow the privatization of about 7,000 enterprises by the end of 1994. It was also intended to involve as many people as possible in the ongoing process of economic transformation.[71]

The Polish government also established a Western-style stock market in April 1991. Initially the only shares available for trading were in five newly privatized enterprises: the Krosno glass works, the Exbud construction company, Tonsil Electronics, the Śląska Fabryka wire-cable company, and the Próchnik clothing company. Though trading was thin, with capital in short supply and limited investment opportunities, the market itself had great symbolic significance. It sent a message abroad to foreign investors that Poland had a capital market in which they could trade. Polish officials hoped that in this market investors would purchase shares in more state-controlled enterprises to be privatized in the next few years.[72]

The Polish government also started up a modern, privately run banking system. In late 1990, Kredyt Bank was founded by a group of private and state-owned Polish companies. Semiprivately run, the bank had the latest electronic banking equipment, making it competitive with state banks for large and small private credit-seeking entrepreneurs. It eventually opened a stock brokerage business and started a foreign-exchange trade. Foreign banks helped Kredyt Bank by providing capital.[73]

Budget Deficits, Inflation, and Unemployment

In the early 1990s, huge annual budget deficits, the result of continuing subsidies to state-controlled industrial dinosaurs that were unprofitable but that employed too many people to shut down all at once, kept Poland from receiving the quantity of Western financial assistance needed to keep up the pace of free-market reform.[74] Inflation, caused partly by the decontrol of prices, also compromised free-market reform by increasing hardship for wage earners. While the supply of goods increased, ending the historic communist phenomenon of long lines and chronic shortages, these goods were priced beyond the reach of average workers, who now found themselves in some cases worse off than they had been under the communists. Making matters worse, production in state-controlled industries declined by about 23 percent to 25 percent as trade with the Soviet Union and its successors dropped off sharply. The Kremlin, itself struggling with a collapsing economy, was selling its valuable natural resources, such as oil and natural gas, to the West for hard currency rather than to the East European countries, which had little or no hard currency to spare. The Russian action, which violated a previously signed trade agreement, caused the shutdown of Polish industries from the Gdańsk shipyards to the Galician metalworks and paralyzed an already enfeebled national economy. It also effectively ended for Poland and other East European countries a long period of cheap energy imports.[75]

Finally, with free-market reformism, in particular, government policy to diminish subsidies to enterprises that could not be privatized and were a drain on scarce public resources, came unemployment, which rose steadily in the early 1990s.

Though less than the 7 percent unemployment rate in the United States in the early 1990s, it shocked and demoralized a society used to providing jobs at any cost to all citizens who wanted to work. It aroused a pervasive popular skepticism about economic liberalization and encouraged a longing for the paternalism of the former communists.[76]

2. Conflict of Approaches: Austerity versus Relaxation

Following the October 1991 parliamentary elections, the Polish leadership was caught between a rock and a hard place on the issue of the scope and pace of economic reform. If it gave in to popular demands for less austerity and more relaxation, the budget deficit would expand, inflation would soar, and the IMF would refuse to make the loans Poland desperately needed to cushion the impact of reform. If, however, the government ignored pressures for relief and followed the IMF's advice, it would risk an explosion of social tensions that could destabilize the fragile democratic process. Polish prime ministers tried to find a middle ground.

Olszewski Favors Relaxation

Olszewski, who took office in November 1991, found it difficult to justify the hardships resulting from the move toward a market economy and opted for less austerity. He guaranteed prices for farmers, provided financial help to potentially profitable state enterprises as an alternative to privatization, lowered interest rates for loans to ailing state industries, assured protection of pensions, and printed more money.[77] But pressure from the IMF for deficit reduction through cuts in spending for the social net forced Olszewski to modify his relaxation. In what has been referred to as a Balcerowicz II Plan, the Olszewski government produced a budget with sharp cuts in government spending in education and health care and canceled plans to rescue some state enterprises and boost farm income.[78]

Suchocka Opts for Austerity

Determined to brook no opposition to plans for privatizing the country's remaining state-controlled enterprises, Olszewski's successor, Prime Minister Suchocka, told angry workers and frustrated managers in September 1992 to decide how to terminate state control. They could try to survive by trimming the workforce and pursuing other cost-cutting procedures or accept closure. Suchocka took the unprecedented step of firing workers who refused to end strikes at a car factory and a coal mine on the verge of collapse.[79] Suchocka also was tough on Poland's 300,000 miners in Silesia who went on strike in mid-December 1992 to protest low wages and the prospect of mine closures. Because

Suchocka refused to be blackmailed into granting inflationary wage increments and threatened the miners with the prospect of cheap imported coal, the strike abated. Finally, in February 1993, Suchocka won parliamentary approval of a tough budget limiting social spending by pointing out how much Poland stood to lose in Western assistance if it rejected austerity. Wałęsa backed her up, threatening a dissolution if the budget were rejected.[80]

Suchocka's austerity paid economic dividends. Polish currency, fully convertible, steadily rose in value against Western hard currencies throughout 1992. The black market in currency vanished. Real wages rose, and a private-sector boom occurred that promised more and better jobs and an eventual easing of price inflation. By early 1993, more than 50 percent of Polish workers were employed in private enterprise.[81] In addition, the IMF acknowledged the progress Poland had made and was trying to make, and, at the end of November 1992, it allowed Poland to draw on about $700 million dollars. This paved the way for additional debt relief from Western creditors, who had promised to forgive 50 percent of Poland's indebtedness provided Warsaw could reach an agreement with the IMF.[82]

The High Political Cost of Austerity

Prime Minister Suchocka's success in the economic sphere, however, cost her dearly in politics. Although public-opinion polls showed her to be immensely popular with the public, and although she had kept up the pace of Poland's rapid movement toward a market economy, winning her support from the West, she had alienated important political groups in the Parliament, notably deputies associated with the left wing of Solidarity representing aggrieved workers. Thus, on April 30, 1993, the Sejm only narrowly passed a privatization bill affecting 600 state-owned enterprises that it had rejected a month earlier. Furthermore, many deputies, especially those representing workers, were infuriated by her refusal to grant pay raises to striking health workers and teachers and to increase pensions despite the lack of funds to pay for these concessions. She also had difficulty even with President Wałęsa, who was concerned about the harshness of her austerity policies and wanted her to pay more attention to the hardship of workers.[83]

By the end of May 1993, Suchocka's political position was untenable. She faced the anger not only of some of her supporters and many parliamentary deputies linked to Solidarity but also of a large conglomeration of opposition parties centered around the former communists called the Left Democratic Alliance.[84] Kwaśniewski suggested that he would support her for the time being if she agreed to some of the pay demands for hard-pressed public workers. But Suchocka refused to compromise on policies she felt were injurious to Poland's long-term health.[85] When Suchocka defended her achievements in Parliament, and President Wałęsa somewhat belatedly supported her, calling her the best prime minister Poland ever had, it appeared she might survive a vote of no-confidence.[86] And she nearly did. When it came, as a result of growing opposition to her policies, she lost by only one vote. She promptly resigned. Wałęsa decided against a cabinet reshuffle. He opted for parliamentary elections, hoping voters would return power to Suchocka, the Democratic Union, and other moderates who had done so much to move the country away from the old socialist order.[87]

The Voters Want Relaxation

Parliamentary elections in late September 1993 gave the parties on the left, which supported economic relaxation, a plurality. The Left Democratic Alliance, made up of former communists, won 20 percent of the popular vote, the left-wing Peasant Party won 15 percent, and a grouping made up of the left wing of Solidarity won 7 percent. Suchocka's Democratic Union won 11 percent.[88] Though Polish voters liked Suchocka personally, they deplored her economic policies, which they blamed for the inflation and unemployment causing them hardship. Farmers especially were infuriated over the failure of the Suchocka government to give them relief from the flood of subsidized agricultural imports from the European Union (EU) and the EU's barriers against Poland's products. Indeed, 51 percent of the electorate voted, a rather high turnout for Poles and a sign of their unhappiness.[89] Miners also were angry. Once among the highest paid workers in the communist system, they clearly were the losers in the transition to capitalism. Disgusted with Suchocka for not protecting them in hard times, they were susceptible to the political left, which was ready to slow down the pace of change toward capitalism.[90] In general, many workers believed that Suchocka could not and did not empathize with their plight. Either she did not know how badly off many workers were, or, despite her awareness, she had decided to stay the course for the sake of completing the transition to capitalism in the short term and of assuring the continued financial support of the West, in particular the IMF.[91] Indeed, some voters thought that the parties supportive of Suchocka had completely ignored the most vulnerable groups in Polish society, namely, pensioners, unskilled workers, and middle-aged unemployed workers. A Polish pensioner, obliged to live on $67.00 a month in Łódź, said she supported the Left because she did not want to have to worry any more about what she would have to eat the next day. She said that under communism she had been able to afford new clothes, but now she had to make do with rags, and even those were stolen when she put them on the clothesline. Not unlike other Central and East European peoples, an overwhelming majority of Polish voters supported the introduction of a free-market economy in the expectation of an overnight improvement in living conditions.[92]

Pawlak Strikes a Balance

Pawlak, who succeeded Suchocka in mid-October 1993, was inclined toward relaxation but was under tremendous pressure to move forward with the transformation to a free-market economy. Fearful of antagonizing the West and jeopardizing the prospects of funding from the Western financial community, the Left Democratic Alliance blocked Pawlak's effort to appoint ministers to key economic posts who wanted to preserve a large amount of state control over the economy. Since the United Peasant Party was the smaller component of the coalition, Pawlak had to consult regularly with Alliance leader Kwaśniewski, who made him appoint people for cabinet posts who favored privatization and continued movement toward a free-market economy.[93] In March 1994, the coalition reaffirmed a commitment to the restoration of a free-market economy, despite popular protests in early February against a reduction of social spending, and came forward with a budget that limited social spending instead of increasing it, as many workers who had voted for the parties on the left in the recent parliamentary election had expected. While the budget did provide for an increase of benefits to the least-well-off groups, particularly pensioners and the unemployed, it did so with the proviso that there would be increases only if revenues were higher than anticipated. The IMF seemed satisfied with this modest appearance of belt tightening and cleared the way for additional credit.[94] But Pawlak discreetly dragged his feet on privatization, where the rate of state selloffs was 25 percent lower in 1994 than it had been in 1993. As a result of his cautious, halting reform policies, which had antagonized Wałęsa and members of the Parliament because they were criticized by the IMF and seen as a weakness of leadership, the elderly, the unemployed, and the less-educated groups in Polish society seemed to be suffering less.[95]

Economic Prospects

By 1995, Poland had made a lot of progress toward economic recovery and the establishment of capitalism, which should facilitate the restoration of the country's economic health and material well-being. Poland had one of the fastest growing economies in Eastern Europe by the end of 1994, with a growth rate in 1994 of 4.5 percent, compared with 2.5 percent in the Czech Republic. Unemployment leveled off and consumer confidence increased.[96] In recognition of the future promise of Polish economic growth and development, Western banks holding Poland's $14 billion of commercial debt, on which it had stopped paying interest and principal in 1990, agreed to a restructuring that reduced the amount of indebtedness by $6.5 billion and a further reduction later on in return for a resumption of Polish payments in early 1995. The agreement should encourage an increase in foreign investment that will stimulate economic growth in the second half of the 1990s.[97] Furthermore, the ascendancy of former communist Oleksy was not considered dangerous to Poland's economic reform program, which was already well established and would have been difficult, if not impossible, to reverse. Many people in Poland today have benefited from the development of a free-market economy and are doing well; indeed, small-scale private enterprise had increased exponentially in the early 1990s. Pawlak's successor, Oleksy, as well as Aleksander Kwaśniewski, reassured both the Polish public and the international community that they had no intention of backtracking on reform. They continued the transition to a free-market economy, though somewhat more slowly than the Right because of their concern to avoid the buildup of social tensions.[98]

Church–State Relations

In their implementation of democracy and a free-market economy, postcommunist Polish governments have had an ally in the Catholic Church, which has enormous credibility with the Polish people because of its long, outspoken opposition to the communists. But the role of the church in Polish democratic development has been problematic. With encouragement from the Vatican, which wants to make Poland a role model for Catholicism in postcommunist Eastern Europe, and a sympathetic audience among Solidarity and the peasant parties, which considered religion an integral part of Polish nationalism, the church has tried to expand its influence over Polish political and social life. For example, the church leadership urged the faithful to vote for candidates of parties and groups that espoused Christian values, opposed abortion, and called for tougher restrictions on divorce. To cultivate the loyalty of young people, the church advocated religious education in the public schools. A government decree in 1990 allowing time and space in public schools for religious teaching accommodated the church on this issue.[99] However, in April 1993, a constitutional tribunal heard a legal challenge to compulsory religious teaching and prayers in public schools brought by Tadeusz Zieliński, the government ombudsman, who argued that the teaching of religion was turning Poland into a theocracy. The tribunal, reflecting the already tremendous political influence of the Catholic Church in Poland, ruled that compulsory religious teaching was constitutional.[100]

There has been a popular reaction against the church's political activism. Many who gladly sent their children to church for religious education were against religious training in the schools. Irritating many was the fact that the religious classes were held in the middle of the school day to discourage absenteeism.[101] While the Warsaw government and, in particular, President Lech Wałęsa, who was very loyal to the church, did not want to antagonize the Vatican, they also could not ignore popular misgivings about the church's effort to influence how they lived. For example, the defeat of the Suchocka government in the September 1993 parliamentary elections, as well as election of President Kwaśniewski in November 1995, represented a rebuke to the Catholic Church and its efforts to expand influence over postcommunist Poland.[102]

1. The Abortion Issue

The complexity of the church–state relationship can be seen in the abortion issue. Under tremendous pressure from the church, the Senate, in early November

1990, enacted a ban on abortions. The bill then went to the Sejm, where it was eventually buried despite efforts to get it enacted into law before the arrival of the Pope in June 1991. When polled, Polish citizens expressed mixed sentiments. While they indicated personal antipathy to abortions, they opposed depriving people of the right to an abortion by imposing a legal ban. As one Polish woman said, the abortion "problem is in the soul, not the penal code." At the same time, while some people insisted that there was too much of the church in their daily lives, others thought that the Pope had a perfect right to speak about abortion and to persuade Polish Catholics to do his bidding on this issue because obeying the Pope was good for them.[103]

The possibility of some legislation against abortion improved with the October 1991 parliamentary elections, when parties supporting the church, such as the Center Alliance and the Christian National Union, together won about 29 percent of the seats. The church and its antiabortion supporters then won something of a victory in December 1991, when the national doctors' guild drafted a new and very controversial code of ethics that sharply restricted abortions, permitting them only in cases of rape or when the life of the mother was threatened. Any doctor who was found guilty of violating the code could lose his or her license.[104] At the beginning of 1993, the Polish Parliament passed a bill into law restricting abortions. Abortions were forbidden except in cases of rape, severe fetus malformation, or serious threat to the mother's life, and only if approved by three doctors. The new law fell short of the church's demand for a total and complete ban on all abortions, affirming again the mixed feelings of Poland's political leadership regarding abortion. Helping the cause of restricting abortions was Prime Minister Hanna Suchocka, who voted for the measure despite opposition to aspects of it in her own party.[105]

The draconian restrictions on abortions led many Polish women to find ways of evading them. There is an illicit network of physicians willing to perform abortions, which are prohibited in state-run hospitals, for a fee that is usually very high. Moreover, people are willing to help those in need, providing the extra funds necessary to pay for an illegal abortion. A dangerous remedy of last resort is a self-induced abortion, which frequently results in death.[106] There were strong misgivings in the Parliament. A new organization, the Women's Caucus in Parliament, actively campaigned for a liberal policy on sex education, freer distribution of contraceptives, and a national referendum on abortion. In 1994, the Sejm and Senate passed a bill somewhat easing restrictions on abortions, though by no means making it easy to get one. The bill allowed a woman to obtain an abortion in cases of difficult material conditions or a demanding personal situation. Wałęsa's veto of it, inspired not only by his closeness to the church but also by his own very conservative personal views, provoked popular anger. Some Polish people likened him to a dictator and his behavior to totalitarianism.[107]

2. The Church and Anti-Semitism

Anti-Semitism is prevalent in postcommunist Poland. It is a bizarre situation, because most Polish Jews died in the World War II Nazi Holocaust and most of the survivors emigrated when the communists took power after the war. Today, there are only 3,000 Jews in a population of 38 million. Yet Polish anti-Semitism is strong and pervasive. In April 1991, a public-opinion poll revealed that one in three Polish citizens believed that "the influence of people they see as Jewish is too great." According to the survey, 5 percent of those polled admitted to being extremely anti-Semitic, 10 percent were strongly anti-Semitic, and 16 percent claimed to be moderately or slightly anti-Semitic. Another poll, in October 1990, showed that the most strongly anti-Semitic statements were made by agricultural and industrial workers, who typically had not advanced past grade school. And four years later, only a very small percentage of those polled said they were aware of the incontrovertible historical fact that 80 percent of Poland's Jewish population had been exterminated by the Nazis in World War II. In that survey, 57 percent of respondents also said that they did not know that Jews constituted less than 1 percent of Poland's population in 1994.[108] Most disturbing has been the appearance of anti-Semitism in political circles. For example, during the Polish presidential campaign in October 1990, Lech Wałęsa asserted that two members of Prime Minister Mazowiecki's cabinet were of Jewish origin, as if this were a crime, and called on voters to support him because he was a "full-blooded Pole." He later admitted that he had been wrong and took steps to improve relations with the small Polish Jewish community.[109]

Cardinal Glemp's Indiscretion

The Polish Roman Catholic primate, Cardinal Józef Glemp, advertently or inadvertently contributed to the resurgence of anti-Semitism in postcommunist Poland.[110] In August 1989, he entered into a dispute over the location of a convent at the site of the Auschwitz death camp. Jews opposed the convent on that site in light of the special significance of Auschwitz for Jews worldwide. Although the church had signed an agreement to remove the convent, Cardinal Glemp declared that Jews were attacking Polish feelings and national sovereignty and were using the "Jewish-controlled" Western media to promote their views.

Glemp not only provoked an angry outcry from Jewish groups in the West, he embarrassed the new noncommunist government of prime minister Mazowiecki, who wanted the friendship and support of Western countries, which had little patience with such intolerance. The Polish government considered Glemp's remarks very damaging to the world prestige of Poland, as well as to the harmony, unity, and peace of an already deeply conflict-ridden Polish society. Nudged by an embarrassed Vatican to take a more conciliatory stand on the issue, Glemp retreated, acknowledging that Catholics in Poland knew too little of the sentiments of the Jews and the wounds that remained from the Holocaust. Eventually, the dispute wound down, but Cardinal Glemp's criticism of the Jews and the slowness of the Vatican's effort to avoid a confrontation aroused the suspicion of many inside as well as outside Poland regarding the church's own prejudices and its readiness to appeal to the prejudices of the Polish people.

Father Jankowski Causes a Stir

Another, similar incident occurred in mid-June 1995, when Reverend Henryk Jankowski, speaking from the pulpit of President Wałęsa's church in Warsaw, declared that the Polish people should not allow those who owe secret allegiance to Israel or Russia to remain in government. He also said that the Jewish Star of David symbol was a part of the communist hammer and sickle and the Nazi swastika. What was even more striking than Jankowski's gratuitous insult to Jews was President Wałęsa's silence. He refused to comment on the cleric's remarks. Some people argued that Wałęsa's silence was linked to his participation in the presidential elections to be held at the end of the year and his reluctance to alienate potential supporters of his possible candidacy. Jankowski was also a strong supporter of Wałęsa against the communists a decade earlier. The fact remains, however, that the Polish head of state lost an opportunity to reinforce his stated opposition to anti-Semitism.

3. The Church and Women

The church's influence on the treatment of women in Polish society today, as well as in the past, is substantial, given the fact that 85 percent of the Polish population is Catholic. Since 1989, the church has aggressively lobbied against efforts of women to gain equality and political advancement and in favor of preserving a stereotypical role of women, as can be seen also in its opposition to abortion, which critics say reflects a church perception of women as "incubators" and "incapacitated persons." The church seems to question the right of women to make independent decisions affecting their daily lives. The church has insisted that a woman's primary responsibility is taking care of home and family.[111]

The church may be motivated in its attitude toward women by power as well as doctrine. The subordination of women could be viewed as part of a large strategy of preserving in postcommunist Poland a patriarchal society and with it the church's own extensive patriarchal role. While this strategy may originate from the Vatican, it seems to have the support of much of the present Polish political establishment, which, of course, is male dominated. And while this strategy is pursued worldwide, its effect is felt more strongly in Poland than elsewhere because of the conservative character of Polish society, in which the role the church assigns to women is considered by most Polish men as the only appropriate role for women. Moreover, the church's position is congenial not only to Polish men but also to many women, who accept the role assigned to them with equanimity and occasionally even with pride.

Of course, church behavior is not the only reason for discrimination against women. As is true elsewhere in Eastern Europe, the hardships caused by the transition from communism to political and economic democracy have both burdened women and undermined the efforts of the few who are so inclined to play an active role outside the home, in a job or in politics. The hardships of inflation and unemployment fell disproportionately on women, especially those who had a job in the communist era, lost it, and have been unable to regain it. Women have suffered far more than men from the consequences of development strategies such as "shock therapy," which Poland adopted to a far greater extent than any other former communist country in Eastern Europe to facilitate the introduction of the free market and which do not adequately take into account the social costs of change.[112]

In addition, many Polish women with an interest in a career outside the home or in the pursuit of political influence and power were disappointed by the failure of former Prime Minister Hanna Suchocka to encourage and assist them. Indeed, some Polish professional women never considered Suchocka a feminist. Quite the contrary, she was regarded as very conservative on women's rights and closely linked to the Catholic Church on such issues as abortion. Some think Suchocka might not have been so conservative on abortion if she had seen more of everyday life in the cramped housing of Poland's cities.[113]

Foreign-Policy Problems

Underlying its postcommunist foreign policy is Poland's need for international security and stability to facilitate the transformation from socialist authoritarianism to capitalist democracy. To these ends, Poland has tried to diversify its foreign policy, strengthening ties with the West, especially Germany and the United States, though with mixed success. At the same time, however, Poland has also sought to keep its diplomatic fences mended with the former Soviet Union and its successors, in particular, Russia, Belarus, Ukraine, and Lithuania, with which it continues to have some serious differences. Finally, Poland has tried to befriend and cooperate with its neighbors in the region, notably Czechoslovakia and Hungary, despite past prejudices that frequently made relations among them tense and conflict ridden.

1. The West

Like other former Soviet satellites, Poland was eager for closer ties with the West, for cultural as well as economic and strategic reasons. Poland needs Western economic, technological, and financial assistance to move forward with the structural reform of the economy and to relieve immediate emergencies such as the scarcity of food and the explosion of unemployment. But the West was cautious with aid because of uncertainty about the political future of Poland and also because the Kremlin had made clear in 1989 that it would react angrily if the West appeared to take advantage of developments in Poland. Postcommunist Russia shares the Soviet uneasiness about growing economic as well as political and other ties between Poland and the West. Also, in the early 1990s, the West entered a recession and faced pressing social needs at home that precluded development of a large aid program for Poland.[114] Nevertheless, the European Union has been responsive to Polish requests for membership. In December 1991, the EU, then called the European Community, admitted Poland to the European Association Agreement, which increased Polish access to the European market. But, more importantly, the agreement envisaged eventual Polish membership in the EU, which would be a boon to the Polish economy by encouraging an expansion of Western investment in Poland.[115]

Relations with Germany

While Poland has difficulty being at ease with a powerful German neighbor, it wants to take advantage of the strong and sincere interest of the German government in "burying the hatchet" and developing close relations between the two countries.[116] But in the early 1990s, it was difficult for Warsaw to strengthen Polish ties to Germany because of two problems, the border between the two countries and the issue of German reparations to Poland arising out of World War II. Indeed, differences over the border issue heightened Polish anxiety over the reunification of Germany in 1990, an event that frightened the Polish people if only because there was little they could do about it.[117]

The border issue had two large aspects. The first concerned Pomerania, a large district in northwestern Poland along the Baltic coast from Szczecin (formerly Stettin) eastward to Gdańsk (formerly Danzig). Poland acquired this territory from a defeated Germany after World War II as compensation for the loss of the eastern part of Poland, including the city of Lvov, to the Soviet Union. In 1990, the Polish leadership was afraid that a unified Germany would demand the return of this territory because many of its inhabitants are ethnic Germans and some at least would prefer German to Polish rule. The Polish leadership also had reason to worry about possible German interest in Silesia, a highly industrialized, coal-rich area in southwestern Poland inhabited by about 800,000 people of ethnic German origin that belonged to Germany before World War II. The Silesian German population was and remains uneasy over Polish rule. Many Silesian Germans believe life was easier and better for them when they were part of Germany than it was under Polish communist rule after World War II. Indeed, in early 1990, the German government was under pressure from a powerful lobby of German "expellees," people now settled in West Germany but originally from Pomerania and Silesia, to leave the door open for an eventual return of

Pomerania and Silesia to German control. The pressure of the expellees on Germany's Chancellor Helmut Kohl was intense because of complaints from people of German cultural background living in Pomeranian and Silesia of discrimination by the Warsaw authorities. In the past, these ethnic Germans in Poland were forbidden to speak German, to practice religion in their own way, or to preserve their folk traditions. Kohl's apparent sympathy for the concerns of the expellee groups disturbed not only Poland but also other West European countries and the United States.[118]

In 1990, these border issues led the Mazowiecki government to demand a role for Poland in the international discussions of German reunification among the four wartime Allies (the Soviet Union, Britain, France, and the United States) and the two German governments in Bonn and East Berlin. Mazowiecki was afraid that clauses in the Basic Law, West Germany's constitution, giving the country a theoretical right to repossess Silesia and Pomerania would provide a basis for future German claims to about a third of Polish territory. Sympathetic to Polish fears, the Allies agreed to include Poland in discussions about the border.[119] In the so-called "two-plus-four talks," the Allies and the two Germanies reached an agreement that somewhat relieved Polish anxiety. It provided for a German commitment to have a border treaty in the shortest possible time after unification, which occurred in the beginning of October 1990.[120] And on November 14, 1990, a Polish–German agreement recognized the Oder–Neisse line as the permanent border between Poland and Germany. In addition, Germany's foreign minister, Hans Dietrich Genscher, pledged that Germany would help Poland and other Central and East European countries to rebuild their economies. It would also lift visa requirements for Polish citizens, allowing them for the first time since World War II to have easy access to a country within the European Union.[121]

Since 1990, relations between Poland and Germany have been good, with the Bonn government living up to promises of help to Poland in its transformation. For example, in early February 1992, it agreed, over the strong objection of German bankers, who thought Poland had not yet established its creditworthiness, to cancel 50 percent of Poland's $5.5 billion debt to the German government and to allow Poland to take eighteen years to pay the remainder.[122] And in March 1992, President Wałęsa visited Bonn, where he was given a warm reception by the German political leadership. The visit had great symbolic significance in punctuating the new friendliness between Poland and Germany in the postcommunist era.[123]

But in the early 1990s, the growth of Silesian German nationalism under Jan Kroll, leader of an ethnic interest group known as the Social and Cultural Society of the German Minority, is a problem for Polish–German relations. The society fields candidates in local and national elections and has won a few seats in the Sejm. The society demands greater recognition by the Warsaw government and by local Silesian Polish authorities of the Silesian German cultural identity and has developed contacts with expellee organizations in Germany, raising fears among Polish officials that someday, somehow, Silesia will revert to Germany.[124] To the relief of Warsaw, Chancellor Kohl in fact paid little attention to the nationalistic actions of the Silesian Germans and showed no interest in claiming their territory for Germany. But the situation could change because of an outbreak of violence between German and Polish youth in Silesia. Moreover, Polish officials in Silesia, as well as in Warsaw, and in particular President Wałęsa, were angered by what they perceived as a gratuitous insult to Poland by some Silesian Germans who decided to hold a public ceremony commemorating the Nazi German army in November 1992.[125]

Nevertheless, a crisis in Polish–German relations over Silesia is not imminent. The Polish government has proceeded very cautiously to avoid prejudicing Poland's good relations with Germany. Moreover, for the moment at least, most Silesian Germans have not given overt support to ethnic radicals, who remain a minority.

The United States

Postcommunist Poland wanted American friendship for both strategic and economic reasons, namely, to counterbalance Russian influence and provide much-needed economic and financial assistance. The American response overall was positive. President George Bush said, shortly after the conclusion of the April 6, 1989, agreement between the Polish Communist government and the political opposition, that "the Poles are now taking concrete steps that require our active support."[126] At the administration's request, Congress eliminated tariffs on selected Polish imports and established a program of American guaranteed loans through the Overseas Private Investment Corporation. Bush also pressed the Commerce Department, the Small Business Administration, and American business organizations to expand the role of American companies in Poland's relatively small private sector. The White House also supported new loans to Poland by the IMF and the International Finance Corporation.[127] In early July 1989, during his visit to Warsaw, Bush offered Poland an outright grant of $100 million and told the Polish Parliament that he would urge the World Bank to move ahead with $325 million in loans and ask the Western allies to support a rescheduling of debts that could amount to $5 billion.[128]

Solidarity leaders, however, reportedly were disappointed by what they considered the modest scope of the American aid gesture, having expected American help of "Marshall Plan" dimensions to see Poland through the transition from socialism to capitalism. But the Bush administration was not inclined to undertake a major aid program for Poland of the scope sought by Jaruzelski and Wałęsa. Caught by surprise when Communist Party rule in Eastern Europe abruptly collapsed, the administration was reluctant to give large amounts of financial assistance without a planned program of aid disbursement with clearly defined goals and methods. Moreover, administration officials in the summer and fall of 1989 also wanted to be sure that Poland really wanted a free-market economy. Aware of the slowness of privatization in Poland and the continued power, by whatever label, of communists in top managerial positions, the Bush administration was determined to wait before considering large grants of aid. The administration also preferred to have the East Europeans help themselves, or, so to speak, "pull themselves up by their own bootstraps," rather than come to rely on massive external support. It was also true that in light of its own economic recession, the United States had "more will than wallet," as Bush put it.[129]

Nevertheless, partly because of much support for increased American help to Poland in Congress and among the voters, especially those of Polish-American origin, Bush agreed in mid-September 1989 to double food aid for Poland that year to $100 million. Bush also agreed to an additional $200 million in economic aid for Poland in early October 1989. In mid-November, after having heard an impassioned appeal for extensive Marshall Plan–like American help by Wałęsa in his address to a joint sitting, Congress went way beyond the president's request and approved an aid package to Poland worth about $852 million. The bill, which was titled "Support for East European Democracy Act of 1989," provided Poland with $125 million in food aid and $240 million in grants to private businesses, including at least $25 million to help modernize Poland's telephone system. The bill also provided up to $200 million to support Poland's currency.[130]

Also, in 1990, Congress urged the Bush administration to be more helpful to Warsaw in dealing with the Germans on the boundary question in the two-plus-four negotiations on German reunification. Congress wanted Kohl to declare the boundary between Germany and Poland as permanent and irrevocable. In response to congressional pressure, Bush did join a chorus of opposition to Kohl's ambiguity on the border issue that undoubtedly persuaded the German leader to accommodate the Poles.[131] The administration also continued to give financial and economic aid throughout 1991 and 1992, but in very small amounts. But, in March 1991, Wałęsa visited Washington and secured an agreement to wipe clean 70 percent of Poland's $3.8 billion debt to the United States. Then in late June, the United States agreed to allocate $15 million to help develop Polish business, agriculture, and health services.[132]

The Clinton administration has been sympathetic to Polish economic and strategic needs but, like the Bush administration, was not overly forthcoming, partly because of a recession and a Congress skeptical of large-scale foreign programs. Moreover, in 1993, Clinton reacted cautiously to Polish demands for full membership in NATO that would bring Poland a Western guarantee of its security and territorial integrity. Clinton met Poland only halfway on this issue in order to avoid compromising U.S. relations with the Russians, who opposed NATO membership for the former Soviet Union's allies in Central and Eastern Europe. Clinton also wanted Russian cooperation in Yugoslavia. He offered Poland an alternative to full membership in the form of participation along with other Central and East European countries and Russia in the Partnership for Peace, which provided for cooperation between NATO and partnership participants but no guarantee of future membership in NATO.

Although Polish relations with the United States remain very good and although Poland received a pledge of $600 million in American aid from Clinton during his speech to the Polish Parliament in July 1994, in which he commended Poland for its impressive strides toward political and economic democracy, the Polish government remains uneasy over American unwillingness to bring Poland into the Western security system at a moment that Polish leaders believe is dangerous for Polish security. The Warsaw government continued throughout 1994 to lobby Washington for full Polish membership in NATO. Its disappointment with American policy on this issue and the evident priority the Clinton administration has given to American–Russian relations remain clouds on the horizon of Polish–American relations in the mid-1990s.

2. The USSR, Russia, and Other Former Soviet Republics

While cultivating the West, it was important for postcommunist Poland to keep its diplomatic fences mended with the Kremlin. This was difficult. The Polish people cannot forget or forgive Soviet treatment of Poland during and after World War II. The Soviet–German nonaggression pact of August 1939 partitioned Poland between its two powerful neighbors. Then, between 1939 and 1945, the Russians deported thousands of Polish citizens from Soviet-occupied eastern Poland to concentration camps in the Soviet heartland and murdered 10,000 Polish officers and enlisted men in 1940 in the Katyń forest. During the forty years of communist rule, the Kremlin added insult to injury by refusing to discuss these incidents or, worse, by denying they ever happened, in the case of the Katyń massacre. To his credit and as part of his new conciliatory approach to Soviet relations with Central and Eastern Europe in the late 1980s, Gorbachev was willing to acknowledge these sad events in Polish–Soviet relations.[133] But the new democratic political leadership in Warsaw was not satisfied. In April 1990, the Sejm adopted a resolution on Katyń stating that, while Poland wanted good relations with the Soviet Union, it expected Soviet compensation to Poland.[134]

Keeping Polish diplomatic fences mended with Moscow was difficult for newly independent Poland also because of the continued presence of 50,000 Soviet troops on Polish soil.[135] The Kremlin agreed to withdraw Soviet troops but did so very slowly, ostensibly because of logistical problems. A rapid withdrawal from Poland would have left Soviet troops in East Germany isolated and vulnerable. The Soviet military dragged its feet also for reasons of pride and strategy: the withdrawal symbolized the loss of influence in a region of historic importance for Soviet territorial security. Finally, legal, financial, and property issues also had to be settled. Moscow wanted compensation from the Polish government for military housing built in Poland, and Warsaw for its part demanded that the Kremlin pay for the damage done to its environment by the long Soviet military presence.[136] Although the troop-withdrawal issue was finally resolved, with the last Russian combat troops departing Świnoujście on October

28, 1993, it vindicated popular distrust and suspicion of the Kremlin and reinforced a preexisting antipathy toward the Russians, which has complicated the efforts of postcommunist Polish leaders to maintain friendly and cooperative relations between Warsaw and Moscow.[137]

In the early 1990s, Poland was concerned by a sharp decline in trade with Russia. In 1992, the government of President Boris Yeltsin sharply reduced gas and oil exports to Poland. Because Polish industry was accustomed to cheap energy sources from the former USSR that had been rarely interrupted by the Kremlin, the Polish economy suffered. Costs of production rose, while the market for the quality of exports Polish industry produced for sale to the former Soviet bloc diminished. This decline in trade with Russia, once Poland's major trade partner, however, was not as serious a problem for Poland as it appeared because trade expanded with the European Union, especially Germany, which replaced Russia in the early 1990s as Poland's chief trade partner. Still, Poland would like the Russians to sell more energy in order to reduce the Polish balance-of-trade surplus, which is likely to continue and possibly increase given obstacles to Russian economic recovery under the Yeltsin government.[138]

In the 1990s, the Russian city and naval base of Kaliningrad, now separated from Russian territory by the independent state of Lithuania, was another problem in Polish–Russian relations. A Russian military buildup in Kaliningrad could threaten Polish territorial security. At the same time, Poland is concerned that Germany might become interested in the fate of Kaliningrad, which belonged to Germany before World War II and was known as Königsberg. Though Warsaw would like Kaliningrad to be part of Poland, if forced to choose, it would prefer a weakened Russia to a strong Germany in Kaliningrad. In any event, for the moment Polish leaders, especially on the Left, are not inclined to make an issue of Kaliningrad's future with either Russia or Germany.[139]

Finally, Poland's well-publicized efforts to join NATO have angered the Kremlin. Although at first Yeltsin did not object to Polish membership in NATO, he subsequently reversed himself in response to pressure from the Russian military leaders who opposed expansion of NATO membership into the former Soviet bloc. This Russian opposition has served merely to increase Warsaw's eagerness to obtain full NATO membership and the security guarantee that goes with it. In the mid-1990s, the growing popularity of the ultranationalist Vladimir Zhirinovskii, who has called for a restoration of Russian influence in the former Soviet republics, has strengthened Polish determination to become a full member of NATO. This issue remains a source of tension between the two countries.

Belarus

Poland's postcommunist governments welcomed the establishment of the independent state of Belarus. They viewed it as a possible buffer between Polish territory and Russia.

The new relationship got off to a promising start with the opening of the Belarus embassy in Warsaw in June 1992. President Stanislav Shushkevich of Belarus came to Warsaw to celebrate the event, which emphasized his country's sovereignty and independence of Moscow.[140] But the Polish minority of about 417,000 people who are permanent citizens of Belarus could cause difficulties between the two neighbors in the future. This Polish minority inhabits territory that once belonged to Poland, and the Belarus government in Minsk worries that someday these people may want their land to become part of Poland. The problem is complicated by the role of the Catholic Church, which the Belarus leadership fears might encourage the Polish minority to embrace separatism. Belarus leaders base their fears of the Catholic Church on its independent behavior. For example, Metropolitan Filaret, the head of the Belarusian Orthodox Church, has complained that the Catholic Church does not consult him as it should in its appointment of high-ranking clerics. After all, he argues, the Orthodox Church is the national church of Belarus and deserves the respect due its position of primacy in Belarusian society. There is little the Warsaw government can do about the behavior of the Catholic Church in western Belarus. The Catholic hierarchy takes orders from Rome, not Warsaw. Still, from the vantage point of Minsk, the cause of Polish nationalism in its westernmost territory is served by this Catholic behavior, and the Belarus leadership does not like it.[141]

Poland also worries about the possibility of strengthened ties between Minsk and Moscow. Aleksandr Lukashenko, who was elected president in the summer of 1994, does not want to move Belarus quickly to a free-market economy. Moreover, he is much more pro-Russian than his predecessor, Shushkevich. Warsaw is afraid that under Lukashenko Belarus will strengthen economic, political, and military ties with the Russians, who have made no secret of their view that Belarus and Russia should be intimately linked, almost as they were in the Soviet period. Indeed, serious economic problems—an inflation that was running at about 40 percent a month in mid-1994 and average workers' wages at $20.00 a month—may well force Belarus to look to Russia for economic assistance in return for cooperation with Russian foreign policy.[142]

Ukraine

Shared problems and perspectives are the basis for a strong relationship between Poland and Ukraine in the postcommunist era. Both had been subservient to the Soviet Union; both are struggling to make a success of the democratic transition, especially in the economic area, where both are committed to raising living standards; and both have ample reason to fear postcommunist Russia and cooperate with one another to resist a possible, though at the moment not probable, Russian threat to their independence. Together they have a population of 90 million people and are rich in natural resources as well as human talent. Together they have the capacity to deter Russian expansion southward and westward.[143]

The Mazowiecki government therefore wasted no time in reaching out to Ukraine as it began to emancipate itself from Moscow. On October 19, 1990, Poland signed a joint declaration recognizing Ukrainian sovereignty. And on May 18, 1992, the two countries concluded a treaty of friendship and cooperation to cement the new relationship between them.[144]

But there are liabilities for Poland in this new relationship with Ukraine. It is implicitly anti-Russian and may suggest to the hypersensitive and defensive Kremlin the imposition of a kind of *cordon sanitaire*. Furthermore, it carries a lot of baggage that may turn out to be burdensome for Poland, notably, Ukraine's territorial, military, economic, and other differences with Russia, which Kiev sees as a threat to Ukrainian security and independence, especially in light of Zhirinovskii's call for a restoration of Russia's control over its Slavic neighbors. Poland would hardly want to become involved in a Russo–Ukrainian confrontation. Furthermore, in the mid-1990s, Poland has to reckon with the possibility that the government in Kiev, despite old fears and prejudices, will turn toward Russia because of its military superiority and energy supplies, especially oil, which Ukrainian factories need to sustain production and because of the Yeltsin government's willingness to use its "oil card" to induce Kiev's cooperation with Russia. For the remainder of the decade, Poland needs to reassure Ukraine that it is not isolated, that its relations with Warsaw could bring it closer to Western Europe, and that it therefore always has an alternative to intimacy with Moscow, with which it continues to have many differences but, in doing so, must tread carefully and cautiously to avoid prejudicing relations with Russia.[145]

Lithuania

Poland has a complex relationship with Lithuania, which is sensitive to once having been part of the Polish nation, with Vilnius, its capital, called Wilno by the Poles, and an important center of Polish culture. At the same time, Poland and Lithuania shared a deep antipathy toward the Soviet Union, which had annexed Lithuania against its will in 1939. In March 1990, Poland encouraged Lithuania's move toward independence, starting with its "declaration of sovereignty," despite the risk of straining its own relations with Moscow. Poland subsequently received Prime Minister Kasimiera Prunskiene in Warsaw and toward the end of the year advocated observer status for Lithuania, Latvia, and Estonia at the Conference for Security and Cooperation in Europe. And when the Soviets assaulted the Lithuanian state television studio in January 1991 in a last, desperate effort to restore control over the rebellious republic, the Polish government reacted strongly, though it did so carefully to avoid confrontation with Moscow. Warsaw wanted to show its support for Lithuanian self-determination but did not want to antagonize Moscow during negotiations about the withdrawal of Soviet troops.[146]

Poland's continuing effort to bond with Lithuania, however, has been difficult. In the early 1990s, Warsaw became worried that the newly independent and highly chauvinistic government of President Vytautas Landsbergis would try to homogenize Lithuanian society at the expense of the large Polish minority of over 300,000, which was made up mainly of workers and poor farmers who had encountered decades of political, economic, and cultural discrimination by the local Lithuanian communist administration. Because of this discrimination, Polish Lithuanians had opposed independence from the Soviet Union, thus inviting the retribution of postcommunist Lithuanian nationalist leaders.[147] Fears of the Polish minority about its future were vindicated when, on September 4, 1991, the Vilnius government dissolved two self-governing Polish regional councils. According to the Lithuanian government, the action was the result of the alleged support by Polish Lithuanian citizens of the failed anti-Gorbachev coup in Moscow in mid-August 1991, as well as their boycott of the 1990 referendum on independence that had been approved overwhelmingly by ethnic Lithuanian voters.[148] But the Warsaw government did not want this problem to get out of hand, compromise the Polish–Lithuanian relationship, and possibly encourage Lithuania to strengthen ties with Moscow. It refused to lobby with the Lithuanian government on behalf of the Polish minority. And Vilnius certainly would have resisted any Polish effort to champion the rights of the Polish minority.

Another problem concerns the Polish–Lithuanian boundary. Because the Soviet government transferred to Lithuania, which it had annexed in April 1940, territories that had belonged to Poland in the interwar period, the Lithuanians fear that Poland might attempt to reclaim these territories, even Vilnius itself.[149] This Lithuanian fear is far-fetched. Poland is unlikely to make border claims against Lithuania or any other of its eastern neighbors, if only because they would open up the question of land acquired by Poland in the west from a defeated Germany. Polish leaders have given oral assurances of their country's disinterest in reclaiming lost land and have acknowledged that Vilnius is now a Lithuanian city. Nevertheless, the border's permanence remains an issue in Polish–Lithuanian relations, given the influence of nationalists in both countries.[150]

3. Relations with the Czech Republic and Hungary

While its relations with the former Soviet republics have continued to be problematic, Poland has been seeking friendship and cooperation with the new democratic governments in Prague and Budapest. All three countries have so much in common: a shared colonial past, an interest in limiting Soviet and Russian influence in Central Europe while continuing to maintain good relations with Moscow, the need to cooperate in solving regional problems such as environmental pollution, German economic expansion, and membership in the European Union and NATO.

Working together, however, has been difficult due to barriers of language and of diverse ethnic and historical conditions. There also have been personality clashes. Polish president Wałęsa did not especially like Czech president Havel, who is an intellectual, while Wałęsa was down-to-earth and close to his working-class roots. Economic diversity reinforced differences among the three, with Hungary the strongest and Poland the weakest. The three countries were introducing economic reform at different rates of speed, with the Poles moving much faster than either the Hungarians or the Czechs. Furthermore, of the three countries, Poland, located between Germany and Russia, is in the most vulnerable situation in terms of security and is likely to have more serious strategic requirements than Hungary or the Czech Republic. Neither Hungary nor the Czech Republic would like to be drawn into a Polish conflict with Russia or Germany. At the same time, with the largest population in Central Europe, almost 40 million people, Poland has the potential to dominate any regional entente, a prospect that somewhat disturbs its neighbors, which have much smaller populations and less resources. Also, Havel on one occasion suggested that Poland should look more to the Baltic countries, with which it has much in common, especially Lithuania, than to the countries of the Danube Basin, which logically look southward to countries like Italy, Austria, and Yugoslavia.[151]

The three countries do, however, have strong incentives to overcome these "asymmetries." They shared in and were affected by the erosion and subsequent dissolution of the Warsaw Pact and CMEA, which has adversely affected their economies. They also were adversely affected by the Persian Gulf War, which jeopardized an important source of energy for Central Europe. Finally, all three suffered from the destabilization of the Soviet Union after the August 1991 anti-Gorbachev coup and its final collapse at the end of December 1991. Moreover, all three countries face the possibility, however remote, of a Russian attempt to regain lost influence in Eastern Europe. In the spring of 1991, for example, some Soviet foreign-policy strategists publicly advocated the use of energy supplies and the manipulation of exports to exert leverage over the foreign policies of the East European countries. Between February and late April 1991, the Kremlin tried to get the new postcommunist governments in Warsaw, Prague, and Budapest to sign a treaty with the USSR pledging to refrain from joining an alliance directed against the USSR, that is, NATO. Such a treaty could also have applied to East European membership in the EU. Poland, Hungary, and Czechoslovakia jointly opposed this move.[152]

In the early 1990s, Polish, Czech, and Hungarian diplomats began a series of trilateral meetings to discuss problems of regional concern. They conferred in Bratislava in April 1990, in Visegrád in February 1991, and in Kraków in October 1991. In Bratislava, they merely agreed to meet again to discuss matters of common interest. Cooperation among the three neighbors got a lift with aggressive Soviet behavior in Lithuania in January 1991, when there was an apparently unauthorized military action in Vilnius to induce a reversal of Lithuania's march to independence. Polish, Hungarian, and Czechoslovak foreign ministers met in Budapest to inaugurate a campaign to dissolve the Warsaw Pact and the

CMEA, which were anachronisms given the collapse of communist rule and with it Soviet influence in Central Europe. And at a trilateral meeting in Visegrád, they agreed to endorse several statements of principle to guide future discussions, in particular, their shared commitment to making their countries part of the European Community. President Wałęsa at Visegrád suggested the importance for Poland, Hungary, and Czechoslovakia of approaching the EU not in competition but in cooperation with each other.[153] In Kraków in October 1991, the three East European leaders discussed their relationship with NATO, taking as a point of departure a statement by Secretary of State Baker of the United States and Foreign Minister Genscher of Germany about the need to develop NATO's relationship with the new democracies of Central and Eastern Europe. They suggested the establishment of more than political links, namely, links similar to those existing among NATO members. In Kraków, the Polish diplomats joined their Hungarian and Czechoslovak colleagues in expressing concern over the expanding civil war in Yugoslavia and insisting on the inviolability of that country's prewar internal boundaries. Finally, they all agreed on common domestic- and foreign-policy objectives, including "total integration into the European political, economic, security, and legislative order."[154]

These regional conferences were of great symbolic importance. They signified a willingness on the part of Poland, Czechoslovakia and its successors, the Czech Republic and Slovakia, and Hungary to forget past disagreements and prejudices and cooperate in economic, social, political, and strategic areas. They offered an opportunity to find collective solutions to common problems in a fragmented and traditionally conflict-ridden region, historically vulnerable to the intrusion of powerful outsiders ready to take advantage of internal disagreements and frictions.

At the same time, however, there are obstacles to further interstate cooperation and alignment. Poland, Hungary, the Czech Republic, and Slovakia have tended to focus on obtaining membership in the European Union as much as on relations with one another and in fact to proceed independently in lobbying with the EU. Another potential drag on regional cooperation in the mid-1990s is the diversity of domestic development in the four countries. In 1993 and 1994, there was a pronounced shift to the left, with the ascendancy of former communists to prime ministerships in Poland and Hungary, while the Czech Republic remained strongly conservative under Prime Minister Václav Havel. Also, Poland has found the Czech Republic, Slovakia, and Hungary more willing than it was to compromise on the issue of full membership in NATO and to accept considerably less than that in the near term. Both Hungary and the Czech Republic responded favorably to the U.S. proposal of the Partnership for Peace as an alternative to NATO membership. Poland, in its disappointment with the Partnership for Peace, became obsessed with the goal of joining NATO and getting its guarantee of security.[155]

Finally, another obstacle to close cooperation, at least between Warsaw and

Prague, is a problem involving a small Polish minority of 44,000 people who live in the Zaolzie region on the Czecho-Slovak frontier with Poland. Worried about the loss of their cultural identity, members of this Polish minority joined a local political organization called Coexistentia, committed to the rights of minorities living in the Czech and Slovak republics. In early February 1992, Stanisław Gawlik, chairman of the executive council of Coexistentia, went to Warsaw to complain that a recently concluded treaty of friendship between Poland and Czechoslovakia failed to guarantee the cultural rights of Poles living in the Zaolzie region. In particular, the treaty said nothing about Polish schools, bilingual geographic names in the region, and the restoration of confiscated Polish property.[156] For the moment the Polish government has not responded openly to Coexistentia's complaint, essentially for the same reason that it has not actively concerned itself with the complaints of the Polish minority in Lithuania. In this instance, Warsaw wants to preserve good relations with Prague and the continuation of a dialogue between the two countries within the Visegrád framework, especially in light of the shared anxiety about a possible resurgence of Russian influence in Central Europe.

Having said all of the above, one can point to a minor achievement in regional cooperation in recent years, namely, the successful trilateral negotiations over the creation of a free trade zone. An agreement was signed in December 1992, despite reservations on the part of the Czechs. The agreement, which calls for a gradual lifting of all tariff barriers by the signatories, is intended to expand multilateral trade and increase foreign investment. However, it remains to be seen whether in fact a true free trade zone will materialize in the near future.[157]

Conclusions

Poland has made much progress in moving toward democracy and a free-market economy. The country has a truly liberal political environment, in which the institutions of government seem to be functioning in accordance with the principles of Western-style parliamentary democracy. State control of the economy has steadily diminished, and small-scale capitalism is flourishing, with good prospects of further development of free enterprise in the industrial sector. Its predominantly homogeneous society seems at peace, with little if any ethnocultural dissent and no visible threat of the turmoil that other, less-unified societies in the region have been experiencing.

But the new democratic institutions are fragile and have yet to demonstrate their staying power. Six years after the collapse of communist rule, the Polish people have very mixed views about democratic government. On the one hand, an overwhelming majority of Polish voters think democracy is preferable to other kinds of government, especially the former communist dictatorship. Indeed, they have no desire to return to the old repressive political order. At the same time, however, many Polish people are inclined to judge democracy on its economic achievements and blame the system as much as its leaders for a deterioration of living conditions. Disappointment tinged with frustration and anger has made many Polish people cynical about democracy. They do not think they can influence its behavior. They also see it as a game among politicians willing to place their own selfish interests ahead of the nation and its interests. Finally, many Polish people crave order and certainty in their lives, which democracy may not be able to provide, at least in the short term. The democratic political system, trying to be responsive as well as efficient, remains under stress.

9

Romania

In the precommunist era of the early twentieth century, an authoritarian monarch subverted the Romanian parliamentary system with the help of an ultraconservative middle class and aristocracy that controlled most of the country's wealth. By the 1930s, the country was a repressive dictatorship strongly influenced by Nazi German totalitarianism, for which Romania's upper classes had much sympathy. They were suspicious of democracy, fearful of Soviet communism, and deeply anti-Semitic. During World War II, Romania was an ally of Nazi Germany and cooperated with its invasion of the Soviet Union in June 1941. After the war and a punishing armistice imposed on Romania by the Kremlin, Romanian communists ousted the monarch, declared a republic, and turned the country into a Soviet-style socialist dictatorship and, eventually, into a satellite of the Kremlin.

Romanian Stalinism

Romania's first communist leader, Gheorghe Gheorghiu-Dej, ruled the country until 1964, when he was succeeded by his long-time confidante Nicolae Ceauşescu. While Dej introduced a neo-Stalinism into Romania reminiscent of the Soviet political system in the 1930s, Ceauşescu consolidated and intensified the dictatorship in ways that would have made Stalin proud. As one authority puts it, "Ceauşescu's despotism united all the elements identified by Friedrich and Brzezinski as typical of totalitarian regimes: ideological uniformity, a single party under a single leader, the use of terror, and the state control of society, communications, and the economy."[1]

Romanian Stalinism was intended not only to promote discipline, obedience, and loyalty to the new communist order but also to modernize Romania, trans-

ROMANIA

Geography

1. Location: southeastern Europe, bordering the Black Sea between Bulgaria and Ukraine
2. Area: total — 237,500 square kilometers; land area — 230,340 square kilometers; comparative area — slightly smaller than Oregon
3. Boundaries: with Bulgaria — 608 kilometers; with Hungary — 443 kilometers; with Moldova — 450 kilometers; with Serbia and Montenegro — 476 kilometers (all with Serbia); with Ukraine — 531 kilometers; coastline along the Black Sea — 225 kilometers

4. Climate: temperate; cold, cloudy, winters with frequent snow and fog; sunny summers with frequent showers and thunderstorms
5. Terrain: central Transylvanian Basin, separated from the plain of Moldova in the east by the Carpathian Mountains and separated from the Walachian Plain in the south by the Transylvanian Alps
6. Land use: arable — 43%; permanent crops — 3%; meadows and pastures — 19%; forest and woodland — 28%
7. Natural resources: petroleum, timber, natural gas, coal and iron, salt
8. Environment: soil erosion and degrada-

tion; air pollution in south from industrial effluents; contamination of Danube Delta wetlands

People
1. Population: 23,198,330 (1995 estimate)
2. Age structure: 0–14 — 21% of population (female — 2,413,933; male — 2,534,019); 15–64 — 67% of population (female — 7,732,038; male — 7,732,038); 65 and over — 12% of population (female — 1,604,210; male — 1,176,599) (1995 estimate)
3. Growth rate: 0.09% (1995 estimate)
4. Life expectancy at birth: total population — 73.13 years; female — 75.35 years; male — 69.31 years (1995 estimate)
5. Ethnic divisions: Romanian — 89.1%; Hungarian — 8.9%; German — 4%; Ukrainian, Serb, Croat, Russian, Turk, and Gypsy — 1.6%
6. Religions: Romanian Orthodox — 70%; Roman Catholic — 6%; Protestant — 6%;
7. Languages: Romanian, Hungarian, German
8. Literacy: total population — 97%
9. Labor force: total — 11.3 million; industry — 38%; agriculture — 28%; other — 34% (1989 estimate)

Government
1. Type: emerging parliamentary democracy
2. Capital: Bucharest
3. Independence: from Turkey in 1881; republic proclaimed 1947
4. Constitution: promulgated December 8, 1991
5. National administration:
   a. Chief of state: President of the Republic (1996 — Ion Iliescu)
   b. Ministerial leadership: Prime Minister and Council of Ministers (1996 — Nicolae Văcăroiu, prime minister)
   c. Legislature: bicameral — House of Deputies (*Adunarea Deputatilor*) and Senate (*Senat*)
   d. Judicial branch: Supreme Court of Justice, Constitutional Court
   e. Political parties: Democratic Party, Social Democratic Party of Romania, Democratic Union of Hungarians in Romania, National Liberal Party, National Peasants' Christian and Democratic Party, Romanian National Unity Party, Socialist Labor Party, Agrarian Democratic Party of Romania, Democratic Convention, Romanian Mare Party, Civic Alliance Party
6. Local administration: unitary system with 40 counties

Economy
1. Gross domestic product: $64.7 billion (1994 estimate)
2. National product real growth rate: 3.4% (1994 estimate)
3. Per-capita national product: $2,790 (1994 estimate)
4. Inflation rate: 62% (1994 estimate)
5. Unemployment rate: 10.9% (1994 estimate)
6. Budget: revenue — $8.3 billion; expenditures — $9.4 billion (1995 estimate)
7. Industrial output: mining, timber, construction materials, metallurgy, chemicals, machine building, food processing, petroleum
8. Agricultural output: wheat and corn, sugar beets, sunflower seed, potatoes, milk, eggs, meat, grapes
9. Exports: $6 billion (1994 estimate) — metal and metal products, mineral products, textiles, electric machines, agricultural goods
10. Imports: $6.3 billion (1994 estimate) — minerals, machinery and equipment, textiles, agricultural products
11. External debt: $4.4 billion (1994 estimate)
12. Trade partners: European Union, Central and Eastern Europe, developing countries, Russia, EFTA, United States, Japan
13. Transportation: railroads — 11,365 kilometers; highways — 461,880 kilometers; ports — Brăila, Constanţa, Galaţi, Mangalia, Sulina, Tulcea; airports — 156 (27 with paved runways)

form it into an industrialized state, and bring a new level of material well-being to Romanian society. In the late 1940s, Romania was predominantly agricultural and underdeveloped, and Stalinist economic centralization and autarchy seemed appropriate for the kind of rapid industrialization the communist leadership wanted for Romania.

Stalinism and Nationalism

Romanian's Stalinistic dictatorship had a unique edge to it. Both Dej and Ceauşescu were intensely nationalistic, paying only lip service to the Soviet concept of international proletarian camaraderie, which called for the unity of the Central and East European socialist systems and their emulation of Soviet domestic and foreign policies. While Dej and Ceauşescu had no problem embracing, as the Kremlin wanted them to do, the Soviet model of communist authoritarianism, which was congenial to Romania's traditionally conservative environment, they deeply resented Moscow's insistence on subservience to Soviet will in domestic and foreign policy making. The Romanian communist leaders were determined to pursue an independent course in economic development and foreign policy based on their perception of what was best for Romania, even if Moscow thought otherwise.

1. Roots of Nationalism

This urge to independence derived from a nationalism based on the pride most Romanians have always had in the historical origins of their society. They trace the history of their country back to the Roman Empire, which had established a political and military outpost in what is today Romania, calling the area Dacia. Romanians believe that this Dacian state predated the establishment of neighboring polities including Russia. Romanians are also proud of other links to Western cultural traditions including their language, which was influenced by Latin and distinguishes them from their Slavic neighbors. Ceauşescu cultivated this sense of "exceptionalism." He insisted that Romanians are a great people with a great destiny. History books used by school children glorified the Romanian people, attributing to them the greatest scientific achievements in the twentieth century.[2]

The Anti-Russian Factor

Romanian nationalism also comes from an historic fear and dislike of the Russians, who made periodic attempts to control Romanian territory during the nineteenth and early twentieth centuries. Romania deeply resented the loss of its northeastern province of Bessarabia to Russia in 1878. Romania regained this province in 1918, only to lose it again to the Soviet Union in 1940, this time permanently. Romanians also could not forgive or forget the harsh, punitive

Soviet armistice in 1944, forcing the surrender once again of Bessarabia and the payment of substantial reparations to Russia, ostensibly in retribution for Romania's participation in the German invasion of the Soviet Union beginning in the summer of 1941, despite Romania's poverty at the end of the war.

The Psychocultural Determinant

The notion of "mythologic overcompensation" helps to explain the development of Romanian nationalism in the 1970s and 1980s, when it reached extremes in the form of official harassment of Hungarians in Transylvania and persecution of the few Jews still living in Romania following the Second World War. The authorities allowed the publication of grotesque accusations against Jews. "Mythologic overcompensation" means the way in which Ceauşescu used nationalism to distract the attention of his people from the increasing harshness of daily life. He used nationalism to help legitimize a regime that was feared and hated by most of his people. Standing up to Moscow helped make him a hero in spite of the failures of his regime in other sectors of Romanian national life.[3]

2. Challenges to Soviet Policy

The first expression of Romanian nationalism under the Communists occurred in 1957 when Gheorghiu-Dej implemented a plan to accelerate the industrialization of the country, a plan opposed by the Kremlin, which wanted Romania to expand agricultural exports to the industrialized countries of the north, notably, East Germany, Poland, Hungary, and Czechoslovakia. In the 1960s and 1970s, Dej complained that the Council for Mutual Economic Assistance (CMEA), which Romania had been forced to join in 1948 and which was led by the Soviet Union, was only a disguised instrument of Soviet control. He insisted on following his own plan for Romanian economic development based on the industrialization of the country and trade links to the West, which the Soviets discouraged.

Both Dej and Ceauşescu challenged the Soviets in other areas. When the Kremlin began its long dispute with the Chinese over ideological, strategic, and territorial issues, the Romanians remained neutral instead of backing the Kremlin. Worse, in Moscow's eyes, Ceauşescu's government tried to strengthen Romanian ties with the Chinese to underline its independence. Indeed, Ceauşescu refused to join Moscow and other Eastern bloc allies in ostracizing the Chinese from the international communist movement. The Ceauşescu regime also frequently criticized the Warsaw Pact, calling it another instrument of Soviet influence building, and refused to allow Warsaw Pact military maneuvers on Romanian territory. Ceauşescu in fact refused to endorse, and did not participate in, the Soviet-led Warsaw Pact intervention in Czechoslovakia in 1968, and he also gave no credence to the Brezhnev Doctrine.[4]

Much as this divergence provoked Soviet resentment toward Romania in the

1960s and 1970s, it never became the serious issue in relations between the two countries that the West, especially the United States, thought it was. Soviet party leader Leonid Brezhnev seemed to recognize that Romania's divergence in foreign policy from Moscow helped to strengthen the Romanian Communist Party's hand by allowing it to score points with the public by catering to the country's deep nationalistic instincts. Moreover, there were many limits on Romanian foreign-policy independence of Moscow, not least of which was Romania's membership in the Warsaw Pact and the CMEA, which greatly restricted its freedom of action at home and abroad. Finally, on the critically important point of maintaining the single-party dictatorship and other aspects of the Soviet political model, the Romanian party was reliable and trustworthy.[5]

Sources of Popular Unrest

While Romanians were pleased by their government's apparent independence of the Russians, they were uneasy over its domestic behavior. Indeed, by the 1980s, many Romanians were angry over the excesses, abuses, and irrationalities of Communist Party rule, which was causing great suffering and hardship.[6]

1. Political Repression and Corruption

The Ceauşescu regime punished the slightest criticism of its policies and its leadership. The police had vast power over the lives of ordinary citizens, with the highest proportion of secret police to population in Eastern Europe. Every Romanian who spoke with a foreigner was required to report the conversation to the Securitate, the secret police, within twenty-four hours. Police could enter people's houses under any number of pretexts and confiscate so-called "illegal possessions," which could mean just about anything. Duplicating machines were banned, and typewriters had to be registered with the police. The regime kept the printed media on a short leash by making paper scarce, as well as by draconian censorship laws.[7]

Ceauşescu practiced a Stalinist-type leadership cult to strengthen his power base. He personally controlled appointments to most top party and government posts. He had at his disposal a powerful and privileged military organization called the Securitate, which protected him against any would-be critics and rivals.[8] Ceauşescu also used the Romanian party daily, Scinteia, to foster the personality cult. At times, Scinteia's propaganda about Ceauşescu became absurd. It called him "the hero among the nation's heroes, eminent fighter, revolutionary patriot and thinker, prominent personality of the international communist and workers movement, hero of peace, and symbol of the struggle for the defense and independence of nations and for the establishment of a new world order" who has single-handedly caused "Romania's name [to be] spoken with admiration and respect everywhere!"[9]

Ceauşescu practiced a vicious nepotism, inspired by a deep distrust of anyone not in his immediate family, to reinforce his power base. Members of Ceauşescu's immediate family occupied key positions of power. He allowed his wife, Elena, to acquire enormous power; it was not unusual for her to participate as almost a coleader in talks with foreign heads of state. In January 1986, on the occasion of Elena's birthday, *Scinteia* paid excessive homage to her "as a providential personality whose birthday was a crucial date in Romanian history, by which the nation in glorifying its chosen ones, glorifies itself."[10] But Ceauşescu's nepotism undermined his leadership. His family isolated him from criticism and deprived him of information about the real state of affairs in his country. It prevented him from learning about popular disaffection with his rule and the pressing need for radical reforms. When he finally realized how widespread this disaffection had become, it was too late to do anything to change the course of events.

Beyond nepotism was Ceauşescu's vicious personal corruption, suspected by many Romanians but unprovable until after he was removed from power at the end of 1989. Ceauşescu and his family had lived in a grotesque luxury, enjoying high-quality food items and living quarters that could easily have belonged to a wealthy monarch while the rest of the country suffered miserably from acute shortages of everything.

2. Economic Hardship

Under Ceauşescu's leadership, Romania had one of the lowest standards of living in Eastern Europe. By the 1980s, living conditions in Romania almost approached those in the Soviet Union in the 1930s. There were chronic shortages of everything people needed to survive, especially food. Meat was a memory to most households by 1989, and eggs had become so valuable that people preferred to exchange them instead of eat them. Western journalists and visiting businessmen in the foreign-currency hotels of Bucharest described how ordinary Romanians in the dead of winter watched hungrily through street-level windows of the dining room while people with dollars and deutsche marks ate their meals.

In part these shortages were the result of the kind of economic underperformance characteristic of all the centrally controlled economic systems in Central and Eastern Europe. But it was also true that the scarcity of food was a result not only of poor-quality farm machinery that kept per-capita output low but also of Ceauşescu's policy of exporting the best of Romanian agricultural output to pay off Romania's foreign debt. By the 1980s, Romania was exporting 90 percent of its food produce.

There also were chronic shortages of heat and light for both consumers and producers. Lights had to be turned off, along with other electrical appliances, early in the evening, adding to the high level of personal discomfort by making many Romanian cities and towns very depressing at night. Romania lost its self-sufficiency in oil as demand soon exceeded supply because of the commitment to industrialization. By the 1980s, Romania had become dependent on Russian oil.

The Ceauşescu leadership blamed the country's mediocre economic performance not on the flaws of the Stalinist administrative system but on the allegedly shoddy work of managers and "indolent" workers. Indeed, Ceauşescu punished workers by loss of pay when output in a particular enterprise fell short of official targets.[11]

In response to the deterioration of living conditions, an unprecedented display of public anger occurred. Despite their fears of retribution by a brutal regime, in November 1987, Romanian workers went on strike in Braşov, an industrial city north of Bucharest, protesting cuts in wages that already barely enabled them to get enough food. Ceauşescu had ordered the cuts to punish them for not producing enough, or what he termed "nonfulfillment" of the plan.[12]

Ceauşescu ruthlessly suppressed the Braşov strike. Local police used specially trained dogs to hunt for the strikers, who were arrested and punished while little was done to improve living conditions. In daring to strike against a regime they knew would retaliate swiftly and harshly toward them, the workers had sent a message to the Ceauşescu leadership that they would not tolerate his policies forever. According to a former economic adviser, Mihai Botez, the strike "highlighted the divorce between the rulers and the ruled . . . and amounted to a severe warning to the leaders from the working class."[13]

3. Abusive Social Policies

One of the most reprehensible social policies of the Ceauşescu regime was its decision to replace ancient towns, villages, and cities with modern, Stalinist-style construction. In Bucharest, people were forced out of their homes into new, shoddily built tenements, while the beautiful and historically irreplaceable ancient quarters of the capital were destroyed. It was Ceauşescu's intention to leave a legacy of his campaign to modernize Romania and introduce Stalinist-style Marxian socialism.[14]

The Ceauşescu regime also had a draconian policy to increase the country's birthrate that caused hardship to women. In the 1960s, Romanian officials had become alarmed about the country's declining birthrate, which by 1965 had dropped below the point needed to sustain a growing labor force. While other East European countries facing a similar problem in the 1960s expanded their social-benefits program, Romania decided to ban abortions. The regime enforced the policy in a draconian fashion. Ceauşescu ordered random gynecological examinations of Romanian women at their places of employment to ensure that they were having their menstrual cycle and, if not, that they carried their pregnancies to term. Divorce became almost impossible, and married couples without children had to pay a special tax.[15]

The regime's policies and punishments to increase the birthrate made an unpleasant life in Romania for young people, who were forced to live with their parents until they were married. They were deprived of a normal privacy, taken for granted in Western societies, and young women in particular were forced into habits of life characteristic of the nineteenth century—they became fearful of men, they suppressed their sexual desires, and they frequently endured an intolerable boredom.[16]

Women clearly suffered the most from the regime's policy to increase the birthrate, especially poor women, by causing them to have illegal and frequently unsafe abortions or simply to abandon babies they could not care for. Many wound up in clinics, where some received AIDS-tainted blood.[17]

Moreover, women who ran afoul of the law in this area were severely punished. They could be imprisoned for a minimum of two years. Married women who refused to have children were humiliated and insulted. They were called shirkers of their responsibility to the nation. The regime also took other steps, such as forbidding couples to share a hotel room, and it was not unusual for police to break into a room unannounced to discover and punish anyone engaged in extramarital sex. If a couple was found together, the woman was charged with prostitution and acquired a criminal record.[18]

4. Ethnic Homogenization

The Ceauşescu regime pursued a policy of "ethnic homogenization," aimed primarily at the large Hungarian-speaking minority in Transylvania, a region acquired from the Hungarian state after World War I. People of Hungarian origin living in Transylvania outnumbered ethnic Romanians. The regime tried to undermine Hungarian identity in Transylvania by replacing the Hungarian language with Romanian. Transylvania was also one of the first areas where the regime applied its modernization policy of replacing ancient buildings with new construction devoid of any Hungarian significance. The Hungarian minority deeply resented the regime's prejudice and discrimination and eventually became an important source of opposition that helped to end Ceauşescu's rule in 1989.[19]

5. Western Opprobrium

In 1988, the Ceauşescu regime's abuse of human rights became a major issue in Romania's relations with the West. At the Review Conference in Vienna of the Conference on Security and Cooperation in Europe, delegates severely criticized Romania's human-rights violations. The Romanian government angrily protested. Western countries then accused Romania of actively seeking to prevent implementation of the human-rights provision of the 1975 Helsinki accords.

By the 1980s, relations with the United States deteriorated as Washington realized that Ceauşescu's independence of the Soviet Union was limited and superficial and that his regime had one of the worst records of human-rights abuse in Europe. In early February 1988, the U.S. deputy secretary of state, John C. Whitehead, visited Bucharest for meetings with top Romanian officials to explain the importance the United States attached to human rights and individual freedom. The timing of the visit was important because the House of Representatives had just voted to suspend most-favored-nation status for Romanian exports to the United States, and Senate consideration of the legislation was imminent.[20] But the Whitehead talks had little impact on Romanian policy: there was no evidence of Romanian willingness to accommodate the United States on the human-rights issue. Shortly afterward, the Senate voted to deny Romania most-favored-nation benefits. Before the legislation became law, however, the Romanian government indicated its intention of renouncing most-favored-nation status.[21] On June 5, 1988, President Reagan announced that he would let Romania's most-favored-nation status expire. The loss of most-favored-nation treatment of its trade with the United States, worth about $588 million in 1988, was costly. The Romanians forfeited a large chunk of the hard-currency earnings they needed to pay off their foreign debt.[22] By midsummer of 1988, Romanian–American relations had reached an all-time low, with Secretary of State George Shultz calling Romania "the worst country" in Eastern Europe "on the scale of internal repressiveness," and the regime's rural modernization program a new and gross abuse of human rights.[23]

Ceauşescu Rejects Change

Gorbachev's reform program in the Soviet Union in the late 1980s offered Ceauşescu a model for change. It was a model that Romania, as much as, if not more than, the Soviet Union itself, desperately needed. In particular, Gorbachev tried to persuade Ceauşescu to adopt a measure of glasnost, especially toward Romania's Hungarian-speaking minority in Transylvania.

Gorbachev also tried to sell his economic reforms to the Romanians, suggesting that they introduce cost accounting and private entrepreneurship. During a visit to Bucharest in May 1987, Gorbachev spoke directly to Romanian workers about the need for perestroika in their country, warning that the Soviet Union would not continue indefinitely to accept inferior Romanian oil- and gas-drilling equipment and shoddy electrical transformers. This was a significant threat because the Soviet Union was Romania's biggest trading partner and also the source of much of its petroleum.[24]

1. Opposition to Perestroika

Ceauşescu rejected Gorbachev's reforms. Perestroika, he warned, had both ideological and administrative flaws. He said, "It is hard to understand how solving the problems of economic development can be left to the vagaries of supply and demand, or how projects can be assured by so-called 'market socialism.'" Ceauşescu also argued that a truly revolutionary party would not let enterprises or economic sectors manage themselves and abdicate its obligations to improve society.[25]

Ceauşescu also had no interest in private entrepreneurship. In November 1985, for example, he asserted that the stimulation in one form or another of certain forms of private property was "completely at variance with socialist principles."[26]

He also insisted that Romania already had undertaken much fundamental reform. Despite the fact that industry was tightly controlled, Ceauşescu said that legally each industrial enterprise was allowed to make its own production and sales decisions, to elect its own management, and to raise its own financing. Romanian leaders said that the country's job was to perfect what already had been put in place.[27]

The Ceauşescu leadership even opposed reform elsewhere in Eastern Europe, notably in Poland and Hungary, seeking Moscow's invocation of the Brezhnev Doctrine to stop the liberalization process in those countries in 1989. Ceauşescu argued that reform abroad threatened Romania's stability. The Romanian press in August 1989 pointed out, for example, that events in Budapest were not the sole concern of Hungary. The Romanian leadership was also agitated by the appointment of Poland's first noncommunist prime minister in August, saying this event jeopardized socialism everywhere. It called upon other socialist countries to oppose this development and help the Polish communists form a government.[28] Considering that the regime had criticized the Brezhnev Doctrine in the past as subversive of the sovereignty of national Communist parties, Ceauşescu's proposal to involve it in 1989 was an act of desperation aimed at stopping the liberalization process in Poland and Hungary before it threatened Romanian socialism.

2. Beginnings of Limited Protest and Dissent

Ceauşescu's stubborn resistance to change had provoked an undercurrent of opposition in the late 1980s, which gained momentum in 1989 with the erosion of communist rule elsewhere in Eastern Europe and the progress of reform under Gorbachev's leadership in the Soviet Union. Romanian opponents of Ceauşescu were getting information about reforms in the Soviet Union, Hungary, and Poland from international broadcasts by Radio Free Europe, the BBC, the Voice of America, and even Radio Moscow, which beamed messages into Romania about what was happening abroad and contradicted the carefully controlled domestic news media. News about radical political change in other socialist countries raised Romanian expectations. Eventually, the example of revolt in other East European countries in the fall of 1989, especially the collapse of the Honecker regime in East Germany, helped provoke resistance to the Ceauşescu regime.

A few brave dissident intellectuals were speaking openly by 1989. For example, Doina Cornea, a university professor in the Transylvanian city of Cluj, at personal peril, openly protested human-rights violations in Romania and called for an end to harassment and repression. Despite isolation and abuse by the *Securitate,* she continued her struggle and received international attention.[29]

In March 1989, former high-ranking party officials Gheorghe Apostol, Alexandru Birladeanu, and the ninety-four-year-old Constantin Pirvulescu, in disgrace for having revealed their disillusionment and disagreement with Ceauşescu, publicly attacked his hard-line policies, accusing him of violating human-rights agreements and condemning him for a gross mismanagement of the economy. They called for an end to Ceauşescu's policy of eliminating villages and moving peasants to new urban centers. They took issue with an unpublished but widely feared law banning Romanians from talking to foreigners.[30]

This dissidence had little impact on the Ceauşescu regime. It lacked organization and leadership and had no strategy for removing the Romanian leader and no program of action to replace communism. Romania never developed anything like Czechoslovakia's Charter 77 or Poland's Committee for Workers' Defense, if for no other reason than that the police terror precluded any attempt to launch such democratic initiatives. Under these circumstances, it is understandable that Ceauşescu could not be removed as easily as some other East European leaders.

In this period, Ceauşescu and his wife, Elena, seemed oblivious to and unaffected by the opposition or by the warnings of Cornea, Apostol, Birladeanu, and others. As late as November 24, 1989, at a party congress meeting in Bucharest, Ceauşescu reportedly vowed not to follow other countries in the region that he accused of "blocking socialism." He insisted that the old order would continue.[31]

The End of Ceauşescu's Rule

But the awakening of the Romanians to the full realization of the regime's incompetence eventually did have an affect. After learning about reforms in other East European countries, Romanian citizens openly challenged Ceauşescu's authority and demanded change.

1. Revolt in Timişoara

In early December 1989, in Timişoara, in the west-central part of Romania, the *Securitate* attempted to arrest a dissident cleric of Hungarian background, László Tőkés of the Reformed Church. When local citizens tried to protect him, the authorities responded with brutality, as they had during the November 1987 strike in Braşov, attacking the crowd protecting Tőkés and killing hundreds of people. Instead of restoring law and order, this brutality provoked further popular demonstrations against the government that soon spread beyond Timişoara to other parts of the country, including Bucharest.[32]

Ceaușescu, still protected from reality by people afraid to tell him how bad things were, seemed oblivious to the mounting popular hostility. At a rally on December 21 to mobilize popular support, he demanded an end to the protests and demonstrations against his government, calling them "counterrevolutionary." In a barely veiled reference to Moscow, he railed against "foreign conspirators" who were supposedly trying to overthrow his socialist regime. As his obedient followers in the square applauded his words on command, a few courageous students suddenly interjected shouts denouncing Ceaușescu. They were immediately arrested, but the events were being televised and viewed throughout the country. Millions of Romanians empathized with the students and were enraged by the arrests. Instead of calming the waters, Ceaușescu had stirred them up even more.[33]

2. The Army Helps the Opposition

At first it looked as if the vicious suppression of antigovernment demonstrators had succeeded in bringing order. But the Romanian army suddenly turned against Ceaușescu, for whom it had little respect and even less loyalty. Army leaders had long despised the lavishly supported *Securitate*. They also were angry over Ceaușescu's decision to make additional cuts in defense expenditures. The army's opposition to Ceaușescu sealed his fate. Army forces confronted *Securitate* personnel defending the government in Bucharest and eventually overwhelmed them, capturing Ceaușescu and his wife. After a brief "show trial," the army executed the Ceaușescus on December 25. It was all done as quickly as possible to undercut the morale of the *Securitate* forces and discourage their continued fighting.[34]

3. Iliescu and the NSF Replace Ceaușescu

The Ceaușescus were eliminated so quickly that the country never had a chance to learn directly from him the reasons for his harsh and eccentric rule. Perhaps his successors, who were communists themselves, wanted it that way, to conceal details about their own political past that could prejudice their claims to leadership in the post-Ceaușescu era.

With Ceaușescu gone, power passed into the hands of a small oligarchy of anti-Ceaușescu Communist Party figures calling themselves the Council of the National Salvation Front (NSF), which seemed to come from out of nowhere at the end of December. The NSF was a broad coalition of former communists, pensioners, and rural and factory workers.

The NSF Council chairman, Ion Iliescu, a former high-ranking Communist Party official, had studied in Moscow in the early 1950s and had been Ceaușescu's protege until 1971, when he had fallen from grace for what the

Ceauşescu leadership called "intellectualism," a code word for divergence from Ceauşescu's ideological line. Though anti-Stalinist, Iliescu was far from being anti-communist. His model was Gorbachev, and his ideal was a reformed version of the one-party system. In a speech never published by the Romanian media but picked up by the Soviet press agency TASS, Iliescu claimed that the NSF advocated a "democratic model without pluralism."[35]

It is possible to view the NSF ascendancy as a conspiracy by disgruntled anti-Ceauşescu people in the Communist Party, the military, and, perhaps, even the *Securitate* to get rid of Ceauşescu, assume power themselves, and institute a new form of party dictatorship behind a facade of democracy. These conspirators may have been working for some time toward their goal of ousting Ceauşescu and taking power. They waited for the right opportunity to make a coup. The episode in Timişoara seems to have provided them this opportunity.[36]

4. The Soviet Role

In late 1989, the Kremlin did nothing to protect Ceauşescu against the wrath of his people. It certainly ignored his disingenuous proposal of a Warsaw Pact intervention to preserve conservative rule in Eastern Europe. Gorbachev undoubtedly considered Ceauşescu's rigid adherence to neo-Stalinism a dangerous liability for the long-term survival of socialism in Romania and hoped that the Communist Party could finesse his replacement with more flexible, rational, and pragmatic leadership. Perhaps the Soviet leader saw such traits in Iliescu. He did nothing to interfere with Iliescu's ascendancy and even may have helped in the formation of the NSF.[37]

This is not to say that the Kremlin lacked leverage with Romania—the Soviet Union had become the country's largest supplier of energy and chief trade partner. And while the price of Soviet oil had been increasing, the Soviets continued to subsidize Romanian oil by purchasing Romanian agricultural exports and poor-quality manufactured goods. Gorbachev could have played the Soviet oil card, so to speak, with the Romanians. He did not, hoping the Romanian Communist Party would deal with Ceauşescu and inaugurate much-needed reform without a risky Soviet interference in Romanian internal politics.

Post-Ceauşescu Political Development

It was hard to know whether the new Iliescu regime was noncommunist or neocommunist. There was much change in the immediate aftermath of its ascendancy. But there was also much that stayed the same and suggested that in many respects Iliescu was following in the footsteps of his predecessor.

1. Limited Relaxation and Change

Romania's post-Ceauşescu leadership promised a break with the discredited past. New policies included the lifting of censorship, the acceptance of new, noncommunist political organizations, the formal abolition of the Communist Party, and the toleration of new freedoms of speech, assembly, and travel. Romanians no longer had to register their typewriters, to address each other as "Comrade," or to obey laws against abortion and the use of birth-control devices.[38]

The new government also announced the immediate cancellation of Ceauşescu's rural modernization program and the termination of his program of economic austerity. It made available many food items that had not been seen by Romanian consumers in many years. Fresh fruits and vegetables and high-quality cuts of meat that had been destined for export to the Soviet Union in payment for oil purchases or to other countries in return for hard currency suddenly appeared in Romanian stores.[39]

2. Conservative Countertendencies

But a closer look at the Iliescu leadership revealed a very conservative, even "neocommunist," bent. The new leaders did not want to open up Romanian society to a full-blown pluralism. They tolerated the existence of other groups, but they had little respect for them and were extremely reluctant to share power. The Iliescu regime maintained a Ceauşescu-like grip over the mass media, obstructing free and vigorous political criticism. Independent newspapers and magazines had difficulty getting newsprint supplies and making distribution arrangements. While the government allowed the number of independent newspapers to increase, it harassed them in a multitude of different ways, sometimes accusing them of circulating false information or disclosing legally protected data, which were grounds for prosecution. The opposition newspaper *Romănia Libera,* which started up in 1990, reached a mass circulation of 1.5 million copies in 1992. Its circulation, however, precipitously dropped in succeeding years to 140,000 copies by mid-1995. And while there was a number of private radio stations in Bucharest and elsewhere in the country, the government severely restricted their penetration, leaving them with only very small audiences.[40] Not surprisingly, opposition political groups and parties had difficulty getting started, despite the NSF's stated willingness to introduce political pluralism. New parties could not easily get office equipment or space, and opposition politicians complained of harassment by security forces.[41]

The NSF regime tried, by a tokenism that changed the appearance but not the reality of the regime's political behavior, to cope with a growing popular perception of Iliescu and his NSF colleagues as little more than communist "hangers on," determined to hold on to power by posing as reformers, and with popular demands in early 1990 for both Iliescu's resignation and the immediate banning of the Communist Party. For example, the NSF Council agreed to ban the Communist Party, but spoke of a Romanian "brand" of democratic development different from the "outmoded Western democracies."[42] It also agreed to share power with opposition groups, and, at the end of January 1990, it replaced the

145-member council with a new body, the Council for National Unity, with 180 members from the NSF and some 30-odd opposition groups.[43] In addition, the NSF dismissed the ministers who had been linked closely with the Ceauşescu regime. It also forced out the ministers of defense and interior, despite the fact that they had supported the removal of Ceauşescu. The government tried and convicted many former Ceauşescu bureaucrats to emphasize its break with the past. Iliescu also officially disbanded the *Securitate,* ostensibly giving its functions to the Defense Ministry, which established a new internal investigation agency modeled after the FBI of the United States. The government arrested 3,000 *Securitate.* But, none of these gestures diluted in any significant way the enormous power of Iliescu and the NSF over the post-Ceauşescu political system.[44]

Indeed, the regime could not resist the temptation to deal with opposition in the Ceauşescu manner. In response to the persistence of anti-NSF demonstrations in Bucharest, the Iliescu leadership staged its own pro-NSF demonstrations. In February, it brought some 3,000 miners into Bucharest from the Jiu Valley to help put down the liberal demonstrations. The miners were willing to support the government on this occasion because of recent pay hikes, improved working conditions, and free transportation to the capital. They eventually broke up the demonstrations and then went home. With this evidence of the government's brutality and attempt to pit Romanians against one another, antigovernment agitation escalated. In April 1990, opposition leaders, principally intellectuals and students, began a long-term protest demonstration in University Square in Bucharest denouncing the government's neocommunist character.[45]

3. The May 1990 Parliamentary Elections

It was in this uncertain political environment that the country prepared for parliamentary and presidential elections. The NSF wrestled with the issue of exactly when to schedule the elections. An early date with a short campaign period would relieve growing international pressure for elections and would exploit the poor organization of the opposition parties. A later date and a long campaign period would allow the opposition to get organized and make a serious challenge to the NSF incumbency. The NSF decided to move swiftly. On March 14, the Romanian Parliament set the date for elections in May.[46]

The NSF Becomes a Political Party

The elections were critical because the NSF had stated shortly after assuming power that it was just an "interim steward," whose members would step down once democratic elections were held. But its behavior in the early months of 1990 suggested that it had every intention of holding on to power. For example, a wing of the NSF led by Iliescu began to transform itself into a political party in a way that calls to mind the splintering of Poland's Solidarity movement. The

Iliescu group fielded candidates, all the while ignoring angry protests by leaders of newly emerging political parties, representatives of student groups and intellectuals, and others, who questioned the NSF's democratic intentions and speculated that it aimed to consolidate its own version of one-party rule. Indeed, because it was all too willing to use force to suppress popular demonstrations against its policies, people feared that, if the Iliescu-led NSF won power, a police state would return under a new name.[47]

Popular Opposition to NSF Rule

During the campaign, the depth of popular hostility to the Iliescu regime was evident. At the end of April, some 40,000 people in Timişoara, the cradle of the anti-Ceauşescu revolution, demanded Iliescu's resignation, accusing him of seeking to reestablish some form of communism in Romania. As the election drew near, the mood was bitter and divisive and the campaign became increasingly violent. Although the NSF was quick to accuse its political opponents of abuse and violence, it engaged in similar behavior, organizing its own campaign of intimidation against the opposition. The NSF-controlled mass media also systematically slandered the democratic parties and their candidates.[48]

Advantages of the NSF

The NSF tried to counter this popular opposition to its rule. Although the elections were advertised as the first free elections in Romania since the end of World War II, in fact they were subject to very undemocratic constraints giving the incumbent NSF the advantage. For example, the electoral law provided that political activity had to be predicated on respect for national independence, sovereignty, and territorial integrity and must affirm the nation's dignity. No one knew what these phrases meant, and their ambiguity enabled the government to take actions prejudicial to the opposition groups, limiting their freedom to campaign.[49]

The NSF appealed to emotion, making good use of many ideas from Ceauşescu's time, including the notion that the other parties were traitors, that they would sell the country to foreigners, and that they had been organized and supported from abroad. NSF supporters in the media accused former dissidents of the same political crimes as Ceauşescu's *Securitate.* In addition, the NSF capitalized on the fact that two of the presidential candidates, Radu Campeanu of the Liberal Party and Ion Ratiu of the Peasants' Party, had lived abroad for many years, and encouraged popular suspicion of them.[50]

NSF candidates also skillfully exploited widespread anxiety over privatization and the reestablishment of property rights advocated by some of the opposition parties. People worried that they would be hurt by these departures from the state-controlled welfare economy of the communist era, in particular unemployment and further increases in the cost of living. The NSF also astutely manipulated anticommunist and nationalist symbols, maintaining that it was a left-of-center party, akin to West European social democracy, while at the same time it ran a rabidly nationalistic and anti-Western campaign. The NSF also benefited from being the incumbent. The authorities created a safe environment for the NSF campaign. They tolerated, and thereby implicitly encouraged, repeated violence against the opposition parties. Opposition gatherings were continually disrupted by the NSF's constituents. The NSF also made effective use of television, which was controlled by the state. Given the fact that most Romanians preferred television to the printed word to get their information about current events, the NSF-controlled government was able to exert a powerful influence over how the public learned about what was going on in the country.[51]

Finally, Iliescu was an aggressive campaigner. He issued numerous public statements characterizing opposition activities as illegal and declaring that, while the government would tolerate them, it could not protect participants.[52] He also exploited the strong anti-intellectual bias among working-class Romanians. Using rhetoric reminiscent of the kind of radical-populist appeal made by fascists in Romania in the pre–World War II period, he struck a responsive chord when he told farmers and miners: "You are at the bottom of society—smash these people in the city who think they are better than you—educated, privileged."[53] Iliescu's campaign also struck a responsive chord with many voters, who reportedly called upon him to "be like a parent."[54] The opposition, supported primarily by university students, the professional intelligentsia, and other groups eager for real political liberalization and a complete break with the communist past, responded with a joint statement criticizing the climate of violence that was interfering with their appeal for popular support. In Bucharest, the opposition tried to discredit the NSF and its leadership.[55]

Success of the NSF

The outcome of the elections was a victory for the NSF, which won about two-thirds of the seats in the Assembly of Deputies and the Senate. Iliescu won 85 percent of the vote for president.[56] Fearful of change, voters in the countryside joined the vast army of conservative bureaucrats to help produce the NSF victory. The opposition was able to get votes only from the city areas, where less than half the country's population resided. The election results reflected the strong conservative instincts of a majority of Romanian voters, who yearned for strong leadership and stability. NSF candidates from Iliescu down had skillfully and successfully exploited this conservative bias.[57]

4. Renewal of Repression

In the aftermath of the elections, the intelligentsia was furious over what appeared as a barely concealed manipulation of the new political system by communists, including many of the former regime's regional party bosses and several former close associates of the late Ceauşescu, who were among the newly elected members of Parliament. Yet to the dismay of the intelligentsia, most ordinary people seemed unaware of or disinterested in this aspect of their new government. Angrily, the opposition launched a massive popular demonstration against the government in the center of Bucharest on June 11, 1990. The Iliescu government responded with a ferocity reminiscent of the Ceauşescu regime's suppression of the November 1987 strikes in Braşov. Police forces, which could have easily controlled the situation on June 12 because of the initially small number of protesters involved, stood aside to allow the demonstration to gather momentum. They also went out of their way to provoke the protesters, and then they responded in force. On June 13, Iliescu declared somewhat hysterically that the legally elected government was in danger of being overthrown by a "legionary rebellion," an oblique reference to the fascist thinking of the pre–World War II Legion of the Archangel Michael, otherwise known as the Iron Guard.[58] Iliescu again called in the miners from northern Romania to help the government put down the demonstrations. About 7,000 miners, among the most hard-pressed of economic groups in Romanian society and still strongly supportive of Iliescu, who they hoped would do something to improve their lot, mercilessly beat down and bloodied the demonstrators.[59]

5. Persistence of Opposition

Opposition to the NSF government persisted despite, and probably because of, the government's heavy-handed repression. It now had a new determination and improved organization. The opposition groups, mainly the reconstituted historical parties—the National Peasant Christian Democratic Party, the National Liberal Party, and the Social Democratic Party—realized the weakness of their situation: they had been continually outmaneuvered in their confrontation with Iliescu. They acknowledged their own deep internal divisions and lack of leadership, cohesion, and unity.

The Civic Alliance

Seeking to achieve strength through unity, the opposition agreed to work together and formed a new organization called the Civic Alliance. In July 1991, the Civic Alliance pledged at its congress in Bucharest to transform itself into a national political party to challenge the NSF in the next parliamentary elections. It claimed several million backers and the support of the antigovernment daily *România Libera*.[60] It was the first noncommunist and nonfascist party in post-Ceauşescu Romania. Its leadership came from the liberal intelligentsia and consisted of university rectors, medical doctors, trade-union leaders, lawyers, student activists, and artists. Furthermore, party leader Nicolae Manolescu had no apparent ties to the communist past. The Civic Alliance advocated the protection of minorities and rejected racist nationalism. It favored an independent media, strict control over the secret police, a free-market economy, and substantial investment in the service industries.[61]

The Democratic Convention

In the autumn of 1991, the Civic Alliance joined an even larger umbrella-type political party organization opposed to the Iliescu regime called the Democratic Convention. While this organization reflected the wide spectrum of opposition to the NSF, the diversity and independence of its membership prevented it from developing the kind of cohesive organization, appealing ideology, and effective leadership needed to challenge the NSF successfully and defeat it in national elections.

The Miners

Romanian miners turned out to be another source of opposition to the Iliescu regime. At the end of September 1991, they were back in Bucharest, blaming Iliescu for unrelenting inflation, food shortages, and unemployment that were keeping their living standards low and causing much suffering. The miners simply wanted relief from the austerity policies of the new government. They believed that the country owed them a debt for the harshness of their daily existence and were angry that life was no better now than it had been under Ceauşescu. Despite sharp class differences between the miners and the middle class in Bucharest, there was an apparent solidarity between the two constituencies around these issues. But unlike city liberals, the miners expressed little understanding of or interest in democracy. Indeed, they saw the myriad of political parties that suddenly appeared after Ceauşescu as little more than anarchy. Their din was so loud, their demands so compelling, and the violence so threatening of anarchy—thousands of protesters of all persuasions and backgrounds penetrated the Parliament and firebombed the main television center—that Prime Minister Petre Roman agreed in the fall of 1991 to step down. He was succeeded by Theodor Stolojan, a former finance minister.[62]

6. The 1992 Presidential and Parliamentary Elections

President Iliescu has shown a remarkable political resilience in the mid-1990s. In parliamentary elections in September 1992, Iliescu's National Salvation Democratic Front, which had split from the parent National Salvation Front following local elections held in February over the president's differences with former Prime Minister Roman, won a plurality of 28 percent of the seats in the Assembly of Deputies. At the same time the new coalition of liberals, the Democratic Convention, won 20 percent. Roman's NSF won only 10 percent. The rest of the seats were divided among five other parties, including the far-right, chauvinistic Romanian National Unity Party. And in the presidential contest, where two ballots were needed because none of the candidates won an absolute majority in the first instance, Iliescu won 48 percent of the popular vote, versus 31 percent for Emil Constantinescu, the rector of Bucharest University, and 11 percent for Gheorghe Funar, the candidate of the Romanian National Unity Party and a rabid nationalist who advocated the suppression of minority rights and a return to a centralized economy. When a runoff was held two weeks after the first ballot, Iliescu obtained a clear victory, with 60.5 percent of the vote versus Constantinescu's 39.5 percent.[63]

The results of the parliamentary and presidential elections signified popular acceptance, at least for the time being, of Iliescu's conservatism. He stood for the retention of many former communists in positions of political influence and only a very gradual reduction of state control over the economic life of the country. While most Romanians were glad to be free of the brutal dictatorship of the late Ceauşescu, they seemed willing to support Iliescu despite his neo-authoritarian style, his excessive sensitivity to criticism, and his willingness to use what power he could to weaken or silence those who opposed him. Beyond the conservatism of the countryside, where many voters supported him because they were fearful of change, Iliescu benefited from a craving on the part of most Romanians for strong leadership that could reassure them about the future in an era of rapid change, which they did not understand and therefore feared. Iliescu's resemblance in many respects to his discredited predecessor was not a liability with many Romanians, who were beginning to take a second and sympathetic look at the communist era, judging many aspects of it, such as full employment and price stability, which were gone in the early 1990s, as good. For many Romanians, Iliescu seemed able to express association with what was good. Voters in the countryside had supported Iliescu because of their fear of change, particularly the dismantling communist paternalism and the freeing up of the country's economic life that were causing widespread hardship. These rural voters appreciated his efforts to ease the difficulties of their daily life by policies of returning land to them and awarding them pensions. Finally, Constantinescu was no match for Iliescu. Although he obtained the support of almost 40 percent of the electorate, mostly in the large urban centers, suggesting that an increasing number of Romanians were ready to back an alternative to the Iliescu regime, he could not carry the countryside, which was essential for victory.[64]

But overall, Iliescu did not do as well in September 1992 as he had in May 1990, when he had won 85 percent of the popular vote. This decline in popularity undoubtedly was the result of popular disappointment over his failure to improve living conditions in the aftermath of Ceauşescu's loss of power. Iliescu indicated sensitivity to this decline, reportedly saying after the elections that he would always bear in mind the views of the large percentage of people who voted for his opponent.[65]

7. Lingering Conservative Tendencies

In the mid-1990s, Romania continued to be conservative in the political sphere and was way behind other countries in the region in terms of democratic development. Remnants of the old regime's authoritarianism were evident in the survival of the *Securitate,* which, despite the initial attacks against it in early 1990, was still very much alive with its network of contacts crisscrossing almost all sectors of Romanian society. Iliescu seemed to be using it as a domestic intelligence agency to monitor and control the political opposition. The state still controlled television, the most influential aspect of the mass media, and the university system.[66] The Iliescu government was willing to use its enormous police power to enforce an almost neocommunist style of political discipline. Moreover, hardly conducive to the evolution of liberal government was a view many Romanians had that for the moment at least the country needed a dictatorship to cope with the chaos of the transition away from communist rule.

The nationalistic obsession of many Romanians and their willingness to tolerate the abuse by Iliescu's government of the human rights of ethnic and political minorities, especially the Hungarian community in Transylvania, were among the biggest obstacles to the emergence of a vibrant and durable Western-style pluralistic democracy. Other tendencies reminiscent of the Ceauşescu era included a revival of anti-Semitism. *România Mare,* or the Greater Romania Party, had a viciously anti-Semitic platform that accused Jews of belonging to a conspiracy against Romania and called for the restoration of an authoritarian dictatorship. It had a newspaper with a circulation of about 500,000. A smaller but no less conservative organization, the Movement for Romania condemned social democracy as contrary to the "cultural and spiritual nature" of Romanian society. These and other rightist political groups collectively are able to attract the support of about 12 percent of the Romanian electorate. Their growing influence suggests they could move from the so-called "lunatic fringe" of postcommunist Romanian politics into the mainstream.[67]

Indeed, radical rightists had representation in Iliescu's coalition in Parliament during 1993, led by Prime Minister Nicolae Văcăroiu. The coalition, collectively known as the Party of Social Democracy, included the Greater Romania party, the Socialist Labor Party, which considered itself the heir to the disbanded Communist Party, and the anti-Hungarian Party of Romanian National Unity under Gheorghe Funar, the militant nationalist whom some in Romania liken to Serbia's president Slobodan Milošević. The Văcăroiu government, arguably the most conservative regime yet to govern Romania in the post-Ceauşescu era, was determined to block any effort of the democratic groups to obtain power. It pressed forward with a campaign to restore the communist bureaucracy at the local level and to a certain extent on the national level as well.[68] By the end of 1993, Prime Minister Văcăroiu's government had lost public and parliamentary support, yet it continued to rule with the backing of President Iliescu. Many people, especially in Bucharest, hated the Văcăroiu regime because it had done little to improve living conditions, which remained the same or deteriorated since Ceaușescu's ouster four years earlier. A report of the World Bank indicated that most Romanians were spending 80 percent of their income on food, while the Ministry of Health acknowledged in December 1993 that infant mortality was climbing.[69]

8. Prospects for Democracy

But there were also institutions taking root in Romania that were supportive of long-term democratic development. Romania's constitution provides for a presidential-parliamentary system that, while endowing the presidency with substantial authority, also assigns the Parliament real power to monitor executive behavior by providing it with the no-confidence vote, which can obligate a cabinet to resign.[70] The postcommunist system thus accommodated a popular craving for strong leadership, which Iliescu to some extent satisfied, while providing for some form of checks and balances to assure against a return to the kind of authoritarian dictatorship developed by the late Ceaușescu.[71] Opposition parties committed to Western-style political liberalism thus survived the regime's frequently harsh treatment of them, and they had adequate freedom to discuss, debate, and criticize government behavior.[72] Romania now has over 900 newspapers and weekly political outlets, of which only a small number are government controlled. Thus, the foundations for democracy were present in Romania. Eventually the opposition would prevail.

Reforming an Economy in Shambles

There was an explosion of popular wrath in mid-December 1993 in Bucharest when thousands of workers took to the streets to demand the Văcăroiu government's resignation. They were disgusted by the leadership's failure to raise the standard of living and by the absence of any promise of improvement in the future. The key to this continuing popular unrest was the economy.

1. The Communist Legacy

Iliescu inherited an economy left in shambles by Ceaușescu. After a year of his leadership, the life of ordinary Romanians still remained hard. Throughout 1990, there were shortages of everything from energy to clothing and light bulbs. At night homes and stores were still dark, adding to the existing dinginess and contributing to a pervasive mental depression. Food that was available in the free-farmers' markets was beyond the reach of most people because prices based on supply and demand were high.[73]

2. Reform Objectives and Policies

On October 18, 1990, Prime Minister Petre Roman called the country's economic performance in the first nine months of the NSF leadership dismal: industrial production was down 28 percent and exports dropped 46 percent. In a speech to the Parliament, he outlined the government's major initiatives in the economic sphere to try to deal with the problems, identifying as goals the introduction of a market economy, in particular, the pursuit of limited privatization and the enactment of agricultural reform to expand food output.[74]

Private Entrepreneurialism and Privatization

The Iliescu regime allowed some private businesses with up to twenty employees to operate freely. But these small efforts at privatization merely led to an increase in prices since production did not increase but declined. Private investors started up businesses simply to exploit shortages for quick profits, after which they closed down and liquidated their firms.[75]

Bureaucrats, most of whom were holdovers from the communist era, stood in the way of an extensive curtailment of state control over the country's economic life, fearful that change would cost them their jobs or, at least, diminish their influence and privileges. Some members of Parliament also had reservations about undoing the paternalistic social order too quickly. And the top leadership of the NSF, including Iliescu, sympathized with this conservative position. They were concerned with the social consequences of privatization, in particular, price increases, unemployment, and speculation. At the same time, bankruptcy of state enterprises was not an option because Romania had no bankruptcy legislation; the Parliament was reluctant to enact it fearing an explosion of unemployment, social tensions, and political disorder should many firms declare bankruptcy. Iliescu continued to subsidize state enterprises at great cost to the national budget and the country's overall economic development. By early 1993, only between 15 percent and 25 percent of Romania's gross domestic product came from private enterprise.[76]

Agricultural Reform

Freeing up the farm sector had mixed results. The Iliescu regime moved forward in 1990, distributing leaseholds to farmers that amounted to almost one-third of the country's arable land, a stunning departure from the nearly 100 percent state-controlled and state-managed agricultural system left by Ceauşescu. And in February 1991, the Romanian Parliament passed a law restoring landed property that had been turned into collective farms to its former owners, with a limit of ten hectares and a minimum of one-half hectare per recipient.[77]

The results of these changes were mixed. For example, although Romanian farmers in many instances responded well to the incentives and with some initiative and persistence increased the supply of meat and fresh produce in the unregulated farmers' markets, prices of commodities in private markets remained much higher than in state stores, which were almost empty because of pent-up demand. Indeed, the sharp increase in prices for such staples as bread, eggs, and meat led the regime, beginning in April 1991, to provide compensatory cash handouts to consumers and to allow wage increases.[78] And a year after the law redistributing land had been put into effect, other problems developed. Restoring land to families that once owned land that was subsequently turned into collective farms caused tensions and conflict in the countryside. Furthermore, as of January 1992, most farmers still were landless, and many chose to remain under the old collective-farm system, preferring to be employees rather than entrepreneurs. Moreover, many of the surviving collective farms, now called "agricultural associations," were still under the management of former communists, who were enriching themselves at everybody else's expense. The government had done little beyond the initial land distribution to help Romanian farmers make the transfer to a free-market agricultural system. For example, the government did little to help impoverished farmers buy necessities such as seed and farm equipment. Existing farm machinery belonged to the old collective, which would not give it up. Worse, there was no gasoline to run the machinery, even if the would-be free farmers had it. And many collective-farm workers were fearful that decollectivization would mean a loss of pensions.[79] In sum, the reform turned out to be only the beginning of private farming. There was a lot of follow-up needed to develop an efficient farm population capable of feeding the country.

3. The Balance Sheet

Romania's economy barely improved over the course of the 1990s. In early October 1991, inflation was running at 70 percent a year and unemployment was rising as many inefficient and unprofitable state-owned factories were closing down. The small private sector just getting started could not absorb the jobless. By the summer of 1993, the average monthly wage of Romanian workers was $50.00, while the average monthly wage of a worker in the Czech Republic was $200.00. In 1993, as unemployment continued to rise, gross national product declined by 15 percent.[80]

These conditions were in part the result of the failure of the Iliescu government to move faster in freeing up the economy from inefficient state control. The Iliescu leadership was divided and confused over how far and how fast to go toward a free-market economy and lacked a coherent strategy for change in this area. It continued to oppose rapid movement toward a free market lest this provoke social unrest. Shock therapy still remained out of the question for Romania's impoverished economy, in which the overwhelming majority of people still lived a marginal existence with little tolerance for added hardship. Making matters worse for the economy was the paucity of foreign investment. It was slow in coming because there was still too much state control over the country's economic life and not enough opportunity for profit making. In 1992 and 1993, Romania also had difficulty getting loans from the International Monetary Fund (IMF), which could have eased the transition away from state-controlled economic life for many poor Romanians by making necessities more accessible. The IMF faulted the Iliescu government for not moving fast enough and not doing enough budgetary belt tightening to bring down inflation.[81]

Social Problems

Postcommunist Romania also had to address serious social problems inherited from the Ceauşescu era. The most important concerned the Hungarian minority in Transylvania, Jews and Roma, the AIDS epidemic among Romanian children, and the hardships endured by women.

1. The Hungarian Minority in Transylvania

Ethnic Romanians in Transylvania resisted the demands of the Hungarian minority for autonomy in the aftermath of the December political upheaval. They set up an organization called *Vatra Românească,* or Romanian Hearth, for the perpetuation of Romanian cultural hegemony in Transylvania. A highly nationalistic organization and somewhat right wing in its political thinking, it recalled the chauvinistic and fascist groups that grew up in Romania on the eve of World War II. The organization encouraged and supported violence against the Hungarians. In late March 1990, aroused by *Vatra Românească* propaganda, crowds of angry Romanian peasants in Tirgu Mureş attacked Hungarians with clubs and sticks, sending many to the hospital. They shattered the windows of stores owned by people with Hungarian names and in so doing intensified a conflict that has shown no signs of abating. This Romanian behavior reflected a deep historic dislike and distrust of the Hungarians fed by myths about their dishonesty and brutality in relations with Romanian people.[82] Gheorghe Funar, elected mayor of Cluj in February 1992, personified the deep prejudice most Romanians felt toward their Hungarian neighbors. He went out of his way to offend the Hungarian citizens of his town by banning street signs in Hungarian and forbidding Hungarians to hold large public meetings.[83]

The Iliescu regime did little to combat this prejudice and violence. Iliescu found the violence a convenient distraction from the country's continuing economic hardships. Moreover, Iliescu in some respects was an old-fashioned Romanian nationalist. Much like his predecessor, he believed that the Hungarians in Transylvania should be assimilated into Romanian society and saw their desire for close links to Hungary and even for an eventual union of their region with the Republic of Hungary as a threat to Romanian unity and territorial integrity, especially if at some future time Hungary should demand a return of Transylvania, which it lost after World War I.[84]

2. Revival of Anti-Semitism

There has been a steady rise in anti-Semitism since the December 1989 revolution. Anti-Semitic articles, which appeared regularly in a number of newspapers, frequently contained the charge that Jews brought communism to Romania and that the communist government was overwhelmingly Jewish. The tabloid press also produced numerous stories blaming Jews for the economic hardships of Romania. These stories also complained about the number of Jews in government, saying there were too many of them, that they held key jobs, that they controlled the Romanian mass media, and that they were exerting an influence over Romanian politics out of proportion to their number. Although these views had no basis in fact in addition to the destruction of the large Jewish community in pre–World War II Romania, the Ceauşescu regime went out of its way on several occasions to remove many Jews from party and state positions—they were believed by many people looking for a scapegoat on which to place the blame for the hard times.[85]

There have been other manifestations of anti-Semitism in postcommunist Romania. The commemoration of the Holocaust was marred by demonstrators. In certain towns the celebration of Jewish holidays had to be canceled because of fears of anti-Semitic attacks. Cemeteries and synagogues have been vandalized. When in the early summer of 1991 Romania dedicated a memorial in Bucharest to the 400,000 Jews who fell victim to the local fascist regime during World War II, people taunted Elie Wiesel, a Nobel laureate who had survived the pogroms in Transylvania.[86]

Meanwhile, in July 1991, the Romanian Parliament paid homage to General Ion Antonescu, the Romanian ally of the Nazis who initiated the mass killings of Romanian Jews in the World War II era. While the rehabilitation of Antonescu, who was executed on orders of the Soviets at the end of the war, may have been intended as a gesture of independence of Moscow by the new Romanian leadership, it is also possible that Parliament was showing its lingering antipathy toward Jews in Romanian society. The Iliescu regime never condemned

Antonescu's fascist beliefs or his blatant anti-Semitism. Nor has it made public the enormous extent of official Romanian cooperation under Antonescu with Nazi policies against Romanian Jews. Furthermore, on October 22, 1993, Romanian government officials attended the unveiling of a statue in the town of Slobozia, near Bucharest, of a statue of Antonescu. The official group included Mihai Ungheeanu, an aid to the late Ceauşescu and secretary of state for culture, and Corneliu Vadim Tudor, a member of the Parliament and reputed to be a vicious anti-Semite. Iliescu, who condemned anti-Semitism and made a point of demonstrating his own personal disdain for it by traveling to Washington, D.C., in the spring of 1993 to participate in the celebrations opening the Holocaust Museum, could have prevented the statue episode but chose to remain aloof, leaving the impression at home as well as abroad that he is intimidated by the power of the anti-Semitic right.[87]

3. Persecution of the Roma People

Worse off than the Jews in Romania is the small minority of Roma, frequently called "Gypsies," who make up less than 1 percent of the country's population. Romanians accuse the Roma of engaging in the black market that is responsible, they say, for the shortages and high prices in Bucharest. The Roma's aversion to work and penchant for begging, so the argument goes, as well as their refusal to integrate into the mainstream of Romanian society, justify the strong prejudice against them. In the early 1990s, the Roma endured attacks by ethnic Romanians, particularly in rural areas. Local administrative authorities did little to punish this behavior, thereby encouraging it. The failure of the authorities to provide security to the Roma may have had a sinister motive: to make living in Romania as uncomfortable for them as possible and to encourage their emigration to other countries to preserve Romanian "racial purity."[88]

The plight of the Romanian Roma people became an international embarrassment in 1992, when Gypsy refugees who had settled in Germany were viciously attacked by radical German youth called skinheads. While most German citizens deplored the violence, they supported the official German response, which consisted of tightening up the country's liberal asylum law and reaching an agreement with Bucharest to repatriate the Roma. The German government argued that the Roma did not qualify for asylum in Germany because they were not internationally recognized victims of political oppression in Romania. But the underlying reason for German behavior was prejudice. Of all the minorities that had taken residence in Germany in recent years, Gypsies were held by many Germans in least regard and were believed to be racially inferior to other ethnic groups. The Romanian government agreed to German deportation of the Roma in return for financial assistance to rebuild and resettle them upon their return.[89]

Whether the Roma will be hospitably received back in Romania remains to be seen. The Roma Union, an advocacy group for the Roma, is working to help them return to their villages. The government in Bucharest has promised to retrain them with the help of German money. But the Roma are still shunted to the margins of society and kept jobless, uneducated, and subject to deep-seated prejudice. It will take a long time before these conditions change, and only then will the circumstances of the Romanian Roma improve.[90]

4. Pediatric AIDS Epidemic

Of all the legacies of the Ceauşescu era, the epidemic of AIDS among newly born Romanian children may be the most grim. According to statistics gathered by Romanian virologists and confirmed by French doctors, Romania has a pediatric epidemic of AIDS concentrated in crowded orphanages and clinics. It was spread by the old-fashioned practice of giving blood transfusions to sickly newborn infants to increase their chance of survival. In many instances, the blood used in this procedure was contaminated by the AIDS virus. Further helping the spread of AIDS was poor equipment, bad medical practices, and the large numbers of abandoned children born as a consequence of the prohibition of birth-control devices and of abortion. All this was first revealed in June 1989, as a result of random testing for other viruses. When the investigating doctors reported their findings to the central Ministry of Health in Bucharest, they were told bluntly by an embarrassed Romanian leadership to stop testing. The doctors at their peril ignored this instruction and continued their investigation at different hospitals in the country. They eventually discovered that children with untreatable AIDS-related infections were everywhere in the hospital system.[91]

The Iliescu government has been hampered in dealing with the AIDS crisis by a continuing shortage of equipment and a sluggish bureaucracy. But the real problem is the regime's unwillingness to invest in an upgrading of the shabby health-care system inherited from the communist era. Five years after Ceauşescu, Romania still had the poorest health-care system in the region. The Iliescu government made clear to health-care professionals that their needs are far down on the list of spending priorities. Consequently, shortages of everything from rubber surgical gloves and soap to complex diagnostic equipment, desperately needed by hospitals and clinics, continue unabated. The regime has told doctors and nurses that medicine is not "productive," so it is not going to get the money it needs.[92]

5. The Predicament of Women

Romanian women have gotten little benefit from the overthrow of Ceauşescu, the development of political democracy, and recent economic reforms. Just as for women in other East European countries, the hardships accompanying the transition to a free-market economy have fallen hardest on Romanian women as homemakers. Although some of the worst pronatalist policies of the Ceauşescu regime have been abandoned, and although the 1991 constitution did establish, at least in theory, the principle of gender equality, guaranteeing legal equality, equal pay for equal work, and paid maternity leave, Romanian women still suffer more than men from the country's impoverished economy, and Romanian women have a long way to go to achieve real equality in the political, economic, and social spheres of national life.

Part of the problem for women in the postcommunist era is their lack of political representation and influence. The new political parties have virtually ignored them and the issues that count most for them, namely, opportunities for a role in politics and a career outside the home. The few women who have been elected to the Romanian national Parliament complain that nobody pays any attention to what they say and that the party agencies in the Parliament keep them from obtaining positions of leadership on matters directly affecting women, such as labor, health, and social welfare, that could enhance their political influence. A parliamentary committee dealing with these matters has a large female membership but is chaired by a man.[93]

But it is also true that many Romanian women are not inclined to push aggressively for greater influence over the postcommunist political system. Some Romanian women have said in effect that they had enough of politics in the Ceauşescu era when they were forced by the regime to take an interest in politics for the sake of strengthening their commitment to building socialism. Some say that they prefer to expand their role in society indirectly and without confrontation, for example, as critical journalists. And most women simply want to focus their energy on home and family in this difficult transition period. Consequently, Romania does not have an active feminist movement.[94]

Foreign Relations Since Ceauşescu

While the post-Ceauşescu leadership has tried to keep its fences mended with the Soviet Union and, after its collapse in December 1991, Russia, it has also tried to strengthen Romanian ties with the West. The Iliescu regime also worried about the explosion of political turmoil in Yugoslavia and is searching for a policy in that area that serves its best interests but does not complicate its relations with Moscow or Washington.

1. The Soviet Union and Russia

Relations with the former Soviet Union improved after the overthrow of Ceauşescu, long an object of the Kremlin's contempt and embarrassment. In the beginning of January 1990, Soviet foreign minister Eduard Shevardnadze said that he found the new atmosphere in Bucharest "absolutely purifying," and he pledged Moscow's support of any political system the Romanians should choose. "Whatever political groups lead Romania is the business of Romanians themselves," he said. Following this declaration, the Soviet Union showed no interest in resuming influence over Romania and sought rather a normal relationship between the two countries based on mutual trust and advantage.[95]

The Future of Moldova

But Romania has had difficulties with President Boris Yeltsin's Russia. The two countries differed over the future of the independent republic of Moldova, formerly known as the Moldavian Soviet Socialist Republic and inhabited primarily by people of Romanian culture. Under Ceauşescu, Romania periodically made oblique claims to Moldavia, which the Kremlin ignored. It had no intention of considering boundary changes with neighboring countries that had real or imagined claims on Soviet territory. Moreover, the Moldavians themselves had no interest in coming under Ceauşescu's repressive regime.[96]

The future of Soviet Moldavia was an issue in the Gorbachev years. With the freedom to speak their minds under Gorbachev's glasnost, many of the non-Russian republics, especially those in the western part of the Soviet state, including Moldavia, expressed a nationalistic assertiveness. Moreover, the Moldovans took a new interest in Romania, especially when Moldavia's frontier with Romania opened following Ceauşescu's overthrow and people could move freely between Moldavia and Romania.[97]

In August 1991, Moldavia declared its independence of the Soviet Union and changed its name to Moldova. It did not, however, raise the issue of a reunification with Romania. While their emotional ties to the Romanian "motherland" remained strong, and while their visits to Romania were welcome, Moldovans did not want annexation and in fact criticized the Iliescu regime for its communist tendencies, its antidemocratic policies, and its delay in reform. Moldovan Jews in particular were wary of reunification. They worried about the long tradition of anti-Semitism before and during communist rule in Romania.[98] But there were Romanians who were anxious to move forward with reunification. In October 1990, some 15,000 Romanians marched through the streets of Bucharest when the Moldovan Republic's Gagauz minority called for separation. The demonstrating Romanians wanted the territorial integrity of Moldova preserved, and they urged closer Romanian ties with Moldova. *Vatra Românescă* was especially active in protests on behalf of the Moldovan resistance to Gagauz separatism.[99]

In the early 1990s, the future of Moldova was a source of tension in Romania's relations with Russia. President Boris Yeltsin's government did not want to see one of the former Soviet republics on Russia's frontier joined to another country. But Romanian president Iliescu was tempted to arouse popular support for his lackluster leadership by playing the nationalist card in policy toward Moldova. At the very least, he had to show some sympathy for the idea of reunification simply to assuage the radical chauvinists whose cooperation he needed in the Romanian Parliament, but he did not push the issue of reunification too hard. He did not want to complicate

Romanian–Russian relations and encourage Moscow to pressure Moldova to strengthen ties with Moscow at the expense of its sovereignty, a situation Moldovan president Mircea Snegur wanted to avoid at all cost.[100]

Trade

Another important issue in Romania's relations with Russia has been trade. Given the dilapidated condition of the Romanian economy and Romania's past dependence on imports of oil and natural gas from the Soviet Union, Iliescu wanted to expand Romanian trade with Russia, as well as with other former Soviet republics, especially neighboring Ukraine. He met with some success, and in early 1990, the new Romanian leadership got a pledge from the Kremlin to ship 390,000 tons of oil and 22 million cubic meters of natural gas daily to Romania. The Kremlin also agreed at that time that Romania might limit exports of meat and dairy products to the Soviet Union and use the scarce commodities at home. But given the unstable economic situation in Russia, the large expansion of Romanian–Russian trade Iliescu wanted is not likely to materialize in the near future.[101]

2. Relations with the West

Romanian relations with the West were also difficult after the collapse of the Ceauşescu regime. The new Romanian leadership was eager to strengthen ties with the West to obtain its economic and financial help in promoting Romania's economic recovery. But this was not easy. The West did not like the Iliescu government's repressive policies, the presence of so many former communists in positions of power, and its slowness in moving away from the old socialist economic order toward a free-market economy. In particular, West European countries and the United States complained to Romanian officials when the government interfered in the May 1990 parliamentary elections and manipulated the press. The Western powers also suspended aid to Romania, and the United States shunned the inauguration of President Iliescu in June 1990 to protest his use of the miners to break up an antigovernment demonstration in Bucharest.[102]

The West resumed aid to Romania in 1991, but it remained skeptical of Romania's commitment to a real break with the communist past. The post-communist government of President Iliescu never made public an account of the role and activities of the hated *Securitate,* and Iliescu acknowledged that the new Romanian intelligence services still employed roughly 4,000 officers of the old *Securitate*, though they were "screened." Under these circumstances, the West did not offer Bucharest the assistance programs given to other former Eastern bloc countries.[103]

Romania, like its neighbors, sought membership in the European Community, now known as the European Union (EU) and NATO. Romania's biggest obstacle to immediate entry into the EU has been the slowness of its movement toward a free-market economy and currency convertibility. By the end of 1994, Romania was in a second tier of countries expected to enter the Union by the end of the decade, after Poland, Hungary, and the Czech Republic, which are further along in the democratization of their economies. Entry into NATO, however, is not imminent, although Romania readily agreed to participate in the U.S.-sponsored Partnership for Peace developed in 1994, which allows the Central and East European countries to join NATO in military exercises, peacekeeping operations, and other activities.[104]

In the spring of 1991, there was an improvement in Romanian relations with the United States, partly in consequence of Romanian support in the Gulf War, a gesture Bucharest intended as fence mending with the West, especially with the Americans. Also, local elections held at the end of February 1991 seemed free and fair, producing, as they did, a setback for the ruling NSF. But Washington was concerned about the success of the anti-Hungarian and chauvinistic Romanian National Unity Party (RNU) in the Transylvanian city of Cluj, inhabited by a large Hungarian ethnic minority. Nevertheless, Washington acknowledged at the end of March 1992 that progress had been made in Romania toward the development of democratic government.[105] But Romania made little progress in its campaign to regain most-favored-nation status for its trade with the United States because of the Bush administration's deep suspicions about the sincerity of postcommunist Romania's commitment to democracy. For example, the administration was still concerned about lingering vestiges of the old authoritarian order and, along with some in Congress, could not forget the government-inspired rampage of the miners in Bucharest in mid-June 1991, which Bush had called "government-inspired vigilante violence."[106] Nor was the Bush administration inclined to dismiss the continuing influence of the state on the electronic media, which were used to discriminate against the political opposition, or reports that the Iliescu regime maintained a domestic political surveillance program.

President Clinton, however, has taken a more indulgent approach toward Romania. Washington could not afford to abandon Romania because of dissatisfaction with its domestic policies. Romania's geographic location made it a key player in the enforcement of the U.N. embargo against the rump state of Yugoslavia in the Bosnian civil war. As the disintegration of Yugoslavia continued to produce one crisis after another in the Balkans, American interest in relations with Bucharest remained important. Also influencing Clinton was Romania's loss of over $8 billion in trade in implementing the United Nations sanctions against Yugoslavia. Moreover, a State Department report on human-rights practices in different countries issued in February 1993 said that "respect for human rights continued to improve in 1992" and that Bucharest had "expressed willingness to comply with Western human rights norms."[107] Clinton therefore responded positively to Iliescu's protestations (during a visit to Washington in the spring of 1993 to participate in the celebrations opening the Holocaust memorial) that Romania had made progress toward the development of democracy and the introduction of a free market. Clinton was inclined to reward and to encourage these apparent liberal tendencies and eventually agreed to sign a new trade agreement with Romania reinstating the most-favored-nation treatment in Romanian–American trade it had lost in 1988 after Ceauşescu's violations of human rights. Normal trade relations were restored in mid-October 1993.[108]

Conclusions

The collapse of the Ceauşescu regime in December 1989 was sudden, precipitous, and, arguably, the most violent of all the anti-communist revolutions in the former Soviet bloc. The long-range consequences of the revolution of December 1989 are far from clear. Nevertheless, there are reasons to be optimistic about future democratic development. The first is the extraordinary electoral victory of Emil Constantinescu, who defeated President Iliescu, and swept anti-communist candidates into office at all levels in Romania, in November 1996 elections. The impact of this change cannot yet be measured.

Second, Romania wants to draw closer to the democratic West; it wants to join the European Union and to become a member of NATO. The West can and will encourage a gradual evolution of democratic government in Romania. Furthermore, other former communist countries, in particular, Poland, Hungary, and the Czech Republic, have made enormous progress toward democracy and can serve as a model for democratization in Romania. And the Romanian people themselves can, if they choose, push their country toward democracy. They can resist, as they have frequently done in recent years, the overbearing and intrusive behavior of would-be autocrats like Iliescu. And the more they become involved in the political system, the more difficult it will be to exclude them, especially if economic conditions improve and popular government thereby gains credibility with them.

10

Yugoslavia— Collapse and Disintegration

Before the present era, there were two Yugoslav states, the constitutional monarchy from 1918 until 1945, and the communist dictatorship from 1945 until 1991.[1] In April 1941, the Kingdom of Yugoslavia was invaded by Nazi Germany, partitioned, and occupied. During the war, an antifascist resistance organization known as the Partisans fought the Germans. Led by Josip Broz Tito, a Croatian Marxist, the Partisan movement consisted of people of different political beliefs but was always controlled by Marxists. In 1944, as German power in Central Europe collapsed, the Partisans were the dominant military and political force in the country.

Yugoslavia's "Patchwork-Quilt" Society

Yugoslavia had a patchwork-quilt society made up of large and small Slavic and non-Slavic ethnocultural groups that had very diverse historical backgrounds, levels of economic well-being, and cultural traditions. One can speak of both macro- and microethnic diversity.

1. Macro- and Microethnic Diversity

Macroethnic diversity refers to five large ethnic groups that had their own administrative units called republics in the post–World War II Yugoslav state: Slovenia, Croatia, Serbia, Macedonia, and Montenegro. In sharp contrast with these republics, Bosnia-Herzegovina had no large majority. Its population con-

Factboxes follow on pages 333–339.

sisted of Muslim Slavs, who comprised 43.7 percent of the total Bosnian population, Orthodox Christian Serbs, who comprised 31.4 percent, and Roman Catholic Croats, who comprised 17.3 percent.

Before the formation of the unified Yugoslav state in 1918, Slovenes, Croats, and Bosnians had been under Austro-Hungarian rule, while the peoples of east-central and southern Yugoslavia—Serbs, Montenegrins, and Macedonians—had been part of the Ottoman Turkish Empire. Austro-Hungarian rule was not liberal, but it was enlightened in the sense of bringing to Slovenia and Croatia western ideas on political individualism and economic progress. Turkish rule, by contrast, tended to be politically and culturally repressive and contributed little to the societal maturation and long-term well-being of the peoples who lived under it. The large ethnic groups also had different levels of economic well-being. Slovenes and Croats were the most economically developed, with a West European standard of living. Their economies consisted of industrial areas with a developed communications and transportation infrastructure. Serbia had an industrial sector but was primarily agricultural with a less modern infrastructure than that of the northern republics, a fact that helps to explain a somewhat lower level of overall economic development and standard of living. Montenegro and Macedonia were primarily agrarian. They had a far less modern infrastructure than Croatia and Slovenia and a much lower standard of living than the other republics. They were far more dependent than the other republics on economic and financial assistance from the central authorities in Belgrade.

Microdiversity refers to the fact that most of the republics that made up Yugoslavia had ethnocultural minorities. For example, Croatia, Bosnia-Herzegovina, Montenegro, and Macedonia had Serb minorities; Serbia had several minorities, notably, Hungarians and Albanians; and Macedonia had small Albanian, Serb, and Bulgarian minorities. Serb minorities seemed to live in almost all the republics, even though the Republic of Serbia was the largest macrogroup. Bosnia-Herzegovina was far more ethnically mixed than the rest of Yugoslavia. Most of the municipalities into which Bosnia-Herzegovina had been divided before the war had been multiethnic in one way or another. In those where one ethnic group had an absolute majority, it was never more than 70 percent. There were no absolutely ethnically homogeneous districts in Bosnia-Herzegovina. It was, more than any other Yugoslav republic, a reflection of the country's extraordinary ethnic diversity, with 5 percent of the republic's population giving their ethnic identification as "Yugoslav."[2]

2. Intergroup Relations

Majorities frequently allowed their historical prejudices against certain minorities to influence national policy, and discrimination was widespread in many republics. This discrimination, moreover, was fueled by the obsession of majorities to unify their society and strengthen their control over territory inhabited by minorities. Thus relations between the Croatian government in Zagreb and the

Serb minority living in the Krajina and Slavonian regions of Croatia, relations between the Serbian government in Belgrade and the Albanian minority in the Serbian province of Kosovo, and relations between the Macedonian government and its Albanian minority in the post–World War II era were at best difficult and at worst confrontational. Although the human rights of the minorities in the former Yugoslavia lacked adequate protection and some groups suffered indignities, they were consoled by their membership in the Yugoslav Federation, which offered them some protection against abuse by local governing authorities.

Furthermore, some consequences of Tito's industrialization of Yugoslavia in the 1950s, 1960s, and 1970s tended to heighten interethnic prejudices and increase the likelihood of interethnic conflict by widening the gap between the country and the city. Rural people, especially the youth, looking for a higher standard of living and a more exciting societal environment left farms in the countryside for jobs in factories and offices in growing urban areas. The people who were left in the rural areas of Yugoslavia in many instances were the elderly, the minimally educated, the culturally inbred (because of isolation from large population centers), and the most religiously oriented with the strongest superstitions, prejudices, and parochialism, which, incidentally, were nurtured by the Church. This rural culture sharply contrasted with the developing urban culture in Tito's Yugoslavia after World War II, which was multicultural, relatively liberal in terms of political and sociocultural and political values, and highly influenced by knowledge about life in Western Europe.[3]

Finally, interethnic differences in central and southern Yugoslavia were exacerbated by the way in which some areas were especially impoverished by government development policies from the early post–World War II years through the 1980s. In the Krajina region of Croatia, in the mountainous center of Bosnia-Herzegovina, in the Posavina (or "Serbian" corridor) in northern Bosnia-Herzegovina, in the Kosovo province of the Republic of Serbia, and in Macedonia, there was an economic decline that contrasted sharply with economic growth in Slovenia, Croatia, and parts of Serbia, such as the Vojvodina and the industrial region surrounding Belgrade. Dominated by extractive mineral and timber industries or military production, these regions were hit hard by uncertain demand abroad as well as at home and by policies favoring export-oriented manufactures that would bring needed hard currency into Yugoslavia. Per-capita income declined, and these regions became increasingly dependent on subsidies from the federation government in Belgrade. These subsidies declined in the late 1980s, when the Federation government began a liberalization of the country's economic life while trying to contain inflation. During the 1980s, unemployment rose far faster in these regions, and especially in Kosovo, than in the more developed parts of the country. By the end of the 1980s, economic deterioration was feeding interethnic prejudices, raising levels of interethnic anger, and increasing the likelihood of interethnic confrontation and conflict over frontiers and land ownership.[4]

3. Sources of National Unity

Having said all of the above, it is also true that many conditions encouraged Yugoslav unity and the development of a true Yugoslav nationality, which, at least temporarily, counteracted the country's ethnocultural centrifugalism. For example, the capital of the country, Belgrade, and to some extent other Yugoslav cities, such as Zagreb in Croatia and Sarajevo in Bosnia-Herzegovina, were cosmopolitan centers made up of people from different parts of the country who thought of themselves first as Yugoslavs and second, if at all, in terms of their specific ethnocultural origins. Many urban families were ethnically mixed, and people of different ethnic backgrounds coexisted peacefully throughout the post–World War II era.

The Yugoslav Communist Party was another unifying force. It always envisaged itself as the leader of all the peoples of Yugoslavia, for whom it wanted to build the socialist paradise. The party, called the League of Yugoslav Communists, paradoxically encouraged unity and loyalty to the central leadership by allowing a discreet decentralization to accommodate the nationalistic instincts of local party leaders. The league had "branches" of the party based in the different republics with substantial independence of the leadership in Belgrade in their control over local affairs. For all intents and purposes, there really were six Yugoslav Communist parties, and the use of the term "league" in the name of the national Communist Party was completely accurate. The Yugoslav national government allowed representation of the interests of the republics in national executive and legislative bodies. Republic governments enjoyed control over local economic development, subject to policy decisions made by the Communist Party leadership in Belgrade, in particular, Tito, as well as control over the media and the publication of school texts. Specific Yugoslav national institutions, such as the federal army and the federal banking system, which was responsible for maintaining the national currency and for helping to manage national economic development, had a vested interest in promoting and protecting a unified Yugoslav state and helped promote national unity.

The different large and small ethnic groups were knit together by an economic interdependence. Each republic had resources and markets essential to the material well-being of its neighbors. Indeed, the national economy depended upon a dense network of interrepublic trade. The country was bonded also by a shared pride in its heroic defense against the imperious Kremlin beginning in 1947; in Yugoslavia's growing political influence abroad, especially in the Third World, where it was recognized as a major international power with enormous economic and military influence; and in its impressive economic expansion in the 1960s and 1970s, which provided many Yugoslav citizens with a standard of living that compared favorably with that in other socialist countries.

Finally, propaganda and indoctrination helped to forge a modest cultural unity. While children learned about the history and culture of their own regions, they were taught shared traditions and values, especially the common purpose in the war against fascism. Finally, Yugoslav foreign policy in the Tito era gave Yugoslav citizens of all ethnocultural backgrounds a shared pride. Unlike most other countries in Central and Eastern Europe, Yugoslavia remained independent of the Soviet Union, developed many influential friends in the developing world, such as India and Cuba, and participated actively in many international organizations.[5]

Arguably the most important source of post–World War II Yugoslav national unity was Tito himself. With military power, communist ideology, and a forceful personality, Tito took control of Yugoslavia after World War II, preventing a restoration of monarchical rule. He ruled Yugoslavia until his death in 1980. In that period he built a new Yugoslav state committed to Marxist-Leninist ideology and the eventual achievement of communism; but he did so with due regard to the unique diversity of Yugoslav society, ingeniously accommodating it without sacrificing its unity. While insisting on political conformity and a Stalinist command economy, and while committed to the principle of a unified, centrally controlled administration of all of Yugoslavia, Tito allowed the large ethnic groups that dominated the six constituent republics that made up the Yugoslav Federation substantial political and administrative autonomy. Tito set up the Yugoslav Federation army to reflect the ethnic diversity of Yugoslav society. The army was divided along regional lines to assure that military personnel in the different republics were under the immediate command of people of their own ethnic background, although the officer corps everywhere was heavily dominated by Serbs.

The success of Tito's economic policies provided an underlying rationale for political and administrative unity. Many unique aspects of his socialist economy were to a degree successful in providing Yugoslavia with a higher standard of living than that in neighboring Balkan countries. For example, in the early 1950s, after having established Soviet-style state control over Yugoslav agriculture, Tito returned some farms to private ownership, thereby enhancing incentives that helped increase productivity. By the end of the 1980s, private-sector dominance of Yugoslav agriculture made Yugoslavia one of the few socialist countries without a serious food problem. In the 1960s, he also increased the autonomy of plant-level managers while curtailing the power of central administrators and planners and introduced a large measure of worker participation in the management of factories and farms. As in agriculture, these changes resulted in greater efficiency and expanded output. By the 1980s, Tito's Yugoslavia had become the seventh largest industrialized nation.[6]

Ironically, efforts to unify Yugoslavia over the long haul contributed to disunity. The Soviet-style federal system that Tito had introduced provided for the cultural autonomy of the constituent republics, which strengthened the ancient and deeply felt cultural identity of each of the Yugoslav peoples and the strong ethnic-based prejudices each had toward others. At the same time, Tito's federation provided for a strong central government, which denied republics the control over local affairs, especially in the economic sphere, they craved. Moreover, the industrialization and urbanization of Yugoslavia before and during the era of communist rule did not significantly diminish its societal diversity and in fact may have accentuated it by widening the gap between the developed republics in the north, such as Slovenia and Croatia, and the underdeveloped republics in the south, such as Macedonia, Montenegro, and the rural portions of Serbia and Bosnia-Herzegovina.[7]

Tito knew that the unity of his country largely depended on him and was concerned about the possibility of conflict and disintegration after he was gone. In a new constitution adopted in 1974, Tito made changes in the structure of the national government in Belgrade to provide the different ethnic groups additional means of reconciling disagreements once he was gone from the scene. The changes included a new executive leadership of nine people, one from each of the country's six constituent republics and two autonomous provinces, and one *ex officio* member. This executive elected a chair annually on a rotational basis, known as the president of Yugoslavia.[8]

But after Tito's death in 1980, the collective presidency he had set up in 1974 never really worked. It never became the consensus-building mechanism for policy making he intended it to be. Indeed, one authority aptly described the 1974 constitution as doing exactly the opposite of what was intended by ratifying the right of the *liberum veto* of the republics in the presidency. In the 1980s, it became just one more forum for the interethnic bickering that eventually paralyzed the presidency and precipitated the country's disintegration.[9] In these years, the republics divided over a variety of issues, including how much influence the central government in Belgrade should have on economic, fiscal, and monetary matters in the republics, in particular, how much or how little of the economic wealth of each republic should be redistributed to assure an equitable balance of wealth throughout the country.[10] The republics also differed over how fast or how slow Yugoslavia should alter its communist dictatorship in light of reforms going on in other communist-ruled countries in Eastern Europe and the Soviet Union.

The most serious interethnic disagreement, and the one that eventually would help precipitate the breakup of Yugoslavia in the early 1990s, was the enormous influence over national politics enjoyed by the Republic of Serbia. The capital of Yugoslavia, Belgrade, was also the capital of the Republic of Serbia. Before World War II, when Yugoslavia was a kingdom, the Yugoslav monarchy was Serb and the Yugoslav civilian and military bureaucracies were heavily populated by Serbs from Serbia and from other republics, especially Croatia. Indeed, Serb influence over the Yugoslav army was especially strong, because 70 percent of the army's officers had always been Serb.

After World War II, Tito tried to diminish the influence of Serbs. He was determined to prevent Yugoslavia from being dominated by one ethnic group.

He redrew Yugoslavia's prewar administrative boundary lines, allocating Serb population to Croatia, Bosnia-Herzegovina, and Macedonia to reduce the size of Serbia's population. He further diluted Serb power by placing two large ethnic minority regions within the newly defined Republic of Serbia: a Hungarian minority in the northern Serbian province of Vojvodina, and Albanians in the south Serbian province of Kosovo. These minorities were guaranteed administrative autonomy.[11]

This dispersion of Serbs and the location of large non-Serb populations within the Republic of Serbia, however, backfired. Instead of diminishing Serb influence, dispersion encouraged an expansion of it by stimulating Serb nationalism in the form of an increasingly compulsive concern about the well-being of Serbs living in Croatia and Bosnia-Herzegovina, which had the largest Serb populations outside Serbia. For all this, some influential Serb intellectuals considered Tito's Yugoslavia "anti-Serb." Serb nationalism became a divisive force in Yugoslav national life.[12]

4. Divisive Impact of Serb Nationalism

With the death of Tito and a growing interest on the part of other republics—especially the more economically developed republics of Slovenia and Croatia, which contributed heavily to the federation budget—in autonomy and eventually independence of Yugoslavia in the late 1980s and early 1990s, the fear grew in Serbia that Serb minorities in Croatia, Bosnia-Herzegovina, and elsewhere were at risk. This fear, nurtured by the Serb Orthodox Church, which saw itself as the guardian of Serb culture and the historical conscience of the Serb people and which blessed the notion that all Serbs should live in a common Serb home under a Serb leader and an all-Serb government, gave rise to an exaggerated sense of persecution and victimization by outsiders going back centuries and became a powerful political force in Serbia. Indeed, Serbs have always had a "pathological image of national suffering," believing that they suffered more than other Yugoslav groups in the first and second world wars and that the outside world never really understood or sympathized with them.[13]

Ascendancy of Slobodan Milošević

Slobodan Milošević, the head of the Serbian branch of the Yugoslav League of Communists in the 1980s, made Serb nationalism his cause. Milošević, elected president of Serbia in 1987,[14] was a rabid nationalist and, as one writer put it, not an attractive man: "He is reclusive, stubborn, vindictive, narrow-minded, and covetous of absolute power."[15] Milošević governed Serbia in a neo-Stalinistic manner. He skillfully manipulated Serbia's mass media, which were the chief source of information for most Serbians, who generally trusted the media and believed what was told them. Milošević harassed political critics and opponents and opposed radical economic reform, the introduction of multiparty pluralism, and administrative decentralization to allow Serbia's large Hungarian and Albanian minorities control over their local affairs.[16]

Milošević's authoritarian and centralizing tendencies inside Serbia initially had popular support, undoubtedly because they were cloaked in a mantle of Serb nationalism. In elections for the Serbian Republic Parliament in early December 1990, Milošević's Communist Party won a comfortable majority, taking 194 out of 250 seats. This majority quickly reelected Milošević as president of the Serbian Republic.[17]

Kosovo

A troublesome aspect of Serb nationalism artfully exploited by Milošević to strengthen his popular appeal involved the large Albanian minority in the province of Kosovo, where Albanians outnumbered Serbs and other ethnic groups nine to one. Serbia considered Kosovo, where the ancient Serb state had been defeated by the Ottoman Turks in 1389, inaugurating a long and brutal occupation of Serbian territory for almost 500 years, as sacrosanct. Between 1987 and 1989, Milošević used the Serbian media to generate a strong Serb hatred of Albanians, which he used to justify a harsh anti-Albanian policy calculated to enhance his popularity.[18] To discourage a growing Albanian interest in self-government and possibly separation from Serbia, in 1989 Milošević deprived Kosovo of the autonomy guaranteed by the 1974 Yugoslav federal constitution, ostensibly to protect Serbs and other minorities from Albanian separatists who were agitating for independence. He pursued a policy of cultural assimilation, involving the imposition of Serbo-Croatian as the official language of Kosovo and the adoption of the Cyrillic alphabet in place of the Latin. With Kosovo under the direct rule of Belgrade, Milošević proceeded to harass Albanian nationalists who advocated the separation of Kosovo from the Serbian Republic, arresting and imprisoning them. In September 1990, a new Serbian constitution formally placed Kosovo directly under the control of Belgrade.[19]

In early 1990, Albanians took to the streets to protest their loss of autonomy. Albanian students and workers also protested against political trials, police brutality, and the detention of political prisoners. They demanded an end to "anti-Albanian" discrimination by the Serbian government, free elections, the lifting of Communist Party censorship of the media, the release of political prisoners, the right to form political associations, and the resignation of hard-line party and government administrators in the province.[20]

Albanian nationalists also formed an antigovernment political organization called the League of Democrats of Kosovo. Its leader, Ibrahim Rugova, was an Albanian intellectual. The league had 300,000 supporters, including former members of the Kosovo branch of the Yugoslav Communist Party angered by Belgrade's denial of Kosovo's administrative autonomy. It called for a multiparty system and an independent judiciary. The league struck many Serbs in

Kosovo as a spearhead for the campaign to separate Kosovo from the Republic of Serbia.[21]

Milošević condemned the league, saying its activity vindicated his anti-Albanian policy. Throughout 1990, he encouraged the formation of vigilante groups made up of radical Serb nationalists to go to Kosovo and help the small and besieged Serb minority fight against the Albanian separatists. He also encouraged the return of some 400,000 Serbs and Montenegrins who had fled since World War II because of Albanian violence, damage to property, and discrimination. In July, the Milošević regime went even further and placed the local provincial government of Kosovo in Priština directly under Serbian authority.[22] By the end of 1990, the province was in the midst of a mini–civil war that deeply disturbed other republics, especially Slovenia, which saw in Kosovo's struggle a reflection of its own aspirations for territorial sovereignty and the right of secession from Yugoslavia. Events in Kosovo seemed to vindicate the suspicion of other Yugoslav peoples that Milošević was ready to do anything to protect Serb interests everywhere. "Kosovo" became a code word throughout Yugoslavia, and especially Slovenia, for Milošević's willingness to expand Serb influence anywhere there were Serb minorities. Slovenia and, subsequently, other Yugoslav republics were determined to oppose further "Serbization" of the Titoist state as a means of preserving its fragile unity.[23]

Vojvodina and Montenegro

Milošević also expanded his influence in the northern province of Vojvodina, inhabited by a large Hungarian minority, and in Montenegro, where there was a lot of popular hostility to the republic government because of economic distress.[24] In 1988, he encouraged nationalist rallies attended by agitators from Serb communities elsewhere in Yugoslavia. He wanted to weaken political leaders in those areas by mobilizing popular hostility toward them and to replace them with figures personally loyal to him. By early 1989, the governments in Vojvodina and Montenegro were completely under his influence. They proceeded throughout 1989 to purge politicians critical of Milošević.[25]

Milošević's control of these areas greatly enhanced his political power in the Yugoslav state. It brought him a step closer to the fulfillment of his dream of a "greater Serbia" encompassing all the Serbs living in the Yugoslav Federation. In amendments to the Serbian constitution in March 1989, the concept of Serb national sovereignty was broadened to include the right to represent Serb communities in other Yugoslav republics. This behavior alarmed leaders of republics with Serb minorities and increased their determination to oppose a Yugoslav state dominated by Milošević.[26]

Milošević tried to use the Serbian Republic's influence in Yugoslavia to fulfill his dream of a "greater Serbia." He opposed reforms, such as the transformation of the Titoist state into a confederation, sought by other republics, above all Slovenia and Croatia. He was afraid that a confederation would undermine

Yugoslav unity along with his own influence and that of Serbia. He soon provoked a conflict with Slovenia and Croatia, which were determined to transform Yugoslavia or to secede.[27]

Slovenia and Croatia Seek Autonomy and Independence

In February 1989, the Slovenian Communist Party, already the most politically tolerant of the republic party organizations in Yugoslavia, responded to popular pressure (knowing that resistance to it would have severely compromised its power) and, inspired by Soviet perestroika and similar reforms in Poland and Hungary beginning in the late 1980s, allowed the formal establishment of new political organizations to compete in republic parliamentary elections. The Slovenian party also relaxed censorship.[28] Another major political reform occurred in the fall of 1989, when the Slovenian Assembly amended the Slovenian constitution to allow free, open, and competitive parliamentary elections. The Assembly also adopted a new electoral law guaranteeing freedom of expression and scheduled parliamentary elections for April 1990.[29]

On April 8, 1990, in Slovenia's first free and competitive parliamentary elections since the beginning of communist rule after World War II, a coalition of democratic groups known as DEMOS won a majority of seats in two of the three chambers of the national Parliament. DEMOS was not only liberal but also nationalist and, along with newly elected President Milan Kučan, formerly president of the League of Communists and a moderate nationalist, wanted a major decentralization of federation authority that would recognize, as he put it, the "political and economic sovereignty of each of Yugoslavia's six republics."[30]

Meanwhile, communist leaders in Croatia, though somewhat less indulgent of pluralistic tendencies than the Slovenes, were also intrigued by the scope of new reforms in the Soviet Union under Gorbachev and the gradual liberalization of the political environment in Poland and Hungary. With a fine instinct for self-preservation, they persuaded the party congress in Zagreb in December 1989 to hold free and open parliamentary elections with other political groups.[31] In these elections, held on April 22, 1990, the Croatian Democratic Union led by Franjo Tudjman won two-thirds of the seats in the Zagreb legislature, while the communists won only 18 seats. Tudjman and his followers campaigned for Croatian autonomy in a decentralized Yugoslav state in which Croatia would have complete control over its internal affairs. Subsequently, Tudjman was elected president of Croatia, the first noncommunist chief executive of a Yugoslav republic, confirming popular support not only for political liberalization but also for administrative independence of Belgrade.[32]

The Slovenian and Croatian drive for autonomy and decentralization was rooted in the belief that Tito's Yugoslav Federation over the years had siphoned off some of their wealth for the benefit of the less developed republics in the south of the country. Slovenia complained that it had been subsidizing Yugoslavia through heavy taxes that provided 27 percent of the Yugoslav national budget with almost nothing in return for this loss of wealth. Moreover, Slovenian leaders were outraged by a Serbian Republic decision to "borrow" $1 billion from the Yugoslav national bank. Slovenians had other grievances against the Federation. For example, they resented efforts by the central authorities to encourage increased use of the Serbo-Croatian language in Slovenian schools as part of a campaign to make it a truly national language by diminishing the use of local languages in public institutions.[33]

Finally, Slovenia and Croatia resented the historic Serb influence over the Yugoslav bureaucracy, army, and central party organs. They feared Milošević's calls for the protection of Serb peoples living outside of Serbia, as well as his strong opposition to their efforts to move away from communism. They deeply distrusted his calls to preserve Tito's Yugoslavia, which meant the preservation of orthodox Soviet-style communist rule in and substantial central influence over republic-level political and economic development. In the post-Tito years, Slovenian and Croatian communist leaders, looking to the future of their party and their own personal political power, longed for the freedom to follow separate and independent paths of development, with more internal reform of the kind beginning to take place elsewhere in the region and in the Soviet Union and with more freedom from, almost independence of, the Yugoslav Federation government in Belgrade.[34]

1. Serbia Opposes Political and Administrative Reform

In 1989 and early 1990, Milošević opposed liberalization on the republic and central levels of Yugoslav administration. He feared that democratization and decentralization would undermine the unity of the Titoist state and Serbia's influence over it. Milošević also believed that the kind of loose confederation of Yugoslav republics sought by Slovenia and Croatia, by weakening republic links with the central authorities in Belgrade, would encourage nationalistic leaders of republics with large Serb minorities, such as Croatia, Bosnia-Herzegovina, and Macedonia, to discriminate against Serb minorities.[35]

Something of a showdown occurred at the Fourteenth Congress of the League of Yugoslav Communists held in January 1990. Serbia proposed to the other republics that the Yugoslav central government's authority over the economy and minority rights be strengthened, not weakened. Milošević also wanted to guarantee Yugoslavia's commitment to socialism and to Communist Party dominance. While Slovenian and Croatian representatives won the support of a majority of delegates from other republics for a limited democratization of the national Yugoslav government involving the legalization of other political parties and a renunciation of the League's historical monopoly of power,[36] they failed to get League approval of decentralization, largely in consequence of the Serbian refusal to transfer Federation control of fiscal, monetary, and defense matters to the republics. The failure of the Fourteenth Congress to resolve this important constitutional issue severely weakened the party's influence and authority, and to that extent undermined the country's unity and cohesion.[37]

Despite the setback at the January League congress, Slovenian and Croatian leaders were still willing to work with other republic leaders throughout 1990 and 1991 to find a way of decentralizing the Federation.[38] The two northern republics had valuable economic links to other republics and realized that, until their exports were competitive in the West, the largest market would remain the rest of Yugoslavia, especially Serbia. But losing hope of ever transforming Yugoslavia into a confederation because of Serbia's near hysterical opposition to any plan other than a recentralized federation, Slovenia and Croatia steadily moved toward secession from Yugoslavia.[39]

2. Slovenia Becomes Independent

Slovenians had accepted membership in the Yugoslav Federation voluntarily in 1943 and argued in the late 1980s that they had the right to withdraw from it. In July 1990, the Slovenian Assembly made a formal declaration of sovereignty, asserting that Slovenia's legislation henceforth would supersede any conflicting Yugoslav laws. Although the Slovenians subsequently drew back from this position, hoping that ongoing discussions with other republics would lead to an agreement to transform Yugoslavia into a confederation that would allow them all a maximum amount of independence in the management of their local affairs, they were in fact well on the way toward complete independence given the unrelenting opposition of Serbia and the lack of any real sympathy in the West for their autonomist aspirations.[40] In October 1990, the Slovenian Parliament adopted a constitutional law partially or completely annulling thirty federal laws in the areas of the economy, politics, and defense. Slovenia was now almost legally independent of the Yugoslav Federation. In a plebiscite held on December 23, 1990, 88 percent of voters opted for an independent and sovereign Slovenia.[41]

With no hope of gaining the administrative autonomy it wanted and little fear that going it alone would cause much economic suffering because of its already extensive commercial ties to Western countries, on June 25, 1991, the government in Ljubljana formally seceded from Yugoslavia. The Slovenian Parliament enacted constitutional changes setting up Slovene control over the local banking system, the patent office, and the collection of customs duties on Slovenia's frontier with Austria.[42]

Even after that date, President Kučan of Slovenia, however, still left the door slightly ajar for compromise. He proposed again that if the Federation government, which really meant Serbian President Milošević, would assure Slovenia the autonomy it wanted in local affairs and would take steps to prevent Serbian aggrandizement, starting with a reversal of repressive Serbian policy toward Kosovo and hostile Serb policies toward the republics of Croatia and Bosnia-Herzegovina, Slovenia would preserve administrative links to the Federation. The Republic of Serbia dismissed the Slovenian overture, closing the door to a compromise that might have kept Slovenia in Yugoslavia.[43]

The Federation government declared the Slovenian independence illegal. The Federation army high command, influenced by the Serbian Republic leadership, decided to force a reversal of Slovenian independence.[44] In June 1991, acting on its own rather than on orders from the Federation presidency, it bombed airports at Ljubljana and Maribor and tried to reimpose Belgrade's control of customs posts on the Slovenian–Austrian frontier. For about ten days there was fierce fighting between Federation forces and the Slovene national guard. But this police action, of questionable legality, did not go well. The unified and well-armed Slovenians effectively defeated the Yugoslav army, which was too far from its power base in Serbia to deal an effective blow against the Slovenians, who had the advantage of fighting on their home territory. But there were also other reasons why the Yugoslav army failed in Slovenia. It was quite unprepared, with soldiers who had been recruited to fight in Slovenia with only one month of service and training. Moreover, some Yugoslav soldiers did not even know why they were in Slovenia and why Slovenes had become their enemy. Federation forces retreated in defeat from Slovenia.[45]

The coercion of Slovenia signalled the primacy of the battlefield over the roundtable as a means of resolving interrepublic differences over constitutional change in the postcommunist era. At its worst, the use of federal forces against Slovenia encouraged the development of a stubborn fanatical nationalism in the republics that reinforced their determination to declare sovereignty and separate from Yugoslavia. In succeeding months, hardened in its determination to separate from Yugoslavia, Slovenia effectively cut all administrative ties to Belgrade. In April 1992, Slovenia received American and West European recognition of its independence.

3. Croatia Becomes Independent

Croatia's break with Yugoslavia began on February 21, 1991, when its Parliament gave the government veto power over federal laws. The Parliament also voted to restore the flag and coat of arms used by the Croatian fascist government in World War II as symbols of its new independence. It renamed streets in Zagreb to honor precommunist conservative Croatian patriots, introduced an oath of loyalty to the Croatian state for all state employees, and required use of the Latin script of the Serbo-Croatian language as opposed to the Cyrillic, which was used elsewhere in Tito's Yugoslavia and was mandatory in all official proceedings. Like Slovenia, however, Croatia left the door open to compromise, reiterating that it would stay in Yugoslavia if the federation were transformed into a loose association of sovereign republics with a capital other than Belgrade to discourage Serbian influence over the new system. Nothing ever came of this offer, and on May 19, Croatians voted overwhelmingly in a referendum in favor of separation from Yugoslavia. At the end of June 1991, the Croatian government declared independence of the Yugoslav Federation.[46]

Croatia's Serb Minority Opposes Independence

Croatia had a special problem separating from Yugoslavia. A large portion of Croatia's Serb minority of about 600,000 people, who constituted 12 percent of the total population of the republic and lived around the south Croatian city of Knin in what was known as the Krajina region, opposed Croatian independence of Yugoslavia. The Krajina Serbs boycotted the May 19 referendum. Impoverished and susceptible to Milošević's radical Serb nationalist preaching in a way that was not true of the small number of assimilated and educated Serbs living in Croatia's large urban centers, in particular Zagreb, Serbs in the Krajina worried that an independent Croatian republic, inspired by old prejudices, would try to repress their culture.[47]

The Krajina Serbs had reason to fear an independent Croatian government. Serbs in southern Croatia believed that during World War II Croatian fascists, known as the Ustaše, had mercilessly tried to exterminate them in an effort to "cleanse" Croatian territory of non-Croat peoples such as Serbs, Jews, Gypsies, Muslims, and others. Memory of this experience was still fresh more than forty years after the end of World War II, and each group could not forgive the outrages of the other.[48]

Further strengthening Serb fears of mistreatment in an independent Croatian state was a decision by the newly elected Parliament in Zagreb to revoke the provision of the Croatian Constitution that required a two-thirds majority for a change in laws concerning the republic's ethnic minorities. Moreover, the revocation occurred as a result of a simple majority, further undermining the confidence of the Krajina Serbs and other minorities in the readiness of the Zagreb government to protect their interests.[49] Also contributing to Serb fears about the future was a new Croatian Constitution adopted in December 1990 containing a forceful expression of Croatian nationalism. The repetition of "Croatian nation" so many times and the provision that the official language and script were the Croatian language and Latin script implied future cultural annihilation to the hypersensitive Serb minority.[50] Croatian Serbs condemned this document, calling it an attack on their national identity saying that the new constitution treated them as second-class citizens. They were especially hostile to the provision that allowed Croatia to secede from Yugoslavia.[51]

Tudjman inadvertently helped arouse Serb fears of him and his government by "off-the-cuff remarks" that seemed to suggest a strong personal prejudice against people who were not Croat. During the campaign leading to the April 1990 parliamentary elections, he is reported to have said "I am doubly happy that my wife is neither a Serb nor a Jew!"[52]

In May 1990, local Serb political leaders, fearing the inevitability of Croatia's separation from Yugoslavia, began their own separatist movement and spoke of annexation to the Republic of Serbia. At the end of July, Jovan Rašković, the head of the Serbian Democratic Party in the Krajina, proposed a referendum on annexation. The Croatian government vigorously opposed the referendum, convinced that if it were held, it would result in an overwhelming vote by the Krajina Serbs for separation, independence, and annexation to Serbia. Despite Zagreb's opposition, the referendum was held in August 1990, with 99 percent of the Serb population in the Krajina voting for administrative autonomy. As the Croatian government continued to oppose administrative autonomy for the Serb minority, some Serbs resorted to violence. In August 1990, Serbs living in and around the town of Knin started blocking rail communication, obstructing highway traffic with timber beams, roughing up journalists and travelers, scaring off foreign tourists vacationing along Croatia's Adriatic coast, and raiding local police stations for arms and ammunition. They were trying to harass the authorities in Zagreb into granting them administrative autonomy.[53]

Meanwhile, the self-styled Serb National Council, a local political organization claiming erroneously to speak for all Serbs living in Croatia, formally declared the territory of the Krajina autonomous of the Croatian Republic government. It is worth noting that Croatian Serbs outside the Krajina did not sympathize with their brethren in the Krajina, recognizing that rebellion in the Krajina would mean nothing but trouble for them.[54]

Milošević and the Krajina Serbs

Serbia's President Milošević was concerned about the fate of Serbs living in the Krajina, given the known Croat prejudice against them, and sympathized with their campaign for autonomy and their aspirations for annexation to the Republic of Serbia. The government-controlled media in the Serbian Republic vilified Tudjman, calling him a reincarnated Ustaša warrior. Belgrade intentionally fed local Serb fear of a Croatian genocide against the Serb minority.[55] Encouraging the Serb communities in southern Croatia to throw over Croatian rule, on March 16, 1991, Milošević observed that "it is the legitimate right and the interest of the Serb people to live in one state" and the following day proclaimed the Krajina a "Serbian autonomous region." At the same time, the nationalist leadership of Krajina Serbs declared that Croatian laws not in accord with the Federation Constitution were invalid and announced their own intention of separation from Croatia.[56]

In late July 1991, Serbian Republic officials publicly acknowledged that they were sending medicine, communications gear, clothing, and food, as well as cash, to the Serb minority. And while these officials insisted that the republic was not sending weapons, they did say that they had no objection to the Krajina Serbs using donated money to buy weapons. In addition, if Croatia became independent of Yugoslavia, the Serbian Republic government said it would demand a Croatian transfer of territory inhabited by Serbs to Serbia.[57] Milošević also surreptitiously supported the training and arming in Serbia of military formations operating in the Krajina led by Serb ultranationalist radicals such as Vojislav Šešelj and Željko Raznjatović, who went by the name of Arkan. These Serb paramilitary forces fought Croatian authority and behaved with brutality that anticipated the ethnic-cleansing policies of the Bosnian Serb insurgents against the Muslim people in Bosnia-Herzegovina in early 1992. The followers of Arkan, called Arkanovići, came from the dregs of Serbian society. They were the victims of growing economic hardship, unemployed, impoverished, and desperate to express their anger. They vented their prejudices and hostilities on Croats in the Serb communities of southern Croatia. It is argued that Arkan and his followers did not reflect the attitudes and beliefs of the majority of Serbs living permanently in Croatia. Although these informal paramilitary organizations were independent of Milošević, they well served his efforts to facilitate the liberation of the Krajina Serbs from Croatian rule.[58]

Croatia Loses Control over Its Serb Communities

As the conflict between the Croatian government in Zagreb and the Serb communities in the Krajina and Slavonia escalated, the Yugoslav army intervened to keep Croatian forces from restoring Zagreb's authority over Knin and other areas controlled by the republic's Serb minority.[59] Fighting between Federation forces and local Serb paramilitary groups on the one hand and Croatian Republic forces soon spread from Glina to Vukovar and Vinkovici along the Sava River toward Zagreb and seemed directed at forcing Tudjman's government to reverse its move toward separation from the Federation. In the latter part of 1991, the Yugoslav army bombed Zagreb. In October and November 1991, Yugoslav naval and land forces and Croatian Serb "irregulars" laid siege to Dubrovnik in an attempt to impose Serbian control over the city and make it the western terminus of a corridor of territory, mostly inhabited by Serbs, extending from Vukovar in the northeast to the Adriatic, even though Dubrovnik was 90 percent Croat. By the end of 1991, Croatia had lost control of 20 percent of its territory in the south, stretching from eastern Slavonia westward through the Krajina and southward along the Dalmatian coast almost to Dubrovnik, to Serb paramilitary forces and the Yugoslav army supporting them.[60]

The Federation Army's Role in Croatia

The initiative for this aggressive military campaign to help the Serb minority in the Krajina and reverse Croatian separatism seems to have come primarily from the Yugoslav army leadership, with the tacit approval of the Federation government in Belgrade and of Milošević. The army leadership regretted the collapse of Yugoslav unity and the erosion of communist rule, the two props on which its power and material well-being had rested throughout the Tito era. Only a unified Yugoslavia that included the wealthy northern republics could provide the army with the enormous resources it needed to protect the country and preserve its privileged and influential position. The army thus had a vested interest in keeping Yugoslavia united under the leadership of a strong central government in Belgrade. Not surprisingly, the army found support from the Republic of Serbia, which shared its commitment to a unified Yugoslav state.[61]

The army also regretted the erosion of communist rule, which more than any other aspect of the Titoist state had kept the country together and promoted its prosperity, as well as that of the army. But it was also true that the army leadership conducted its campaigns against both Slovenia and Croatia for ideological reasons. In the long period of Tito's rule, the army had been thoroughly indoctrinated with Marxist-Leninist teachings. The army leadership had little sympathy for wasteful and greed-motivated capitalism, especially when it was accompanied by pluralistic democracy, which would encourage diversity and disunity.[62]

Finally, the Yugoslav army was to a degree an instrument of Serb nationalism. At the beginning of the 1990s, a few high-ranking officers in leadership positions, such as General Ratko Mladić, who was in charge of the Federation forces fighting in the Krajina, were fanatical Serb nationalists. Others in the army leadership, in particular General Blagoje Adzić, who became chief of staff in the autumn of 1989, were unabashed Serb nationalists ready to use the army to help the cause of beleaguered Serb minorities in Croatia and Bosnia-Herzegovina.[63] Mladić, Adzić, and other similarly inclined officers, especially with family ties to Serb communities outside the Serbian Republic, had close contacts with Milošević and enjoyed his support. Milošević wanted to protect his kinsmen living in other parts of Yugoslavia against perceived local tyrannies but could do so legally only through the Federation, which had the constitutional responsibility for dealing with republic-level discrimination against minorities when it chose to do so (there was little Federation complaint against Milošević's discriminatory behavior toward the Albanian minority in Kosovo).[64]

Impact of War on Croatia

The Serb insurrection in the Krajina and Slavonia tended to strengthen the Tudjman regime's authoritarian political tendencies. The attempt of Croatian Serbs to establish their own independent republic in the Krajina provided Tudjman with a pretext to intensify government control over the media, especially independent newspapers, critical of his policies. Journalists were harassed and journals and newspapers closed down. The University of Zagreb also did not escape Tudjman's vendetta against people who disagreed with him. The regime dismissed faculty and administrators for showing the slightest evidence of multiethnic views and nostalgia for the old Yugoslavia.[65]

The war in the Krajina also hurt the Croatian economy and slowed market reforms. The Croatian military campaign in the Krajina and along the Dalmatian coast in 1991 destroyed about 40 percent of the country's economic capacity. The infrastructure in the war zone was badly hit, with about 38 percent of the total road network made unusable by the fighting. Dozens of important bridges were destroyed, and severe damage was inflicted on the port facilities at Dubrovnik, Šibenik, and Zadar. Beyond that, the Croatian tourist industry along the Adriatic, which had been the country's biggest source of foreign currency, lost about 90 percent of its business in 1991 and did not fare much better in 1992, though in 1993 and 1994 foreign tourists started returning to the coastal resorts.[66]

As a result of the expense of producing and purchasing military equipment, Zagreb had spent, according to one estimate, about $250 million on weapons by the end of 1992. Almost 700,000 refugees, half of whom were Croats who fled Serb-controlled areas in the Krajina, and most of the remainder were Muslim refugees from Bosnia-Herzegovina, caused additional stress on the Croatian economy. To meet the escalating costs of housing, feeding, and caring for these people, the Zagreb government printed money, which fueled inflation, reaching 250 percent in early 1993 and further depressing real income and living standards.[67]

On the other hand, the war led to a strengthening of the Croatian army. Massive defections of Croat officers and enlisted men from the Yugoslav army, who had valuable technical expertise that enabled them to manage the latest weaponry, joined Croatia's National Guard and provided the republic with the nucleus of a new, modern, and efficient military organization, enabling Tudjman within a few years to turn the tide against the Serb side, restore Croatian authority in Slavonia and Krajina, and put Milošević and the Bosnian Serb insurgents on the defensive. The war helped the fledgling Croatian military in still another way. It provided Croatia with the opportunity to acquire possession of weapons from the huge Yugoslav arsenals built during the Tito era.[68]

4. Reactions of the West

There was no coherent Western response to the independence movements in Slovenia and Croatia. On the one hand, the European Community (EC), now called the European Union (EU), wanted to protect its security, was concerned about violations of the Helsinki principles in the Serbian–Croatian conflict over the Krajina, and, at least initially, was committed to the preservation of Yugoslavia's territorial integrity. On the other hand, the EC and the United States were hampered in the development of policy toward the precipitous disintegration of the Yugoslav state during 1991 by their preoccupation with events elsewhere, in particular, the reunification of Germany, the outbreak of the Persian Gulf War, and the rapidly deteriorating political situation inside the Soviet Union, climaxed by its disintegration at the end of 1991. Moreover, the Western powers considered the march to independence of the Yugoslav republics an internal Yugoslav affair that the Yugoslav peoples should address. Eventually, the West looked to the United Nations to restore and maintain peace, charging it with one of the most difficult international responsibilities it has had since its founding.[69]

The European Community

The EC responded promptly to the fighting in Slovenia, determined to end it as soon as possible to avoid the explosion of a refugee problem on the Slovenian frontier with Austria and Italy and to prevent the conflict from spreading. In early July, an EC-sponsored conference at Brioni produced an agreement calling for an immediate cease-fire and a three-month moratorium on Slovenian independence of Yugoslavia, to be accompanied by a complete withdrawal of Yugoslav forces. President Kučan accept the Brioni Agreement because in reality it provided a clear track to independence should Slovenia want it, which it now did. The Yugoslav military leadership also accepted it in order to quit Slovenia, given the failure to achieve its military and political objectives. Moreover, trouble in the Krajina was imminent, and the army was needed there to help the Serb minority defend itself against the wrath of Zagreb.[70]

In the latter half of 1991, however, the EC was much less successful in Croatia than it had been in Slovenia. EC diplomats proposed conferences and cease-fires to end the fighting in the Krajina. Invariably they were broken by Federation forces and their Krajina Serb allies. Blaming the Serbian Republic for the continued warfare in Croatia, Chancellor Kohl of Germany warned the Milošević leadership in August 1991 that there would be no economic aid to Yugoslavia if the right to self-determination was crushed by tanks. The war continued, leading the EC to invite leaders of the warring parties to a peace conference in September 1991 at the Hague. EC officials came forward with a compromise to end the fighting in Croatia: the Yugoslav state would remain intact, as Serbia wanted, but it would be transformed into a very loose confederation of quasi-independent republics, as sought by Slovenia, Croatia, and other republics.[71]

But this compromise pleased nobody in Yugoslavia and nothing came of it. President Kučan of Slovenia said his republic was not interested in any compromise because it was no longer part of Yugoslavia. President Tudjman of Croatia, however, said he might accept the compromise if Yugoslav troops were withdrawn from the Krajina. Milošević condemned the compromise outright, insisting that Serbia could not agree to an alteration of Yugoslavia's centralized political system.[72]

In September 1991, to break this stalemate, the EC imposed sanctions on the Yugoslav Federation government. Hoping to induce a withdrawal of its forces from Croatia, the EC froze arms sales and financial aid to Yugoslavia, suspended a 1980 trade and cooperation agreement with Yugoslavia, imposed new limits on imports of Yugoslav textiles, terminated GATT benefits, and excluded Yugoslavia from participation in an economic recovery program for Eastern Europe backed by twenty-four countries.[73]

These gestures, however, did not stop the fighting. Moreover, following the August 1991 anti-Gorbachev coup, there was less worry in Western Europe, particularly in Germany, about a possibility that the Soviet Union might support the Yugoslav army's war against Croatia to preserve a unified, centralized Yugoslav state under the influence of the left-leaning Milošević. Eventually the EC gave up hope of keeping Yugoslavia together and began to consider recognition of the independence of Slovenia, Croatia, Macedonia, and Bosnia-Herzegovina. But EC members were divided on whether to recognize the independence of the breakaway Yugoslav republics now or later.[74]

Germany

With historical and cultural links to Slovenia and Croatia, Germany favored immediate international recognition of their independence if they could demonstrate effective control over their territories, which, of course, they could. At the same time, the German government was annoyed by the Yugoslav government's aggressive behavior toward these republics and its indifference to German attempts to promote peace. German leaders also believed that early recognition of Slovenia and Croatia would help the cause of democratic development in the Balkans, since both of the republics had moved firmly away from communism. Moreover, powerful German Catholic politicians, sympathetic to the large Catholic populations of Slovenia and Croatia, encouraged Kohl to give immediate recognition. Kohl was determined to go ahead with unilateral recognition of Croatia and Slovenia, asserting that German recognition would come before Christmas 1991. He was as good as his word. Germany formally announced recognition of Slovenia and Croatia on December 24, 1991.[75]

Germany's unilateral recognition of Croatia's independence was precipitous in the extreme. The Germans ignored the criteria for recognizing the independence of former Yugoslav republics set forth by the EC's Badinter Commission of international jurists, in particular, acceptance of the principles of democratic rule, human rights, and inviolable borders. In effect, Germany gave President

Tudjman's government recognition without requiring Zagreb to guarantee fair and equitable treatment of its Serb minority, without requiring it to pledge that it would not seek to expand its existing territory at the expense of other republics, and without requiring it to swear allegiance to the concept of liberal democracy and respect for the human rights of all its citizens. The Germans apparently ignored or gave no credence to Tudjman's frequent assertions that Croatia's true boundaries included parts of Bosnian territory.[76]

Britain, France, and Spain

Other members of the EC, notably, Spain, France, and Britain, were more circumspect than the Germans and favored a postponement of recognition. Apart from wanting to salvage Yugoslav unity and discourage the accentuation of growing regional particularism and separatism, Britain and France favored a delay of Western recognition also because of alleged human-rights violations by the Zagreb government. They were inclined to take more seriously than the Germans the recommendation that, prior to receiving international recognition of its independence, Croatia should provide constitutional guarantees of human and minority rights.[77] The British and French also suspected that Germany's readiness to recognize Slovenia and Croatia was an attempt to reassert historical Germanic influence in the Balkans.[78]

Britain in particular showed little sympathy for the cause of Slovenian and Croatian independence. When the war in Croatia escalated rapidly in the fall of 1991, Britain declined to send a special diplomatic mission to Zagreb to find out what was going on. Partly, of course, Britain was sympathetic to the preservation of Yugoslav unity and had no great affection for Tudjman's authoritarian political style and perceived nostalgia for Croatia's fascist, pro-German past. But Britain also feared that the endorsement of independence movements in Yugoslavia could have an impact on Northern Ireland and embolden the Irish Republican Army and its political wing, Sinn Fein, to emulate the Slovenian and Croatian nationalists by intensifying their challenge to British authority. Indeed, the Republic of Ireland made no secret of its sympathy for the cause of national self-determination in Yugoslavia.[79]

From mid-1991 onward, however, the international backers of Yugoslav unity inadvertently undercut their position. For example, at the Brioni conference in early July, EC officials in effect had acknowledged the Slovenian victory in a cease-fire agreement and in a statement declaring that "it is up to the Yugoslav peoples to decide their future." Moreover, by early 1992, the British and French were weary of opposing Germany. Reluctant to divide the Community, they finally decided in favor of recognition. In mid-January 1992, they and other EC countries recognized the independence of Slovenia and Croatia.[80]

The decision to recognize Croatia's independence of Yugoslavia before a settlement of the republic's "Serb question," especially the question of Serb political rights, turned out to be a bad mistake.[81] The omission provided implicit encouragement of the Tudjman government's ambition to regain control of the Krajina and Slavonia from the rebellious Serb communities as soon as possible. And, worse, it opened the door, so to speak, for Croatian retribution against Serbs for their separatism. It may also have encouraged Serb nationalists in Bosnia in their determination not to be a minority in a Muslim-led independent republic of Bosnia-Herzegovina.[82]

The United States

Committed to the preservation of Yugoslavia's territorial integrity, the United States was also reluctant to recognize the independence of Slovenia and Croatia, knowing that recognition would doom any chances of keeping the old Yugoslav state together.[83] But members of Congress and others opposed this approach. They complained that the policy of preserving Yugoslav unity inadvertently put the United States on the side of Serbia and its opposition to the national self-determination of the other republics. In their view, the behavior of the Serbian Republic was the root cause of the continuing civil war.[84]

By September 1991, the Bush administration began to move away from trying to save the old Yugoslavia and to focus on peacemaking to prevent the Yugoslav army from dismembering Croatia and possibly other republics with Serb minorities. The administration was also intent on blocking Serbia's ambition to build a greater Serb state out of the ruins of the Yugoslav Federation. On December 6, the United States imposed its own sanctions against Yugoslav exports to the United States, which had amounted to $776 million in 1990. The State Department also suspended assistance for Yugoslavia under its program Support for East European Democracies, which promoted institutions such as political parties and independent news organizations.[85]

As hope for any chance of Yugoslavia's survival vanished in early 1992, the Bush administration began to consider how and when it would grant recognition, insisting that the warring parties must reach a peaceful settlement through negotiation and with firm protection for minorities before recognition would be granted. But in April 1992, the administration proceeded with formal recognition of Slovenia, Croatia, and Bosnia-Herzegovina without obtaining guarantees of minority rights from Croatia.

The United Nations

The United Nations became actively involved in Yugoslavia on September 25, 1991, when the Security Council expressed concern about the fighting on Croatian territory and called for an embargo of all weapons to Yugoslavia.[86] By

October 1991, both the EC and the United States looked increasingly to the United Nations to bring about peace in the Krajina. On October 8, Secretary-General Javier Pérez de Cuéllar appointed former U.S. Secretary of State Cyrus Vance as his personal envoy to Yugoslavia to establish contact with the EC and other interested parties to the conflict in Croatia to help bring about peace. With Western encouragement and support, the UN brokered cease-fires between the combatants and agreed to deploy forces in the Krajina to discourage a resumption of fighting once a cease-fire was in place.[87]

None of the first fourteen cease-fires lasted long enough for the ink to dry on them. Yugoslav army leaders in the field initially opposed a UN presence, seeing it as an obstacle to finishing off once and for all Croatian rule in the Krajina. The Croatian leadership in Zagreb also opposed UN intervention, fearful that a cease-fire and deployment of UN peacekeepers would undermine its sovereignty in the region. And the Krajina Serbs opposed any arrangement that would require using UN forces, which they distrusted, to replace Yugoslav forces, which they trusted to protect them against the Croatians.

But Vance tried very hard during November to bring about a permanent cease-fire, and the Security Council indicated a willingness to send a peacekeeping force of up to 10,000 soldiers to prevent a resumption of fighting.[88] Using "shuttle diplomacy" between Zagreb and Belgrade to get all three elements—the Yugoslav army, its Krajina allies, and the Croatian government military forces—to lay down their arms, Vance tried toward the end of 1991 for a durable cease-fire. In early January 1992, he was successful.[89]

All the combatants eventually accepted a UN presence in the Krajina and Slavonia. Yugoslav and Krajina Serb authorities eventually concluded that a UN presence could work to their advantage by eventually weakening Croatia's sovereignty in the disputed region, strengthening Serb chances of emancipation from Zagreb's control. Croatia also was sympathetic to a United Nations peacekeeping effort in the Krajina, partly for the opposite reason, believing that a temporary UN peacekeeping effort, by preventing Yugoslav and local Serb military forces from consolidating their position in the Krajina, could lead eventually to a restoration of Croatia's control over the region. In January 1992, the Croatian government appointed local officials and police in areas to be occupied and protected by UN forces to maintain at least a semblance of Croatian authority and to discourage local Serb efforts to rebel.[90]

But the UN deployment was held up in the early weeks of 1992 because some Krajina Serbs refused to give up their weapons unless Croatian police authorities also disarmed. The Croatians balked. After all, the Krajina was still legally part of the Croatian Republic and subject to the jurisdiction of Zagreb. In addition, some Serb officers in the Federation army, skeptical of a UN presence and convinced they could eventually conquer the region, said they would not forcibly disarm the local Serb population without its approval.[91] Moderate Krajina Serbs backed by President Milošević, who now wanted peace in order to focus attention on the Serbs in Bosnia-Herzegovina, prevailed over radicals. On February 9, 1992, two-thirds of a self-styled Krajina Serb Parliament voted to support the UN deployment. At the same time, Croatian leaders, hoping that the Krajina eventually would return to them, reluctantly agreed that rebel Serb governments recently set up in places occupied by Yugoslav forces could remain until a general political solution was worked out. On February 21, the Security Council established the United Nations Protection Force (UNPROFOR) for deployment in Croatia.[92]

The arrival of UNPROFOR personnel brought a fragile peace to the Krajina. But the ambiguity of the cease-fire, which helped get it accepted by the parties involved, was its most serious weakness, in that a failure to require the Republic of Croatia to respect the rights of its Serb minority made inevitable, when the opportunity presented itself, a resumption of fighting over the Krajina.[93]

By early 1992, on the eve of the explosion of civil war in Bosnia-Herzegovina, the West undoubtedly had done more harm than good in its efforts to mediate and manage the crisis of Yugoslavia's collapse. While it had brought peace for the time being to the Krajina, it had failed to tame the growth of radical ethnic-based nationalism by its acceptance of national self-determination, despite misgivings and a predilection for preserving Yugoslav unity. Indeed, Western support of Slovenian and Croatian independence in the latter part of 1991 encouraged other Yugoslav republics, such as Macedonia and Bosnia-Herzegovina, to seek independence. Worse, the West also inadvertently encouraged Serb minorities, such as the Krajina Serbs, also to seek independence, which not only accelerated the disintegration of Yugoslavia but also increased the likelihood of sustained interethnic conflict.

Macedonia Becomes Independent

While Slovenia and Croatia were cutting their ties to Belgrade, the Yugoslav Republic of Macedonia also was moving toward independence. Like the Croatians and Slovenians, the Macedonians initially had mixed feelings about complete separation from Yugoslavia. The least economically developed of the Yugoslav republics, Macedonia had the most to gain from maintaining links with a central government in Belgrade, which could provide economic help. But popular pressure for independence increased in 1990, with a lifting of censorship, an acceptance of multiparty pluralism, and free and competitive parliamentary elections scheduled for November by the local communist leadership looking to curry favor with voters.[94]

By the end of the year, at least four large Macedonian political organizations had emerged: a reconstituted Communist Party seeking to preserve communist control of the republic; the Alliance of Reformist Forces of Yugoslavia, which was led by Prime Minister Ante Marković of the Yugoslav Federation and was committed to preserving the existing Yugoslav federal union; a coalition of radically nationalist groups, including the All-Macedonian Movement for Action (MMA) and the Internal Macedonian Revolutionary Organization (IMRO); and an ethnic Albanian party supported by Macedonia's Albanian minority. These parties fielded candidates in parliamentary elections held in November.[95]

Appealing to popular prejudice, communists attacked the Albanian minority, which had been growing steadily in recent years and was suspected of wanting a union with kinsmen in Kosovo or, at the very least, increased influence over local affairs in Macedonia. The communists also made common cause with the Reform Party of Ante Marković, the last prime minister of Yugoslavia before its collapse in 1992, since both parties wanted Macedonia kept closely linked with the rest of Yugoslavia. In the elections, the big winner turned out to be IMRO, which favored decommunization and independence. As in other Central and East European countries, the communists had lost credibility among voters, who, given a chance to express their feelings openly, voted for decommunization and autonomy.[96]

1. Independence

With the failure of the republic leaders in discussions held in 1991 to agree on a plan for transforming Yugoslavia into a confederation, the Macedonian government planned for complete independence. In early September 1991, it held a national referendum on independence, in which Macedonians voted overwhelmingly for separation from Yugoslavia.[97] In November 1991, Macedonia formalized its new status and a commitment to democratic processes when it approved a new constitution. Although the preamble was similar to the preamble of the Croatian constitution in that it emphasized historical aspirations for national independence, the constitution also called for "cohabitation" between Macedonian and non-Macedonian people and therefore was somewhat less ethnically chauvinistic than the Croatian document. To serve the interests of the ethnic minorities, the constitution provided for the establishment of a Council for Interethnic Relations within the legislature.[98]

The new document nevertheless alarmed Macedonia's Albanian minority, which made up 23 percent of the republic's population and opposed independence. They were worried that, despite provisions that appeared to guarantee minority rights, the Skopje government, which was controlled by ethnic Macedonians fearful of an outbreak of Albanian separatism, would discriminate against them and get away with it because of the failure of the constitution to identify them as a "nation." The Albanian minority wanted assurances, which they never received from the Macedonian political leadership, that once Macedonia was independent of Yugoslavia the new republic would not violate their cultural rights and try to assimilate them. By 1992, local Albanian leaders were demanding autonomy for Ilirida, as they called the territory in northwest Macedonia where the bulk of Albanian-speaking people resided. The demands of Macedonian Albanians and their talk of the possibility of joining kinsmen in Kosovo and in the Republic of Albania to create a "Greater Albania" began to resemble the situation of Croatia's Serb minority in the Krajina.[99] Albanian politicians in Macedonia urged the EC not to recognize the independence of Yugoslav Macedonia on the grounds that it failed to meet the Union's human- and civil-rights standards. Other ethnic minorities, notably, Greeks, Bulgarians, and Serbs, shared the worry of the Albanians. The problem for an independent Macedonia was to make sure that its powerful neighbors would not use the protection of these minorities as a pretext for interference in its internal affairs and possibly even some landgrabbing.

2. Recognition

By the end 1991, Macedonia tried to get Western recognition of its independence, since it had met all of the preconditions for such recognition. For example, the November 1991 constitution precluded territorial claims against neighboring territories. It called for respect for human rights. Moreover, President Kiro Gligorov of Macedonia was a moderate democrat, who, most Western diplomats believed, was the only reliable and trustworthy leader among the various Yugoslav heads of state.[100] Western recognition of Macedonia, however, was delayed by problems with its neighbors. The Republic of Serbia claimed Macedonian territory it called "South Serbia," which was located along Macedonia's border with Serbia, was inhabited mostly by Serbs, and was taken from Serbia after World War II by Tito as part of his policy to disperse Serbs and thereby weaken Serbia's influence in the new Yugoslavia.[101]

The most serious obstacle to Western recognition of Macedonia's independence came from Greece. In April 1992, Greek Prime Minister Mitsotakis asked his NATO allies not to extend recognition to the Yugoslav Republic of Macedonia. Greece questioned the right of the new state to use the name "Macedonia," which was the name of its northern province. The Greek government worried that an independent Macedonia might eventually lay claim to Greek Macedonia inhabited by people of ethnic Macedonian stock. Greek fears seemed vindicated when some Macedonian communist leaders referred to Greek territory inhabited by Macedonians as "Aegean Macedonia" and characterized it as "occupied." Greece also worried that the recognition of an independent state for Macedonians called Macedonia would require an acknowledgment that Greece had "non-Greek" minorities, that is, that its society was not homogeneous, as it claimed, but multinational, and require Athens to subject itself to EC regulations governing the treatment of minorities.[102]

Initially the Western allies accommodated Greece on this issue, despite the legal advice that Macedonia met their conditions for recognition. The allies considered an independent Macedonia vulnerable to the territorial pretensions of its Balkan neighbors, notably, Greece, Bulgaria, and Serbia. The Bush administration also was afraid that the pro-American, pro-NATO government of Prime Minister Mitsotakis might fall if it did not prevail on this issue. Its successor would surely be composed of anti-American Greek socialists. In addition, the West was concerned that the Albanian minority in Macedonia had been systematically underrepresented in the republic's Parliament, justifying Albanian fears of extensive discrimination by an independent Macedonian state. Nevertheless, the allies eventually recognized Macedonia's independence, provoking the wrath of the government in Athens, which imposed a trade embargo on the new state that lasted four years.[103]

Bosnia-Herzegovina Becomes Independent

The government of Bosnia-Herzegovina would also have preferred to remain part of the Yugoslav Federation if it could have been transformed to allow member republics complete autonomy over their local affairs. But with strong opposition to a confederation from Milošević's Serbia, with the secession of Croatia, whose membership in a Yugoslav state was essential for Bosnia to offset Serbian influence, and with the movement throughout 1991 and early 1992 of the Western powers toward recognition of the independence of Slovenia, Croatia, and Macedonia, President Alija Izetbegović of Bosnia believed his country must achieve independence.[104]

On October 15, the Bosnian Parliament declared the republic a sovereign and independent state. But the Serb minority in Bosnia-Herzegovina, which was about 31 percent of the republic's population, preferred to keep Bosnia-Herzegovina within Yugoslavia. Serb members of the Bosnian Parliament refused to participate in the vote and called it unconstitutional because it lacked the legal consensus of the three ethnic groups that made up the republic. The Serbian Democratic Party of Bosnia subsequently created a Parliament to represent Bosnian Serb communities and in November 1991 held a plebiscite in areas inhabited primarily by Serb people. The Bosnian-Serb politicians also threatened the Sarajevo government that, if it proceeded with independence, the regions inhabited by Serbs as well as other regions without Serb majorities but important to the local Serb population because of their geographic proximity to the Republic of Serbia would secede from Bosnia-Herzegovina.[105]

In November, Izetbegović appealed to the UN for peacekeeping forces and continued a campaign begun in October for Western recognition of Bosnia-Herzegovina's independence. He wanted not only to legitimize the new state but also to strengthen it vis-à-vis the newly independent Croatia and Serbia, which he correctly suspected of wanting to partition Bosnia-Herzegovina along ethnic lines.[106] At the end of February 1992, at the request of the EC, Izetbegović put the issue of independence to the Bosnian people in a referendum. Bosnian Muslims and

Croats, who together constituted a majority of the population, voted overwhelmingly in support of independence. Bosnia's Serb population boycotted the referendum and began a wave of violent actions against the authority of Sarajevo, with local Arkanovići raiding Bijeljina on April 2.[107]

On April 6–7, 1992, the European Community and the United States recognized the independence of Bosnia-Herzegovina, provoking the Serb minority to begin its long campaign for independence of Sarajevo.[108] On April 7, the Bosnian Serbs retaliated by proclaiming their independence, setting up their own military command under General Ratko Mladić of the Yugoslav National Army (JNA).[109]

The Western recognition of Bosnian independence without first having addressed the concerns of the Serb minority was seriously flawed. The EC had ignored the advice of its own commissions that a vote on independence would be valid only if there were a substantial turnout of voters, an event that had not occurred as a result of the Serb minority's refusal to vote. Just as bad was the failure of the Western powers to insist on acceptance by the Izetbegović government of guarantees of political and cultural rights for the Serb minority in an independent Bosnia-Herzegovina.[110]

The Final Collapse of Tito's Yugoslavia

By early 1992, Tito's Yugoslav Federation was gone, despite heroic efforts by Ante Marković, the Federation's last prime minister, to save it. He was in the early 1990s, despite his Croatian background, the best example of a true "Yugoslav" person. With the breakup of the League of Yugoslav Communists after its January 1990 congress, Marković and his government in Belgrade became solely responsible for holding Yugoslavia together in the face of escalating conflict among the republics. But as a result of republic-level parliamentary elections in 1990 and 1991 that led eventually to declarations of sovereignty and movements toward secession, he could not even speak about strengthening the central government to republic leaders terrified by the prospect of Serb dominance. The march to independence of the Yugoslav republics in 1991 coincided with a gradual but steady disintegration of the Federation economy, the central administrative system in Belgrade, and the JNA.

1. Economic Disintegration

Federal military campaigns in Slovenia and Croatia in 1991 bankrupted the federal treasury and disrupted interrepublic trade. By the end of 1991, the Yugoslav economy was in a shambles. The war precipitated a collapse of the central banking system as the republics began helping themselves to money from the national banking system without authorization. For example, in 1990 Serbia took the equivalent of about $1.7 to $1.8 billion dollars, by far the largest amount.[111]

The war also disrupted commercial links among the republics. A debilitating trade war had developed between Serbia and Slovenia. Stores in Belgrade refused to sell televisions and other consumer appliances manufactured in Slovenia. Slovenes were depicted in Serbia as clever exploiters taking the artificially low-priced energy, food, and minerals from Serbia and other regions and selling manufactured goods at inflated prices. Lacking fuel supplies from refineries such as that in Sisak 30 miles south of Zagreb, Serbia had to purchase crude oil abroad at world market prices. In addition, the absence of deliveries from mills and factories throughout Croatia and Slovenia severely hurt Serbian plants, especially those producing automobiles. Shortages of everything sent prices skyrocketing and provoked an inflation made worse by the Federation government's recourse to the printing press to pay debts and continue subsidies to inefficient and bankrupt industries.[112]

With industry paralyzed by the breakdown of distribution, hundreds of thousands of Yugoslav workers lost their jobs or were not paid for several months. Many more received only minimum wages. Even well-off Slovenia suffered, with a 10 percent unemployment rate in mid-1991, a degree of joblessness unheard of since World War II. Workers' incomes everywhere in Yugoslavia declined from $450.00 a month to $100.00. And making matters worse was the reluctance of Yugoslav workers abroad to send money home because of the country's turmoil. An important source of national income and revenue dried up as the Yugoslav tourist industry, which had always been a lucrative source of hard foreign currency, disappeared because of the spread of conflict to the Adriatic coast, especially the popular resort of Dubrovnik.[113]

A brutal trade war between Slovenia and Croatia on the one hand and Serbia on the other accelerated economic disintegration. Beginning in October 1990, Milošević started taxing imports from the northern republics and nationalized Slovenian and Croatian commercial property in Serbia in the name of economic reform. Slovenia and Croatia reciprocated, and trade among the republics almost came to a standstill, increasing economic distress all around.[114]

The Federation was quickly going bankrupt. Beyond the Serbian Republic's theft of over $1 billion from the Federation treasury, Croatia, Slovenia, Vojvodina, and Kosovo refused to transfer revenue to the central government in Belgrade. By the end of November 1990, the Federation was receiving only one-third of the revenue it expected. Bankruptcy was imminent.[115]

Finally, a significant footnote to all of this was the highly negative impact of the Persian Gulf crisis and the imposition of sanctions on Iraq. Ten thousand Yugoslav citizens had been employed in Iraq at the time of its invasion of Kuwait, and another 50,000 were working in Yugoslavia on contracts with Iraq. All economic activity with Iraq was interrupted, costing Yugoslavia several billion dollars, at the worst possible time for the country.[116]

2. Political and Administrative Disintegration

The outbreak of civil strife in 1990 and 1991 helped facilitate administrative disintegration of Tito's Yugoslavia in giving each of the six republics virtual veto power over national decision making. Prime Minister Marković lacked the political wherewithal to assert leadership and move forward with a program of economic reform that he hoped would keep the country together by improving living conditions and giving the different Yugoslav peoples a stake in preserving the country's unity. Parliamentary elections in the republics in 1990 and 1991 undermined his authority, which rested on majority support in a conflict-ridden federal Parliament. He never fully developed his own noncommunist party, which might have bolstered his leadership of the country. The so-called Alliance of Reformist Forces of Yugoslavia he eventually launched in July 1990 had little following in most of the republics and virtually none in Slovenia, Croatia, and Serbia.[117]

The scope of political and administrative disintegration was evident also in March 1991 following the resignation of Federation president Borislav Jović.[118] Next in line for this position was Stipe Mesić, a Croat who was opposed by Serbia's President Milošević. Mesić had been the first prime minister of an independent Croatia and advocated independence for Croatia and the end of the Titoist federation. For two months the country was without a president, as Serbia refused to endorse Mesić.[119] Finally allowed to take office, Mesić did not last long. The division over his selection eventually split the collective federation presidency into two groups, one led by Branko Kostić, a Serb supported by Serbia, Vojvodina, Kosovo, and Montenegro. The other group was led by Mesić and was supported by Slovenia, Croatia, Bosnia-Herzegovina, and Macedonia. The presidency was now paralyzed and unable to control the explosion of nationalism among the republics and their relentless drive for independence. By the end of 1991, the presidency and its chair were no longer meeting.[120]

3. Military Disintegration

By the summer of 1991, during the fighting in Slovenia, the JNA had begun to experience the same divisions that were breaking up the Federation. The deployment of Serb officers in command positions in army units stationed in Slovenia and Croatia aroused local ethnic-based resentments. Officers of Slovene and Croat background saw their Serb colleagues as tools of the Milošević regime.[121]

There was a wave of desertions by Croat and Slovene personnel and of evasions of the draft. Draftees from Serbia and elsewhere seemed to have little stomach for battle. By the end of 1991, the JNA was relying on irregular troops, who were poorly trained.

Although the composition of the JNA senior officer corps of the army had in the past followed strictly the rule of national parity, with citizens of Slovenia and Croatia as well as other republics promoted to command positions, Serbian influence over the army increased. Serb officers became increasingly independent of Federation President Mesić, who was legally commander in chief. Indeed, led by its predominantly Serb officer corps, the Yugoslav army displayed an unauthorized aggressiveness in fighting Croatian self-defense forces in the Krajina. Yugoslav field commanders displayed a special sympathy for the independence efforts of the Krajina Serbs. Furthermore, Serb officers in the JNA shared the interest of the Milošević regime in preserving Tito's centralized and authoritarian Yugoslav state in which the army had always enjoyed a special place of honor and had been well rewarded for its loyalty with high wages and generous pensions.[122]

The army also turned out to be a poor defender of Yugoslavia's unity. After too much time and materiel and too many casualties, its campaign to reverse Slovenia's march to independence in the first half of 1991 ended in ignominious failure. The army's handling of the campaign in Croatia was not much better. The army took eighty-six days, despite its superiority in weapons, to defeat Croatian forces. Yugoslav commanders also lost control over their Krajina Serb allies, who were determined to conquer as much territory in southern Croatia as they could. The Krajina Serb irregulars, not the army, were responsible for the relentless shelling of Dubrovnik and the enormous damage to the city's historical center.[123]

4. Serbia and Montenegro Form a New Yugoslav State

In late 1991, as the old Yugoslavia was disintegrating, Serbia had strong incentives to forge a close union with Montenegro. A Croatian decision on September 11, 1991, to shut off the Adria oil pipeline feeding Serbia as well as other parts of Central Europe meant that Serbia needed access to the Adriatic through Montenegro. But the Republic of Montenegro government was not enthusiastic about intimacy with the Milošević regime and tried in subtle ways to distance itself from aggressive Serbian policies toward Croatia and Bosnia-Herzegovina in which it had little stake.[124] Unfortunately for the Montenegrins, they were too weak to protect their independence. They already had close economic ties with Serbia on which their material well-being relied. For example, Montenegro's transportation routes and energy grids were linked to Serbia. Moreover, they always had been dependent on the Federation government for subsidies to help maintain needed social spending and were forced to look to Serbia in early 1992 with the collapse of central authority. Finally, there was no support from the West for Montenegro's resistance to Serbia's pressure for union, which Milošević had no misgivings about applying in the form of overnight hikes in the price of Serbian electricity.[125]

In April 1992, Serbia and Montenegro formed a new, small Yugoslav federation preserving most of the federal administrative apparatus of the former Yugoslavia, including the president, the prime minister, the cabinet, and the Assembly. Serbian and Montenegrin leaders declared that their new state would be a democracy based on respect for human rights and on the principles of a market economy. In adopting the new Yugoslavia's constitution, the leadership said that it had no claims on the territory of its neighbors. The government pledged to avoid force and to use diplomacy in the settlement of any outstanding differences with neighboring republics. This new Yugoslav state, which had a population of 10.5 million people, most of whom lived in the Republic of Serbia, was heavily influenced by President Milošević, who made sure that the newly constituted federal Yugoslav government was led by people congenial to Serbian interests. Indeed, the new Yugoslavia was little more than an enlarged Serbia. Montenegro's small population was for all intents and purposes without influence and was growing increasingly resentful of the overbearing Milošević, whose policies frequently were not in the best interest of the Montenegrin people.

Conclusions

The Milošević leadership of Serbia must be blamed for the speed and trauma of Yugoslavia's disintegration: it opposed reforms that might have preserved Yugoslavia; it opposed economic and political liberalization; and it opposed democratization, decommunization, and decentralization in Yugoslavia. Partly the reasons for Serbian conservatism were ideological, a faith in the efficacy of the socialist system bequeathed by Tito in bringing a measure of prosperity to the Yugoslav peoples. But mainly, the Milošević leadership opposed perestroika-style reforms in Yugoslavia for reasons of narrow self-interest. Serbia enjoyed a privileged position of wealth and influence in a united Yugoslavia that would be severely curtailed if the country were transformed into a confederation of independent states, as most of the republics wanted because of their resentment of Serb dominance. The Republic of Serbia resisted change and in so doing compromised the survival of the Titoist state.

But once Milošević realized that preserving a unified Yugoslavia was impossible given the determination of Slovenia, Croatia, Macedonia, and Bosnia-Herzegovina to have independence, he decided to look to Serbia's national interest, which consisted primarily of the ambition to bring all the Serb minorities in neighboring republics, along with the territory they inhabited, under the control of the Serbian government in Belgrade. This ambition brought Serbia into direct conflict with its neighbors, especially Croatia and Bosnia-Herzegovina, where the large Serb minorities outside Serbia lived. With Serbia's comparative superiority of resources and military power, Milošević was able to throw Yugoslavia into civil war. In so doing, he finished off once and for all any chances of keeping the country together. The other republics no longer had any doubt of Serbia's aggressiveness and brutality and certainly not the slightest interest in reconstituting any Yugoslav system sure to be dominated by Serbia.

But beyond the behavior of Serbia were other circumstances responsible for the disintegration of Yugoslavia having to do with the peculiar features of the Yugoslav state bequeathed by Tito. The Yugoslav Federation lasted as long as it did largely because of Tito's commanding and charismatic leadership, which literally forced unity among the diverse and conflict-ridden ethnic groups that for his sake sublimated their historical and deep-seated prejudices toward one another. Not long after his death in 1980, the Yugoslav peoples started fighting one another, first politically and eventually militarily. The intensity of their combativeness testified to the failure of Tito, despite his best efforts, to build a true Yugoslav nationality that would unify the country's multinational society.

Indeed, it could be argued that Tito inadvertently encouraged the persistence of the ethnic particularism that would lead to separatist movements and the disintegration of his country. For reasons of expediency, he kept alive the separate cultural identities of the different groups by his policies of political and administrative decentralization. He did little to diminish the economic gap between the developed north and the underdeveloped south, reinforcing interethnic prejudices and animosities. And he certainly provided a catalyst for the expression of a vehement, belligerent, aggressive nationalism in the Republic of Serbia with his crude effort to diminish Serbia's influence by dispersing Serbs throughout the country instead of allowing them all to be administered by the Serbian Republic.

If the republics of Tito's Yugoslavia could have had a federation in which all members were equal in the enjoyment of self-rule with no member having the kind of primacy Serbia had since 1918, they would have been willing to belong. They all had strong incentives to preserve some kind of federation because of the benefits, especially in the economic sphere, gained from unity in the Tito years. Tito's Yugoslavia had brought to the different geographic regions development, some modernization, and improved living conditions for many, if not most, Yugoslav peoples.

In the early 1990s, the disintegration of Yugoslavia began to undermine the economic gains the republics had made and eventually reversed them. The outbreak of the Bosnian civil war and its ripple effects in neighboring republics discussed in the next chapter further weakened the Yugoslav economy, slowing down and in some places halting or reversing economic expansion, which will take decades to remedy.

SLOVENIA

Geography

1. Location: southeastern Europe, bordering the Adriatic Sea between Croatia and Italy
2. Area: total — 20,296 square kilometers; land area — 20,296 square kilometers; comparative area — slightly larger than New Jersey
3. Boundaries: with Austria — 262 kilometers; with Croatia — 501 kilometers; with Italy — 199 kilometers; with Hungary — 83 kilometers; coastline along Adriatic Sea — 32 kilometers
4. Climate: Mediterranean climate on the coast, continental climate with mild to hot summers and cold winters in the plateaus and valleys to the east
5. Terrain: a short coastal strip on the Adriatic Sea; alpine mountain region adjacent to Italy; mixed mountains and valleys to the east
6. Land use: arable — 10%; permanent crops — 2%; meadows and pastures — 20%; forest and woodland — 45%
7. Natural resources: lignite coal, lead, zinc, mercury, uranium, silver
8. Environment: Sava River polluted with domestic and industrial waste; pollution of coastal waters with heavy metals and toxic chemicals; forest damage near Koper from air pollution originating at metallurgical and chemical plants and resulting acid rain

People

1. Population: 2,051,522 (1995 estimate)
2. Age structure: 0–14 — 19% of population (female — 191,318; male — 200,957); 15–64 — 69% of population (female — 701,082; male — 708,482); 65 and over — 12% of population (female — 160,662; male — 89,021) (1995 estimate)
3. Growth rate: 0.24% (1995 estimate)
4. Life expectancy at birth: total population — 74.73 years; female — 78.76 years; male — 70.91 years (1995 estimate)
5. Ethnic divisions: Slovene — 91%; Croat — 3%; Serb — 2%; Muslim — 1%
6. Religions: Roman Catholic — 96%; Muslim — 1%; other — 3%
7. Languages: Slovenian — 91%; Serbo-Croatian — 7%; other — 2%
8. Labor force: total — 786,036; manufacturing and mining — 46%; agriculture — 28%

Government

1. Type: emerging parliamentary democracy
2. Capital: Ljubljana
3. Independence: June 25, 1991, from Yugoslavia
4. Constitution: promulgated December 23, 1991
5. National administration:
   a. Chief of state: President of the Republic (1996 — Milan Kučan)
   b. Ministerial leadership: Prime Minister and Council of Ministers (1996 — Janez Drnovšek, prime minister)
   c. Legislature: bicameral — National Assembly, consisting of State Assembly and State Council
   d. Judicial branch: Supreme Court, Constitutional Court
   e. Political parties: Liberal Democratic, Slovene Christian Democrats, Social Democratic Party of Slovenia, Slovene People's National Party, United List, Slovene People's Party, Democratic Party, Greens of Slovenia
6. Local administration: unitary system with 60 provinces

Economy

1. Gross domestic product: $16 billion (1994 estimate)
2. National product real growth rate: 4% (1994 estimate)
3. Per-capita national product: $8,110 (1994 estimate)
4. Inflation rate: 20% (1994 estimate)
5. Unemployment rate: 9% (1994 estimate)

6. Budget: revenue — $9.9 billion; expenditures — $9.8 billion (1993 estimate)
7. Industrial output: ferrous metallurgy and rolling-mill products, aluminum reduction and rolled products, lead and zinc smelting, electronics, trucks, electric power equipment, wood products, textiles, chemicals, machine tools
8. Agricultural output: sheep and cattle raising, dairy products, potatoes, hops, hemp, flax
9. Exports: $6.5 billion (1994 estimate) — machinery and transport equipment, intermediate manufactured goods, chemicals, food, raw materials, consumer goods
10. Imports: $6.5 billion (1994 estimate) — machinery and transport equipment, intermediate manufqactured goods, chemicals, raw materials, fuels and lubricants, food (1993 estimate)
11. External debt: $2.1 billion (1994 estimate)
12. Trade partners: Germany, Italy, other former Yugoslav republics, France, Italy, Austria
13. Transportation: railroads — 1,201 kilometers; highways — 14,726 kilometers; ports — Izola, Koper, Piran; airports — 14 (10 with paved runways)

CROATIA

Geography
1. Location: southeastern Europe, bordering the Adriatic Sea, between Bosnia-Herzegovina and Slovenia
2. Area: total — 56,538 square kilometers; land area — 56,410 square kilometers; comparative area — slightly smaller than West Virginia
3. Boundaries: with Bosnia-Herzegovina — 923 kilometers; with Hungary — 329 kilometers; with Serbia and Montenegro — 266 kilometers (241 kilometers with Serbia and 25 kilometers with Montenegro); with Slovenia — 501 kilometers; mainland coastline along the Adriatic Sea — 1,778 kilometers
4. Climate: Mediterranean and continental — continental climate predominant, with hot summers and cold winters; mild winters, dry summers along coast
5. Terrain: geographically diverse — flat plains along Hungarian border, low mountains and highlands near Adriatic Coast
6. Land use: arable — 32%; permanent crops — 20%; meadows and pastures — 18%; forest and woodland — 15%
7. Natural resources: oil, some coal, bauxite, low-grade iron ore, calcium, natural asphalt, silica, mica, clays, salt
8. Environment: air pollution from metallurgical plants and resulting acid rain is damaging forests; coastal pollution from industrial and domestic waste; widespread casualties and destruction of infrastructure in border areas affected by civil strife

People
1. Population: 4,665,821 (1995 estimate)
2. Age structure: 0–14 — 19% of population (female — 418,272; male — 442,064); 15–64 — 68% of population (female — 1,592,187; male — 1,588,455); 65 and over — 13% of population (female — 394,650; male — 230,193) (1995 estimate)
3. Growth rate: 0.13% (1995 estimate)
4. Life expectancy at birth: total population — 74.02 years; female — 77.65 years; male — 70.59 years (1995 estimate)
5. Ethnic divisions: Croat — 78%; Serb — 12%; Muslim — 0.9%; Hungarian — 0.5%; Slovenian — 0.5%
6. Religions: Catholic — 76.5%;

Orthodox — 11.1%; Muslim — 1.2%; Protestant — 0.4%
7. Languages: Serbo-Croatian — 96%
8. Literacy: total population — 97%
9. Labor force: total — 1,509,489; industry — 38%; agriculture — 28%; other — 34% (1989 estimate)

Government

1. Type: emerging parliamentary democracy
2. Capital: Zagreb
3. Independence: June 25, 1991, from Yugoslavia
4. Constitution: promulgated December 22, 1990
5. National administration:
   a. Chief of state: President of the Republic (1996 — Franjo Tudjman)
   b. Ministerial leadership: Prime Minister and Council of Ministers (1995 — Nikica Valentić, prime minister)
   c. Legislature: bicameral — Assembly (*Sobor*), consisting of House of Representatives (*Predstavnicke*) and House of Districts (*Zupanije Dom*)
   d. Judicial branch: Supreme Court, Constitutional Court
   e. Political parties: Croatian Democratic Union, Croatian Democratic Independents, Croatian Social Liberal Party, Croatian Democratic Peasant Party, Croatian Party of Rights, Croatian Peasants Party
6. Local administration: unitary system with 21 counties

Economy

1. Gross domestic product: $12.4 billion (1994 estimate)
2. National product real growth rate: 3.4% (1994 estimate)
3. Per-capita national product: $2,640 (1994 estimate)
4. Inflation rate: 3% (1994 estimate)
5. Unemployment rate: 17% (1994 estimate)
6. Industrial output: chemicals and plastics, machine tools, fabricated metal, electronics, pig iron and rolled steel products, aluminum reduction, paper, wood products (including furniture), building materials (including cement), textiles, shipbuilding, petroleum and petroleum refining, food processing, and beverages
7. Agricultural output: surplus production with most farms in private hands; wheat, corn, sugar beets, sunflower, alflafa, and clover in Slavonia; cereal production, orchards, vineyards, livestock breeding, dairy farming, olives, citrus fruits, and vegetables in Adriatic coastal and island areas
8. Exports: $3.9 billion (1994 estimate) — machinery and transport equipment, chemicals, food, live animals, raw materials, fuels and lubricants
9. Imports: $4.7 billion (1993 estimate) — machinery and transport equipment, fuels and lubricants, food and live animals, chemicals, manufactured goods, raw materials, beverages, and tobacco (1990)
10. External debt: $2.9 billion (1994 estimate)
11. Trade partners: European Union, Slovenia, CIS
12. Transportation: railroads — 2,699 kilometers; highways — 27,368 kilometers; ports — Dubrovnik, Omiš, Plŏce, Pula, Rijeka, Šibenik, Split, Zadar; airports — 76 (66 with paved runways)

FEDERAL REPUBIC OF YUGOSLAVIA:
SERBIA AND MONTENEGRO

Geography

1. Location: southeastern Europe, bordering the Adriatic Sea, between Albania and Bosnia-Herzegovina
2. Area: total — 102,350 square kilometers; land area — 102,136 square kilometers; comparative area — slightly larger than Kentucky (Serbia has a total land area of 88,412 square kilometers, making it slightly larger than Maine; Montenegro has a total land area of 13,724 square kilometers, making it slighly larger than Connecticut)
3. Boundaries: with Albania — 287 kilometers (114 kilometers with Serbia and 173 kilometers with Montenegro); with Bosnia-Herzegovina — 527 kilometers (312 kilometers with Serbia and 215 kilometers with Montenegro); with Bulgaria — 318 kilometers; with Croatia — 239 kilometers in the north and 15 kilometers in the south; with Hungary — 151 kilometers; with Macedonia — 221 kilometers; with Romania — 476 kilometers; the internal boundary between Serbia and Montenegro is 211 kilometers; with the Adriatic Sea — 199 kilometers (all with Montenegro)
4. Climate: in the north, cold winters and hot, humid summers with well-distributed rainfall; central portion has continental and Mediterranean climate; south has Adriatic climate along the coast, with hot, dry summers and autumns and cold winters with heavy snowfalls inland
5. Terrain: extremely varied — rich, fertile plains in the north; limestone ranges in the east; mountains and hills in the southeast; high shoreline in the southwest
6. Land use: arable — 30%; permanent crops — 5%; meadows and pastures — 20%; forest and woodland — 25%
7. Natural resources: oil, coal, gas, antimony, copper, lead, zinc, nickel, gold, pyrite, chrome
8. Environment: pollution of coastal waters from sewage outlets, especially in tourist areas such as Kotor; air pollution around Belgrade and other industrial cities; water pollution from industrial wastes dumped into the Sava River, which flows into the Danube River

People

1. Population: total — 11,101,883; Serbia — 10,393,585; Montenegro — 708,248 (1995 estimate)
2. Age structure: Montenegro: 0–14 years — 22% of population (female — 17,498; male — 82,005); 15–64 years — 68% of population (female — 236,987; male — 241,397); 65 and over — 10% (female — 41,625; male — 28,736) (1995 estimate); Serbia: 0–14 years — 22% (female — 1,095,121; male — 1,173,224); 15–64 years — 66% (female — 3,431,823; male — 3,483,066); 65 and over — 12% (female — 699,488; male — 510,863) (1995 estimate)
3. Growth rate: Montenegro — 0.79%; Serbia — 0.15% (1995 estimate)
4. Life expectancy at birth: Montenegro: total population — 79.56 years (female — 82.61 years; male — 76.69 years) (1995 estimate); Serbia: total population — 73.94 years (female — 76.68 years; male — 71.4 years) (1995 estimate)
5. Ethnic divisions: Serbs — 63%; Albanians — 14%; Montenegrins — 6%; Hungarians — 4%
6. Religions: Orthodox — 65%; Muslim — 19%; Roman Catholic — 4%; Protestant — 1%
7. Languages: Serbo-Croatian — 95%; Albanian — 5%
8. Labor force: total — 2,640,909; industry and mining — 40%

Government

1. Type: republic (quasi-parliamentary democracy)
2. Capital: Belgrade
3. Independence: April 11, 1992, from Yugoslavia
4. Constitution: promulgated April 27, 1992
5. National administration:
   a. Chief of state: Yugoslavia — President of the Republic (1995 — Zoran Lilić); Serbia — Slobodan Milošević; Montenegro — Momir Bulatović
   b. Ministerial leadership: Yugoslavia — Prime Minister and Council of Ministers (1995 — Radoje Kontić, prime minister)
   c. Legislature: bicameral — Federal Assembly, consisting of Chamber of Citizens and Chamber of Republics
   d. Judicial branch: Federal Court, Constitutional Court
   e. Political parties: Serbian Socialist Party, Serbian Radical Party, Serbian Renewal Movement, Democratic Party, Democratic Party of Serbia, Democratic Party of Socialists of Montenegro, People's Party of Montenegro, Liberal Alliance of Montenegro, Democratic Community of Vojvodina Hungarians, League of Communists–Movement for Yugoslavia, Democratic Alliance of Kosovo, Party of Democratic Action, Civic Alliance of Serbia, Socialist Party of Montenegro
6. Local administration: Yugoslavia — federal system with two republics; Serbia — unitary system with two quasi-autonomous provinces (Kosovo and Vojvodina); Montenegro — unitary system

Economy

1. Gross domestic product: $10 billion (1994 estimate)
2. Per-capita national product: $1,000 (1994 estimate)
4. Inflation rate: 20% (1994 estimate)
5. Unemployment rate: 40% (1994 estimate)
6. Industrial output in Kosovo, Serbia proper, Vojvodina, and Montenegro: machine building (aircraft, trucks, automobiles, armored vehicles, weapons), electrical equipment, agricultural machinery, metallurgy (steel, aluminum, copper, lead, zinc, chromium, antimony, bismuth, cadmium), mining (coal, bauxite, nonferrous ore, iron ore, limestone), consumer goods (textiles, footwear, foodstuffs, appliances), electronics, petroleum products, chemicals, pharmaceuticals
7. Agricultural output in Kosovo, Serbia proper, Vojvodina, and Montenegro: cereals, cotton, oil seeds, chicory, olives, sheep and goat husbandry, fruits, livestock, grapes, dairy farming, tobacco
8. No current data on exports, imports, revenue, and expenditures
9. Trade partners prior to international sanctions (1991): European Union, mainly Italy and Germany; other Yugoslav republics; CIS countries
10. Transportation: railroads — 3,960 kilometers; highways — 46,019 kilometers; ports — Bar, Belgrade, Kotor, Novi Sad, Pančevo, Tivat; airports — 54 (38 with paved runways)

MACEDONIA

Geography

1. Location: southeastern Europe, north of Greece
2. Area: total — 25,333 square kilometers; land area — 24,856 square kilometers; comparative area — slightly larger than Vermont
3. Boundaries: with Albania — 151 kilometers; with Bulgaria — 148 kilometers; with Greece — 228 kilometers; with Serbia and Montenegro — 221 kilometers (all with Serbia)
4. Climate: hot, dry summers and autumns; cold winters with heavy precipitation
5. Terrain: mountainous territory covered with deep basins and valleys; three large lakes with division of the country by the Vardar River
6. Natural resources: chromium, nickel, lead, zinc, manganese, tungsten, low-grade iron ore, asbestos, sulphur, timber
7. Land use: arable — 5%; permanent crops — 5%; meadows and pastures — 20%; forest and woodland — 30%
8. Environment: air pollution from metallurgical plants

People

1. Population: 2,159,503 (1995 estimate)
2. Age structure: 0–14 — 25% of population (female — 257,876; male — 277,314); 15–64 — 67% of population (female — 711,810; male — 733,903); 65 and over — 8% of population (female — 97,475; male — 81,125) (1995 estimate)
3. Growth rate: 0.9% (1995 estimate)
4. Life expectancy at birth: total population — 74 years; female — 76.3 years; male — 71.87 years (1995 estimate)
5. Ethnic divisions: Macedonian — 65%; Albanian — 22%; Turkish — 4%; Serb — 2%; Gypsy — 3%
6. Religions: Eastern Orthodox — 67%; Muslim — 30%
7. Languages: Serbo-Croatian — 96%
8. Literacy: total population — 97%
9. Labor force: total — 1,509,489; industry — 38%; agriculture — 28%; other — 34% (1989 estimate)

Government

1. Type: emerging parliamentary democracy
2. Capital: Skopje
3. Independence: September 17, 1991, from Yugoslavia
4. Constitution: promulgated November 20, 1991
5. National administration:
   a. Chief of state: President of the Republic (1996 — Kiro Gligorov)
   b. Ministerial leadership: Prime Minister and Council of Ministers (1995 — Branko Crvenkovski)
   c. Legislature: unicameral — Assembly (*Sobranje*)
   d. Judicial branch: Judicial Court of the Republic; Constitutional Court
   e. Political parties: Social Democratic Alliance of Macedonia, Party for Democratic Prosperity, National Democratic Party, Alliance of Reform Forces of Macedonia/Liberal Party, Socialist Party of Macedonia, Internal Macedonian Revolutionary Organization/Democratic Party for Macedonian National Unity, Party of Yugoslavs in Macedonia, Democratic Party, Democratic Party of Serbs, Democratic Party of Turks, Party for Democratic Action
6. Local administration: unitary system with 34 counties

Economy

1. Gross domestic product: $1.9 billion (1994 estimate)
2. National product real growth rate: – 15% (1994 estimate)
3. Per-capita national product: $900 (1994 estimate)
4. Inflation rate: 54% (1994 estimate)
5. Unemployment rate: 30% (1994 estimate)
6. Industrial output: low levels of technol-

ogy predominate (such as in oil refining); basic liquid fuels, coal, metallic chromium, lead, zinc, ferronickel, basic textiles, wood products, tobacco

8. Agricultural output: labor-intensive production of rice, tobacco, wheat, corn, millet, cotton, sesame, mulberry leaves, citrus fruits, vegetables

9. Exports: $1.06 billion (1993 estimate)
— machinery and transport equipment, manufactured goods, raw materials

10. Imports: $1.2 billion (1993 estimate)
— machinery and transport equip-

ment, fuels and lubricants, food and live animals, chemicals, manufactured goods, raw materials, beverages, tobacco

11. External debt: $840 million (1992 estimate)

12. Trade partners: Serbia and Montenegro, other former Yugoslav republics, Germany, Greece, Albania, Bulgaria

13. Economic aid recipient: $10 million

14. Transportation: railroads — 922 kilometers; highways — 10,591 kilometers; airports — 16 (13 with paved runways)

11

Yugoslavia—
The Bosnian Civil War

One of the first challenges to the newly independent Republic of Bosnia-Herzegovina was an explosion of civil war. The war threatened the well-being, even the survival, of the new state, absorbing most of its attention, resources, and energy.

Roots and Causes

At the root of the conflict, though by no means the main cause of it, was the anti-Muslim nationalism of the republic's Serb minority exacerbated by its move to independence, which left Serbs under the leadership of a Muslim-dominated central government in Sarajevo. Cut off administratively from the federation government in Belgrade and the Yugoslav Republic of Serbia, the Bosnian Serbs were fearful of the future. Christian Serb prejudices toward Muslim Slavs persisted for centuries, long after the two groups had learned to coexist peacefully with each other.

1. Historical Roots

Serbs in Bosnia, as well as in the Republic of Serbia and other parts of Yugoslavia, pointed to the Muslim Turkish conquest of Bosnia-Herzegovina's Slavic people in the late fourteenth century, which ended with the establishment of Sarajevo as a predominantly Muslim city. In that period, when many Slavic

Inset: After Dayton

BOSNIA-HERZEGOVINA

Geography

1. Location: southeastern Europe, bordering the Adriatic Sea, Croatia, Serbia, and Montenegro
2. Area: total — 51,233 square kilometers; land area — 51,233 square kilometers; comparative area — slightly larger than Tennessee
3. Boundaries: with Croatia — 932 kilometers; with Serbia and Montenegro — 527 kilometers (312 kilometers with Serbia, 215 with Montenegro); with the Adriatic Sea — 20 kilometers
4. Climate: hot summers and cold winters; areas of high elevation have short, cool summers and long, severe winters
5. Terrain: mountains and valleys
6. Land use: arable — 20%; permanent crops — 2%; meadows and pastures — 25%; forest and woodland — 36%
7. Natural resources: coal, iron, bauxite, manganese, timber, wood products,

copper, chromium, lead, zinc

8. Environment: air pollution from metallurgical plants; sites for disposing of urban waste are limited; water shortages; destruction of infrastructure resulting from war

People

1. Population: 3,201,823 (1995 estimate)
2. Age structure: 0–14 — 22% of population (female — 337,787; male — 370,966); 15–64 — 68% of population (female — 1,082,357; male — 1,085,610); 65 and over — 10% of population (female — 190,992; male 134,111) (1995 estimate)
3. Growth rate: 0.65% (1995 estimate)
4. Life expectancy at birth: total population — 75.47 years; female — 78.37 years; male — 72.75 years (1995 estimate)
5. Ethnic divisions: Slavic Muslim — 38%; Serb — 40%; Croat — about 22%
6. Religions: Muslim — 40%; Orthodox — 21%; Catholic — 15%; Protestant — 4%
7. Languages: Serbo-Croatian — 99%
8. Labor force: total — 1,026,254

Government

1. Type: emerging parliamentary democracy
2. Capital: Sarajevo
3. Independence: April 1992, from Yugoslavia
4. Constitution: promulgated in 1974; amended 1989, 1990, 1991, and 1994 to establish a federation including Slavic Muslim– and Croatian-held territories

5. National administration:
   a. Chief of state: President of the Republic (1996 — Alija Izetbegović)
   b. Ministerial leadership: Prime Minister and Council of Ministers (until February 1996 — Haris Silajdžić)
   c. Legislature: bicameral — National Assembly, consisting of Chamber of Citizens and Chamber of Municipalities
   d. Judicial branch: Supreme Court, Constitutional Court
   e. Political parties: Party of Democratic Action, Croatian Democratic Union of Bosnia and Herzegovina, Serbian Democratic Party of Bosnia and Herzegovina, Liberal Bosnian Organization, Democratic Party of Socialists, Party of Democratic Changes, Serbian Movement for Renewal, Alliance of Reform Forces of Yugoslavia for Bosnia and Herzegovina
6. Local administration: unitary system with 109 districts

Economy

1. No recent information available in 1996 for gross domestic product, national product real growth rate, inflation rate, budget revenue and expenditures, unemployment, industrial output, agricultural output, exports, imports, external debt
2. Transportation: railroads — 1,021 kilometers; highways — 21,168 kilometers; ports — Bosanski Brod; airports — 27 (18 with paved runways)

---

people chose to adopt Islam as a means of survival under Turkish rule, other Slavic people kept their Christian faith and were persecuted by the Turks. Nor could Serbs today forget or forgive the way in which their ancestors were slaughtered by Muslims who had joined forces with Croat fascists allied to Nazi Germany during World War II.

2. Ascendancy of Radovan Karadžić

Radovan Karadžić, the political leader of Serbs in Bosnia-Herzegovina, personified the anti-Muslim nationalism of the Bosnian Serbs and played a central role in mobilizing Serb opposition to independence. Karadžić was an articulate advocate of the Bosnian Serb cause, pointing out that the Muslim population had a higher birthrate than other ethnic groups in the republic and soon would be an absolute majority. When that happened, Karadžić insisted, they would enjoy a permanent political dominance, transform Bosnia-Herzegovina into an Iran-like fundamentalist state, and discriminate against the Christian Serb population. To buttress this argument, Karadžić called attention to the "Islamic Declaration" Bosnian president Alija Izetbegović, a Muslim, had made twenty years earlier, in which he had spoken of the superiority of Islam.[1]

Karadžić and the nationalist Serbs who supported him ignored the fact that in 1992 Izetbegović could hardly be considered an Islamic militant and in fact had become over the years a political moderate. They also ignored repeated assurances by Muslim leaders of their commitment to a "citizens' state" with equal rights for all. Karadžić also dismissed the long-standing reality of coexistence between Serbs and Muslims, who had intermarried and represented a truly cosmopolitan and productive part of the republic's society and economy in the twentieth century, especially in the areas of business and commerce.[2]

Indeed, Serb nationalist rhetoric in Bosnia-Herzegovina paid no attention to the fact that many Muslims, especially in the developed urban areas, matched a Western rather than an Eastern profile, adopting Western dress and lifestyles, and could by no far stretch of the imagination be considered the followers of Iranian theocracy that Karadžić accused them of being. Sarajevo's population, in particular, was ethnically mixed and cosmopolitan, with a high level of political and sociocultural sophistication dating back at least to the First World War. It was one of the few places in Tito's Yugoslavia where the "Yugoslav idea" seemed to have taken root and where people of different ethnic backgrounds for the most part coexisted peacefully.[3]

Karadžić's anti-Muslim nationalism in Bosnia-Herzegovina nevertheless found a ready audience, especially in the countryside, where interethnic prejudice had always existed just below the surface of Bosnian society and where people were more conservative, superstitious, and ignorant of the world around them than people living and working in cities like Sarajevo. Widespread mutual distrust surfaced in the remarks of ordinary people, such as, "those Croats, Muslims, and Serbs" are "always sticking together"; in the furtive glances of Serbs or Croats at Muslims going to the mosque in a largely Christian village or at Christians going to church in predominantly Muslim towns; and in the confidential acknowledgment by people of different ethnic backgrounds of their fear of other ethnic groups. Many inside the local culture preferred to ignore or dismiss this fear.[4]

Led by Karadžić, Serbs quit their posts in the Sarajevo government. Karadžić called upon the local Serb population to emancipate themselves from Muslim rule given the absence of any official Bosnian guarantee of political and other rights of the Serb minority.[5] In early April 1992, only a few days after international recognition of Bosnia-Herzegovina, Karadžić and his political supporters, with the enthusiastic backing of most Serbs in the republic, declared the Serb community's independence of Sarajevo and announced the establishment of a "Serb Republic of Bosnia." Following the example of the Serbs in the Krajina region of Croatia, Bosnian Serb leaders also claimed the right to associate their lands with the Republic of Serbia.

Outbreak of Violence

1. Bosnian Serb Strategy

The Serb communities went on the warpath in Bosnia-Herzegovina in the early months of 1992 to establish their independence of Sarajevo, the capital, which they wanted to capture and control because it symbolized the multiethnic coexistence they opposed. The Serbs wanted a division of the capital into two separate administrative units, one controlled by Muslims and the other by Serbs. To force the Muslim government to negotiate a partition, they started a long and unrelenting bombardment of the city's Muslim population with artillery deployed on the mountainous outskirts of the city, where they set up a military command post. They eventually blocked all entries into the city, including the airport, to incoming food and medical supplies. They further tried to make life hellish in the city by cutting off supplies of fresh water and electricity.

Although there were moments when the Bosnian Serbs seemed on the threshold of conquering the city, they never did. The people and leaders of Sarajevo showed a miraculous resilience. Moreover, before long Sarajevo became a symbol of the suffering the Muslim side was enduring and helped the city gain the kind of international attention and sympathy that would lead to eventual Western help in keeping it from falling into the hands of the Serb insurgents.

2. "Ethnic Cleansing"

Perhaps the most dramatic and provocative aspect of Bosnian Serb strategy to seize control of territory inhabited by Serbs, including areas where Serbs were in a minority in eastern and northern Bosnia, was "ethnic cleansing," or the permanent removal of Muslim inhabitants. Serb nationalist leaders like Karadžić and General Mladić were convinced, and convinced other Serbs skeptical of this tactic, that, in order to assure permanent Serb control, the Muslims must be driven from land where they had lived peacefully with Serbs. Thus ethnic cleansing was based as much on a competition for land and political power as on primordial ethnic prejudices and hostility.

Ethnic cleansing involved not only the torture, rape, and murder of thousands of Muslim civilians but also the wanton destruction of their property and livestock in a deliberate pattern of abuse calculated to drive Muslim people from their homes and discourage their return, even if that meant ruining the land so that no one else, not even Serb farmers, could live on it. Moreover, by the late summer of 1992, Serb nationalist forces had set up Nazi-like concentration camps in places like Omarska, Trnoplolje, Manazca, and elsewhere in Bosnia-Herzegovina into which they herded many thousands of innocent, mostly Muslim, civilians. Ethnic cleansing also involved the obliteration of Turkish–Muslim architecture and cultural life, such as the National Library in Sarajevo, which was fired on by Serb gunners outside the city even though it had no military importance. The Serb insurgents were determined also to deprive the Muslims of any incentive to return or hope that they could someday pick up life where they had left it. There also seemed to be a conscious effort by the Bosnian Serbs to murder as many of the Muslim educated elite as possible to discourage the successful rejuvenation of a Muslim government, which would lack the elite needed to make it work successfully.[6]

In part the source of this barbarous Serb behavior lay in the cultural background of the fighters who carried out the ethnic cleansing. Many Bosnian Serb guerrillas were from the countryside and were inspired by traditional rural values, especially fear of Islamic fundamentalism, which, they believed, threatened family and property. Bosnia Serb leaders, notably, Karadžić, fueled these fears and it is believed that Milošević encouraged ethnic cleansing as the only means of decisively defeating the Muslims.

3. The Refugee Problem

Serb "ethnic cleansing" caused a horrendous refugee problem, the worst since the end of World War II. By July 1992, roughly 2.3 million people had fled from towns and villages of the former Yugoslavia. Of the 2.3 million refugees, more than 400,000 fled to countries outside the former Yugoslavia's borders, while the rest were living precariously within parts of the former Yugoslavia. Croatia had the largest number of refugees, 630,000, while Serbia had 375,000 and Bosnia 598,000. In addition, 850,000 people were trapped in their homes in four Bosnian towns being attacked by the Serbs: Sarajevo, Bihać, Tuzla, and Goražde.[7]

The refugees were vulnerable to hunger and disease, especially during the brutal winters in the mountainous terrain of Bosnia-Herzegovina. But worse was the military threat from Serb gunners determined to kill as many Muslims as possible. By 1994, the refugee problem became more sinister. For example, starting in January, the governments of Croatia and Serbia began forcing refugees from Bosnia to fight on the war front.[8] The refugees may turn out to be the most long-lasting legacy of the civil war. It will certainly take a long time to resettle them and restore normality to their lives.

4. Support from the Republic of Serbia

In their campaign for annexation to Serbia, the Bosnian Serbs initially had the enthusiastic and dedicated support of President Milošević of the Serbian Republic, who saw an opportunity in the Serb insurgency to move ahead with his policy to create a "greater Serbia." Support for the Bosnian Serbs was popular in Serbia, and it was easy for Milošević to ship weapons to them because they were just across the frontier. Moreover, the Milošević regime had sent Serbian agents to Bosnia to stir up nationalist feelings in predominantly Serb communities in much the same way as it had done in Kosovo, Vojvodina, and Montenegro. Indeed, even before widespread violence had begun in early 1992, at least two Serb communities had openly challenged the authority of Sarajevo and called for annexation to Serbia.[9]

Serbian Republic support of the Bosnian Serb insurgency escalated quickly in the early months of 1992. Eventually, soldiers of the Yugoslav army who were Bosnian citizens (about 80,000 out of a total force of 140,000) joined the Bosnian Serb army as the Yugoslav army was officially withdrawing from Bosnian territory. Former Yugoslav personnel who remained in Bosnia kept their equipment, which included some of the latest and most sophisticated weapons in Eastern Europe.[10]

5. An Abundance of Weapons

Indeed, Bosnia-Herzegovina had been "the" arsenal of Tito's Yugoslavia since the end of World War II. The Yugoslav army in the postwar era called Bosnia its "Dinaric Fortress" when the country was threatened by the prospect of a Soviet intervention in 1948 in consequence of the conflict between Stalin and Tito over ideological, developmental, and foreign policy issues. By the 1980s, much of Bosnian industry was connected with armaments, and much of the army's resources, such as weapons suppliers, airfields, stockpiles, training schools, and oil depots were located in parts of Bosnia inhabited primarily by Serbs. On the eve of the war, about 68 percent of the federation's forces were stationed in Bosnia.[11]

The Bosnian arsenal thus explains not only the sources of Bosnian Serb military strength and the ability of the insurgents to continue fighting for many years. It also explains Milošević's strong interest in Bosnia and his expectation that eventually the Bosnian Serbs would join their emancipated territory to Serbia. They would bring a significant dowry to Belgrade.

Weaknesses of the Muslim Side

Bosnian Serbs were initially successful in seizing control of land because of the weaknesses of the Bosnian government in Sarajevo. Aside from an inferiority in weapons capability, the Bosnian government was chaotic in almost every respect, political, economic, and military. The defection of the Croat minority in 1992, however, was another source of the Bosnian government's weakness in fighting the Serb insurgency.

1. Administrative Disarray

In the early months of the war against the Serb insurgency, Bosnian government decisions were made on the spur of the moment without benefit of careful discussion and deliberation. Most Serb members of the government who had left were not replaced, leaving huge gaps in chains of responsibility. Serb policemen set up parallel police forces in Serb-held territory, driving out the legitimate law-enforcement authorities over most of the republic.

The Muslim side also suffered from acute shortages of food and medicines. The Serb insurgents blocked normal food and medicine deliveries to Sarajevo and disrupted communications facilities, forcing government leaders and EC and UN personnel to negotiate with representatives of the Serb army over television or radio, with amateur radio operators providing the government's only communications links with most of the republic. The banks had no money, forcing practically everyone to work voluntarily, since there was no way to pay them.[12]

2. Problems in the Bosnian "Army"

The Bosnian government's so-called "army" was initially a militia-style defense force made up of Muslims, Croats, and some Serbs hastily thrown together without even common uniforms. Criminals joined the military ranks, and many people used their weapons to fight private wars. A weapons shortage soon became apparent, especially after the United Nations declared an international embargo on weapons shipments to either side in May 1992, a gesture that hurt the Muslims more than the Serbs, who already were well armed with weapons obtained from Yugoslav federal arsenals and who had easy access to additional weapons from the Serbia.

3. Defection of the Croat Minority

A decisive weakness of the Bosnian government in responding to the Serb insurgency was the eventual defection of the Croat minority. Although the Croat minority initially had joined the Muslims in supporting Bosnian independence in late 1991, it had been divided over what to do about the Serb insurgency. Moderate Croats who lived close to Muslims in ethnically mixed communities, including Sarajevo, considered themselves as much Bosnian as Croat and favored the preservation of Bosnian unity and territory. But Croats who lived in communities mainly in western Herzegovina near the Republic of Croatia, where they were in a majority, were more nationalist and favored the creation of a Croat administrative entity with substantial autonomy of Sarajevo and close links to the Republic of Croatia.

In 1992 and 1993, the nationalists had the upper hand. Many Bosnian Croats resented the failure of the government in Sarajevo in 1991 to show any real interest in the Serb insurgency in the Krajina and in Slavonia and its reluctance to cooperate with Croatia against the Yugoslav army's support of the Serb insurgency against Croatian authority in those regions and incursions into northern Bosnia. On May 7, 1992, leaders of Bosnia's Croat and Serb minorities met in Graz, Austria, and agreed to divide Bosnia-Herzegovina between them, leaving only a small amount of territory to the Muslims, whose leaders did not attend this meeting.[13] Next, on July 3, 1992, the Bosnian Croat nationalist leader Mate Boban, with encouragement from Zagreb, declared the establishment in areas of Bosnia inhabited primarily by Croats of the Croat community of Herzeg-Bosna with its own government.[14]

Bosnian Croats were encouraged to make common cause with the Serbs by President Tudjman. In early 1992, Tudjman shared Milošević's view of the inevitability of Bosnia's disintegration and wanted Croatia to annex territory in northwestern Bosnia inhabited by Croats.[15] Tudjman allegedly argued, and many Croats in Croatia as well as in Bosnia apparently agreed, that Croatia was the defender of Croatian–Catholic civilization against the Muslims and that Croatia had historical claims to territory in Bosnia-Herzegovina. Indeed, Tudjman had made no secret of his belief that, as far as he was concerned, Croatia's "real" boundaries were those in the World War II era, when an independent Croatian state included a substantial amount of northern Bosnia-Herzegovina inhabited predominantly by Croats.[16]

For two years into the war with the Serbs, the Bosnian government had to cope with a Croat insurgency that severely taxed its limited resources. The fighting between Croats and Muslims was occasionally very harsh, as in Mostar, which was devastated. Both sides fought bitterly for control of the city where the two communities had lived peacefully for many years. Eventually the historic bridge across the Neretva River built by the Turks centuries earlier, one of the most famous historical sites in central Yugoslavia, was destroyed.[17]

4. The Problem of Fikret Abdić

A distraction more than a weakness was the appearance in the early 1990s of autonomist groups seeking their own independence of Sarajevo. They were Muslim, and some were active in western Bosnia and in the region around Tuzla. The most prominent consisted of the followers of Fikret Abdić, a popular Muslim businessman in the northwestern Bosnian town of Velika Kladuša not far from Bihać. Abdić actually fought against Bosnian Muslim forces as they were battling Serb insurgents. He declared his town of about 50,000 Bosnian-

Muslims autonomous of Sarajevo at the end of 1993 and proceeded to conclude separate treaties of peace with Serb insurgent forces, which allowed him to trade with Zagreb and Belgrade and turn his Velika Kladuša into a commercial gold mine.[18]

The Izetbegović leadership was enraged by the divisive behavior of Abdić, seeing it as a boon to the Serb side. It refused to tolerate these rebellious coreligionists and on several occasions engaged in fierce hand-to-hand combat with them. It certainly ignored Abdić in any discussions with either the West or with Tudjman and Milošević about the constitutional future of the Bosnian state.

The International Dimension

The United Nations, Western Europe, and the United States deplored the outbreak of war in Bosnia-Herzegovina. It was the first large-scale conflict since World War II and in many respects replicated its brutality. While the UN was willing to become directly involved militarily as well as in other ways to promote peace and dispense humanitarian assistance to the beleaguered civilian population, the West tried hard to do the same without interference in the fighting, though on many occasions the Americans, at least, were sorely tempted to take the Muslim side against the Serbs. The development of Western policy was complicated by the need to deal with Bosnia's powerful neighbors, Serbia and Croatia, who tried to exploit the conflict in Bosnia for their own benefit and for that reason helped to prolong it.

1. The United Nations

The United Nations tried to promote peace among Serbs, Muslims, and Croats in Bosnia-Herzegovina by brokering cease-fires and by formulating peace plans. The UN also tried to provide humanitarian relief and protect civilians under the most difficult conditions and punish those who obstructed its peacemaking and humanitarian endeavors by imposing economic and military sanctions on Yugoslavia.

Cease-Fires

Almost all the UN-sponsored cease-fire agreements in Bosnia-Herzegovina were broken as quickly as they were made, sometimes by the Muslim side but mostly by the Serbs. The Muslim side always demanded Serb evacuation of captured territory, while the Serbs insisted that the Muslims accept the permanent loss of territory and recognize their so-called Serb Republic of Bosnia-Herzegovina. It did not take long for the Serb side to learn that disregard of UN cease-fires carried no threat of retribution. UN Secretary-General Boutros-Ghali insisted that

UN forces in Bosnia, like those already deployed in Croatia, were not to get involved in the fighting and were to shoot only in self-defense. UN military personnel soon became "clay pigeons" for the belligerents, especially the Serbs, who rarely missed an opportunity to ridicule, humiliate, and assault them. UN efforts to achieve a permanent cease-fire between the belligerents turned out to be futile. The deep-seated hostility and unrelenting suspicion and distrust each side had toward the other were simply too much for the best efforts of the UN to overcome.

Peace Plans

The so-called Vance–Owen Peace Plan, endorsed by the Security Council on April 17, 1993, and presented to the combatants by UN special envoy to Yugoslavia Cyrus Vance and European Community (EC) mediator David Owen, would have divided Bosnia-Herzegovina into ten largely autonomous ethnic-based provinces under a confederated central government in Sarajevo. None of the enclaves were to be ethnically pure: Muslims were to predominate in three, Serbs in one, and power would be shared in five by Muslims and Croats or Muslims and Serbs. Sarajevo, the tenth province, would preserve its traditional ethnic mix. Bosnia-Herzegovina was to be demilitarized, with the United Nations responsible for collecting heavy artillery, a provision that mostly affected the Serb side because it had the bulk of heavy weaponry. The plan also required the Serbs to give up any idea of joining their territory in Bosnia to the Republic of Serbia. To enforce the plan, Vance and Owen proposed a UN peacekeeping force of 25,000 troops supported by U.S. and NATO warplanes and the use of American-supplied satellite communications.[19]

Karadžić signed the plan in April 1993 in response to pressure from the West but also from President Milošević, who was concerned about the damage to his country by the international trade embargo and diplomatic ostracism. By this time Milošević also believed that the Bosnian Serbs had obtained as much territory, actually 70 percent of Bosnia-Herzegovina, as the international community would let them have.[20]

President Izetbegović of Bosnia, however, rejected the plan. Acceptance of the plan, in his view, amounted to an endorsement of Bosnian Serb "ethnic cleansing policies" and in effect would result in the dissolution of his country. Many citizens of Sarajevo of Muslim, Croat, and Serb backgrounds criticized the plan, saying it divided power on the basis of nationality and creed, effectively destroying Bosnia's unique centuries-old multicultural ethnic mix of populations.[21] Izetbegović, moreover, found solace in his opposition to Vance–Owen from former British prime minister Margaret Thatcher, who was convinced that it would leave the Muslims powerless and turn them into a radicalized irredentist refugee population driven to terrorism in Europe to get back their land. The new Clinton administration also objected to the plan because it accepted illegal Serb seizures of territory.[22]

Owen urged the Muslim side to accept his plan because it was the best deal he and Vance could get given Serb military superiority. The plan had many advantages for the Muslim side. Under the plan, the Serbs would have had to return 27 percent of the land they had seized and would be autonomous in only three of the ten provinces. Territory inhabited by Muslims and Croats would have included most of the country's mines and industry. And another advantage of the plan for the Muslim side was that it would have kept the Bosnian state intact. A new constitution, while granting a high degree of autonomy to each province, specifically forbade any province from declaring its independence and annexing itself to another state. In May 1993, convinced that the plan did in fact favor the Muslims, Serb military leaders overruled Karadžić and rejected the plan. And in a referendum in May, Bosnian Serb voters upheld the decision of the military.[23]

Another UN plan, somewhat more favorable to the Serb side, quickly followed. In June 1993, former Norwegian foreign minister Thorwald Stoltenberg, Vance's successor as chief UN mediator in Yugoslavia, and Owen proposed the partition of Bosnia-Herzegovina into three ethnic-based ministates with a weak central authority to regulate trade and foreign policy. The Owen–Stoltenberg Plan assigned the Bosnian Serbs up to 50 percent of the republic's territory, the Croats about 30 percent, and the Muslims 20 percent. The Croat and Serb ministates were allowed, if they wished, to link up eventually with the Croatian and Serbian republics that they bordered. Sarajevo was to be demilitarized and placed under United Nations administration for two years.[24]

Izetbegović denounced this plan as well, saying it was tantamount to genocide for the Muslims. Bosnia's Muslim-dominated Parliament agreed with Izetbegović and eventually rejected the plan at the end of August 1993, saying that it would bring about the destruction of the Bosnian state and was a step toward the creation of a "Greater Serbia" and a "Greater Croatia."[25]

The Bosnian Serbs also rejected the new plan, even though it was more favorable to them than the Vance–Owen Plan had been. They refused to give back additional territory sought by Izetbegović, including the towns of Foča, Višegrad, Bratunac, Rogatica, and Zvornik, which, they said, was and would remain Serbian, since Serbs had been a majority in the area before many had been killed during World War II. The Owen–Stoltenberg Plan had failed, and the fighting continued for the remainder of 1993 and into 1994.[26]

Humanitarian Relief

The UN had more success in providing relief to areas that were cut off from the outside world by fighting and were short of food, medicines, and other necessities of daily life, although there were problems. In many instances Bosnian Serb forces intercepted and delayed these convoys to prevent food and medicines from reaching Muslim areas under siege. From the point of view of Bosnian

Serbs, the UN was undermining their efforts to drive Muslims from territory they wanted to control. Eventually, the Serbs saw the UN's humanitarian efforts as part of a pro-Muslim bent, despite the organization's insistence that its policies in Bosnia-Herzegovina were neutral and objective. Muslims also contributed to the difficulties of UN relief efforts. In response to Serb attacks from artillery positions on the outskirts of Sarajevo, Muslim forces threatened attacks on UN supply efforts. The Muslims also disrupted UN aid deliveries because they wanted conditions to become so desperate in Sarajevo that the West would have to become militarily involved out of sheer embarrassment at the suffering. This Muslim behavior suggested how maddeningly difficult the UN relief mission had become. Furthermore, to defend its convoys, the UN had to deploy troops throughout Bosnia who were prevented from using heavy force to defend themselves. Worse, their deployment, which made them potential hostages, prevented effective UN retaliation for Serb interference.[27]

"Safe Havens"

The UN tried to protect the hundreds of thousands of refugees, mostly Muslims forced from their homes, by establishing, in May 1993, so-called "safe havens" in Sarajevo, Tuzla, Zepa, Goražde, Bihać, and Srebrenica, where more than a million Muslims lived.[28] When Bosnian Serb forces were on the outskirts of Srebrenica, threatening to decimate its predominantly Muslim population, the Security Council passed the "safe havens" resolution, declaring that these cities should be free from armed attacks and from any other hostile act.[29]

The "safe havens" resolution was difficult to enforce. No mention was made of how the UN would get the Serbs to recognize the "safe havens" and refrain from attacking them. The UN deployed far fewer troops than was deemed necessary by its own military command in Bosnia.[30] The Serbs therefore were able to attack the "safe havens," especially Sarajevo, Srebrenica, and Bihać, with impunity. In response, the Security Council in July 1993 authorized the doubling of the 9,000 UN peacekeeping forces protecting the Muslims and the delivery of food and medicine. But West European countries would not commit more ground troops to UN peacekeeping forces, insisting that the United States help.[31] Eventually the Bosnian Serbs entered and occupied some of the safe havens, among them Srebrenica, and continued their bombardment of Sarajevo.

Sanctions

When the Bosnian Serbs ignored an ultimatum to end the fighting and continued to interfere with UN agencies delivering humanitarian aid, the Security Council, on May 30, 1992, imposed a universal blockade of all trade and all scientific, cultural, and sports exchanges with the rump Yugoslavia created by President Milošević in April 1992.[32] Persistent violations of the sanctions led to a significant toughening of enforcement procedures. On April 17, 1993, the Security Council banned transshipment of goods through Serbia and Montenegro by land and transshipment on the Danube River unless UN inspectors were present. The Council also impounded Yugoslav transport and cargo outside its borders and froze its financial assets abroad.[33]

The weapons embargo had a psychological as well as a military impact on the Bosnian Muslim side. Given the existing military superiority of the Serbs, the Bosnian government felt betrayed by the international community, and especially by the West, which so recently had recognized its independence. In effect, the embargo gave the Serb side a permanent superiority that could be undone only by a massive infusion of weapons and other kinds of military assistance. And, worse, it opened the way for the brutal Serb military campaigns against Muslim civilians, whose army lacked the wherewithal to defend them.

On the other hand, while sanctions on trade did not cripple the Serbian economy, they severely debilitated it in the next few years, causing severe shortages of everything and imposing intolerable hardships on Serb society, in particular, inflation and unemployment, which especially affected city areas, including Belgrade. For a while Serbia endured the strain. There were ways to ease it. The Milošević regime, which had been preparing for the trade blockade for several months, leased additional oil barges from Czechoslovakia and Ukraine and used its own and Romanian vessels to bring oil up the Danube River from Romanian ports to refineries near Belgrade.[34]

The trade sanctions also radicalized Serbian nationalism, discouraging compromise and providing an incentive to fight on indefinitely regardless of the cost in loss of lives, damage to property, and dislocation of people. By closing off supplies from abroad, the sanctions made Serbs rely more on themselves and united them in their response to the common danger to their survival. Moreover, the more hardship there was among the Serbs, the greater the appeal of the radical nationalism of Milošević and Karadžić, who took satisfaction in using the sanctions to vindicate their most extreme views, in particular, that the outside world was against them and sought their subjugation. Moreover, the sanctions provided Milošević with a justification for accentuating his informal repression of non-Serbs through the expansion of the police and the frequent disregard of human rights in the name of order and security.[35]

The sanctions did not strengthen, as was hoped, the liberal opposition to war and to Milošević's leadership. Rather, the hardships they caused encouraged an exodus of middle-class moderates from Serbia to escape the increasing harshness of daily life as well as a radicalization of Serbs outraged over the way economic sanctions tended to hurt the Serb side more than the Muslim side.

Eventually the sanctions did significantly debilitate Serbia's economy and demoralize its leadership, inducing Milošević to accommodate Western demands to rein in the Bosnian Serbs. But this did not happen until after a horrendous loss of Bosnian lives and a mind-boggling devastation of the central Yugoslav terrain, which may well take many decades to reverse. By 1994, as economic conditions in Serbia deteriorated with no relief in sight because of the UN determination to give no quarter until Milošević obliged his allies in Bosnia to compromise, the sanctions posed an increasingly serious political risk for Milošević.

The arms embargo, however, ironically did benefit the Bosnian Serb side, enabling it to maintain military superiority until well into 1995, which emboldened it to reject territorial compromise that could have led to peace. The arms embargo denied the Muslim side access to weapons that could have evened the military playing field and possibly induced the Bosnian Serbs to compromise early on in the war. Indeed, the Muslims had little in the way of weapons beyond what they could steal or capture from their enemies or obtain from sympathetic Islamic states in the Middle East.[36]

In October 1992, in response to Bosnian Serb use of air power against Muslim population centers, the UN imposed another sanction when it banned all military flights over Bosnia-Herzegovina. Although this UN action lacked explicit enforcement procedures, UN officials were in contact with the military commanders of all sides and were hopeful—though there was little reason for them to be so—that the Serbs would comply with the ban.[37]

The Bosnian Serbs, however, all but ignored the no-fly zone because they knew they would not be punished. Although the ban was toughened at the end of March 1993, when the UN authorized individual members to act on their discretion to intercept violators, the Bosnian Serbs, after a period of compliance, subsequently continued to disregard the ban.[38]

Another UN sanction to induce a cutoff of Belgrade's assistance to the Bosnian Serb insurgents was the decision at the end of April 1993 to deny the two republics membership as the Federal Republic of Yugoslavia. The Security Council noted that henceforth Yugoslavia would no longer be able to participate in the activities of the Economic and Social Council.[39] This gesture was a psychological blow to Milošević, deepening Serbia's isolation from the international community and underlining international opprobrium toward a people who were already hypersensitive about their perceived rejection by the community of nations.

War Crimes Prosecution

In response to world outrage at Serb atrocities, including rape, murder, and the genocide of ethnic-cleansing policies against the Muslim population in Bosnia-Herzegovina, the UN decided in October 1992 to set up a war crimes commission. Modeled loosely on the Allied War Crimes Commission in World War II, the commission was charged to look for breaches of the 1949 Geneva Conventions, which define the rights of prisoners of war and civilians caught in war zones. The commission would also look for violations of principles of international law recognized in the Charter of the Nuremberg Tribunal. These principles define three sets of international crimes: crimes against peace, which include planning or waging a war of aggression; war crimes, which include mistreatment of civilians or prisoners of war; and crimes against humanity, which include murder, extermination, enslavement, deportation, or other inhuman acts done against any civilian population.[40] By mid-February 1993, with endless reports of atrocities by all belligerents—Serbs, Croats, and Muslims—against civilians, the UN decided to convene a war crimes trial. The support for such a move was strong among the West European nations and the United States. They saw Milošević in particular as an international criminal, responsible for the ethnic-cleansing policies pursued by the Bosnian Serbs, despite his assertions of neutrality in the Bosnian war.[41]

At the end of May 1993, the Security Council set up the war crimes tribunal, and by mid-September 1993, the General Assembly had completed the election of the eleven judges who would serve on it. Although Muslims were the victims of many of the atrocities committed in Bosnia-Herzegovina, none of the members of the tribunal were Muslim, though judges were selected from three countries with Muslim majorities: Pakistan, Egypt, and Malaysia. This court had no authority to compel nations to hand over accused criminals or evidence.[42]

By the end of 1993, however, the likelihood of international punishment seemed slight, and little has happened since then to suggest that it will ever materialize in any meaningful way, especially in the case of prominent and patently guilty political figures like Milošević, Karadžić, and Mladić. The obstacles to arresting, trying, convicting, and sentencing known perpetrators of war crimes were daunting. The whole project has received little financial support from the international community, especially Western Europe. Gathering evidence against these and other potential defendants is at best difficult, at worst impossible. The evidence lies in places beyond the control of the international community. Perhaps the biggest obstacle to the materialization of the kind of international justice meted out by the Nuremberg War Crimes Trials is a fear among UN members that going after the real culprits of "ethnic cleansing," people like Karadžić, Mladić, and Milošević, could discourage and prevent a permanent peace settlement that must be accepted by these figures. On the other hand, some have argued that eventually these people will receive justice. Karadžić, for example, is afraid to leave Bosnian territory lest he be arrested and held for prosecution, and Mladić went into hiding to escape arrest. Nevertheless, the West has made clear that any agreement ending the war cannot affect any charges of war crimes made against people like Karadžić, Mladić, and others responsible for ethnic cleansing and other violations of human rights of which they are accused by the international community.[43]

2. Western Europe

West European governments individually and collectively within the European Union (EU) shared the international goal of restoring peace in Bosnia-Herzegovina. But they consistently refused to use military force and were determined to avoid a direct involvement to help one side against the other. While they deplored the ethnic-cleansing policies of the Bosnian Serbs, they had little affection for the Muslim side, which they saw as stubborn and unrealistic in its refusal to compromise on political and territorial issues despite the military superiority of their enemy. Moreover, use of force against the Serb side and the arming of the Muslim side, which would have involved a lifting of the arms embargo, would have invited retaliation against British and French ground troops participating in UN humanitarian operations in Bosnia. The EU shied away from direct involvement because, as its president, Jacques Delors, put it, the transition away from the cold war had produced a plethora of demands that the EU was hard put to accommodate. It was unrealistic, so this argument ran, to expect the EU to respond effectively to the Bosnian crisis.[44]

EU nations, rather, used political and economic diplomacy to bring about peace in Bosnia and, at the end of August 1992, convened an international conference in London to discuss a peace settlement. What happened at this conference set a pattern for future diplomatic efforts. The conference included Owen, UN Secretary-General Boutros-Ghali, the warring factions in Bosnia, their patrons in Zagreb and Belgrade, and a delegation of American officials led by Acting Secretary of State Lawrence Eagleberger. The conference gave priority to ending the war in Bosnia by mediation. It also mandated that any settlement must halt ethnic cleansing, bar the acquisition of territory by force, and allow refugees to return home.[45]

The conference was stalemated from the outset. The Muslim side demanded that the Serbs cease their aggression and asked for international support of Bosnia's territorial integrity. The Serb side demanded independence of Sarajevo and control over all the Bosnian territory they had won thus far. Representatives of Croatia, Slovenia, and Macedonia called for a Western military intervention, if necessary, to end the war in Bosnia. And Croatia demanded the return of the 30 percent of its territory in the south, notably the Krajina, now in the hands of the local Serb population. No agreement on anything was possible.[46]

The EC, however, did endorse the Vance–Owen and Owen–Stoltenberg peace plans for Bosnia in 1993, hoping, with futility, as it turned out, that its imprimatur would help persuade the warring parties to accept the plans and negotiate peace. Also, as the war continued throughout the remainder of 1993, some EU countries, in particular, France and Germany, took another approach, proposing a gradual easing of the sanctions against Yugoslavia in return for Belgrade's help in persuading the Bosnian Serbs to compromise on their all-or-nothing territorial ambitions. Opposition by the United States and other EU members to this proposal killed it.[47]

The most dramatic and significant aspect of EU involvement was the deployment of British and French troops in the UNPROFOR to help distribute humanitarian aid. Ironically, the deployment of British and French forces discouraged the EU from taking any coercive measures, such as a lifting of the arms embargo to allow the Muslim government to obtain weapons from abroad, lest such action widen and further brutalize the war by provoking Serb retaliation. The British and French threatened to withdraw their troops if the arms embargo were suspended. In 1994, the EU, contributed little toward peacemaking in Bosnia.

The fifty-three–member Conference on Security and Cooperation in Europe (CSCE) initially tried to get involved in the Bosnian situation, starting with its July 1992 conference in Helsinki, where it suspended Yugoslavia from participation and agreed to participate in efforts to bring about peace. The CSCE sent observer missions to Bosnia to assist in sanctions monitoring and to underline the concern of the larger European community over the brutality of the war, in particular, the establishment of Serb concentration camps where Muslim civilians were interned and many murdered in ways that called to mind the Nazi concentration camps fifty years earlier.[48] But the CSCE was simply too large an organization and too diverse in its membership to exert influence on events in Bosnia, to say nothing of engineering a peace agreement among the combatants. In 1994 and 1995, the CSCE played a marginal role in the Yugoslav crisis.

NATO, on the other hand, did get directly involved, helping the UN enforce its edicts. For example, NATO agreed in early November 1992 to help the UN enforce the trade embargo in coordination with the Western European Union (WEU). But its enforcement action, as well as that of the WEU, was limited to monitoring maritime traffic in the Adriatic Sea and did not involve halting and searching ships suspected of breaking the embargo. Smugglers ignored the trade ban and continued to supply Serbia with oil and other needed items from Malta, Greece, Italy, and Egypt. NATO also had no authority to stop the substantial smuggling that was taking place overland from Greece.

In December 1992, NATO agreed to help enforce the no-fly zone in Bosnia-Herzegovina. But, again, it did little to constrain the Serbs. The British and French insisted that NATO avoid confrontation with the Serbs. President Yeltsin of Russia also did not want to have NATO enforce the UN ban aggressively to avoid provoking his conservative rivals, who were pro-Serb. As a result, NATO did not respond to violations of any side until the UN Security Council had acted on an enforcement resolution. Even then, NATO planes were not authorized to bomb antiaircraft positions or surface-to-air missile positions even if attacked. The UN in fact waited over three months to call for enforcement of the no-fly zone. Not until the end of March 1993 was NATO authorized to shoot down planes and helicopters in the no-fly zone. And even then NATO proceeded with great caution and restraint in enforcing the no-fly zone, firing on Serbian aircraft that violated the ban only as a last resort.[49]

NATO also agreed to help the UN maintain the safe havens for Muslims set up in May 1993, but only under special circumstances designed to avoid a confrontation with the Serbs. NATO planes could be used only if UN ground forces protecting the enclaves called for air strikes. Although NATO planes from the United States, Britain, France, and the Netherlands stood poised for action from July 1993 onward, there were no air strikes until early 1994. But the prospect of NATO air strikes did not deter the Serbs from continuing their attacks on the safe havens, including Sarajevo.[50]

NATO intervened in February 1994 in response to an escalation of Bosnian Serb shelling of Sarajevo, which reached a climax on February 6, when a 120-millimeter mortar was fired into a central market in Sarajevo, killing about 68 people and wounding over 100. The Western powers, especially the United States, were enraged and through NATO, on February 9, ordered the Serbs to end their siege of Sarajevo by withdrawing or regrouping under UN control all heavy weapons from a so-called "exclusion zone" within ten days or suffer the consequences of air strikes. UN diplomats approved the NATO ultimatum in the hope that it would give momentum to their latest efforts to negotiate a cease-fire.[51]

This NATO action had some success. The Serb leadership met most of the conditions of the ultimatum, partly out of fear and partly in response to the good offices of the Russian special envoy to Yugoslavia, Vitalii Churkin, who met with Karadžić to persuade him to do whatever was necessary to avoid a punishing NATO attack that Russia as well opposed.[52] There was a temporary lull in the fighting over Sarajevo, and the conclusion of a cease-fire gave its citizens a respite and an appearance of peace returned. The cease-fire eventually was broken. The Bosnian Serbs soon resumed their bombardment of Sarajevo, and the war continued throughout the remainder of 1994 and during the first half of 1995.

NATO finally had a decisive impact in its extensive shelling of several Bosnian Serb ammunition depots and command and control centers in the late spring and during the summer of 1995 to force a removal of heavy artillery around the outskirts of Sarajevo that had been used to bombard the capital in violation of the UN safe-havens edict. NATO air strikes on these occasions were sufficiently destructive to force the Bosnian Serbs to withdraw their heavy guns out of firing range of Sarajevo and eventually to weaken decisively Bosnian Serb military capability, helping the Muslim government to regain control over a substantial amount of territory in the northwest held by the Serbs, roughly the equivalent of what the West had been asking the Serbs to return to the Muslims as part of a comprehensive peace settlement.[53]

All in all, however, up until the summer of 1995, NATO had contributed little more than the EU and the UN to restoring peace. Worse, throughout 1993 and 1994, its restraint undoubtedly encouraged the Bosnian Serbs to continue their landgrabbing war against the Muslims and convinced the hypernationalistic Mladić that he was fighting not only Muslims but also the West.

3. The United States

The Americans were forever in a quandary over what to do about the Bosnian civil war. On the one hand, national self-interest dictated caution and restraint, because there was no convincing evidence that the benefits of an activist policy involving the use of military power outweighed its substantial risks and costs. On the other hand, considerations of morality encouraged a strong impulse to respond with force to Serb outrages and help the Muslim side, which was seen as the underdog.[54]

The Bush Administration

Inspired by its stated commitment to a new world order in which the West would keep rogue governments from aggressive behavior, the Bush administration condemned the Serb insurgency and at times contemplated U.S. military intervention to halt Serb ethnic cleansing. There were compelling arguments in favor of an American military intervention. Strong U.S. action to curb Bosnian Serb landgrabbing might send a clear message to other ethnic groups elsewhere in the world in areas with similarly aggressive ambitions dangerous to international peace and security. Moreover, there had always been a large reservoir of public as well as official sympathy for the Muslim side, which was seen not only as the underdog because of its military inferiority vis-à-vis the well-armed Serbs but also as the hapless victim of grotesque excesses in the form of Serb ethnic-cleansing policies that bordered on genocide. Many in Congress urged a firm policy after the Serbs began to bombard Sarajevo in the spring of 1992, notably, Senate minority leader Bob Dole, Republican of Kansas.[55]

In response to congressional pressure, as well as its own pangs of conscience over the horrors of the war brought home in televised pictures, the administration encouraged the UN to strengthen enforcement of its sanctions against Serbia and Montenegro. Especially concerned with the military inferiority of the Muslim side, Washington urged a naval blockade by NATO ships in the Adriatic to prevent the unloading of embargoed goods at Montenegrin ports. It also proposed a ban on military flights over Bosnia similar to the one imposed on portions of Iraq to protect the Kurds against aggression by Saddam Hussein following the conclusion of the Persian Gulf War.[56]

But the administration refused to go any further. Arguments against direct American military involvement in Bosnia from Congress, from Joint Chiefs of Staff chairman Colin L. Powell, and from other influential sources were overwhelming. These people said involvement in Bosnia would lead to a Vietnam-like sinkhole, with more and more troops being required and not much being accomplished. Congressional opposition to military intervention cut across party and ideological lines and was especially fierce among some legislators who had fought in Vietnam. Representative Robert G. Torricelli, a senior member of the House Foreign Affairs Committee, summed up a widely held congressional point of view when he said that Congress would follow the president to war only when "there is a clear American interest, an identifiable foe, and a sense that victory can be gained at an acceptable price and in an acceptable amount of time."[57] And General Powell consistently argued against force in places like Bosnia, saying U.S. vital interests in Yugoslavia were not clear and efficient use of power to protect those limited interests was not assured. Because of the deep interethnic animosities driving the war between the Muslims and the Serbs, he declared, only a political solution was viable.[58]

Ultimately, the Bush administration decided against a military involvement in the Bosnian conflict, telling President Alija Izetbegović on one occasion that "we are not the world's policeman."[59] Relying on diplomacy to promote peace in Bosnia, the administration sent Ralph R. Johnson, deputy assistant secretary of state for European affairs, to Bosnia to signal both the Bosnian Serbs and the Serb Republic of American anxiety. The Bush administration also exerted pressure directly on the Milošević regime, which it considered largely responsible for the civil war because of its military assistance to the Bosnian Serbs, by withholding recognition of the new Yugoslav state formed by Serbia and Montenegro in April 1992. The administration recalled Ambassador Warren Zimmerman to Washington and tried to ostracize Serbia, proposing that the Conference on Security and Cooperation in Europe meeting in April 1992 in Helsinki suspend Yugoslavia from membership unless it withdrew its forces from Bosnia within a two-week period. And, on May 22, 1992, with no change in policy by Milošević, the administration announced new American sanctions against the Serbian-dominated rump Yugoslavia, closing Yugoslav consulates in New York and San Francisco and expelling Yugoslav military attachés in Washington.[60]

The administration also tried to undermine Milošević's political position inside Serbia during the Serb Republic presidential elections in December 1992 by obliquely endorsing the candidacy of Milan Panić, the prime minister of Yugoslavia and a person who was critical of Belgrade's role in Bosnia, and by accusing Milošević and other Serb nationalists of being war criminals who should be prosecuted. This interference, however, backfired, strengthening the inclination of many Serbian voters to view Milošević as a hero able to stand up to the Americans and to support his reelection.[61]

By the beginning of 1993, when Bush left office, however, the United States had little to show for its opposition to Serb aggression in Bosnia. Bush's failure to do something tangible to bring peace to Bosnia-Herzegovina contributed to a prolongation of the war, undermined his credibility as a foreign-policy leader, and hurt his campaign for the presidency in the summer and fall of 1992.

The Clinton Administration

President Bill Clinton said he was outraged by abusive Serb policies like ethnic cleansing and Serb refusal to make peace. He made an issue of Bush's refusal to do something against the Bosnian Serbs in the 1992 presidential campaign. After his election, on several occasions, usually following some egregious Serb act of brutality against Muslim civilians, Clinton would threaten the use of American military power against the Serb side to make the Bosnian Serb leadership heed UN resolutions and induce a move to the peace table. The administration considered three military options: air strikes to knock out Serb artillery bombarding Sarajevo and other Muslim population centers; lifting the UN arms embargo to allow arms to go to the Bosnians; and the deployment of U.S. ground combat troops to help the UN enforce its peace plans or withdraw its military personnel.[62]

Clinton favored the so-called lift-and-strike options (lifting the arms embargo and striking the Serbs from the air) because they would benefit the underdog, because they would not require an American troop deployment, because there was strong bipartisan support from Congress for lifting the arms embargo, and because of support for air strikes from influential people, such as Jean Kirkpatrick, Zbigniew Brzezinski, and former President Jimmy Carter.[63]

But in 1993 and 1994 there was strong opposition to the lift-and-strike option and even stronger opposition to any move involving a deployment of American troops in Bosnia, despite sympathy for the Muslim side and outrage over Bosnian Serb ethnic-cleansing policies. The American involvement in Somalia in 1993, not to mention the memory of the brief American deployment in Lebanon in the early 1980s, reminded Americans of the risks and dangers of deploying troops in difficult situations like Bosnia-Herzegovina. As Congress pushed for a withdrawal of U.S. troops from Somalia by March 1994, there was little reason to believe it would agree to another and probably more costly and dangerous involvement in Bosnia. Indeed, recalling Vietnam, many in Congress from both parties told Clinton what Bush had been told, that there were not enough votes for armed action in Bosnia. Dimitri Simes, senior associate at the Carnegie Endowment for International Peace, echoed the arguments of Colin Powell that the United States should stay out of Bosnia because there was no oil there. Simes insisted that the United States had no good reason to defend the former Yugoslavia's internal administrative borders created by Tito's communist regime "and based neither on history nor on current demography."[64]

Furthermore, some American experts doubted the efficacy of arming the Muslim side, arguing that many months would be needed to train Muslim troops to use antitank weapons. How, the experts asked, would the arms arrive? Bosnia was landlocked, and the only nearby ports were in Croatia, which would demand compensation for the transit of weapons. The Croatians would steal some weapons, perhaps as much as half, greatly enhancing Croatian military strength, a development that Washington initially opposed.[65]

The Clinton administration also had to take into account the continuing British and French opposition to arming the Muslims. They feared Serb retribution against their troops serving with the UN. Indeed, Prime Minister John Major of

Britain reportedly told Secretary of State Christopher of his fear that his government might fall if Washington implemented the lift-and-strike options.[66] The West Europeans, moreover, were still convinced that military action against the Serbs would widen and prolong the war and increase casualties. There was also a sense in Western Europe that the Serbs had won their war against the Muslim government in Sarajevo, and nothing short of a massive allied invasion of Yugoslavia could reverse their victory.

Russia also opposed arming the Muslims, with the Yeltsin government insisting that the introduction of more weapons into Bosnia would simply escalate the killings and increase the risk of casualties for UN peacekeepers. There was much Russian sympathy for the Serb side, especially in the Parliament. For example, at the end of February 1993, the Russian Supreme Soviet demanded that the Yeltsin government tell the UN that, if sanctions against Yugoslavia were not eased, Russia would withdraw its support for them.[67]

Moreover, despite occasional threats to exercise the lift-and-strike option and statements of interest in sending U.S. combat troops to Bosnia to help the UN enforce a peace plan accepted by the combatants, Clinton always shied away from these options, especially a troop deployment, when it looked as if he might have to exercise them. Indeed, he always seemed to be looking for a way to avoid a deployment of U.S. forces. For example, while pledging that U.S. troops would help enforce a peace plan accepted by the combatants, he insisted he could not redeem such a pledge without explicit assurances that Serb military forces in fact would abide by a peace plan accepted by its leadership, an unlikely prospect since they had violated almost every past cease-fire they had pledged to respect. Clinton also said that Congress would have to give explicit approval before any deployment could begin.[68] Indeed, contradicting promises he had made during the presidential campaign that he would take positive action, Clinton eventually settled on a policy of caution and restraint in Bosnia, much like that of Bush, because, as Christopher declared on June 3, 1993, the situation in Bosnia-Herzegovina did not involve American vital interests.[69]

What Clinton was prepared to do was provide American humanitarian assistance to ease the sufferings of several hundred thousand Muslim civilians stranded in eastern Bosnia. For example, to break a Serb blockade of Muslim enclaves in February 1993, Clinton proposed to the allies and to the UN to conduct an airlift of emergency food and medicine and carried it through in the beginning of March 1993.[70] A three-day airlift, which dropped about fifty-eight tons of food and medicine, however, was more significant as a symbol than as an effective relief mission because little of the supplies reached Muslim towns under siege. Nevertheless, the airlift sent a message of American concern and of a strong will to do something to ease the suffering of war victims and could have been interpreted as criticism of the West European nations for not doing more to help the Muslims. Subsequently, there were more U.S. airlifts to central Bosnia in cooperation with the UN, which welcomed the American gesture though the allies criticized it as diplomatic grandstanding.[71]

By the end of 1993, the Clinton Administration had little to show for its rhetoric of anger at and threats to the Serb side in the Bosnian war. The ephemeral response of the administration to the Bosnian civil war in 1993 arguably helped prolong it into 1994 and 1995 by encouraging the Serb side to think that it could continue its war against the Muslims without impunity.

The Muslim Side Gains Strength in 1994 and 1995

In the first eighteen months of the war, it seemed that the Bosnian Serbs would eventually triumph. But by the latter half of 1993, a Bosnian Serb military victory was less certain. The Muslim side benefited from its own resilience, seen in the failure of the Serbs, despite their military superiority in weapons, to defeat Muslim forces decisively on the battlefield; from a reconciliation with the Croat minority and the formation of a federation with them supported by both the United States and the Republic of Croatia; and from an intensification of Western diplomatic efforts, especially on the part of the Clinton administration, reinforced by an increase of military pressure on the Serb side, to bring the warring parties to agreement on a territorial compromise on territorial issues that would open the way to a peace agreement.

1. Sources of Muslim Resilience

Despite the arms embargo, weapons did trickle into Bosnia from sympathetic countries, especially in the Arab-Islamic Middle East. The Muslim superiority in manpower, moreover, was finally beginning to counterbalance the initial Serb superiority in heavy weaponry. At the same time, the Muslim side benefited from the growing weaknesses of the Serb side. For example, after two years of fighting what was perceived to be an enfeebled enemy, the Bosnian Serbs had failed to score a decisive victory, largely because of their hit-and-run strategy against Muslim population centers. While causing much damage to civilian property and many civilian casualties, Serb strategy, especially ethnic cleansing, did not bring effective permanent Serb control of contested territory. As the Bosnian Serb forces gradually experienced a decline in morale, just the opposite was happening on the Muslim side, which was imbued with a fanatic determination to recapture lost territory containing the towns and villages that were home to many Muslim soldiers. Indeed, the Muslim lack of heavy weapons encouraged the development of a high degree of mobility that eventually contributed to a leveling of the battlefield.[72]

2. Muslim Reconciliation with the Croat Minority

The Muslim side was also strengthened by a reconciliation with the Croat minority, encouraged by the United States. In the latter part of 1993, the Clinton administration proposed, and began working with Bosnian Croat and Muslim officials for, a federation of Muslims and Bosnian Croats to end the war between them, isolate and weaken the Serbs, and, conceivably, induce their willingness to compromise on a territorial settlement that would bring peace and diminish the possibility of a large American troop deployment that neither Clinton nor Congress wanted. The federation, which envisaged eventual linkage with the Republic of Croatia, had the support of President Tudjman of Croatia, who saw the possibility of creating a "greater Croatia" consisting of the Krajina and a portion of northwestern Bosnia inhabited by Croats. Moreover, he may well have reasoned that, if he supported the federation, the United States and other Western powers, which also backed the federation in the hope that it would eventually include the Bosnian Serbs and provide the basis for ending the civil war, would allow him the free hand in the Krajina and Slavonia he needed to recover control of the territory.[73]

In mid-March 1994, Bosnian government officials and the political leadership of the Croat minority formally agreed to the federation, as well as a constitution providing for a presidency, a Parliament, and a decentralized cantonal system of local government. Governments at both the central and the cantonal levels would be ethnically mixed. Central and cantonal governments would share responsibility for human rights, transport, and repatriation of refugees. Croat and Muslim military leaders agreed to a joint military command. Foreign policy, defense based on joint Croat-Muslim armed forces, and trade, fiscal, monetary, and reconstruction policy would be handled by a mixed Muslim–Croat central government.[74]

By bringing the Bosnian Croats back to the Muslim side, the federation considerably strengthened the Bosnian government psychologically, and to a degree militarily, helping it in the fall of 1994 to make some deep inroads into Serb-held territory and regain control of some of it in the region around Kupres to the north and west of Sarajevo.[75] The federation also benefited the Bosnian Croats by acknowledging their equality with the Muslims and by guaranteeing their right as a constituent nation with the option of confederating with the Republic of Croatia. Moreover, the Croats won these advantages despite the military ascendancy of the Muslim side by the time of the agreement.[76]

The federation also provided advantages to the Republic of Croatia, the reason why Tudjman went along with it. Apart from American readiness to reward Zagreb for its cooperation with reconstruction aid once the war was over, the federation opened a legal avenue for eventual administrative linkage between the Republic of Croatia and the Croat community in Bosnia. Tudjman thus obtained implicit American backing for a restoration of Croatia's pre-war boundary in the south.

The advantages for the Bosnian Croats, however, may eventually work to the detriment of the Muslims. If the Muslims have a falling-out with the Croats and if the Bosnian Croats do decide to join the Republic of Croatia, as may well be the case, the Muslims will be confined to a narrow strip of territory between a greater Croatia and either a Bosnian Serb state protected by Serbia or a greater Serbia, should the Serbian Republic eventually annex the territory of the Bosnian Serbs.

In any event, in the latter part of 1994, the Muslim–Croat federation and the momentary Muslim military success against the Bosnian Serbs provoked a sharp response from the Bosnian Serbs and from Serbs in the Krajina, who were fearful that the restoration of Muslim control over Bosnian territory neighboring the Knin region of southwestern Croatia would weaken their independence of Zagreb. In October 1994, the Krajina Serbs joined with Bosnian Serbs to force a retreat of Bosnian government forces from the territory just captured. The Bosnian Serbs and their allies eventually threatened the predominantly Muslim city of Bihać, which had been a UN-declared safe haven. By the end of 1994, Bosnian Serb forces had successfully recaptured all the territory temporarily lost to the Muslim side and were on the threshold of occupying Bihać. At this point, there was a temporary cessation of fighting between the Muslim–Croat and the Serb forces as a result of a cease-fire arranged in December 1994 by former President Jimmy Carter. It provided for a truce, UN monitoring of heavy weapons, and the opening of routes for relief convoys. But it did not lead to a peace agreement, and within four months fighting resumed in northwest Bosnia, especially over Bihać. The Serbs reneged on opening roads for UN relief deliveries, and there was no progress toward a political settlement.[77]

3. Western Diplomacy: The "Contact Group"

Given the failure throughout 1993 and early 1994 of the UN/EU–sponsored peace plans, Britain, France, and Germany, along with the United States and Russia, decided to try their own hand at getting the Bosnian Serbs to the peace table. In May 1994, they formed the so-called "Contact Group," which proposed a territorial compromise in which the Bosnian Serb side would get 49 percent of Bosnian territory and the Bosnian government side would get 51 percent. The powers also agreed that the Bosnian Serbs, after the conclusion of peace with the Bosnian government, could, if they wanted, join their territory to Serbia. It was not a bad deal for the Serbs or for the Republic of Serbia.[78]

The Bosnian government accepted it, though with some hesitation, because it obviously meant a substantial reduction of the territory it controlled when it became independent in early 1992. By the end of 1994, however, the Serb side had firmly rejected it. Serb political and military leaders and Bosnian Serb voters opposed surrendering territory they had conquered in the preceding two years.

The Contact Group was divided over what to do next. The United States seemed willing to exert strong pressure on the Serb side to accept the 51/49 proposal. For example, with an eye to the strong pro-Muslim sentiment in Congress, Clinton publicly declared that, if the Bosnian Serbs did not accept the plan by October 15, 1994, he would seek a UN resolution lifting the arms embargo. And in November, as support for lifting the arms embargo increased with the Republican landslide in the congressional elections, the administration announced that the United States would no longer help to enforce the arms embargo or provide intelligence on apparent violations of it to other NATO allies.[79]

The West European members of the Contact Group, on the other hand, seemed less willing to push the Bosnian Serbs hard to accept the 51/49 plan and were inclined to give diplomacy more time to influence decision making in Belgrade and Pale (the capital of the self-styled "Serb Republic of Bosnia." They opposed the strong American gestures. The British and French threatened to withdraw or reduce their forces in UNPROFOR if the United States unilaterally lifted the arms embargo on Yugoslavia. The Russians were adamantly opposed to "strong-arming" the Bosnian Serbs.

Russia and the Contact Group

Russia was a serious threat to the unity of the Contact Group because of its sympathy for the Serb side. Apart from opposing Western coercion of the Serbs, Russia called for a lifting of UN sanctions against the Serbian Republic. Russia's position doubtlessly helped embolden the Bosnian Serb leadership to reject the Contact Group plan.

While the Yeltsin government wanted to belong to the Contact Group and supported its 51/49 compromise, it was unwilling to coerce the Serbs to accept it, largely because throughout 1994 Yeltsin had been under relentless pressure from conservatives and nationalists, notably, Vladimir Zhirinovskii, whose Liberal Democratic Party had garnered about 25 percent of the popular vote in the December 12, 1993, parliamentary elections, to look out for Serb interests and resist Western pressures on the Serbs. The nationalists insisted that Russia should stand by the Serbs, as Russia had done in the past. They insisted also that the Yeltsin government not kowtow to U.S. policy, which was pro-Muslim and anti-Serb, simply to ingratiate itself with Washington for the sake of getting economic and financial concessions.

Yeltsin, however, resisted conservative pressures and agreed to Russian membership in the Contact Group and to support for its 51/49 proposal. Yeltsin had never been comfortable with a strongly pro-Serb position. Indeed, the Kremlin sometimes had found it very difficult, even distasteful, to support the Bosnian Serbs as strongly as the nationalist politicians urged. Quite apart from Bosnian Serb brutality condemned by the international community—at no time did Moscow ever condone ethnic cleansing—the Kremlin found the Bosnian Serb leaders unreliable, willing to make promises and then equally willing to break them. For example, just when the Yeltsin government thought it had won a diplomatic victory in getting the Bosnian Serb leaders to show restraint in order to deter a threatened Western military action against them, they would escalate their bombardment of Muslim population centers, including Sarajevo. This Bosnian Serb behavior embarrassed the Yeltsin government, which was trying to show the West it had clout in the Serb side and therefore should be consulted and treated as an equal in the development of Western policy toward Bosnia.[80]

At the same time, however, Yeltsin could not and did not ignore nationalist sentiment, especially since it had a substantial degree of popular support. Thus, while willing to cooperate with some Western policies toward Bosnia, he consistently opposed coercing of the Serb side. The Russian government also was lenient with President Milošević, far more so than the Clinton administration liked, asking him throughout the summer of 1994 to persuade the Bosnian Serbs to accept the Contact Group's proposal but refusing to pressure him to do so.

New American Initiatives

With the Contact Group seemingly immobilized by its differences over approach, the Clinton administration had an opportunity in 1995 to get involved, encouraged no doubt by criticism from the Republican opposition of its perceived passivity in dealing with the Bosnian crisis. The administration also may have been goaded by the aggressive behavior of the Bosnian Serbs toward United Nations personnel. One especially provocative gesture in the late spring of 1995 involved the taking of UN personnel as hostages to discourage NATO air strikes. The Clinton administration offered U.S. assistance should the UN decide to withdraw its military personnel and offered to contribute about 20,000 U.S. troops to a NATO peacekeeping force to replace the departing UN forces, despite opposition to any American military involvement in Bosnia and Clinton's own misgivings. But the prospect of sending troops to a war-torn Bosnia terrified the administration and was another reason for the decision to bring the warring parties to the negotiating table.[81]

The American diplomatic campaign in 1995 focused on Milošević and involved getting him to persuade the Bosnian Serbs to compromise and settle for the 51/49 territorial formula put forward by the Contact Group. The Americans proposed that Bosnia be divided into two self-governing, separate administrative entities, the Muslim-Croat Federation and the Serb Republic of Bosnia, united in a confederation in which the balance of central executive and legislative authority in Sarajevo, which would remain the capital of Bosnia-Herzegovina, would be tilted toward the Muslims and Croats. But, unlike earlier UN peace plans, the American proposal envisaged an eventual linking of the two Bosnian entities to their powerful neighbors: the Muslim-Croat federation to Croatia, and the Bosnian Serb Administration to the Republic of Serbia. The United States asked Tudjman, Izetbegović, and Milošević to discuss its proposition at conferences in Geneva and New York at the end of the summer of 1995.[82]

The American proposal appealed to Milošević who, more than anybody else, held the key to a final settlement and a restoration of peace in Bosnia-

Herzegovina. Moreover, following the November 1994 congressional elections, which brought Republican majorities to both the House of Representatives and the Senate, Milošević had to confront the reality of a toughening U.S. policy toward Serbia and the Bosnian Serbs. Senate majority leader Bob Dole and House of Representatives speaker Newt Gingrich had stated publicly their support for a unilateral American abandonment of the arms embargo as a means of forcing the Bosnian Serbs to accept a territorial compromise that would end the war. Moreover, the Clinton administration took the lead in opposing any relief of the trade embargo and other aspects of the international isolation of Serbia. Yeltsin, too, wanted Milošević to use his influence on the Bosnian Serbs to make peace so as to relieve pressure being exerted on him by nationalists, always ready to confront the United States in Bosnia and risk an unraveling of three years of careful Russian diplomacy to strengthen ties to the United States. Also, public opinion in Serbia was becoming critical of Milošević's supporting of the self-determination of Serb minorities in neighboring republics because of the high cost to the country. Indeed, after three years of direct involvement in the Bosnian civil war, Milošević wanted relief from its burdens on Serbia, and that, more than any other consideration, provided the Serb president with a strong incentive for peacemaking. The key to Milošević's decision to cooperate with U.S. diplomacy lay in the impact of the continuing conflict in Bosnia-Herzegovina on the politics, society, and internal administration of the Serb Republic.[83]

The War and Serbia

The Bosnian civil war had taken its toll on Serbia. The war weakened the Serbian economy. It undermined Milošević's leadership, had a negative impact on Serbia's minorities in Vojvodina and Kosovo, and strained Serbia's union with Montenegro in the new Yugoslav state forged in April 1992. By 1994, President Milošević apparently tired of trying to fulfill his dream of a "greater Serbia" and, in what turned out to be a diplomatic volte-face, started looking for ways to back off from his past support of self-determination among the Serb minorities in both the Krajina and Bosnia-Herzegovina. The United States took advantage of this opportunity to further the cause of peace.

1. A Weakened Economy

By 1993, war and international economic sanctions, had drained the country of so much wealth that the standard of living of most ordinary Serbians had dropped precipitously.[84] By 1993, the international sanctions and the costs of supporting the Bosnian war led to scarcity and hyperinflation in Serbia. The dinar fell to one million to the U.S. dollar, and the German mark had replaced the dinar as the medium of exchange. Banking activity had nearly ceased, with

90 percent of domestic loans outstanding. Average monthly incomes had declined precipitously, some from $1,000 to $100.00; and few people could buy the few goods that were available. There was massive unemployment in the Belgrade region, with factories shut down for lack of supplies. By the summer of 1993, industrial activity had dropped 40 percent, after a 30 percent plunge in 1992; 50 percent of the Belgrade workforce was without a job, while others spent months on forced vacations. Nowhere was the shortage of supplies more apparent than among the sick. Although medicines were allowed into Serbia under the embargo, the raw materials to manufacture them were not, and few medical facilities had the money to buy what they needed.[85]

2. Challenges to Milošević's Leadership

There was always some opposition to Milošević, coming mainly from the urban intelligentsia and other sectors of the professional middle class, which disliked his heavy-handed dictatorial rule and wanted Serbia to adopt the kind of liberalization going on elsewhere in Eastern Europe. When he arrested and imprisoned the popular and charismatic opposition leader Vuk Drašković in early 1991, there was an explosion of antigovernment demonstrations by Drašković's supporters that included calls for Milošević's resignation and the introduction of democracy. While this activity momentarily put the regime on the defensive and led to the release of Drašković, nothing else changed. Milošević continued to rule Serbia with an iron hand.[86]

The Bosnian conflict exacerbated the opposition to Milošević. Despite his skillful use of propaganda, telling Serbian citizens fed up with what they viewed as the worst shortages since World War II that the West was to blame, opposition to his policies mounted in 1993 and 1994. People, especially in the country's urban centers, weary of the war and especially the drain on the economy caused by sanctions and resentful of the regime's tight control over the media that denied them information as well as an opportunity to complain about a loss of political freedom and an increase in economic hardships, called for a softening of policy at home and abroad.

While there was a number of prominent and outspoken intellectuals who condemned Milošević's political excesses, two important Serbian leaders, former Serbian prime minister Milan Panić and former Yugoslav president Dobrica Ćosić, were the most notable critics. Panić, a Belgrade-born successful American businessman whom Milošević had invited to serve as prime minister in 1992 in the hope that he would be helpful in restoring Yugoslav relations with the United States, soon was arguing for a more democratic Yugoslavia through the establishment of a free press, of open and competitive parliamentary elections, of a free-market economy, and of peace in Bosnia even if the Bosnian Serbs had to give back some captured territory. Six months after taking office, Panić challenged Milošević in Serbia's December 1992 presidential elections. He appealed to the so-called "silent Serbian majority" suffering from Milošević's policies of dictatorship at home and aggression abroad. But Panić's bid to oust Milošević failed. He was no match for the dictator, who did everything possible to undermine his rival's campaign. While in spite of this Panić won 90 percent of Belgrade's vote, Milošević won in the conservative countryside and kept the presidency, with 55 percent of the national vote to Panić's 33 percent. With the support of the Yugoslav Parliament, which was dominated by his supporters, Milošević soon finessed the ouster of Panić.[87]

In 1992, another critic of Milošević was Yugoslav president Dobrica Ćosić. At first sympathetic to Milošević's strategy to enhance Serbia's influence in Yugoslavia, Ćosić had become alarmed by the country's international isolation and the punitive sanctions by the United States and UN. Ćosić also realized that under Milošević Serbia had little chance of getting the $3 billion IMF loan he wanted to resuscitate the Yugoslav economy. In the December 1992 presidential elections, Ćosić held back his support of Milošević, who never forgave him for this and forced his resignation from the presidency in June 1993.[88]

On the other side of the Serbian political pendulum were ultraconservatives who championed Milošević's goal of a "greater Serbia," but to a fault. They demanded a tough protective policy toward Serb minorities in Bosnia, Croatia, and Macedonia, seeking emancipation and eventual annexation to Serbia.

The most notorious of these ultraconservatives was Vojislav Šcšelj, leader of the Serbian Radical Party. Hoping to capture Milošević's place as Serbia's "first patriot," Šešelj advocated all-out support of Serbs in Bosnia in the expectation of having their territory be part of a greater Serbia. He saw in Milošević's eventual disenchantment with this policy an opportunity to challenge the Serbian leader. What made him especially dangerous to Milošević was the way in which he styled himself the conscience of the country, urging the Serbian president to stand by kinsmen in Bosnia and the Krajina. Delighted by the ouster of Panić and Ćosić and seemingly indifferent to the hardships caused by the international sanctions, Šešelj condemned the Contact Group's proposed 51/49 split of territory between the Muslim-Croat Federation and the Bosnian Serb Administration. He was incensed by the award of the larger part of Bosnia-Herzegovina to the Muslim government while the Bosnian Serbs controlled most of the country. Šešelj was also critical of Milošević's refusal to stand by the Serb minority in the Krajina as Tudjman was gradually strengthened Croat control over the disputed territory with a view to reimposing Zagreb's rule.

To make his point, Šešelj withdrew his party's support of Milošević in the Serbian Parliament, presenting the Serbian president with the prospect of a vote of no-confidence in late 1993. Milošević struck back. He dissolved the Serbian Parliament and scheduled elections for mid-December, three years before they were supposed to be held. Milošević believed that elections would strengthen his Socialist Party's grip on the Parliament, allowing him a freer hand to solve domestic and international problems without having to worry about being pushed too far too fast by the Šešelj radicals. The elections gave Milošević's party a solid victory. But the wily and sanctimonious Šešelj was not so easily dealt with. Still unmoved by Western pressures, Šešelj continued to badger Milošević throughout 1994, lobbying for Belgrade's continued support of Serb nationalist insurgencies in Bosnia and the Krajina. Šešelj's danger to Milošević in 1994 increased as a result of sympathy for him from Serb officers in the Yugoslav army with family in Bosnia-Herzegovina who opposed pressure on the Bosnian Serb forces to give up conquered territory.[89]

Indeed, the army remained a potential source of support for Šešelj and other ultranationalist politicians. It resented the decline of prestige, deteriorating living conditions, and poor pay. It was especially hostile to the diversion of precious resources to local Serbian police forces, partly to increase their readiness for a confrontation with ethnic minorities, especially the Albanians in Kosovo, that might otherwise have gone to the army.[90]

3. Minority Problems in the Vojvodina and Kosovo

Milošević had to deal with some of the consequences of his own ethnonationalist propaganda and the fierce passions it unleashed in Serbia's northwest province of Vojvodina, which had a Hungarian minority of about 340,000 people. Historically tolerant of the different groups in the region, Vojvodina citizens chafed under restrictive laws introduced by Belgrade in 1990 and 1991, including the suspension of autonomy guaranteed to the province in the 1974 Yugoslav Constitution. Most troublesome to Vojvodina was a Serbian law declaring Serbo-Croatian the national language. Henceforth it was forbidden to use Hungarian in the local administration of Vojvodina. Adding to the discomfort of the Hungarians was the effort of Šešelj's Radical Party and other Serb nationalists to stir up anti-Hungarian feeling in Vojvodina during 1993. The Radical Party in particular began to attract popular support and became influential in the local administrations of Novi Sad, the capital of Vojvodina, and of other cities and towns. Milošević increased the prospects of political instability in Vojvodina by encouraging the settlement of ethnic Serb refugees from the Krajina in predominantly Hungarian neighborhoods. To some in the Hungarian community it appeared that Milošević was laying the ground for a new episode of ethnic cleansing in Vojvodina.[91]

While tension grew in Vojvodina, Milošević faced more problems in Kosovo. Furious over their loss of the administrative autonomy guaranteed in the 1974 Yugoslav Constitution, the Albanian community in Kosovo tried to establish its own version of autonomy by setting up their own schools in private homes, having Albanian doctors care for patients in their own makeshift clinics, and electing their own Kosovo Parliament in May 1992, which chose Ibrahim Rugova as "President of Kosovo." Serb authorities responded by throwing Albanian teachers and students out of schools and universities, by closing hospitals to Albanians, and by firing more than 100,000 Albanians from state jobs.[92]

Terrified by the prospect of coercion in the enforcement of a policy to make Kosovo more "Serbian," Albanians voted overwhelmingly on May 24, 1992, in favor of separation from the Serbian Republic. Serbian authorities declared the vote illegal, reminded Albanians of Kosovo's historic significance for the Serb nation in its war with the Turks centuries ago, and pledged to keep Kosovo a part of Serbia forever. Unlike the breakaway of Slovenes, Croats, Bosnians, and Macedonians from Yugoslavia, the separation of Albanians would involve a loss of Serbia's own territory, which the Serbian Republic would never tolerate. Even critics of Milošević said they would fight, and would send their children to fight, to keep Serbian control of Kosovo.[93]

The volatility of Kosovo's internal political situation after the separation vote increased with the arrival in the province in the spring of 1993 of Željko Raznjatović. Identified as a war criminal in the United States, he was also wanted for armed robbery in Sweden. Known as Arkan, this Bosnian Serb militia leader in the pay of the Milošević government had openly murdered people in Bosnia and Croatia and was suspected of atrocities against Muslims during the Serbian takeover of Zvornik, Bijeljina, and other Bosnian towns. Swaggering around Priština followed by gun-toting bodyguards, his presence enraged the local Albanian population, which saw it as a signal of Belgrade's preparation to intervene in Kosovo to strengthen Serb control.[94]

Milošević's determination to keep the Albanians subordinated politically, economically, and culturally produced an explosive impasse. War between the Serbian government and Kosovo's Albanian majority was not only possible, according to Rugova, it was inevitable. Militant Serb nationalists were adamant about maintaining political control over Kosovo and were quite ready, in the Albanian view, for a war to keep Kosovo part of Serbia. The Serb minority in Kosovo had a monopoly of firepower and was using it to intimidate the Albanians. Priština was surrounded by artillery ranges that belonged to the old Yugoslav army.[95]

A Serbian military takeover of Kosovo could ignite a Balkan war. If Serbs and Albanians in Kosovo start fighting, the Albanian state and the large Albanian minority in the Macedonian Republic might join in.[96] If that happened, Serbia would probably have to invade Macedonia, which some Serbs call "South Serbia." In that event, Greece and Bulgaria would join the fray to take their shares of Macedonian territory. Eventually Turkey might come into such a war on behalf of Muslim Albanians threatened by Serbs, Greeks, and Bulgarians.[97]

4. Montenegro's Disenchantment

In the early 1990s, another problem that came directly from the ongoing war in Bosnia was Montenegro's growing dissatisfaction with Serb dominance of the new Yugoslav state. Montenegrins believed they got little benefit from their close administrative relationship with Serbia. Though they had little direct interest in the Bosnian civil war, they helped pay for it. The Liberal Alliance, a major political party in Montenegro led by Slavko Perović, opposed Serb policy in Bosnia and wanted complete autonomy of Belgrade. President Momir Bulatović of Montenegro and the ruling Democratic Party of Socialists also wanted a substantial distance between their government and the Serbian Republic leadership. Bulatović would prefer a very loose federation of autonomous Yugoslav republics, which Belgrade has always opposed.[98]

Complicating Montenegro's relationship with Serbia is the situation of Muslims in the region of the Sandžak, once a province of the Turkish Empire but eventually split between Serbia and Montenegro. Eighty percent of the Sandžak's population is Muslim. The Sandžak Muslims in Montenegro's jurisdiction have been equitably treated by the Bulatović government, whereas the Muslims who were unfortunate enough to come under Serbian rule have been harassed by the Milošević government, which has worried about the support they might give to their coreligionists in Bosnia-Herzegovina. Ironically, the more the Serbian authorities badger the Muslim population in ways that call to mind their treatment of the Albanian population in Kosovo, the more inclined the Sandžak Muslims are to cooperate in a holy war against Belgrade or join their kinsmen living in Macedonia. The sharply different approaches to the Sandžak Muslims of Skopje and Belgrade have contributed to an underlying tension in the relations between Serbia and Montenegro.[99]

Finally, Montenegro's discomfort over intimacy with Serbia is also the result of culture. Though the Montenegrins speak the same language as Serbs and officially belong to the same church, ethnic Montenegrins feel strongly about their separate historical identity, which has evolved over centuries. The Montenegrins consider themselves as different than Serbs in much the same way Austrians see themselves as different than Germans. Thus, three years after their alliance with Serbia to create the small Yugoslav Federation, Montenegrins have become uncomfortable.[100]

Milošević is not likely to allow Montenegro to loosen its ties with Belgrade. Montenegro provides Serbia with access to the Adriatic Sea, a strategic advantage the Milošević regime would not easily give up. Also, a full-blown secessionist movement probably would encourage Montenegro's Serb minority in districts bordering the Serbian Republic to look to Milošević for protection, encouraging him to help them with weapons and money in much the same way as he helped Bosnian Serb separatists. In the event of a Bosnian-style civil war in Montenegro, ethnic Montenegrins, following the example of Bosnian Muslims, would fight to preserve the territorial integrity of their country.

5. *Milošević's Volte-Face on Bosnia*

By the summer of 1995, Milošević was inclined to compromise over the future of Bosnia-Herzegovina. He was annoyed by the independence of his protégés in

Bosnia, especially General Mladić, who was bent on making a last-ditch effort to capture Sarajevo and unwisely dismissed signals and warnings from the West as well as from Milošević to show restraint. Why should Serbia, at great cost to itself, continue to back a leader who had excessive and dangerous nationalist ambitions? At the same time, the West had been escalating pressure on Milošević, for example, promising him an abatement of the international sanctions against Yugoslavia if he would cooperate in getting the Bosnian Serbs to accept the Contact Group's proposal. Also, Russia was hard put to support continued Serb intransigence without risking a major confrontation with the West, which Yeltsin was determined to avoid.[101]

The further deterioration of the refugee problem for Serbia as a result of Croatia's reconquest of the Krajina provided still another incentive for Milošević to push the Bosnian Serbs to compromise. Thousands of Serb refugees from the Krajina, terrified by the prospect of violent Croat retribution against them, crossed into Serbia in the latter half of 1995. The Serbian economy was in no position to sustain them for any length of time. Living conditions for many of them put the lie to Milošević's promises of a good life in his country. Some went to the Vojvodina, where their embittered nationalism stirred up tensions. Other refugees were told to settle in Kosovo. Their arrival, which impoverished Albanians viewed as a maneuver by the Belgrade government to provoke them and justify a draconian suppression, intensified interethnic tensions.

By mid-1995, a change in Milošević's policy toward the Serb insurgencies in both the Krajina and in Bosnia was evident. In August, Milošević was ready to tell the Bosnian Serb leaders that they must accept the Contact Group's territorial proposal or else suffer a loss of Serbian backing that would severely undermine their military capabilities. He also persuaded them to allow him to speak for them in the American-sponsored negotiations for a territorial agreement on Bosnia with Tudjman and Izetbegović held in Geneva and New York at the end of the summer of 1995. Other evidence of his retreat was a refusal to interfere with the Republic of Croatia's successful campaign to regain control of the Krajina in the summer of 1995. His behavior shocked the Krajina Serb leadership, weakening its bid for independence and in effect ordaining the return of the Serbs in the Krajina to the rule of Zagreb. Finally, Milošević's refusal to interfere with NATO's decision in September to go forward with air strikes against Bosnian Serb military depots seemed to punctuate the Serbian Republic's decision to back off in Bosnia. The NATO action, intended to force General Mladić to remove the heavy artillery deployed in the mountainous outskirts of Sarajevo, which had been forbidden by the UN and was being used to bombard the city, with substantial civilian casualties, severely weakened the Bosnian Serb military capability. Indeed, within a month the Bosnian Serb side had lost to the Bosnian Muslim and Croat armies 20 percent of the territory held at the beginning of the summer, the equivalent of what the Contact Group wanted the Bosnian Serb side to return to the Muslims.

The War and Macedonia

In 1994, fallout from the war in Bosnia-Herzegovina put the independent former Yugoslav Republic of Macedonia (FYRM), as the country is now called, in peril. The new independent government of Macedonia faced serious economic problems, experienced a potentially dangerous ethnic-based political instability, and remained vulnerable to external interference.

1. Economic Problems

The UN sanctions against the Serbs in both Serbia and Bosnia hurt the Macedonian economy, which suffered also from a blockade by Greece because of Greek opposition to the republic's use of the term "Macedonia." The Greek blockade, imposed in February 1994, was estimated to have cost Macedonia more than $100 million. The government in Skopje had to shelve plans for free-market reforms because living standards dropped sharply. Before the sanctions and the Greek blockade, Macedonia's per-capita GNP reportedly was $1,800. By 1995, it was $760 and unemployment stood at 30 percent. The West had provided insufficient aid to assure the economy's survival. For example, total annual U.S. aid in 1993 and 1994 was only about $25 million.[102]

2. Political Instability

Desperate economic conditions contributed to a radicalization of internal Macedonian politics as the Albanian minority, which comprised about 21 percent of the total population, was becoming more nationalistic and was seeking increased influence over the government in Skopje. Some radical Macedonian Albanians called for the autonomy of the territory of the Albanian community located in the western part of the country. They made no secret of their dream of an eventual union with the Republic of Albania and with kinsmen in the Republic of Serbia's Kosovo province to make a greater Albanian state.[103]

For the first time, Macedonian nationalists who supported the Democratic Party for Macedonian National Unity, led by Ljupčo Georgievski, campaigned for popular support with the slogan "Macedonia for the Macedonians," which intimidated the Albanian minority and threatened future discrimination against them. Radical Macedonian nationalists thought that President Kiro Gligorov already had given too much recognition to Albanian demands for increased control over their local affairs, saying that he was trying to make Macedonia into another Yugoslavia, a strategy that inevitably would lead to civil war. The fears of the Macedonian nationalists were understandable. In the early and mid-1990s, the Albanian minority was fed up with discrimination, especially in the area of education. They wanted their own university that instructed in Albanian and their own local Parliament. In some respects, they were imitating the Serb minorities in Croatia and Bosnia. They also wanted the option to join kinsmen in the Republic of Albania. They received some encouragement from the Berisha government in Tirana.[104]

Should the Albanian minority implement this revolutionary agenda, Macedonia would face the same kind of civil war that has occurred in Croatia and Bosnia. Furthermore, such a war would certainly become fierce were Serbia's Milošević to crack down on Kosovo and provoke a massive emigration of Kosovan Albanians into Macedonia. Such an emigration would destabilize Macedonia, given the considerable anti-Albanian prejudice.

Macedonia's Albanian minority has remained a wild card in the post-independence period. Albanians in western Macedonia have said that if kinsmen in Kosovo were threatened by Milošević, they would have no choice but to come to their aid. In preparation for the possibility of a showdown in Kosovo, Macedonia's Albanian community began stockpiling weapons for what was termed "communal self-defense." By 1994 the government in Skopje had become alarmed and started legal proceedings against local Albanian politicians accused of arms smuggling and the formation of paramilitary groups.[105]

A majority of Macedonians of all ethnic backgrounds, however, still supported Gligorov's moderate strategies toward the country's ethnic problems.[106] They reelected him president in October 1994. But in early 1995, Macedonia was on the verge of civil war and vulnerable to outside pressures by countries that, each for their own reasons, had a strong interest in Macedonian internal affairs and would not find it difficult to carve the country up into spheres of influence. These countries have been and will remain Serbia, Greece, Albania, and Bulgaria.[107]

3. A Threat from Serbia?

During 1992, it appeared that Serbia might try to expand its influence into Macedonia on the pretext of concern for the well-being of the small Serb minority, about 2.2 percent of the population, now that Macedonia was out of Yugoslavia, beyond the influence of Serbia, and governed by nationalist political leaders. Anticipating this danger, Washington sent several hundred marines to Macedonia to signify its interest in the territorial integrity and political independence of this country. The threat of Serbian Republic influence building in Macedonia was real.[108] Some extreme Serb nationalists, with the blessing of the Orthodox Church, lobbied for autonomy for the Serb community in Macedonia. There was already a lot of Serb influence in Skopje. Gligorov was surrounded by former communists with ties to colleagues in Belgrade, with whom they had close relations. Macedonian Serbs who would like someday to see their country join the Yugoslav Federation, now dominated by the Republic of Serbia, hold influential positions in the Macedonian military. There is some reason to believe that this Serb clique has the tacit support of the European Union, which sees Macedonian independence as a strategic liability and would prefer to see the country part of the new Yugoslavia.[109]

The War and Croatia

As 1995 drew to a close, it looked as if the one former Yugoslav republic that might come out on top after four years of civil war would be Croatia. The Tudjman regime succeeded in regaining control of most of the region in southern Croatia seized by the Serb minority in 1990 and 1991. And it also appeared that Croatia might eventually obtain a modest slice of western Bosnia, inhabited largely by a Croat minority, if the peace settlement based on the Contact Group's May 1994 territorial proposal dividing the country into two separate self-govern-ing regions, the Muslim-Croat Federation and the Serb Republic of Bosnia, was accepted.

1. Reconquest of the Krajina

Following the initial deployment in early 1992 of UNPROFOR personnel in the Krajina and other areas seized by the local Serb population, the Tudjman regime never abandoned the goal of restoring Croatian authority. It never recognized the so-called "Serb Republic of the Krajina," not to mention its claims to territory in eastern Slavonia adjacent to the Republic of Serbia, western Slavonia in the central part of Croatia, and a region wedged between Bosnia and Croatia's coastal area of Dalmatia with its capital at Knin, a farming center amid barren mountains about 270 miles southwest of Zagreb. Especially irritating to Zagreb was the failure of UNPROFOR to oblige Serbs to surrender their heavy weapons, in particular, tanks and artillery, and to allow expelled Croat refugees to return to their homes. Tudjman took advantage of UNPROFOR's difficulty in maintaining law and order by escalating military pressure on the Serbs in the Krajina to bring them to heel. During 1993, there were frequent and violent clashes between Croatian authorities and the local Serb population.[110] In addition, Tudjman ex-ploited the international embargo against Serbia, Montenegro, and the Bosnian Serbs to weaken the Krajina Serbs, literally by starving them in the expectation that they eventually would capitulate to Zagreb and accept the reimposition of Croatian authority or flee into Serbia.[111]

Tudjman eventually decided to reinforce Zagreb's authority in Krajina, telling UNPROFOR in late 1994 either to do something to quiet the Serbs or to vacate and allow Zagreb to restore its authority. Bothered by the failure of UNPROFOR to heed his warning, Tudjman announced on January 12, 1995, that Croatia would terminate UNPROFOR's mandate in the Krajina when it expired at the end of March.[112] Tudjman worried that the Krajina Serbs would present

Milošević with a *fait accompli* the Serbian leader could not resist: a vote to annex themselves to Serbia. Also, conservative Croatian nationalists, in particular, the Croatian Party of Rights, were pressuring Tudjman to recover the Krajina by force, if necessary.[113]

Tudjman undoubtedly was encouraged to move aggressively in the Krajina by remarks made by Peter Galbraith, the American ambassador to Croatia, and German foreign minister Klaus Kinkel to the Krajina Serbs that their demands for an independent state could not be met and that their aspirations to join the Republic of Serbia could never be realized. These messages seemed to imply Western recognition of Croatia's control over at least the Krajina portion of its territorial domain lost to its rebellious Serb communities in 1991.[114]

Tudjman eventually agreed to allow "for the time being" the continued deployment of UNPROFOR along Croatia's frontier with Bosnia-Herzegovina and Serbia, with certain alterations in the makeup of the deployment.[115] But in early May 1995, he launched a major military action to restore Zagreb's control in the Krajina and western Slavonia. He was encouraged by Milošević's willingness to refrain from interfering in the Krajina on behalf of the Serb minority and its independent government. Tudjman was influenced also by oblique signals of approval from Washington to bring the Krajina Serbs to heel to discourage their cooperation with the Bosnian Serbs and thus "level the playing field" in Bosnia.

By the end of the summer of 1995, Croatia was successful beyond its expectations, as well as those of outsiders, in reimposing Zagreb's authority over most of the territory taken by Serbs in 1991. The successful Croatian offensive in Krajina also strengthened the Bosnian Muslim military position in the north, encouraging the Bosnian army to try to regain territory under Serb control. By the end of August 1995, with a wink from Washington, Republic of Croatia army units joined with Bosnian Croat and Muslim forces against the Serbs.

2. Croatia the Winner in the Bosnian War?

The success of its military campaign with Krajina increased Croatia's chances of eventually obtaining a portion of northern Bosnia inhabited by Bosnian Croats. Bosnian government control of the region adjacent to Croatia virtually had disappeared. The local currency of the Bosnian Croats was Croatian, and few Muslims had returned to the homes they had been forced to flee by the Croats in 1992 and 1993, when they were doing some ethnic cleansing of their own while Sarajevo's military forces were fighting the Serbs elsewhere in the republic. By the end of 1995, Croatia controlled all access into Bosnia-Herzegovina from the West, assuring its economic dependence on Croatia. It is not unreasonable to assume that the federation of Bosnian Croats and Muslims formed in 1994 will inevitably draw closer to, if not become a part of, the Republic of Croatia in response to an equally inevitable movement toward Belgrade of the Serb Republic of Bosnia.

Peace at Last? The Dayton Agreement

Meeting in Paris in early December 1995, presidents Izetbegović of Bosnia-Herzegovina, Tudjman of Croatia, and Milošević of Serbia ratified the provisions of the peace agreement signed in Dayton, Ohio, in October 1995. Credit for the success of the negotiations in Dayton goes to the Clinton administration for bringing the three presidents to the bargaining table and getting the Serbian leadership to represent the Bosnian Serb side, which did not participate, and for getting the three presidents to accept a territorial compromise and other political arrangements that made possible a cessation of hostilities in Bosnia-Herzegovina.

The terms of the Dayton agreement affirmed a unified Bosnian state. But the new Bosnia-Herzegovina was to be divided into two separate self-governing administrative entities: the Muslim-Croat Federation created in March 1994; and the Serb Republic of Bosnia, proclaimed in early 1992. This division required that the Bosnian Serb military forces transfer the control of about 20 percent of the territory captured in the past four years to the new state, which is to say the central government of Bosnia in Sarajevo.

The two administrative entities were to be linked together very loosely by this central government which was in charge of foreign relations and other national business, including a central constitutional court. The signatories agreed that both the Federation and the Serb Republic of Bosnia were to hold free democratic elections within about nine months, to guarantee freedom of movement, to allow displaced persons to repossess their property or receive just compensation, and to respect the principles of freedom of speech and freedom of the press and human rights. The Dayton agreement provided that two-thirds of the membership of a national parliament would come from the Muslim-Croat Federation and one-third from the Serb Republic of Bosnia, and that all parliamentary decisions would require a majority vote, with a minimum of one-third of votes from each entity. A multimember collective presidency would represent Muslims, Serbs, and Croats in the same way they were represented in the Parliament.[116]

Under the agreement, both Federation and Bosnian Serb military forces were to withdraw to agreed-upon positions and NATO was to send a multinational force of about 60,000 troops, one-third of them from the United States, to act as peacekeepers. The NATO mission was to keep Bosnia's rival armies separated and to redeploy them to new lines identified in the Dayton agreement. Under plans agreed upon by troop-contributing countries, including NATO and non-NATO members like Russia, the peacekeeping, or International Protection Force (IFOR), as it was called, was to deal primarily with military matters and to limit its involvement in civilian issues.[117]

The Dayton agreement also provided for a civilian mission to assure the security of Bosnian civilians and their right to travel freely, as well as to prepare the country for the parliamentary elections to be held in the latter part of 1996.

This mission was placed under the command of Carl Bildt, the former Swedish prime minister, who was to recruit an international police force to help him carry out his mandate. Bildt was to report to individual governments, the European Union, and the UN Security Council. He had no significant liaison with the NATO peacekeeping command with which he would have to cooperate for the success of his mission. Indeed, he was only supposed to give advice to NATO, which in turn had no obligation to share intelligence with him, work with him, or accept his advice.[118]

In addition, persons indicted by the War Crimes Tribunal in the Hague, in particular, the Bosnian Serb president Radovan Karadžić and General Ratko Mladić, were excluded from holding office in the government of the Bosnian Serb Republic. The agreement was not clear as to how the tribunal should proceed to apprehend indicted war criminals and, in particular, what kind of action, if any, NATO peacekeepers should take to prevent Karadžić and Mladić from participating in the politics of the Bosnian Serb Republic.[119]

Finally, the Dayton agreement addressed the difficult question of what was to happen to eastern Slavonia, a region of about 100 square miles inhabited by 68,000 Serbs, 125,000 Croats, and other groups. The agreement required the return of eastern Slavonia to Croatian authority within a year. In the interim, the region was to be under UN control, with UN peacekeepers responsible for maintaining peace by demilitarizing the region and preparing it for the transfer of authority to Zagreb.[120]

While the agreement brought an immediate cessation of hostilities and the restoration of a tentative peace throughout Bosnia-Herzegovina, there were many problems in implementing it. Moreover, the Dayton agreement had an impact on politics in Croatia, insofar as it affected eastern Slavonia, and in Serbia, where it seemed to strengthen Milošević and focus attention on Kosovo.

1. Withdrawal of Foreign Military Personnel

Withdrawal of foreign military personnel was difficult. For example, European military officers and Bosnian government officials acknowledged the ease with which personnel of the Croatian regular army, who had intermingled with the local Croat population in northern Bosnia, ostensibly on instructions from Zagreb to facilitate the integration of that area with the republic of Croatia, could simply change insignias on their uniform and avoid identification and removal. Much the same could be said about Serbian personnel belonging to the Yugoslav Army. It was almost impossible to obtain a complete withdrawal of military personnel belonging to the armies of Croatia and Yugoslavia.[121]

2. Bosnian Muslim Ties to Iran

In addition, NATO accused the Bosnian government of hiring Iranians to instruct Bosnian military personnel, a violation of the Dayton agreement. Revelation of growing ties between Bosnian Muslim authorities and Teheran tended to vindicate the suspicion of Bosnian Serbs, nourished by their nationalist leaders, of the spread of Islamic fundamentalist influence in southeastern Europe. While some Iranians were obliged to leave Bosnia, the problem of Iranian influence continued as the Sarajevo government in early 1996 sent officers from its army to Teheran to get instruction on terrorist tactics. And at the end of March 1996, Iran offered to train and equip the Bosnian army.[122]

3. Obstacles to Interethnic Coexistence

Equally serious were obstacles to coexistence of different ethnic communities throughout Bosnia that threatened the unity of Bosnia that the Dayton agreement was supposed to forge. In the early months of 1996, IFOR tried but failed to get Serbs to stay in their homes located in territory administered by the Federation and to get Croats and Muslims to remain where they lived, regardless of the ethnic group in administrative control, or to return to homes in territory administered by the Serbs.[123] Typical was the situation in Sarajevo, which under the Dayton agreement was to come under the authority of the Muslim-Croat Federation by March 19, 1996. Serbs were terrified by the prospect of retribution by Muslims and began an exodus. Many Serb families went to the length of disinterring buried relatives for reburial in places under Bosnian Serb authority. Bosnian Serb leaders, in particular President Karadžić, seeking to foster ethnically pure Serb communities, were partly responsible for the exodus.[124] Mostar was another Bosnian city deeply divided between different ethnic communities, in this case Muslims and Croats. Croats on one side of the city refused to allow Muslims on the other to cross over. While Muslim citizens said they wanted a reunited city, the Croat population was all but unanimous in keeping its side of the city ethnically pure and segregated and rejected a plan to create a multiethnic city center with a mixed Croat–Muslim population. Indeed, what was becoming increasingly evident throughout most of Bosnia was a tendency of each ethnic group to withdraw into its own space.[125]

4. Deterioration of Muslim–Croat Relations

Meanwhile, another challenge to Dayton and to the preservation of Bosnian unity was a growing deterioration of Muslim–Croat relations within the Federation.[126] For example, Federation president Krešimir Zubak, a Croat, in early March 1996, refused to fulfill a pledge signed in February to turn over Croat-administered districts in Sarajevo to Federation control, because he was afraid that Croats would lose influence over the local administration.[127]

At the heart of strained relations between the two communities were the intractable views of local Croat political and religious leaders in western Bosnia, who never really liked the Federation and considered the Federation a betrayal of Croatian values, calling attention to the deep religious and cultural differences they believe separate Muslims from Catholic Croats, despite common Slavic ethnic origins. An equally important source of antagonism was the memory of the World War II Croatian Ustashe movement which Croats everywhere saw in a positive light, believing it had defended wartime Croatia against Serb and Muslim threats.

Finally, the Croatian government in Zagreb contributed to separatist thinking among Bosnian Croats, making little secret of its ambition to create a greater Croatia consisting of the Republic of Croatia and territory adjacent to it in Bosnia-Herzegovina known as Herzeg-Bosna, inhabited primarily by Croats. Indeed, Croatia maintained strong economic, sociocultural, and military links to the Bosnian Croat minority. In early 1996 it encouraged local Bosnian Croat leaders to resist American efforts to strengthen the Federation.[128]

The Clinton administration tried to reinforce the Federation by getting Muslim and Bosnian Croat leaders to sign an agreement at the end of March 1996, with Tudjman's reluctant approval, providing for a strengthening of the Federation's administrative structure. Both sides agreed to jointly collect customs duties, to fuse financial structures, to form local governing bodies throughout Federation territory, and to have a new green, white, and red flag.[129] But, this agreement was less than it appeared to be. There was major disagreement between the two communities on treatment of refugees, the formation of a federation-wide police force, and other aspects of joint administration. By the summer of 1996 it appeared almost doubtful that the Federation would survive through the year.

5. Karadžić and Mladić

Important to the overall success of the Dayton agreement in preserving the territorial integrity and political viability of postwar Bosnia-Herzegovina was the exclusion of Karadžić and Mladić from political leadership in Serb-controlled regions. Both were indicted war criminals, subject to arrest on sight. Both had made public their dislike of the Dayton agreement. But IFOR officials did not attempt to arrest Karadžić and Mladić. Although IFOR said that apprehension of war criminals was not its job, the real reason for its restraint was fear that the arrest of Karadžić and Mladić, still very popular among Bosnian Serbs, would provoke an explosion of local violence. Another consideration involved Serbian president Milošević who was in no hurry to punish Karadžić and Mladić and thereby make then "martyrs." Moreover, Milošević was afraid that if these two Bosnian Serb leaders were turned over to the Hague Tribunal they would give testimony about ethnic cleansing, implicating the Serbian president.

The NATO high command in Bosnia also had reason to believe that Karadžić would soon fade away politically. Despite his popularity with many Bosnian Serbs, Karadžić faced substantial opposition in places throughout the Serb

Republic of Bosnia like Banja Luka, a university town with a population of well-educated middle-class professionals who had suffered materially and psychologically from the civil war. The people of Banja Luka, who had supplied a good portion of the troops in Mladić's army, as well as other Bosnian Serbs, in early 1996 increasingly blamed Karadžić for bringing them to the brink of ruin and of isolating them from not only the Western world but also from Russia and other Slavic countries through the pursuit of a brutal, obsessive hypernationalism. Some political opponents of Karadžić accused him and his supporters in the Bosnian Serb Parliament in Pale of corruption—of having profited enormously from the shortages caused by the long war by smuggling into the country scarce commodities, including oil from Romania and Bulgaria. Many also believed that Karadžić lacked the credibility and the capacity to lead the new Bosnian Serb state in a process of reconstruction that would depend very much on help from the West, which Karadžić had vehemently denounced. The West now refused to have any dealings with him.[130]

6. Economic Collapse and Widespread Poverty

By the spring of 1996, it was clear that one of the most important obstacles to the implementation of the Dayton agreement was the pervasive poverty throughout Bosnia, caused in no small way by more than three years of fighting that had ravaged Bosnia's transportation and communications infrastructure, destroyed factories and farms, and provoked an exodus of professionals and skilled workers from the electronics and food processing industries. By early 1996, the country's industry was producing at only 5 percent of prewar levels. Also, the banking system had been virtually immobilized for four years. Bosnia's economic collapse was also the result of economic collapse in neighboring republics that had been its trade partners in the highly interconnected prewar Yugoslav economy. Bosnia's external markets, an important source of national income, had all but disappeared as a result of the war.[131]

The human impact of this economic collapse was of special concern to local authorities as well as to the West. Many parts of the rural economy were cash-short as bankrupt factories had to pay workers with paper they could use only at local stores at greatly discounted rates. Personal income either declined precipitously or in some cases simply disappeared, causing many families to accept charity from the UN or other sources to survive. Unemployment increased as demobilized soldiers from all sides returned home looking for work.[132] And making matters worse in this regard was the impact of interethnic prejudices. For example, Karadžić hindered economic recovery in his country by rejecting economic contacts with non-Serb regions. Bosnian Serb authorities also refused to allow Muslims to work in enterprises located in their jurisdiction.

Muslim authorities acted in the same way toward Serbs, abruptly and arbitrarily dismissing them from government posts in Sarajevo and elsewhere. This behavior encouraged strong local anti-Serb prejudice. In some places, Muslims simply refused to work with Serbs and would walk off the job in protest against the hiring of Serbs. This kind of behavior impeded economic recovery, impoverishing local ethnic communities and exacerbating interethnic hostility.

A key to Bosnia's economic and especially industrial revival was infusion of foreign capital, but potential investors from Germany and Italy interested in putting money into the economic recovery of Bosnia were scared off by the risks and difficulties of restarting a factory and making it profitable given the level of continuing violence and political instability. Money from foreign governments that did enter Bosnia was only a trickle. The West, by the spring of 1996, still had not yet provided the massive sums needed to help get the Bosnian economy functioning again so that it could support the local population. Western nations were discouraged by the strong prospect of a resumption of war despite the Dayton agreement. They also had their own domestic problems that discouraged large-scale disbursement of aid money—Germany was coping with the huge cost of rebuilding the eastern part of the country formerly under communist rule, while Washington was influenced by intense domestic pressure to cut expenditures on foreign aid.

7. Punishment of War Criminals

In early 1996, the Hague war crimes tribunal faced new and very difficult problems fulfilling its mandate to prosecute and punish those guilty of war crimes in Bosnia-Herzegovina and elsewhere in central Yugoslavia. The tribunal still had no physical means at its disposal to arrest those it indicted and could not rely on NATO to broaden its military mission to include the apprehension of international criminals. In February 1996, IFOR announced that it could go no further in assisting the Hague tribunal than collecting evidence.[133] At the same time, the tribunal had difficulty getting presidents Milošević, Tudjman, and Izetbegović to send protégés identified as war criminals, whom they had been harboring, to the Hague. Tudjman and Milošević argued that the tribunal was biased in favor of Muslims because, as of the beginning of March 1996, of 53 indictments issued, none were of Muslims.[134] Moreover, it was clear that Milošević was certainly not going to help the tribunal if Tudjman didn't. Milošević ignored tribunal requests to arrest Karadžić and Mladić, and was even reluctant to allow the tribunal to open a liaison office in Belgrade.

Other obstacles impeded the Hague tribunal, in particular, a lack of information about crimes and the whereabouts of those who had committed them. In the beginning of 1996, the tribunal still had very little investigatory staff to do the extensive legwork to identify and collect specific evidence about those guilty of criminal acts in connection with the pursuit of ethnic cleansing. And then there were problems of procedure. The tribunal's eleven judges, who came from eleven different countries with different kinds of legal systems and trial procedures, were bound to have difficulty acting in concert and coming to shared conclusions.[135]

By the spring of 1996, the tribunal was stymied, with only a small number of lower level officials indicted and extradited to the Hague. The big fish, as Karadžić, Mladić, and Milošević were called, were being let off the hook. The tribunal's mission in other words seemed undermined by what appeared to be a pragmatic trade-off by the West to get peace in Bosnia: support of some of those most responsible for carrying out the war, such as Serbian president Milošević, in return for their willingness to end the war and keep the peace and tolerance of others clearly guilty of war crimes, because pursuing them would cause more trouble than their punishment was worth.

8. Eastern Slavonia and Croatia

At the end of 1995, an impatient Tudjman made no secret of his determination to regain control of eastern Slavonia, by military force if necessary, before the 1997 deadline for reintegration provided in the Dayton agreement. This impatience was born of overt Serb resistance in eastern Slavonia to a restoration of Croatian authority. The Serb minority in eastern Slavonia was terrified by the prospect of revenge by Zagreb, once its authority was reestablished in the region, for its revolt in 1990 and 1991. In early 1996, local Serb politicians in eastern Slavonia waged an unrelenting propaganda war against reintegration and invited home refugees who had fled in the summer and fall of 1995, when a restoration of Zagreb's control seemed imminent. Serb authorities in eastern Slavonia hoped that an increase in the region's Serb population might discourage an influx of Croats and Muslims who had fled in 1991 and delay the completion of Zagreb's administrative control.[136]

Croatian Republic leaders responded angrily to this Serb resistance with Foreign Minister Granić intoning at the end of January 1996 that if the Serb population refused to accept the Dayton agreement, the Croatian government would seize control of the region by force. In the spring of 1996, the situation in eastern Slavonia did not change for the better with the arrival of UN peacekeepers to demilitarize the region and superintend the restoration of Croatian control over aspects of local administration. Eventually, on the eve of the official reintegration of eastern Slavonia into the Croatian administrative system, UN peacekeepers were supposed to hold local elections. The Dayton agreement stipulated that the initial twelve-month period in which this reorientation of administrative life is supposed to occur could be extended. The irony of this situation was that while officials in Zagreb were making elaborate plans in 1996 for the restoration of

Croatian authority in eastern Slavonia, even plotting a local budget and providing money for rebuilding homes and resettling Croatian refugees, the local Serb population lived the illusion that this scenario would never occur and that somehow they would be able to retain their independence, possibly with the help of President Milošević.

9. Milošević and Political Dictatorship

The Dayton agreement enhanced Milošević's stature at home. Serbian citizens were impressed by his new friendship with the United States, which many welcomed for the benefits it would bring to Serbian society demoralized and depressed by its international isolation. The Serbian leader was now not only an ally of Washington and a participant in the formulation and implementation of the Dayton agreement, he was also positioned to obtain trade and other concessions from the West that would benefit Serbia materially.[137] But the strengthening of Milošević's political image and authority had a downside as well. Milošević was still running an authoritarian political system, drafting opposition leaders into the army to silence them and consolidating his control over television by nationalizing a privately owned and operated station.[138] In December 1995, the government outlawed demonstrations in the center of Belgrade. And at a congress of his Socialist Party in early March 1996, Milošević announced policies that seemed like a throwback to the communist era. In fact, the pro-Milošević demonstrations at the congress were so excessive as to call to mind Ceauşescu's Romania and the development of a Ceauşescu-style leadership cult. Moreover, in a gesture reminiscent of the harsh Chinese crackdown on democracy demonstrators in Beijing's Tiananmen Square in the beginning of June 1989, Milošević sent tanks to disperse a very modest popular demonstration against his government in Belgrade's Republic Square in early March 1996, by his irrepressible antagonist Vuk Drašković, still leading the country's most prominent anti-Milošević party, the Serbian Renewal Movement. Drašković was in effect asking for Milošević's removal, and there was a lot of popular support for this, with people calling Milošević "Slobo Saddam."[139]

Although the Dayton agreement did not mention Kosovo, an American summary of the negotiations said "an outer wall" of sanctions will remain in place until Serbia addresses a number of areas of concern including Kosovo. But the Milošević government continued to resist self-rule for the Albanian minority. Milošević refused even to discuss conditions in Kosovo at Dayton, or afterward, and continued in early 1996 to administer Kosovo in a harsh and repressive manner.[140]

Whether Milošević would continue to support the Dayton agreement, put aside dreams of creating a greater Serbia, soften Belgrade's relations with Kosovo, work for good relations with the United States, and indeed, maintain his hold on power—all were uncertain at the end of 1996. Certainly he appeared more inclined than at any earlier time to accept peace at any price in Bosnia, enjoy the fruits of Serbia's improved ties with the West, and postpone for the future expansionist ambitions at least in Bosnia. At the least, Milošević showed little sympathy for Karadžić and did what he could to weaken the Bosnian Serb leader's influence at home, short of handing him over to the Hague.

The Slovenian Exception

Slovenia has remained relatively unscathed by the Bosnian civil war and, indeed, has prospered. It is geographically distant from the fighting, and internal economic and political conditions remained stable. Gone are the subsidies to the less-developed parts of the former Yugoslavia that burdened the pre-independence Slovene economy. The inflation of the early 1990s was brought down to 20 percent a year and was under 5 percent by late 1993 thanks to a tight fiscal policy and control over imports. Slovenes, however, are experiencing some of the problems accompanying transition to a free-market economy present in other East European countries. Free-market reforms have caused unemployment, real income for most workers has remained unchanged as prices gradually increased with the curtailment of state control over the country's economic life, and a small minority of very wealthy individuals has emerged while many poor people have suffered as a result of the curtailment of state management of the economy.[141]

Nevertheless, Slovenia's stable currency and strong export industries have contributed to a measure of economic health and led to membership in the IMF. But, however better off materially Slovenes may be than people in neighboring parts of the former Yugoslavia, they have not achieved the Western living standards they want. Nor are they likely to in the near future. Independence has brought new economic burdens. The cost to Slovenia of maintaining its own military establishment is higher than its share of the former Yugoslavia's defense budget, and it has had to invest in additional administrative agencies, such as a new foreign office and diplomatic establishment.

The Slovenian political system remains stable, in contrast to extremist tendencies in other former Yugoslav states. The strong democratic instincts of the Slovene people, as seen in the very high voter turnout for the December 1992 parliamentary elections, account in part for the steady evolution of parliamentary government in Ljubljana in the early 1990s, in contrast to the appearance of distinctly authoritarian tendencies in the political life of neighboring Croatia.[142]

Slovenia's independence also has brought it closer to Western Europe and the more prosperous former communist countries in the north, notably, Poland, Hungary, and the Czech Republic. But dear to the hearts of the Slovene people is the prospect of close association with the European Union. Admission of Slovenia as a full member would move the country toward the fulfillment of its dream of achieving a Western level of material well-being, one that was impossible as long as its was in the old Yugoslavia with its fate linked closely to Serbia.

But there is a cloud in Slovenia's political sky. It is a small but potentially significant ethnic problem. Slovenia was over 90 percent homogenous, in sharp contrast to its multiethnic neighbors in the former Yugoslavia. But, while the government in Ljubljana was willing to acknowledge the special cultural identity of its small Hungarian community, it refused to act equivalently toward Slovenian citizens of Serb or Croat origin. The result was growing interethnic tensions in the early 1990s. While this situation did not threaten a crisis in Slovenia's relations with Croatia and Serbia, it could lead to difficulties with those countries, where there is some resentment over the way in which Slovenia escaped the worst of the wars attending Yugoslavia's disintegration and, indeed, prospered while they suffered.[143]

Conclusions

The explosion of civil war in Bosnia-Herzegovina was truly the *coup de grâce* for Tito's Yugoslavia. Divided as it was among three large minorities—Muslims, Serbs, and Croats—two of which, the Croats and the Serbs, had powerful and mutually antagonistic patrons outside the republic, namely, Croatia and Serbia, Bosnia-Herzegovina was an eternal land mine in Yugoslavia. It was in many respects an artificial administrative entity that had survived as long as it did because it was part of Yugoslavia, which was responsible for its territorial integrity and political stability. Once Tito was gone, and once the Yugoslav state started disintegrating, Bosnia's survival became precarious. As Yugoslavia disintegrated, a partition of Bosnia between Croatia and Serbia became logical, if not inevitable. Resentful of control by a predominantly Muslim government in Sarajevo, the Serb and Croat minorities looked to their patrons abroad. With the Serb Republic's response, which was immediate and took the form of active encouragement of the Bosnian Serbs to emancipate themselves from Muslim control and join Serbia, civil war exploded in Bosnia-Herzegovina.

The Bosnian civil war was the worst of the conflicts attending the disintegration of Yugoslavia for five major reasons: (1) the opposition of the Serb minority to Bosnia-Herzegovina's independence under the leadership of a central government dominated by a Muslim plurality and its use of violence to escape Muslim control; (2) the determination of the Muslim-dominated government of Bosnia-Herzegovina to preserve the republic's territorial integrity or as much of it as they could without destroying themselves in the process; (3) Milošević's substantial help, especially in the form of weapons, to the Bosnian Serb campaign for independence; (4) the political, economic, military, and diplomatic weaknesses of the Bosnian government, denying it victory over the Serb side, accompanied by a strong emotional commitment to continue the fight until a time when such a victory may be possible; and (5) the failure of the international community to stop the fighting, force the combatants to the peace table, and pledge whatever commitment of force was necessary to prevent a resumption of the fighting.

While the Serb side must bear chief responsibility for the outbreak of the war and for its most brutal aspects, the Muslim side also carries blame. It has shown the same stubbornness in its determination to restore the territorial status quo and at times the same brutality. Both sides seemed determined to fight each other to the bitter end with no room for territorial compromise and despite the efforts of outsiders to end the conflict. Each side was convinced that time is on its side and that it will eventually be victorious. The Serbs believed this because they had military superiority and the support of a powerful outsider, the Republic of Serbia, and, indirectly, the Russian Federation. The Muslim side believed that the future would bring the military superiority they lacked because outsiders, in particular, the United States and oil-rich Islamic countries, would come to support them and shift the balance of strategic power in their favor.

The Bosnian war had a destructive impact on most of the Yugoslav peoples. It caused them severe economic hardship and psychological trauma. It prevented them from making the transition to a new, more liberal economic and political order in the postcommunist era. It will take decades for them to recover from the war. No other country in Central and Eastern Europe has experienced the violence and conflict Yugoslavia has, suggesting that Tito's communist rule was more flawed than anyone had suspected and that his achievements in bringing unity and a comparative economic well-being to Yugoslavia after World war II must be reappraised in light of what has happened to his country since his death.

Conclusions

The collapse of Communist Party rule and of Soviet influence and power beginning in 1989 in Central and Eastern Europe, one of the most profound political upheavals of the late twentieth century, took the West, as well as the people in the region, by surprise. The collapse was sudden, unexpected, and traumatic. Conventional wisdom held that communism, despite its flaws, would give way only if the Kremlin were willing to let that happen. Everybody assumed that the Kremlin was determined that the region remain under communist control indefinitely because of its importance to the Soviet Union's domestic stability and external security, especially vis-à-vis the West.

Causes of Collapse

But when the collapse occurred, its causes were no mystery. The Soviet-style communist systems in place, with minor variations, in all the countries of Central and Eastern Europe shared serious flaws. Communist leaders seemed incapable of responding in a timely fashion. Some did not acknowledge or, in some cases, did not understand the system's weaknesses. And the few who did see the problems feared that if they undertook extensive reform they risked not only weakening their authority and undermining socialism but also incurring the anger of the Kremlin, which was suspicious of change, especially if it led to a weakening of the Communist Party's repressive grip and its own extensive influence in the region. All this suggests that communist leaders looked to their own personal needs while turning away from the needs of their society. They had their heads in the sand, so to speak, bent on preserving the status quo and relying on Soviet power to support and protect them.

This behavior of the Central and East European communist leaders turned out to be a disaster for them. Their conservatism provoked the wrath of their citizens, who knew of changes taking place in the Soviet Union under Gorbachev and who insisted that those changes, especially political liberalization, be adopted at home. Then, when some of the leaders relented and allowed reform, it got out of hand and eventually overwhelmed them and their socialist system, bringing both down to the ground in 1989 and 1990, just as they had suspected it would.

Moreover, when in the fall of 1989 those leaders who continued to oppose political change were besieged by angry citizens participating in unprecedented protests, they found to their shock and dismay that the Kremlin was unwilling to do what it had done in the past, namely, help preserve the status quo by military means if necessary. This Soviet behavior was a striking reversal of traditional Soviet policy toward Central and Eastern Europe. It was implicit in Gorbachev's historic announcement in July 1989 abrogating the so-called Brezhnev Doctrine, which had been used to justify the Soviet-led Warsaw Pact intervention in Prague to suppress the 1968 Czechoslovak reform movement, believed by the Kremlin to be a threat both to communist power and to Soviet influence not only in Czechoslovakia but elsewhere in Eastern Europe.

When it became clear to the Central and East European peoples, and especially those leading the popular demonstrations for reform, that the Brezhnev Doctrine would no longer apply, the rate of political and economic change accelerated throughout the region. In 1989 and the early 1990s, in one country after another, noncommunist reform figures successfully forced the resignation of communist leaders, even reformist ones willing to embrace in full measure the political and economic dimensions of perestroika, and replaced them. And the Kremlin looked on, eventually becoming reconciled to the collapse of communist rule and with it the system of satellization that had guaranteed Soviet power in the region since the end of the Second World War.

In addition, Western policies were having an effect. These policies worked to weaken communist rule and with it Soviet power and influence in the region by discrediting communist leaders at home and isolating them abroad. Varied and at times imaginative Western initiatives pointed to human-rights violations and other forms of repressive behavior intended to embarrass communist leaders and encourage domestic opposition to them. The United States in particular tried to weaken communist systems in Central and Eastern Europe by punishing them with trade sanctions that contributed to economic hardship and increased popular discontent. Finally, the West tried to encourage a relaxation of Soviet control over the region by improving relations with the Kremlin and convincing it that there was no threat to its security and therefore little logic to riding herd on its Central and East European allies.

Character of Collapse

Because of differences in national character and the history of communist rule in a given country, the peoples of Central and Eastern Europe challenged the socialist system in different ways. For example, Polish and Hungarian Communist

Party leaders were willing to accommodate public pressure for political liberalization. They were not prepared to use massive force to resist change. Rather, they hoped—mistakenly, as it turned out—that in accommodating demands for reform they could strengthen the party's frayed credibility and give it a new lease on life. Moreover, an influential reforming wing of the Polish and Hungarian parties, which allowed such people a home instead of repressing them, sympathized with Soviet perestroika and acknowledged the need for some change to reinvigorate the socialist system and assure its longevity. But once Polish and Hungarian voters received new opportunities for free choice in national elections, instead of rewarding party leaders who had given them this concession, voters punished the communists by voting overwhelmingly against them enabling noncommunist groups to assume leadership.

In East Germany and Czechoslovakia, however, communist leaders Erich Honecker and Miloš Jakeš firmly rejected popular demands for political reform. Frightened of change but also ideologically committed to the Soviet-style system and expecting Soviet support for their loyalty, they provoked an explosion of popular anger and were forced to resign. The stubbornness and rigidity of these leaders destroyed any chances Communist parties may have had in those countries of salvaging a leadership role or of playing some kind of political role in the postcommunist era. Romania's president and party leader Nicolae Ceauşescu was even more stubbornly opposed to change than his conservative colleagues in East Berlin and Prague. Determined to preserve the flawed status quo and prepared to use force against anyone demanding change, Ceauşescu provoked a mini–civil war that ended with his public execution. In Romania people seemed more hostile to Ceauşescu himself than to communist rule and tolerated a continuation of many policies Ceauşescu had pursued. Finally, conservative Bulgarian and Albanian communist leaders, torn between a preference for the status quo and recognition that if they did not make timely changes demanded by reform elements they would be forced out, eventually gave way to reformers who introduced sweeping liberalization of the political and economic systems while preserving the Communist Party's leadership. But Bulgarians and Albanians also showed the same dislike of communist rule as other peoples in Central and Eastern Europe and replaced communists with noncommunists in free and competitive party elections. While communist reformers were unable to save the party's historic leadership role, the changes they introduced made possible a transition from communist to noncommunist rule that was gradual and nonviolent and in so doing laid the groundwork for a future political role.

Problems of Postcommunist Development

In the postcommunist era, the peoples of Central and Eastern Europe have experienced a revolution of rising expectations. They assumed that political, economic, and societal democracy would transform their lives. In the years that have passed since the political upheavals of 1989 and 1990, disenchantment has set in, with people expressing skepticism about their postcommunist political, economic, and social order. They are confused and frustrated by the slow-moving, conflict-ridden character of democratic government, which they are inclined to blame for a lack of real improvement in living standards and new threats to social stability. All of the postcommunist systems in Central and Eastern Europe have serious problems, almost as serious as those of communist rule. These problems concern democratic development, the introduction of a free market, and the revival of intergroup conflict that is dividing and in some instances traumatizing some of the societies of the region.

1. Limits and Constraints on Democracy

While most Central and East European countries have made great strides toward Western-style parliamentary democracy, they still have a long way to go before they can compare favorably with the governments of the West. For example, heads of state in many Central and East European countries have developed distinctly authoritarian styles of behavior, which have been criticized by some as reminiscent of the communist political order but have nonetheless been tolerated, particiularly in Slovakia, Romania, and Serbia. Such leaders say they are committed to democracy but use undemocratic means to develop democracy in societies that traditionally have been difficult to govern and are particularly so in the postcommunist era. The new pluralistic societies lack the discipline needed to reform themselves, especially in the economic area. In these countries, and in others as well, free and open communications media, an important prerequisite of democracy, have not yet materialized. Leaders use the press and television to control their societies, especially at election time. They practice censorship, which sometimes reaches the level maintained by the communist dictatorships. Free and open media in Serbia and Slovakia are seen as threats to public order, the pursuit of policy, and the power of leadership.

There is a pervasive popular tolerance, if not acceptance and encouragement, of this behavior because the social support base of democracy remains largely limited to the intelligentsia and urban professionals. Most people seem to be growing tired of the participation that is essential to successful democracy. They are impatient with parliaments that debate issues and nonissues endlessly without coming to decisions. In short, they are just beginning to learn what Westerners have known for a long time, that democracy is messy, time-consuming, not always the most dignified kind of government, and by no means the most efficient.

Despite these difficulties, however, democracy *is* developing in Central Europe and the Balkans. The former communist dictatorships have all given way to systems of political pluralism. There have been regular and frequent elections for national parliaments and local governing bodies. Parties have moved in and out of power with no violent upheavals. Leaders are more sensitive than they ever were under communist rule to public opinion. Most countries have embraced Western-style civil liberties. Communist-style censorship that was all-inclusive has significantly diminished. Opposition newspapers are at least allowed to exist, even if life is made difficult for them when they become too critical of government policy. The degree to which democracy has taken hold, however, varies from one part of the region to another and from country to country. The contrasts in political development suggest an enormous diversity of postcommunist political, economic, and social development.

Central Europe

For the most part, the countries of Central Europe, Poland, Hungary, and the Czech Republic, have made significant progress in developing democratic government and a politically pluralistic environment. Working to their advantage is their historic closeness to West European cultural values, a brief democratic tradition before World War II, and a history of democratic opposition under communism.

These countries differ, however, in the stability of their postcommunist democratic systems. For example, through the summer of 1996, Poland has had eight prime ministers since the ascendancy of the first noncommunist leadership in August 1989. The inability of a single party to win a majority, or even a large plurality, has required government by coalitions, which tend to be extremely fragile. In response to parliamentary weakness, President Lech Wałęsa tried without much success to strengthen the office of the presidency to increase the efficiency of government. But, while Polish voters crave strong and decisive leadership to help the country raise living standards, they are determined to avoid anything reminiscent of a political dictatorship and were suspicious of Wałęsa, convinced he would like to become a modern-day Piłsudski. Popular misgivings about Wałęsa help explain the victory of his rival, Aleksandr Kwaśniewski, in the October 1995 presidential elections. On the other hand, to get elected Kwaśniewski had to reassure voters, as he tried to do during his campaign, of his commitment and that of his political supporters to the preservation of Poland's newly achieved political and economic democracy.

In the early 1990s, Czechoslovakia enjoyed a somewhat greater degree of political stability under the leadership of President Václav Havel and Prime Minister Václav Klaus. At that time, the problem for postcommunist Czechoslovak democracy, however, was what appeared to be the undemocratic way in which the state split into two separate and independent entities at the end of 1992, the Czech Republic and Slovakia, because of seemingly irreconcilable differences between the two large ethnic groups over many public-policy issues, including the constitutional structure of the postcommunist Czechoslovak state. Czech and Slovak political leaders seemed to have ignored the will of a majority of their constituents to keep the country together by means of some sort of compromise. And since the split, most Slovaks have made no secret of their regret, as promises of a better life after independence have not been fulfilled. Indeed, since the beginning of 1993, Czech and Slovak leaders have led their new countries along different paths of development. While the government of the Czech Republic in Prague remains firmly committed to Western political and economic liberalism, the Slovak government in Bratislava has displayed authoritarian tendencies in monitoring the press very closely to discourage criticism and dissent and in moving at a snail's pace toward a free market.

While Hungary seems liberal and stable enough on the surface, its political leaders and voters have displayed a disquieting nostalgia for authoritarian styles of governmental behavior. Politicians like István Csurka, a neo-fascist nationalist and anti-Semite, attract a substantial public audience. The spirit of liberal democratic government to which most Hungarians still swear allegiance is at risk as a rightist authoritarian constituency pushes for more political order. At the same time, Hungarian voters, like their Polish counterparts, have begun to look to former communists at election time as an alternative to noncommunist parties that failed to remain sensitive to the hardships of ordinary citizens during the transition to a free-market economy. Like Poland, Hungary in 1994 had, and still has in late 1996, a former communist as prime minister. He insists on his party's commitment to political and economic democracy as he tries to provide more responsive leadership than his predecessors. But, the political ascendancy of the former communist left in Hungary, as in Poland, is a political wild card in future democratic development.

The Balkans

Balkan countries, in particular Romania, Bulgaria, Albania, Croatia, and Yugoslavia, have moved very slowly toward the kind of Western-style democracy seen in their neighbors to the north. Limits on political party pluralism, on freedom of thought, assembly, and the press, and on leadership accountability to Parliament still exist. Some Balkan leaders rely on authoritarian styles of behavior, which are not widely condemned. A majority of the people in these countries, especially those who live in the countryside, do not seem to mind conservative political rule and even display a certain sympathy for politicians who advocate or practice it. In some ways this is fortunate, allowing for a gradual evolution toward democratic government in countries where democracy does not have historic roots and where communist authoritarianism had a degree of legitimacy and acceptability nonexistent in Central Europe. Poverty also has been a barrier to democratic development. The hardships of moving away from a state-controlled economy to a free market have been more severe in the Balkans than in the more highly developed Central European countries, and people therefore have been more willing to accept strong leaders with authoritarian instincts for the sake of a more efficient problem-solving system. Thus, in supporting President Ion Iliescu, who showed little tolerance for public ciriticism of his policies, many Romanians seemed to have said that they preferred more authority than liberty if that kind of political balance would cushion the social and economic dislocation caused by the move away from socialist paternalism to a capitalist order. Many people in other Balkan countries, in particular, Yugoslavia and Croatia, seem to have accepted the same kind of trade-off, one that encourages authoritarian styles of leadership and impedes movement toward Western-style liberal democracy in return for a measure of security and stability.

2. Economic Achievements

The record of economic achievement in the transition from dictatorship to democracy has been mixed. Although reform economists in all the former communist-ruled countries argued in favor of diminishing state control over economic life and increasing opportunities for private entrepreneurship, the degree to which postcommunist governments have accepted and implemented these changes has varied sharply throughout the region.

Six years after the collapse of communist rule, Poland, the Czech Republic, Hungary, and eastern Germany have gone further and faster in diminishing state control over the economy than Romania, Bulgaria, Albania, and Yugoslavia. The percentage of privately owned enterprises is higher in the north than in the south, where privatization has barely started. The state still controls most of the national economy in the Balkan countries.

Moreover, the problems attending the transition from a command to a market economy, in particular unemployment, inflation, and the decline of productivity in agriculture and industry, have been more severe in the south than in the north. While inflation initially was high everywhere in Central and Eastern Europe as state control of prices was lifted and prices floated in response to supply and demand, a slowdown of price rises occurred in Poland, Hungary, and the Czech Republic in 1993. But the rate of inflation remained high in the Balkans, especially Albania, where it was 210 percent in early 1994. Unemployment is in the double digits, except for the Czech Republic, where the free sector of the economy has gradually absorbed labor forced out of work when inefficient, loss-making state enterprises were closed down.

Different levels of achievement in the economic sphere, as in the political sphere, in different parts of Central and Eastern Europe result from particular conditions in each country. For example, in the late 1980s, economic reformers in Poland and Hungary had access to Western economic literature. Therefore, in the early postcommunist era, many economists as well as politicians could deal with free-market concepts. They produced their own Western-style economists and freely used consultants from capitalist economies. But in Bulgaria, Romania, and Albania, there was little familiarity with or sympathy for liberal economic models. In the early 1990s, leaders of those countries and voter constituencies that supported them preferred to retain much of the paternalistic economic order developed by the communists—to which workers throughout the region had become accustomed —to minimize hardship as private entrepreneurship was allowed to expand and state control over economic life was diminished.

Improvement in living conditions has been slower than most people expected and wanted in almost all of Central and Eastern Europe because of the slowness of foreign investment. Foreign investors are put off by a lax work ethic, by enormous amounts of bureaucratic red tape, and by a primitive infrastructure that interferes with business expansion. These conditions are, not surprisingly, worse in the Balkans, where foreign investment has been marginal, than in Central Europe, where it has in fact increased in recent years, though only in a limited way. Given the shortage of domestic capital for economic expansion, economic growth in Central and Eastern Europe has not been great enough to make a real difference in living standards, which have remained unchanged or in some instances have fallen since the collapse of communist rule at the end of the 1980s. It is not unusual for some Central and East European consumers to be heard saying that things were actually better under the communists than they were in the early 1990s.

By contrast, eastern Germany has made the greatest progress in replacing the socialist economy of the communist era with Western-style capitalism thanks to the enormous financial help coming from western Germany. The German federal government and private investment have infused the equivalent of about $3 billion into eastern Germany to modernize its infrastructure and foster economic development, which eventually will bring eastern Germany's living standards up to Western levels, probably well before other former communist countries in the region achieve such levels. No other former communist country today has the equivalent of eastern Germany's wealthy western German patron. But eastern Germans are no different from the other peoples of Eastern Europe in missing the security and certainty of the paternalistic state of the communists that had guaranteed them a minimum material well-being including shelter, medical care, and employment. Indeed, the eastern Germans increasingly see themselves as western Germany's "charity case" and many are psychologically depressed.

Finally, efforts to clean up the environment have had mixed results. On the one hand, factory emissions have somewhat declined because of a concerted government antipollution effort. Indeed, the installation of anti-pollution devices has barely begun, while energy is still being produced largely from highly polluting brown coal. Rather, if the air is a bit cleaner in some industrial areas, it is thanks to the closure of pollution-making factories because of their inefficiency and failure to show a profit on investment. In the main, the current leaders of the Central and East European countries still assign a low-level priority to the expenditure of scarce public funds on the environment. There are more pressing needs, they say, and the environment must wait. Furthermore, as the free market develops, it will be increasingly difficult for governments to police the environment. Finally, the West has been niggardly in dispensing needed assistance for the expensive clean-up job, for much the same reasons that other forms of Western aid have not been forthcoming in the amount expected and needed to help in the economic transformation of Central and Eastern Europe.

3. Threats to Societal Unity and Tranquility

The collapse of communist rule helped revive many societal problems that were ignored and, arguably, made worse under the communists. Perhaps the most potentially dangerous of these problems for the well-being of the postcommunist societies in Central and Eastern Europe is the explosion of ethnocultural nationalism. With the personal freedom to speak out, people have given vent to long-held and deeply sublimated cultural prejudices, which have fueled a vicious nationalism the communists had tried hard to suppress. This nationalism, pitting neighbor against neighbor in the postcommunist era, has severely taxed democratic systems, interfered with economic growth and development, and undermined the stability and harmony of the diverse societies that compromise the Central and East European region.

At its worst, ethnocultural nationalism produced violence and civil war in Yugoslavia, where different ethnic groups went to war against one another rather than resolve their differences peacefully. By contrast, differences between Czechs and Slovaks in the early 1990s were resolved peacefully, as seen in the so-called "velvet divorce" between Czechs and Slovaks, who went their own political ways without violence. But even though the split was peaceful, many people had been against it, and it may be argued that both countries are the weaker, with the Slovaks suffering the most. Severe ethnic conflicts also exist in Romania and Bulgaria, where the prejudice of the majority against the minority (Hungarians in Romania and Turks in Bulgaria) is strong but so far has not led to violent civil conflict.

Political culture helps explain why ethnic conflict has played out differently in the Central and East European countries. Large ethnocultural groups in Yugoslavia had far less in common, despite their membership in a Yugoslav community, than Czechs and Slovaks in Czechoslovakia, who identified more as individuals than as members of a particular ethnic group. While Tito had forged administrative unity in Yugoslavia, he never was able to homogenize its society, and only a small portion of the Yugoslav peoples, mainly those who were educated and lived in the large cosmopolitan urban centers of the country, thought of themselves first as Yugoslav citizens and only secondarily as members of a particular ethnocultural group. Leadership is also critical in understanding the explosions of ethnocultural nationalism. Nationalist leaders in the former Czechoslovakia, notably, Václav Klaus and Vladimír Mečiar, never descended to the level of Serbia's Milošević in fanning intergroup hatred. Havel's conciliatory leadership was also important. While he could not keep Czechoslovakia together, he must be given credit for having helped to discourage an explosion of civil conflict. Havel was admired and respected by both Slovaks and Czechs and exercised a moderating influence over both. By contrast, leaders of Yugoslavia's large ethnocultural groups, notably, Serbia's Milošević, Croatia's Tudjman, and Bosnia-Herzegovina's Izetbegović, distrusted and disliked one another. They are angry and aggressive leaders ready to display their hostility to one another openly and forcefully.

The effects of ethnocultural conflicts in postcommunist Central and Eastern Europe have been uniformly negative. They have increased the difficulty the new democratic systems already have in building the consensus needed for stable government. They are subversive of democratic values in that they involve a denial of rights and freedoms to small groups. They impede economic growth and development by encouraging political separatism that leads to economic separatism. They can eventually, as some already have done, destroy the unity of a state. And they can complicate the relations of a country experiencing ethnic conflict with its neighbors in the region and other countries with an interest in the region's stability.

Another social problem, less dramatic but equally important for social stability in Central and Eastern Europe, is the continuing political marginalization of women. They remain only a small fraction of the political elite. In 1995, they were outnumbered by men in the parliaments of Poland, Hungary, and East Germany 9 to 1, and they have even less political influence in the Balkan societies. The economic situation for women remains bleak, as the advantages of the shift to a free-market economy seem to be passing them by. For example, in Poland, 58 percent of the country's unemployed are women, and in Poland and Hungary, on average women continue to earn between 20 percent and 25 percent less than men in comparable jobs. And women with children find it most difficult to get employment, because privately owned companies see welfare costs for them adversely affecting profit margins. While most women do not want to go back to communism, they remain disappointed and disillusioned with capitalism, which they see as a boon only for men.

Finally, health care has severely deteriorated, with state-employed doctors paid less than bus drivers and state-owned medical clinics lacking some of the most basic supplies, from pills to syringes. Financially strapped governments continue to refuse to put scarce financial resources into the debilitated health-care system for much the same reasons they give minimum attention to the environment. It is a matter of priorities, with health maintenance considered far less important than the expansion of the economic infrastructure. The consequences of this neglect are devastating. The death rate for adult males from heart disease and cancer has surged in almost all the former communist countries, except the Czech Republic, to the point where some argue the economic competitiveness of the country is threatened. And increasingly people who thought they were insured find they have to pay out of pocket for medicines and procedures once paid by government, which is gradually shifting the cost of health maintenance to individuals, many of whom cannot afford the new financial burden. Finally, only through extensive bribery of poorly paid health-care personnel can people get the quality of health care they need.

Like the marginalization of women, the deterioration of health maintenance has become a serious social problem in the postcommunist era. It is becoming an identifiable source of popular frustration and anger that eventually could contribute to a backlash against the postcommunist era and to political destabilization injurious to the development of democracy.

4. Postcommunist Diplomatic Achievements

One area of national life where most of the former communist countries of Central and Eastern Europe have similar interests is foreign relations. They all are reorienting their foreign policies westward. They want closer links to the West and need some Western help to manage their economies. The Balkans need the most help because they are starting from such a low point of development. They have received the least help because the West is dissatisfied with the authoritarian overtones of their postcommunist governments. Ironically, however, for this very reason the West should pay more attention to them if it wants to keep them on the democratic path. Like the northern countries, the Balkans see themselves as part of a common European home in which they claim to share most of the same values as the West.

But there are some distinctions among the East European countries in their approaches to the West. Former Warsaw Pact countries (Yugoslavia and Albania were not members of the Warsaw Pact) seem especially eager for the intimacy with the West that had been denied them by the Soviet Union. Those countries most bent on drawing closer to Western Europe are Poland, the Czech Republic, Slovakia, and Hungary because of their historic links to Western Europe and because all experienced and remember with bitterness Soviet military and political coercion during the communist era. Of these four, perhaps Poland, because of its historic rivalry with czarist Russia and the Soviet Union, has been especially aggressive in its drive for close military ties with Western Europe. For Poland, closeness to the West is a matter of territorial security vis-à-vis a superpowerful neighbor that frequently threatened the survival of the Polish people in recent history.

Throughout the region, however, there is disappointment with the meager response of the West. The new postcommunist leaders in Eastern Europe believe their countries have earned and are entitled to substantial financial and strategic backing from the West because they finally threw out the communists and established their independence of the Soviet Union and Russia, as the West had always wanted them to do. In the view of many former communist countries in Central and Eastern Europe, the West, and especially the United States, the wealthiest and most powerful member of the Western community, has failed to meet its obligation to help the new governments of Central and Eastern Europe make a success of breaking with communism and developing new democratic political and economic orders. Poland in particular has been annoyed by the failure of the West to be more forthcoming. President Lech Wałęsa did little to conceal his frustration over the unwillingness of NATO to admit Poland in the early and mid-1990s as a full member. He was upset over the unwillingness of the West, as he saw it, to recognize Poland's need for security arising out of its location between two great competitive powers, Germany and Russia.

The failure of the West to accommodate the demands of Poland and its neighbors for guarantees of their security, in particular their territorial integrity, especially in light of the growing influence of nationalists in Russian politics, jeopardizes the integrity and survival of the new democratic systems. No one knows Russia better than its neighbors in Central and Eastern Europe. They fear for their future independence, remembering that in recent history the countries that now make up Central and Eastern Europe had far shorter and fewer periods of freedom from foreign control than most other countries on the European continent.

The East European countries, of course, have made some progress in finding alternative ways to promote their security. They have turned to one another for cooperation and consultation to resolve problems of mutual concern, such as security, the environment, and trade. Leaders of the northern countries have been meeting at regular intervals. Known as the Visegrád Group, Poland, the former Czechoslovakia, and Hungary have established good working relations despite some sharp differences on interstate issues, including the environment. Romania, Bulgaria, Serbia, Albania, and some of the former Soviet republics, including Russia, have also taken steps to promote cooperation among themselves and with Turkey in the economic and cultural areas. In the end, these gestures of intraregional cooperation may become as important as relations with Western Europe in preserving the new postcommunist system of independent states.

5. Prospects of a Communist Revival

In most Central and East European countries, the uncertainties of the postcommunist era have translated into anger, which the former communist parties or socialists have harnessed for their own purposes. Voter support for former communists in parliamentary elections increased, in Poland, Hungary, and to a lesser extent in eastern Germany. As a result of the May 1994 parliamentary elections, Gyula Horn, a former communist who was foreign minister in the last Hungarian communist government, became prime minister. And in early March 1995, Józef Oleksy, a former communist, became prime minister of Poland. Former communists also expect to score gains in upcoming parliamentary elections in Bulgaria and Albania.

With their advocacy of a slow rate of economic change that will minimize hardships like unemployment and inflation and with their apparent willingness to go into debt to maintain a substantial social net, the message of former Communist parties is a popular one, which free-market-oriented leaders are beginning to take seriously. But the former communists insist that they do not want a return to an authoritarian political system and show no special affection for Russia, at least publicly.

The revival of popular interest in communists in some countries so shortly after the end of their long period of repressive and inept rule is worrisome. With the ascendancy of the former communists and parties aligned with them, the rate of change to a free market is likely to slow down. The former communists can also be expected to show an interest in fostering greater political discipline in the name of more efficient administration. They could even reach out to and make common cause with like-minded groups in Russia, in particular, the Russian Communist Party.

The Czech Republic seems to be the only country in the region where former communists remain weak as a party and unlikely to return to positions of leadership. The reason for this may lie in the comparative health of the Czech economy, which has maintained an extraordinary stability as it implements free-market reforms. Another obstacle to a communist revival in the Czech Republic is popular acceptance of and loyalty to the postcommunist democratic leadership of President Václav Havel, arguably a national hero because of his heroic resistance to communist rule in the late 1980s and his very liberal and humane political philosophy and political behavior. Czechoslovakia's nearest neighbors, Poland and Hungary, as well as the Balkan countries, lack this kind of credible and competent leadership.

Notes

Chapter 1

1. Recent studies of communist political systems in Central and Eastern Europe include Ghita Ionescu, *The Politics of the European Communist States* (New York: Praeger, 1967); Robert Wesson, *The Aging of Communism* (New York: Praeger, 1980); Ivan Volgyes, *Politics in Eastern Europe* (Chicago, IL: The Dorsey Press, 1986); J.F. Brown, *Eastern Europe and Communist Rule* (Durham, NC: Duke University Press, 1988); Leslie Holmes, *The End of Communist Power: Anti-Corruption Campaigns and Legitimation Crises* (New York: Oxford University Press, 1993), especially chap. 3, pp. 97–98, 102, 105–7, 110–17; Thomas W. Simmons, *Eastern Europe in the Postwar World*, 2nd ed. (New York: St. Martin's Press, 1993); Michael G. Roskin, *The Rebirth of Eastern Europe*, 2nd ed. (Englewood Cliffs, NJ: Prentice Hall, 1994).

2. See Seweryn Bialer, "Perestroika and the Future of the Cold War," in *Central and Eastern Europe: The Opening Curtain?* ed. William E. Griffith (Boulder, CO: Westview Press, 1989), pp. 406–12; Zbigniew Brzezinski, *The Grand Failure: The Birth and Death of Communism in the Twentieth Century* (New York: Scribners, 1989), p. 132. See also Jan Vanous, "East European Economic Slowdown," *Problems of Communism*, vol. 31, no. 4 (July–August 1982): 1–19.

3. *Christian Science Monitor*, April 25, 1991, cited in *Eastern Europe: Transformation and Revolution 1945–1991*, ed. Lyman H. Legters (Lexington, MA: D.C. Heath, 1992), p. 608; Roger Mansur, *Failed Transitions: The Eastern European Economy and Environment Since the Fall of Communism* (New York: The Free Press, 1993), pp. 26–38; Hillary French, "East Europe's Clean Break with the Past," *World Watch* (March–April 1991): 22.

4. See Zbigniew Brzezinski, *The Soviet Bloc: Unity and Conflict*, revised and enlarged (Cambridge, MA: Harvard University Press, 1971). See also Karen Dawisha, *East Europe, Gorbachev, and Reform* (Cambridge: Cambridge University Press, 1988), chap. 4, pp. 60–101.

5. See Paul Marer, "The Political Economy of Soviet Relations with Eastern Europe" in *Soviet Policy in Eastern Europe*, ed. Sarah M. Terry (New Haven, CT: Yale University Press, 1984), pp. 158–60.

6. Brzezinski, *The Grand Failure*, p. 141.

7. Academician Oleg T. Bogomolov, head of the Institute for the Economics of the World Socialist System in 1988, said at the time that sooner or later all socialist countries

would have to undertake profound systemic reform to deal with the crisis of stagnation common to all of them, including the Soviet Union. See Ronald D. Asmus, J.F. Brown, and Keith Crane, *Soviet Foreign Policy and Revolutions in Eastern Europe* (Santa Monica, CA: RAND, 1991), p. 6.

8. Asmus, Brown, and Crane, *Soviet Foreign Policy*, p. 19.

9. Allen Lynch, *Gorbachev's International Outlook: Intellectual Origins and Political Consequences* (New York: Institute for East-West Studies, 1989), pp. 43–52. See also Mikhail Gorbachev, *Perestroika: New Thinking for Our Country and the World* (New York: Harper and Row, 1987), pp. 161–70.

10. Charles Gati, *The Bloc That Failed* (Bloomington: Indiana University Press, 1990), p. 169; Asmus, Brown, and Crane, *Soviet Foreign Policy*, p. 9.

11. Stephen R. Bowers, "The East European Revolution," *East European Quarterly* 25, no. 2 (Summer 1991): 138; Sharon Wolchik, *Czechoslovakia in Transition: Politics, Economics, and Society* (London: Pinter, 1990), pp. 42–44.

12. Gati, *The Bloc That Failed*, p. 194.

13. See "Press Conference in Milan," *Pravda*, December 3, 1989, p. 2, cited from *Current Digest of the Soviet Press* 41, no. 48 (December 3, 1989): 5–6; "Press Conference by M.S. Gorbachev and H. Kohl," *Pravda*, July 18, 1990, pp. 1, 5, cited from *Current Digest of the Soviet Press* 42, no. 29 (July 18, 1990): 3–6.

14. See Angela Stent, "Technology Transfer to Eastern Europe: Paradoxes, Policies, Prospects," in *Central and Eastern Europe*, ed. Griffith, pp. 86–95.

15. See Wolfgang Berner and William E. Griffith, "West German Policy Toward Central and Eastern Europe," in *Central and Eastern Europe*, ed. Griffith, pp. 338–52.

16. James M. Markham, "Gorbachev in France Pursues Drive for European Support," *The International Herald Tribune*, July 3, 1989. See also Dominique Moisi, "French Policy Toward Central and Eastern Europe," in *Central and Eastern Europe*, ed. Griffith, pp. 353–65.

17. See Michael Mandelbaum, "The United States and Eastern Europe," in *Central and Eastern Europe*, ed. Griffith, pp. 366–87; Karl W. Ryavec, *United States–Soviet Relations* (New York: Longman, 1989), pp. 241–46.

18. For the origins and development of dissent in Eastern Europe in the 1960s and 1970s see Walter D. Connor, "Dissent in Eastern Europe: A New Coalition?" *Problems of Communism*, vol. 29, no. 1 (January–February 1980): 1–17. See also Brzezinski, *The Grand Failure*, p. 138; Bowers, "The East European Revolution," p. 135; Gale Stokes, *The Walls Came Tumbling Down: The Collapse of Communism in Eastern Europe* (New York: Oxford University Press, 1993), pp. 12–45.

19. Jeffrey Goldfarb, *After the Fall: The Pursuit of Democracy in Central Europe* (New York: Basic Books, 1992), p. 197.

20. Brzezinski, *The Grand Failure*, p. 138.

Chapter 2

1. Jan Ake Dellenbrant, "Parties and Party Systems in Eastern Europe," in *Developments in East European Politics*, ed. Stephen White, Judy Batt, and Paul G. Lewis (Durham, NC: Duke Univertsity Press, 1994), pp. 158–62; for a recent large overview of postcommunist development in Central and Eastern Europe, see Geoffrey Pridham and Tatu Vanhannen, *Democracy in Eastern Europe: Domestic and International Perspectives* (New York: Routledge, 1995).

2. Judy Batt, *East Central Europe: From Reform to Transformation* (New York: Council on Foreign Relations Press, 1991), p. 55; Gale Stokes, *The Walls Came Tumbling Down: The Collapse of Communism in Eastern Europe* (New York: Oxford University

Press, 1993), p. 170; Sharon Wolchik, *Czechoslovakia in Transition: Politics, Economics, and Society* (London: Pinter, 1990), p. 51. See also J.F. Brown, *Hopes and Shadows: Eastern Europe after Communism* (Durham, NC: Duke University Press, 1994), pp. 32–33; Dellenbrant, "Parties and Party Systems in Eastern Europe," pp. 151–55.

3. Batt, *East Central Europe*, pp. 48–49.

4. Krzyzstof Jasewiecz, "Structures and Representation," in *Developments in East European Politics*, ed. White, Batt, and Lewis, pp. 142–45.

5. Dellenbrant, "Parties and Party Systems in Eastern Europe," pp. 156–58.

6. Jasewiecz, "Structures and Representation," pp. 136–40. See also Raymond Taras, "Leadership and Executives," in *Developments in East European Politics*, ed. White, Batt, and Lewis, pp. 163–66.

7. "Eastern Europe: The Old World's New World," *The Economist*, March 13, 1993, p. 4.

8. *The Boston Globe*, December 5, 1993 (hereafter cited as *BG*).

9. Batt, *East Central Europe*, pp. 54–55; "Eastern Europe: The Old World's New World," *The Economist*, March 13, 1993, p. 5; Stephen Fischer-Galati, "The Political Right in Eastern Europe in Historical Perspective," in *Democracy and Right Wing Politics in Eastern Europe in the 1990s*, ed. Joseph Held (New York: Columbia University Press, 1993), p. 10.

10. Giuseppi Di Palma, "Eastern Europe After Leninism: Democracy Can Work," *Current*, June 1, 1991, p. 35; George Schopflin, "Central and Eastern Europe Over the Last Year: New Trends, Old Structures," in *Eastern Europe: Transformation and Revolution 1945–1991*, ed. Lyman H. Legters (Lexington, MA: D.C. Heath, 1992), p. 649; J. Brian Atwood, "Reflections on the Transition in Eastern and Central Europe," in *The New Democratic Frontier: A Country by Country Report on Elections in Central and Eastern Europe*, ed. Larry Garber and Eric Bjornlund (Washington, DC: National Democratic Institute for International Affairs, 1992), p. 223.

11. Brown, *Hopes and Shadows*, pp. 26–29.

12. Di Palma, "Eastern Europe after Lenninism," p. 35. See also Ralf Dahrendorf, "Road to Freedom: Democratization and Its Problems in East-Central Europe," in *Uncertain Futures: Eastern Europe and Democracy*, ed. Peter Volten (New York: Institute for East-West Security Studies, 1990), p. 13–15.

13. Batt, *East Central Europe*, pp. 46–47; "Eastern Europe: The Old World's New World," *The Economist*, March 13, 1993, p. 4; Jolanta Babiuch, "Church and Society in Post-Communist Eastern Europe," *The World Today*, vol. 56, no. 11, November 1994, p. 213; David S. Mason, "Attitudes Toward the Market and Political Participation in Post-Communist States," *Slavic Review* 54, no. 2 (Summer 1995): 397.

14. Schopflin, "Central and Eastern Europe over the Last Year," in *Eastern Europe*, ed. Legters, p. 649.

15. Richard C. Longworth, "Eastern Europe: The Party's Over," *Bulletin of the Atomic Scientists* (January–February 1992): 23.

16. Zoltan D. Barany, "East European Armed Forces in Transition and Beyond," *East European Quarterly* 26, no. 1 (March 1992): 16.

17. Mason, "Attitudes Toward the Market and Politics in the Post-Communist States," pp. 387–89.

18. Jan S. Prybyla, "The Road from Socialism: Why, Where, What, and How," *Problems of Communism*, vol. 40, no. 1–2 (January–April 1991): 2, 7–8; Goldfarb, *After the Fall*, pp. 174, 178. See also *The New York Times*, January 29, 1990 (hereafter cited as *NYT*).

19. Prybyla, "The Road from Socialism," p. 8.

20. Yali Pang, "Privatization in East European Countries," *East European Quarterly*

26, no. 4 (January 1993): 476; "Eastern Europe: The Old World's New World," *The Economist*, March 13, 1993, p. 14; Wolchik, *Czechoslovakia in Transition*, p. 252; Brown, *Hopes and Shadows*, pp. 160–61.

21. Brown, *Hopes and Shadows*, pp. 150–51; Bob Deacon, "Social Change, Social Problems, and Social Policy," in *Developments in East European Politics*, ed. White, Batt, and Lewis, pp. 236–37.

22. Pang, "Privatization in East European Countries," pp. 472–73; Judy Batt, "The Politics of Economic Transition," in *Developments in East European Politics*, ed. White, Batt, and Lewis, pp. 220–21.

23. Pang, "Privatization in East European Countries," p. 475; Wolchik, *Czechoslovakia in Transition*, pp. 249–52.

24. Batt, "The Politics of Economic Transition," p. 222.

25. Pang, "Privatization in East European Countries," pp. 475–76; "Business in Eastern Europe," *The Economist*, September 21, 1991, pp. 18–19.

26. Pang, "Privatization in East European Countries," p. 477; *NYT*, May 19, 1992; Roger Mansur, *Failed Transitions: The Eastern European Economy and Environment Since the Fall of Communism* (New York: The Free Press, 1993), p. 64.

27. Pang, "Privatization in East European Countries," p. 481.

28. Dezo Kovacs and Sally Ward Maggard, "The Human Face of Political, Economic, and Social Change in Eastern Europe," *East European Quarterly* 27, no. 3 (September 1993): 337–38.

29. Stokes, *The Walls Came Tumbling Down*, p. 189; John M. Kramer, "Eastern Europe and the 'Energy Shock' of 1990–1991," *Problems of Communism*, vol. 40, no. 3 (May–June 1991): 87–91.

30. Stokes, *The Walls Came Tumbling Down*, p. 189; *NYT*, May 6, June 29, 1991. See also Wolchik, *Czechoslovakia in Transition*, p. 248; Brown, *Hopes and Shadows*, pp. 151–52.

31. Mansur, *Failed Transitions*, pp. 52–56.

32. Brown, *Hopes and Shadows*, pp. 145–47.

33. See George Schopflin, "The Prospects of Democracy in Central and Eastern Europe," in *Uncertain Futures*, ed. Volten, p. 26; *BG*, February 4, 1990.

34. Brown, *Hopes and Shadows*, p. 169; Mansur, *Failed Transitions*, p. 80; see also Barbara Jancar Webster, ed., *Environmental Action in Eastern Europe: Responses to Crisis* (Armonk, NY: M.E. Sharpe, 1993), passim; Colin Woodard, "A Terrible Communist Legacy," *Transition*, vol. 2, no. 15 (July 26, 1996), pp. 50–52.

35. Erich G. Frankland, "Green Revolutions? The Role of Green Parties in Eastern Europe's Transition, 1989–1994," *East European Quarterly* 29, no. 3 (Fall 1995): 341.

36. Brown, *Hopes and Shadows*, p. 170; Mansur, *Failed Transitions*, pp. 86–92; Frankland, "Green Revolutions?" p. 341; Ghita Bisschop, "Optimism Wanes for a Prompt Cleanup," *Transition*, vol. 2, no. 10 (May 17, 1996), pp. 42–45; Colin Woodard, "The Western Aid Cavalry Is Not Coming," ibid., vol. 2, no. 15 (July 26, 1996), p. 53.

37. Mason, "Attitudes Toward the Market and Politics in Post-Communist States," p. 391.

38. Todoritchka Gotovska-Popova, "Nationalism in Post-Communist Eastern Europe," *East European Quarterly* 27, no. 2 (June 1993): 117–18; Monty G. Marshall, "States at Risk: Ethnopolitics in the Multinational States of Eastern Europe," in *Minorities at Risk: A Global View of Ethnopolitical Conflicts*, ed. Ted Robert Gurr (Washington, DC: United States Institute of Peace Press, 1993), chap. 7, pp. 173–83; Paul Latawski, ed., *Contemporary Nationalism in East-Central Europe* (New York: St. Martin's Press, 1995), pp. 15–22.

39. Marshall, "States at Risk," p. 209; for background on the Roma people in Czecho-

slovakia, see Wolchik, *Czechoslovakia in Transition*, pp. 182–84; and Brown, *Hopes and Shadows*, pp. 172–78; for a historical overview of ethnocultural nationalism in Central and Eastern Europe in the twentieth century see *East European Nationalism in the Twentieth Century*, ed. Peter Sugar (Washington, DC: American University Press, 1995) and *Nationalism and Nationalities in the New Europe*, ed. Charles Kupchan (Ithaca, NY: Cornell University Press, 1995).

40. Steven L. Burg, "Nationalism Redux: Through the Glass of the Post-Communist States Darkly," *Current History* (April 1993): 164–65. See also Robert M. Hayden, "Constitutional Nationalism in the Formerly Yugoslav Republics," *Slavic Review* 51, no. 4 (Winter 1992): 673.

41. Deborah Lipstadt, "Anti-Semitism in Eastern Europe Rears Its Ugly Head Again," *USA Today*, September 1993, pp. 50–51; Katherine Verdery, "Nationalism and National Sentiment in Post-Socialist Romania," *Slavic Review* 52, no. 2 (Summer 1993): 199.

42. Lipstadt, "Anti-Semitism in Eastern Europe," p. 51.

43. Ibid., p. 53.

44. *NYT*, November 17, 1993; Zoltan Barany, "Living on the Edge: The East European Roma in Post-Communist Politics and Society," *Slavic Review*, 53, no. 2 (Summer 1994): 327–28; Verdery, "Nationalism and National Sentiment in Post-Socialist Romania," p. 197; Alaina Lemon, "No Land No Contracts for Romani Workers," *Transition*, vol. 2, no. 13 (June 28, 1996), pp. 28–30.

45. *NYT*, November 17, 1993. See also Barany, "Living on the Edge," pp. 330–32.

46. Barany, "Living on the Edge," p. 334.

47. See Chris Corrin, "People and Politics," in *Developments in East European Politics*, ed. White, Batt, and Lewis, p. 199.

48. For a recent study of the role of women in postcommunist Eastern Europe, see Marilyn Rueschemeyer, ed., *Women in the Politics of Postcommunist Eastern Europe* (Armonk, NY: M.E. Sharpe, 1994). See also Corrin, "People and Politics," pp. 199–203.

49. *BG*, February 13, 1991; *NYT*, June 19, 1991; Brown, *Hopes and Shadows*, p. 282; see also F. Stephen Larabee, *East European Security After the Cold War* (Santa Monica, CA: RAND, 1993), pp. 121–40.

50. *NYT*, September 15, 1991; see also Larabee, *East European Security*, pp. 141–52.

51. "Eastern Europe: The Old World's New World," p. 21; Janusz Bugajski, *Nations in Turmoil: Conflict and Cooperation in Eastern Europe* (Boulder, CO: Westview Press, 1993), p. 211.

52. *BG*, November 23, 1991; the EU also has stipulated as a prerequisite for membership establishment of a proven stable democracy. Bugajski, *Nations in Turmoil*, p. 211.

53. *The International Herald Tribune*, June 23, 1993.

54. Stokes, *The Walls Came Tumbling Down*, pp. 189–90; Bugajski, *Nations in Turmoil*, p. 209.

55. *NYT*, September 30, 1994.

56. See Larabee, *East European Security*, pp. 53–80.

57. *NYT*, October 17, 1993; Bugajski, *Nations in Turmoil*, p. 221.

58. *BG*, June 7, 1991; *NYT*, June 7, 1991.

59. *NYT*, October 22, 1993.

60. Bugajski, *Nations in Turmoil*, p. 221.

61. Larabee, *East European Security*, pp. 169–72.

62. The Russian perspective is discussed in *Ibid.*, pp. 160–64.

63. CMEA in particular had outlived its usefulness with the adoption of market reforms, industrial restructuring, reduction and elimination of subsidies to unprofitable state-run enterprises, and the rapid economic merger of East Germany with the German Federal Republic. Bugajski, *Nations in Turmoil*, pp. 187–88.

64. The precipitous decline of Russian energy exports on which East European industry depended in the communist era was accompanied by a steady loss of markets in the former Soviet Union for East European exports. Ibid., p. 188.

65. For a full discussion of the region's changing views about military security see Ibid., pp. 193–99.

66. Larabee, *East European Security*, pp. 158–60.

67. *NYT*, October 21, 1994.

68. See Andrew Cottey, *East-Central Europe after the Cold War: Poland, the Czech Republic and Hungary in Search of Security* (New York: St. Martin's Press, 1995).

69. Larabee, *East European Security*, pp. 109–14.

Chapter 3

1. Elez Biberaj, "Albania: The Last Domino," in *Eastern Europe in Revolution*, ed. Ivo Banac (Ithaca, NY: Cornell University Press, 1992), pp. 191–92.

2. *Yearbook on International Communist Affairs 1989* (Stanford, CA: Hoover Institution Press, 1990), p. 241 (hereafter cited as *YICA*).

3. Ibid.

4. Biberaj, "Albania: The Last Domino," pp. 191–92.

5. Louis Zanga, "A Watershed Year," in *Eastern Europe: Transformation and Revolution 1945–1991*, ed. Lyman H. Legters (Lexington, MA: D.C. Heath, 1992), pp. 542–43.

6. Biberaj, "Albania: The Last Domino," pp. 192–93

7. Elez Biberaj, "Albania at the Crossroads," *Problems of Communism*, vol. 40, no. 5 (September–October 1991): 2–4.

8. Biberaj, "Albania: The Last Domino," pp. 192–93.

9. Biberaj, "Albania at the Crossroads," pp. 2–4.

10. Ibid., p. 4; Biberaj, "Albania: The Last Domino," pp. 193–94. See also *YICA 1989*, p. 299.

11. Zanga, "A Watershed Year," p. 545; *YICA 1991*, p. 256.

12. Biberaj, "Albania at the Crossroads," pp. 2–4; *YICA 1991*, p. 256.

13. United States Department of State, Foreign Broadcast Information Service, *Daily Report Eastern Europe* 90–239 (December 12, 1990), pp. 5–6 (hereafter cited as *FBIS-EEU*). See also Zanga, "A Watershed Year," p. 548; Biberaj, "Albania at the Crossroads," pp. 5–7; *YICA 1991*, p. 257; Biberaj, "Albania: The Last Domino," pp. 199–200.

14. *FBIS-EEU* 90–239 (December 12, 1990), pp. 5–6.

15. Ibid.; Zanga, "A Watershed Year," p. 549; Biberaj, "Albania at the Crossroads," p. 7; *YICA 1991*, p. 258; Biberaj, "Albania: The Last Domino," p. 200.

16. Zanga, "A Watershed Year," p. 549; Biberaj, "Albania: The Last Domino," pp. 200–201.

17. Biberaj, "Albania: The Last Domino," p. 196.

18. Ibid., p. 202; Biberaj, "Albania at the Crossroads," p. 7.

19. Biberaj, "Aibania at the Crossroads," pp. 7–8.

20. Ibid., p. 8.

21. Ibid.

22. Elez Biberaj, "Albania," in *Democracy and Right-Wing Politics in Eastern Europe in the 1990s*, ed. Joseph Held (New York: Columbia University Press, 1993), p. 213.

23. Biberaj, "Albania: The Last Domino," p. 203.

24. *The Boston Globe*, April 2, 1991; April 22, 1991 (hereafter cited as *BG*).

25. Biberaj, "Albania at the Crossroads," pp. 8–9; Biberaj, "Albania: The Last Domino," p. 294. See also *The New York Times*, April 2, April 4, 1991 (hereafter cited as *NYT*).

26. Biberaj, "Albania at the Crossroads," pp. 9–10.

27. Ibid., pp. 10–11.
28. Ibid., p. 12.
29. Ibid., p. 9.
30. Ibid.
31. Ibid., p. 14.
32. Ibid.
33. *The Christian Science Monitor*, August 13, 1991 (hereafter cited as *CSM*).
34. *The International Herald Tribune*, July 11, July 16, 1990; *NYT*, August 9, August 18, 1991.
35. *CSM*, August 13, 1991.
36. Ibid.
37. *BG*, June 13, 1991; *NYT*, September 3, 1991; October 29, 1992.
38. *FBIS-EEU* 92–006 (January 9, 1992), p. 2; *FBIS-EEU* 92–040 (February 28, 1992), p. 2; *NYT*, March 1, March 12, 1992.
39. *NYT*, December 5, December 10, December 13, 1991; *BG*, December 15, 1991.
40. *FBIS-EEU* 91–235 (December 6, 1991), p. 3.
41. *NYT*, December 5, December 10, December 13, 1991; *BG*, December 15, 1991; Biberaj, "Albania," pp. 217–18.
42. *FBIS-EEU* 92–041 (March 2, 1992), p. 2.
43. Ibid.
44. *FBIS-EEU* 92–063 (April 1, 1993) pp. 2, 3.
45. *NYT*, October 29, 1992; Elez Biberaj, "Albania's Road to Democracy," *Current History* (November 1993): 382.
46. *FBIS-EEU* 92–057 (March 24, 1992), p. 5.
47. Biberaj, "Albania's Road to Democracy," p. 383.
48. Ibid.
49. Ibid.
50. Tina Rosenberg, "Albania: The Habits of the Heart," *World Policy Journal* 11 (Winter 1994): 91.
51. Ibid., p. 92.
52. Ibid.
53. *NYT*, November 13, December 1, 1994.
54. Marianne Sullivan, "Socialists on the Campaign Trail," *Transition*, vol. 2, no. 11 (May 31, 1996), p. 38.
55. Ibid.
56. Ibid., p. 39.
57. Ibid.; Fabian Schmidt, "Election Fraud Sparks Protest," *Transition*, vol. 2, no. 13 (June 28, 1996), pp. 38–39; *NYT*, May 28, 29, 1996.
58. *NYT*, August 3, 1993. See also Louis Zanga, "Albanian President Defends His First Year in Office," *Radio Free Europe/Radio Liberty Research Report* 2, no. 29 (July 16, 1993): 24; Rosenberg, "Albania: The Habits of the Heart," pp. 87–88.
59. *NYT*, August 2, 1993; Zanga, "Albanian President Defends His First Year in Office," p. 24.
60. Biberaj, "Albania's Road to Democracy," p. 382; Zanga, "Albanian President Defends His First Year in Office," pp. 24, 25.
61. Zanga, "Albanian President Defends His First Year in Office," p. 24.
62. Ibid.; Biberaj, "Albania's Road to Democracy," p. 382.
63. *NYT*, August 3, 1993.
64. Ibid.
65. Colin Woodward, "Albania's Academic Revival," *The Chronicle of Higher Education*, April 25, 1995, p. A43.

66. Ibid.
67. Ibid.
68. Fatos Tarifa, "Albania," in *Women in the Politics of Postcommunist Eastern Europe*, ed. Marilyn Rueschemeyer (Armonk, NY: M.E. Sharpe, 1994), pp. 144–45.
69. Ibid., pp. 145–150.
70. Rosenberg, "Albania: The Habits of the Heart," p. 89.
71. See Fabian Schmidt, "Albania's Tradition of Pragmatism," *Transition*, vol. 2, no. 7 (April 5, 1966), pp. 33–35, 63, especially p. 63.
72. *BG*, June 7, 1990.
73. *NYT*, March 13, 1991.
74. *NYT*, June 23, 1991.
75. Ibid.
76. *NYT* (June 16, 1992); see also Janusz Bugajski, *Nations in Turmoil: Conflict and Cooperation in Eastern Europe* (Boulder, CO: Westview Press, 1993), p. 133.
77. *NYT*, June 13, 1993.
78. Ibid.
79. Ibid.
80. Biberaj, "Albania's Road to Democracy," p. 385
81. Ibid.
82. Robert Austin, "Albanian-Greek Relations: The Confrontation Continues," *Radio Free Europe/Radio Liberty Research Report* 2, no. 33 (August 20, 1993): 32–33; Bugajski, *Nations in Turmoil*, pp. 178–79.
83. Austin, "Albanian-Greek Relations," pp. 32–33; see also Rosenberg, "Albania: The Habits of the Heart," p. 90; Bugajski, *Nations in Turmoil*, pp. 179–80.
84. Ibid., p. 33.
85. Rick E. Bruner, "Albania: Balkan Time Bomb," *The World and I* (February 1995): 68.
86. Ibid., pp. 31, 68.
87. Biberaj, "Albania's Road to Democracy," p. 384; Austin, "Albanian-Greek Relations," pp. 33–34; *FBIS-EEU* 93–137 (July 20, 1993), pp. 7–9.
88. Biberaj, "Albania's Road to Democracy," p. 384
89. Austin, "Albanian-Greek Relations," p. 34.
90. *NYT*, October 6, December 19, 1994.
91. Austin, "Albanian-Greek Relations," p. 34. See also Zanga, "Albanian President Defends His First Year in Office," p. 25.

Chapter 4

1. For a brief review of Bulgaria under communist rule, see J.F. Brown, *Eastern Europe under Communist Rule* (Durham, NC: Duke University Press, 1988); for more details on communist rule in Bulgaria see Nissan Oren, *Revolution Administered* (Baltimore: The Johns Hopkins Press, 1973).
2. Janusz Bugajski, *Nations in Turmoil: Conflict and Cooperation in Eastern Europe* (Boulder, CO: Westview Press, 1993), pp. 171–72.
3. Gale Stokes, *The Walls Came Tumbling Down: The Collapse of Communism in Eastern Europe* (New York: Oxford University Press, 1993), pp. 50–51: Duncan M. Perry, "Bulgarian Nationalism: Permutations of the Past," in *Contemporary Nationalism in East Central Europe*, ed. Paul Latawski (New York: St. Martin's Press, 1995), pp. 46–51, 54–55.
4. *The New York Times*, October 7, 1987 (hereafter cited as *NYT*).
5. Ibid.

6. Karen Dawisha and Jonathan Valdez, "Socialist Internationalism in Eastern Europe," *Problems of Communism*, vol. 36, no. 2 (March–April 1987): 5–6; *Yearbook on International Communist Affairs 1987* (Stanford, CA: Hoover Institution Press, 1988), pp. 278–79 (hereafter cited as *YICA*).

7. *NYT*, October 3, October 7, 1987; February 3, 1988; John D. Bell, "Post-Communist Bulgaria," in *Eastern Europe: Transformation and Revolution 1945–1991*, ed. Lyman H. Legters (Lexington, MA: D.C. Heath, 1992), p. 490; John D. Bell, "Bulgaria," in *Developments in East European Politics*, ed. Stephen White, Judy Batt, and Paul G. Lewis (Durham, NC: Duke University Press, 1995), p. 84.

8. *NYT*, January 28, 1988; *YICA 1987*, p. 279.

9. Bell, "Post-Communist Bulgaria," pp. 491–92; Rada Nicolaev, "A Year of Crucial Change in Bulgaria," in *Eastern Europe*, ed. Legters, pp. 502–3; Maria M. Todorova, "Improbable Maverick or Typical Conformist: Seven Thoughts on the New Bulgaria," in *Eastern Europe in Revolution*, ed. Ivo Banac (Ithaca, NY: Cornell University Press, 1992), pp. 155–56; Stokes, *The Walls Came Tumbling Down*, p. 144; Perry, "Bulgarian Nationalism," p. 52.

10. Nicolaev, "A Year of Crucial Change in Bulgaria," p. 503; Stokes, *The Walls Came Tumbling Down*, p. 144; Perry, "Bulgarian Nationalism," p. 52.

11. *NYT*, October 3, October 7, 1987; February 3, 1988.

12. Stokes, *The Walls Came Tumbling Down*, pp. 50–51.

13. Bell, "Post-Communist Bulgaria," p. 490.

14. Stokes, *The Walls Came Tumbling Down*, pp. 146–47; Bell, "Bulgaria," pp. 83–84.

15. Stokes, *The Walls Came Tumbling Down*, pp. 146–47; Bell, "Bulgaria," p. 85.

16. Stokes, *The Walls Came Tumbling Down*, pp. 146–47; Bell, "Post-Communist Bulgaria," p. 490; Nicolaev, "A Year of Crucial Change in Bulgaria," p. 501; Stokes, *The Walls Came Tumbling Down*, p. 147.

17. Stokes, *The Walls Came Tumbling Down*, pp. 145–46; Bell, "Bulgaria," pp. 85–86.

18. Charles Gati, *The Bloc That Failed* (Bloomington, IN: Indiana University Press, 1990), p. 182; Nicolaev, "A Year of Crucial Change in Bulgaria," pp. 498–99; *YICA 1989*, p. 303; *YICA 1990*, pp. 313–14; Stokes, *The Walls Came Tumbling Down*, pp. 147–48.

19. *YICA 1990*, p. 316; *YICA 1991*, p. 262.

20. *YICA 1991*, p. 262; Larry Garber, "Bulgaria: June 10, 1990," in *The New Democratic Frontier: A Country by Country Report on Elections in Central and Eastern Europe*, ed. Larry Garber and Eric Bjornlund (Washington, DC: National Democratic Institute of International Affairs, 1992), pp. 139–40.

21. *YICA 1990*, p. 316; Bell, "Post-Communist Bulgaria," p. 492; Bell, "Bulgaria," pp. 87–89.

22. Bell, "Post-Communist Bulgaria," p. 492; Rada Nicolaev, "The Bulgarian Communist Party After Its 'Congress of Renewal,'" in *Eastern Europe*, ed. Legters, pp. 510–12; Bell, "Bulgaria," pp. 86–87;

23. Ibid.

24. Nicolaev, "The Bulgarian Communist Party After Its 'Congress of Renewal,'" pp. 507–9, 514.

25. Perry, "Bulgarian Nationalism," p. 55.

26. Bell, "Post-Communist Bulgaria," p. 492; Nicolaev, "A Year of Crucial Change," p. 501; Garber and Bjornlund, eds., *The New Democratic Frontier*, p. 138; *YICA 1990*, pp. 315–16; Bell, "Bulgaria," p. 89.

27. *YICA 1991*, p. 263; Marek Bankowicz, "Bulgaria: The Continuing Revolution," in

The New Democracies of Eastern Europe: Party Systems and Political Cleavages, ed. Sten Berglund and Jan Ake Dellenbrant, 2nd ed. (Brookfield, VT: Edward Elgar, 1994), pp. 232–33; Bell, "Bulgaria," pp. 89–90.

28. Bell, "Post-Communist Bulgaria," p. 495, Nicolaev, "The Bulgarian Communist Party after Its 'Congress of Renewal,' " p. 508; Garber, "Bulgaria: June 10, 1990," p. 148; *YICA 1991*, p. 263; Luan Troxel, "Socialist Persistence in the Bulgarian Elections of 1990–1991," *East European Quarterly* 26, no. 4 (January 1993): 409.

29. In February 1990, political leaders of Bulgaria's Turkish minority established the MRF, which campaigned for educational, religious, and linguistic rights as well as minority representation in the national government in Sofia. Although it appealed to a diverse constituency, 90 percent of its membership came from the Turkish minority. By mid-1990 it had become the country's fourth largest party. See Bugajski, *Nations in Turmoil*, pp. 172–73.

30. *The International Herald Tribune*, July 24, 1990 (hereafter cited as *IHT*); *The London Times*, July 23, 1990 (hereafter cited as *LT*).

31. *NYT*, June 16, 1990; Troxel, "Socialist Persistence in the Bulgarian Elections," pp. 411–12; Luan Troxel, "Political Spectrum in Post-Communist Bulgaria," in *Democracy and Right-Wing Politics in Eastern Europe in the 1990s*, ed. Joseph Held (New York: Columbia University Press, 1993), pp. 195–96.

32. Plamen S. Tzvetkov, "The Politics of Transition in Bulgaria: Back to the Future?" *Problems of Communism*, vol. 41, no. 3 (May–June 1992): 34; Garber, "Bulgaria: June 10, 1990," pp. 146–47, 149, 150, 153.

33. Troxel, "Socialist Persistence in the Bulgarian Elections," p. 413.

34. Ibid., pp. 414–416.

35. White, Batt, and Lewis, eds., *Developments in East European Politics*, p. 90.

36. Perry, "Bulgarian Nationalism," pp. 56–57.

37. *NYT*, June 10, 1990; *IHT*, July 24, 1990; *LT*, July 23, 1990; J.F. Brown, *Hopes and Shadows: Eastern Europe after Communism* (Durham, NC: Duke University Press, 1994), pp. 109–10.

38. Garber, "Bulgaria: June 10, 1990," p. 156; *YICA 1991*, p. 264; Bell, "Bulgaria," pp. 87, 90.

39. *YICA 1991*, p. 265; Brown, *Hopes and Shadows*, p. 108.

40. Within a year, however, Bulgarians had lost interest in Zhivkov. Moreover, his trial and conviction did not lead to a massive prosecution of former communist rulers. See C. Charles Bertschi, "Lustration and the Transition to Democracy: The Cases of Poland and Bulgaria," *East European Quarterly* 28, no. 4 (Winter 1994): 442–43.

41. *NYT*, April 4, November 4, 1990.

42. *YICA 1991*, p. 266

43. Ibid.; Garber, "Bulgaria: June 10, 1990," p. 155.

44. *YICA 1991*, p. 266; Troxel, "Socialist Persistence in the Bulgarian Elections," pp. 417–18.

45. *YICA 1991*, p. 266; Troxel, "Socialist Persistence in the Bulgarian Elections," pp. 416–17.

46. Ibid.; Brown, *Hopes and Shadows*, p. 106; Bell, "Bulgaria," p. 90.

47. *YICA 1991*, p. 267; *NYT*, December 4, 1990.

48. *NYT*, January 24, January 30, 1991.

49. Jose-Alon Fralon, "Bulgarians See Glimpses of Better Days to Come," *The Guardian Weekly*, April 7, 1991, cited from *Eastern Europe*, ed. Legters, p. 522.

50. *The Boston Globe*, August 21, 1991 (hereafter cited as *BG*).

51. Luan Troxel, "Bulgaria: Stable Ground in the Balkans?" *Current History* (November 1993): 388; Brown, *Hopes and Shadows*, pp. 142–44.

52. Ibid.

53. Troxell, "Socialist Persistence in the Bulgarian Elections," pp. 423–25; Brown, *Hopes and Shadows*, pp. 108–9; Bell, "Bulgaria," p. 91.

54. Tzvetkov, "The Politics of Transition in Bulgaria," p. 35; *NYT*, January 12, January 13, January 20, 1992; Bankowicz, "The Continuing Revolution," p. 234, Department of State, Foreign Broadcast Information Service, *Daily Report Eastern Europe* 92–013 (January 21, 1992), p. 9 (hereafter cited as *FBIS-EEU*).

55. *The Washington Post*, October 14, 1991 (hereafter cited 25 *WP*); Brown, *Hopes and Shadows*, p. 108.

56. Richard Davy, "Eastern Europe III: Pragmatism in Bulgaria," *The World Today*, May 1, 1992, p. 85.

57. White, Batt, and Lewis, eds., *Developments in East European Politics*, p. 93.

58. Davy, "Pragmatism in Bulgaria," p. 86.

59. Ibid. See also *NYT*, December 12, 1991; Bell, "Bulgaria," p. 94.

60. See Bell, "Bulgaria," pp. 92–93.

61. Postcommunist Bulgarian leaders continued to insist that the country had no ethnic minorities, a claim that antagonized the Turkish government. See Bugajski, *Nations in Turmoil*, p. 176.

62. Bankowicz, "The Continuing Revolution," pp. 234–35; Bell, "Bulgaria," p. 94.

63. Brown, *Hopes and Shadows*, pp. 112–13.

64. *NYT*, July 22, 1993.

65. *BG*, December 18, 1994; *NYT*, December 19, 1994.

66. *NYT*, December 19, 1994; *BG*, December 20, 1994.

67. *WP*, March 6, 1992; Bell, "Bulgaria," p. 95.

68. Davy, "Pragmatism in Bulgaria," p. 86; Bell, "Bulgaria," p. 95.

69. Troxel, "Stable Ground in the Balkans?" pp. 388–89.

70. *NYT*, December 8, 1992.

71. Dimitrina Petrova, "The Winding Road to Emancipation in Bulgaria," *Gender Politics and Post-Communism*, ed. Nanette Funk and Magda Mueller (New York: Routledge, 1993), pp. 22 23.

72. Ibid., p. 27.

73. Maria Todorova, "The Bulgarian Case: Women's Issues or Feminist Issues," *Gender Politics and Post-Communism*, ed. Funk and Mueller, pp. 35–37; for a more detailed discussion of the situation of women in postcommunist Bulgaria by this author see Maria Todorova, "Historical Tradition and Transformation in Bulgaria: Women's Issues or Feminist Issues," *Journal of Women's History*, vol. 5, no. 3 (Winter 1994), pp. 129–143.

74. An important incentive for good Bulgarian–Greek relations is the shared concern about a perceived growth of Turkish influence in the Balkans reinforced by a fear of an Islamic-oriented Balkan *entente*. See Bugajski, *Nations in Turmoil*, p. 177.

75. Stephan Lefebvre, "Bulgaria's Foreign Relations in the Post-Communist Era: A General Overview and Assessment," *East European Quarterly*, vol. 28, no. 4 (Winter 1994), p. 458; for a detailed review of postcommunist Bulgaria's interests in the former Yugoslav Republic of Macedonia, see Perry, "Bulgarian Nationalism," pp. 57–62; church leaders in Sofia have called Macedonia the cradle of Bulgarian culture and religions. See Bugajski, *Nations in Turmoil*, pp. 145–46.

76. Tzvetkov, "The Politics of Transition in Bulgaria," p. 4; for a discussion of the possibility of a Serbian strike against Macedonia, see Bugajski, *Nations in Turmoil*, pp. 148–49.

77. *YICA 1990*, p. 320; Lefebvre, "Bulgaria's Foreign Relations," p. 462; some Bulgarian commentators complained about the size of the Turkish army in eastern Thrace in comparison with Bulgarian forces deployed in the region, and questioned the logic of

Western military aid to Turkey, which could threaten Bulgarian security. See Bugajski, *Nations in Turmoil*, p. 166.

78. Stokes, *The Walls Came Tumbling Down*, pp. 208–9.

79. *YICA 1991*, p. 268.

80. The success of the MRF aroused suspicion among ethnic Bulgarian politicians that Turkey was helping the party expand its influence as a prelude to fostering a separatist movement on the part of the Turkish minority. See Bugajski, *Nations in Turmoil*, pp. 173–74.

81. *WP*, June 26, 1992.

82. Tzvetkov, "The Politics of Transition in Bulgaria," p. 42.

83. A cloud on the horizon of Bulgarian–Russian relations in the mid-1990s, is the steady Russian influence building in the neighboring former Soviet republics and a perceived effort of the Kremlin to lure Bulgaria as well into a Russian sphere of influence. When Russian president Boris Yeltsin suggested on March 29, 1996, following the conclusion of integration agreements with Belarus, Kazakhstan, and Kyrgyzstan, that Bulgaria might eventually be included in this new relationship, Bulgarian president Zhelev reacted vehemently, calling Yeltsin's statement an infringement of Bulgarian sovereignty. Zhelev obliquely accused the Socialist government of encouraging Russian forwardness toward Bulgaria behind his back. See Victor Gomez, "Close But Not Too Close," *Transition*, vol. 2, no. 9 (May 3, 1996), p. 3.

84. *FBIS-EEU* 91–202 (May 28, 1991), p. 9.

85. *YICA 1990*, p. 320.

86. *BG*, January 23, 1991.

87. *NYT*, March 5, 1992.

88. *BG*, February 11, 1990; *NYT*, February 11, 1990.

89. *YICA 1991*, pp. 275–76.

90. *NYT*, March 5, 1992; *FBIS-EEU* 92–000 (March 13, 1992), p. 2.

91. Troxel, "Stable Ground in the Balkans?" p. 389; Lefebvre, "Bulgaria's Foreign Relations," p. 456.

92. Since 1994, the BSP government has shown as "undemocratic" sensitivity to political criticism, condoning a policy of official discrimination against the opposition in its management of the national electronic media considered by some a form of censorship reminiscent of communist rule before 1989. See Maria Koinova and Stefan Krause, "Protesting State Meddling in the National Media," *Transition*, vol. 2, no. 7 (April 5, 1996), pp. 52–55.

Chapter 5

1. See Tad Szulc, *Czechoslovakia Since World War II* (New York: Grosset and Dunlap, 1971), pp. 5–216; Sharon Wolchik, *Czechoslovakia in Transition: Politics, Economics, and Society* (London: Pinter, 1991); Jan Adam, *Why Did Socialism Collapse in Central and Eastern Europe? The Case of Poland, Hungary, and Czechoslovakia* (New York: St. Martin's Press, 1995).

2. H. Gordon Skilling, *Czechoslovakia's Interrupted Revolution* (Princeton, NJ: Princeton University Press, 1976), pp. 45–450.

3. Ibid., pp. 617–812; Jiri Valenta, *Soviet Intervention in Czechoslovakia, 1968: Anatomy of a Decision* (Baltimore, MD: Johns Hopkins University Press, 1979), pp. 40–122.

4. Ronald D. Asmus, J.F. Brown, and Keith Crane, *Soviet Foreign Policy and Revolutions in Eastern Europe* (Santa Monica, CA: RAND, 1991), p. 110

5. Ibid., pp. 120–22; *Yearbook on International Affairs 1987* (Stanford, CA: Hoover

Institution, 1988), p. 285 (hereafter cited as *YICA*); Karen Dawisha and Jonathan Valdez, "Socialist Internationalism in Eastern Europe," *Problems of Communism*, vol. 36, no. 2 (March–April 1987): 10.

6. Gale Stokes, *The Walls Came Tumbling Down: The Collapse of Communism in Eastern Europe* (New York: Oxford University Press, 1993), pp. 67–68.

7. Asmus, Brown, and Crane, *Soviet Foreign Policy*, p. 114.

8. *YICA 1990*, p. 328; *The New York Times*, December 1, 1990 (hereafter cited as *NYT*).

9. *YICA 1990*, pp. 327–29.

10. See Peter Martin and Kevin Devlin, "Religious Struggle in Czechoslovakia," in *Soviet/East European Survey 1987–1988*, ed. Vojtec Mastny (Boulder, CO: Westview Press, 1989), p. 194, hereafter cited as *SEES*; Asmus, Brown, and Crane, *Soviet Foreign Policy*, p. 131; Stokes, *The Walls Came Tumbling Down*, pp. 149, 151–53.

11. Asmus, Brown, and Crane, *Soviet Foreign Policy*, p. 132; Stokes, *The Walls Came Tumbling Down*, p. 153.

12. Asmus, Brown, and Crane, *Soviet Foreign Policy*, pp. 132–33; Stokes, *The Walls Came Tumbling Down*, p. 154; *NYT*, December 11, 1988; *The Boston Globe*, December 14, 1988 (hereafter cited as *BG*).

13. Jiri Pehe, "Czechoslovakia: An Abrupt Transition," in *Eastern Europe: Transformation and Revolution 1945–1991*, ed. Lyman H. Legters (Lexington, MA: D.C. Heath, 1992), p. 349; *YICA 1990*, pp. 323–24; Asmus, Brown, and Crane, *Soviet Foreign Policy*, p. 134; Stokes, *The Walls Came Tumbling Down*, p. 155; Bernard Wheaton and Zdenek Kavan, *The Velvet Revolution 1988–1991* (Boulder, CO: Westview Press, 1992), pp. 27–29.

14. Vladimir Kusin, "Vaclav Havel's First Term," in *Eastern Europe*, ed. Legters, p. 378; Tony Judt, "Metamorphosis: The Democratic Revolution in Czechoslovakia," in *Eastern Europe in Revolution*, ed. Ivo Banac (Ithaca, NY: Cornell University Press, 1992), pp. 98–99, 101. The popular demonstrations in November 1989 that led to the resignation of Party First Secretary Miloš Jakeš are discussed at length in Wheaton and Kavan, *The Velvet Revolution 1988–1991*, pp. 39–126.

15. Pehe, "Czechoslovakia: An Abrupt Transition," p. 347; Stokes, *The Walls Came Tumbling Down*, p. 157; Marek Bankowicz, "Czechoslovakia: From Masaryk to Havel," in *The New Democracies of Eastern Europe: Party Systems and Political Cleavages*, ed. Sten Berglund and Jan Ake Dellenbrant, 2nd ed. (Brookfield VT: Edward Elgar, 1991), pp. 156–59.

16. Pehe, "Czechoslovakia: An Abrupt Transition," pp. 346–47; *YICA 1990*, pp. 325. See also Wheaton and Kavan, *The Velvet Revolution 1988–1991*, pp. 130–39.

17. Pehe, "Czechoslovakia: An Abrupt Transition," pp. 346–47;

18. See Asmus, Brown, and Crane, *Soviet Foreign Policy*, pp. 141–42; *YICA 1990*, p. 325; *BG*, January 31, 1990; Judt, "The Democratic Revolution in Czechoslovakia," pp. 99–100.

19. *YICA 1990*, p. 325; Judt, "The Democratic Revolution in Czechoslovakia," pp. 99–100; *NYT*, March 31, 1990.

20. Judt, "The Democratic Revolution in Czechoslovakia," p. 103

21. Robin Carnahan and Judith Corley, "Czechoslovakia: June 8 and 9, 1990," in *The New Democratic Frontier: A Country by Country Report on Elections in Central and Eastern Europe*, ed. Larry Garber and Eric Bjornlund (Washington, DC: National Democratic Institute for International Affairs, 1992), p. 123–25.

22. Otto Ulc, "The Bumpy Road of Czechoslovakia's Velvet Revolution," *Problems of Communism*, vol. 41, no. 3 (May–June 1992): 19–21; Carnahan and Corley, "Czechoslovakia: June 8 and 9, 1990," p. 132; Judt, "The Democratic Revolution in Czechoslovakia," pp. 106–7; Gordon Wightman, "The Czech and Soviet Republics," in *Developments*

in East European Politics, ed. Stephen White, Judy Batt, and Paul G. Lewis (Durham, NC: Duke University Press, 1994), pp. 54–56.

23. See Asmus, Brown, and Crane, *Soviet Foreign Policy*, pp. 141–42.

24. Charles Gati, *The Bloc That Failed* (Bloomington: Indiana University Press, 1990), pp. 178–80, 182.

25. David M. Olsen, "The Sundered State: Federalism and Parliament in Czechoslovakia," in *Parliaments in Transition: The New Legislative Politics in the Former USSR and Eastern Europe*, ed. Thomas F. Remington (Boulder, CO: Westview Press, 1994), pp. 104–5.

26. Jiri Pehe, "The Civic Forum Splits into Two Groups," in *Eastern Europe*, ed. Legters, pp. 393–94; Judy Batt, *East Central Europe: From Reform to Transformation* (New York: Council on Foreign Relations Press, 1991), pp. 60–61.

27. United States Department of State Foreign Broadcast Information Service, *Daily Report Eastern Europe* 92–007 (January 10, 1992), pp. 12–13; 92–009 (January 14, 1992), pp. 8–10 (hereafter cited as *FBIS-EEU*); Batt, *East Central Europe: From Reform to Transformation*, pp. 98, 100; John Morison, "The Road to Separation: Nationalism in Czechoslovakia," in *Contemporary Nationalism in East Central Europe*, ed. Paul Latawski (New York: St. Martin's Press, 1994), p. 81.

28. Pehe, "The Civic Forum Splits into Two Groups," pp. 387–88; Ulc, "The Bumpy Road of Czechoslovakia's Velvet Revolution," p. 27; Batt, *East Central Europe: From Reform to Transformation*, pp. 63–64; Sharon Wolchik, "The Right in Czechoslovakia," in *Democracy and Right-Wing Politics in Eastern Europe in the 1990s*, ed. Joseph Held (New York: Columbia University Press, 1993), pp. 68–70; Wheaton and Kavan, *The Velvet Revolution*, p. 167.

29. Batt, *East Central Europe: From Reform to Transformation*, pp. 60–61; Wolchik, *Czechoslovakia in Transition*, pp. 70–71.

30. Ulc, "The Bumpy Road of Czechoslovakia's Velvet Revolution," p. 28.

31. Wheaton and Kavan, *The Velvet Revolution*, pp. 160–61; J.F. Brown, *Hopes and Shadows: Eastern Europe after Communism* (Durham, NC: Duke University Press, 1994), p. 133.

32. Ulc, "The Bumpy Road of Czechoslovakia's Velvet Revolution," pp. 23–24.

33. Ibid.

34. Ibid., p. 26.

35. Ibid., pp. 24–25; Wheaton and Kavan, *The Velvet Revolution*, pp. 156–57.

36. Stokes, *The Walls Came Tumbling Down*, pp. 198–99.

37. Ulc, "The Bumpy Road of Czechoslovakia's Velvet Revolution," pp. 25–26; Vaclav Klaus, "Transition—An Insider's View," *Problems of Communism*, vol. 41, nos. 1–2 (January–April 1992): 74. See also *NYT*, January 21, 1992; Wheaton and Kavan, *The Velvet Revolution*, pp. 157–58; Thomas W. Hazlett, "The Czech Miracle," *Reason*, April 1995, pp. 33–34.

38. *NYT*, January 5, 1992; Batt, *East Central Europe: From Reform to Transformation*, p. 92.

39. *NYT*, January 21, 1992; Batt, *East Central Europe: From Reform to Transformation*, p. 96; Stokes, *The Walls Came Tumbling Down*, pp. 199–200.

40. *NYT*, October 17, 1993.

41. *NYT*, April 16, 1991; for a detailed discussion of recent Czechoslovak and Czech Republic policies involving agricultural decollectivization see Alina Darbellay, "Farmers and Entrepreneurs in Poland and the Czech Republic," *Transition*, vol. 2, no. 15 (July 16, 1996), pp. 17–20.

42. *NYT*, June 3, 1992.

43. Wolchik, *Czechoslovakia in Transition*, pp. 282–84.

44. Ulc, "The Bumpy Road of Czechoslovakia's Velvet Revolution," pp. 23–24.

45. Ibid.

46. *NYT*, October 17, 1993.

47. Judt, "The Democratic Revolution in Czechoslovakia," pp. 104–5.

48. *NYT*, January 21, April 23, July 17, 1992.

49. See the Atlantic Council of the United States (ACUS), "Post–Cold War Communists in Central and Eastern Europe: The Challenges to Reform. Seminar Report and Policy Recommendations" (Washington DC: ACUS, 1993), p. 6.

50. Ulc, "The Bumpy Road of Czechoslovakia's Velvet Revolution," p. 32; Jeffrey Goldfarb, *After the Fall: The Pursuit of Democracy in Central Europe* (New York: Basic Books, 1992), p. 71.

51. *NYT*, February 19, April 13, 1992; *BG*, November 18, 1992; *The Washington Post*, July 26, 1992 (hereafter cited as *WP*).

52. Wheaton and Kavan, *The Velvet Revolution*, pp. 144–45; *NYT*, February 28, March 31, 1990; Wolchik, *Czechoslovakia in Transition*, pp. 297–300.

53. *FBIS-EEU* 91–200 (October 16, 1991), p. 11; *NYT*, October 14, 1991; see also Otto Ulc, "The Role of the Political Right in Post-Communist Czechoslovakia," in *Democracy and Right-Wing Politics in Eastern Europe*, ed. Held, pp. 99–100; Victor Gomez, "Specter of Racism," *Transition*, vol. 1, no. 10 (June 23, 1995), p. 18.

54. Judt, "The Democratic Revolution in Czechoslovakia," pp. 112–113; "Street Crime Hits Prague Daily Life," *NYT*, December 18, 1991; Ulc, "The Role of the Political Right in Post-Communist Czechoslovakia," pp. 100–101.

55. Sharon L. Wolchik, "Women in Transition in the Czech and Slovak Republics: The First Three Years," *Journal of Women's History*, vol. 5, no. 3 (Winter 1994), pp. 102–5; for additional information on the status of Czech and Slovak women in the early 1990s, see Alena Heitlinger, "The Impact of the Transition from Communism on the Status of Women in the Czech and Slovak Republics," in *Gender Politics and Post-Communism*, ed. Nanette Funk and Magda Mueller (New York: Routledge, 1993), pp. 95–108.

56. Wolchik, "Women in Transition," p. 103.

57. Heitlinger, "The Impact of the Transition," p. 104.

58. Ibid., p. 105.

59. *NYT*, October 17, 1993.

60. *NYT*, February 7, 1990.

61. *NYT*, February 21, February 22, 1990.

62. *NYT*, October 23, 1991; *WP*, October 23, 1991.

63. *NYT*, April 7, 1990.

64. *NYT*, February 22, 1990.

65. *NYT*, October 23, 1991.

66. *WP*, October 23, 1991.

67. Judt, "The Democratic Revolution in Czechoslovakia," p. 115; *BG*, January 3, 1990; *NYT*, January 3, January 14, March 16, 1990.

68. *NYT*, February 28, 1992.

69. *WP*, February 10, 1992.

70. *FBIS-EEU* 90–037 (February 23, 1990), pp. 17–18; *FBIS-SOV* 91–123 (June 26, 1991), p. 18.

71. *WP*, February 16, 1991; David Shumaker, "The Origins and Development of Central European Cooperation: 1989–1992," *East European Quarterly* 27, no. 3 (September 1993): 362–63.

72. *WP*, May 22, 1992; Roger Mansur, *Failed Transitions: The East European Economy and Environment Since the Fall of Communism* (New York: The Free Press, 1993), pp. 140–42; *NYT*, December 5, 1990; *WP*, May 22, 1992.

73. Morison, "The Road to Separation," pp. 73–75. For a detailed review of Czech–Slovak relations in the interwar period, see Carol Skalnik Leff, *National Conflict in Czechoslovakia: The Making and Remaking of a State, 1918–1987* (Princeton: Princeton University Press, 1988), pp. 45–85, 181–211.

74. Morison, "The Road to Separation," pp. 73–75. See also Stanislav J. Kirschbaum, *A History of Slovakia: The Struggle for Survival* (New York: St. Martin's Press, 1995), pp. 196–200.

75. Morison, "The Road to Separation," pp. 77–78.

76. Ibid.; see also Kirschbaum, *A History of Slovakia*, pp. 245–46; Leff, *National Conflict in Czechoslovakia*, pp. 86–128; 212–40; Robert Dean, *Nationalism and Political Change in Eastern Europe: The Slovak Question and the Czechoslovak Reform Movement* (Denver, CO: University of Denver Press, 1973), passism.

77. Pavol Fric, "Slovakia on Its Way Toward Another Misunderstanding?" *Sisyphus* 8, no. 2 (1992): 117. See also Ulc, "The Role of the Political Right in Post-Communist Czechoslovakia," pp. 94–95; Wheaton and Kavan, *The Velvet Revolution*, p. 169; Brown, *Hopes and Shadows*, pp. 136.

78. Wheaton and Kavan, *The Velvet Revolution*, p. 169; Brown, *Hopes and Shadows*, p. 137; Morison, "The Road to Separation," p. 81; Kirschbaum, *A History of Slovakia*, p. 261. See also Leff, *National Conflict in Czechoslovakia*, pp. 45–85, 181–211.

79. *NYT*, April 19, 1992.

80. Kirschbaum, *A History of Slovakia*, p. 255; see also Peter Martin, "Relations Between Czechs and Slovaks," in *Eastern Europe*, ed. Legters, pp. 382–83.

81. Peter Martin, "Relations Between the Czechs and the Slovaks," in *Eastern Europe*, ed. Legters, pp. 382–83; Ulc, "The Role of the Political Right in Post-Communist Czechoslovakia," p. 96.

82. Kirschbaum, *A History of Slovakia*, pp. 263–64.

83. Judt, "The Democratic Revolution in Czechoslovakia," pp. 104–5.

84. Janusz Bugajski, *Nations in Turmoil: Conflict and Cooperation in Eastern Europe* (Boulder, CO: Westview Press, 1993), pp. 68–69.

85. Paul Wilson, "Czechoslovakia: The Pain of Divorce," *The New York Review of Books*, December 17, 1992, p. 72.

86. *FBIS-EEU* 92–002 (January 3, 1992), pp. 8–9; *FBIS-EEU* 92–134 (July 13, 1992), pp. 20–21; Wilson, "The Pain of Divorce," p. 72.

87. *FBIS-EEU* 90–238 (December 11, 1990), p. 10.

88. *YICA 1991*, p. 277; Batt, *East Central Europe: From Reform to Transformation*, p. 99; *FBIS-EEU* 90–238 (December 11, 1990), p. 10; *FBIS-EEU* 90–239 (December 12, 1990), p. 20; *FBIS-EEU* 92–024 (February 5, 1992), pp. 13–24.

89. *FBIS-EEU* 91–222 (November 18, 1991), pp. 7–8.

90. Kirschbaum, *A History of Slovakia*, pp. 268–69. For comments on the influence of ethnic issues, see *FBIS-EEU* 92–108 (June 4, 1992), p. 17; *FBIS-EEU* 92–110 (June 8, 1992), pp. 14–17.

91. *FBIS-EEU* 92–024 (February 5, 1992), pp. 13–14; *FBIS-EEU* 92–115 (June 15, 1992), p. 8. See also Bankowicz, "Czechoslovakia: From Masaryk to Havel," pp. 164–65.

92. *FBIS-EEU* 92–117 (June 17, 1992), pp. 6–7; *FBIS-EEU* 91–119 (June 19, 1992), pp. 3–4.

93. Wilson, "The Pain of Divorce," p. 70.

94. *FBIS-EEU* 91–118 (June 18, 1992), p. 5; *FBIS-EEU* 91–119 (June 19, 1992), p. 3; *FBIS-EEU* 92–120 (June 22, 1992), pp. 12–17.

95. *FBIS-EEU* 92–113 (June 11, 1992), p. 11.

96. Fric, "Slovakia on Its Way to Another Misunderstanding?" p. 118; *WP*, July 16, 1992; Brown, *Hopes and Shadows*, pp. 62–63.

97. *FBIS-EEU* 92–112 (June 10, 1992), p. 17.

98. *NYT*, July 4, July 5, 1992; *WP*, July 4, 1992.

99. Kirschbaum, *A History of Slovakia*, p. 269.

100. *FBIS-EEU* 92–230 (November 30, 1992), pp. 17–18.

101. *FBIS-EEU* 93–010 (January 15, 1993), p. 15; *FBIS-EEU* 93–216 (November 10, 1993), p. 18.

102. *NYT*, July 30, 1993.

103. *The Prague Post*, June 23–29, 1993 (hereafter cited as *PP*).

104. *NYT*, January 31, 1994; *FBIS-EEU* 94–068 (April 8, 1994), pp. 8–9.

105. *FBIS-EEU* 93–038 (March 1, 1993), p. 18. See also *NYT*, July 30, 1993; *BG*, July 12, 1994.

106. *FBIS-EEU* 94–053 (March 18, 1994), p. 6.

107. *NYT*, March 17, 1994.

108. Judt, "Metamorphosis: The Democratic Revolution in Czechoslovakia," p. 112; Brown, *Hopes and Shadows*, p. 202; Bennett Kovrig, "Hungarian Minorities in East Central Europe," *Occasional Paper Series of the Atlantic Council of the United States* (March 1994), p. 19; see also Matthew Rhodes, "National Identity and Minority Rights in the Constitutions of the Czech Republic and Slovakia," *East European Quarterly*, vol. 29, no. 3 (Fall 1995), pp. 358–63; Bugajski, *Nations in Turmoil*, pp. 75–80.

109. *PP*, June 23–29, 1993; "Slovakia Targets Imports," *IHT*, July 3–4, 1993. See also *FBIS-EEU* 93–114 (June 16, 1993), p. 17; *FBIS-EEU* 93–118 (June 22, 1993), p. 14.

110. *NYT*, March 17, 1994.

111. See Daniel Munich and Vit Storm, "The Czech Republic as a Low-Unemployment Oasis," *Transition*, vol. 2, no. 13 (June 28, 1996), pp. 21–25.

112. Bugajski, *Nations in Turmoil*, pp. 73–74.

113. Rhodes, "National Identity and Minority Rights," pp. 353–57.

114. *BG*, June 2, 3, 1996; *NYT*, June 2, 3, 1996; Jiri Pehe, "Elections Result in Surprise Stalemate," *Transition*, vol. 2, no. 13 (June 28, 1996), 36–37.

115. Pehe, "Elections Result in Surprise Stalemate," p. 36.

116. Ben Slay, "Elections Unlikely to Affect Economic Transformation," *Transition*, vol. 2, no. 15 (July 26, 1996), pp. 38–41.

117. *IHT*, July 7, 1993.

118. *PP*, June 23–29, 1993.

119. *NYT*, August 23, 1993.

Chapter 6

1. See Damon A. Terrill, "Tolerance Lost: Disaffection, Dissent, and Revolution in the German Democratic Republic," *East European Quarterly* 28, no. 3 (September 1994): 356–65.

2. *Yearbook on International Communist Affairs 1989* (Stanford, CA: Hoover Institution Press, 1990), pp. 326–27 (hereafter cited as *YICA*).

3. Marshall Goldman, *Gorbachev's Challenge: Economic Reform in the Age of High Technology* (New York: Norton, 1987), p. 169; *YICA 1987*, p. 298; *The New York Times*, March 8, 1988 (hereafter cited as *NYT*).

4. J.F. Brown, *Eastern Europe and Communist Rule* (Durham, NC: Duke University Press, 1988), pp. 249–50.

5. Goldman, *Gorbachev's Challenge*, p. 170; *YICA 1989*, pp. 326–27; *YICA 1990*, pp. 338–40; see also Barbara Donovan, "Benefits to the GDR from FRG," in *Soviet/East European Survey 1987–1988*, ed. Vojtech Mastny (Boulder, CO: Westview Press, 1989), pp. 318–22; hereafter cited as *SEES*.

6. Karen Dawisha and Jonathan Valdez, "Socialist Internationalism in Eastern Europe," *Problems of Communism*, vol. 36, no. 2 (March–April 1987): 6; *YICA 1986*, p. 289; Charles Gati, *The Bloc That Failed* (Bloomington: Indiana University Press, 1990), p. 175.

7. Dawisha and Valdez, "Socialist Internationalism," p. 8; Goldman, *Gorbachev's Challenge*, pp. 167–70; Norman Naimark, " 'Ich will hier raus': Emigration and the Collapse of the German Democratic Republic," in *Eastern Europe in Revolution*, ed. Ivo Banac (Ithaca, NY: Cornell University Press, 1992), p. 81; see also Thomas A. Baylis, "East Germany's Economic Model," *Current History* (November 1987), pp. 377–81, 393–94.

8. Naimark, "The Collapse of the German Democratic Republic," p. 81; Ronald D. Asmus, J.F. Brown, and Keith Crane, *Soviet Foreign Policy and Revolutions in Eastern Europe* (Santa Monica, CA: RAND, 1991), pp. 103–4.

9. Asmus, Brown, and Crane, *Soviet Foreign Policy*, pp. 99–100.

10. *NYT*, February 18, 1987; Vladimir Tismaneanu, "Nascent Civil Society in the German Democratic Republic," *Problems of Communism*, vol. 36, no. 2 (March–April 1989): 95–98, 101–3; Janusz Bugajski and Maxine Pollack, "East European Dissent: Impasses and Opportunities," *Problems of Communism*, vol. 37, no. 2 (March–April 1988): 64.

11. Brown, *Eastern Europe and Communist Rule*, pp. 256–58; Asmus, Brown, and Crane, *Soviet Foreign Policy*, pp. 99–100; Jeffrey Gedmin, *The Hidden Hand: Gorbachev and the Collapse of East Germany* (Washington, DC: American Enterprise Institute Press, 1992), pp. 68–69; see also Barbara Donovan, "East German State Debates Church Policy," *SEES 1987–1988*, ed. Mastny, pp. 200–5.

12. *NYT*, May 31, 1987; *YICA 1988* (1989), p. 217.

13. *YICA 1989*, p. 324.

14. Brown, *Eastern Europe and Communist Rule*, pp. 256–58.

15. *YICA 1989*, p. 328.

16. "Speech by M.S. Gorbachev to the Eleventh Congress of the (East German) Socialist Unity Party of Germany," *Pravda*, April 19, 1986, cited from *Current Digest of the Soviet Press* 38, no. 16 (May 21, 1986): 7–9.

17. Asmus, Brown, and Crane, *Soviet Foreign Policy*, pp. 103–4.

18. Brown, *Eastern Europe and Communist Rule*, p. 234.

19. "Life in the Unpromised Land," *World Press Review* (November 1988): 17; Barbara Donovan, "East Germany in 1989," in *Eastern Europe: Revolution and Transformation 1945–1991*, ed. Lyman H. Legters (Lexington, MA: D.C. Heath, 1992), pp. 411–16; Asmus, Brown, and Crane, *Soviet Foreign Policy*, p. 108; Naimark, "The Collapse of the German Democratic Republic," pp. 83–84.

20. Donovan, "East Germany in 1989," pp. 415–16; Naimark, "The Collapse of the German Democratic Republic," pp. 85–86; Sten Berglund, "The Breakdown of the German Democratic Republic," in *The New Democracies of Eastern Europe: Party Systems and Political Cleavages*, ed. Sten Berglund and Jan Ake Dellenbrant (Brookfield, VT: Edward Elgar, 1994), p. 132.

21. *YICA 1990*, pp. 334–35; Daniel I. Gordon and Fred W. Reinke,"East Germany: March 18, 1990," in *The New Democratic Frontier: A Country by Country Report on Elections in Central and Eastern Europe*, ed. Larry Garber and Eric Bjornlund, (Washington, DC: The National Democratic Institute for International Affairs, 1992), p. 24; Naimark, "The Collapse of the German Democratic Republic," p. 90.

22. Gedmin, *The Hidden Hand*, pp. 104–5.

23. *YICA 1990*, pp. 334–35; Asmus, Brown, and Crane, *Soviet Foreign Policy*, p. 109; Naimark, "The Collapse of the German Democratic Republic," pp. 91–92. See also Gedmin, *The Hidden Hand*, pp. 105–11.

24. Donovan, "East Germany in 1989," p. 413.

25. Gordon and Reinke, "East Germany: March 18, 1990," p. 24; *YICA 1990*, p. 337–38; Naimark, "The Collapse of the German Democratic Republic," pp. 93–94.

26. *YICA 1991*, pp. 293–95; Gale Stokes, *The Walls Came Tumbling Down: The Collapse of Communism in Eastern Europe* (New York: Oxford University Press, 1993), p. 183.

27. Donovan, "East Germany in 1989," p. 414; *YICA 1990*, pp. 334–35; Gedmin, *The Hidden Hand*, pp. 106, 111.

28. Stokes, *The Walls Came Tumbling Down*, p. 182

29. *YICA 1990*, p. 342.

30. Berglund, "The Breakdown of the German Democratic Republic," p. 133; Gordon and Reinke, "East Germany: March 18, 1990," p. 25.

31. Ibid., p. 27; Stokes, *The Walls Came Tumbling Down*, p. 184.

32. Gordon and Reinke, "East Germany: March 18, 1990," pp. 30, 36.

33. *YICA 1991*, p. 296.

34. *NYT*, March 19, 1990; Stephen R. Bowers, "The East European Revolution," *East European Quarterly* 25, no. 2 (Summer 1991): 138.

35. *YICA 1991*, pp. 303–4; Stokes, *The Walls Came Tumbling Down*, pp. 185–186.

36. For a detailed discussion of the abortion issue see Nanette Funk and Magda Mueller, "Abortion and German Unification," *Journal of Women's History*, vol. 5, no. 4 (Winter 1994), pp. 194–206; for West German practice see ibid., pp. 195–96.

37. *Boston Globe* (September 30, 1990), hereafter cited as *BG*.

38. Ibid.

39. Ibid.

40. Funk and Mueller, "Abortion and German Unification," pp. 195–96.

41. *YICA 1991*, pp. 301–2.

42. Stokes, *The Walls Came Tumbling Down,* p.187.

43. Ibid., p. 186.

44. Ibid.

45. Ibid.

46. *NYT*, March 12, November 3, 1991; John Hall and Udo Ludwig, "Creating Germany's *Mezzogiorno*," *Challenge* (July–August 1993): 40–42.

47. *NYT*, August 7, 1991.

48. Ibid.

49. Peter Neckerman, "What Went Wrong in Germany After Unification?" *East European Quarterly* 26, no. 4 (Winter 1992): 456–57.

50. *NYT*, September 29, 1991; Neckerman, "What Went Wrong in Germany After Unification?" p. 458.

51. *YICA 1991*, p. 301; *NYT*, September 9, 1990.

52. *The International Herald Tribune*, July 12, 1990.

53. *NYT*, August 9, September 29, 1990.

54. *NYT*, August 21, 1990; June 13, 1991.

55. Stephen Kinzer, "East Germans Face Their Accusers," *The New York Times Magazine*, April 12, 1992; Neckerman, "What Went Wrong in Germany After Unification?" p. 455.

56. Kinzer, "East Germans Face Their Accusers."

57. Ibid.

58. Stephen Brockmann, "Living Where the Wall Was: What Still Divides the Germans," *Commonweal*, September 24, 1993, p. 18.

59. For a brief discussion of the impact of reunification on East German women see Hannelore Scholz, "East-West Women's Culture in Transition: German Women the Losers in Reunification?" *Journal of Women's History*, vol. 5, no. 4 (Winter 1994), pp. 108–16.

60. Marilyn Rueschemeyer, "Women in the Politics of East Germany," in *Women in the Politics of Postcommunist Eastern Europe*, ed. Marilyn Rueschemeyer (Armonk, NY: M.E. Sharpe, 1994), pp. 92–93, 98–101.

61. *NYT*, October 14, 1994; see also Scholz, "East-West Women's Culture in Transition," pp. 110–11.

62. *NYT*, October 27, 1990.

Chapter 7

1. *Yearbook on International Communist Affairs 1987* (Stanford, CA: Hoover Institution Press, 1988), pp. 305–7 (hereafter cited as *YICA*); Ivan Volgyes, "Hungary Before the Storm Breaks," *Current History* (November 1987): 373–75; Sandor Agocs, "Collapse of Communist Ideology in Hungary—November 1988 to February 1989," *East European Quarterly* 27, no. 2 (June 1993): 202.

2. Rudolf L. Tokes, "Hungary's New Political Elites: Adaptation and Change," *Problems of Communism*, vol. 39, no. 6 (November–December 1990): 47–49. See also Marian Grzybowski, "The Transition to Competitive Pluralism in Hungary," in *The New Democracies in Eastern Europe: Party Systems and Political Cleavages*, ed. Sten Berglund and Jan Ake Dellenbrant, 2nd ed. (Brookfield, VT: Edward Elgar, 1994), pp. 185–86.

3. William Echikson, "Bloc-Buster," in *Eastern Europe: Transformation and Revolution*, ed. Lyman H. Legters (Lexington, MA: D.C. Heath, 1992), pp. 432–33; *YICA 1990*, p. 354. See also *The New York Times*, March 12, July 30, 1987; February 6, 1989 (hereafter cited as *NYT*); George Schopflin et al., "Leadership Change and Crisis in Hungary," *Problems of Communism*, vol. 37, no. 5 (September–October 1988): 23–25, 27.

4. Agocs, "The Collapse of Communist Ideology in Hungary," p. 195.

5. Tokes, "Hungary's New Political Elites," pp. 47–49.

6. See Rudolf L. Tokes, "Hungarian Reform Imperatives," *Problems of Communism*, vol. 33, no. 5 (September–October 1984): 1–23; Schopflin et al., "Leadership Change and Crisis in Hungary," p. 24. See also Alfred Reisch, "Mounting Pressures for Change" and "The Fall of Kadar," in *Soviet/East European Survey 1987–1988*, ed. Vojtec Mastny (Boulder, CO: Westview Press, 1989), pp. 269–76.

7. Schopflin et al., "Leadership Succession and Crisis in Hungary," p. 24; *The Boston Globe*, September 27, 1987 (hereafter cited as *BG*).

8. *NYT*, September 27, October 23, 1987.

9. *NYT*, October 23, 1987.

10. *NYT*, October 6, October 10, December 18, 1988.

11. Alfred Reisch, "The Growth of Civil Society in Hungary," *Soviet/East European Survey 1987–1988*, ed. Mastny, p. 245; *YICA 1989*, pp. 332–34.

12. Thomas O. Melia, "Hungary: March 25, 1990," in *The New Democratic Frontier: A Country by Country Report of Elections in Central and Eastern Europe*, ed. Larry Garber and Eric Bjornlund (Washington, DC: National Democratic Institute for International Affairs, 1992), p. 45; Judy Batt, *East Central Europe: From Reform to Transformation* (New York: Council on Foreign Relations Press, 1991), pp. 64–65; Grzybowski, "The Transition to Competitive Pluralism in Hungary," pp. 189–90.

13. Melia, "Hungary: March 25, 1990," pp. 45–46; Grzybowski, "The Transition to Competitive Pluralism in Hungary," p. 189.

14. Batt, *East Central Europe: From Reform to Transformation*, p. 66.

15. Agocs, "The Collapse of Communist Ideology in Hungary," pp. 197–99; Joe C. Davis, "The Splintering of the Hungarian Labor Movement," *East European Quarterly* 29, no. 3 (Fall 1995): 373, 376.

16. Tokes, "Hungary's New Political Elites," pp. 53–54.

17. Bennett Kovrig, "Kadarism Without Kadar," in *Soviet/East European Survey 1987–1988*, ed. Mastny, pp. 276–79. See also Schopflin et al., "Leadership Succession and Crisis in Hungary," pp. 27–39; Agocs, "The Collapse of Communist Ideology in Hungary," p. 188.

18. Agocs, "The Collapse of Communist Ideology in Hungary," p. 190.

19. Laszlo Bruszt and David Stark, "Remaking the Political Field in Hungary: From the Politics of Confrontation to the Politics of Competition," in *Eastern Europe in Revolution*, ed. Ivo Banac (Ithaca, NY: Cornell University Press, 1992), p. 29.

20. Charles Gati, *The Bloc That Failed* (Bloomington: University of Indiana Press, 1990), pp. 170–71; *YICA 1990*, pp. 349–50.

21. *YICA 1990*, p. 350.

22. Timothy Garten Ash, "Budapest: The Last Funeral," in *Eastern Europe*, ed. Legters, p. 436.

23. *YICA 1990*, pp. 349–51; Alfred Reisch, "Hungary in 1989: A Country in Transition," in *Eastern Europe*, ed. Legters, p. 444; Gati, *The Bloc That Failed*, pp. 170–71; *YICA*, pp. 349–51, 353; *NYT*, October 10, 1989.

24. Melia, "Hungary: March 25, 1990," pp. 50–51; Ronald D. Asmus, J.F. Brown, and Keith Crane, *Soviet Foreign Policy and Revolutions in Eastern Europe* (Santa Monica, CA: RAND, 1991), pp. 73–79, 80–81; Bruszt and Stark, "Remaking the Political Field in Hungary," pp. 45–49.

25. Melia, "Hungary: March 25, 1990," p. 52; Reisch, "Hungary in 1989," p. 445.

26. Gati, *The Bloc That Failed*," p. 174; Reisch, "Hungary in 1989," p. 444.

27. Melia, "Hungary: March 25, 1990," p. 53; Grzybowski, "The Transition to Competitive Pluralism in Hungary," pp. 191–92.

28. Melia, "Hungary: March 25, 1990," pp. 57–59; Grzybowski, "The Transition to Competitive Pluralism in Hungary," pp. 192–193. See also Andras Koresenyi, "The Hungarian Parliamentary Elections, 1990," in *Post-Communist Transition: Emerging Pluralism in Hungary*, ed. Andras Bozoki, Andros Korosenyi, and George Schopflin (London: Pinter, 1992), pp. 25–78; Eva Fodor and Ivan Szelenyi, "Left Turn in Post-Communist Politics—The Case of Hungarian Elections 1990 and 1994," Working Papers Series No. 6, Advance Study Center, International Institute, University of Michigan, 1994–95, pp. 11–12.

29. Zoltan D. Barany, "The Hungarian Democratic Forum Wins National Elections Decisively," in *Eastern Europe*, ed. Legters, pp. 450–52; Melia, "Hungary: March 25, 1990," pp. 58–59; Fodor and Szelenyi, "Left Turn in Post-Communist Politics," pp. 10, 13–14.

30. Melia, "Hungary: March 25, 1990," pp. 56–57.

31. Ibid., pp. 57–58.

32. *The International Herald Tribune*, June 19, 1989 (hereafter cited as *IHT*); *YICA 1990*, p. 357.

33. *NYT*, September 1, September 4, 1988, respectively; Joseph Kun, *Hungarian Foreign Policy: The Experience of a New Democracy* (Westport, CT: Praeger, 1993), p. 39.

34. Kun, *Hungarian Foreign Policy*, p. 40; *NYT*, September 1, September 4, 1988; Agocs, "The Collapse of Communist Ideology in Hungary," pp. 204–5.

35. *BG*, September 15, 1987; *NYT*, September 20, 1987.

36. Ibid.

37. *NYT*, September 19, 1989; *BG*, September 19, 1989.

38. *NYT*, September 8, September 16, 1988; *YICA 1990*, p. 356.

39. Batt, *East Central Europe: From Reform to Transformation*, p. 94; Ivan T.

Berend, "*Jobbra At* [Right Face]: Right-Wing Trends in Post-Communist Hungary," in *Democracy and Right-Wing Politics in Eastern Europe in the 1990s*, ed. Joseph Held (New York: Columbia University Press, 1993), p. 110.

40. Jeffrey Goldfarb, *After the Fall: The Pursuit of Democracy in Central Europe* (New York: Basic Books, 1992), p. 118. See George Schopflin, "From Communism to Democracy in Hungary," in *Post-Communist Transition*, ed. Bozoki, Korosenyi, and Schopflin, pp. 103–4.

41. Dezso Kovacs and Sally Ward Maggard, "The Human Face of Political, Economic, and Social Change in Eastern Europe," *East European Quarterly* 27, no. 3 (September 1993): 333; Davis, "The Splintering of the Hungarian Labor Movement," pp. 373, 380–81.

42. Melia, "Hungary: March 25, 1990," pp. 60–61; Grzybowski, "The Transition to Competitive Pluralism in Hungary," p. 194; Kovacs and Maggard, "The Human Face of Political, Economic, and Social Change in Eastern Europe," pp. 323–25.

43. Kovacs and Maggard, "The Human Face of Political, Economic, and Social Change in Eastern Europe," p. 325; Berend, "*Jobbra At* [Right Face]: Right-Wing Trends in Post-Communist Hungary," p. 133.

44. Batt, *East Central Europe: From Reform to Transformation*, p. 91; Berend, "*Jobbra At* [Right Face]: Right-Wing Trends in Post-Communist Hungary," p. 133.

45. Batt, *East Central Europe: From Reform to Transformation*, pp. 67–68; Robert Bigler, "Back in Europe and Adjusting to the New Realities of the 1990s in Hungary," *East European Quarterly*, vol. 30, no. 2 (Summer 1996), pp. 223–24.

46. Berend, "*Jobbra At* [Right Face]: Right-Wing Trends in Post-Communist Hungary," pp. 117, 120–21, 128; J.F. Brown, *Hopes and Shadows: Eastern Europe After Communism* (Durham, NC: Duke University Press, 1994), pp. 87–90; Rebecca Ann Haynes, "Hungarian National Identity," in *Contemporary Nationalism in East Central Europe*, ed. Paul Latawski (New York: St. Martin's Press, 1995), pp. 96–97.

47. Brown, *Hopes and Shadows*, p. 90; see also Szofia Szilagyi, "Parliament Backs Law to Punish Extremist Rhetoric," *Transition*, vol. 2, no. 11 (May 31, 1996), p. 46.

48. In the May 1994, parliamentary elections, Csurka's Hungarian Justice and Life Party and two other like-minded right-wing fringe groups received together only 1.75 percent of the popular vote. Szilagyi, "Parliament Backs Law to Punish Extremist Rhetoric," p. 46.

49. United States Department of State, *Foreign Broadcast Information Service Daily Report Eastern Europe* 93–171 (September 7, 1993), pp. 24–25 (hereafter cited as *FBIS-EEU*).

50. *FBIS-EEU* 92–172 (September 3, 1992), pp. 9–12; *FBIS-EEU* 93–127 (July 6, 1993), p. 13; *FBIS-EEU* 93–130 (July 9, 1993), p. 13.

51. *NYT*, May 30, May 31, June 5, June 25, June 26, 1994.

52. Rudolf Andorka, "Hungary: Disenchantment After Transition," *The World Today*, vol. 50, no. 12 (December 1994), p. 235.

53. Fodor and Szelenyi, "Left Turn in Post-Communist Politics," pp. 21–22, 31.

54. Ibid., pp. 28–29.

55. *NYT*, June 26, 1994.

56. *NYT*, May 8, 1994.

57. *FBIS-EEU* 90–068 (April 9, 1990), pp. 32–33; *FBIS-EEU* 91–016, (December 24, 1991), p. 41; *FBIS-EEU* 92–233 (December 3, 1992), pp. 12–14. See also Berend, "*Jobbra At* [Right Face]: Right-Wing Trends in Post-Communist Hungary," p. 110; Batt, *East Central Europe: From Reform to Transformation*, p. 67.

58. *FBIS-EEU* 93–075 (April 21, 1993), pp. 17–18.

59. *NYT*, May 8, May 9, 1994.

60. *FBIS-EEU* 93–108 (June 8, 1993), pp. 15–16; *The Prague Post*, June 23–29, 1993 (hereafter cited as *PP*); Brown, *Hopes and Shadows*, p. 138.

61. *NYT*, February 27, 1990. See also Kovacs and Maggard, "The Human Face of Political, Economic, and Social Change in Eastern Europe," p. 335; *FBIS-EEU* 92–232 (December 2, 1992), p. 18.

62. Gale Stokes, *The Walls Came Tumbling Down: The Collapse of Communism in Eastern Europe* (New York: Oxford University Press, 1993), pp. 200–201; Brown, *Hopes and Shadows*, pp. 138–39.

63. *NYT*, May 3, 1990.

64. Batt, *East Central Europe: From Reform to Transformation*, p. 92; some exceptions were the energy and media sectors of the Hungarian economy. By the beginning of 1996, book publishing and the print media had been fully privatized and substantial progress had been made in the privatization of energy-producing public utilities. See Zsofia Szilagyi, "Hungary Has a Broadcast Media Law," *Transition*, vol. 2, no. 8 (April 19, 1996), p. 24; Jeff Freeman, "Hungarian Utility Privatization Moves Forward," ibid., vol. 2, no. 11 (May 3, 1996), pp. 27–29.

65. *BG*, June 5, 1990; Girard C. Steichen, "Lean Times Ahead in Hungary," in *Eastern Europe*, ed. Legters, p. 455.

66. James Angresano, "Political and Economic Obstacles Inhibiting Comprehensive Reform in Hungary," *East European Quarterly* 26, no. 1 (March 1992): 69; *NYT*, May 6, 1993.

67. *NYT*, February 21, 1995.

68. *NYT*, August 30, 1993.

69. *NYT*, February 20, 1990.

70. Kovacs and Maggard, "The Human Face of Political, Economic, and Social Change in Eastern Europe," pp. 335–36; *FBIS-EEU* 92–232 (December 2, 1992), p. 18; Brown, *Hopes and Shadows*, pp. 139–40.

71. Kovacs and Maggard, "The Human Face of Political, Economic, and Social Change in Eastern Europe," p. 337.

72. Angresano, "Political and Economic Obstacles Inhibiting Comprehensive Reform in Hungary," p. 68.

73. Striking progress had been made in the controversial area of public utilities where by 1996, Hungary had sold more of its energy sector on a per-capita basis to foreign interests than any other former communist country in the region. Indeed, in 1996, with the exception of the Czech Republic, Hungary's Visegrád group partners have had to privatize their energy sectors. See Freeman, "Hungarian Utility Privatization Moves Forward," p. 27.

74. Kovacs and Maggard, "The Human Face of Political, Economic, and Social Change in Eastern Europe," p. 336.

75. Andorka, "Disenchantment After Transition," pp. 234–35.

76. Ibid.

77. *NYT*, November 29, 1992.

78. Andorka, "Disenchantment After Transition," p. 235.

79. *NYT*, October 23, 1990.

80. Ibid.

81. Robert M. Bigler, "From Communism to Democracy: Hungary's Transition Thirty-Five Years After the Revolution," *East European Quarterly* 25, no. 4 (January 1992): 446; Berend, "*Jobbra At* [Right Face]: Right-Wing Trends in Post-Communist Hungary," p. 126.

82. *NYT*, August 9, 1991.

83. Bigler, "From Communism to Democracy," p. 446; Berend, "*Jobbra At* [Right Face]: Right-Wing Trends in Post-Communist Hungary," p. 129.

84. Ibid.

85. Robert M. Bigler, "Back in Europe and Adjusting to the New Realities of the 1990s in Hungary," *East European Quarterly*, vol. 30, no. 2 (Summer 1996), p. 216.

86. Deborah Lipstadt, "Anti-Semitism in Eastern Europe Rears Its Ugly Head," *USA Today*, September 13, 1993, p. 53.

87. Eva Fodor, "The Political Woman: Women in Politics in Hungary," in *Women in the Politics of Postcommunist Eastern Europe*, ed. Marilyn Rueschemeyer (Armonk, NY: M.E. Sharpe, 1994), pp. 182–83.

88. *FBIS-EEU* 90–049 (March 13, 1990), p. 38; *NYT*, January 19, 24, 1990; *BG*, June 17, 1990. See also Kun, *Hungarian Foreign Policy*, pp. 76–79. Janusz Bagajski, *Nations in Turmoil: Conflict and Cooperation in Eastern Europe* (Boulder, CO: Westview Press, 1993), p. 196.

89. *FBIS-EEU* 91–082 (April 29, 1991), pp. 29–30.

90. In June 1991, the governments of Budapest and Moscow signed a protocol providing for Soviet compensation for Hungary's construction of the Yamburg pipeline. Hungary's contribution was to be repaid in 1992 through the delivery of 14.6 billion cubic meters of natural gas. See Bugajski, *Nations in Turmoil*, p. 190.

91. *NYT*, December 30, 1990; Kun, *Hungarian Foreign Policy*, pp. 98–100. One cloud on the horizon of Hungarian relations with Ukraine is the Kiev government's treatment of its small Hungarian minority, which has demanded increased autonomy that Budapest implicitly condones. See Bugajski, *Nations in Turmoil*, p. 53.

92. *FBIS-EEU* 89–083 (May 2, 1989), p. 15.

93. See Kun, *Hungarian Foreign Policy*, pp. 124–25.

94. Bennett Kovrig, "Hungarian Minorities in East Central Europe," *Occasional Paper Series: The Atlantic Council of the United States* (March 1994): 17–18; Haynes "Hungarian National Identity," p. 98.

95. Haynes, "Hungarian National Identity," pp. 98–99.

96. *FBIS-EEU* 93–034 (February 23, 1993), p. 24, 93–037, February 26, 1993, p. 11; Berend, "Jobbra At (Right Face): Right-Wing Trends in Post-Communist Hungary," Held (ed.), *Democracy and Right-Wing Politics in Eastern Europe*, pp. 122, 125; Kun, *Hungarian Foreign Policy*, pp. 42–43, 107; Haynes, "Hungarian National Identity," p. 99. Belgrade accused Budapest of raising claims to Yugoslav territory and of working against its efforts to preserve the Federation's unity. See Bugajski, *Nations in Turmoil*, p. 140.

97. Haynes, "Hungarian National Identity," pp. 98–99.

98. Ibid.; see also Bugajski, *Nations in Turmoil*, pp. 52–53.

99. *NYT*, July 29, 1995.

100. See Sharon Fisher, "The Gabukovo-Nagymaros Dam Controversy Continues," *Radio Free Europe/Radio Liberty Research Reports*, vol. 2, no. 37 (September 17, 1993), pp. 7–12.

101. Robert J. Gutman, "The View from Hungary," *Europe*, November 1993, p. 31; Bugajski, *Nations in Turmoil*, p. 141.

102. Shumaker, "The Origins and Development of Central European Cooperation," p. 361; in January 1991, Hungary and Czechoslovakia agreed to exchange information on military movements along their frontier as part of a new bilateral security framework in response to the Soviet Union's aggressive behavior in early January 1991 toward the Lansbergis government in Vilnius. See Bugajski, *Nations in Turmoil*, p. 198.

103. Shumaker, "The Origins and Development of Central European Cooperation," p. 361.

Chapter 8

1. Wlodzimierz Wesolowski, "Transition from Authoritarianism to Democracy," in *Eastern Europe: Transformation and Revolution 1945–1991*, ed. Lyman H. Legters (Lex-

ington, MA: D.C. Heath, 1992), p. 302; Frances Millard, *The Anatomy of the New Poland: Post-Communist Policy in Its First Phase* (Brookfield, VT: Edward Elgar, 1994), pp. 27–28, 36–41.

2. Voytek Zubek, "Walesa's Leadership and Poland's Transition," *Problems of Communism*, vol. 40, nos. 1–2 (January–April 1991): 70; Gale Stokes, *The Walls Came Tumbling Down: The Collapse of Communism in Eastern Europe* (New York: Oxford University Press, 1993), pp. 104, 110–11, 115–17.

3. *Yearbook on International Communist Affairs 1989* (Stanford, CA: Hoover Institution Press, 1990), pp. 344–345 (hereafter cited as *YICA*); *YICA 1990*, p. 361. See also Ronald D. Asmus, J.F. Brown, and Keith Crane, *Soviet Foreign Policy and Revolutions in Eastern Europe* (Santa Monica, CA: RAND, 1991), pp. 52–53; J.F. Brown, *Eastern Europe and Communist Rule* (Durham, NC: Duke University Press, 1988), p. 196.

4. Stokes, *The Walls Came Tumbling Down*, pp. 118–19.

5. Ibid.

6. *The New York Times*, April 28, April 30, May 3, May 5, August 17, August 24, August 25, 1988 (hereafter cited as *NYT*).

7. Asmus, Brown, and Crane, *Soviet Foreign Policy*, p. 60. See also *The Boston Globe*, August 27, 1988 (hereafter cited as *BG*); *NYT*, August 29, 1988.

8. Jan T. Gross, "Poland: From Civil Society to Political Nation," in *Eastern Europe in Revolution*, ed. Ivo Banac (Ithaca, NY: Cornell University Press, 1992), pp. 58–59; Stokes, *The Walls Came Tumbling Down*, p. 122.

9. Zubek, "Walesa's Leadership and Poland's Transition," pp. 71–72; *YICA 1989*, pp. 341–42; *YICA 1990*, p. 365; Stokes, *The Walls Came Tumbling Down*, p. 123.

10. Stokes, *The Walls Came Tumbling Down*, pp. 14–125.

11. Wesolowski, "Transition from Authoritarianism to Democracy," pp. 303–4; *YICA 1990*, pp. 366–69; Asmus, Brown, and Crane, *Soviet Foreign Policy*, pp. 69–70; Wojciech Sokolewicz, "The Legal-Constitutional Bases of Democratization in Poland: Systemic and Constitutional Change," in *Democratization in Poland, 1989–1990: Polish Voices*, ed. George Sanford (New York: St. Martin's Press, 1992), p. 77. For an extensive discussion of the political reforms that came out of the roundtable negotiations, see Stanislaw Gebethner, "Political Reform in the Process of Roundtable Negotiations," in *Democratization in Poland 1989–1990*, ed. Sanford, pp. 50–68; Stokes, *The Walls Came Tumbling Down*, pp. 125–26; Leszek Garlicki, "The Development of the Presidency in Poland: Wrong Institutions or Wrong Persons?" in *Poland in a World of Change*, ed. Kenneth W. Thompson (Washington, DC: University Press of America, 1992), pp. 83–86.

12. Maya Latynski, "Poland: May 27, 1990," in *The New Democratic Frontier: A Country by Country Report on Elections in Central and Eastern Europe*, ed. Larry Garber and Eric Bjornlund (Washington, DC: National Democratic Institute for International Affairs, 1992), pp. 98–99.

13. Ibid., pp. 99–100; Zubek, "Walesa's Leadership and Poland's Transition," p. 72.

14. Sokolewicz, "The Legal-Constitutional Bases of Democratization in Poland," p. 80; Stokes, *The Walls Came Tumbling Down*, p. 127; Raymond Taras, "Voters, Parties, and Leaders," in *The Transition to Democracy in Poland*, ed. Richard F. Staar (New York: St. Martin's Press, 1993), p. 23.

15. Latynski, "Poland: May 27, 1990," pp. 101–2; Millard, *The Anatomy of the New Poland*, pp. 64–70.

16. *YICA 1990*, p. 369; Zubek, "Walesa's Leadership and Poland's Transition," pp. 72–73; Charles Gati, *The Bloc That Failed* (Bloomington: Indiana University Press, 1990), p. 168; Wesolowski, "Transition from Authoritarianism to Democracy," p. 304; *YICA 1990*, pp. 370–72.

17. *YICA 1990*, p. 369; Stokes, *The Walls Came Tumbling Down*, p. 128. Jaruzelski

apparently received some indirect encouragement from President George Bush, who was skeptical of Wałęsa and believed that Wałęsa would not be a good transitional leader.

18. Sokolewicz, "The Legal-Constitutional Bases of Democratization in Poland," p. 81; Stokes, *The Walls Came Tumbling Down*, pp. 128–29. See also Jaroslav Kurski, *Lech Walesa: Democrat or Dictator* (Boulder, CO: Westview Press, 1993), pp. 79–81.

19. *YICA 1990*, p. 363.

20. Gati, *The Bloc That Failed*, p. 168; *YICA 1990*, pp. 372. See also Asmus, Brown, and Crane, *Soviet Foreign Policy*, p. 71.

21. Sokolewciz, "The Legal-Constitutional Bases of Democratization in Poland," pp. 82–83.

22. *YICA 1990*, p. 374.

23. *YICA 1991*, pp. 325–26; Wlodzimierz Wesolowski, "The Role of Political Elites in Transition from Communism to Democracy: The Case of Poland," *Sisyphus* 8, no. 2 (1992): 86; J.F. Brown, *Hopes and Shadows: Eastern Europe After Communism* (Durham, NC: Duke University Press, 1994), pp. 127–28; James Bjork, "The Use of Conditionality: Poland and the IMF," *East European Quarterly* 29, no. 1 (Spring 1995): 98.

24. *YICA 1990*, pp. 375–76; Millard, *The Anatomy of the New Poland*, pp. 80–82.

25. *YICA 1991*, pp. 325–26.

26. *YICA 1990*, pp. 376–77; Bjork, "Poland and the IMF," pp. 98–99.

27. Latynski, "Poland: May 27, 1990," p. 108. See also "Market Myths and Polish Realities: An Interview with Jan Olszewski," *Multinational Monitor* (September 1993): 21–23.

28. Wesolowski, "The Role of Political Elites in Transition from Communism to Democracy," p. 86.

29. *YICA 1991*, pp. 316–17.

30. United States Department of State, Foreign Broadcast Information Service, *Daily Report Eastern Europe* 90–182 (September 19, 1990), p. 50 (hereafter cited as *FBIS-EEU*).

31. Judy Batt, *East Central Europe: From Reform to Transformation* (New York: Council on Foreign Relations Press, 1991), p. 57–58; Millard, *The Anatomy of the New Poland*, pp. 119–28. See also Kurski, *Lech Walesa*, pp. 86–101, passim.

32. Frances Millard, "Nationalism in Poland," in *Contemporary Nationalism in East Central Europe*, ed. Paul Latawski (New York: St. Martin's Press, 1995), pp. 122–23.

33. *FBIS-EEU* 90–122 (June 25, 1990), p. 45; *FBIS-EEU* 90–125 (June 28, 1990), p. 46; *FBIS-EEU* 90–142 (July 24, 1990), pp. 51–52.

34. George Sanford, "The Polish Road to Democratization: From Political Impasse to the 'Controlled Abdication' of Communist Power," in *Democratization in Poland, 1989– 1990*, ed. George Sanford (New York: St. Martin's Press, 1992), p. 25.

35. *FBIS-EEU* 90–189 (September 28, 1990), p. 35. See also Sokolewciz, "The Legal-Constitutional Bases of Democratization," pp. 88–89; Garlicki, "The Development of the Presidency in Poland," p. 67.

36. *FBIS-EEU* 90–210 (October 30, 1990), p. 34; *FBIS-EEU* 90–221 (November 15, 1990), pp. 48–50.

37. *FBIS-EEU* 90–175 (September 10, 1990), pp. 48–50. See also Jeffrey Goldfarb, *After the Fall: The Pursuit of Democracy in Central Europe* (New York: Basic Books 1992), pp. 90–91; *YICA 1991*, pp. 322–23.

38. *FBIS-EEU* 90–230 (November 28, 1990), pp. 37–39; *FBIS-EEU* 90–232 (December 3, 1990), pp. 41–42. See also Zubek, "Walesa's Leadership and Poland's Transition," pp. 81–83. Andrzej Korbonski has suggested that Polish voters supported Tymiński for the same reasons many French voters supported Pierre Poujade in the 1954 French parliamentary elections, namely, to express their frustration with the government of the time.

See Andrzej Korbonski, "The Revival of the Political Right in Post-Communist Poland: Historical Background," in *Democracy and Right-Wing Politics in Eastern Europe in the Early 1990s*, ed. Joseph Held (New York: Columbia University Press, 1993), p. 28; Sarah M. Terry, "What's Left, What's Right, and What's Wrong in Polish Politics?" in *Democracy and Right-Wing Politics*, ed. Held, p. 50; and Millard *The Anatomy of the New Poland*, p. 129.

39. *FBIS-EEU* 90–235 (December 6, 1990), p. 21. For more detail on the results of the first ballot, see Sanford, "The Polish Road to Democratization," pp. 26–27.

40. *FBIS-EEU* 90–237 (December 10, 1990), p. 35; *FBIS-EEU* 90–241 (December 14, 1990), pp. 40–42; Sanford, "The Polish Road to Democratization," p. 27; *YICA 1991*, pp. 323–24; Millard, *The Anatomy of the New Poland*, pp. 131–32; Taras, "Voters, Parties, and Leaders," pp. 24–25.

41. Zubek, "Walesa's Leadership and Poland's Transition," pp. 75–76.

42. Goldfarb, *After the Fall*, pp, 191–192.

43. *NYT*, March 18, 1991; *FBIS-EEU* 91–179 (September 16, 1991), p. 22; Millard, *The Anatomy of the New Poland*, pp. 86–87.

44. *International Herald Tribune*, July 14–15, 1990; *NYT*, October 29, December 30, 1990, respectively; *FBIS-EEU* 90–251 (December 31, 1990), p. 33.

45. *NYT*, October 27, 28, 1991; *BG*, October 28, 1991; Tomasz Zukowski, "Polish Parliamentary Elections," *Politicus*, Bulletin of the Institute of Political Studies, Polish Academy of Sciences, Warsaw (1992): 33–35. For a detailed analysis of the elections, see Miroslawa Grabowska, "The Party System Under Construction: The Parliamentary Elections in 1991," *Politicus*, Bulletin of the Institute of Political Studies, Polish Academy of Sciences, Warsaw (1992): 12–26; *FBIS-EEU* 91–212 (November 1, 1991), p. 80. See also Terry, "What's Left, What's Right, and What's Wrong in Polish Politics?" pp. 46, 47–50; Marian Grzybowski, "Poland: Toward Overdeveloped Pluralism," in *The New Democracies in Eastern Europe: Party Systems and Political Cleavages*, ed. Sten Berglund and Jan Ake Dellenbrant (Brookfield, VT: Edward Elgar, 1994), pp. 62–63; Millard, *The Anatomy of the New Poland*, pp. 136–40.

46. *FBIS-EEU* 91–214 (November 5, 1991), p. 25; *FBIS-EEU* 91–216 (November 7, 1991), pp. 15–16.

47. *NYT*, December 6, December 18, 1991; *FBIS-EEU* 91–222 (November 18, 1991), p. 22; Millard, *The Anatomy of the New Poland*, pp. 136–40.

48. *NYT*, June 6, 1992; *FBIS-EEU* 92–109 (June 5, 1992), p. 24; Millard, *The Anatomy of the New Poland*, pp. 97–104; Andrew A. Michta, "The Presidential Parliamentary System," in *The Transition to Democracy in Poland*, ed. Staar, pp. 64–67.

49. *FBIS-EEU* 92–109 (June 5, 1992), pp. 24–25; *FBIS-EEU* 92–110 (June 8, 1992), p. 32; *FBIS-EEU* 92–129 (July 6, 1992), p. 23. See also Michta, "The Presidential Parliamentary System," p. 67–68.

50. *FBIS-EEU* 92–129 (July 6, 1992), p. 23; *FBIS-EEU* 92–130 (July 7, 1992), pp. 26–27; *FBIS-EEU* 92–132 (July 9, 1992), p. 24; *FBIS-EEU* 92–134 (July 13, 1992), p. 31. See also Michta, "The Presidential Parliamentary System," pp. 68–69.

51. Michta, "The Presidential Parliamentary System," pp. 69–70; Janine P. Hole, "Competing Visions of Polish Parliament 1989–1993," *East European Quarterly* 29, no. 1 (Spring 1995): 70–71.

52. Ibid., pp. 71–72.

53. Ibid., pp. 72–73.

54. Ibid., p. 71.

55. Jolanta Babiuch, "Church and Society in Post-Communist Eastern Europe," *The World Today*, vol. 50, no. 11 (November 1994), p. 213.

56. *NYT*, January 8, January 15, 1995.

57. *NYT*, February 5, February 7, 1995; *BG*, February 6, 1995.

58. *NYT*, February 8, February 9, 1995.

59. *FBIS-EEU* 90–241 (December 14, 1990), p. 42; Hole, "Competing Visions of Polish Parliament," pp. 70–71.

60. Jan B. deWeydenthal, "The First Hundred Days of Walesa's Presidency," in *Eastern Europe*, ed. Legters, pp. 335–36; Taras, "Votes, Parties, and Leaders," pp. 33–34.

61. Grzybowski, "Toward Overdeveloped Pluralism," pp. 68–70; Hole, "Competing Visions of Polish Parliament," pp. 72–73.

62. deWeydenthal, "The First Hundred Days of Walesa's Presidency," pp. 336–37; Goldfarb, *After the Fall*, pp. 92–93.

63. *NYT*, July 6, 1994.

64. Kurski, *Lech Walesa*, 64–65.

65. *NYT,* November 20, 1995.

66. Ibid., *NYT*, November 23, 1995.

67. *NYT,* November 12, 20, 25, 1996; see also Anne Nivat, "Convincing Polish Voters That Kwasniewski Is 'The Choice of the Future,' " *Transition*, vol. 2, no. 8 (April 19, 1996), pp. 32–33.

68. *NYT*, November 25–26, 1995; *BG*, November 28, 1995; see Pawel Swieboda, "In NATO's Waiting Room," *Transition*, vol. 2, no. 8 (April 19, 1996), pp. 52–55.

69. Lucja Swiatkowski Cannon, "Privatization Strategy and Its Political Context," in *The Transition to Democracy in Poland*, ed. Staar, p. 138.

70. See *YICA 1991*, p. 325; *NYT*, February 26, June 17, October 29, 1990; June 3, 1991; February 23, 1993. See also Swiatkowski Cannon, "Privatization Strategy and Its Political Context," pp. 122–41, especially pp. 130–31, 133, 139–41.

71. "Business in Eastern Europe," *The Economist*, September 21, 1991, pp. 18–19; *BG*, June 28, 1991. See also Swiatkowski Cannon, "Privatization Strategy and Its Political Context," pp. 131–32.

72. *NYT*, April 17, 1991; *FBIS-EEU* 91–072 (April 15, 1992), *FBIS-EEU* 91–076 (April 19, 1991), p. 18.

73. *FBIS-EEU* 91–072 (April 15, 1991), pp. 32–33; *FBIS-EEU* 90–133 (July 11, 1990), pp. 45–46; *FBIS-EEU* 93–226 (November 26, 1993), p. 25.

74. *NYT*, November 19, 1990; April 19, 1991; February 9, 1992.

75. *NYT*, October 25, 1991; Zbigniew M. Fallenbuchl, "Poland: The Case for Cautious Optimism," *The World Today*, vol. 47, no. 11 (November 1991), p. 187; Bjork, "Poland and the IMF," p. 106.

76. *NYT*, January 11, January 30, and February 6, 1992, respectively; *BG*, January 26, 1992; Bjork, "Poland and the IMF," p. 106.

77. *NYT*, February 21, 1992; *FBIS-EEU* 92–029 (February 12, 1992), pp. 16–18.

78. *FBIS-EEU* 92–038 (February 26, 1992), p. 18; *FBIS-EEU* 92–039 (February 27, 1992), pp. 12–15; *BG*, March 3, 1992; *NYT*, March 6, March 19, March 24, 1992; Brown, *Hopes and Shadows*, p. 130. See also Bjork, "Poland and the IMF," p. 109.

79. *NYT*, September 6, 1992; *FBIS-EEU* 92–170 (September 1, 1992), p. 31; *FBIS-EEU* 92–171 (September 2, 1992), p. 17.

80. Bjork, "Poland and the IMF," p. 111.

81. *NYT*, October 15, 1991; Brown, *Hopes and Shadows*, pp. 130–31.

82. *NYT*, February 29, November 25, 1992; Bjork, "Poland and the IMF," p. 111.

83. Stephen Engelberg, "Her Year of Living Dangerously," *The New York Times Magazine* (September 12, 1993), pp. 38ff; *FBIS-EEU* 93–082 (April 30, 1993), pp. 33–34.

84. *FBIS-EEU* 93–094 (May 18, 1993), pp. 15–16; *FBIS-EEU* 93–095 (May 19, 1993), p. 20.

85. *FBIS-EEU* 93–099 (May 25, 1993), pp. 22–24; *FBIS-EEU* 93–102 (May 28, 1993), pp 13–15.

86. *FBIS-EEU* 93–102 (May 28, 1993), p. 73; Bjork, "Poland and the IMF," pp. 113–114.

87. *NYT*, May 28, May 29, 1993; *BG*, May 29, 1993. See also Bjork, "Poland and the IMF," pp. 114–15.

88. *FBIS-EEU* 93–184 (September 24, 1993), p. 19; Grzybowski, "Toward Overdeveloped Pluralism," p. 69.

89. *FBIS-EEU* 93–184 (September 24, 1993), p. 19.

90. *NYT*, December 18, December 24, 1992.

91. *NYT*, June 9, September 21, 1993. See also *BG*, November 26, 1992.

92. *NYT*, September 15, September 21, 1993; *FBIS-EEU* 93–182 (September 22, 1993), pp. 14–16; Terry, "What's Right, What's Left, and What's Wrong in Polish Politics?" p. 40.

93. *NYT*, September 21, October 15, 1993; *FBIS-EEU* 93–198 (October 25, 1993), p. 18; *FBIS-EEU* 93–206 (October 26, 1993), p. 13; *FBIS-EEU* 93–226 (November 26, 1993), pp. 24–25.

94. *BG*, March 6, 1994.

95. *NYT*, February 5, 1995.

96. Ibid.

97. *NYT*, September 15, 1994.

98. *FBIS-EEU* 93–182 (September 27, 1993), pp. 20–21; *FBIS-EEU* 93–183 (September 23, 1993), pp. 24–25; *FBIS-EEU* 93–189 (October 1, 1993), pp. 20–21.

99. Goldfarb, *After the Fall*, p. 166. See also *FBIS-EEU* 90–161 (August 20, 1990), pp. 32–33; *NYT*, June 2, June 11, October 21, 1991.

100. *NYT*, April 22, 1993; *The Christian Science Monitor*, May 26, 1993.

101. *NYT*, June 2, June 11, October 21, 1990.

102. See Jakub Karpinski, "Poles Divided over Church's Renewed Political Role," *Transition*, vol. 2, no. 7 (April 5, 1996), pp. 11–13.

103. *NYT*, June 11, 1991.

104. *NYT*, April 21, 1992.

105. *FBIS-EEU* 93–019 (February 1, 1993); *NYT*, March 11, 1993, pp. 35–36.

106. *NYT*, December 28, 1992; April 22, 1993; Wanda Nowicka, "Two Steps Backward: Poland's New Abortion Law," *Journal of Women's History* 5, no. 3 (Winter 1994): 153.

107. *NYT*, February 10, July 2, 1994; *BG*, July 5, 1994.

108. Deborah Lipstadt, "Anti-Semitism In Eastern Europe Rears Its Ugly Head Again," *USA Today*, September 13, 1993, p. 52; Lawrence Wechsler, *The Passion of Poland* (New York: Pantheon Books, 1982), pp. 16–24; *NYT*, January 26, 1995.

109. Lipstadt, "Anti-Semitism in Eastern Europe Rears Its Ugly Head," p. 52; Brown, *Hopes and Shadows*, p. 222–23; Goldfarb, *After the Fall*, p. 157.

110. Lipstadt, "Anti-Semitism in Eastern Europe Rears Its Ugly Head," p. 52; Brown, *Hopes and Shadows*, pp. 222–23; *YICA 1990*, p. 379–80. See also *NYT*, August 29, September 1, 1989.

111. Anna Titkov, "Polish Women in Politics: An Introduction to the Status of Women in Poland," in *Women in the Politics of Postcommunist Eastern Europe*, ed. Marilyn Rueschemeyer (Armonk, NY: M.E. Sharpe, 1994), p. 32; Nowicka, "Two Steps Backward," p. 151.

112. Joanna Regulska, "Women in Polish Politics," in *Women in the Politics of Postcommunist Eastern Europe*, ed. Rueschemeyer, p. 57; Elzbieta Pakszys and Dorota Mazurczak, "From Totalitarianism to Democracy in Poland: Issues in the Socio-Political Transition 1989–1993," *Journal of Women's History* 5, no. 3 (Winter 1994): 147–48;

Renata Siemienska, "Women in the Period of Systemic Change in Poland," *Journal of Women's History* 5, no. 3 (Winter 1994): 74–79.

113. See Regulska, "Women in Polish Politics," pp. 51–56.

114. *NYT*, August 23, 1989.

115. Bartlomiej Kaminski, "Emerging Patterns of Foreign Trade," in *The Transition to Democracy in Poland*, ed. Staar, p. 118.

116. Arthur R. Rachwald, "National Security Relations," in *The Transition to Democracy in Poland*, ed. Staar, p. 241.

117. Ibid.

118. *NYT*, February 22, February 23, February 28, March 4, 1990; see also Janusz Bugajski, *Nations in Turmoil: Conflict and Cooperation in Eastern Europe* (Boulder, CO: Westview Press, 1993), pp. 85–88.

119. *The London Times*, July 18, 1990.

120. Ibid.; see also Bugajski, *Nations in Turmoil*, pp. 83–84.

121. *NYT*, November 9, November 15, 1990.

122. *FBIS-EEU* 92–023 (February 4, 1992), p. 22; *NYT*, February 20, 1992.

123. *NYT*, April 3, 1992; *FBIS-EEU* 92–061 (March 30, 1992), pp. 10–11. See also Michael R. Beschloss and Strobe Talbott, *At the Highest Levels: The Inside Story of the End of the Cold War* (Boston, MA: Little Brown, 1993), pp. 191, 192.

124. Brown, *Hopes and Shadows*, pp. 211–13; Rachwald, "National Security Relations," pp. 243–44.

125. Brown, *Hopes and Shadows*, pp. 211–13.

126. "Remarks to Citizens . . . of Michigan, April 17, 1989," *Weekly Compilation of Presidential Documents* 25, no. 16: 564 (hereafter cited as *WCPD*).

127. *NYT*, April 8, April 9, April 18, April 23, 1989.

128. "Remarks to the National Assembly in Warsaw, Poland (July 10, 1989)," *WCPD* 25, no. 29: 1071–72. See also Beschloss and Talbott, *At The Highest Levels*, pp. 85–89.

129. *YICA 1990*, p. 383; *The International Herald Tribune*, July 15–16, July 26, 1989; *NYT*, August 19, August 20, August 25, 1989. See also Beschloss and Talbott, *At the Highest Levels*, pp. 85–89.

130. *NYT*, September 15, October 5, November 16, November 19, 1989; *FBIS-EEU* 89–174 (September 17, 1989), p. 31; *FBIS-EEU* 89–192 (October 5, 1989), p. 43. For the provisions of the *Support for East European Democracy (SEED) Act of 1989*, see United States Code, Public Law 101–179 (HR 3402, November 28, 1989, 101st Congress, First Session) (St. Paul, MN: West Publishing Co., 1989), vol. 1, 103 stat. pp. 1298–1307.

131. *NYT*, February 28, 1990.

132. *BG*, March 21, June 23, 1991.

133. *YICA 1990*, p. 381.

134. *YICA 1990*, pp. 381–82; *YICA 1991*, p. 330; *NYT*, April 14, 1990; *FBIS-EEU* 90–057 (March 23, 1990), pp. 66–67.

135. *NYT*, January 17, February 15, 1991; Kurski, *Lech Walesa*, p. 86.

136. *YICA 1991*, pp. 330–31; *NYT*, April 10, 1991; Rachwald, "National Security Relations," p. 246; Bugajski, *Nations in Turmoil*, pp. 34–36.

137. *FBIS-EEU* 91–196 (October 9, 1991), p. 19; *FBIS-EEU* 91–173 (September 6, 1991), p. 22.

138. Bugajski, *Nations in Turmoil*, p. 36.

139. Brown, *Hopes and Shadows*, pp. 209–10; Rachwald, "National Security Relations," p. 246; Bugajski, *Nations in Turmoil*, pp. 44–45.

140. Brown, *Hopes and Shadows*, pp. 206–7; Bugajski, *Nations in Turmoil*, p. 41.

141. Brown, *Hopes and Shadows*, pp. 206–7; Bugajski, *Nations in Turmoil*, p. 42.

142. *BG*, June 25, 1994; *NYT*, July 12, 1994.

143. Rachwald, "National Security Relations," p. 248.

144. Ibid.

145. Ibid.

146. Stephen R. Burant, "Polish-Lithuanian Relations," *Problems of Communism*, vol. 40, no. 3 (May–June 1991), pp. 69–74; Bugajski, *Nations in Turmoil*, p. 39.

147. Burant, "Polish-Lithuanian Relations," pp. 79–83; Brown, *Hopes and Shadows*, pp. 204–6.

148. Burant, "Polish-Lithuanian Relations," pp. 79–83; *FBIS-EEU* 91–177 (September 12, 1991), pp. 23, 91–179; (September 16, 1991), pp. 23, 91–187; (September 26, 1991), pp. 18, 91–191; (October 2, 1991), pp. 22–23; Bugajski, *Nations in Turmoil*, pp. 39–41.

149. Burant, "Polish-Lithuanian Relations," p. 83. According to the secret protocols of the pact, Lithuania and eastern Poland were to become a Soviet sphere of influence. After the Soviet Union's conquest of eastern Poland in September 1939, Stalin gave Vilnius to Lithuania. In the fall of 1940, after Lithuania was annexed by the Soviet Union, Lithuania received additional Polish territories that Stalin had originally given to Belarus. The postwar Polish–Soviet border, which was imposed on Poland by Stalin, was confirmed in an August 16, 1945, Polish–Soviet treaty.

150. Burant, "Polish-Lithuanian Relations," pp. 83–84.

151. Sarah M. Terry, "Prospects of Regional Cooperation," in *The Transition to Democracy in Poland*, ed. Staar, pp. 205–8.

152. Rudolph L. Tokes, "From Visegrád to Kraków: Cooperation, Competition, and Coexistence in Central Europe," *Problems of Communism*, vol. 40, no. 6 (November–December 1991): 100–114; Terry, "Prospects of Regional Cooperation," pp. 211–12.

153. Tokes, "From Visegrád to Kraków," p. 111; David Shumaker, "The Origins and Development of Central European Cooperation: 1989–1992," *East European Quarterly* 27, no. 3 (September 1993): 360–61. For further information about the Bratislava and Visegrád summits, see *FBIS-EEU* 90–070 (April 11, 1990), pp. 1–2; *FBIS-EEU* 92–089 (May 7, 1992), pp. 2–4.

154. Tokes, "From Visegrád to Kraków," pp. 112–13; Shumaker, "The Origins and Development of Central European Cooperation," pp. 361–62; Terry, "Prospects of Regional Cooperation," pp. 214, 216. For additional information on the Kraków summit, see *FBIS-EEU* 91–195 (October 8, 1991), pp. 4–6.

155. Terry, "Prospects of Regional Cooperation," pp. 218–23.

156. *FBIS-EEU* 92–023 (February 4, 1992), p. 23.

157. Terry, "Prospects of Regional Cooperation," p. 224.

Chapter 9

1. Martyn Rady, "Nationalism and Nationality in Romania," in *Contemporary Nationalism in East Central Europe*, ed. Paul Latawski (New York: St. Martin's Press, 1995), p. 127. Studies of communist rule in Romania include Aurel Braun, *Romanian Foreign Policy Since 1965: The Political and Military Limits of Autonomy* (New York: Praeger, 1978); Stephen Fischer-Galati, *The New Rumania: From People's Democracy to Socialist Republic* (Cambridge, MA: MIT Press, 1967); Ghita Ionescu, *Communism in Rumania 1944–1962* (London: Oxford University Press, 1964); Trond Gilberg, *Nationalism and Communism in Romania: The Rise and Fall of Ceauşescu's Personal Dictatorship* (Boulder, CO: Westview Press, 1990); Tom Gallagher, *Romania After Ceauşescu* (Edinburgh: Edinburgh University Press, 1995), pp. 45–71.

2. Rady, "Nationalism and Nationalisty in Romania," pp. 129, 133–34.

3. Ibid., p. 128.

4. See David Floyd, *Rumania: Russia's Dissident Ally* (New York: Praeger, 1965).

5. See Braun, *Romanian Foreign Policy Since 1965*.

6. Vladimir Tismaneanu, "In Romania: Between Euphoria and Rage," in *Eastern Europe: Transformation and Revolution 1945–1991*, ed. Lyman H. Legters (Lexington, MA: D.C. Heath, 1992), p. 468.

7. Tira Shubart, "Arrested in Romania," in *Eastern Europe*, ed. Legters, p. 464.

8. Gale Stokes, *The Walls Came Tumbling Down: The Collapse of Communism in Eastern Europe* (New York: Oxford University Press, 1993), p. 56. See also Roger Mansur, *Failed Transitions: The East European Economy and Environment Since the Fall of Communism* (New York: The Free Press, 1993), pp. 27–38.

9. Zbigniew Brzezinski, *The Grand Failure: The Birth and Death of Communism in the Twentieth Century* (New York: Scribners, 1989), pp. 134–35; Stokes, *The Walls Came Tumbling Down*, p. 54.

10. Anneli Maier, "Ceauşescu Family Succession," in *Eastern Europe*, ed. Legters, p. 460; *Yearbook on International Communist Affairs 1989* (Stanford, CA: Hoover Institution Press, 1990), p. 351 (hereafter cited as *YICA*); *YICA 1990*, p. 388; J.F. Brown, *Eastern Europe and Communist Rule* (Durham, NC: Duke University, 1988), pp. 280–81; Stokes, *The Walls Came Tumbling Down*, p. 54.

11. *YICA 1989*, pp. 353–54; *YICA 1990*, pp. 390–91; Shubart, "Arrested in Romania," p. 463; Brown, *Eastern Europe and Communist Rule*, pp. 282–87; Stokes, *The Walls Came Tumbling Down*, p. 58.

12. Stokes, *The Walls Came Tumbling Down*, pp. 159–60.

13. Vladimir Socor, "Social Protests in Romania," in *Soviet/East European Survey 1987–1988*, ed. Vojtech Mastny (Boulder, CO: Westview Press, 1989), pp. 208–10.

14. Shubart, "Arrested in Romania," p. 465; *YICA 1989*, pp. 354–55; Stokes, *The Walls Came Tumbling Down*, pp. 160–61; Gilberg, *Nationalism and Communism in Romania*, pp. 237–39.

15. Stokes, *The Walls Came Tumbling Down*, p. 158.

16. Mary Ellen Fischer and Doina Pasca Harsanyi, "Women in Romania," in *Women in the Politics of Postcommunist Eastern Europe*, ed. Marilyn Rueschemeyer (Armonk, NY: M.E. Sharpe, 1994), p. 206.

17. *The Boston Globe*, March 25, 1990 (hereafter cited as *BG*); *The New York Times*, January 17, 1991 (hereafter cited as *NYT*); Stokes, *The Walls Came Tumbling Down*, pp. 57–58.

18. Fisher and Harsanyi, "Women in Romania," pp. 207–8.

19. *YICA 1990*, p. 392; *NYT*, March 21, 1990; Stokes, *The Walls Came Tumbling Down*, pp. 161–62; Jonathan Eyre, "Transylvania Discord," *The World Today*, vol. 44, nos. 8–9 (August–September 1988), p. 130; Janusz Bugajski, *Nations in Turmoil: Conflict and Cooperation in Eastern Europe* (Boulder, CO: Westview Press, 1993), p. 160.

20. For a detailed discussion of the U.S. position on Romania's alleged violations of human rights, see Roger Kirk and Mircea Raceanu, *Romania versus the United States: Diplomacy of the Absurd 1985–1989* (New York: St. Martin's Press, 1994), pp. 65–86. See also Joseph Harrington, Edward Karns, and Scott Karns, "American-Romanian Relations 1989–1994," *East European Quarterly* 29, no. 2 (Summer 1995): 207.

21. Kirk and Raceanu, *Romania Versus the United States*, p. 182; Harrington, Karns, and Karns, "American-Romanian Relations," p. 207.

22. *YICA 1989*, p. 357; Harrington, Karns, and Karns, "American-Romanian Relations," p. 207–8.

23. Ibid., p. 359.

24. Ibid.

25. Ceauşescu quoted in *BG*, December 15, 1987; see also Karen Dawisha and Jona-

than Valdez, "Socialist Internationalism in Eastern Europe," *Problems of Communism,* vol. 36, no. 2 (March–April 1987), p. 10; Charles Gati, "Gorbachev and Eastern Europe," *Foreign Affairs* 65, no. 5 (Summer 1987): 962.; *YICA 1989,* pp. 351–452; Gilberg, *Nationalism and Communism in Romania,* pp. 229–34.

26. *YICA 1986,* p. 330; *YICA 1990,* p. 389.

27. *NYT,* December 2, 1987.

28. *YICA 1990,* p. 395.

29. Ibid., p. 391; Gallagher, *Romania After Ceauşescu,* p. 65; Madalina Nicolaescu, "Post-Communist Transition: Romanian Women's Response to Changes in the System of Power," *Journal of Women's History,* vol. 5, no. 4 (Winter 1994): 120–21.

30. *NYT,* March 14, 1989. See also *YICA 1990,* pp. 389, 393.

31. *NYT,* November 25, 1989; Kirk and Raceanu, *Romania Versus the United States,* pp. 175–76.

32. Thomas Carothers, "Romania: May 20, 1990," in *The New Democratic Frontier: A Country by Country Report on Elections in Central and Eastern Europe,* ed. Larry Garber and Eric Bjornlund (Washington, DC: National Democratic Institute for International Affairs, 1992), pp. 77–78; Stokes, *The Walls Came Tumbling Down,* p. 163; Nestor Ratesh, *Romania: The Entangled Revolution* (New York: Praeger, 1991), pp. 17–43; Martyn C. Rady, *Romania in Turmoil: A Contemporary History* (London: I.B. Taurus, 1992), pp. 99–115.

33. Carothers, "Romania: May 20, 1990," pp. 77–78; *YICA 1990,* p. 401

34. Tismaneanu, "In Romania: Between Euphoria and Rage," p. 467; *YICA 1990,* pp. 402–4; Stokes, *The Walls Came Tumbling Down,* pp. 163–66. See also Ratesh, *Romania: The Entangled Revolution,* pp. 44–47, 73–77; Rady, *Romania in Turmoil,* pp. 114–20; Larry L. Watts, "The Romanian Army in December Revolution and Beyond," in *Romania After Tyranny,* ed. Nelson, pp. 95–98, 105–7.

35. Tismaneanu, "In Romania: Between Euphoria and Rage," p. 471; Ratesh, *Romania: The Entangled Revolution,* pp. 47–57; Rady, *Romania in Turmoil,* pp. 122–25; Steven D. Roper, "The Romanian Party System and the Catch-All Party Phenomenon," *East European Quarterly* 28, no. 4 (Winter 1994): 527.

36. Carothers, "Romania: May 20, 1990," p. 78; "Bulgaria and Romania: No End of Trouble," *The Economist,* September 1, 1990, p. 44.

37. Charles Gati, *The Bloc That Failed* (Bloomington: Indian University Press, 1990), p. 185; *YICA 1990,* p. 394.

38. *YICA 1990,* pp. 404–6.

39. Ibid.

40. Mary Ellen Fischer, "The New Leaders and the Opposition," in *Romania After Tyranny,* ed. Nelson, pp. 49–53; *NYT,* June 8, 1995.

41. Fischer, "The New Leaders and the Opposition," pp. 54–58; Stokes, *The Walls Came Tumbling Down,* p. 173; Rady, *Romania in Turmoil,* pp. 136–38.

42. Carothers, "Romania: May 20, 1990," p. 79.

43. Ibid.

44. *YICA 1991,* p. 335.

45. Ibid.; Rady, *Romania in Turmoil,* pp. 186–88.

46. Carothers, "Romania: May 20, 1990," p. 80; Katherine Verdery and Gail Kligman, "Romania after Ceausescu: Post Communist Communism?" in *Eastern Europe in Revolution,* ed. Ivo Banac (Ithaca, NY: Cornell University Press, 1992), p. 123.

47. Carothers, "Romania: May 20, 1990," p. 79.

48. *YICA 1991,* p. 337. See also Verdery and Klingman, "Romania after Ceausescu," pp. 123–24

49. Carothers, "Romania: May 20, 1990," p. 79.

50. Matei Calinescu and Vladimir Tismaneanu, "The 1989 Revolution and Romania's Future," *Problems of Communism*, vol. 40, nos. 1–2 (January–April 1991), p. 57; Carothers, "Romania: May 20, 1990," p. 82; Verdery and Klingman, "Romania after Ceausescu," pp. 123–25.

51. Verdery and Kligman, "Romania after Ceausescu," pp. 123–24; Ioan Mihailescu, "Mental Stereotypes in the First Years of Post-Totalitarian Romania," *Government and Opposition* (Autumn 1993): 318.

52. Carothers, "Romania: May 20, 1990," p. 86.

53. *The International Herald Tribune*, May 18, June 21, 1990 (hereafter cited as *IHT*); Stokes, *The Walls Came Tumbling Down*, pp. 174–75.

54. *IHT*, May 18, 1990.

55. *YICA 1991*, p. 338.

56. Carothers, "Romania: May 20, 1990," pp. 80–81, 89–90; Gallagher, *Romania After Ceausescu*, pp. 103–4.

57. Carothers, "Romania: May 20, 1990," pp. 80–81, 89–90; Michael Shafir, "The Political Right in Post-Communist Romania," in *Democracy and Right-Wing Politics in Eastern Europe in the 1990s*, ed. Joseph Held (New York: Columbia University Press, 1993), p. 157; Rady, *Romania in Turmoil*, pp. 167–70.

58. *YICA 1991*, p. 339; Ratesh, *Romania: The Entangled Revolution*, p. 134; Gallagher, *Romania After Ceausescu*, pp. 104–5.

59. Calinescu and Tismaneanu, "The 1989 Revolution and Romania's Future," pp. 57; Carothers, "Romania: May 20, 1990," pp. 92–93; *YICA 1991*, pp. 338–39; Verdery and Kligman, "Romania after Ceausescu," pp. 130–35; Stokes, *The Walls Came Tumbling Down*, p. 175; Ratesh, *Romania: The Entangled Revolution*, p. 135.

60. Department of State, Foreign Broadcast Information Service, *Daily Report Eastern Europe* 91–136 (July 16, 1991), pp. 26 (hereafter cited as *FBIS-EEU*). See also Gallagher, *Romania After Ceausescu*, pp. 156–57.

61. Calinescu and Tismaneanu, "The 1989 Revolution and Romania's Future," pp. 57–59; *FBIS-EEU* 91–138 (July 18, 1991), pp. 27–28; *FBIS-EEU* 90–219 (November 13, 1990), p. 63.

62. *FBIS-EEU* 91–187 (September 26, 1991), pp. 22–24; *FBIS-EEU* 91–191 (October 2, 1991), pp. 38–39. See also Gallagher, *Romania After Ceausescu*, pp. 115–17.

63. *FBIS-EEU* 92–193 (October 5, 1992), p. 9. See also Jan Ake Dellenbrant, "Romania: The Slow Revolution," in *The New Democracies in Eastern Europe: Party Systems and Political Cleavages*, ed. Sten Berglund and Jan Ake Dellenbrant (Brookfield, VT: Edward Elgar, 1994), p. 213; Roper, "The Romanian Party System," p. 526; Henry F. Carey, "Irregularities or Rigging," *East European Quarterly* 29, no. 1 (Spring 1995): 43–44.

64. *BG*, September 29, 1992; *NYT*, October 13, October 14, 1992; J.F. Brown, *Hopes and Shadows: Eastern Europe After Communism* (Durham, NC: Duke University Press, 1994), pp. 96–97.

65. *NYT*, October 14, 1992.

66. Dan Ionescu, "Tele-Revolution to Tele-Evolution in Romania," *Transition*, vol. 2, no. 8 (April 19, 1996), pp. 42–43.

67. Rady, "Nationalism and Nationality in Romania," pp. 137–38; Gallagher, *Romania after Ceausescu*, pp. 155–56. It is worth nothing that in 1995, according to public opinion polls, the national army and the Orthodox Church, hardly known for their democratic instincts and organization, were the most popular institutions in Romania. See Dan Ionescu, "Romanian Orthodox Leaders Play the Nationalist Card," *Transition*, vol. 2, no. 7 (April 5, 1996), p. 25.

68. Nestor Ratesh, "Romania: Slamming on the Brakes," *Current History* (November 1993): 391; Brown, *Hopes and Shadows*, pp. 197–98; "Romania in Trouble," *The Econo-*

mist, October 3, 1992, p. 55; Dellenbrant, "Romania: The Slow Revolution," pp. 214–15; Brown, *Hopes and Shadows*, pp. 99–100.

69. *NYT*, November 24, December 17, 1993.

70. More reason for cautious optimism about the future of democracy in postcommunist Romania is a law promulgated on April 25 that deprives small parties with little or no organization, funding, or national backing of eligibility to compete in election campaigns. This curtailment of multiparty "political inflation" is expected to strengthen Romanian democracy by making it more efficient and lessening its vulnerability to single-party tendencies encouraged by excessive partisan conflict that can fatigue and disillusion Romanian voters with democratic processes. See Michael Shafir, "Political Engineering and Democratization in New Law on Parties," *Transition*, vol. 2, no. 14 (July 12, 1996), pp. 60–63.

71. Shafir, "The Political Right in Post-Communist Romania," p. 157; Trond Gilberg, "Romanians and Democratic Values: Socialization After Communism," in *Romania After Tyranny*, ed. Nelson, pp. 83–89, 90–93.

72. For example, see Victor Gomez, "Local Victories for the Opposition," *Transition*, vol. 2, no. 14 (July 12, 1996), p. 2.

73. Rady, *Romania in Turmoil*, pp. 181–82; "Romania: Another Winter of Discontent," *The Economist*, October 27, 1990, p. 54; Brown, *Hopes and Shadows*, p. 140.

74. *YICA 1990*, p. 347.

75. *YICA 1991*, pp. 346–47; *NYT*, February 6, 1990; *The London Times*, July 26, 1990.

76. *YICA 1991*, p. 348; Rady, *Romania in Turmoil*, pp. 183–84; Ratesh, "Slamming on the Brakes," p. 392; Verdery and Klingman, "Romania after Ceausescu," p. 140. See also Mugur Isarescu, "The Prognoses for Economic Recovery," in *Romania After Tyranny*, ed. Nelson, 149–66.

77. Katherine Verdery, "The Elasticity of Land: Problems of Property Restitution in Transylvania," Working Papers Series 9, Advanced Study Center, International Institute, University of Michigan, 1994 95, pp. 2 4, 6.

78. Verdery and Kligman, "Romania after Ceausescu," pp. 140–41; "Romania Undermined," *The Economist*, October 5, 1991, p. 5.

79. Verdery and Kligman, "Romania after Ceausescu," pp. 140–41.

80. *The Christian Science Monitor* (June 8, 1993), hereafter cited as *CSM*; Ursula Bayreuther and Andreas Gummick, "Romania: Economic Reform Still Walking the Tightrope," *Focus: Eastern Europe*, no. 81, (Frankfurt am Main: Deutsche Bank Research, June 17, 1993); postcommunist Romania has also failed to diminish its vulnerability to the periodic energy crises that have plagued the country's economic life and depressed living standards since the late 1970s. These crises continue to occur and they are worse in the 1990s than twenty years earlier, with factories paralyzed and apartments cold and dark in Bucharest and other urban centers, because the postcommunist government cannot arbitrarily limit consumption as its communist predecessor frequently did. See Dan Ionescu, "Romanian Energy Crisis Turns Political," *Transition*, vol. 2, no. 9 (May 3, 1996), pp. 20–22.

81. See Robert Corzine and Virginia March, "Feet Drag on Road to Market: Change Goes Against Grain for Many in Government," *The Financial Times*, July 27, 1993; *NYT*, November 24, 1993.

82. Juliana Geran-Pilon, "Post-Communist Nationalism: The Case of Romania," *The World and I* (February 1992), pp. 111–14; Carothers, 89; *YICA 1991*, pp. 353–56; Stokes, *The Walls Came Tumbling Down*, p. 174; Bugajski, *Nations in Turmoil*, p. 166.

83. Shafir, "The Political Right in Post-Communist Romania," pp. 161; Rady, *Romania in Turmoil*, pp. 146–48; Brown, *Hopes and Shadows*, pp. 192–99, especially pp. 196–98; Gallagher, *Romania After Ceausescu*, p. 213.

84. Bugajski, *Nations in Turmoil*, pp. 159–60; Mary Szabo, "We (The Leaders of Hungarian Churches in Romania) Demand Our Rights," *Transition*, vol. 2, no. 7 (April 5, 1996), pp. 26–27.

85. Deborah Lipstadt, "Anti-Semitism in Eastern Europe Rears Its Ugly Head," *USA Today*, September 1993, p. 53; Katherine Verdery, "Nationalism and National Sentiment in Romania," *Slavic Review* 52, no. 2 (Summer 1993): 199; Shafir, "The Political Right in Post-Communist Romania," p. 162; Gallagher, *Romania After Ceausescu*, p. 147.

86. *NYT*, July 5, 1991; Deborah Lipstadt, "Anti-Semitism in Eastern Europe Rears Its Ugly Head," p. 53.

87. *NYT*, July 5, 1991; December 7, 1993. For background on Antonescu, see Ghita Ionescu, *Communism in Rumania* (London: Oxford University Press, 1964), pp. 54–76, passim.

88. *YICA 1991*, p. 353; *NYT*, July 5, 1991; Verdery, "Nationalism and National Sentiment in Romania," pp. 197–98.

89. Jonathan Kaufman, "Germany Hastens Exit of Gypsies," *The Boston Sunday Globe*, November 1, 1992.

90. *NYT*, October 18, 1992.

91. *NYT*, February 8, 1990; *BG*, March 25, 1990; Rady, *Romania in Turmoil*, pp. 80–81.

92. *NYT*, November 23, 1994.

93. Fischer and Harsanyi, "Women in Romania," Reuschemeyer (ed.), *Women in the Politics of Post-Communist East Europe*, pp. 212–13. See also Doina Pasca Harsanyi, "Romania's Women," *Journal of Women's History*, vol. 5, no. 3 (Winter 1994), pp. 47–52; Nicolaescu, "Post-Communist Transition: Romanian Women's Response to Changes in the System of Power," pp. 117–28; Marianne Hausleitner, "Women in Romania: Before and After the Collapse," *Gender Politics and Post-Communism*, ed. Nanette Funk and Magda Mueller (New York: Routledge, 1993), pp. 58–59.

94. Fischer and Harsanyi, "Women in Romania," pp. 212–13.

95. *FBIS-EEU* 90–005 (January 8, 1990), pp. 73–75.

96. *YICA 1991*, p. 356. For brief comments on Moldova in Romanian–Soviet relations, see William Crowther, "Romania and Moldavian Political Dynamics," in *Romania After Tyranny*, ed. Nelson, pp. 240–43.

97. *YICA 1991*, p. 357; *BG* (May 7, 1990); Brown, *Hopes and Shadows*, p. 189; see also Charles King, "Moldovan Identity and the Politics of Pan-Romanianism," *Slavic Review*, vol. 53, no. 2 (Summer 1994), p. 351; Bugajski, *Nations in Turmoil*, pp. 56–57.

98. *FBIS-EEU* 91–167 (August 28, 1991), pp. 102–104; Brown, *Hopes and Shadows*, pp. 190–91; King, "Moldovan Identity," pp. 352–53; Bugajski, *Nations in Turmoil*, p. 60.

99. *YICA 1990*, p. 357; *FBIS-EEU* 90–207 (October 25, 1990), p. 43; Brown, *Hopes and Shadows*, p. 191; King, "Moldovan Identity," p. 355; Bugajski, *Nations in Turmoil*, p. 57.

100. King, "Moldovan Identity," p. 365.

101. *NYT*, January 7, 1990. See also *FBIS-EEU* 90–033 (February 16, 1990), p. 65.

102. *FBIS-EEU* 90–120 (June 21, 1990), p. 44; *IHT*, July 4, 1990; Harrington, Karns, and Karns, "American-Romanian Relations," pp. 207–8.

103. *YICA 1990*, p. 359; *IHT*, June 26, 1990; *BG*, June 20, September 1, 1990. See also *NYT*, June 11, 1993.

104. Susan Caskie, "Pushing Toward NATO as Russia Grumbles," *Transition*, vol. 2, no. 8 (April 19, 1996), p. 62.

105. *FBIS-EEU* 92–000 (March 13, 1992), pp. 12–13; *NYT*, April 18, 1991.

106. Harrington, Karns, and Karns, "American-Romanian Relations," pp. 213–15.

107. Ibid., p. 221.

108. *FBIS-EEU* 93–196 (October 13, 1993), pp. 21–22; *FBIS-EEU* 93–204 (October 25, 1993), p. 20. See also Harrington, Karns, and Karns, "American-Romanian Relations." pp. 221–24.

Chapter 10

1. Christopher Bennett, *Yugoslavia's Bloody Collapse: Causes, Course, and Consequences* (New York: New York University Press, 1995), pp. 33–50.

2. For a brief review of the political, economic, and sociocultural characteristics of the Yugoslav peoples, see Paul Mojzes, *Yugoslavian Inferno: Ethno-Religious Warfare in the Balkans* (New York: Continuum, 1994), pp. 14–46; Bogdan Denitch, *Ethnic Nationalism: The Tragic Death of Yugoslavia* (Minneapolis: University of Minnesota Press, 1994), pp. 22–50; Bennett, *Yugoslavia's Bloody Collapse*, pp. 2–32, 180; Susan L. Woodward, *Balkan Tragedy: Chaos and Dissolution After the Cold War* (Washington, DC: Brookings Institution, 1995); Leonard Cohen, *Broken Bonds: The Disintegration of Yugoslavia*, 2nd ed. (Boulder, CO: Westview Press, 1995), pp. 36–38.

3. Woodward, *Balkan Tragedy*, p. 238; Bennett, *Yugoslavia's Bloody Collapse*, pp. 62–64.

4. Woodward, *Balkan Tragedy*, p. 247

5. Ibid., pp. 26–45, passim; Bennett, *Yugoslavia's Bloody Collapse*, pp. 7–8, 64.

6. Gale Stokes, *The Walls Came Tumbling Down: The Collapse of Communism in Eastern Europe* (New York: Oxford University Press, 1993), pp. 225–28; Dusko Doder, "Yugoslavia: New War, Old Hatreds," *Foreign Policy* 91 (Summer 1993): 13; Bennett, *Yugoslavia's Bloody Collapse*, pp. 56–62, 67–70.

7. Stokes, *The Walls Came Tumbling Down*, pp. 228–30; Cvijeto Job, "Yugoslavia's Ethnic Furies," *Foreign Policy* 92 (Fall 1993): 58, 67; J.F. Brown, *Hopes and Shadows: Eastern Europe After Communism* (Durham, NC: Duke University Press, 1991), p. 250.

8. Stokes, *The Walls Came Tumbling Down*, pp. 225–28; John R. Lampe, "Nationalism in the Former Yugoslavia," in *Contemporary Nationalism in East Central Europe*, ed. Paul Latawski (New York: St. Martin's Press, 1995), p. 160; Bennett, *Yugoslavia's Bloody Collapse*, pp. 70–77.

9. Denitch, *Ethnic Nationalism*, pp. 104–5.

10. Woodward, *Balkan Tragedy*, pp. 169–70.

11. *The United Nations and the Situation in the Former Yugoslavia*, Reference Paper, Revision 4 (Department of Public Information), pp. 65–69 (hereafter cited as *UNSFY*). See also Brown, *Hopes and Shadows*, pp. 235–36; Woodward, *Balkan Tragedy*, p. 243.

12. Woodward, *Balkan Tragedy*, p. 238; Bennett, *Yugoslavia's Bloody Collapse*, p. 81.

13. Mojzes, *Yugoslavian Inferno*, pp. 135–41; Woodward, *Balkan Tragedy*, pp. 109–10; Denitch, *Ethnic Nationalism*, p. 113.

14. Bennett, *Yugoslavia's Bloody Collapse*, pp. 90–91; Cohen, *Broken Bonds*, pp. 51–52.

15. For a detailed biographical statement about Milošević, see Aleksa Djilas, "A Profile of Slobodan Milosevic," *Foreign Affairs* 72, no. 3 (Summer 1993): 81–96; Jeffrey Gedmin, "Comrade Slobo," *The American Spectator* (April 1993): 28–33. See also Sabrina P. Ramet, *Nationalism and Federalism in Yugoslavia 1962–1991* (Bloomington: Indiana University Press, 1994), pp. 225–39; Denitch, *Ethnic Nationalism*, pp. 112–13; Brown, *Hopes and Shadows*, pp. 238–39.

16. Bennett, *Yugoslavia's Bloody Collapse*, p. 95.

17. Woodward, *Balkan Tragedy*, pp. 90–93; Misha Glenny, *The Fall of Yugoslavia:*

The Third Balkan War (New York: Penguin, 1992), pp. 40–41; Bennett, *Yugoslavia's Bloody Collapse*, pp. 83–85; see also Cohen, *Broken Bonds*, pp. 52–55.

18. Denitch, *Ethnic Nationalism*, pp. 113–15; Bennett, *Yugoslavia's Bloody Collapse*, pp. 85–90, 97–98, 107–8.

19. Glenny, *The Fall of Yugoslavia*, p. 68; Stokes, *The Walls Came Tumbling Down*, pp. 230–32; see also Branka Magas, "The Curse of Kosovo," *New Internationalist* (September 1993), pp. 8–10; Brown, *Hopes and Shadows*, pp. 255–57; Ramet, *Nationalism and Federalism in Yugoslavia*, pp. 187–201; Laslo Sekelj, *Yugoslavia: The Process of Disintegration* (New York: Columbia University Press, 1993), pp. 189–95; Derek Hall, *Albania and the Albanians* (New York: St. Martin's Press, 1994), p. 209; Miron Rezun, *Europe and War in the Balkans: Toward a New Yugoslav Identity* (Westport, CT: Praeger, 1995), pp. 116–21.

20. Brown, *Hopes and Shadows*, pp. 256–57; Denitch, *Ethnic Nationalism*, pp. 117–20; Rezun, *Europe and War in the Balkans*, p. 170.

21. Cohen, *Broken Bonds*, pp. 121–24; see also Stokes, *The Walls Came Tumbling Down*, pp. 230–232; Janusz Bugajski, *Nations in Turmoil: Conflict and Cooperation in Eastern Europe* (Boulder, CO: Westview Press, 1993), p. 129.

22. In July 1990, Milosevic suspended Kosovo's provincial assembly days after it had declared Kosovo independent of Serbia and a sovereign republic of Yugoslavia. Bugajski, *Nations in Turmoil*, p. 129.

23. *The New York Times*, February 16, March 15, 1990 (hereafter cited as *NYT*); *The London Times*, July 6, 1990; Woodward, *Balkan Tragedy*, p. 98; Glenny, *The Fall of Yugoslavia*, pp. 34–35; Bennett, *Yugoslavia's Bloody Collapse*, pp. 11, 99–100.

24. For a brief review of political development in Vojvodina in the late 1980s, especially with regard to the Hungarian minority, see Bugajski, *Nations in Turmoil*, pp. 137–38.

25. Bennett, *Yugoslavia's Bloody Collapse*, pp. 98–99.

26. Ibid., p. 115.

27. Woodward, *Balkan Tragedy*, pp. 94–95, 97–98.

28. *Yearbook on International Communist Affairs 1989* (Stanford, CA: Hoover Institution Press, 1990), p. 408 (hereafter cited as *YICA*); Stokes, *The Walls Came Tumbling Down*, pp. 236–37, 238; Ramet, *Nationalism and Federalism in Yugoslavia*, pp. 207–11; Dimitry Rupel, "Slovenia's Shift from the Balkans to Central Europe," in *Independent Slovenia: Origins, Movements, Prospects*, ed. Jill Benderly and Evan Kraft (New York: St. Martin's Press, 1994), p. 189.

29. Woodward, *Balkan Tragedy*, p. 110; Sabrina P. Ramet, "War in the Balkans," *Foreign Affairs*, vol. 71, no. 4 (Fall 1992): 84; Edward McMahon, "Slovenia: April 7 and 21, 1990," in *The New Democratic Frontier: A Country by Country Report on Elections in Central and Eastern Europe*, ed. Larry Garber and Eric Bjornlund (Washington, DC: National Democratic Institute for International Affairs, 1992), pp. 69–70.

30. Cohen, *Broken Bonds*, pp. 89–94; Dennison Rusinow, "Yugoslavia: Balkan Breakup," *Foreign Policy* 83 (Summer 1991), p. 154; McMahon, "Slovenia: April 7 and 21, 1990," pp. 70–73; Rezun, *Europe and War in the Balkans*, p. 125; Woodward, *Balkan Tragedy*, p. 119; United States Department of State, Foreign Broadcast Information Service, *Daily Report Eastern Europe* 90–127 (July 2, 1990), p. 69 (hereafter cited as *FBIS-EEU*).

31. *FBIS-EEU* 90–037 (February 23, 1990), p. 88.

32. Cohen, *Broken Bonds*, pp. 94–102; see also Rusinow, "Yugoslavia: Balkan Breakup," p. 155; Banac, "Post-Communism as Post-Yugoslavism: The Yugoslav Non-Revolutions of 1989–1990," in *Eastern Europe in Revolution*, ed. Ivo Banac, p. 180; Woodward, *Balkan Tragedy*, p. 119; Bennett, *Yugoslavia's Bloody Collapse*, pp. 123–24. See also *FBIS-EEU* 90–127 (July 2, 1990), p. 69.

33. Bagomil Ferfila, "Yugoslavia: Confederation or Disintegration." *Problems of Communism*, vol. 40, no. 4 (July–August 1991): 23; McMahon, "Slovenia: April 7 and 21, 1990," pp. 67–69; *NYT*, February 13, 1990; *FBIS-EEU* 90–227 (November 26, 1990), p. 73.

34. *YICA 1989*, pp. 407–8; Banac, "Post-Communism as Post-Yugoslavism," p. 169; Stokes, *The Walls Came Tumbling Down*, pp. 237–38; Rupel, "Slovenia's Shift from the Balkans to Central Europe," p. 190; Sekelj, *Yugoslavia: The Process of Disintegration*, pp. 250–51.

35. Brown, *Hopes and Shadows*, pp. 244–45.

36. Rusinow, "Yugoslavia: Balkan Breakup," p. 152; Bennett, *Yugoslavia's Bloody Collapse*, p. 110.

37. Woodward, *Balkan Tragedy*, pp. 115–16; Bennett, *Yugoslavia's Bloody Collapse*, p. 110. Cohen, *Broken Bonds*, p. 84; Rezun, *Europe and War in the Balkans*, p. 132.

38. Cohen, *Broken Bonds*, pp. 198–200.

39. Glenny, *The Fall of Yugoslavia*, p. 64.

40. Cohen, *Broken Bonds*, pp. 120–21.

41. *FBIS-EEU* 90–156 (August 13, 1990), p. 55; 90–247 (December 24, 1990), p. 55; see also Cohen, *Broken Bonds*, pp. 118–121; Woodward, *Balkan Tragedy*, pp. 138–39; Rezun, *Europe and War in the Balkans*, p. 133.

42. *FBIS-EEU* 91–122 (June 25, 1991), pp. 35–36; *FBIS-EEU* 91–123 (June 26, 1991), pp. 42–43. See also Rupel, "Slovenia's Shift from the Balkans to Central Europe," p. 190; Bennett, *Yugoslavia's Bloody Collapse*, pp. 13, 142–43.

43. Bennett, *Yugoslavia's Bloody Collapse*, pp. 143–44; Cohen, *Broken Bonds*, pp. 121, 198–200; Rezun, *Europe and War in the Balkans*, p. 134.

44. Members of the Federation High Command were enraged by statements of Slovene Defense Minister Janes Jansa that Slovene military recruits should serve only in Slovenia, that Slovene funds supporting the military should no longer be sent to the Federation, and that Federation military property should be divided among the republics and help to explain its own professional interest in suppressing Slovene separatism; Cohen, *Broken Bonds*, p. 188.

45. Glenny, *The Fall of Yugoslavia*, pp. 96–97; Woodward, *Balkan Tragedy*, pp. 166–67; Bennett, *Yugoslavia's Bloody Collapse*, pp. 156–59; Rezun, *Europe and War in the Balkans*, pp. 140–41; Bugajski, *Nations in Turmoil*, pp. 110–11; see also *NYT*, June 28, July 4, 1991; *BG*, July 2, 1991.

46. *FBIS-EEU* 91–106 (June 3, 1991), pp. 38–39; Woodward, *Balkan Tragedy*, pp. 120, 140, 143.

47. Glenny, *The Fall of Yugoslavia*, p. 87; Woodward, *Balkan Tragedy*, p. 120; Bennett, *Yugoslavia's Bloody Collapse*, pp. 125, 129, 135; Cohen, *Broken Bonds*, pp. 128–30.

48. Doder, "Yugoslavia: New War, Old Hatreds," pp. 10–11; Bennett, *Yugoslavia's Bloody Collapse*, pp. 126, 129.

49. Bennett, *Yugoslavia's Bloody Collapse*, p. 141.

50. Robert M. Hayden, "Constitutional Nationalism in the Formerly Yugoslav Republics," *Slavic Review* 51, no. 4 (Winter 1993), p. 657; Rezun, *Europe and War in the Balkans*, pp. 133–34; Cohen, *Broken Bonds*, pp. 130–32; see also *FBIS-EEU* 90–245 (December 20, 1990), p. 57; 90–247 (December 24, 1990), pp. 56–57.

51. *FBIS-EEU* 90–247 (December 24, 1990), p. 57.

52. Bennett, *Yugoslavia's Bloody Collapse*, p. 141; for more details about Tudjman's ethnic prejudice that alarmed Croatia's Serb minority see Cohen, *Broken Bonds*, p. 208.

53. Banac, "Post-Communism as Post-Yugoslavism," in *Eastern Europe in Revolution*, ed. Banac, p. 182; Woodward, *Balkan Tragedy*, p. 141; Bennett, *Yugoslavia's Bloody Collapse*, p. 148; Cohen, *Broken Bonds*, pp. 128–32.

54. *FBIS-EEU* 90–150 (August 3, 1990), p. 37, 90–166 (August 27, 1990), p. 48; Bugajski, *Nations in Turmoil*, p. 102.

55. Bennett, *Yugoslavia's Bloody Collapse*, p. 136; for the roots of Serbia's suspicion and dislike of Croatia see Alex Dragnich, *Serbs and Croats: The Struggle for Yugoslavia* (New York: Harcourt Brace Jovanovich, 1992).

56. Glenny, *The Fall of Yugoslavia*, pp. 37–38, 121–22; Woodward, *Balkan Tragedy*, pp. 141–42; Bennett, *Yugoslavia's Bloody Collapse*, p. 146; Bugajski, *Nations in Turmoil*, p. 103.

57. Stephen Engelberg, "Carving out a Greater Serbia," *The New York Times Magazine* (September 1, 1991), p. 20; *NYT*, November 22, 1991; see also Bugajski, *Nations in Turmoil*, p. 102.

58. Bennett, *Yugoslavia's Bloody Collapse*, pp. 150, 164.

59. Ibid., p. 131; Rezun, *Europe and War in the Balkans*, p. 137.

60. Bennett, *Yugoslavia's Bloody Collapse*, pp. 165–69.

61. Ibid., pp. 132–33; Rezun, *Europe and War in the Balkans*, p. 141; Bugajski, *Nations in Turmoil*, p. 105.

62. Bennett, *Yugoslavia's Bloody Collapse*, pp. 132–33.

63. Adzić is also reported to have favored an "extermination of tens of thousands of Croats [that] would provoke 'some grumbling' around the world but would be soon forgotten." Rezun, *Europe and War in the Balkans*, p. 139.

64. Bennett, *Yugoslavia's Bloody Collapse*, p. 133.

65. Woodward, *Balkan Tragedy*, pp. 231–32; Cohen, *Broken Bonds*, pp. 271–73.

66. Ian Kearns, "Croatia: The Politics Behind the War," *The World Today*, vol. 49, no. 4 (April 1993), pp. 62–63; see also Cohen, *Broken Bonds*, pp. 266–77.

67. Kearns, "Croatia," pp. 62–63.

68. Bennett, *Yugoslavia's Bloody Collapse*, p. 166.

69. Woodward, *Balkan Tragedy*, pp. 146–47.

70. Bennett, *Yugoslavia's Bloody Collapse*, p. 160.

71. Ibid., pp. 175–76; *NYT*, September 4, 1991.

72. *FBIS-EEU* 91–167 (August 28, 1991), p. 39; *FBIS-EEU* 91–173 (September 6, 1991), p. 30; Woodward, *Balkan Tragedy*, pp. 177–78; Bennett, *Yugoslavia's Bloody Collapse*, p. 177.

73. *FBIS-EEU* 91–183 (September 20, 1991), pp. 33–34.

74. David Haglund, S. Neil McFarlane, and Joel J. Sokolsky, eds., *NATO's Eastern Dilemma* (Boulder, CO: Westview Press, 1994), pp. 164–65; Woodward, *Balkan Tragedy*, p. 177. In the latter half of 1991, European public opinion lost interest in the preservation of a unified Yugoslav state. Many voters throught the Yugoslav peoples should be left alone to pursue self-determination. See Cohen, *Broken Bonds*, pp. 230–31.

75. Rezun, *Europe and War in the Balkans*, pp. 142, 147, 149; Cohen, *Broken Bonds*, pp. 233–34.

76. *FBIS-EEU* 91–214 (November 5, 1991), p. 28; 91–217 (November 8, 1991), p. 35; Rezun, *Europe and War in the Balkans*, p. 181; Glenny, *The Fall of Yugoslavia*, pp. 179–80; Woodward, *Balkan Tragedy*, pp. 153, 159, 164, 183–87, 190–91.

77. Woodward, *Balkan Tragedy*, p. 183; *NYT*, January 16, 1992.

78. Woodward, *Balkan Tragedy*, p. 176; John Newhouse, "The Diplomatic Round: Dodging the Problem in Yugoslavia," *The New Yorker*, August 24, 1992, p. 63.

79. Bennett, *Yugoslavia's Bloody Collapse*, p. 178.

80. Woodward, *Balkan Tragedy*, p. 169.

81. In December 1991, Croatia's Parliament passed a law on minority autonomy providing that in predominantly Serb areas, schools, courts, the police, and media would

be left in Serb hands once Croatia achieved formal independence. The local Serb population was not satisfied by this gesture and continued to fight for its own complete political
independence of Zagreb. See Bugajski, *Nations in Turmoil*, p. 108.

82. Ibid., p. 279.

83. Steven J. Woehrel and Julius Kim, "Yugoslavia Crisis and U.S. Policy," *CRS
Issue Brief*, IB91089 (Washington, DC: Congressional Research Service, Library of Con-
gress, 1993), p. 13; Woodward, *Balkan Tragedy*, p. 161; Bennett, *Yugoslavia's Bloody
Collapse*, p. 175; administrative officials also were concerned that the disintegration of
Yugoslavia would have a negative impact on the efforts of Gorbachev to preserve Soviet
unity threatened by an escalation of interethnic tensions throughout Soviet society. See
Cohen, *Broken Bonds*, pp. 215, 218.

84. *NYT*, September 27, November 9, December 7, 1991.

85. *FBIS-EEU* 91–236 (December 9, 1991), p. 41; *FBIS-EEU* 91–237 (December
10, 1991), p. 60.

86. "Resolution 713" (September 25, 1991), *UNSFY*, p. 104.

87. "Resolution 721, 724" (November 27, December 15, 1991, respectively), *UNSFY*
pp. 105–7.

88. *BG*, November 10, November 24, 1991; *NYT*, November 14, November 27,
1991.

89. *UNSFY*, p. 2.

90. Woodward, *Balkan Tragedy*, pp. 188–90.

91. *FBIS-EEU* 92–084 (April 30, 1992), pp. 31–32.

92. "Resolution 743" (February 21, 1992), *UNSFY*, pp. 110–11.

93. *FBIS-EEU* 92–110 (June 8, 1992), p. 46; Woodward, *Balkan Tragedy*, pp. 189–
90.

94. Bugajski, *Nations in Turmoil*, pp. 144–45.

95. Ibid., p. 145; *FBIS-EEU* 90–219 (November 13, 1990), pp. 66–67.

96. Brown, *Hopes and Shadows*, p. 26; Woodward, *Balkan Tragedy*, pp. 121–22;
Cohen, *Broken Bonds*, pp. 147–51; see also *FBIS-EEU* 90–219 (November 13, 1990), p.
22, *FBIS-EEU* 90–223 (November 19, 1990), p. 83.

97. *FBIS-EEU* 91–176 (September 11, 1991), p. 39. See also Loring Danforth, *The
Macedonian Conflict: Ethnic Nationalism in a Transnational World* (Princeton, NJ:
Princeton University Press, 1995), pp. 141–44.

98. Hayden, "Constitutional Nationalism in the Formerly Yugoslav Republics," pp.
659–60.

99. *FBIS-EEU* 91–174 (September 9, 1991), p. 45; Woodward, *Balkan Tragedy*, pp.
341–42; Bugajski, *Nations in Turmoil*, p. 135.

100. *FBIS-EEU* 91–212 (November 1, 1991), p. 27.

101. Brown, *Hopes and Shadows*, p. 182.

102. Woodward, *Balkan Tragedy*, pp. 344–45; Glenny, *The Fall of Yugoslavia*, pp.
71–72; Bennett, *Yugoslavia's Bloody Collapse*, pp. 220–21; Danforth, *The Macedonian
Conflict*, pp. 147–49.

103. Woodward, *Balkan Tragedy*, p. 358; Bennett, *Yugoslavia's Bloody Collapse*, p.
221.

104. Bennett, *Yugoslavia's Bloody Collapse*, p. 186.

105. Steven J. Woehrel, "Bosnia-Herzegovina: Background to the Conflict," *CRS
Report for Congress*, 93–106F, January 21, 1993, p. 3; Woodward, *Balkan Tragedy*. pp.
172, 181, 193, 344.

106. In the summer of 1991, allegations of secret meetings between Serb Republic
and Croatian leaders gave rise to fears in Sarajevo of a conspiracy between Tudjman and
Milošević to partition Bosnia-Herzegovina. Fear of partition increased with efforts of

local Serb communities throughout the country and especially in eastern Bosnia to establish communal autonomy in ways that suggested an eventual renunciation of Sarajevo's administrative control over them. See Bugajski, *Nations in Turmoil*, pp. 113–14.

107. Bennett, *Yugoslavia's Bloody Collapse*, pp. 186–87; Cohen, *Broken Bonds*, pp. 237, 240.

108. Cohen, *Broken Bonds*, p. 238.

109. Glenny, *The Fall of Yugoslavia*, pp. 122, 162–63.

110. It has been suggested that the West underestimated the depth of interethnic tensions and prejudices in Bosnia, ". . . accepting naively the glib media claims that the area had been an oasis of intergroup harmony for hundreds of years." Cohen, *Broken Bonds*, p. 239. For a thorough review of Bosnian political culture see Robert Donia, *Bosnia-Herzgovina: A Tradition Betrayed* (New York: Columbia University Press, 1994).

111. *FBIS-EEU* 90–227 (November 26, 1990), p. 72; Bennett, *Yugoslavia's Bloody Collapse*, p. 121.

112. *NYT*, April 20, August 15, September 5, October 13, 1991; February 9, 1992; Woodward, *Balkan Tragedy*, pp. 129–30; Bennett, *Yugoslavia's Bloody Collapse*, p. 118.

113. *NYT*, April 20, August 15, September 5, October 13, 1991; February 2, 1992.

114. Bennett, *Yugoslavia's Bloody Collapse*, p. 122.

115. Ramet, *Nationalism and Federalism in Yugoslavia*, p. 249.

116. James Gow, *Legitimacy and the Military: The Yugoslav Crisis* (New York: St. Martin's Press, 1992), p. 134.

117. Bennett, *Yugoslavia's Bloody Collapse*, pp. 119–20; see also Cohen, *Broken Bonds*, pp. 176–181.

118. *FBIS-EEU* 91–052 (March 18, 1991), p. 36.

119. *FBIS-EEU* 91–097 (May 20, 1991), p. 43; Woodward, *Balkan Tragedy*, p. 143; Bugajski, *Nations in Turmoil*, p. 104.

120. *FBIS-EEU* (May 24, 1991), p. 35.

121. Brown, *Hopes and Shadows*, pp. 253–54.

122. Milan Andrejevich, "The Yugoslav Crisis: No Solution in Sight," Legters (ed.), *Eastern Europe*, p. 576; Glenny, *The Fall of Yugoslavia*, pp. 135–37; Ramet, *Nationalism and Federalism in Yugoslavia*, p. 249; see also Cohen, *Broken Bonds*, pp. 181–83; Bugajski, *Nations in Turmoil*, p. 106–7.

123. *NYT*, November 14, December 23, 1991; January 9, 1992; Mojzes, *Yugoslavian Inferno*, p. 164.

124. Montenegran president Momir Bulatović actually called for the withdrawal of Montenegran recruits from the Croatian battlefront in the latter part of 1991. Growing dissatisfaction with subservience to Serbia reached a climax with a public demonstration in Titograd in February 1992 of 10,000 people. See Bugajski, *Nations in Turmoil*, p. 118.

125. Woodward, *Balkan Tragedy*, p. 265.

Chapter 11

1. Noel Malcolm, *Bosnia: A History* (New York: Columbia University Press, 1994), p. 217; Christopher Bennett, *Yugoslavia's Bloody Collapse: Causes, Course, and Consequences* (New York: New York University Press, 1995), p. 184.

2. See, for example, Karadžić's comments about recent visits by President Izetbegović to Sudan, Libya, and Iran, in United States Department of State, Foreign Broadcast Information Service, *Daily Report Eastern Europe* 92–077 (April 21, 1992), p. 14 (hereafter cited as *FBIS-EEU*). See also David Rieff, *Slaughterhouse: Bosnia and the Failure of the West* (New York: Simon and Schuster, 1995), pp. 73–74; Bennett, *Yugoslavia's Bloody Collapse*, p. 184.

3. Malcolm, *Bosnia: A History*, pp. 218–22; Susan L. Woodward, *Balkan Tragedy: Chaos and Dissolution after the Cold War* (Washington DC: The Brookings Institution, 1995), pp. 234–35.

4. Cvijeto Job, "Yugoslavia's Ethnic Furies," *Foreign Policy* 92 (Fall 1993): 68–69; Bennett, *Yugoslavia's Bloody Collapse*, pp. 181–82.

5. *FBIS-EEU* 92–067 (April 7, 1992), p. 40.

6. Rieff, *Slaughterhouse*, pp. 111–13; Woehrel, "Bosnia-Herzegovina," p. 7; Bennett, *Yugoslavia's Bloody Collapse*, pp. 189–91: Miron Rezun, *Europe and War in the Balkans: Toward a New Yugoslav Identity* (Westport, CT: Praeger, 1995), pp. 156, 159, 161, 163.

7. *The New York Times*, July 24, 1992 (hereafter cited as *NYT*).

8. Woodward, *Balkan Tragedy*, pp. 364–65.

9. Bennett, *Yugoslavia's Bloody Collapse*, p. 183.

10. John Newhouse, "The Diplomatic Round: Dodging the Problem in Yugoslavia," *The New Yorker*, August 24, 1992, p. 65; Rieff, *Bosnia and the Failure of the West*, pp. 81, 158; Paul Mojzes, *Yugoslavian Inferno: Ethno-Religious Warfare in the Balkans* (New York: Continuum, 1994), p. 165.

11. Woodward, *Balkan Tragedy*, p. 259.

12. *NYT*, May 8, 1992.

13. Leonard Cohen, *Broken Bonds: The Disintegration of Yugoslavia* (Boulder, CO: Westview Press, 1993), p. 241.

14. Woehrel, "Bosnia-Herzegovina: Background to the Conflict," p. 6; Woodward, *Balkan Tragedy*, p. 284; Bennett, *Yugoslavia's Bloody Collapse*, p. 199.

15. Woehrel, "Bosnia-Herzegovina: Background to the Conflict," p. 6.

16. Woodward, *Balkan Tragedy*, pp. 212, 279; Bennett, *Yugoslavia's Bloody Collapse*, pp. 199–200. It is reasonable to assume that Tudjman knew and tacitly approved of the Graz agreement. See Cohen, *Broken Bonds*, p. 241.

17. Bennett, *Yugoslavia's Bloody Collapse*, p. 201.

18. Woodward, *Balkan Tragedy*, p. 345; *NYT*, July 4, 1994; see also Victor Gomez, "Bihac Kingpin on the Stump," *Transition*, vol. 2, no. 10 (May 17, 1996), p. 2.

19. *FBIS-EEU* 93–077 (April 23, 1993), pp. 36–37; "Resolution 820" (April 17, 1993), *The United Nations and the Situation in the Former Yugoslavia*, Reference Paper, Revision 4 (Department of Information), p. 162 (hereafter cited as *UNSFY*).

20. Cohen, *Broken Bonds*, pp. 249–51.

21. *FBIS-EEU* 93–064 (April 6, 1993), pp. 24–25. See also John J. Mearsheimer and Robert A. Pape, "The Answer: A Partition Plan for Bosnia," *The New Republic*, June 14, 1993, p. 24.

22. Mearsheimer and Pape, "A Partition Plan for Bosnia," pp. 22–24.

23. *FBIS-EEU* 93–094 (May 18, 1993), p. 21; *UNSFY*, pp. 55–56.

24. *FBIS-EEU* 93–123 (June 29, 1993), pp. 52–54; Woodward, *Balkan Tragedy*, 310–11.

25. *FBIS-EEU* 93–117 (June 21, 1993), p. 26; Woodward, *Balkan Tragedy*, pp. 311–12.

26. *NYT*, September 9, 1993.

27. *UNSFY*, pp. 61–65.

28. "Resolution 824" (May 6, 1994), *UNSFY*, p. 94.

29. Steven J. Woehrel and Julie Kim, "Yugoslavia Crisis and U.S. Policy," *CRS Issue Brief* IB91089 (Washington DC: Congressional Research Service, Library of Congress, September 2, 1993), p. 9; Rieff, *Bosnia and the Failure of the West*, p. 187.

30. Steven J. Woehrel and Julie Kim, "Bosnia–Former Yugoslavia: Ongoing Conflict and U.S. Policy," *CRS Issue Brief*, IB91089, Congressional Research Service, Library of Congress, Washington, DC, January 19, 1995, p. 6.

31. Woehrel and Kim, "Yugoslavia Crisis and U.S. Policy," p. 9; Rieff, *Bosnia and the Failure of the West*, p. 173.

32. Bennett, *Yugoslavia's Bloody Collapse*, pp. 196–97; Woodward, *Balkan Tragedy*, p. 294. See also "Resolution 757" (May 30, 1992), *UNSFY*, pp. 116–20.

33. Woehrel and Kim, "Bosnia–Former Yugoslavia," p. 10; Susan L. Woodward, "Yugoslavia: Decline and Fall," *The Bulletin of the Atomic Scientists* (November 1993): 24. See also Milica Zarkovich Bookman, *Economic Decline in the Balkans* (New York: St. Martin's Press, 1994), pp. 111–14; "Resolution 757" (May 30, 1992), *UNSFY*. pp. 116–20.

34. Lawrence Freedman, "Why the West Failed," *Foreign Policy* 97 (Winter 1994–95): 61.

35. Woodward, *Balkan Tragedy*, p. 386; Bennett, *Yugoslavia's Bloody Collapse*, pp. 208–9.

36. Woodward, "Yugoslavia: Decline and Fall," pp. 26–27.

37. Mearsheimer and Pape, "A Partition Plan for Bosnia," p. 25; "Resolution 781" (October 9, 1992), *UNSFY*, pp. 135–36.

38. "Resolution 816" (March 31, 1995), *UNSFY*, pp. 152–53.

39. "Resolution 821" (April 28, 1993), *UNSFY*, pp. 161–63.

40. Woehrel and Kim, "Bosnia–Former Yugoslavia," pp. 10–11; "Resolution 779" (October 6, 1992), *UNSFY*, pp. 133–34.

41. Wochrel and Kim, "Yugoslavia Crisis and U.S. Policy," p. 9; "Resolution 808" (February 22, 1993), *UNSFY*, pp. 147–48.

42. "Resolution 827" (May 25, 1993), *UNSFY*, pp. 146–47; *NYT*, September 19, 1993.

43. *The Washington Post*, November 12, 1993 (hereafter cited as *WP*).

44. Woodward, *Balkan Tragedy*, pp. 274–75.

45. *FBIS-EEU* 92–141 (July 22, 1992), pp. 25–26.

46. *FBIS-EEU* 92–164 (August 24, 1992), p. 41; Woodward, *Balkan Tragedy*, pp. 302–3; Bennett, *Yugoslavia's Bloody Collapse*, pp. 183–84; *NYT*, August 27, 1992.

47. Woehrel and Kim, "Bosnia–Former Yugoslavia," p. 10; See also "Resolution 981" (March 31, 1995), *UNSFY*, pp. 219–22.

48. Woehrel and Kim, "Bosnia–Former Yugoslavia," pp. 10–12.

49. Ibid.; "Resolution 816" (March 31, 1993), *UNSFY*, pp. 152–53.

50. *NYT*, June 5, 1993; *The International Herald Tribune*, July 15, 1993. See also "Resolution 836" (June 19, 1993), *UNSFY*, pp. 168–70.

51. *UNSFY*, pp. 22–23.

52. *NYT*, May 25, May 27, August 31, September 6, September 8, September 11, September 15, 1995.

53. Woodward, *Balkan Tragedy*, p. 314; Sergei Sidorov, "Our Country Sends 400 Soldiers to the Sarajevo Area," *Krasnaia zvezda*, February 19, 1994, cited from *Current Digest of the Soviet Press* 46, no. 7: 4–5 (hereafter cited as *CDOSP*); *UNSFY*, pp. 23–24.

54. See Rezun, *Europe and War in the Balkans*, pp. 176–78.

55. *NYT*, August 6, 1992.

56. Woodward, *Balkan Tragedy*, p. 296.

57. *Congressional Record*, April 29, 1993: H2132.

58. *NYT*, October 8, 1992.

59. *Weekly Compilation of Presidential Documents* 28, no. 24: 1035 (hereafter cited as *WCPD*).

60. *NYT*, April 16, April 17, May 23, 1992.

61. *U.S. Department of State Despatch* 13, no. 52: 913, 914.

62. Mark Lowenthal, "Bosnia: U.S. Objectives, Military Options, Serbian Responses," *CRS Report for Congress*, 93–408S, April 14, 1993, pp. 3–5.

63. *NYT*, February 19, 1993.

64. *NYT*, March 10, 1993.

65. *NYT*, April 18, April 22, 1993; *BG*, May 2, 1993.

66. Bennett, *Yugoslavia's Bloody Collapse*, p. 203.

67. Maksim Yusin, "Russian Parliament's Resolution on Yugoslavia Pushes Moscow Toward International Isolation," *Izvestia*, February 20, 1993, cited from *CDOSP* 45, no. 8 (February 20, 1993): 17–18.

68. *WCPD* 29, no. 18: 740.

69. *NYT*, June 4, 1993.

70. *WCPD* 29, no. 8: 271, 318.

71. *NYT*, March 2, March 3, 1993.

72. Bennett, *Yugoslavia's Bloody Collapse*, pp. 225–26.

73. Woodward, *Balkan Tragedy*, pp. 314–15.

74. Woehrel and Kim, "Bosnia–Former Yugoslavia," p. 5; Bennett, *Yugoslavia's Bloody Collapse*, pp. 226–27, 230.

75. Woehrel and Kim, "Bosnia–Former Yugoslavia," p. 5.

76. Woodward, *Balkan Tragedy*, p. 392.

77. *NYT*, December 17, December 20, December 21, December 24, 1994; *WP*, December 20, December 22, 1994. See also Jim Wooten, "The Conciliator," *The New York Times Magazine*, January 29, 1995.

78. Woehrel and Kim, "Bosnia–Former Yugoslavia," p. 5.

79. Ibid.

80. See, for example, Maksim Yusin, "Serbs Deal a Cruel Blow to the Prestige of Russian Diplomacy," *CDOSP* 46, no. 16 (April 20, 1994): 1–2.

81. *NYT*, June 1, June 2, June 4, June 8, 1995.

82. *The International Herald Tribune*, August 9, 11, and 15, 1995.

83. *NYT*, September 1, September 2, 1995.

84. Bookman, *Economic Decline in the Balkans*, pp. 114–18; Cohen, *Broken Bonds*, p. 277.

85. Cohen, *Broken Bonds*, pp. 232, 277; Bennett, *Yugoslavia's Bloody Collapse*, p. 207; *NYT*, October 22, 1993.

86. Woehrel, "Bosnia-Herzegovina: Background to the Conflict," p. 6.

87. Douglas Schoen, "How Milošević Stole the Election," *The New York Times Magazine* (February 14, 1993), pp. 32, 39–40; Cohen, *Broken Bonds*, p. 278.

88. *NYT*, November 12, December 19, 1992; June 1, 1993; see also Cohen, *Broken Bonds*, p. 249.

89. Woodward, *Balkan Tragedy*, p. 356; *NYT*, October 25, 1994.

90. *NYT*, October 25, 1994.

91. J.F. Brown, *Hopes and Shadows: Eastern Europe After Communism* (Durham, NC: Duke University Press, 1994), pp. 185–88; Bennet Kovrig, "Hungarian Minorities in East Central Europe," *Occasional Paper Series: The Atlantic Council of the United States* (March 1994): 20.

92. Woodward, *Balkan Tragedy*, pp. 340–41; Bennett, *Yugoslavia's Bloody Collapse*, pp. 216–17; "Kosovo: The Quiet Siege," *Cultural Survival Quarterly* (Summer 1995): 37–39; *NYT*, June 23, 1992; May 30, 1993.

93. Brown, *Hopes and Shadows*, p. 257; Bennett, *Yugoslavia's Bloody Collapse*, pp. 220–21.

94. Bennett, *Yugoslavia's Bloody Collapse*, p. 185; *BG*, August 1, 1993.

95. "The Serbs' Next Target?" *The Economist*, May 29, 1993, p. 54.

96. Bennett, *Yugoslavia's Bloody Collapse*, p. 217.

97. Ibid.; Newhouse, "Dodging the Problem in Yugoslavia," p. 68; *NYT*, October 10, 1993.

98. Bennett, *Yugoslavia's Bloody Collapse*, p. 213; *BG* (August 13, 1993); *NYT* (October 20, 1993); see also Stan Markotich, "Tensions Rise over Montenegro's Moves," *Transition*, vol. 2, no. 15 (July 26, 1996), pp. 59–61.

99. See Fabian Schmidt, "Sandzak Muslims Pin Hopes on Elections," *Transition*, vol. 2, no. 14 (July 12, 1996), pp. 39, 71.

100. Bennett, *Yugoslavia's Bloody Collapse*, pp. 212–13.

101. *NYT*, September 17, September 21, 1995.

102. *BG*, August 21, October 16, November 1, 1994; *NYT*, September 4, October 31, 1994. See also James Pettifer, "Macedonia: Still the Apple of Discord," *The World Today*, vol. 51, no. 3 (March 1995), pp. 56–57.

103. Woodward, *Balkan Tragedy*, pp. 341, 357–58; see also Bugajski, *Nations in Turmoil*, p. 134.

104. *NYT*, March 4, 1995; Bugajski, *Nations in Turmoil*, pp. 134–35; Dusko Doder, "Albania Language University in Macedonia Is Facing Serious Ethnic Tensions," *The Chronicle of Higher Education* (February 24, 1995), p. A43; Pettifer, "Macedonia," pp. 56–57; Hall, *Albania and the Albanians*, p. 211; Bugajski, *Nations in Turmoil*, pp. 134–35.

105. Woodward, *Balkan Tragedy*, pp. 337–41.

106. Ibid., p. 342.

107. Pettifer, "Macedonia," p. 56.

108. In April 1996, Yugoslavia and Macedonia signed a mutual recognition agreement in which both pledged respect for the principles of equality, noninterference in internal affairs, sovereignty, independence, and territorial integrity. Whether the Serb Republic will live with this agreement and refrain from influence building in Macedonia remains to be seen. For the moment at least, Serbia seems ready to strengthen ties, especially in the economic sphere, with Macedonia on the basis of equality. See Stefan Krause and Stan Markotich, "Rump Yugoslavia and Macedonia Deal the Cards of Mutual Recognition," *Transition*, vol. 2, no. 11 (May 31, 1996), pp. 54–57.

109. Pettifer, "Macedonia, p. 56; Bennett, *Yugoslavia's Bloody Collapse*, p. 219.

110. Woodward, *Balkan Tragedy*, pp. 354–55; *The International Herald Tribune*, June 21, 1993.

111. Woodward, *Balkan Tragedy*, p. 387.

112. Woehrel and Kim, "Bosnia–Former Yugoslavia," p. 2; *UNSFY*, p. 40.

113. Woehrel and Kim, "Bosnia–Former Yugoslavia," p. 2.

114. Woodward, *Balkan Tragedy*, p. 346.

115. *UNSFY*, p. 41.

116. *NYT*, November 22, 23, December 15, 1995; for an analysis of the provisions of the Dayton Agreement, see Susan Woodward, "The United States Leads, Europe Pays," *Transition*, vol. 2, no. 14 (July 12, 1996), pp. 14–15.

117. *NYT*, November 22, 23, December 15, 1995.

118. Ibid.

119. Ibid.

120. Ibid.

121. *NYT*, February 17, 1996.

122. *NYT*, December 10, 1995, March 2, 1996; see also Tom Warner, "Bosnia Balances the West and Middle East," *Transition*, vol. 2, no. 7 (April 5, 1996), pp. 61–62; *BG* (March 27, 1996).

123. Patrick Moore, "The Chess Player Peace," *Transition*, vol. 2, no. 14 (July 12, 1996), pp. 7–8.

124. *NYT*, January 12, February 3, 21, 15, March 11, 12, 17, May 28, 1996; *BG*, January 25, May 30, 1996.

125. *NYT*, January 7, 1996; *IHT*, February 17–18, 1996; for a discussion of the sources of interethnic conflict in Mostar see Daria Sito Sucic, "The Disunited Colors of Mostar," *Transition*, vol. 2, no. 14 (July 12, 1996), pp. 42–44, 47.

126. *NYT*, February 13, March 20, 1996.

127. *BG*, March 5, 1996.

128. See Marinko Culic, "Herzegovinian Croats Steer Croatian Politics," *Transition*, vol. 2, no. 14 (July 12, 1996), p. 32.

129. *NYT*, April 1, 1996; *BG*, April 1, 1996.

130. *NYT*, January 4, 1996; see also Ana Trisic-Babic, "Changes Brewing in Bosnian Serb Politics," *Transition*, vol. 2, no. 14 (July 12, 1996), pp. 33–34.

131. *NYT*, February 4, 1996.

132. *NYT*, May 5, 1996.

133. *IHT*, February 15, 1996.

134. *BG*, March 8, 1996; Stan Markotich, "Belgrade Unwilling to Arrest War Criminals," *Transition*, vol. 2, no. 14 (July 12, 1996), pp. 35–36.

135. *NYT*, January 28, 1996; additional procedural problems are discussed in Minna Shrag, "Assessing the War Crimes Trials," *Transition*, vol. 2, no. 14 (July 12, 1996), pp. 51–53.

136. *NYT*, February 1, 1996.

137. *NYT*, November 22, December 19, 1995.

138. Victor Gomez, "Smearing the Opposition," *Transition*, vol. 2, no. 9 (May 3, 1996), p. 2; Tom Warner, "A Plea to Support a Democratic Serbia," ibid., p. 62; Eva Rybkova, "Shutting Out Criticism in Serbia," ibid., 14 (July 12, 1996), p. 69.

139. *NYT*, March 4, 1996; *BG*, March 19, 1996.

140. *NYT*, March 11, 1996; see also Fabian Schmidt, "Teaching the Wrong Lesson in Kosovo," *Transition*, vol. 2, no. 14 (July 12, 1996), pp. 37–39.

141. Karl W. Ryavec, "Slovenia: The Origins of Independence and an Outline of the Present Situation," unpublished paper presented at a meeting of an international faculty seminar at Wesleyan University, April 23, 1994, pp. 7, 10–14; Karl Ryavec, "Recent Developments in Slovenia," unpublished paper presented at the annual meeting of the New England Slavic Association, Providence College, Providence, RI, April 3, 1993, pp. 8–9, 12; Evan Kraft, Milan Modovipec, and Milan Cvikl, "On Its Own: The Economy of Independent Slovenia," in *Independent Slovenia: Origins, Movements, Prospects*, ed. Jill Benderly and Evan Kraft (New York: St. Martin's Press, 1994), pp. 207–13; Bennett, *Yugoslavia's Bloody Collapse*, p. 234.

142. Ryavec, "Slovenia: The Origins of Independence," pp. 7, 10–14; Ryavec, "Recent Developments in Slovenia," pp. 8–9, 12. The first parliamentary elections since December 1992 were scheduled for December 1996. In the interim, Slovene democracy flourished by comparison with other parliamentary governments elsewhere in the former Yugoslavia that were experiencing authoritarian tendencies. There was, however, some instability at the top where cabinets had to rely on coalitions in the Parliament. These coalitions tended to be somewhat conflict-ridden as a result of interparty bickering that became especially pronounced in 1996, as the date of elections approached. The two governing parties, the Liberal Democrats and Christian Democrats, were posturing throughout the year to establish their separate identities, each hoping to gain the majority needed to govern without the other. See Stan Markotich, "An Unstable Government Faces an Election Year," *Transition*, vol. 2, no. 12 (June 14, 1996), pp. 54–56; Cohen, *Broken Bonds*, pp. 275–76.

Bibliography

Newspapers

The Boston Globe.
The Boston Sunday Globe.
The Christian Science Monitor.
Current Digest of the Soviet Press.
The Financial Times.
The International Herald Tribune.
The London Times.
The New Republic.
The New York Times.
The Prague Post.
The Washington Post.
USA Today.

Documents

Congressional Record.
Support for East European Democracy (SEED) Act of 1989. United States Code, "Public Law 101–179 (HR 3402, November 28, 1989, 101st Congress, First Session). St. Paul, MN: West Publishing Co., 1989. Vol. 1, 103 stat. pp. 1298–1307.
The United Nations and the Situation in the Former Yugoslavia (UNSFY). Reference Paper, Revision 4. Department of Public Information.
United States Department of State, Foreign Broadcast Information Service. *Daily Report Eastern Europe (FBIS-EEU).*
United States Department of State, Foreign Broadcast Information Service. *Daily Report Soviet Union (FBIS-SOV).*
U.S. Department of State Despatch 13, no. 52: 913, 914.
Weekly Compilation of Presidential Documents (WCPD).

Monographs, Biographies, and Edited Studies

Adam, Jan. *Why Did Socialism Collapse in Central and Eastern Europe? The Case of Poland, Hungary, and Czechoslovakia* (New York: St. Martin's Press, 1995).

453

Asmus, Ronald D.; Brown, J.F.; and Crane, Keith. *Soviet Foreign Policy and Revolutions in Eastern Europe*. Santa Monica, CA: RAND, 1991.

The Atlantic Council of the United States (ACUS). "Post–Cold War Communists in Central and Eastern Europe: The Challenges to Reform. Seminar Report and Policy Recommendations." Washington, DC: ACUS, 1993.

Banac, Ivo, ed. *Eastern Europe in Revolution*. Ithaca, NY: Cornell University Press, 1992.

Batt, Judy. *East Central Europe: From Reform to Transformation*. New York: Council on Foreign Relations Press, 1991.

Benderly, Jill, and Kraft, Evan, eds. *Independent Slovenia: Origins, Movements, Prospects*. New York: St. Martin's Press, 1994.

Bennett, Christopher. *Yugoslavia's Bloody Collapse: Causes, Course, and Consequences*. New York: New York University Press, 1995.

Berglund, Sten, and Dellenbrant, Jan Ake, eds. *The New Democracies of Eastern Europe: Party Systems and Political Cleavages*. 2nd ed. Brookfield, VT: Edward Elgar, 1994.

Beschloss, Michael R., and Talbott, Strobe. *At the Highest Levels: The Inside Story of the End of the Cold War*. Boston: Little, Brown, 1993.

Bookman, Milica Zarkovich. *Economic Decline in the Balkans*. New York: St. Martin's Press, 1994.

Bozoki, Andras; Korosenyi, Andras; and Schopflin, George, eds. *Post-Communist Transition: Emerging Pluralism in Hungary*. London: Pinter, 1992.

Braun, Aurel. *Romanian Foreign Policy Since 1965: The Political and Military Limits of Autonomy*. New York: Praeger, 1978.

Brown, James F. *Eastern Europe and Communist Rule*. Durham, NC: Duke University Press, 1988.

———. *Hopes and Shadows: Eastern Europe after Communism*. Durham, NC: Duke University Press, 1994.

Brzezinski, Zbigniew. *The Soviet Bloc: Unity and Conflict*. Revised and enlarged. Cambridge, MA: Harvard University Press, 1971.

———. *The Grand Failure: The Birth and Death of Communism in the Twentieth Century*. New York: Scribners, 1989.

Bugajski, Janusz. *Nations in Turmoil: Conflict and Cooperation in Eastern Europe*. Boulder, CO: Westview Press, 1993.

———. *Ethnic Politics in Eastern Europe: A Guide to Nationality Policies, Organizations, and Parties*. Armonk, NY: M.E. Sharpe, 1994.

Cohen, Leonard. *Broken Bonds: The Disintegration of Yugoslavia* 2nd ed. Boulder, CO: Westview Press, 1995.

Danforth, Loring. *The Macedonian Conflict: Ethnic Nationalism in a Transnational World*. Princeton, NJ: Princeton University Press, 1995.

Dawisha, Karen. *East Europe, Gorbachev, and Reform*. Cambridge, MA: Cambridge University Press, 1988.

Dean, Robert. *Nationalism and Political Change in Eastern Europe: The Slovak Question and the Czechoslovak Reform Movement*. Denver, CO: University of Denver Press, 1973.

Denitch, Bogdan. *Ethnic Nationalism: The Tragic Death of Yugoslavia*. Minneapolis: University of Minnesota Press, 1994.

Donia, Robert J. *Bosnia-Herzegovina: A Tradition Betrayed*. New York: Columbia University Press, 1994.

Dragnich, Alex. *Serbs and Croats: The Struggle in Yugoslavia*. New York: Harcourt Brace Jovanovich, 1992.

Fischer-Galati, Stephen. *The New Rumania: From People's Democracy to Socialist Republic*. Cambridge, MA: MIT Press, 1967.

Floyd, David. *Rumania: Russia's Dissident Ally*. New York: Praeger, 1965.

Funk, Nanette, and Mueller, Magda, eds. *Gender Politics and Post-Communism: Reflections from Eastern Europe and the Former Soviet Union*. New York: Routledge, 1993.

Gallagher, Tom. *Romania After Ceausescu*. Edinburgh: Edinburgh University Press, 1995.

Garber, Larry, and Bjornlund, Eric, eds. *The New Democratic Frontier: A Country by Country Report on Elections in Central and Eastern Europe*. Washington, DC: National Democratic Institute for International Affairs, 1992.

Gati, Charles. *The Bloc That Failed*. Bloomington: Indiana University Press, 1990.

Gedmin, Jeffrey. *The Hidden Hand: Gorbachev and the Collapse of East Germany*. Washington, DC: American Enterprise Institute Press, 1992.

Gilberg, Trond. *Nationalism and Communism in Romania: The Rise and Fall of Ceauşescu's Personal Dictatorship*. Boulder, CO: Westview Press, 1990.

Glenny, Misha. *The Fall of Yugoslavia: The Third Balkan War*. New York: Penguin, 1992.

Goldfarb, Jeffrey. *After the Fall: The Pursuit of Democracy in Central Europe*. New York: Basic Books, 1992.

Goldman, Marshall. *Gorbachev's Challenge: Economic Reform in the Age of High Technology*. New York: Norton, 1987.

Gorbachev, Mikhail. *Perestroika: New Thinking for Our Country and the World*. New York: Harper and Row, 1987.

Gow, James. *Legitimacy and the Military: The Yugoslav Crisis*. New York: St. Martin's Press, 1992.

Griffith, William E., ed. *Central and Eastern Europe: The Opening Curtain?* Boulder, CO: Westview Press, 1989.

Gurr, Ted Robert, ed. *Minorities at Risk: A Global View of Ethnopolitical Conflicts*. Washington, DC: United States Institute of Peace Press, 1993.

Haglund, David; McFarlane, S. Neil; and Sokolsy, Joel J. *NATO's Eastern Dilemma*. Boulder, CO: Westview Press, 1994.

Hall, Derek. *Albania and the Albanians*. New York: St. Martin's Press, 1994.

Held, Joseph, ed. *Democracy and Right-Wing Politics in Eastern Europe in the 1990s*. New York: Columbia University Press, 1993.

Holmes, Leslie. *The End of Communist Power: Anti-Corruption Campaigns and Legitimation Crises*. New York: Oxford University Press, 1993.

Ionescu, Ghita. *Communism in Rumania 1944–1962*. London: Oxford University Press, 1964.

———. *The Politics of the European Communist States*. New York: Praeger, 1967.

Jancar-Webster, Barbara, ed. *Environmental Action in Eastern Europe: Responses to Crisis*. Armonk, NY: M.E. Sharpe, 1993.

Kirk, Roger, and Raceanu, Mircea. *Romania Versus the United States: Diplomacy of the Absurd 1985–1989*. New York: St. Martin's Press, 1994.

Kirschbaum, Stanislav J. *A History of Slovakia: The Struggle for Survival*. New York: St. Martin's Press, 1995.

Kun, Joseph. *Hungarian Foreign Policy: The Experience of a New Democracy*. Westport, CT: Praeger, 1993.

Kurski, Jaroslav. *Lech Walesa: Democrat or Dictator*. Boulder, CO: Westview Press, 1993.

Larabee, Stephen. *East European Security After the Cold War*. Santa Monica, CA: RAND, 1993).

Latawski, Paul, ed. *Contemporary Nationalism in East-Central Europe*. New York: St. Martin's Press, 1995.

Leff, Carol Skalnik. *National Conflict in Czechoslovakia: The Making and Remaking of a State, 1918–1987*. Princeton: Princeton University Press, 1988.

Legters, Lyman H., ed. *Eastern Europe: Transformation and Revolution 1945–1991*. Lexington, MA: D.C. Heath, 1992.

Lynch, Allen. *Gorbachev's International Outlook: Intellectual Origins and Political Consequences.* New York: Institute for East-West Studies, 1989.

Magas, Branko. *The Destruction of Yugoslavia: Tracking the Breakup 1980–1982.* New York: Verso Publishing Company, 1993.

Malcolm, Noel. *Bosnia: A History.* New York: New York University Press, 1994.

Mansur, Roger. *Failed Transitions: The Eastern European Economy and Environment Since the Fall of Communism.* New York: The Free Press, 1993.

Mastny, Vojtec, ed. *Soviet/East European Survey 1987–1988.* Boulder, CO: Westview Press, 1989.

Millard, Frances. *The Anatomy of the New Poland: Post-Communist Policy in Its First Phase.* Brookfield, VT: Edward Elgar, 1994.

Mojzes, Paul. *Yugoslavian Inferno: Ethno-Religious Warfare in the Balkans.* New York: Continuum, 1994.

Nelson, Dan N., ed. *Romania After Tyranny.* Boulder, CO: Westview Press, 1992.

Nissan, Oren. *Revolution Administered.* Baltimore: Johns Hopkins Press, 1973.

Prust, Jim. *The Czech and Slovak Federal Republic: An Economy in Transition.* Washington, DC: The International Monetary Fund, 1994.

Rady, Martyn C. *Romania in Turmoil; A Contemporary History.* London: I.B. Taurus, 1992.

Ramet, Sabrina P. *Balkan Babel: Politics, Culture and Religion in Yugoslavia.* Boulder, CO: Westview Press, 1992.

———. *Nationalism and Federalism in Yugoslavia 1962–1991.* Bloomington: Indiana University Press, 1994.

Ratesh, Nestor. *Romania: The Entangled Revolution.* New York: Praeger, 1991.

Remington, Thomas F., ed. *Parliaments in Transition: The New Legislative Politics in the Former USSR and Eastern Europe.* Boulder, CO: Westview Press, 1994.

Rezun, Miron. *Europe and War in the Balkins: Toward a New Yugoslav Identity.* Boulder, CO: Westview Press, 1995.

Rieff, David. *Slaughterhouse: Bosnia and the Failure of the West.* New York: Simon and Schuster, 1995.

Roskin, Michael G. *The Rebirth of Eastern Europe.* 2nd ed. Englewood Cliffs, NJ: Prentice Hall, 1994.

Rueschemeyer, Marilyn, ed. *Women in the Politics of Postcommunist Eastern Europe.* Armonk, NY: M.E. Sharpe, 1994.

Ryavec, Karl W. *United States–Soviet Relations.* New York: Longman, 1989.

Sanford, George, ed. *Democratization in Poland, 1989–1990: Polish Voices.* New York: St. Martin's Press, 1992.

Sekelj, Laslo. *Yugoslavia: The Process of Disintegration.* New York: Columbia University Press, 1993.

Simmons, Thomas W. *Eastern Europe in the Postwar World.* 2nd ed. New York: St. Martin's Press, 1993.

Skilling, H. Gordon. *Czechoslovakia's Interrupted Revolution.* Princeton, NJ: Princeton University Press, 1976.

Staar, Richard F., ed. *The Transition to Democracy in Poland.* New York: St. Martin's Press, 1993.

Stokes, Gale. *The Walls Came Tumbling Down: The Collapse of Communism in Eastern Europe.* New York: Oxford University Press, 1993.

Szulc, Tad. *Czechoslovakia Since World War II.* New York: Grosset and Dunlap, 1971.

Terry, Sarah M., ed. *Soviet Policy in Eastern Europe.* New Haven: Yale University Press, 1984.

Thompson, Kenneth W., ed. *Poland in a World of Change.* Washington, DC: University Press of America, 1992.

Valenta, Jiri. *Soviet Intervention in Czechoslovakia, 1968: Anatomy of a Decision.* Baltimore: Johns Hopkins University Press, 1979.

Volgyes, Ivan. *Politics in Eastern Europe.* Chicago: The Dorsey Press, 1986.

Volten, Peter, ed. *Uncertain Futures: Eastern Europe and Democracy.* New York: Institute for East-West Security Studies, 1990.

Weschler, Lawrence. *The Passion of Poland.* New York: Pantheon Books, 1982.

Wesson, Robert. *The Aging of Communism.* New York: Praeger, 1980.

Wheaton, Bernard K., and Kavan, Zdenek. *The Velvet Revolution 1988–1991.* Boulder, CO: Westview Press, 1992.

White, Stephen; Batt, Judy; and Lewis, Paul G., eds. *Developments in East European Politics.* Durham, NC: Duke University Press, 1994.

Wolchik, Sharon. *Czechoslovakia in Transition: Politics, Economics and Society.* London: Pinter, 1990.

Woodward, Susan L. *Balkan Tragedy: Chaos and Dissolution After the Cold War.* Washington, DC: Brookings Institution, 1995.

Yearbook on International Communist Affairs (YICA). Stanford, CA: Hoover Institution Press, 1988–92.

Chapters in Books, Periodicals, and Reports

Agocs, Sandor. "Collapse of Communist Ideology in Hungary—November 1988 to February 1989." *East European Quarterly* 27, no. 2 (June 1993): 187–218.

Andorka, Rudolf. "Hungary: Disenchantment After Transition." *The World Today,* vol. 12, no. 12 (December 1994): 233–37.

Andrejevich, Milan."The Yugoslav Crisis: No Solution in Sight." In *Eastern Europe: Transformation and Revolution 1945–1991,* ed. Legters, pp. 566–78.

Angresano, James. "Political and Economic Obstacles Inhibiting Comprehensive Reform in Hungary." *East European Quarterly* 26, no. 1 (March 1992): 55–76.

Atwood, J. Brian. "Reflections on the Transition in Eastern and Central Europe." In *The New Democratic Frontier: A Country by Country Report on Elections in Central and Eastern Europe,* ed. Garber and Bjorlund, pp. 221–35.

Austin, Robert. "Albanian-Greek Relations: The Confrontation Continues." *Radio Free Europe/Radio Liberty Research Report* 2, no. 33 (August 20, 1993): 32–34.

Babiuch, Jolanta. "Church and Society in Post-Communist Eastern Europe." *The World Today,* vol. 50, no. 11 (November 1994): 211–15.

Banac, Ivo. "Post-Communism as Post-Yugoslavism: The Yugoslav Non-Revolutions of 1989–1990." In *Eastern Europe in Revolution,* ed. Banac, pp. 168–87.

Bankowicz, Marek. "Bulgaria: The Continuing Revolution." In *The New Democracies of Eastern Europe: Party Systems and Political Cleavages,* ed. Berglund and Dellenbrant, pp. 219–37.

———. "Czechoslovakia: From Masaryk to Havel." In *The New Democracies of Eastern Europe,* ed. Berglund and Dellenbrant, pp. 136–59.

Barany, Zoltan D. "East European Armed Forces in Transition and Beyond." *East European Quarterly* 26, no. 1 (March 1992): 1–30.

———. "Living on the Edge: The East European Roma in Post-Communist Politics and Society." *Slavic Review* 53, no. 2 (Summer 1994): 321–44.

———. "The Hungarian Democratic Forum Wins National Elections Decisively." In *Eastern Europe: Transformation and Revolution 1945–1991,* ed. Legters, pp. 450–53.

Basom, Kenneth E. "Prospects for Democracy in Serbia and Croatia," *East European Quarterly,* vol. 29, no. 4 (Winter 1995), pp. 509–28.

Batt, Judy. "The Politics of Economic Transition." In *Developments in East European Politics,* ed. White, Batt, and Lewis, pp. 205–24.

Baylis, Thomas A. "East Germany's Economic Model." *Current History* (November 1987): 377–81, 393–94.

Bayreuther, Ursula, and Gummick, Andreas. "Romania: Economic Reform Still Walking the Tightrope." *Focus: Eastern Europe* (Deutscher Bank Research, Frankfurt am Main), no. 81 (June 17, 1993).

Bell, John D. "Post-Communist Bulgaria." In *Eastern Europe: Transformation and Revolution 1945–1991*, ed. Legters, pp. 488–97.

———. "Bulgaria." In *Developments in East European Politics*, ed. White, Batt, and Lewis, pp. 83–97.

Berend, Ivan. "*Jobbra At* [Right Face]: Right-Wing Trends in Post-Communist Hungary." In *Democracy and Right-Wing Politics in Eastern Europe in the 1990s*, ed. Held, pp. 105–34.

Berglund, Sten. "The Breakdown of the German Democratic Republic." In *The New Democracies of Eastern Europe: Party Systems and Political Cleavages*, ed. Berglund and Dellenbrant, pp. 107–33.

Berner, Wolfgang, and Griffith, William E. "West German Policy Toward Central and Eastern Europe." In *Central and Eastern Europe: The Opening Curtain?* ed. Griffith, pp. 338–52.

Bertschi, C. Charles. "Lustration and the Transition to Democracy: The Cases of Poland and Bulgaria." *East European Quarterly* 28, no. 4 (Winter 1994): 435–51.

Bialer, Seweryn. "Perestroika and the Future of the Cold War." In *Central and Eastern Europe: The Opening Curtain?* ed. Griffith, pp. 401–38.

Biberaj, Elez. "Albania: The Last Domino." In *Eastern Europe in Revolution*, ed. Banac, pp. 188–206.

———. "Albania at the Crossroads." *Problems of Communism*, vol. 40, no. 5 (September–October 1991): 1–16.

———. "Albania." In *Democracy and Right-Wing Politics in Eastern Europe in the 1990s*, ed. Held, pp. 203–22.

———. "Albania's Road to Democracy." *Current History* (November 1993): 382–85.

Bigler, Robert M. "From Communism to Democracy: Hungary's Transition Thirty-Five Years After the Revolution." *East European Quarterly* 25, no. 4 (January 1992): 437–61.

Bigler, Robert M. "Back in Europe and Adjusting to the New Realities of the 1990s in Hungary," *East European Quarterly*, vol. 30, no. 2 (Summer 1996), pp. 205–34.

Bisschop, Gita. "Optimism Wanes for a Prompt Cleanup," *Transition*, vol. 2, no. 10 (May 17, 1996), pp. 42–45.

———. "Unhealthful Water and Air in the Visegrád Countries," *Transition*, vol. 2, no. 12 (June 14, 1996), pp. 39–41.

Bjork, James. "The Use of Conditionality: Poland and the IMF." *East European Quarterly* 29, no. 1 (Spring 1995): 89–120.

Bowers, Stephen R. "The East European Revolution." *East European Quarterly* 24, no. 2 (Summer 1991): 129–43.

Brockmann, Stephen. "Living Where the Wall Was: What Still Divides the Germans." *Commonweal*, September 24, 1993, pp. 16–19.

Bruner, Rick E. "Albania: Balkan Time Bomb." *The World and I* (February 1995): 64–69.

Bruszt, Laszlo, and Stark, David. "Remaking the Political Field in Hungary: From the Politics of Confrontation to the Politics of Competition." In *Eastern Europe in Revolution*, ed. Banac, pp. 13–55.

Bugajski, Janusz, and Pollack, Maxine. "East European Dissent: Impasses and Opportunities." *Problems of Communism*, vol. 37, no. 2 (March–April 1988): 59–67.

"Bulgaria and Romania: No End of Trouble." *The Economist*, September 1, 1990, pp. 44–45.

Burant, Stephen R. "Polish-Lithuanian Relations." *Problems of Communism*, vol. 40, no. 3 (May–June 1991): 67–84.

Burg, Steven L. "Nationalism Redux: Through the Glass of the Post-Communist States Darkly." *Current History* (April 1993): 162–66.

"Business in Eastern Europe." *The Economist*, September 21, 1991, pp. 18–19.

Calinescu, Matei, and Tismaneanu, Vladimir. "The 1989 Revolution and Romania's Future." *Problems of Communism*, vol. 40, no. 2 (January–April 1991): 42–59.

Carey, Henry F. "Irregularities or Rigging." *East European Quarterly* 29, no. 1 (Spring 1995): 43–66.

Carnahan, Robin, and Corley, Judith. "Czechoslovakia: June 8 and 9, 1990." In *The New Democratic Frontier: A Country by Country Report on Elections in Central and Eastern Europe*, ed. Garber and Bjorlund, pp. 112–34.

Carothers, Thomas. "Romania: May 20, 1990." In *The New Democratic Frontier: A Country by Country Report on Elections in Central and Eastern Europe*, ed. Garber and Bjorlund, pp. 75–94.

Caskie, Susan. "(Romania) Pushing Toward NATO as Russia Grumbles," *Transition*, vol. 2, no. 18 (April 19, 1996), p. 62.

Connor, Walter D. "Dissent in Eastern Europe: A New Coalition?" *Problems of Communism* 19 (January–February 1980): 1–17.

Corrin, Chris. "People and Politics." In *Developments in East European Politics*, ed. White, Batt, and Lewis, pp. 186–204.

Corzine, Robert, and March, Virginia. "Feet Drag on Road to Market: Change Goes Against Grain for Many in Government." *The Financial Times*, July 27, 1993.

Crowther, William. "Romania and Moldavian Political Dynamics." In *Romania After Tyranny*, ed. Nelson, pp. 239–60.

Čulić, Marinko. "Herzegovinian Croats Steer Croatian Politics," *Transition*, vol. 2, no. 14 (July 26, 1996), pp. 31–32.

Dahrendorf, Ralf. "Road to Freedom: Democratization and Its Problems in East-Central Europe." In *Uncertain Futures: Eastern Europe and Democracy*, ed. Volten, pp. 5–18.

Darbellay, Alina. "Farmers and Entrepreneurs in Poland and the Czech Republic," *Transition*, vol. 2, no. 15 (July 26, 1996), pp. 26–28.

Davis, Joe C. "The Splintering of the Hungarian Labor Movement." *East European Quarterly* 29, no. 3 (Fall 1995): 371–88.

Davy, Richard. "Eastern Europe III: Pragmatism in Bulgaria." *The World Today*, vol. 10, no. 5 (May 1, 1992), pp. 85–87.

Dawisha, Karen, and Valdez, Jonathan. "Socialist Internationalism in Eastern Europe." *Problems of Communism* (March–April 1987): 1–14.

Deacon, Bob. "Social Change, Social Problems, and Social Policy." In *Developments in East European Politics*, ed. White, Batt, and Lewis, pp. 225–39.

Dellenbrandt, Jan Ake. "Parties and Party Systems in Eastern Europe." In *Developments in East European Politics*, ed. White, Batt, and Lewis, pp. 147–62.

———. "Romania: The Slow Revolution." In *The New Democracies in Eastern Europe: Party Systems and Political Cleavages*, ed. Berglund and Dellenbrant, pp. 203–18.

Di Palma, Giuseppe. "Eastern Europe After Leninism: Democracy Can Work." *Current*, June 1, 1991, pp. 34–39.

Djilas, Aleksa. "A Profile of Slobodan Milošević." *Foreign Affairs* 72, no. 3 (Summer 1993): 81–96.

Doder, Dusko. "Yugoslavia: New War, Old Hatreds." *Foreign Policy* 91 (Summer 1993): 3–23.

————. "Albania Language University in Macedonia Facing Serious Ethnic Tensions." *The Chronicle of Higher Education*, February 24, 1995, p. A43.

Donovan, Barbara. "East German State Debates Church Policy." In *Soviet/East European Survey 1987–1988*, ed. Mastny, pp. 200–205.

————. "Benefits to the GDR from the FRG." In *Soviet/East European Survey 1987–1988*, ed. Mastny, pp. 318–22.

————. "East Germany in 1989." In *Eastern Europe: Transformation and Revolution 1945–1991*, ed. Legters, pp. 411–16.

"Eastern Europe: The Old World's New World." *The Economist*, March 13, 1993, pp. 4, 14.

Echikson, William. "Bloc-Buster." In *Eastern Europe: Transformation and Revolution 1945–1991*, ed. Legters, pp. 427–34.

Engelberg, Stephen. "Carving out a Greater Serbia." *The New York Times Magazine*, September 1, 1991, p. 20.

————. "Her Year of Living Dangerously." *The New York Times Magazine*, September 12, 1993, p. 38.

Eyal, Jonathan. "Transylvania Discord." *The World Today*, vol. 44, nos. 8–9 (August–September 1988): 130–32.

Fallenbuchl, Zbigniew M. "Poland: the Case for Cautious Optimism." *The World Today*, vol. 50, no. 11 (November 1991): 185–89.

Ferfila, Bagomil. "Yugoslavia: Confederation or Disintegration." *Problems of Communism*, vol. 40, no. 4 (July–August 1991): 18–30.

Fischer, Mary Ellen. "The New Leaders and the Opposition." In *Romania After Tyranny*, ed. Nelson, pp. 45–66.

Fischer, Mary Ellen, and Harsanyi, Doina Pasca. "Women in Romania." In *Women in the Politics of Post-Communist Eastern Europe*, ed. Rueschemeyer, pp. 201–23.

Fischer-Galati, Stephen. "The Political Right in Eastern Europe in Historical Perspective." In *Democracy and Right-Wing Politics in Eastern Europe in the 1990s*, ed. Held, pp. 1–12.

Fodor, Eva, and Szelebyi, Ivan. "Left Turn in Post-Communist Politics—The Case of Hungarian Elections 1990 and 1994." Working Papers Series No. 6. Advance Study Center, International Institute, University of Michigan, 1994–95, pp. 10–14, 21–22, 28–29, 31.

————. "The Political Woman: Women in Politics in Hungary." In *Women in the Politics of Post-Communist Eastern Europe*, ed. Rueschemeyer, pp. 171–99.

Fralon, Jose-Alon. "Bulgarians See Glimpses of Better Days to Come." *The Guardian Weekly*, April 7, 1991. Cited from *Eastern Europe: Transformation and Revolution 1945–1991*, ed. Legters, pp. 521–23.

Frankland, Erich G. "Green Revolutions? The Role of Green Parties in Eastern Europe's Transition, 1989–1994." *East European Quarterly* 29, no. 3 (Fall 1995): 315–45.

Freedman, Lawrence. "Why the West Failed." *Foreign Policy* 97 (Winter 1994–95): 53–69.

French, Hillary. "East Europe's Clean Break with the Past." *World Watch* (March–April 1991): 21–27.

Fric, Pavol. "Slovakia on Its Way Toward Another Misunderstanding?" *Sisyphus* 8, no. 2 (1992): 115–20.

Funk, Nanette, and Mueller, Magda. "Abortion and German Unification," *Journal of Women's History*, vol. 5, no. 3 (Winter 1994), pp. 194–206.

Garber, Larry. "Bulgaria: June 10, 1990." In *The New Democratic Frontier: A Country by Country Report on Elections in Central and Eastern Europe*, ed. Garber and Bjorlund, pp. 135–60.

Garlicki, Leszek. "The Development of the Presidency in Poland: Wrong Institutions or Wrong Persons?" In *Poland in a World of Change*, ed. Thompson, pp. 67, 83–86.

Garton Ash, Timothy. "Budapest: The Last Funeral." In *Eastern Europe: Transformation and Revolution 1945–1991*, ed. Legters, pp. 435–43.

Gati, Charles. "Gorbachev and Eastern Europe." *Foreign Affairs* 65, no. 5 (Summer 1987): 958–75.

Gebethner, Stanislaw. "Political Reform in the Process of Roundtable Negotiations." In *Democratization in Poland, 1989–1990: Polish Voices*, ed. Sanford, pp. 50–68.

Gedmin, Jeffrey. "Comrade Slobo." *The American Spectator* (April 1993): 28–33.

Geran-Pilon, Juliana. "Post-Communist Nationalism: The Case of Romania." *The World and I* (February 1992): 111–14.

Gilberg, Trond. "Romanians and Democratic Values: Socialization After Communism." In *Romania After Tyranny*, ed. Nelson, pp. 83–94.

Gomez, Victor. "Bihac Kingpin (Firket Abdic) on the Stump," *Transition*, vol. 2, no. 10 (May 17, 1996), pp. 54–56.

———. "Close, But Not That Close (to Russia)," *Transition*, vol. 2, no. 9 (May 3, 1996), p. 3.

———. "Local Victories for the Romanian Opposition," *Transition*, vol. 2, no. 14 (July 12, 1996), p. 2.

———. "Shady Dealings in Campaign Finance (in the Czech Republic)," *Transition*, vol. 2, no. 12 (June 14, 1996), p. 3.

———. " 'Sorry' Seems to be the Hardest Word (in the Czech Republic)," *Transition*, vol. 2, no. 9 (May 3, 1996), pp. 2–3.

———. "Specter of Racism in the Czech Republic," *Transition*, vol. 1, no. 10 (June 23, 1995), p. 1.

Gordon, Daniel I., and Reinke, Fred W. "East Germany: March 18, 1990." In *The New Democratic Frontier: A Country by Country Report on Elections in Central and Eastern Europe*, ed. Garber and Bjorlund, pp. 20–38.

Gotovska-Popova, Todoritchka. "Nationalism in Post-Communist Eastern Europe." *East European Quarterly* 27, no. 2 (June 1993): 171–86.

Grabowska, Miroslawa. "The Party System Under Construction: The Parliamentary Elections in 1991." *Politicus*, Bulletin of the Institute of Political Studies, Polish Academy of Sciences, Warsaw (1992): 12–26.

Gross, Jan T. "Poland: From Civil Society to Political Nation." In *Eastern Europe in Revolution*, ed. Banac, p. 56–71.

Grzybowski, Marian. "Poland: Toward Overdeveloped Pluralism." In *The New Democracies in Eastern Europe: Party Systems and Political Cleavages*, ed. Berglund and Dellenbrant, pp. 40–70.

———. "The Transition to Competitive Pluralism in Hungary." In *The New Democracies of Eastern Europe: Party Systems and Political Cleavages*, ed. Berglund and Dellenbrant, pp. 161–94.

Gutman, Robert J. "The View From Hungary." *Europe*, November 1993, pp. 30–31.

Hall, John, and Ludwig, Udo. "Creating Germany's *Mezzogiorno*." *Challenge*, July–August 1993, p. 38–44.

Harrington, Joseph; Karns, Edward; and Karns, Scott. "American-Romanian Relations 1989–1994." *East European Quarterly* 29, no. 2 (Summer 1995): 207–35.

Harsanyi, Doina Pasca. "Romania's Women." *Journal of Women's History* 5, no. 3 (Winter 1994): 30–54.

Hayden, Robert M. "Constitutional Nationalism in the Formerly Yugoslav Republics." *Slavic Review* 51, no. 4 (Winter 1992): 654–73.

Haynes, Rebecca Ann. "Hungarian National Identity." In *Contemporary Nationalism in East Central Europe*, ed. Latawski, pp. 96–99.

Hazlett, Thomas W. "The Czech Miracle." *Reason*, April 1995, pp. 33–34.

Hole, Janine P. "Competing Visions of Polish Parliament 1989–1993." *East European Quarterly* 29, no. 1 (Spring 1995): 69–87.

Ionescu, Dan. "Romanian Energy Crisis Turns Political," *Transition*, vol. 2, no. 9 (May 3, 1996), pp. 20–22.

————. "Romanian Orthodox Leaders Play the Nationalist Card," *Transition*, vol. 2, no. 7 (April 5, 1996), pp. 24–28.

————. "Tele-Revolution or Tele-Evolution in Romania," *Transition*, vol. 2, no. 8 (April 19, 1996), pp. 42–44.

Isarescu, Mugur. "The Prognoses for Economic Recovery." In *Romania After Tyranny*, ed. Nelson, pp. 149–66.

Jasewiecz, Krzyzstof. "Structures and Representation." In *Developments in East European Politics*, ed. White, Batt, and Lewis, pp. 125–46.

Job, Cvijeto. "Yugoslavia's Ethnic Furies." *Foreign Policy* 92 (Fall 1993): 52–74.

Judt, Tony. "Metamorphosis: The Democratic Revolution in Czechoslovakia." In *Eastern Europe in Revolution*, ed. Banac, pp. 96–116.

Kaminski, Bartlomiej. "Emerging Patterns of Foreign Trade." In *The Transition to Democracy in Poland*, ed. Staar, p. 181–201.

Karpinski, Jakub. "Poles Divided over Church's Renewed Political Role," *Transition*, vol. 2, no. 7 (April 5, 1996), pp. 28–31.

Kearns, Ian. "Croatia: The Politics Behind the War." *The World Today*, vol. 49, no. 4 (April 1993): 62–64.

Kideckel, David A. "Peasants and Authority in the New Romania." In *Romania After Tyranny*, ed. Nelson, pp. 67–82.

King, Charles. "Moldovan Identity and the Politics of Pan-Romanianism." *Slavic Review* 53, no. 2 (Summer 1994): 345–68.

Kinzer, Stephen. "East Germans Face Their Accusers." *The New York Times Magazine*, April 12, 1992.

Klaus, Vaclav. "Transition—An Insider's View." *Problems of Communism*, vol. 41, nos. 1–2 (January–April 1992): 73–75.

Koinova, Maria. "Protesting Meddling in the National Media," *Transition*, vol. 2, no. 8 (April 19, 1996), pp. 2–3.

Korbonski, Andrzej. "The Revival of the Political Right in Post-Communist Poland: Historical Background." In *Democracy and Right-Wing Politics in Eastern Europe in the 1990s*, ed. Held, pp. 13–31.

Korosenyi, Andras. "The Hungarian Parliamentary Elections, 1990." In *Post-Communist Transition: Emerging Pluralism in Hungary*, ed. Bozoki, Korosenyi, and Schopflin, pp. 25–78.

"Kosovo: The Quiet Siege." *Cultural Survival Quarterly* (Summer 1995): 37–39.

Kovacs, Dezo, and Maggard, Sally Ward. "The Human Face of Political, Economic, and Social Change in Eastern Europe." *East European Quarterly* 27, no. 3 (September 1993): 317–45.

Kovrig, Bennett. "Hungarian Minorities in East Central Europe." *Occasional Paper Series: The Atlantic Council of the United States* (March 1994): 17–20.

————. "Kadarism Without Kadar." In *Soviet/East European Survey 1987–1988*, ed. Mastny, pp. 276–79.

Kraft, Evan; Modovipec, Milan; and Cvikl, Milan. "On Its Own: The Economy of Independent Slovenia." In *Independent Slovenia: Origins, Movements, Prospects*, ed. Benderly and Kraft, pp. 207–13.

Kramer, John M. "Eastern Europe and the 'Energy Shock' of 1990–1991." *Problems of Communism*, vol. 40, no. 3 (May–June 1991): 85–96.

Krause, Stefan, and Markotich, Stan. "Rump Yugoslavia and Macedonia Deal the Cards of Mutual Recognition," *Transition*, vol. 2, no. 11 (May 31, 1996), pp. 54–57.

Kusin, Vladimir. "Vaclav Havel's First Term." In *Eastern Europe: Transformation and Revolution 1945–1991*, ed. Legters, pp. 377–81.

Lampe, John R. "Nationalism in the Former Yugoslavia." In *Contemporary Nationalism in East Central Europe*, ed. Latawski, p. 160.

Latynski, Maya. "Poland: May 27, 1990." In *The New Democratic Frontier: A Country by Country Report on Elections in Central and Eastern Europe*, ed. Garber and Bjorlund, pp. 95–111.

Lefebvre, Stephane. "Bulgaria's Foreign Relations in the Post-Communist Era: A General Overview and Assessment." *East European Quarterly* 28, no. 4 (Winter 1994): 443–66.

Lemon, Alaina. "No Land, No Contracts for Romani Workers," *Transition*, vol. 2, no. 13 (June 28, 1996), pp. 28–30.

"Life in the Unpromised Land." *World Press Review* (November 1988): 17.

Lipstadt, Deborah. "Anti-Semitism in Eastern Europe Rears Its Ugly Head Again." *USA Today*, September 13, 1993, pp. 50–53.

Longworth, Richard C. "Eastern Europe: The Party's Over." *Bulletin of the Atomic Scientists* (January–February 1992): 22–29.

Lowenthal, Mark. "Bosnia: U.S. Objectives, Military Options, Serbian Responses." *CRS Report for Congress*, 93–408S, April 14, 1993, pp. 3–5.

Magas, Branka. "The Curse of Kosovo." *New Internationalist* (September 1993): 8–10.

Maier, Anneli. "Ceausescu Family Succession." In *Eastern Europe: Transformation and Revolution 1945–1991*, ed. Legters, pp. 457–62.

Mandelbaum, Michael. "The United States and Eastern Europe." In *Central and Eastern Europe: The Opening Curtain?* ed. Griffith, pp. 366–87.

Marer, Paul. "The Political Economy of Soviet Relations with Eastern Europe." In *Soviet Policy in Eastern Europe*, ed. Terry, pp. 155–88.

"Market Myths and Polish Realities: An Interview with Jan Olszewski." *Multinational Monitor* (September 1993): 21–23.

Markotich, Stan. "An Unstable Government (in Slovenia) Faces an Election Year," *Transition*, vol. 2, no. 12 (June 14, 1996), pp. 54–56.

———. "Tension Rises over Montenegro's Independent Moves," *Transition*, vol. 2, no. 15 (July 26, 1996), pp. 58–61.

Marshall, Monty G. "States at Risk: Ethnopolitics in the Multinational States of Eastern Europe." In *Minorities at Risk: A Global View of Ethnopolitical Conflicts*, ed. Gurr, chap. 7, pp. 173–83.

Martin, Peter. "Relations between Czechs and Slovaks: The Hyphen Controversy." *Radio Free Europe: Report on Eastern Europe* (September 7, 1990), no. 36, pp. 1–5.

———. "Relations Between the Czechs and the Slovaks." In *Eastern Europe: Transformation and Revolution 1945–1991*, ed. Legters, pp. 381–87.

Martin, Peter, and Devlin, Kevin. "Religious Struggle in Czechoslovakia." In *Soviet/East European Survey 1987–1988*, ed. Mastny, pp. 194–200.

Mason, David S. "Attitudes Toward the Market and Political Participation in Post-Communist States." *Slavic Review* 54, no. 2 (Summer 1995): 385–406.

Mathis, Eric, and Swinnen, Jo. "Agricultural Privatization and Decollectivization in Central and Eastern Europe," *Transition*, vol. 2, no. 15 (July 26, 1996), pp. 12–16.

McMahon, Edward. "Slovenia: April 7 and 21, 1990." In *The New Democratic Frontier: A Country by Country Report on Elections in Central and Eastern Europe*, ed. Garber and Bjorlund, pp. 67–73.

Mearsheimer, John J., and Pape, Robert A. "The Answer: A Partition Plan for Bosnia." *The New Republic*, June 14, 1993, pp. 22–25.

Melia, Thomas O. "Hungary: March 25, 1990." In *The New Democratic Frontier: A Country by Country Report on Elections in Central and Eastern Europe*, ed. Garber and Bjorlund, pp. 39–64.

Michta, Andrew A. "The Presidential Parliamentary System." In *The Transition to Democracy in Poland*, ed. Staar, pp. 57–76.

Mihailescu, Ioan. "Mental Stereotypes in the First Years of Post-Totalitarian Romania." *Government and Opposition* (Autumn 1993): 315–24.

Millard, Frances. "Nationalism in Poland." In *Contemporary Nationalism in East Central Europe*, ed. Latawski, pp. 122–23.

Moisi, Dominique. "French Policy Toward Central and Eastern Europe." In *Central and Eastern Europe: The Opening Curtain?* ed. Griffith, pp. 353–65.

Moore, Patrick. "The Chess Players' Peace" (Dayton at Midpoint), *Transition*, vol. 2, no. 14 (July 12, 1996), pp. 6–9.

———. "Waiting and Watching in the Wake of Western Slavonia," *Transition,* vol. 1, no. 10 (June 23, 1995), pp. 28–31.

Morison, John. "The Road to Separation: Nationalism in Czechoslovakia." In *Contemporary Nationalism in East Central Europe*, ed. Latawski, pp. 73–75, 81.

Mroziewicz, Dagmar. "Polish Economic Reform Marred by High Unemployment," *Transition*, vol. 2, no. 13 (June 28, 1996), pp. 26–27.

Munich, Daniel, and Sorm, Vit. "The Czech Republic as a Low-Unemployment Oasis," *Transition*, vol. 2, no. 13 (June 28, 1996), pp. 21–25.

Naimark, Norman. " 'Ich will hier raus': Emigration and the Collapse of the German Democratic Republic." In *Eastern Europe in Revolution*, ed. Banac, pp. 81, 83–86, 90–94.

Neckerman, Peter. "What Went Wrong in Germany After Unification?" *East European Quarterly* 26, no. 4 (Winter 1992): 456–57.

Newhouse, John. "The Diplomatic Round: Dodging the Problem in Yugoslavia." *The New Yorker*, August 24, 1992, pp. 63, 65, 68.

Nicolaesca, Madalina. "Post-Communist Transition: Romanian Women's Response to Changes in the System of Power." *Journal of Women's History* 5, no. 3 (Winter 1994): 117–28.

Nicolaev, Rada. "A Year of Crucial Change in Bulgaria." In *Eastern Europe: Transformation and Revolution 1945–1991*, ed. Legters, pp. 498–503.

———. "The Bulgarian Communist Party after Its 'Congress of Renewal.' " In *Eastern Europe: Transformation and Revolution 1945–1991*, ed. Legters, pp. 507–15.

Nivat, Anne. "Convincing Polish Voters that Kwasniewski Is 'The Choice of the Future,' " *Transition*, vol. 2, no. 8 (April 19, 1996), pp. 32–33.

Nowicka, Wanda. "Two Steps Backward: Poland's New Abortion Law." *Journal of Women's History* 5, no. 3 (Winter 1994): 151–55.

Olson, David M. "The Sundered State: Federalism and Parliament in Czechoslovakia." In *Parliaments in Transition: The New Legislative Politics in the Former USSR and Eastern Europe*, ed. Remington, pp. 97–123.

Orenstein, Mitchell. "The Failures of Neo-Liberal Social Policy in Central Europe," *Transition*, vol. 2, no. 13 (June 28, 1996), pp. 16–20.

Pakszys, Elzbieta, and Mazurczak, Dorota. "From Totalitarianism to Democracy in Poland: Issues in the Socio-Political Transition 1989–1993." *Journal of Women's History* 5, no. 3 (Winter 1994): 144–50.

Pang, Yali. "Privatization in East European Countries." *East European Quarterly* 26, no. 4 (January 1993): 471–84.

Parrish, Scott. "Russia's Marginal Role" (Dayton at Midpoint), *Transition*, vol. 2, no. 14 (July 12, 1996), pp. 17–20.

Pehe, Jiri. "Czechoslovakia: An Abrupt Transition." In *Eastern Europe: Transformation and Revolution 1945–1991*, ed. Legters, pp. 346–51.
———. "The Civic Forum Splits into Two Groups." In *Eastern Europe: Transformation and Revolution 1945–1991*, ed. Legters, pp. 387–94.
———. "Election Results in Surprise Stalemate" (in the Czech Republic), *Transition*, vol. 2, no. 13 (June 28, 1996), pp. 36–37.
Perry, Duncan M. "Bulgarian Nationalism: Permutations of the Past." In *Contemporary Nationalism in East Central Europe*, ed. Latawski, pp. 46–52, 54–57.
Pettifer, James. "Macedonia: Still the Apple of Discord." *The World Today*, vol. 51, no. 3 (March 1995), pp. 55–58.
Poulton, Hugh. "Playing the Kinship Card in the Balkans," *Transition*, vol. 2, no. 12 (June 14, 1996), pp. 16–21.
Prybyla, Jan S. "The Road from Socialism: Why, Where, What, and How." *Problems of Communism* (January–February 1991): 1–17.
Rachwald, Arthur R. "National Security Relations." In *The Transition to Democracy in Poland*, ed. Staar, pp. 235–55.
Rady, Martyn. "Nationalism and Nationality in Romania." In *Contemporary Nationalism in East Central Europe*, ed. Latawski, pp. 127, 129, 133–34.
Ramet, Sabrina P. "War in the Balkans." *Foreign Affairs*, vol. 71, no. 4 (Fall 1992): 79–98.
Ratesh, Nestor. "Romania: Slamming on the Brakes." *Current History* (November 1993): 390–95.
Regulska, Joanna. "Women in Polish Politics." In *Women in the Politics of Post-Communist Eastern Europe*, ed. Rueschemeyer, pp. 35–62.
Reisch, Alfred. "Mounting Pressures for Change." In *Soviet/East European Survey 1987–1988*, ed. Mastny, pp. 264–69.
———. "The Fall of Kadar." In *Soviet/East European Survey 1987–1988*, ed. Mastny, pp. 269–76.
———. "Hungary in 1989: A Country in Transition." In *Eastern Europe: Transformation and Revolution 1945–1991*, ed. Legters, pp. 443–49.
———. "The Growth of Civil Society in Hungary." In *Soviet/East European Survey 1987–1988*, ed. Mastny, pp. 244–45, 249–52.
Rhodes, Mathew. "National Identity and Minority Rights in the Constitutions of the Czech Republic and Slovakia." *East European Quarterly* 29, no. 3 (Fall 1995): 347–69.
"Romania: Another Winter of Discontent." *The Economist*, October 27, 1990, p. 54.
"Romania in Trouble." *The Economist*, October 3, 1992, p. 55.
"Romania Undermined." *The Economist*, October 5, 1991, p. 5.
Roper, Steven D. "The Romanian Party System and the Catch-All Party Phenomenon." *East European Quarterly* 28, no. 4 (Winter 1994): 519–30.
Rosenberg, Tina. "Albania: The Habits of the Heart." *World Policy Journal* 11 (Winter 1994): 33, 85–94.
Rueschemeyer, Marilyn. "Women in the Politics of East Germany." In *Women in the Politics of Post-Communist Eastern Europe*, ed. Rueschemeyer, pp. 87–116.
Rupel, Dimitry. "Slovenia's Shift from the Balkans to Central Europe." In *Independent Slovenia: Origins, Movements, Prospects*, ed. Benderly and Kraft, pp. 183–200.
Rusinow, Dennison. "Yugoslavia: Balkan Breakup." *Foreign Policy* 83 (Summer 1991): 143–59.
Rybkova, Eva. "Shutting Out Criticism in Serbia," *Transition*, vol. 2, no. 14 (July 12, 1996), p. 69.
Sanford, George. "The Polish Road to Democratization: From Political Impasse to the

'Controlled Abdication' of Communist Power." In *Democratization in Poland, 1989–1990*, ed. Sanford, pp. 25–27.

Schmidt, Fabian. "Election Fraud Sparks Protest (in Albania)," *Transition*, vol. 2, no. 13 (June 28, 1996), pp. 38–39.

———. "Sadzak Muslims Pin Hopes on Elections," *Transition*, vol. 2, no. 14 (July 12, 1996), pp. 39, 71.

———. "Teaching the Wrong Lesson in Kosovo," *Transition*, vol. 2, no. 14 (July 12, 1996), pp. 37–39.

———. "Tradition of Pragmatism (in Albania)," *Transition*, vol. 2, no. 7 (April 5, 1996), pp. 33–35.

Schoen, Douglas. "How Milošević Stole the Election." *The New York Times Magazine*, February 14, 1993, pp. 32, 39–40.

Scholz, Hannelone, "East-West Women's Culture Transition: German Women the Losers in Reunification?" *Journal of Women's History*, vol. 5, no. 3 (Winter 1994), pp. 108–16.

Schopflin, George. "Central and Eastern Europe over the Last Year: New Trends, Old Structures." In *Eastern Europe: Transformation and Revolution 1945–1991*, ed. Legters, pp. 646–51.

———. "From Communism to Democracy in Hungary." In *Post-Communist Transition: Emerging Pluralism in Hungary*, ed. Bozoki, Korosenyi, and Schopflin, pp. 96–110.

———. "The Prospects of Democracy in Central and Eastern Europe." In *Uncertain Futures: Eastern Europe and Democracy*, ed. Volten, pp. 19–34.

Schopflin, George, et al. "Leadership Change and Crisis in Hungary." *Problems of Communism*, vol. 37, no. 5 (September–October 1988): 23–46.

"The Serbs' Next Target?" *The Economist*, May 29, 1993, p. 54.

Shafir, Michael, "Political Engineering and Democratization in New Law on Parties," *Transition*, vol. 2, no. 14 (July 12, 1996), pp. 60–63.

———. "The Political Right in Post-Communist Romania." In *Democracy and Right-Wing Politics in Eastern Europe in the 1990s*, ed. Held, pp. 153–74.

Shrag, Minna. "Assessing the War Crimes Tribunal," *Transition*, vol. 2, no. 14 (July 12, 1996), pp. 51–53.

Shubart, Tira. "Arrested in Romania." In *Eastern Europe: Transformation and Revolution 1945–1991*, ed. Legters, pp. 462–67.

Shumaker, David. "The Origins and Development of Central European Cooperation: 1989–1992." *East European Quarterly* 27, no. 3 (September 1993): 351–73.

Sidorov, Sergei. "Our Country Sends 400 Soldiers to the Sarajevo Area." *Krasnaya zvesda*, February 19, 1994. Cited from *Current Digest of the Soviet Press* 46, no. 7: 4–5.

Siemienska, Renata. "Women in the Period of Systemic Change in Poland." *Journal of Women's History* 5, no. 3 (Winter 1994): 74–79.

Sito Sučić, Daria. "The Disunited Colors of Mostar," *Transition*, vol. 2, no. 14 (July 12, 1996), pp. 42–44.

Slay, Ben. "Elections Unlikely to Affect Economic Transformation," *Transition*, vol. 2, no. 15 (July 26, 1996), pp. 38–41, 62.

"Slovakia Targets Imports." *The International Herald Tribune*, July 3–4, 1993.

Socor, Vladimir. "Social Protests in Romania." In *Soviet/East European Survey 1987–1988*, ed. Mastny, pp. 208–10.

Sokolewicz, Wojciech. "The Legal-Constitutional Bases of Democratization in Poland: Systemic and Constitutional Change." In *Democratization in Poland, 1989–1990: Polish Voices*, ed. Sanford, pp. 77, 80–83, 88–89.

"Speech by M.S. Gorbachev to the Eleventh Congress of the (East German) Socialist Unity Party of Germany." *Pravda*, April 19, 1986. Cited from *Current Digest of the Soviet Press* 38, no. 16 (May 21, 1986): 7–9.

Steichen, Girard C. "Lean Times Ahead in Hungary." In *Eastern Europe: Transformation and Revolution*, ed. Legters, pp. 454–55.

Stent, Angela. "Technology Transfer to Eastern Europe: Paradoxes, Policies, Prospects." In *Central and Eastern Europe: The Opening Curtain?* ed. Griffith, pp. 74–101.

"Street Crime Hits Prague Daily Life." *The New York Times*, December 18, 1991.

Sullivan, Marianne, "Socialists on the Campaign Trail (in Albania)," *Transition*, vol. 2, no. 11 (May 31, 1996), pp. 38–39.

Swiatkowski-Cannon, Lucja. "Privatization Strategy and Its Political Context." In *The Transition to Democracy in Poland*, ed. Staar, pp. 122–41.

Swieboda, Pawel. "(Poland) In NATO's Waiting Room," *Transition*, vol. 2, no. 8 (April 19, 1996), pp. 52–55.

Szabo, Mary. "We (Leaders of the Hungarian Churches in Romania) Demand Our Rights," *Transition*, vol. 2, no. 7 (April 5, 1996), pp. 26–27.

Szilagyi, Zsofia. "Hungary Has a Broadcast Media Law," *Transition*, vol. 2, no. 8 (April 19, 1996), pp. 22–25.

———. "Parliament Backs Law to Punish Extremist Rhetoric," *Transition*, vol. 2, no. 11 (May 31, 1996), pp. 46–48.

Taras, Raymond. "Leadership and Executives." In *Developments in East European Politics*, ed. White, Batt, and Lewis, pp. 163–85.

———. "Voters, Parties, and Leaders." In *The Transition to Democracy in Poland*, ed. Staar, pp. 15–39.

Tarifa, Fatos. "Albania." In *Women in the Politics of Postcommunist Eastern Europe*, ed. Rueschemeyer, pp. 135–51.

Terrill, Damon A. "Tolerance Lost: Disaffection, Dissent, and Revolution in the German Democratic Republic." *East European Quarterly* 28, no. 3 (September 1994): 356–65.

Terry, Sarah M. "What's Left, What's Right, and What's Wrong in Polish Politics?" In *Democracy and Right-Wing Politics in Eastern Europe in the 1990s*, ed. Held, pp. 33–53.

———. "Prospects for Regional Cooperation." In *The Transition to Democracy in Poland*, ed. Staar, pp. 203–37.

Tismaneanu, Vladimir. "Nascent Civil Society in the German Democratic Republic." *Problems of Communism*, vol. 38, no. 2 (March–April 1989): 90–111.

———. "In Romania: Between Euphoria and Rage." In *Eastern Europe: Transformation and Revolution 1945–1991*, ed. Legters, pp. 467–73.

Titkow, Anna. "Polish Women in Politics: An Introduction to the Status of Women in Poland." In *Women in the Politics of Post-Communist Eastern Europe*, ed. Rueschemeyer, pp. 29–34.

Todorova, Maria M. "Improbable Maverick or Typical Conformist: Seven Thoughts on the New Bulgaria." In *Eastern Europe in Revolution*, ed. Banac, pp. 148–67.

———. "Historical Tradition and Transformation in Bulgaria: Women's Issues or Feminist Issues." *Journal of Women's History* 5, no. 3 (Winter 1994): 129–43.

Tokes, Rudolf L. "Hungary's New Political Elites: Adaptation and Change." *Problems of Communism*, vol. 39, no. 6 (November–December 1990): 44–65.

———. "Hungarian Reform Imperatives." *Problems of Communism*, vol. 33, no. 5 (September–October 1984): 1–23.

———. "From Visegrád to Kraków: Cooperation, Competition, and Coexistence in Central Europe." *Problems of Communism*, vol. 40, no. 6 (November–December 1991): 100–114.

Trišić-Babić, Ana. "Changes Brewing in Bosnian Serb Politics," *Transition*, vol. 2, no. 14 (June 12, 1996), pp. 33–34.

Troxel, Luan. "Socialist Persistence in the Bulgarian Elections of 1990–1991." *East European Quarterly* 26, no. 4 (January 1993): 407–30.

————. "Political Spectrum in Post-Communist Bulgaria." In *Democracy and Right-Wing Politics in Central and Eastern Europe in the 1990s*, ed. Held, pp. 191–202.

————. "Bulgaria: Stable Ground in the Balkans?" *Current History* (November 1993): 142–44, 388–89.

Tzvetkov, Plamen S. "The Politics of Transition in Bulgaria: Back to the Future?" *Problems of Communism*, vol. 41, no. 3 (May–June 1992): 34–43.

Ulc, Otto. "The Bumpy Road of Czechoslovakia's Velvet Revolution." *Problems of Communism*, vol. 41, no. 3 (May–June 1992): 19–33.

————. "The Role of the Political Right in Post-Communist Czechoslovakia." In *Democracy and Right-Wing Politics in Eastern Europe in the 1990s*, ed. Held, pp. 89–103.

Vanous, Jan. "East European Economic Slowdown." *Problems of Communism*, vol. 31, no. 4 (July–August 1982): 1–19.

Verdery, Katherine. "Nationalism and National Sentiment in Post-Socialist Romania." *Slavic Review* 52, no. 2 (Summer 1993): 197–99.

————. "The Elasticity of Land: Problems of Property Restitution in Transylvania." Working Papers Series 9. Advanced Study Center, International Institute, University of Michigan, 1994–95, pp. 2–4.

Verdery, Katherine, and Kligman, Gail. "Romania after Ceausescu: Post Communist Communism?" In *Eastern Europe in Revolution*, ed. Banac, pp. 117–47.

Volgyes, Ivan. "Hungary Before the Storm Breaks." *Current History* (November 1987): 373–76.

Warner, Tom. "Bosnia Balances the West and the Middle East," *Transition*, vol. 2, no. 7 (April 5, 1996), pp. 61–62.

Watts, Larry L. "The Romanian Army in December Revolution and Beyond." In *Romania After Tyranny*, ed. Nelson. pp. 95–126.

Wesolowski, Wlodzimierz. "Transition from Authoritarianism to Democracy." In *Eastern Europe: Transformation and Revolution 1945–1991*, ed. Legters, pp. 302–4.

————. "The Role of Political Elites in Transition from Communism to Democracy: The Case of Poland." *Sisyphus* 8, no. 2 (1992): 77–100.

deWeydenthal, Jan B. "The First Hundred Days of Walesa's Presidency." In *Eastern Europe: Transformation and Revolution 1945–1991*, ed. Legters, pp. 336–40.

Wightman, Gordon. "The Czech and Slovak Republics." In *Developments in East European Politics*, ed. White, Batt, and Lewis, pp. 1–65.

Wilson, Paul. "Czechoslovakia: The Pain of Divorce." *The New York Review of Books*, December 17, 1992, pp. 69–75.

Woehrel, Steven J. "Bosnia-Herzegovina: Background to the Conflict." *CRS Report for Congress*, 93–106F, January 21, 1993, pp. 3, 6.

Woehrel, Steven J., and Kim, Julius. "Yugoslavia Crisis and U.S. Policy." *CRS Issue Brief*, IB91089, Congressional Research Service, Library of Congress, Washington, DC, September 2, 1993, pp. 9–13.

————. "Bosnia–Former Yugoslavia: Ongoing Conflict and U.S. Policy." *CRS Issue Brief*, IB91089, Congressional Research Service, Library of Congress, Washington, DC, January 19, 1995, pp. 2–15.

Wolchik, Sharon. *Czechoslovakia in Transition: Politics, Economics, and Society*. London: Pinter, 1990.

————. "The Right in Czechoslovakia." In *Democracy and Right-Wing Politics in Central and Eastern Europe in the 1990s*, ed. Held, pp. 61–87.

————. "Women in Transition in the Czech and Slovak Republics: The First Three Years." *Journal of Women's History* 5, no. 3 (Winter 1994): 100–107.

Woodard, Colin. "Albania's Academic Revival," *The Chronicle of Higher Education*, April 25, 1995, p. A43.

———. "A Terrible Communist Legacy," *Transition*, vol. 2, no. 15 (July 26, 1996), pp. 50–52.

———. "The Western Aid Cavalry Isn't Coming," *Transition*, vol. 2, no. 15 (July 26, 1996), p. 53.

Woodward, Susan. "Yugoslavia: Decline and Fall." *The Bulletin of the Atomic Scientists* (November 1993): 24–27.

———. "The United States Leads, Europe Pays," *Transition*, vol. 2, no. 14 (July 12, 1996), pp. 12–16.

Wooten, Jim. "The Conciliator." *The New York Times Magazine*, January 29, 1995, pp. 28–33, 42, 48, 54.

Yusin, Maksim. "Russian Parliament's Resolution on Yugoslavia Pushes Moscow Toward International Isolation." *Izvestia*, February 20, 1993. Cited from *Current Digest of the Soviet Press* 45, no. 8 (February 20, 1993): 17–18.

———. "Serbs Deal a Cruel Blow to the Prestige of Russian Diplomacy." *Current Digest of the Soviet Press* 46, no. 16 (April 20, 1994): 1–2.

Zanga, Louis. "A Watershed Year." In *Eastern Europe: Transformation and Revolution 1945–1991*, ed. Legters, pp. 541–49.

———. "Albanian President Defends His First Year in Office." *Radio Free Europe/Radio Liberty Research Report* 2, no. 29 (July 16, 1993): 24.

Zubec, Voytek. "Walesa's Leadership and Poland's Transition." *Problems of Communism*, vol. 40, nos. 1–2 (January–April 1991): 69–83.

Zukowski, Tomasz. "Polish Parliamentary Elections." *Politicus*, Bulletin of the Institute of Political Studies, Polish Academy of Sciences, Warsaw (1992): 33–38.

Unpublished Papers

Ryavec, Karl W. "Recent Developments in Slovenia." Paper presented at the annual meeting of the New England Slavic Association, Providence College, Providence, RI, April 3, 1993.

———. "Slovenia: The Origins of Independence and an Outline of the Present Situation." Paper presented at a meeting of an international faculty seminar at Wesleyan University, April 23, 1994.

Data presented in the "factboxes" for each country are from Central Intelligence Agency, *The World Factbook,* and *The Statesman's Year-Book,* both issued annually.

Index

Minton F. Goldman teaches political science at Northeastern University in Boston, Massachusetts, and is a past recipient of the university's Excellence in Teaching award. He has done extensive field research throughout Central and Eastern Europe and presented papers at professional conferences in the United States and abroad. In addition to scholarly articles and book chapters on topics in diplomacy, foreign policy, and area studies, Professor Goldman has published a sixth edition of his *Global Studies* volume *Russia, the Eurasian Republics, and Central/Eastern Europe* (1996).